THE CANADIAN POLITICAL SYSTEM

ENVIRONMENT, STRUCTURE & PROCESS

Suggested further reading from McGraw–Hill Ryerson:
The McGraw–Hill Ryerson Series in Canadian Politics
General Editor: P.W. Fox

McGraw–Hill Ryerson Limited

Toronto   Montreal   New York   London   Sydney

Johannesburg   Mexico   Panama   Düsseldorf   Singapore

São Paulo   Kuala Lumpur   New Delhi   Auckland

RICHARD J. VAN LOON
Department of Political Science
Carleton University

MICHAEL S. WHITTINGTON
Department of Political Science
Carleton University

THE CANADIAN POLITICAL SYSTEM

ENVIRONMENT, STRUCTURE & PROCESS

SECOND EDITION

TO OUR STUDENTS

THE CANADIAN POLITICAL SYSTEM, Second Edition

4 5 6 7 8 9 0 HR 5 4 3 2 1 0 9

ISBN 0–07–082262-X

Printed and bound in Canada

CONTENTS

APPENDIX

Preface To The Second Edition

In 1969, when we began the first edition of The Canadian Political System, we were aware that in many ways our efforts could be judged premature. More important, even than the fact that the authors were fresh from graduate school, was the problem that in many sub-fields of Canadian political science there was little published material available and little really substantial research. Thus, for example, while there were dozens of articles on political parties, there had been only one national voting study completed to the point of publication of its findings. There was virtually no material on political socialization and little with a substantial empirical base on political culture. This list of problems could be multiplied by many other sub-fields.

In the years since, the authors have grown older and (we hope) a bit wiser. More importantly, we have benefited not only from a substantial body of criticism of the *Canadian Political System* but also from a veritable explosion of published research in many of the fields where the greatest gaps had existed in the past. All of this has resulted in some very major changes between the first and second editions. The book is set in a revised framework. While we have retained some elements and the very basic concepts of systems analysis where we thought them useful, we have tried much more consciously in this edition to relate our material to the policy process. Thus, with every topic discussed we have tried to ask ourselves "what has this to do with the making of public policy in Canada?" We have added much new material to the chapters on the economic and social environment in which our political system operates, and we have tried to apply new interpretations to the impact of environment on process. Thus, for example, there is much new material on political socialization and on our economic relationships with the United States, and there is an attempt to use consociationalism in linking political culture with policy making.

Federal–provincial relations and the constitution have been accorded a new, dual treatment; the constitution and the historical dimension of federal–provincial relations are treated as environmental constraints on the policy process, and today's federal–provincial relations are treated in a separate chapter as an integral (and perhaps even the central) part of the policy process.

Our material on political parties and voting has been updated but is essentially unchanged in concept from the first edition. Interest groups, however, have been accorded a more central role in the analysis, and the material on them had nearly doubled in volume. Except for federal–provincial conferences, the major institutional actors at the core of the policy process (cabinet, parliament and the bureaucracy) are accorded the same type of treatment given them in the first edition, although all material has been completely updated. On the whole, it was our feeling that those sections of the first edition were fairly successful and we should concentrate our efforts elsewhere. The person who has read both editions may notice, however, that in the second more power is attributed to the elected actors and their personal appointees *vis à vis* the bureaucratic actors. This represents not so much a recantation of our original views as what we perceive to have been a real trend in Ottawa over the last five years.

The bibliography, one of the most popular features of the first edition, was completely updated in the summer of 1974. Most articles and books published after that date do not appear but we hope that we have achieved fairly complete coverage of significant sources up to at least the end of 1973 or to mid-1974. Any glaring omissions are errors and not to be viewed as an attempt on our part to pass judgement on the merits of the work of our colleagues.

While we have been greatly assisted by our many critics, we have naturally been unable to meet all of their criticisms. Sometimes, we simply felt, on the basis of our own experience and reading, that they were wrong. In some cases, our critics have been in opposition to each other. For example, some have said we spend too much time dealing with the historical development of federalism, and others have complained that we neglect history. Other of our critics have attacked us for not doing some things that we had no intention of doing. We agree that there is a striking lack of literature dealing with provincial governments and with urban politics, but without pressing our text to a thousand pages we cannot begin to fill such gaps in the literature; nor is it the responsibility of a textbook which is avowedly about politics at the national level to do so. We have been criticized by some as being too negative or pessimistic about the Canadian political system and by others as being apologists for the Canadian system. On the whole, we are rather proudly and unrepentently guilty of the latter; although we certainly do not refrain from criticism where we think it appropriate. Finally, it should be recognized that no textbook can *exhaustively* cover all, or even most areas of a discipline. Thus, for example, almost anyone who is an expert on political parties can find places in our treatment where we have not covered all of the available literature or where they might have added qualifications that we did not. Again we are to a considerable degree prisoners of the limitations of space. The place for such embellishment, important as it is, is in the lecture theatre or the seminar room.

A further reminder which may be of value to teachers and students alike is that there is a substantial lead time involved in the preparation of a book of this size. Thus, although the book first appears in early 1976, the bulk of the work on the original manuscript was completed by mid-1974. In some areas (political culture comes first to mind) there has been a great expansion of the literature since that time. The users of the book should be aware of this unavoidable limitation.

We have been assisted in the preparation of this edition by too many people to thank them all individually. We possess a lengthy file of letters from people in the discipline, many of whom we have never met personally and yet who took the time to point out some error they picked up in the first edition. Our friends and colleagues at Carleton have been consistently helpful to us in making revisions. We are most grateful to Mrs. Pearl Fisher and the secretarial staff in the Department of Political Science at Carleton who somehow managed to get our draft chapters typed as fast as we could produce them. Jean Van Loon deserves a special thanks for long hours spent revising both the substance and the prose of many chapters of this edition. Margaret Kipp spent much time in updating the bibliography. Finally, as with the first edition, this version owes much to the comments and criticisms of our students. In the final analysis their opinions are a major test of a textbook.

Ottawa, Ontario, 1975

RICHARD J. VAN LOON
MICHAEL S. WITTINGTON

1
Introduction

In 1971, governments in Canada collected and spent approximately $35 billion, an amount approaching 40% of the Gross National Product.[1] In that same year, one Canadian worker in five was employed by some level of government. Federal, provincial and municipal governments in Canada today provide a myriad of services ranging from the preservation of order in society to the redistribution of income. Government regulates industry, labour and the professions; it provides the roads we drive on, the water we drink, national communications networks, public education, medical care and low cost housing; it engages in commercial enterprises ranging from running airlines to producing synthetic rubber; it even engages in such seemingly godlike activities as the deliberate manipulation of the national economy through fiscal, monetary and exchange rate policies.[2]

However, while the provision of such goods and services and the redistribution of material resources represent the major activities of government, these are not the only functions governments perform. They also provide symbols such as flags and anthems with which we can identify or against which we can vent hostility. Moreover, through their antics, posturings and sincere concerns, our politicians provide us with psychological stimuli which may have little direct relevance for the political system, but which form a significant dimension of modern life.

In sum, governments are the dominant actors on the world's stage today, and their activities constantly affect the economic, social and psychological dimensions of our everyday lives. This book is about how government works at the national level in Canada. The relevance of this inquiry is clear enough given the importance of government in the modern world. But if that is not reason enough to study it, the subject and the

[1]See: Canadian Tax Foundation, *The National Finances 1972–73*, *(Toronto, 1972)*, *p.* 21. It is interesting to note as well that government expenditure as a percentage of the GNP amounted to but 16.8% in 1926. For a good analysis of government growth, with projections see also: Economic Council of Canada, *Ninth Annual Review: The Years to 1980*, (Information Canada, 1972), pp. 33 ff.
[2]See: Economic Council of Canada, *Eighth Annual Review: Design for Decision Making*, (Information Canada, 1971), esp. pp. 5–16, for a brief but succinct discussion of the increased role of government.

questions it poses are also inherently fascinating: What is the real meaning of our electoral process? How do our political parties work? What is the nature and importance of relations between the provinces and Ottawa? How do other Canadians think and feel about our political process? What difference does it make whether the government has a majority or not? And most important of all, how do the needs of society get translated into the policies of governments; what are the inner workings of that sometimes mysterious process in capital cities and council chambers? Before attempting to answer some of these questions, it is necessary to provide some framework within which such processes can be systematically analysed.

THE POLITICAL FUNCTION

All societies,[3] however primitive, possess some form of government. It is logical, therefore, to assume that there must be some common underlying function[4] (or set of functions) which is performed by such institutions. There are two simple reasons for the existence and nature of the governmental or political function: first human beings have a multitude of basic needs and wants which must be satisfied if the species is to survive and if individuals are to attain happiness; second, the resources necessary for the satisfaction of these needs and wants must be extracted from an environment which is limited. The combination of virtually unlimited human wants and limited resources produces a situation where man must compete with his fellows in order to maximize his personal satisfaction. The function of government is to resolve the conflict which arises over who gets what resources in a given society.

The Limited Environment Canadians are immensely lucky in where they live. Although our climate is hard on people, automobiles and brass monkeys, the natural resources available to Canadians are so abundant that our economic standard of living and the general quality of life here are the second or third highest in the world. No matter how abundant our resources, however, they are still limited. No one would argue that the Canadian economy produces enough material goods to satisfy every Canadian, and, in fact, because our expectations tend to rise with our standard of living the elimination of material scarcity may be an impossible dream. Furthermore, as we will see in the next chapter, our material

---

[3]By "society" we mean the network of social relationships that exists among individuals and is continuous through successive generations. This rather perfunctory definition is intended merely as a starting point for the reader and will be elaborated as the discussion unfolds. See: Marion J. Levy, *The Structure of Society*, (Princeton University Press, Princeton, 1952), p. 113; and J.W. Vander Zanden, *Sociology*, (The Ronald Press, New York, 1965), p. 153.

[4]Marion Levy defines the term as well as anybody: ". . .a function is a condition or state of affairs resultant from the operation. . .of a structure through time. . .a structure is a pattern, i.e., an observable uniformity of action or operation. . . ." in Roland Young, *Approaches to the Study of Politics*, (Northwestern, Evanston, 1958), p. xv.

well-being is offset by significant inequalities in the distribution of what is available.

But material scarcity is only one dimension of the limited environment. Even if there were no limit to the material resources of a society, there are other situations where scarcity cannot be eliminated or even significantly reduced. Status, for instance, is a psychological need which can be satisfied only relative to other people.[5] One's status is high because that of others is lower. It is illogical therefore to speak of eliminating scarcity in such a resource. The inequality of the allocation of psychological goods such as status can be reduced only if people can be conditioned not to need them.

Conflict and Cooperation The result of a limited environment is that in Canada, as in all societies, people must compete with others for the resources they require to survive and to be content. This competition occurs at several levels. At one level, man may compete directly with other men. In spite of some halting evidence of changing values in North America, getting a promotion or raise, finding a job in the first place, winning a scholarship and, in general, "keeping up with the Joneses" is still a central concern of life. But competition often transcends the individual level. Groups of people with interests in common are also in competition with other groups; labour unions compete with management, farmers compete with non-agricultural occupational groups, and dentists compete with denturists. Intergroup competition is a sort of bargaining game where the "prize" is the larger share of an available but limited resource.

But competition among groups in society is transcended by an even broader "intersector" conflict. In our post-industrial society, some would argue that traditional interpersonal and intergroup conflict has been superseded by a "balance of bigness," with big business, big labour and big government as the main protagonists.[6] Moreover, in federal systems such as Canada's, intergovernmental conflict itself is an important dimension of the competition for scarce resources.

Finally, of course, whole societies are perpetually in conflict, not only in the international arena, where governments are the actors, but also even within the confines of a single state where, for example, national or cultural groups are the adversaries. The French-English conflict which colours so much of Canadian politics is our most obvious example of the

---

[5]Whether the need for status is biologically determined and common to other animals than man, or whether it is a culturally determined feature of human society, is an interesting debate but is not really germane here. The point here is that Canadians do seem to have a need for status and that their political behaviour is influenced by this need. Those interested in the debate itself may wish to peruse Robert Ardrey, *The Social Contract*, (Delta, New York, 1970).

[6]This thesis is set forth most succinctly in J.K. Galbraith's *The New Industrial State*, (Houghton Mifflin, Boston, 1969) and in *Economics and the Public Purpose*, (Thomas Allen & Son Ltd., New York, 1973). For a different perspective, see articles in M.D. Hancock and G. Sjoberg (eds.), *Politics in the Post-Welfare State*, (Columbia University Press, New York, 1972), esp. pp. 37–55.

latter, and the increasing demands of our native peoples might also be viewed in this way.

So far conflict has been our central focus. Conflict is inherently neither good nor bad, but simply an inevitable state of affairs which occurs when man's boundless appetites are loosed on a limited environment. As inevitable as conflict in society, however, is cooperation. The very fact that human beings do live in societies and not alone testifies to the fundamentally cooperative side of man's nature. Cooperation is useful because man can accomplish with others more than he could alone. Within the context of a modern industrial society this has led to highly developed systems of cooperation called organizations, which permit the division of labour which vastly increases the capacity of a society to reduce material scarcity. Furthermore, as pointed out earlier, many of man's psychological needs can be satisfied only in relation to other men. While the drive to satisfy these needs results in interpersonal competition, without cooperation there would be no social resources for which to compete. In sum, while conflict is likely more interesting and more visible, particularly to political scientists, the cooperative mechanisms which permit a society to come into existence in the first place are at least equally significant.[7]

Conflict Resolution and Resource Allocation While conflict over the allocation of the scarce resources of a society is inevitable, it must be controlled in order to hold the society together. Conflict may be a useful tool for stimulating change, but if the social fabric is not to be destroyed, if we are not to have a continual state of war between each man and all other men, decisions must be made as to "who gets what, when, and how."[8] There must be some process or set of processes for distributing or allocating the scarce resources of a society.

In any society there are a number of different *systems*[9] or sets of human relationships which perform the function of resource allocation. For example, in Canadian society the economic system, through a medium of exchange we call money and by a complex process of bargaining we call prices, does much to determine what material resources individuals and groups will possess. Resources may also be allocated by our system of beliefs and values. For example, the value our society places upon competi-

[7]When we come to analyse the bases of conflict and cooperation within Canadian society we will use the terms *cleavage* and *consensus*. A cleavage is a line of conflict between two groups which are in competition for the same resources. Hence, for example, we will often speak of French–English cleavage, class cleavage, or regional cleavage. *Consensus* is a state of agreement among a group of people over the desirability of some end. Consensus is the foundation for cooperation among individuals, within groups, and within societies.

[8]H. Lasswell, *Politics: Who Gets What, When, How*, (McGraw-Hill Book Company, New York, 1936).

[9]The examination of society as a group of systems and sub-systems has a history too long to be traced in a footnote. Most recently the concept has been promoted by Talcott Parsons in most of his voluminous writings, and in political science by Gabriel Almond, David Easton and Karl Deutsch, among others. A listing of the relevant books is to be found in the bibliography and in other footnotes in this chapter.

tive sports means that an outstanding athlete receives greater rewards in terms of status and money than an outstanding clergyman or professor. While the way in which these different systems interact in the process of resource allocation will vary from society to society and from time to time, the allocative function always is performed.

Government too is a system for allocating resources, but it is unique. Unlike the other allocative systems in society it can be viewed as the master system; there are virtually no limits on what resources government can allocate. Furthermore, all persons in a given society are subject to the allocative decisions of government whether they choose to be or not. The jurisdiction of government is general rather than specific.

Government can also be viewed as the "master" allocative system in a society because it is empowered to control the functioning of the other allocative systems. For example, the family may be regarded as an allocative system. In most societies the head of the family will be permitted to distribute allowances to the children, but prohibited by laws enacted by government from killing unwanted infants. Similarly, the operation of the economic system is limited by laws prohibiting unfair employment practices and regulating labour relations. Thus, government is different from other allocative systems in a society in that its jurisdiction or sphere of control, while limited territorially by national boundaries, is comprehensive.

However, there are reasons for not taking this description of the government as the "master" system too far. Governments in Canada may be formally omnipotent, but they are constrained by the distribution of economic power, the prevailing value system of the society, and by the values and beliefs of the decision-makers themselves. For example it is inconceivable that a government in Canada could decree that all Roman Catholics be summarily executed or that all corporations of any type be nationalized. The prevailing ideology and the prevailing distribution of economic power would obviously prohibit the untrammelled exercise of governmental power in these areas. We will discuss in depth later the realistic limitations on governmental activity in Canada. Still government, if not omnipotent, is certainly the single most powerful and ubiquitous allocative system in any modern society.

Legitimacy and Authority Another distinguishing characteristic of governments is that the decisions they make are *authoritative*.[10] In part, this means that government possesses a monopoly over the use of the collective coercive power of the society to back up its decisions. The exclusive ability to employ coercion obviously lends a great deal of authority to governmental enactments; but a system which relied only on coercion in order to make its allocations effective would be neither stable nor efficient. Too large a percentage of the available resources would be utilized in merely keeping the citizenry in line, and the slightest let-up in the use of force would leave the system vulnerable to overthrow or collapse. For a governmental system to persist, it must acquire *legitimacy*. The members of

[10]David Easton, *A System's Analysis of Political Life*, (John Wiley & Sons, New York, 1965), ch. 1.

the society must accept the system not merely because they have to but also because there is some agreement that it is good, or at least adequate.

A system becomes legitimate in many ways. Often it happens simply because people accept it out of habit or because it is easier to accept the existing regime than to rebel against it. But whatever the origins of a system's legitimacy, it can persist only if the values and norms the system supports through its actions are basically acceptable to the society as a whole. It must resolve conflicts and allocate resources in such a way as to gain and retain the support of most of the members of society.

Our original conception of the political function as the resolution of conflict can now be filled out somewhat in the light of what has been said about the allocative role of government, the authoritative nature of governmental decisions, and the comprehensiveness of the sphere of control of government. A more complete statement of the political function is: *conflict resolution through the authoritative allocation of the scarce resources of a society.* *"Politics"* can then be defined as the process[11] by which the political function is performed; it is the way that authoritative decisions concerning the allocation of scarce resources are made and carried out in a society.

GOVERNMENT AS A SYSTEM: ENVIRON-MENT AND STRUCTURE

While we have so far avoided the use of the term, we view government as a system, specifically as that system which performs the political function. Moreover, because the political function has been defined in terms of "what government does for society" our political system is an open one: it exists in and is influenced by an environment.[12] The environment of the political system includes not only the society for which it performs the allocative function, but other societies as well. On a still wider plane, the environment of the system includes non-human factors (such as topography, climate and vegetation) which directly affect the lot of human beings. However, the important thing to remember when considering the environment of the political system is that it is composed of things that have varying relevance to politics, ranging from the virtually irrelevant, such as sun-

[11]Note: it is necessary to make an analytical distinction here between the concepts of function and process. *Function* is viewed as outcome, effect or result of organizational activity. *Process* is viewed as the activity that produces outcomes, effects or results.

[12]While open system theory has been popularized for political scientists, most notably by the works of David Easton and Gabriel Almond, it has been far more completely developed in other disciplines. See particularly: L. von Bertalanffy, "The Theory of Open Systems in Physics and Biology," *Science* 1950, V. III, pp. 23–28; J.G. Miller, "Toward a General Theory for the Behavioral Sciences," *American Psychologist*, V. 10, 1955, pp. 513–531; T. Parsons, *The Social System* (Free Press, New York, 1951); and more recently D. Katz, and R.L. Kahn, *The Social Psychology of Organizations* (John Wiley & Sons, New York, 1966). There are as well innumerable articles in *General Systems: The Yearbook of the Society for the Advancement of General Systems Theory.*

spots and quasars, to the very relevant, such as voters and the mass media.

But if we define the environment of the political system as everything other than the system itself, must we not ask where the system-environment boundary lies? Until now we have made no attempt to speak of politics or of the political system in other than functional terms, that is, we have said what the political system does without bothering about what it is. When we want to define it in structural terms, we can state that the political system is a social structure or set of institutions that performs the political function, and because the basic unit of social structure is the *role*, it follows that the political system must be seen ultimately as a complex of interrelated roles.

A role is a pattern of behaviour that is defined by the expectations a society has of one who is occupying that position. Thus, the Prime Minister performs a set of interrelated roles which includes, among other things, acting as chairman of cabinet meetings, chief advisor to the Governor General, Privy Councillor, party leader and member of parliament. The way in which a Prime Minister behaves in each of these roles is determined largely by what society expects his behaviour to be. Sometimes, as in the case of the Prime Minister's more formal roles, the society has made its expectations explicit through constitutional conventions and statutes. The Prime Minister is, in this manner, constrained to behave according to the expectations implicit in the role itself, and not according to his own predispositions.

But unfortunately role theory is not as neat in practice as it seems in the abstract. In the first place, most roles are defined partly by the man playing them. It is only roles which are defined legally or constitutionally that leave little room for improvisation on the part of the incumbent himself. Moreover, each person occupies many roles in life, and all of these become interrelated. For example, the fact that Mrs. Trudeau accompanied her husband on his diplomatic visit to China modified both his behaviour and that of his hosts even though, strictly speaking, his role as "husband" has little connection with his role as Canadian Prime Minister. The roles themselves may not be connected, but the fact that the same man occupies all of them will probably cause them to impinge on each other in many ways.

Nevertheless, despite the limitations of role theory, it is still useful to refer to the political system, structurally, as a complex of interrelated political roles. What makes a role political is the fact that it directly concerns the authoritative allocation of resources.

There are also roles such as the "voter" role which are relevant to politics but which cannot be said to affect the authoritative allocation of resources directly and immediately. Such *politically relevant* roles are probably best considered as part of the environment of the political system and not part of the system itself. However, the boundary between the political and the politically relevant cannot be drawn distinctly, and the boundary between the politically relevant and the apolitical is similarly impossible to define.

While recognizing this thorny problem of boundaries, it is still possible to say that certain roles and complexes of roles which we refer to as *institutions* are definitely political, and that certain others are definitely not. By looking then at the roles and institutions of the "gray area" in terms of their relationship to roles and institutions that are either clearly political or clearly not, we will come to understand their overall significance for the political process. It does not matter whether we decide that an interest group is a part of the political system or a politically relevant part of the environment—we will come to understand the political functions of interest groups through looking at their place in the process of politics. Thus, in our discussion of interest groups, we will point out that they perform both political and non-political activities. They are acting politically when their agents attempt to "lobby" Cabinet Ministers or bureaucrats, but they are acting apolitically when they publish a monthly news letter devoted to new methods and techniques which may assist their members in the day-to-day performance of their jobs. The key to the subsequent analysis of the Canadian political system is that it is to be viewed in terms of processes and not in terms of structures per se.

What follows is an overview or model of the political process which will be utilized as a framework for our detailed description of the Canadian system. This model has a purely pedagogical function. It should be used as a mental peg board on which to organize information. To use another metaphor, this chapter provides a rough map of the Canadian political process, without which the subsequent masses of information might be but an array of disjointed facts. Later chapters can be regarded as the "real world" topography which is rather imperfectly represented and over-simplified on our map.

GOVERNMENT AS A SYSTEM: AN INFORMATION FLOW MODEL

For the political system to be responsive to a changing environment, and for it to be able to affect changes in that environment, there must be a two-way flow of communication. This communication takes the form of information flow referred to as *input*, *output* and *feedback*.[13] These categories of information flow are illustrated in Figure 1-1.

Input An input is an incoming communication between the political system and the environment. One basic class of input is the *demand* input. This takes the form of information indicating to the political decision makers that a certain allocation or reallocation of resources is needed. In one sense demands can be perceived in the literal sense of the word—firmly stated requests by interested parties for allocative outputs which will be to their advantage. At the local level, the request by a developer for a re-zoning bylaw would be such a demand; at the national level, a request by the Canadian Manufacturers' Association for a reduction in

[13]The terminology utilized here is that of David Easton. See: *A Systems Analysis of Political Life*.

Figure 1-1

AN INFORMATION FLOW MODEL

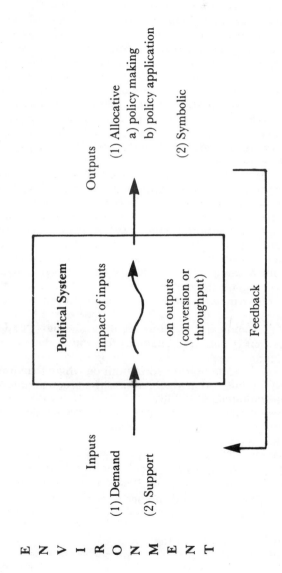

Adapted from David Easton, *A Systems Analysis of Political Life*, Chapter 1.

the level of corporate income tax would be another. Demand inputs can also be information actively sought by the political decision makers regarding the need for certain allocations. The essential characteristic is that there is an input of information which leads the political decision makers to consider making an output.

A second class of incoming communication between the system and the environment is the *support* input. A support input is information which indicates a positive orientation towards the system; such inputs function as a barometer which tells the political decision makers in the system whether or not the members of the society are satisfied with the system's performance. If there is an indication that the public is withdrawing its support, the political decision makers will attempt to alleviate the situation by making new allocative decisions. If the system continues to lose support, it is said to be in a situation of *stress*, which, if not relieved, can ultimately lead to its breakup.

There is often a difficulty in conceptualizing support for the system as an input, for it exists only in the form of attitudes or orientations toward the system held by persons in its environment. The Canadian political system employs a number of mechanisms to gauge the level of support. Elections, party policy conventions, field offices in various government departments, the receipt of briefs from interest groups, the monitoring of demonstrations, and the use of public opinion polls are all techniques to facilitate support inputs.

We have stated that the withdrawal of support, if left unchecked, could lead to the breakup of the political system. That statement must now be qualified. There are three objects or aspects of the political system towards which one can give support. The basic object of support is the *political community*, or the society itself. In the case of the Canadian system, for instance, the political community is the Canadian "nation" and its significance is that it permits Canadians to identify themselves as politically "other" than the rest of the world. Support for the political community involves the attitude that the social unit on which the political system is built is a viable one—that there is indeed a true community and not merely an artificial or coerced unity.

A second fundamental object of support is the *regime*. The regime is the set of structures, norms and values which define the form of the state. It not only sets broad system goals and defines the limits of legitimate governmental activity, but it also provides the institutional mechanisms and the "rules of the game" of politics in a given country. In Canada the regime is composed of our political institutional arrangements such as federalism, parliamentary government, and cabinet responsibility. Support for the regime involves the belief that the values implicit in the particular form of political system are good.

Finally, the *authorities* of the system can be an object of support as well. Support for the authorities means support for the individuals occupying the positions or roles of the political system—the incumbents to whom we have been referring as the political decision makers.

For a society to be stable, it is important that support for the political community and the regime be sustained at a relatively high level. If there is a withdrawal of support for the political community, one of the results can be separation of the dissatisfied section. For example, separatism in the Province of Quebec represents a withdrawal of support for the political community of Canada by some of its members. Unless the Canadian political system can produce outputs which will maintain the support of the Québecois for the Canadian political community, there is a strong possibility that Quebec will break away from Canada and set up a separate political system. Similarly, if there is withdrawal of support for the regime, the result can be the destruction of or the radical alteration of the existing system. The Communist Party of Canada, for instance, accepts the Canadian political community but rejects the liberal democratic form of the regime. This party would like to see the present regime supplanted by one similar to that of the Soviet Union.

While the stability and persistence of a political system depends on the retention of support for the political community and the regime, in liberal democratic systems the regime explicitly provides institutional devices for expressing the withdrawal of support from the authorities. In fact, such systems could be said to encourage the periodic withdrawal of support for one set of authorities and their replacement by another set through elections.

Outputs The basic form of outgoing communication from the system to the environment is the *allocative* output. This takes the form of information which produces allocations of resources in the environment. Allocative outputs, however, are of two basic types. First there are general statements known as *laws*. Laws state "who gets what, when and how" in general terms. Second, there are outputs which apply the laws to individuals in society—statements which tell individual X how the law affects him and what his rights and obligations are *vis-à-vis* that law. It should be noted at this stage that these two basic types of allocative output correspond roughly to the more traditional classification of governmental functions: the first kind of allocative output corresponds to *rule making*, the second to *rule application*, which includes the executive and adjudicative functions.[14]

There is a second form of output of the political system which is not allocative in any direct sense. This is an output of information which is aimed at educating, informing, or propagandizing, and which can be styled a *symbolic output*. The usual function of symbolic outputs is to communicate information about the outputs of the system to those who might be affected by them. In this sense symbolic outputs tell us about new laws which must be obeyed, about new opportunities created for us through government policies, and about the day-to-day activities of government that may be of interest to us. However, another important function of symbolic outputs is to increase support for the system without having to make any new allocative decisions. In this sense the government attempts to con-

[14]See: Chapters 5 and 6.

vince us of the "goodness" and legitimacy of the system simply by extolling its virtues to us.

Feedback Once an allocative or symbolic decision is made there will normally be some sort of reaction to it from people in the environment. As time passes, it will become apparent whether or not the allocation has had the desired effect and the decision makers in the system can modify their future decision making accordingly. This process is known as feedback. In a primitive system this is a simple process, because direct personal contact is possible between decision makers and the environment. Indeed, in a simple system the decision maker leaves his meeting and becomes a major part of the social environment. In Canada the decision maker also has roles—such as his role in his family—which make him a part of the environment, and he will have some limited opportunity to gain feedback in that way. However, our political system relies primarily on those parts of its institutions which operate on the "input side" of the process to gather information about the impact of its policies on society.

INSIDE THE SYSTEM: POLICY MAKING

While we have briefly described how the political system interacts with its environment, we have so far left untouched what is really the core concern for the political scientist: the *conversion process*,[15] whereby the decision makers in the political system decide upon outputs. The resolution of conflicts that arise over the distribution of resources is the operational goal of the political system, and the activities which directly contribute to the attainment of that goal are the central process of politics. The part of the process which is internal to the system is policy making, and it forms the dominant focus of this book.

However, in selecting policy making as our central theme we must recognize that other processes of politics have great relevance as well. For the political system effectively to pursue its operational goal of conflict resolution it must persist over time. In other words, while the attainment of operational goals is the "job" government does on a day-to-day basis, there are functions related directly to the maintenance of the system which must be performed first.

Goal Attainment and System Maintenance In one sense, the maintenance of the system is very closely related to its effectiveness in attaining operational goals, for if the "clients"[16] of the system are not

---

[15]In Fig. 1-1 this is described as the impact of input on outputs. It is the process of converting demands into outputs which are directed at meeting those demands. It is also sometimes referred to as "throughput."

[16]The term "clientele" has been developed and utilized most in the literature of administrative theory and policy analysis, although the concept is implicit in the notion of legitimacy. See: L.C. Freeman, *et al.*, "Role of Community and Clientele Leaders: Identifying Community Leaders in Decision-Making"; B.L. Bible and E.J. Brown, "Role of Community and Clientele Leaders: Coopting Clientele in

satisfied with the standard of service being performed for them they will not continue to support it. In this way the legitimacy of a system is achieved at least in part through effective goal attainment. Similarly, if the system is to continue to perform its allocative function effectively, it will be necessary from time to time for the system to initiate structural changes and sometimes even to redefine goals[17] in response to environmental changes. It is the adaptive mechanisms of a political system that permit it to persist even when faced with large scale social and economic changes or major shifts in the predominant value system of a population.[18]

Other aspects of the process of system maintenance, however, are linked less closely to policy making. For instance, because the political system is goal directed, the persons who occupy roles must be induced to engage in activity which is directed at the attainment of system goals. Because the goals of the system will likely not be identical to the personal goals of the occupants of system roles, the actors within the system must be made willing to put off the satisfaction of their immediate preferences in the interest of working towards the attainment of system goals. This *integrative function* is a critical dimension of system maintenance and it is achieved through a number of processes related to political recruitment, socialization and the manipulation of material and non-material rewards. All of these facets of system maintenance will be discussed in the chapters that follow.

To summarize, our aim is to look at political institutions and processes primarily in terms of their relationship to goal attainment. Because goal attainment activity within the context of the political system amounts to policy making, that will be our central concern. While it is our inten-

Decision-Making"; and R.G. Mason, "Securing Clientele Acceptance and Cooperation"—all articles in F.J. Lyden, *et al.* (eds.) *Policies, Decisions and Organization*, (Appleton-Century-Crofts, New York, 1969), pp. 66–87, 214–228.

[17]While Roberto Michels is normally credited with origination of the concept of *goal displacement*, there is a large body of literature today which has developed the concept and applied it to specific organizations. This phenomenon is discussed briefly and clearly in A. Etzioni, *Modern Organizations*, (Prentice–Hall Inc., Englewood Cliffs, 1964), pp. 10–14. See also R.J. Merton, *Social Theory and Social Structure*, (the Free Press of Glencoe, 1957), pp. 197 ff. and P. Selznick "An Approach to a Theory of Bureaucracy", *American Sociological Review*, Vol. 8, No. 1, 1943, pp. 47–54. The redefinition of goals in the interest of the survival of the organization is elaborated in a case study of the Salvation Army by S.D. Clark. See: *Church and Sect in Canada*, (University of Toronto Press, Toronto, 1948).

[18]Note here that there are some value parameters beyond which a system may not adapt without becoming a new system entirely. The maintenance of these is referred to as "pattern maintenance" and is described as protecting ". . .the basic ordering principles of the system with regard to both the value of such patterns and the commitment of system units to them. . . ." T. Parsons, "The Political Aspect of Social Structure and Process", in D. Easton (ed.), *Varieties of Political Theory*, (Prentice–Hall Inc., Englewood Cliffs, 1966), p. 105. In other words, whereas adaptation is the dynamic element in the system, pattern maintenance is the conservative element. The "raw material" of pattern maintenance can be found in the fundamental values of the members of the society, and/or the "clientele" of the system.

tion neither to ignore nor to de-emphasize the processes of politics related to the maintenance of the system, these will be viewed primarily in terms of their relationship to effective policy making.

The Policy Concept A *policy* can best be defined as a course of action that the authorities of the political system have decided should become an output. In other words a policy is the intention to produce a certain allocative output, and the process of policy making involves deciding what that output should be. However, while such a definition is simple enough on the surface it includes a number of implications that need elaboration.

In the first place, it is possible to think of policy and the process of policy making within the context of any organization, not just the political system. It is quite reasonable to speak of "company policy" and "party policy" without implying any connection to the political system, and if the structural focus is specified, the above definition of policy is compatible with all of these usages of the term.[19] However, unless otherwise specified, the term "policy" within the context of this book will refer only to public policy or governmental policy.

The second implication of this definition of policy is that the policy process consists of decision-making activity. Because political decision making is in the end the prerogative of individual minds acting in complex organizations, in order to understand the policy process completely it would be necessary to consider social-psychological factors as well as a host of influences that arise because of the organizational context within which decisions are made. But our concern is more with the question of which people occupying which political roles have the power to make various kinds of political decisions than with the process whereby a human mind in the organizational setting perceives a problem, looks for alternative solutions to the problem, and then chooses one of the alternatives.[20] This is not to assert that the social-psychological and organizational imperatives are not vital, but rather that they are too complex to be discussed extensively in a basic text.

Finally, this definition of policy recognizes that there is a distinction between "policy" and "output". While the outputs of a political system are always a reflection of policy decisions taken within the system, the conversion of a policy to an output often requires formal steps which legitimize or render authoritative the internal decisions. For example, a bill passed by parliament does not become a legislative output until it has

[19]"Company policy," for instance, may be viewed as decisions by the people who occupy authority positions within a company that a certain course of action should be expressed as an organizational "output."

[20]Herbert Simon refers to these stages of decision making as "intelligence activity," "design activity," and "choice activity." See: *The Scope of Automation: For Men and Management*, (Harper & Row, New York, 1965), pp. 53–54. J.G. March and H.A. Simon, *Organizations*, (John Wiley & Sons Ltd., New York, 1958), chs. 6–7. We do make extensive use of organization theory when discussing cabinets and the bureaucracy in Canada.

been assented to by the Governor General, proclaimed, and printed in the Canada Gazette. Because "being the government" in Canada to a large extent means having control over these formal legitimizing procedures, the conversion of government policy to outputs is a routine matter. The decision to employ those procedures is in reality the final step in the policy process; what occurs subsequently is virtually automatic and not strictly a part of policy making. Thus, while we will occasionally speak of "outputs" and "policies" as synonymous terms, and while it would be rare empirically for one to occur without the other, it must be recognized that there is an analytical distinction.

There have been many attempts to define policy in more restrictive terms than ours. For instance, policy decisions are frequently viewed as those more properly taken by politicians than by administrators or bureaucrats. In this view a distinction is made between "political" decisions, which involve "policy," and "administrative" decisions, which do not.[21] While the distinction between policy making and policy implementation or between deciding and doing may be analytically appealing, empirically the distinction very quickly breaks down. The decision to pass a piece of major legislation may be more important than the decision of a customs official to inspect or not to inspect someone's luggage, but each of these activities does involve making a governmental decision. To say that one process is policy and the other is not is to introduce an artificial distinction.

While it is artificial to attempt to classify "political" decisions as policy and administrative decisions as some lower species, it is useful to classify policy into different types. The simplest yet one of the most useful classifications is to divide outputs into those generated by the legislative process, those by the executive or administrative process and those by the judicial process. By describing legislative, executive and adjudicative decisions by the common term "policy," we can avoid a good deal of semantic debate about what is a policy, while still being able to relate each type of output back to a particular, analytically distinct process.

These three types of process and output are themselves very closely interrelated. Both the executive and adjudicative outputs depend upon the preexistence *laws*, with the former having the effect of implementing and the latter of interpreting them. Consequently, there is a certain primacy about legislation which has caused the lawmaking process to be viewed traditionally as the "master" allocative function of government. In conformity with this, our analysis of the Canadian political system will focus primarily on the decision-making processes which result in the formation of legislation and secondarily on the processes which result in the executive and judicial implementation of law.

Our analytical focus on the legislative policy process is not intended to minimize the importance of executive processes.[22] Because the

[21]Peter Drucker speaks of a split between the "deciders and the doers" in the political system and sees a clear delineation of these functions as a solution to some of the problems of the "age of discontinuity." Peter Drucker, *The Age of Discontinuity*, (Harper & Row, New York, 1969), p. 233.

[22]The judicial process will be discussed in a separate chapter. While judicial deci-

effectiveness of the political system in meeting the demands of a diverse clientele may to a large extent depend upon how the vast tax revenues of the system are spent, executive decision making within the political system, particularly that related to the preparation of the budget and the expenditure of public funds, has an increasingly important influence on the impact of government on society. Over 90% of the money spent by the Canadian government each year is spent on already existing programs and hence is allocated primarily through executive and administrative decisions. Thus such decision making must be viewed as an important type of policy making. Nevertheless, because each of the continuing programs was generated originally by new legislation and because the key issues of politics today still involve new policies and not the ongoing ones, our main focus must be the process whereby decisions about new legislation are taken.

The Policy Process in a Technological Age

The theory of parliamentary democracy posits an ideal system of government where legislative outputs prevail over all other outputs of the system and where the power to legislate is vested in an elected parliament. Furthermore, the executive power in a perfect parliamentary system resides with the Prime Minister and his cabinet, who are in turn responsible directly to parliament. Thus, in an ideal parliamentary democracy, ultimate power rests with the people who elect the parliament, which in turn controls the Prime Minister and his cabinet. The administrative arm of the government, the bureaucracy, is responsible directly to the cabinet and indirectly, through the budgetary process, to parliament. The bureaucracy is responsible for the implementation or application of the laws passed by parliament, and such responsibilities are totally divorced from the legislative process.

While it seems unlikely that this theoretical version of parliamentary democracy was ever a fact, it is part of the conventional wisdom that there was a "Golden Age" of parliamentary democracy when reality conformed much better to the ideal than it does today. One major factor associated with this trend away from the hypothetical ideal of parliamentary democracy is technological change, although in large part it is not technology but the social and economic consequences of technology which have altered the policy process most startlingly.

Technological advances precipitated industrialization which has been the single most important variable in determining the nature of modern societies. The movement from a pre-industrial or agricultural society produced social discontinuities which were so great that existing mechanisms of social adaptation could not cope. Industrialization, for instance, created in Canada the phenomenon of the employable unemployed. The problem of welfare within the pre-industrial system had concerned the care of those unable to find employment because of physical or mental disability, a problem which could be dealt with by agencies such as the church and local charities. With the massive unemployment that resulted from economic fluctuations in industrial society, the traditional agencies

sions are important, it is analytically simple to view them as auxiliary and subsequent to policy making, rather than as a form of policy making.

were no longer capable of carrying the burden of welfare. By default, more than anything else, government was forced to step into the field of income redistribution and social insurance in order to alleviate the intense economic hardships of depression and unemployment.

Similarly, because an industrial society is complex and very sensitive to the activities of individuals who control large amounts of capital, economic stability can be maximized only if there is a degree of control and planning of the economy. Governments were the natural structures in society to step in and regulate the economic system, with anti-combines, labour relations, fair employment practices and other legislation. The "unseen hand" of Adam Smith did not effectively keep the economy in a state of equilibrium, and government stepped in to attempt to restore the balance.

Technology not only made industrialization possible in the first instance, but through development in the field of economics also made possible the intervention of government as a planner and regulator of the industrial economy:

> Even in the most conservative of the industrial states, technology has steadily expanded governmental activity in the fields once left exclusively to the private entrepreneurs. . . .[23]

Technology and industrialization thus stimulated a change in the role of the political system in society. Where governments had once been very passive and negative, they assumed positive and active roles in society. Where the public attitude to the role of government had once been that the government that governed least was the best form of government, the political system was now expected as a matter of course to perform broad regulatory and redistributive functions heretofore left to economic and social mechanisms.

The immediate implications of this changing role of government for the political system were three. First, the number of outputs of government increased because the role of government expanded. There has been a linear increase in the quantity of governmental activity which means that the number of policies considered in any given year will normally be greater than in the year before.[24]

Second, the complexity of legislation increased enormously after the turn of the century. The amount of detail required in legislation that spells out the procedures and formulae in a national pension plan, for instance, is much greater than that required in legislation to amend a criminal code, and an increasing percentage of legislation deals with subjects like pension plans.

Finally, not only have governmental outputs increased in number and complexity, but their content has increased in technological sophistication as well. Policies dealing with subjects such as defense research and

---

[23]E.G. Mesthene, *Technological Change*, (Harvard University Press, Cambridge, 1970), pp. 64–65, and V.C. Ferkiss, *Technological Man*, (Braziller, New York, 1969), p. 177.
[24]V.C. Ferkiss, *Technological Man*, p. 178.

taxation must of necessity be highly technical, reflecting as they do the most advanced levels of knowledge in the given field. The combination of increased volume, complexity and technological sophistication of governmental activity has made a high level of specialization and technical expertise necessary for public policy making. This has had important consequences for the ideal of parliamentary democracy.

In the first place, parliament, being neither specialized nor highly expert, is disqualified in practical terms from taking a central part in the legislative policy process. In part, the law-making power in the Canadian political system has shifted to the cabinet, for it is this body which has acquired and retains the *de facto* authority to set goals or establish priorities for governmental action. Through party discipline and through its access to the expertise within the various government departments, the cabinet member is placed in a position of considerable advantage over the backbench M.P.

In part, however, the policy function has moved out of the cabinet as well and into the hands of the thousands of experts throughout the public service. These experts are entrusted with the responsibility of tendering policy advice to the ministers. The power to advise, which sounds harmless enough, becomes a very real political power when the advice given is highly technical in nature and when the man being advised is not himself an expert. In Peter Drucker's terms, knowledge has become power; it is the "central capital" of modern society:

> . . .scientists and scholars are no longer merely "on tap" they are "on top". . . .They largely determine what policies can be considered seriously in such crucial areas as defence or economics. . . .[25]

While in a formal sense, the power to decide policy still resides with political office holders such as the Prime Minister and the cabinet, this is in many ways *positional* power. That is to say, it derives from the role an individual occupies and is only secondarily affected by the character and ability of the individual himself. Because rational decision making in a modern system necessitates the use of specialized and technical information which the politician does not possess, the real power that accrues to him through his position is significantly reduced. As Jacques Ellul has pointed out:

> The task of the expert is to furnish the politician with information and estimates on which he can base a decision. . . .When the expert has effectively performed his task of pointing out the necessary ways and means, there is generally *only one* logical and admissible solution. The politician will then find himself obliged to choose between the technician's solution, which is the only reasonable one and other solutions which he can indeed try out at his own peril, but which are not reasonable. . . .In fact, *the politician no longer has any real choice; decision follows automatically from the preparatory technical labours*. . . .[26]

While the above generalization likely applies fairly accurately to

[25]Drucker, Peter, *The Age of Discontinuity*, (Harper & Row, New York, 1969), p. 372.
[26]E.G. Mesthene, *Technological Change, op. cit.*, pp. 64–65.

the Canadian situation, the fact remains that cabinet ministers and the Prime Minister himself will from time to time make decisions which go contrary to the advice of their technical hired hands. Whether they are inspired by sincere doubts about the validity of the advice tendered, by political opportunism, or by simple whim, our politicians still possess the positional power to make policy decisions against the advice of technicians. However, for the most part technical advice to our political leaders does have a profound influence on their decisions.

The outcome of the shift in policy-making power from those who occupy political authority roles to those who possess technical knowledge or information is that the institutions that concentrate expertise will tend to dominate the institutions, such as parliament, that do not. *Prima facie*, there is no reason why concentrations of expertise in non-governmental locales such as industry, the universities and pressure groups could not provide important sources of policy influence to compete with the governmental bureaucracy. In some instances they do. However, ". . .the development and the application of technology seem necessarily to require large scale and complex social concentration. . . ."[27] which occurs most commonly in government. There are few if any non-governmental organizations which control sufficient resources to gather expertise and technological information on a scale that would permit them to compete effectively with the governmental bureaucracy. Thus, in terms of the public policy process in Canada, the conclusion must be not only that power has shifted from the political to the technical level, but also that it has shifted within government rather than to non-governmental institutions.[28]

Public servants can also influence governmental outputs more directly through the instrument of delegated power. It is frequently necessary, because of the complexity of the matters being dealt with by government, for legislation to leave a great deal of discretion to the public servants who implement it. In other words, the power to work out the details of a particular government program is often delegated to the administrative agency charged with the responsibility for administering it in such a way that the administrators become, in a limited way, legislators. This presents serious problems of political control. The bureaucrats, unlike the politicians, are not elected. Perhaps the most effective way of preventing the abuse of delegated power today is through judicial process, which provides remedies through civil action for an individual who is harmed by misuse of administrative discretion.

The foregoing paints a picture quite different from the traditional one of a supreme parliament, responsible to an informed and active electorate, making policy on the basis of a grand concept of "national interest." Nevertheless, while the policy process in the positive state does not match our classical image of parliamentary democracy, the system does seem to work after a fashion. Furthermore, it is important to emphasize

---

[27]J. Ellul, *Technological Society*, (Alfred A. Knopf, Inc., New York), pp. 258-9.
[28]For an opposite point of view see M. Lamontagne, "The Influence of the Politician", *Canadian Public Administration*, 11, No. 3, pp. 263-71.

that there is no blame to be assigned for this shift in power within our system. Power is moving from parliament to the cabinet and from the cabinet to the bureaucracy simply because the environment of the political system is such that experts in large information-gathering organizations are the ones most likely to find solutions to current problems. The bureaucrats and technocrats have not deliberately wrested policy-making power from the hands of those who should rightfully possess it. There has been no *coup d'état!*

THE POLICY PROCESS IN CANADA: A MODEL

The Initiation of Policies The policy process has been defined as internal to the political system. It is the process whereby persons "inside" the system decide what should become system outputs. A distinction has already been made between policy and output, but little has been said about the "input side" of the process. The authorities do not make policy decisions on a random or whimsical basis (even though this sometimes appears to be the case). The policy process is triggered by information from outside the system, specifically by information about problems which can be solved by governmental action. Hence, given that the origins of public policy lie in information about environmental circumstances, the process whereby that information comes to the attention of the policy makers is the first stage in the formation of policy.

The key problem in initiating or triggering the policy process is in finding channels through which demand inputs can be brought to the attention of men occupying policy roles. Points of access occur naturally where people within the system are paying attention to what is going on outside; in order to insure continued attentiveness, MPs and cabinet ministers are subject to periodic evaluation through the institutional device of elections. Institutions such as political parties and pressure groups have come to play a key role in rationalizing and articulating to parliament and cabinet the wants and needs of people in the environment. However, given the diversity of problems that exist in modern societies and given the overall movement of decision-making power from the political institutions to bureaucratic ones, newer, less traditional channels of access to the political system have developed at the bureaucratic level.

Many government departments have as their organizational *raison d'être* a specific clientele. For instance, the Department of Agriculture exists to serve agricultural interests and to solve agricultural problems, and the Department of Veterans' Affairs exists to serve the interest of ex-servicemen. The survival and growth of these departments depends almost entirely on their success in representing the interests of their clienteles. The more problems they can define and begin to solve, the greater will be their budgetary allocations and manpower establishment. As a result clientele-oriented departments constantly seek environmental information in an effort to anticipate the needs and problems of their clientele. Because of this bureaucratic attentiveness, important channels of access to the policy process have been created within the public service.

Today even large interest groups focus their attention on bureaucratic channels, frequently by seeking the establishment of a separate department that will serve their clientele. Close symbiotic relationships exist today between organizations such as the Canadian Legion or the Canadian Federation of Agriculture and departments such as Veteran's Affairs or Agriculture. While bureaucratic channels of access have not completely replaced the traditional ones through parliament and cabinet, they are often more effective for policy initiation. Because so many bureaucratic agencies are clientele oriented, and because they possess the expertise that makes them more effective than political institutions in ferreting out problems among their clientele, the political channels are increasingly in competition with the bureaucratic ones.

Nor is this situation confined to the federal government. There are similar points of access at the provincial level in Canada. The trends there are similar to those at the federal level: decision-making power generally has been moving from the political to the bureaucratic institutions, with the consequent increase in the importance of provincial departments as channels of policy initiation. The trend is more marked in larger provinces than in smaller ones, but it exists everywhere.

The Establishment of Policy Priorities The inflow of information from the environment is a necessary condition for policy making. If that flow of information should cease for some reason, the policy process would grind to a halt. In the modern political system, however, the central problem is not in garnering information but in coping with vast amounts of it. The problems of modern societies are so numerous and so complex that the greatest threat to the stability of the system lies in information overload. The first internal step in the policy process therefore involves weeding out, reducing, and ordering in importance the vast quantity of information with which the priority setters are constantly bombarded.[29]

The core institutions or the key authorities involved in the establishment of policy priorities in the Canadian system are the Cabinet, the Prime Minister and federal-provincial conferences. It is the cabinet that possesses the formal authority to set the broadest directions of public policy. Because of the vast bulk of inputs, however, much of the initial reduction of policy demands and the preliminary weeding out of information must be prformed elsewhere. The channels of input themselves act as "gatekeepers" in filtering policy information even before it comes to the attention of the cabinet and PM. Pressure groups, for instance, establish priorities among the objectives of their membership in order to maximize policy influence. Not all of the needs of the entire clientele of an interest group can be met simultaneously, so the organizational leaders must decide

[29]Victor Thompson speaks of "the knowledge explosion" and of "information affluence". See: *Bureaucracy and Innovation*, (University of Alabama, 1969), pp. 1–6.

which policy objectives are most important and which, within a given time, are achievable. Similarly, a clientele-oriented government department must limit and order the policy demands of its clientele; in doing so it reduces the number of choices facing the political decision makers.

At a point closer to the cabinet and PM still more reduction and ordering of information occurs. The "gatekeepers" here are found among the advisory staff of the PM and cabinet, located primarily in the Prime Minister's Office (PMO) and to a lesser degree in Privy Council Office (PCO). While the PM and his cabinet can bypass the PMO and PCO in seeking information, most information flowing from the bureaucracy and interest groups is in fact filtered through these offices. By deciding which information that they receive is important enough to be passed on to their cabinet "masters", by summarizing information so as to brief the ministers, and by helping to set the agenda for cabinet and cabinet committee meetings, the people in the PMO and PCO play a significant role in determining what policy demands will even be considered by the priority setters. However, whether gleaned independently, or filtered through the various information "gatekeepers", a great many policy ideas ultimately do come to the attention of the cabinet; it is these that make up the raw material of cabinet-level priority decisions.

The initial cabinet-level decision in the process is whether to reject a policy idea outright or to consider it further. For those deemed important enough to be considered further, the cabinet must then decide which should be dealt with first and which government agency should be given the responsibility for formulating specific operational alternatives. The rejection of a policy idea outright can be considered as a negative output of the system and can have important consequences not only in terms of support for the system but also in terms of future inflow of information.

Most policy decisions at this stage will inevitably be negative ones. Although the number of demands being made on the system is potentially limitless, the resources of the system are severely limited. These resources, calculated in terms of human energy and finance, must be parsimoniously allocated to a very few policy suggestions that are deemed most "worthy." These negative priority decisions are often not noticed by the media or the public but they are important since they are effectively the same as opting for the status quo.[30]

While these cabinet-level choices as to what should be done and when may seem relatively simple, given the reduction and ordering that has already taken place, they may not be so. Because of the complex and technical nature of most subjects of governmental concern today, further information is usually necessary, first in order to establish value criteria and standards and second, to measure the various choices against those standards. This information can be examined within a four-fold classification system.

    i) The first type is *normative information*. This involves knowledge

[30]See P. Bachrach and M.S. Baratz, *Power and Poverty*, (Oxford University Press, New York, 1970), pp. 39–51.

about the basic values of the system, which set the broadest parameters for governmental action. Such information will be possessed by virtually all participants in the policy process as part of their personal value systems, acquired through the process of socialization. It is this type of information that provides vague criteria such as justice, human dignity, freedom, and equality, against which people in modern western democracies automatically measure all policies. The problem with normative information is that it sets only very broad limits on governmental activity. Thus, for example, if someone suggests that we exterminate the Jews, the basic values of Canadian policy makers will prohibit consideration of such a policy alternative. However, if someone suggests nationalizing automobile insurance, the answer is not implicit in a set of shared values but must be weighed against less fundamental criteria.

Normative information is not drawn from specialized institutions but from the shared values of virtually all Canadians. This means that at this level of policy determination, the political authorities in the Cabinet and Parliament do possess real decision-making power. This is more an apparent than a real power, however, since such fundamental decisions arise only very infrequently.

ii) *Political information* is the second type of information necessary in establishing policy priorities. This is information concerning the political feasibility or advisability of undertaking various policies. The criteria that must be employed in measuring the political advisability of a policy are shaped by the political institutions themselves. Thus, in the Canadian system, which features elections with a "universal" franchise, the criterion is simply how many votes will a policy ultimately win and lose for the current political office holders.

The main institutions tendering political advice to the cabinet are the Prime Minister's Office and the political party organization. By monitoring information flowing from political parties, pressure groups, the press and the provincial governments, the people in the PMO and party organizations keep themselves attuned to political developments across the country. The bureaucracy also pays considerable attention to political information, for senior bureaucrats are well aware that there is no point in tendering politically unrealistic advice to the cabinet and Prime Minister. Political information is very often intuitive information based on the "gut" feelings of politicians or senior officials, but more recently social science techniques of data gathering have begun to replace at least some of the more intuitive methods used in the past.

iii) *Technical information* is that possessed by the line departments of the public service. These governmental technicians are called upon to advise the politicians of the technical feasibility of various possible policy suggestions and to make estimates of cost. While technical information may be available from non-governmental sources, at the level of cabinet decisions concerning broad policy priorities, the most significant competition for the federal departments will come from the provincial bureaucracies, through the provincial cabinets and senior bureaucrats.

iv) *Financial information* concerns the fundamental problem of funding governmental projects. When an estimate of the cost of undertaking a certain policy is provided by a line department, the financial advisors to the government, in the Department of Finance and the Treasury Board Secretariat, must provide information as to the financial feasibility of the suggested policy. In broad terms, the financial experts within the bureaucracy must advise the government of the day whether they can "afford" the suggested policy and whether implementing this policy will necessitate the increase of taxes or the cancellation of existing programs.

Having obtained political, technical and financial information about the policy proposal under consideration, the Cabinet must ultimately decide whether to act. When there is conflicting advice, the cabinet must make a choice. If the experts do not agree as to the feasibility of the policy suggestion, the most common response for the cabinet is simply not to act at all. The immediate effect here is the same as if a negative decision had been taken.

Another common response to conflicting technical information is for the cabinet to refer the matter to a specialized body for further study. Royal commissions and task forces can often provide a vehicle through which difficult decisions can be postponed, and at the same time new technical information can be gathered.

Perhaps the most common form of conflicting advice at the level of priority setting is that which occurs between political and technical information. In private, technocrats are very quick to accuse the politicians of "playing politics" when pet projects have been rejected. What often has happened, of course, is that their technical advice has been rejected because of competing advice from the "political technocrats." In that case, as Jacques Ellul points out,

> . . .the conflict is not between politicians and technicians, but among technicians of differing categories. . . .[31]

If the advice of the various categories of experts does point in generally the same direction, the cabinet will usually follow that advice. While it is always conceivable that a Prime Minister and cabinet can assert their positional power and refuse to heed advisors, most evidence indicates that Prime Ministers and cabinets do, with a few exceptions, act according to the advice of those with superior information.

Once a number of policy ideas is adopted by the cabinet, the next step is determining which of the policies should be tackled first. This decision is normally implicit in the advice from the technical, political and financial experts, and can be made without further information. Finally, the decision must be made as to who will formulate the specific alternatives for putting the policy idea into effect. In other words, the cabinet must decide which department or agency will take the responsibility for the next stage in the process, *policy formulation*.

The Formulation of Policy

Until this stage the concern has been with the broad directions of public policy rather than with the

[31]Ellul, *Technological Society*, p. 257.

specifics. At the formulation stage of the process the object is to narrow down the number of specific choices to a few "best" ones from which the final choice can be made.

There are two analytically separate steps in the formulation of policy alternatives. First, the myriad experts within the public service must design a few workable schemes; second, the politicians must choose the one that appears to be best.

Design activity[32] initially involves narrowing down the number of possible approaches to a workable few; this becomes the responsibility of the more senior "generalists" in a department, likely in consultation with other departments and possibly with other levels of government as well. Then, those few viable choices must be "fleshed out" through the activity of a great many technocrats often with very specialized expertise. In Galbraith's terms:

> . . .knowledge is brought to bear on the ultimate microfraction of the task; then on that in combination with some other fraction; then, on some further combination and thus on to final completion. . . .[33]

In this sense, only very broad direction is given at the more senior bureaucratic and ministerial levels. The bulk of the responsibility for the ultimate detail of policy resides with the many highly specialized technocrats at lower levels of the hierarchy. The end product, which may be presented after cabinet approval as a "White Paper," is produced incrementally as many individuals make small technical decisions.

Given the incremental nature of the process of policy design the choice of the politician is seriously curtailed. Departmental proposals have been produced through a hierarchy of decisions, beginning with the most highly specialized at the middle levels and proceeding to ever more general ones at the higher levels. At each higher level of decision making, there is less choice than at the previous one, because there is proportionately less information transmitted with the proposals. By the time the politician, who is at the top of the hierarchy, comes to make his "choice" it often will be simply to accept or reject the incrementally generated and monolithic conclusion of "the department." The choice, in other words, will be determined largely through the design process itself.

Politicians sometimes appear to reject "irrationally" a detailed policy proposal that has been meticulously produced by the technocrats in a department. Normally, however, policies are significantly altered or rejected at this stage only because of new political circumstances. But while a policy must continue to meet important political criteria and while political or budgetary circumstances may temporarily stall the process, in most cases some form of output is inevitable once the formulation process has commenced.

The complicated process we have spelled out here is, in fact, a simplified version of reality; at both the priority and the formulation stages of the policy process innumerable complications can occur. The most perva-

[32]H.A. Simon, *op. cit.*
[33]J.K. Galbraith, *The New Industrial State*, (Houghton Mifflin, Boston, 1969), p. 13.

sive result from the unavoidable lack of clarity in the jurisdictional boundaries between the federal and the provincial governments and among departments within those governments. As we discuss the policy process in more detail we will see that the Canadian political system has developed an array of devices to handle these complications as well as those already mentioned here.

The Refinement of Policy At this stage in the policy process, the detailed policy proposal formulated by the bureaucracy and approved formally by the cabinet must be translated into "legalese." The technical details of the policy proposal must be put into the language of legislative outputs. This task is performed by legislative draftsmen in the Department of Justice, after which the draft legislation must be introduced in Parliament as a bill.

The basic problem at this stage of the process is to insure that the legislative proposal accurately reflects the aims of the priority setters and that there are no ambiguities in the bill that might lead to administrative problems in its implementation. It is the standing committees in the House of Commons that play the major role in refining the legislation before it is converted to output. As well, at this time, through discussion and through opposition probing the government is forced to justify its policy publicly. The legislation is thus legitimized by receiving the "seal of approval" of the people's representatives.

Because of party discipline and because of the complex and technical nature of most legislation, the MP can usually have little impact on the substance of policy at this stage. Faced with a proposal that has taken years of full-time attention on the part of perhaps a few hundred specialists of different types, the overworked MP, who is himself not an expert in the field in question, and who must deal with a large number of proposals per session, is unlikely to be able to make substantive criticisms that cannot be answered by the government and its advisors. There has never been a piece of government legislation defeated by the House of Commons in a majority situation, and even with a minority government, government legislation has only been defeated on rare occasions. While the opposition may stall government legislation temporarily because of their control over a considerable amount of time in the House of Commons, this does not happen often. Furthermore, even granting that a parliament could in legal terms reject a government policy proposal, the power here is only negative; the initiative to introduce legislation still resides with the Cabinet.

Limitations of the Model Any model abstracts from reality. Accordingly, it distorts some of the features of reality. One weakness of the policy model posited above is that it attempts to represent a complex and multidimensional process in what is admittedly a linear framework. The "stages" in the policy process are established arbitrarily. In the real world formulation begins while priorities are being established, new policy ideas emerge in the process of formulating other ones, and governmental priorities occasionally change so drastically during the process of formulation that a policy proposal may die at an advanced stage in its development. Government and, by implication, the governmental policy process is so complex that it cannot accurately be described in such simple terms. A second major weakness of the policy model is that it fails to deal with the policy process in multi-jurisdictional systems, a failing which we will attempt to cure as we discuss the process in more detail.

But though our model oversimplifies, it does direct our attention to certain patterns which can be observed in the real world. Most of the phenomena we have described as clustering in "stages" do occur at some point in the evolution of any policy. To understand the whole panorama at once would be an impossible task. It is quite simply convenient to view logically related activities as occurring at distinct stages. We are distorting reality in order to understand it! The rest of this text is, in effect, an elaboration of this model in the direction of greater reality.

Part 1
The Cultural and
Demographic
Environment

2
Environment:
Social and Economic Context

The summer of 1973 was a period of rapidly rising food prices in Canada and throughout the western world. The price of steak rose from $1.29 a pound a year earlier to as high as $2.49, and hamburger meat rose from 69¢ to $1.09 a pound. The price of wheat more than doubled in a short time, and the price of a loaf of bread rose by over 33 per cent. In the same summer, gasoline which had been available for 40¢ a gallon at discount service stations in June rose to 55¢ in September to over 60¢ in December. Canada—and indeed all of the western world—was caught in the intitial grip of a spiralling inflation. Under circumstances such as these the cry for the government to do something grew louder as individual Canadians felt more and more pinched by the inflation.

But an inflationary situation is not bad for everyone. The farmer felt that he was finally getting something approaching a just return for his labour. Unemployment, while not low by historical standards, was declining. The economy was booming and Canada's trade picture had seldom looked better. The oil companies were showing record profits and both the federal and provincial governments were enjoying record levels of revenues produced by rapidly growing incomes.

For government, the boom and inflation of 1973 produced sets of demands which were typically difficult to reconcile. The farmers wanted food price rises to continue and so did grocery store operators. The housewife did not. The oil exploration companies were all for higher oil prices. The motorist and home owner were not. Unemployment was low, but the overheated economy might race too fast and eventually fall on its face in a disastrous recession or depression. People on fixed incomes were suffering, but businessmen were wreathed in smiles as they looked at sales figures. How could a government reconcile the conflicting demands and pressures? And what could it realistically be expected to do in view of its firm belief that high food prices were the result of world-wide shortages brought on by several years of unusual climatic conditions and growing demands from developing countries?

The problems faced by Canadian governments in 1973 illustrate the type of influence the physical and economic environment can have on the political process. The demands generated by the Canadian people in

1973 forced several policy responses from the federal government. The domestic price of wheat was pegged (to keep food prices down) while a base price was guaranteed (to keep farm incomes up should wheat surpluses develop again). Old age security payments and family allowances were raised (to help poorer families cope with price rises). A "two-price" policy on oil was established (which ensured that Canada's relatively low-priced crude oil would not all be exported to U.S. markets) while much of the revenue derived from the export levy involved was returned to Alberta (to soothe that province's ruffled feelings). A Food Prices Review Board was established (to please the consumers), but it was left largely toothless (so as not to alienate food producers and distributors). Beef exports were restricted until beef prices began to fall then imports were restricted when they threatened to fall too far.

The cynic will suggest that in trying to please everyone, the federal government pleased no one, and that its raft of self-contradictory policies was bound to founder. The optimist will assert that the problem was alleviated somewhat and that no government did a better job than Canada's. We need not take either position here to point out the difficulty of the problem; yet this is a very typical illustration of the type of conflicting demands which can be generated by the environment of a political system.

Another illustration of influences from the environment can be found in the federal response to pressures from French Canada. Since Confederation, the federal public service in Canada has been basically unilingual and, particularly over the last fifty years, there have been relatively few French Canadians in the upper levels of the service. This made it difficult for French-speaking Canadians to communicate with the federal public service and was thought by federal politicians to be partially responsible for the increase in unrest in Quebec in the 1960s. No one attributed French Canada's "quiet revolution" and the growth of its unquiet aspects solely to this cause, but the situation in Quebec in the early 1960s did put pressure upon federal political decision makers and created a strain within the Canadian political system which could only be alleviated by structural change. One of the structural changes has been that, in the mid-1960s, the federal government decided to make the federal service bilingual by establishing training programs for its employees and by emphasizing bilingualism in its recruitment programs. The success of these programs in creating a truly bilingual civil service and in allaying discontent in Quebec is still in doubt, but the programs demonstrate the type of change which may be induced within a political system through stress generated by its own social environment.

Few of the stresses generated by the environment of a political system are simple. What pleases French-speaking Quebeckers may not please English-speaking Albertans, and what pleases farmers may not please consumers. Moreover, the more complex the environment of a political system, the more complex the demands it generates. The reconciliation of these various demands, the balancing of one against another, is at the heart of the political process. In some cases the competition can be reconciled through the economic system or other social systems, but in Canada today it is more and more often the political system which must allocate the available resources among competing groups. Thus the nature of the environment of the political system is a vital determinant of the nature of the system itself.

One way in which the environment affects the political system is through *cleavages*. Cleavages may result from any number of things, not all of which are significant politically. For instance, the difference between blue-eyed and brown-eyed people does not normally have any effect on the political system, though the difference between black-skinned and white-skinned people often does. The term cleavage is used rather loosely in political science, sometimes referring to differences of opinion over specific issues and other times referring to generalized splits created by differences in the environment. In this book we will use the term in the latter sense, to mean a line of conflict between two groups which are in competition for the same resources. Specific differences over particular items will be referred to simply as *issues*. Thus we shall speak of a "cleavage" between French and English Canadians in general. A specific difference between French and English Canadians over a particular matter such as educational institutions within Quebec would be referred to as an "issue."

Cleavages created by one factor are often reinforced by another. For example, the cultural cleavage between French- and English-speaking Canadians is reinforced by the fact that most French Canadians live in one province (creating a geographical cleavage) and that that province is one of the less well developed in Canada (creating an economic cleavage). When cleavages are reinforced by a number of factors they naturally tend to become more serious for the political system because they generate more issues.

We have described politics as a process of both conflict and cooperation. The conflict arises from cleavage: from what does the cooperation arise? Consider for a moment what happens within a group of people who are in conflict with another group over some issue. A *consensus* will form within the group over the issue in question and possibly over a common stance to adopt. We defined it earlier as a state of agreement among a group of people over the desirability of some end. For instance, among prairie farmers in Canada there is a near-unanimous agreement that it is appropriate government policy to subsidize the wheat farmer. This consensus is further strengthened by the fact that many issues based upon geographic and economic cleavages divide the prairie wheat farmers from Ontario business associations or other economic interests in Canada.

A consensus is often specific to a particular issue. It is therefore not simply the opposite of a cleavage. There may be substantial disagreement within a group such as prairie wheat farmers over other issues. Farmers in areas with abundant rainfall may be considerably less enthusiastic about irrigation projects than those in dry areas. However, the consensus created by one issue may spill over into other areas as well, simply because the people involved come to know each other or because their leaders find the coalitions so created to be useful. Moreover, conflict between large groups tends to create large areas of consensus. A war can do wonders to unify a divided nation, and locally depressed economic conditions can do a great deal to solidify one area when it faces the rest of the country.

There is another type of consensus which is perhaps more important than that within sub-groups of a society about particular issues. It is a consensus not so much about what is to be done as about how things are to be done. It is particularly important when applied to politics because its implication is that even if a group does not agree with the political decisions that have been made, it will abide by them because they have been made in keeping with the accepted rules of the game. Even if there is not consensus over the content of the outputs of a political system, there may be consensus over the process by which the outputs are produced. This *procedural consensus* is closely linked to the concept of legitimacy. If there is a fairly broad agreement on the process by which decisions are made, the political system attains an important element of stability and legitimacy not present in systems which lack procedural consensus.

To sum up, where there is unity over either one item or a broad range of items or procedures, we speak of a consensus. Where there is a division over one item we speak of that item as an issue. A cleavage is a division in society caused by cultural, economic or geographical factors which may cause differences between groups over any number of issues.

In the rest of this chapter we will look at the three most important types of cleavage in the environment of Canadian politics: geographical and general economic cleavages, cleavages based on stratification, and ethnic cleavages. We shall ask two questions about any cleavage: 1. Of what does it consist? 2. What are its political consequences?

GEOGRAPHIC AND ECONOMIC CLEAVAGES

Canada's Global Position Canada is unusual among nations in that she shares a land border with only one other nation and that a giant with ten times her population. She is separated from all the rest of the world by thousands of miles of water, land or ice. This geographic situation has led Canada to rely on trade patterns which are overwhelmingly dominated by exchanges with the United States. Thus, in 1971, 67.5 per cent of Canada's exports went to the United States and 70.2 per cent of imports came from there. Our next biggest trading partner was the United Kingdom, which took less than 8 per cent of Canada's exports, and the European Common market took only a little over 6 per cent.[1] During each year of the last nine, Canada has had a balance of trade surplus,[2] but that

[1]*Canada 1973*, Statistics Canada, Ottawa, 1972, pp. 308–10. Canada's trade ties with the U.S. have been tightening in recent years but they have also come into closer balance. In 1964 the U.S. provided 68.9 per cent of Canada's imports and took only 52.7 of Canadian exports; in that year, Britain bought 14.8 per cent of Canadian exports. See André Raynauld, *The Canadian Economic System* (Macmillan Co., Toronto, 1967) p. 369.
[2]*Canada 1973*, p. 304.

surplus tends to be counterbalanced by the outflow of Canadian dollars as dividends and interest payments to foreign sources, particularly the United States, which hold much of the ownership of Canadian industry.

Canada is the sixth largest trading nation in the world.[3] It ranks behind the United States, West Germany, England, Japan and France. In terms of trade per capita, it ranks tenth. Less populous countries tend to have higher per capita figures than larger ones, so that in this respect Canada is outranked by such nations as the Netherlands, Belgium, Switzerland and Sweden.

Canada is in a more difficult position than such countries in two important respects. First, she does not belong to any regional trading bloc. Other nations with small populations heavily dependent upon trading do, which gives them access to large and stable markets with relatively low or non-existent tariff barriers. Canada, without any such agreements (beyond the relatively unimportant Commonwealth Preference), is exposed to rapidly changing world conditions in a way that they are not. In part this problem has been overcome through the negotiation of a series of special agreements with the United States, and this again makes Canada heavily dependent upon the goodwill of her southern neighbour. The abrogation of a special pact such as the automotive products agreement, whereby cars and car parts may cross the border duty-free, would do little harm to the American economy but would create considerable dislocation in Canada.

Canada is principally an exporter of primary goods and an importer of secondary or manufactured goods. Thus in 1971 only 35.7 per cent of Canadian exports were fully manufactured "end products" whereas 62.9 per cent of imports were fully manufactured. American exports are usually about 37 per cent primary goods and European Economic Community exports are usually about 33 per cent primary goods.[4] Primary goods such as lumber, agricultural products and metals are far more susceptible to international competition than are manufactured goods, because the latter often depend upon specialized knowledge and techniques specific to one particular nation. Exports of primary goods may be suddenly and drastically affected by many different and unpredictable factors, such as rainfall in Russia and China, or the discovery of nickel deposits in New Caledonia. For example, the effects of the depression were worsened in Canada not only by a prolonged drought in our own wheat-growing area but by good growing conditions in some other wheat-producing areas of the world. On the other hand, it is becoming clear as the 1970s progress that primary products are becoming very scarce and the rapidly rising prices for primary goods have put the Canadian economy in a relatively strong position. Paradoxically, this may make it increasingly easy for Canadian governments to promote secondary industry at home at the same time as they realize greater benefits from the sale of primary goods abroad.

[3]*Ibid, loc. cit.*
[4]1971 Canadian figures are from *Canada 1973*, pp. 306–7. Comparative data is available in United Nations, *Yearbook of International Trade Statistics* and is summarized in A. Raynauld, *The Canadian Economic System*, pp. 359–61.

In sum, Canada's global position forces her to be more heavily dependent on the United States for her trade relationships than her political decision makers and many of her citizens might prefer. However, unlike such countries as Britain and Japan, Canada trades largely for luxuries. Whereas without trade Britain could scarcely produce enough food to survive, very few of the most basic necessities of diet or shelter need be imported into Canada. Canada does have some flexibility, then, which may not be available to other nations.

Canada and the United States The Canadian preoccupation with the United States is readily understandable in view of the foregoing trade figures. During a visit to Washington early in 1969, Prime Minister Trudeau suggested that sharing a continent with the United States was rather like sleeping with an elephant—he may not know you're there, but you must be sensitive to his every twitch.[5] The elephant in this case is some ten times as large as Canada in population and twelve times as large in terms of gross national product.[6] With Newfoundland excepted, 94 per cent of Canadians live within 300 miles of the American border and most of these live in a narrow strip within 100 miles of the border.[7] The presence of Canada is of relatively little consequence to the United States, but the presence of the United States is of immense consequence to Canada.

This geographic position has had consequences for Canada's defence policy. As recently as 1895 the Canadian military made substantial defence preparations against the U.S. Even between the two World Wars, the only defence plans drawn up by the Canadian military were for defence from an attack from the south. Fears of a direct attack have finally vanished—or at least Canadians have recognized the dubious benefits of defence against an immensely improbable military enemy which, in any case, could not be resisted.

In another sense, however, Canada's proximity to the U.S. still shapes Canadian defence policy. It makes Canada strategically one target with the United States; an attacker would hardly discriminate between these two parts of North America. In the period prior to 1941, when America was not particularly active in world affairs, this was not too important. But since the end of World War II American involvement in world politics has led to, among other things, the formation of regional alliances such as NATO (the North Atlantic Treaty Organization) and NORAD (the North American Air Defence Command) in which Canada has of necessity participated. Whether the necessity was felt because of American pressure on the Canadian government or because of some real conviction on the part of Canadian politicians is not necessarily vital; the American presence on our doorstep would in any case have made abstention difficult. Changing world circumstances and changing American commitments

[5]Prime Minister Trudeau in a speech to the Washington Press Club, March 25, 1969.
[6]Figures adopted from *The Financial Post*, Oct. 28, 1972, p. d–1.
[7]T.R. Weir, "The People," in John Warkentin (ed.), *Canada: A Geographic Interpretation*, (Methuen, Toronto, 1968), p. 138.

may be more important than anything Canada can do in determining a valid Canadian defence and foreign policy.[8]

Probably much more important in the long run than the various military and foreign policy ramifications of American proximity to Canada are cultural and economic encroachments. A number of factors facilitate the imposition of American culture on Canada and most of them derive basically from our geographical proximity. American television reaches almost everyone in Canada. English-Canadian stations carry a great deal of American programming; well over half of the prime-time television in English Canada is American in origin. Moreover, most Canadians are in direct range of American television stations, and in areas where both Canadian and American sources are available the latter are often preferred. For example, Colborne, Ontario, a town of about 1,400 located some 80 miles from Toronto, receives at least two Canadian and three American television stations. In October of 1968 an extensive survey was conducted of all of the town's students in Grades 4, 5, 6, and 7. Eighty-two per cent of the children interviewed claimed to watch the news on television sometimes or every day, and of these over 56 per cent usually watched American news broadcasts.[9] Children and adults alike pick up cultural images from television and consequently are socialized by it.[10] This is one of the ways in which the values of American culture may be imported into Canada.[11]

Much of French Canada is also within range of American television, but fewer French Canadians watch American channels because of the language barrier. The Canadian content of the French network of the CBC is much higher than that of the English network, so the television exposure of French Canadians to foreign culture has been less than that of

[8]For further discussions and elaborations of Canada's role in world affairs and in particular her place in NORAD and NATO see: P.V. Lyon, *The Policy Question* (McClelland and Stewart, Toronto, 1963); J.W. Holmes, *The Better Part of Valour: Essays on Canadian Diplomacy*, (Carleton Library, Toronto, 1970) and *Canada and the United States: Political and Security Issues*, (Canadian Institute of International Affairs, Toronto, 1970); J.L. Granatstein, *Canadian Foreign Policy Since 1945: Middle Power or Satellite?*, (Copp Clark, Toronto, 1969); Jan B. McLin, *Canada's Changing Defense Policy*, 1957–63, (Copp Clark, Toronto, 1967); L. Hertzman, John Warnock, and Thomas Hockin, *Alliances and Illusions: Canada and the NATO-NORAD Question*, (Hurtig, Edmonton, 1969); J. Eayrs, *The Art of the Possible: Government and Foreign Policy in Canada*, (University of Toronto Press, Toronto, 1961); J. Eayrs, *Northern Approaches: Canada and the Search for Peace*, (Macmillan, Toronto, 1961).
[9]John Hill, "The Political Socialization of Children in a Rural Environment," (Unpublished B.A. thesis, Queen's University, 1969), p. 52.
[10]Political socialization is the learning of the political values and behaviour patterns of a society. Canadian political socialization will be discussed at some length in chapter 4.
[11]There is recognition of this fact at many levels in Canadian government and there are even occasional attempts to counteract the problem. For example, in 1970 the Canadian Radio Television Commission (CRTC) announced a series of steps to increase the Canadian content of radio, prime-time television, and cablevision services.

English Canadians. The difference is compounded when the effects of radio, magazines, and other segments of the mass media are added in. The language barrier has been instrumental in helping to preserve French-Canadian culture from the overwhelming geographical proximity of the United States.

While the military implications of proximity to the United States are often viewed by Canadians with resignation if not applause, and while cultural domination is frequently decried, the area of United States-Canadian relations which usually receives the most publicity is the economic area. We have already indicated the closeness of trade ties between the two neighbours; now let us look a bit more closely at Canadian-United States economic relations and their effect on the political system.

The Foreign Investment Question Table 2-1 indicates two basic trends in the picture of foreign investments (which are very nearly equal to gross international liabilities) in Canada. First, the proportion of foreign investment to gross national product has been decreasing, which at first hand would appear to suggest that the situation is improving. Second, the proportion of foreign investment held by Americans has steadily increased and that held by Britons has steadily decreased. We will examine below the ramifications of the latter point.

The first point is deceptive because the nature of foreign investment

TABLE 2-1: CANADIAN BALANCE OF INTERNATIONAL INDEBTEDNESS 1926–69 (PORTFOLIO AND DIRECT INVESTMENT)

	1926	1939	1949	1959	1967	1969
Gross Liabilities (in billions of dollars)	6.4	7.4	9.3	23.8	40.2	46.9
Per cent held in U.S.	55	61	69	71	74	74
Per cent held in U.K.	42	35	19	14	10	10
Gross National Product (in billions of dollars)	5.1	5.6	16.3	32.3	65.7	78.6
Foreign Indebtedness as per cent of GNP	125	132	57	74	61	60

Source: *Canada Year Book*, 1972, pp. 1177 and 1211, adapted. Reproduced by permission of Information Canada.

has changed significantly since 1926. The more normal form of investment before the Second World War was "portfolio" investment—in bonds or debentures which give the investor relatively little managerial control over the firm. Since 1945, investment has been increasingly "direct," that is in stock of a firm, which may give the investor considerable control over what the company actually does.[12]

Table 2-2 indicates the growth in the percentage of Canadian industry controlled by non-residents and by United States residents. Once again it provides evidence of the increasing control of Canadian industry by Americans. While the figures stop at 1963, there is no evidence that the trend has been reversed since that time.[13]

TABLE 2-2: NON-RESIDENT CONTROL* AS A PERCENTAGE OF SELECTED CANADIAN INDUSTRIES; 1926–1963

Percentage of Total Controlled by All Non-Residents	1926	1939	1948	1963
Manufacturing	35	38	43	60
Petroleum and natural gas	—	—	—	74
Mining and smelting	38	42	40	59
Railways	3	3	3	2
Other utilities	20	26	24	4
TOTAL	17	21	25	34
Percentage of Total Controlled by U.S. Residents				
Manufacturing	30	32	39	46
Petroleum and natural gas	—	—	—	62
Mining and smelting	32	38	37	52
Railways	3	3	3	2
Other utilities	20	26	24	4
TOTAL	15	19	22	27

*Control is computed as percentage of total output in that sector from companies over 50 per cent foreign-owned.
Source: Dominion Bureau of Statistics, *Canadian Balance of International Payments 1963, 1964 and 1965*, August 1967, p. 127; Reproduced in K. Levitt, *Silent Surrender*, (Student Edition, Macmillan, Toronto, 1971), p. 61. These figures are essentially the same as those presented in *Foreign Ownership and the Structure of Canadian Industry*, (Ottawa, Queen's Printer, 1965), pp. 9–10. Reproduced by permission of Information Canada.

[12]See I.A. Litvak, C.J. Maule and R.O. Robinson, *Dual Loyalty* (McGraw–Hill, Toronto, 1971), p. 2. In 1926 there was twice as much portfolio investment as direct investment. The situation has now reversed.
[13]*Ibid.*, pp. 9–10.

Not all Canadian industries have fallen under foreign control. For example, at various times Canadian governments have decided that banking and finance, railways, communications, insurance and uranium mining were too vital to be allowed to fall into the control of foreigners.[14] But foreign control is concentrated in many of Canada's most profitable and fastest growing manufacturing and resource industries.

A number of questions follow from these facts. How did ownership of Canadian industry get that way? What is wrong with foreign ownership? What have Canadian responses been?

The complete story of how so much of Canadian industry came to be owned by foreigners cannot be covered in an elementary text, but a couple of explanations are of interest.[15] Firstly, some responsibility for the situation must be laid squarely on a policy which was designed to avoid American domination. Macdonald's famous "National Policy" of the 19th century had three prongs: build railways, encourage immigration and erect tariff barriers. The first two components of the policy did serve the purpose of pre-empting United States settlement in the Northwest and preserving that territory for Canada. The third component, designed to encourage Canadian industry, backfired. What happened was that foreign firms—first British and later American—seeing a lucrative territory for their investments, moved in behind the tariff barriers which protected them from competition. They then set up miniature replicas of their home operations. Meanwhile, other foreign entrepreneurs, who must be given credit for seeing more possibilities in Canadian resource industries than did Canadians themselves, invested in primary industry and exported the primary goods to their own home bases to provide jobs for workers in other nations. It is extremely difficult for governments to foresee all the consequences of the policies they make and in this case, one consequence of the national policy was exactly the opposite of what was intended.

Another argument often advanced to explain the prevalence of American ownership in the Canadian economy is that Americans have provided necessary capital which was not otherwise available. Table 2-3 indicates, however, that Canada's need for foreign investment to ensure her economic growth is largely fictional: the capital that has been used to expand Canadian industry is Canadian, not foreign. At no time since records have been kept has foreign capital ever been more than 30 per cent of the total invested in a given year.[16] Kari Levitt has put the case bluntly:

---

[14]*Ibid.*, p. 7.

[15]There is an immense economics literature on the effect of foreign ownership in Canada and it cannot all be cited here. However the key works are *The Report of the Task Force on Foreign Ownership and the Structure of Canadian Industry* (The Watkins Report), Queen's Printer, Ottawa, 1965; A.E. Safarian, *Foreign Ownership of Canadian Industry*, (McGraw–Hill, Toronto, 1966); A. Rotstein (ed.) *The Prospect of Change*, (McGraw–Hill, Toronto, 1965); Kari Levitt, *Silent Surrender*, (Liveright, New York; published in Canada by Macmillan, Toronto, 1970), (Student Edition, 1971); and I.A. Litvak, C.J. Maule and R.D. Robinson, *Dual Loyalty*, (McGraw–Hill, Toronto, 1971).

[16]I.A. Litvak, *et al.*, *Dual Loyalty*, pp. 21–2.

. . .it is simply not true that Canada is short of capital. The expensive infrastructure required by her peculiar geography has long been put in place and paid for. . . .The brutal fact is that acquisition of control by U.S. companies over the commodity producing sectors of the Canadian economy has largely been financed from corporate savings deriving from the sale of Canadian resources, extracted and processed by Canadian labour, or from the sale(s) of branch plant manufacturing businesses to Canadian consumers at tariff protected prices. Thus over the period 1957 to 1964 U.S. direct investments in manufacturing, mining and petroleum secured 73 per cent of their funds from retained earnings and depreciation reserves, a further 12 per cent from Canadian banks and other intermediaries and only 15 per cent in the form of new funds from the United States. Furthermore, throughout the period, payout of dividends, interest, royalties and management fees exceeded the inflow of new capital.[17]

TABLE 2-3: USE OF FOREIGN AND DOMESTIC RESOURCES IN GROSS CAPITAL FORMATION IN CANADA, SELECTED YEARS 1950–1965

	1950	1955	1960	1965
Gross Capital Formation (in billions of dollars)	4.5	6.6	8.7	13.7
Per cent from Domestic Sources	84	74	74	79

Source: Adapted from D.B.S. *The Canadian Balance of International Payments, 1963, 1964, 1965 and International Investment Position*, Queen's Printer, Ottawa, p. 76, and cited in I.A. Litvak *et al.*, *Dual Loyalty*, p. 3.

The question then arises—so what? What difference does it make if a considerable proportion of Canadian industry is U.S.-controlled? The easy answer is that it diminishes Canada's sovereignty, but this is no answer at all for it begs the question of why sovereignty is considered to be necessary.

There are economic reasons why sovereignty is considered to be desirable. Foreign control may be undesirable for reasons related to both economic growth and economic stability.[18] To the extent that Canada depends on the investment decisions of foreign-controlled corporations she could be susceptible to changes in her growth patterns depending on how these corporations see their growth prospects elsewhere in the world. Since 1950 United States corporations have concentrated their foreign investments (some of which are financed by the earnings of Canadian subsidiaries) in Europe rather than Canada to the possible detriment of the Cana-

[17]Kari Levitt, *Silent Surrender*, Student Edition, pp. 63–64.
[18]A. Litvak, *et al.*, *Dual Loyalty*, pp. 21–2.

dian growth rate. The economic stability of Canada can be influenced by the decisions of foreign firms to put more or less money into Canada, to increase or decrease employment in Canadian operations, or to change plant locations. If these decisions are taken contrary to Canadian economic needs they may destabilize the Canadian economy.

With regard to individual firms, concern has been expressed that research and development activities are not carried out in Canada, that Canadians are not adequately employed in management roles, that exports to third countries are usually from the home base plant, that supplies are not purchased in Canada and that the firms evade taxation by various subterfuges.[19] Yet, "with regard to most of these activities, researchers have found that, in fact, American affiliates perform as well, if not better, than comparable Canadian firms but worse than comparable American firms in the U.S."[20]

"[However] the problems posed by foreign subsidiaries cannot be understood or dealt with solely in economic terms. The problems must be viewed within a broader frame of response which includes political, legal and social-cultural parameters as well as the economic."[21] Perhaps the major political problem is that of extra-territoriality—the application of the laws of one nation within the boundaries of another. In 1957 a Canadian trader charged that Ford Canada had refused to ship trucks to China because of fear that the parent company would be penalized under the United States Treasury's Foreign Assets Control Regulations and the United States' Trading with the Enemy Act. That case was never satisfactorily resolved, but in 1958 John Diefenbaker obtained assurances from President Eisenhower that, to quote Diefenbaker:

> If cases arose in the future where the refusal of orders by companies operating in Canada might have an effect on Canadian economic activity, the U.S. government would consider favourably exempting the parent company in the U.S. from the application of foreign asset control regulations with respect to such orders.[22]

Yet incidents continued and some Canadian subsidiaries shied away from trade with North Vietnam, North Korea and Cuba for fear of the U.S. Trading with the Enemy Act or of adverse U.S. reaction which might affect their markets.[23]

The United States regulations were changed in 1969 to permit U.S. subsidiaries to trade with China, but as some analysts point out: "This change in policy clearly confirms that these policies do have an extra-territorial reach."[24] A recent example further confirmed the fact that the Trading with the Enemy Act still hampers the activity of Canadian firms which are subsidiaries of American ones. In 1974, a Montreal locomotive

---

[19]*Ibid.*, p. 22.
[20]*Ibid.*, p. 22.
[21]*Ibid.*, p. vii.
[22]*Canada House of Commons Debates (Hansard)*, July 11, 1958, p. 2142 and quoted in I.A. Litvak *et al*, *Dual Loyalty*, p. 25.
[23]*Ibid.*, pp. 25–6.
[24]*Ibid.*, p. 26.

company, MLW-Worthington Ltd., had arranged to build twenty-five locomotives for Cuba, a transaction estimated as worth $18 million. Trouble arose, however, when the American parent company, Studebaker-Worthington, Inc., felt obliged under the Trading With the Enemy Act to seek a license for the transaction from the American government. For weeks the American government made no decision on the matter.[25] Ultimately, after considerable controversy in the Canadian press, the Canadian subsidiary's board of directors did vote to go ahead with the sale, although the American members of the board voted against it in the hope of avoiding personal prosecution by the U.S. government.[26] The chronology of this case indicates that even though the U.S. government chose not to intervene directly to block the sale to Cuba, the policy defined by the Trading With the Enemy Act did affect the behaviour of the Canadian company.

There have been several other instances when U.S. regulations have been applied to the Canadian political system through U.S.-controlled firms operating in Canada. For example, in January 1968 the U.S. introduced mandatory controls on foreign investment by U.S. companies. This resulted in an outflow of Canadian funds to the U.S., and it was not until March that Canada was able to gain some exemptions to avoid too much damage to her economy. Despite the existence of a U.S.–Canada consultative committee to discuss problems such as these, the Canadian government had no forewarning of the move or of similar and even more drastic moves by the U.S. in August 1971. Balance of payment difficulties in the U.S. are thus often transmitted to Canada via subsidiaries of U.S. firms.

Aside from these problems there have also been less major but equally upsetting instances of misbehaviour by individual U.S. firms in Canada, aided by the U.S. government. Two examples have been particularly glaring. The first involved the purchase of the Mercantile Bank of Canada by the New York-based Rockefeller interests. Canadian officials warned the Rockefellers that the Canadian government would act retroactively to limit foreign holdings of Canadian banks if U.S. interests purchased more than 25% of the Mercantile. The Rockefellers went ahead with this purchase and then were able to apply sufficient economic and political pressure through the U.S. State Department to ensure that the Canadian government did not act.[27]

The second involved a Canadian decision no longer to allow businesses to deduct from their taxes expenditures on advertising in foreign-owned periodicals even if these had a Canadian supplement and were printed in Canada. The idea was to encourage the Canadian magazine industry. The publications which stood to lose most by the regulation were *Time* and *Reader's Digest*, and the owner of the former, Henry Luce, was

[25]Geoffrey Stevens, "Like the Bad Old Days," *Globe and Mail*, February 27, 1974, p. 6.

[26]*Globe and Mail*, Saturday, March 9, 1974.

[27]Peter Newman, *The Distemper of Our Times* (McClelland and Stewart, 1968), pp. 418–23, 511–518.

able to apply sufficient pressure, again through the State Department in Washington, to ensure that the Canadian government did not carry out its policy.[28]

It should be apparent by now that foreign investment has not been an unmixed blessing for Canadians. Canadian policy makers feel inhibited, at least to some extent, in promoting economic policies aimed at achieving Canadian political interests. Their international trade policies must constantly take account of U.S. interests, as must their taxation and monetary policies. The promotion of east-west ties is made difficult by the prevalence of north-south economic relationships, and the provision of distinctive Canadian wage and social security policies may be made more difficult by the presence of both multinational corporations and international unions.[29] The desire to provide more employment for Canadians in secondary industry using Canadian raw materials may be subverted, not necessarily intentionally, by the decisions of firms whose primary loyalty is to workers in another country.

Canada has attempted to counter these problems. There are laws relating to the level of foreign investment in key sectors, there is a 15% withholding tax on interest and dividends to foreigners, and much of the financial disclosure legislation currently on the books in Canada is aimed at foreign companies. In December 1973 the federal government passed legislation which set up a Foreign Takeover Review Board to rule on the takeover of Canadian companies by Americans and on future foreign investments in Canada. There have been several bilateral agreements with the U.S. government such as that made by Diefenbaker and Eisenhower in 1958. But the effect of these, with the exception of the automobile agreements, has not been great.

> To date the bilateral consultations and arrangements between Canada and the U.S. have rarely realized Canadian objectives because the political bargaining takes place between two very unequal partners. Canada is fully able to articulate the problems to the U.S. government but it lacks the political power to negotiate mutually beneficial solutions. . . .In short, as the two economies become more closely integrated along "continentalist" (North American) lines, the threat to Canadian political sovereignty is escalated. . . .Experience to date has shown that Canada *alone* has little political bargaining power, vis-à-vis the U.S. in cases where the loci of decision-making power are centered in U.S. multinational corporations, and where the U.S. government has been unwilling to renounce the extraterritorial reach of its laws.[30]

Thus one of the most vital features of the environment of the Canadian political system is its geographic and economic ties with the United States. Canadians have reaped many benefits from this relationship, but

---

[28]*Ibid.*, pp. 224–6. By 1975 the federal government was apparently finally ready to act by amending the appropriate section of the Income Tax Act, although at the time of this writing, the legislation had not been passed and the periodicals in question were still protesting.

[29]I.A. Litvak, *et al.*, pp. 134–5.

[30]*Ibid.*, p. 154.

there have been problems too. What Canadian decision makers can and cannot do is clearly conditioned by this relationship.

Canada's Internal Geographical and Economic Environment

In the years since Confederation Canada's population has risen from 3.5 million to over 22 million. Many features of the population have changed but many have remained the same. For example, in 1867, 75 per cent of all Canadians lived in that part of Southern Ontario and Quebec called the St. Lawrence Lowlands; in 1973 over 60 per cent still did.

Within these areas, as elsewhere in Canada, there has been a general movement off the farms and into urban centres. In 1871 only 3.3 per cent of Canadians lived in centres of over 100,000 population (Montreal was the only one). By 1971 there were 22 urban areas larger than Montreal had been in 1871, and 65 per cent of Canadians lived in such centres.[31] In 1959-1961 only 5.1 per cent of the gross domestic product (that part of the GNP consumed within the country) came from agriculture.[32] By 1970, only about 6.5 per cent of the Canadian labour force worked on a producing farm.[33] In short, Canada has changed rapidly from a rural agricultural society to an urban industrialized one and is now one of the most highly urbanized of Western societies.[34] The rapid adjustments necessary have often put strains on the political system as people moved from farms to cities faster than the structures of Canadian politics could move to accommodate them.

Yet although Canada is an urban society with manufacturing and service industries accounting for the largest portion of its GNP, it is still in many ways a resource-based society.[35] Many of Canada's larger industrial complexes are still in the primary sector of the economy, in industries like mining or pulpwood production. In terms of numbers of workers, secondary and service industries far outrank primary industries, but Canada exports a very high proportion of its primary products and imports a relatively high proportion of its manufactured goods. Thus, the standard of living enjoyed by Canadians today is largely dependent upon her natural resources.[36]

[31]Statistics Canada, *Canada 1973*, p. 113.
[32]T.R. Weir, "The People," in John Warkentin (ed.), *Canada: A Geographical Interpretation*, (Methuen, Toronto, 1967), p. 154.
[33]Statistics Canada, *Canada Year Book 1972*, p. 527.
[34]One must be careful not to underemphasize the importance of agriculture in Canada. In one way or another agriculture and agriculture-related activities account for more than 25 per cent of the country's economic activity and in 1971 agricultural exports accounted for about 11 per cent of the value of the country's total exports. In that year more than twice as many workers were engaged in agriculture as in all other primary industries combined. See Statistics Canada, *Canada 1973*, pp. 227 ff.
[35]In 1963 only 11.8 per cent of Canada's domestic product came from primary industries whereas 25.6 per cent came from manufacturing and 36.6 per cent from service industries. See Raynauld, *The Canadian Economic System*, p. 14.
[36]Canada's economic growth possibly *could* have been based on other than primary

Canada has a more severe climate than most countries. This has been one reason for the concentration of her population along her southern boundary. When to a harsh climate is added a land whose largest areas are covered by marsh, rock, or permafrost, the picture emerges of a difficult environment indeed.

For the political system, a number of stresses result from the climate. Seasonal unemployment in outdoor and construction industries often adds a quarter of a million to the list of Canada's unemployed and constitutes an expensive wastage of human resources; short construction periods add much to the cost of large outdoor projects; low-cost transportation of bulk cargoes to and from the interior depends on the St. Lawrence Seaway, but this route is closed by ice for four months of the year; it costs over ten dollars a year for every man, woman and child in Canada just to scrape the snow off the streets.[37]

Finally and above all, Canada is big. Distances between the major industrial centres in the St. Lawrence Lowlands are relatively small, but in the rest of the country Canadians must maintain communication links between units of population separated by vast distances. Indeed, paradoxically, one reason for the high level of urbanization in Canada may be its vast size. The maintenance of adequate communications and services in small population centres widely separated from each other is much more costly per capita than the maintenance of similar services in centres which are close together. One way around this problem is to concentrate population in large centres which can collectively afford the costly communication links involved. Thus, small, densely populated nations can afford to be less urbanized than Canada.

From what has been said so far, we can piece together a partial picture of the internal geographical and economic environment within which the Canadian political system must operate. It operates in a highly urbanized nation which, in order to uphold its standard of living, depends on resources based far from the urban centres. There is a high concentration of the population in one small corner of a huge territory, but lines of communication must be kept up throughout the whole space. The climate and the physical structure combine to make much of the land scenic, but not well suited to permanent habitation, and to make transportation and construction very expensive. We live next door to a giant which acknowledges our presence seldom and then often in a fit of pique. We import more manu-

industries but it *was* based on resource industries. See J.K. Galbraith, "The Causes of Economic Growth: The Canadian Case," *Queen's Quarterly*, Summer, 1958. The argument that Canada's growth did depend on resource industries is usually called the staple products theory. The numerous works of H.A. Innis represent the most complete statement of the theory. See also M.H. Watkins, "A Staple Theory of Canada's Economic Growth," *Canadian Journal of Economics and Political Science*, May, 1963, in favour of the theory and K. Buckley, "The Role of Staple Industries in Canada's Economic Development," *The Journal of Economic History*, vol. 18, 1958, against it.

[37]Roy I. Wolfe, "Economic Development," in Warkentin, *Canada: A Geographical Interpretation*, pp. 189–191.

factured goods than we export, and thus we depend upon trade to support us in the style to which we are accustomed.

The consequences of all this for our political system are immense. Transportation projects have always required government assistance; indeed, much of the politics of the first fifty years of Confederation was concerned directly with railway construction.[38] Settlement and development of our territory has depended on vast expenditures and intervention by all levels of government, for only governments have large enough resources to be able to take on the risks involved in such projects as the extensive development of the North. The harsh climate produces cyclical economic effects which only the powers of very large governmental units can hope to overcome. In short, the scattering of a small population over a large area early accustomed Canadians to "big government" and prepared the way naturally for the welfare programs of the mid-twentieth century.[39]

Regional Disparity in Canada So far the focus of analysis has been on factors which are common to most of Canada. Now the discussion will turn to cleavages in the geographical and economic environment—in particular those regional differences which generate very different and often conflicting demands on the political system.

Table 2-4 gives some indication of the great discrepancies in income across Canada. A person living in Ontario is likely to have twice the annual income of one living in Newfoundland and 60 per cent more income than one living in New Brunswick. The Maritimes as a whole have levels of income only about 75 per cent of the national average, while those of British Columbia and Ontario are far above it. What is perhaps even more alarming is the stubborn resistance of these patterns to change.

With the exception of minor fluctuations caused by strikes in key industries or by variations in the price of agricultural commodities, there have been no changes in the relative positions of provinces since the mid-60s, and there has been very little change for as long as the Canadian government has kept records. By contrast, regional disparities in the United States have been steadily reduced over the same period and are now only about half as great as they were in the 1920s.

These regional economic cleavages put stress on the Canadian political system. Thus, for example, there is a constant cry expressed at every federal-provincial conference that Canada's poorer regions should get more of Canada's goods and services, and there is a constant resistance from richer areas to any quick move in the direction of equality. With the exception of the Maritimes, the poorer regions frequently spawn protest movements—often in the form of minor political parties—and in their protests usually accuse the richer regions of exploiting the poorer. The "Bar-

[38]See Pierre Berton, *The National Dream* (McClelland and Stewart, Toronto, 1971) and *The Last Spike* (McClelland and Stewart, Toronto, 1972); W.T. Easterbrook and M.G. Aitken, *Canadian Economic History* (Macmillan, Toronto, 1965), ch. 18 and D. Creighton, *John A. Macdonald*, vol. II, *The Old Chieftain* (Macmillan, Toronto, 1955).
[39]See Creighton, *John A. Macdonald*, vol. II, *The Old Chieftain*, ch. 14.

TABLE 2-4: GEOGRAPHICAL DISTRIBUTION OF PER CAPITA INCOME IN CANADA, 1973

Province	Per Cent of National Average	$ Per Capita Per Year
Newfoundland	65	2760
P.E.I.	69	2922
Nova Scotia	78	3332
New Brunswick	73	3089
Quebec	90	3839
Ontario	114	4840
Manitoba	96	4071
Saskatchewan	89	3803
Alberta	102	4325
British Columbia	108	4581
TOTALS	100	4254

Source: Statistics Canada, *National Income and Expenditure Accounts.* Figures include government transfer payments.

ons of Bay Street" and the "Robbers of St. James Street" are familiar Canadian villains.[40]

To some extent Canadian policies have favoured the central regions over the peripheral. For instance, corporation tax collected from a firm whose head office is in Toronto is split only between the federal and Ontario governments in spite of the fact that the corporate earnings may come from anywhere in Canada. The effects of this are now mitigated by equalization payments from the federal government to poorer provinces, but this has not always been the case, and in some instances the head start given the richer central areas cannot be overcome by the payment of present-day equalization settlements. Too, the Maritimes and Prairies frequently claim that the tariff barriers set up as early as the mid-nineteenth century protected industry in the central provinces but did nothing to protect the resources of the poorer areas from the fluctuations of world markets. The central provinces counter by suggesting that their own resource industries do not appear to have been badly harmed by world competition, and the argument goes on.

Part of the problem in poorer areas in Canada stems from the type

[40]S.M. Lipset, *Agrarian Socialism*, (Anchor Books, N.Y. 1968); C.B. MacPherson, *Democracy in Alberta*, (University of Toronto Press, Toronto, 1953), and M. Pinard, *The Rise of a Third Party*, (Prentice–Hall, Englewood Cliffs, 1971). There are many other sources covering third party protest movements. These are covered extensively in Chapter 10.

of industry located there. Relative to the rest of Canada, the Maritimes have a very low proportion of their production in manufacturing industries and a very high proportion in primary industries such as mining, fishing and forestry. These industries are less likely to create jobs and more likely to hide under-employment—the employment of people in jobs which do not really need to be done or the employment of people for longer periods than are necessary to do the job.[41]

However important government policies may have been in creating regional disparities, geographical factors have been much more important.[42] Differences of terrain, climate, and the distribution of mineral and forest resources by themselves create regional disparities. Of these three factors, climate is probably the least troublesome for, in spite of the overall harshness of the weather, there are fairly large areas of Canada where rainfall and mean temperatures are sufficient to grow productive crops if the soil is fertile enough.[43] Growing seasons vary greatly from region to region, so that the southern tip of Ontario and interior British Columbia can safely grow soft fruits while northern Ontario, large parts of the Maritimes and northern Quebec have seasons barely long enough to grow oats.[44] But if climate were the only determinant, regional disparities would not be as great as they are.

Another of Canada's problems is that most of the country has only shallow, young soil spread over rocky terrain. In the west the Cordillera rises to spectacular heights more suited to viewing than farming. Most of Manitoba, Ontario, Quebec and the Northwest Territories and much of Saskatchewan are covered by the Canadian Shield, whose old, low hills and valleys were scoured nearly clean of soil during the last Pleistocene ice age. Much of the Atlantic region is covered by the rocky northern extension of the Appalachian mountains. Only on the Prairies and in the Great Lakes-St. Lawrence Lowlands is there any extensive region of fertile soil combined with a climate conducive to agriculture. The regions which do possess good climate and good soil tend to have higher population, better per-capita income and superior services, while other regions are more sparsely populated—if at all.

Canada's vast size and her expanses of bare Precambrian rock have not been entirely a curse, for they have provided her with at least four resources—water, trees, petroleum and minerals. Water has enabled Canada to generate large amounts of electricity cheaply and has consequently made electrical energy one of her most plentiful commodities.[45] This in turn has provided the basis for industrial development she might not otherwise have had and has helped to temper the effects of the energy short-

[41]André Raynauld, *The Canadian Economic System*, p. 57.
[42]For a general description see P.B. Clibbon and L.E. Hamelin, "Landforms," in Warkentin, pp. 57–77.
[43]See F.B. Watts, "Climate, Vegetation, Soil," in Warkentin, pp. 77–111.
[44]Detailed maps are included in F.B. Watts, "Climate, Vegetation, Soil" in Warkentin.
[45]See G. Wilson, S. Gordon and S. Judek, *Canada, An Appraisal of Its Needs and Resources* (University of Toronto Press, Toronto, 1965).

ages of the 1970s. Water has also provided the basis for one of Canada's largest industries, tourism. The oil and gas reserves in Alberta and perhaps in the north and off the East Coast have helped Canada avoid the brunt of the oil shortages which have afflicted most industrial nations. Trees have made Canada the western world's largest producer of newsprint and one of the largest producers of paper.[46] Mineral deposits have made isolated areas of the Canadian Shield and the Cordillera pockets of prosperity.

However, Canada's primary resources are not evenly distributed. Significant amounts of hydroelectric power can be generated only in large watersheds, and mineralization occurs in isolated pockets in the rock. The best forest stands tend to be in provinces already better off than the others. Ontario, whose secondary industries are Canada's largest, also has the largest mineral production. British Columbia, with fertile interior valleys, also has the best timber stands and large deposits of minerals; and Alberta, already agriculturally advanced, has the largest reserves of oil. The Maritimes, with poor agricultural prospects, also lack the large mineral deposits, stands of timber and hydroelectric power resources of central and western Canada.

Geography has also contrived to cut off one section of Canada from another. The Maritimes are separated from the rest of Canada by the Northern Appalachians, and the Canadian Shield cuts off Ontario and Quebec from the Prairies, which are in turn separated from British Columbia by the Cordillera. This often leads to the observation that Canada is really five distinct regions, and that Canadian nationhood has been achieved in spite of physical barriers which should have lined us up along a north-south rather than an east-west axis.[47] The difficult geographical environment has meant that the building of communication lines had to be a cooperative venture, national in scope. The lessons learned about cooperation and about the uses to which government can be put to overcome big obstacles may have done much to help in building Canadian attitudes towards government.

At any rate, it is clear that regional disparity is one of the most significant factors producing cleavages in the Canadian political system, and that peculiar Canadian geographical problems have brought about responses by the Canadian political system which make it distinctive. Aside from the vital problems of ethnic cleavage, which we will discuss shortly, perhaps the greatest problems of Canadian federalism derive from regional cleavages caused by geographical discrepancies.

For the men who must make political decisions, the difficulties posed by regional disparities are intensified by the fact that even among specialists in the field there is not unanimous agreement on what must be

[46]The manufacture of pulp and paper is Canada's leading industry in terms of employment, salaries and wages paid and in value added by manufacture. Statistics Canada, *Canada 1971*, p. 245.

[47]The number of regions into which Canada should be divided for economic analysis is the subject of some debate. For example, one text has suggested that 68 regions is a more appropriate number than five. See P. Camu, E.P. Weeks, and Z.Q. Sametz, *Economic Geography of Canada*, (Macmillan, Toronto, 1964).

done to solve the problem. For example, can the Maritimes best be helped by a decrease in national tariffs combined with economic aid to industries already there, or would they be helped more by encouraging new and growing industries to locate there while letting the older ones die a natural death? Or might the problem best be attacked by encouraging greater mobility of the labour force while leaving industry alone to locate where it can grow fastest—usually in Southern Ontario or Quebec?[48]

In general, policy makers have adopted the policy of encouraging growth in certain "designated areas" which are presently depressed but in which the application of capital might be expected to produce significant growth. Most provincial governments have their own legislation. The federal government has attacked the problem in many ways: through the Agricultural and Rural Development Act (ARDA), the Fund for Rural Economic Development, the Atlantic Development Board, The Area Development Agency, and most recently, through the amalgamation of many of these plans under the Department of Regional Economic Expansion.[49]

Finally, we should re-emphasize that in a very large and very sparsely settled territory like Canada, solutions which may be appropriate elsewhere do not always fit. For example, the methods of transportation development which were successful in the United States could not be applied in Canada. Because transportation links to remote areas of low population density do not pay, most major developments in Canada have been carried out by government alone or by private enterprise with huge government subsidies. Examples include the national railways and more recently the Trans-Canada Pipeline. Later, when the links themselves create a market for their own use it may be possible to make a profit, and in that situation private business can be induced to invest capital; but for many such projects, private enterprise is simply not appropriate. Broadcasting could be suggested as another example: in the early days of radio there were not enough customers to allow a national network to pay its own way, yet a national network could obviously be useful in fostering national unity. The solution adopted was for the government to step in and create the Canadian Radio Broadcasting Commission. In fact, the Commission and its successor, the Canadian Broadcasting Corporation, have never been profitable because they have had to provide services to remote areas and on topics with little sponsor appeal. The Canadian situation in this respect can be contrasted with the American one where there are no publicly owned railways (although the U.S. Federal government has recently moved into the operation of rail passenger services) and where public

[48]Two articles epitomizing the different sides of this debate are W.J. Woodfine, "Canada's Atlantic Provinces, A Study in Regional Economic Retardation," *The Commerce Journal*, 1962 and T.W. Wilson, "Financial Assistance with Regional Development," in J.H. Deutsch *et al.* (eds.), *The Canadian Economy*, (Macmillan, Toronto, 1965), p. 402 ff.

[49]See T.N. Brewis, "Regional Development," in T.N. Brewis *et al.*, *Canadian Economic Policy*, (Macmillan, Toronto, 1965), p. 316 ff. The most important single governmental response has been the extensive use of equalization payments.

broadcasting is still a fledgling. Higher population density, a richer environment and, occasionally, a lower level of service can make such enterprises profitable in the United States, so private industry operates them.

SOCIAL STRATIFICATION: CLASS CLEAVAGE IN CANADA

In addition to the *horizontal cleavages* we have discussed, most societies have *vertical lines of cleavage* which cut across regional boundaries. Sociologists describe these vertical lines of cleavage as *social stratification* or *class cleavages.*[50]

One's place in the class structure is by no means wholly tied to money or possessions.[51] In pre-industrial societies there were many criteria other than the possession of property by which a person's social position could be determined, and even in North American society money or possessions are not the only ways in which high status is reflected. For example, priests usually have almost no personal possessions and little income, yet their status is usually thought of as being higher than, say, that of plumbers, who may make a great deal more money.

There are a number of criteria that may be used to measure a person's socio-economic status. One scale proposed for the Canadian setting depends upon a ranking of occupations based on a combination of factors such as years of education or annual income. Another depends upon a survey of people's perceptions of other people's occupations.[52] These *objective* systems of measurement can be buttressed by *subjective* systems, in which a person is asked to rate his own status. No one of these scales is perfect, and occasionally someone like the priest, who ranks fairly low on the income scale, will rank fairly high on some of the other scales. For the most part, however, all of them are highly interrelated. A person who ranks high on one is likely to rank high on others as well. For this reason it is fairly safe to use any scale, whether of occupation, education, or income, as an index of social class in Canada. Since income data are the most readily collected and the most widely available, we will base most of our discussions on the income scale. The terms "upper class," "middle class," and "lower class," however, also connote distinctions based on education and life style as well as on income.

---

[50]The authors will use the terms *class cleavage, vertical cleavage* and *social stratification* virtually synonymously, although if one were to delve deeper into the literature it might become clear that there are subtle distinctions that can be made between these terms.
[51]Bernard R. Blishen, "A Socio-Economic Index for Occupations in Canada," *Canadian Review of Sociology and Anthropology*, vol. 4, No. 1, February, 1967.
[52]Peter C. Pineo and John Porter, "Occupational Prestige in Canada," *Canadian Review of Sociology and Anthropology*, vol. 4, No. 1, pp. 24–40, February, 1967.

Poverty in Canada[53] The question of just how unequal the distribution of income is in Canada can be answered by reference to Figure 2-1. This figure is a *Lorenz curve* which shows, graphically, inequalities of income.[54] If all people had equal income, then the curve, which expresses the cumulative per cent of income received versus the cumulative percent-

Figure 2-1

DISTRIBUTION OF FAMILY AND UNATTACHED INDIVIDUAL NONFARM INCOME IN CANADA, 1965

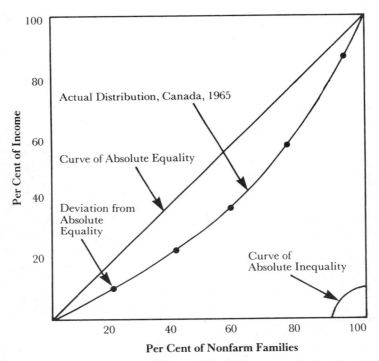

Source: Paul A. Samuelson and Anthony Scott, *Economics*, 3rd Canadian edition (McGraw–Hill Ryerson, Toronto, 1971), p. 150.

[53]The "discovery" by social scientists in the mid-1960s that the affluent society had a very large poverty component produced a deluge of literature on the subject. There are too many recent books on poverty in Canada for use to cite them all here. However, in addition to the sources cited elsewhere in this section, see Special Senate Committee on Poverty, *Poverty in Canada*, (Ottawa, Information Canada, 1971); Ian Adams *et al.*, *The Real Poverty Report*, (M.G. Hurtig, Edmonton, 1971); T.E. Reid, *Canada's Poor*, (Holt, Rinehart and Winston, Toronto, 1972).

[54]For a more detailed explanation and a comparison of Canada with other countries, see Paul Samuelson and Anthony Scott, *Economics*, 3rd Canadian ed., (McGraw–Hill, Toronto, 1971) pp. 145–153.

age of individuals, would be a straight line with a slope of 45 degrees. In that case 50 per cent of the families would have 50 per cent of total income, and the lowest 1 per cent of the families would have the same proportion of income as the highest 1 per cent (in which case, of course, there would be no "highest" and "lowest"). From this diagram and from Table 2-5 it can be seen that in 1965 the lowest 20 per cent of families in Canada received only 6.7 per cent of all income, while the upper 20 per cent received 38.4 per cent. Put otherwise this means that the families in the lowest 20 per cent of the population received only about one-sixth the income of the families in the upper 20 per cent.

TABLE 2-5: LOW INCOME FAMILIES IN CANADA

Percentile	Percent of Total Income				Mean Income/Family	
	1951	1961	1965	1973	1965	1973
1 to 20	6.1	6.6	6.2	6.1	$ 2,263	$4,306
21 to 40	12.9	13.4	13.1	12.9	4,542	8,793
41 to 60	17.4	18.2	18.0	18.1	6,102	11,978
61 to 80	22.5	23.4	23.5	23.9	7,942	15,653
81 to 100	41.1	38.4	39.0	38.9	13,016	25,654

Source: Economic Council of Canada, *Fifth Annual Review*, (Queen's Printer, Ottawa, 1968), p. 107, and Statistics Canada, Cat. 13-207, 1973. p. 117. Reproduced by permission of Information Canada.

This situation is highly resistant to change. The distribution of income in Canada today is little different from what it was in 1945, although it has improved since the 1920s. Table 2-5 indicates the distribution of income in Canada in each of four postwar years.[55] It can be seen that these figures have changed only slowly over the 22-year period covered. The right-most column of the table indicates the mean income per family for families in each group in 1973. Thus, for example, the mean income of families in the fourth group (having that income below which 80 per cent of families fall) is $15,653. Expressed otherwise, the average family in the lowest 20 per cent of the population earned $4,306 in 1973, while the average family in the highest 20 per cent earned $25,654.

Table 2-5 shows the picture in broad outline. More detailed figures reveal an even greater inequality of income in Canada. In its *Fifth Annual Review*, the Economic Council of Canada pointed out that in 1961 some 916,000 families and 416,000 single individuals in urban centres in Can-

[55]A percentile is defined as the figure below which that percentage of cases lie. Thus the 20th percentile of family income is that income below which 20 per cent of the incomes in Canada lie.

ada were living below what it considered to be the poverty line. When the 150,000 farm families who were in similar circumstances are added in, it appears that in 1961 some 4.75 million people in Canada were below the poverty line. This was 29 per cent of the entire Canadian population. In 1965, at the height of a boom, the figure dropped to 24.5 per cent, but it probably rose again at the end of the 1960s.[56] If we adopt a higher estimate of what constitutes economic discomfort and suggest that $3,000 is a barely adequate income for a single person and $6,000 for a family of four, the figure is even more surprising, for in that case fully 40 per cent of Canadians are below at least a "discomfort" line.[57]

Where are the poor? Why do other Canadians not see more of them and consequently become more aware of the problem? To a large extent, poverty can be hidden in modern society. Clothing has become cheaper so that the poor no longer live in rags even if they do suffer from dietary deficiencies and live in condemned and overcrowded homes. Expressways may cross over poor neighbourhoods but the sixty-mile-per-hour commuter never sees them. The poor have been and continue to be collectively inarticulate so that unless someone speaks for them or organizes them they are unheard.

The poor in Canada do not live only in depressed areas of the country. We often think of the Maritimes and Eastern Quebec as being Canada's poorest regions, and indeed they are, but between one-third and one-half of all poor people in Canada live west of Three Rivers.[58] In Canada the poor are often thought of as living in rural areas, and it is true that the concentration of poor people is higher in those areas, but 62 per cent of low income families live in urban areas and over 30 per cent live in supposedly affluent metropolitan areas.[59] While we think of the poor as being unemployed, the heads of 68 per cent of poor families were employed for at least part of the year. While we think of the poor as tending to be elderly, the heads of 77 per cent of poor families were under 65. Eighty-seven per cent of poor families are headed by men although there is a higher concentration of poverty in female-headed households.[60]

In Canada one of the largest groups of the poor is to be found among the native peoples.[61] The Economic Council reports that in 1965,

[56]The Economic Council of Canada, *Fifth Annual Report*, p. 109. The Council defined low-income (impoverished) individuals or families as having less than $1,-500 per year income for an individual or $3,500 for a family of four. These figures may have been valid in 1965 but inflation since then suggests that in 1975 we should add at least 60 per cent to all numbers, making the 1975 equivalents $2,400 and $5,600 respectively.

[57]The average college student in 1974 probably "makes do" fairly decently on less than $3,000 per year and hence may have difficulty in seeing such an income as barely adequate. However, picture living the rest of your life on that income and without the various subsidies in the form of heat, light, etc., which governments provide to students.

[58]The Economic Council of Canada, *Fifth Annual Report*, p. 104.

[59]The Economic Council of Canada, *Fifth Annual Report*, p. 112.

[60]The Economic Council of Canada, *Fifth Annual Report*, p. 112.

[61]Among Canadian native peoples there were 18,000 Eskimos and 297,000 Indians

78.2 per cent of Indian households had incomes of less than $3,000 per year, and over half of them had incomes less than $2,000. The average life expectancy of an Indian woman in 1965 was 25 years, and infant mortality among Indians was ten times that of the general population. In spite of this, the Indian population is the fastest growing in Canada. But fewer than one-third of present reservation lands could be made capable of supporting even their present populations in reasonable fashion.[62]

Undoubtedly the greatest handicap the poor face in modern society is simply low income. The problem goes deeper than that, though, for poverty creates a sub-culture within the larger Canadian culture—a sub-culture with its own norms and values. Some of these norms, such as a lack of respect for education or a lack of belief in its necessity, make it extremely difficult for the poor to escape their situation. Poverty leads as well to crime, disease and low productivity and constitutes a vast waste of potential talent within Canadian society.[63]

The existence of such large numbers of impoverished people in Canada puts a tremendous strain on the Canadian political system. The stress is felt everywhere in the system but probably most acutely at the provincial and local levels, which are responsible under the British North America Act for welfare and for otherwise alleviating many of the problems caused by poverty. However, lack of financial resources on the part of many of the provinces and municipalities prompted Ottawa to take over the unemployment insurance scheme by constitutional amendment in 1940 and has increasingly led the federal government into financing other welfare programs such as family allowances and health insurance.

In addition to the direct costs of poverty, there are a number of indirect or potential stresses which it may place on the political system. In addition to the costs of wasted talent, crime and disease, there is the possibility of a political upheaval which could be precipitated if the poor ever became a coherent group in society. If that 40 per cent of Canada's population were ever to be mobilized simultaneously, the Canadian political system would be subjected to extreme stress. On the other hand, the poor have traditionally been impossible to organize in large numbers. Recently, social animation projects and other forms of community organization have occasionally succeeded on a local level, but there is so far little reason to anticipate much in the way of national mobilization of the poor in Canada.

The Canadian Elite So far our discussion of stratification in Canada has been far from complete. If 40 per cent of Canadians are below

in 1971, (*Canada Year Book*, 1973, page 215). The Economic Council of Canada, (*Fifth Annual Report*, p. 121) estimates that there were about 60,000 Métis in 1961, and a reasonable guess for 1971 would be 80,000.

[62]The Economic Council of Canada, *Fifth Annual Report*, p. 122. See also Harold Cardinal, *The Unjust Society*, (Hurtig, Edmonton, 1969).

[63]See Ian Adams, *The Poverty Wall*, (McClelland and Stewart, Toronto, 1970) and W.E. Mann (ed.), *Poverty and Social Policy in Canada*, (Copp Clark, Toronto, 1970) and, as a general bibliographical work, Freda Paltiel (ed.), *Poverty*, (Canadian Welfare Council, Ottawa, 1966).

the discomfort line, then 60 per cent are above it; and these constitute a heterogeneous group. On the top end of the scale is a very small group holding the top positions in industry, business, the professions and the bureaucracy. Estimates of the size of this "elite" vary depending on the criteria used to describe it, but at most it comprises only some two or three per cent of the population. We will focus on the political and bureaucratic elite when we discuss decision-making processes in Canadian politics, but we can ask a broader question here: what influence has this small elite in making the major decisions that guide Canadian society?

Undoubtedly the key work in this area is Professor John Porter's *The Vertical Mosaic*.[64] Porter first addresses himself to the question of whether or not there is a Canadian elite and, having decided that there is, he examines its characteristics. He suggests that the top positions in a number of hierarchies such as business, religion, education, politics and the bureaucracy are likely to be occupied by men with similar backgrounds. These include British or possibly French ethnic origin, a middle-class or higher upbringing, and Catholic, Anglican or United Church religious affiliations. There are also similarities in educational background in this group and tendencies toward other social interconnections.

But if these men are potentially a "ruling class," do they actually behave as one? It seems unlikely. The great complexity of the decision-making process in Canada ensures that control by any one small group would be extremely difficult. Furthermore, the fact that members of the various elites may share a similar outlook on life is no guarantee that under the complex pressures which come to bear on any particular decision they will act as a uniform class. On the other hand, given that the decision makers are primarily middle and upper class in origin and that most inputs from the environment are channelled through middle-class organizations, it seems probable that the voice of lower-class citizens is, at best, somewhat muffled.[65]

The Swollen Middle If the various elites make up only two or three per cent of the population and those below the poverty line about forty per cent, obviously the middle income group of the population, made up of the middle class and better-off members of the working class, constitutes a majority of the Canadian population.[66] It must not be supposed that this middle-income group is by any means homogeneous, for there are wide variations in behavioural patterns which may lead to differences in political behaviour and in the type of demands fed into the political system.

[64](University of Toronto Press, Toronto, 1965). See also Wallace Clement, *The Canadian Corporate Elite*, (McClelland and Stewart, Toronto, 1975) for an updating and re-interpretation of Porter's work.

[65]The whole question of elites and decision making is discussed in much more detail in chapter 15. Its brief consideration here is not intended to suggest that the question is unimportant.

[66]In 1972 the mean income of all Canadian families was $11,311 and in Ontario it was $12,632. Thus the middle groups live at least comfortably if not lavishly. *Globe and Mail*, Toronto, Nov. 9, 1973.

Within this middle-income group, the dividing line between the middle class and the working class depends not so much on income as on type of occupation. Many skilled tradesmen such as plumbers or electricians earn more money than many junior executives, yet the junior executive tends to emulate the life style of his corporate seniors while the tradesman does not.[67] The differences in behaviour appear to derive mainly from family traditions, for working-class families tend to remain working class for many generations, and from job security, for the junior executive is less subject to the vagaries of the business cycle than is the tradesman or industrial worker.

Stratification and Canadian Politics There are obviously deep class differences among Canadians. Presumably these deep differences could be translated into deep political cleavages. There are, indeed, reasons to suggest that class-based cleavages are important to the Canadian political system. When we discuss political participation among Canadians we will see that lower-class Canadians take little interest in the political system, have little awareness of its relevance to them, and do very little to attempt to influence it. The higher up the status hierarchy we go, the greater the amount of political participation. Viewed this way, it would seem that stratification-based cleavages are significant for the political system.

On the other hand, we will soon see that class is not a vital determinant of Canadian voting behaviour or party identification. There have been attempts to establish class-based parties, but these have been less than overwhelmingly successful. The Independent Labour Party flashed briefly across Ontario politics in the 1920s and died. The Canadian Communist party has never been anything but a weak joke, and even the more broadly based CCF–NDP movement has had trouble establishing itself as a viable party with a real chance of gaining national power. In fact the CCF–NDP has tended to succeed in inverse proportion to the amount of attention it has paid to class cleavages.

Whatever the influence of social class on the political behaviour of Canadians, the presence of inequalities of opportunity and of large scale poverty has called forth many responses from the political decision makers. Thus in 1968-69 direct welfare expenditures by Canadian governments totalled 3.7 billion dollars or nearly 16 per cent of all expenditures by all levels of government that year.[68] If we include spending on health care and education (which have less redistributive effect than direct welfare spending but which *may* contribute in some measure to the equalization of opportunity), the sum expended in 1965 was some 42 per cent of total government outlays and over 13 per cent of Canada's GNP.[69] By 1971–72

[67]See the interesting summary of different behaviour patterns in Nariman K. Dhalla, *These Canadians: A Sourcebook of Marketing and Socio-Economic Facts*, (McGraw–Hill, Toronto, 1966), pp. 177–84.
[68]Canadian Tax Foundation, *The National Finances*, 1971–72, p. 16.
[69]Richard Bird, *The Growth of Government Spending in Canada*, (National Tax Foundation, Toronto, 1970), p. 160. Bird's analysis of why spending in this area has risen

federal expenditures on purely welfare items had risen to 4.2 billion or 28 per cent of the federal budget and the rapid rise in unemployment insurance payments has since added another jump to the total.

There are literally hundreds of federal, provincial and municipal welfare programs, ranging from the Old Age Security payments, which resulted in the payment of 2.2 billion dollars in 1971–72, down to local welfare programs in the smallest municipal governments.[70] The last 40 years have seen a rapid and steady growth in the size of such programs, both in absolute terms and as a proportion of GNP. For whatever reasons, these appear to be a recognition, though belated and still modest, that not all Canadians have shared equally in post-war affluence and that those who miss out on affluence in good times also suffer disproportionately in more difficult times. The responses of the political system to this problem cannot be labelled adequate by humanitarian standards, but they illustrate that political systems will adapt even if slowly, to major demands from their environments.

FRENCH–ENGLISH RELATIONS IN CANADA

For much of the period since the British conquest in 1760, the most obvious of Canada's cleavages has been one between Canadians of French origin and the rest of Canada—"English" Canada, so called. French Canadians do form a substantial minority. In 1971 Canadians of French origin constituted nearly 30 per cent of the Canadian population. About 29 per cent of our people learned French as their first language and still understand it. But the rest of Canada is not an undifferentiated "majority." About 25 per cent of Canadians are of neither British nor French ethnic background, and some 13.5 per cent learned some language other than English or French in childhood and still understand it. Why, then, does the cleavage between French and English constantly confront Canadian politicians while the potential cleavage between the "other" Canadians and the two original groups of Canadians remains largely in the background? What are the reasons for the importance of the French–English cleavage in Canada and how does this major environmental factor affect Canada's political process?

The Causes of French–English Cleavage Undoubtedly the main reason why the French–English cleavage is the major one in Canada and why other ethnic groups tend to fade into merely local political significance is that no single one of the other groups is very large. About 6

rapidly is among the best short treatments of this subject. See pp. 160–167.

[70]Whether justifiably or not, Canadian governments are fairly proud of their welfare programs and go to great lengths to describe them to the public. Thus detailed information on the structure of welfare programs can be found in any provincial government bookstore or in Information Canada outlets. Useful brief descriptions are available in *The Canada Year Book* or *Canada 1973*, both Information Canada publications or in The Canadian Tax Foundation's annual review called *The National Finances*.

per cent of the Canadian population is of German origin, and Ukrainians, Italians, Dutch and Scandinavians each constitute between two and three per cent of the total population. Thus, the French Canadians are over five times as numerous as the biggest of the other ethnic groups. Each of the other groups seems to feel as close to the English Canadians as to any of the other small ethnic groups, and for the majority of Canadians of other ethnic origin, one of the primary goals in ethnic relations appears to be to assimilate with the English Canadians.[71]

There are other factors in addition to simple numbers which tend to increase the English–French cleavage in Canada. One is that the great majority of French Canadians live in one area. In 1971, over 80 per cent of the residents of Quebec listed French as their mother tongue, while only 13 per cent listed English as the language they had first learned.[72] Outside of the Montreal area, the proportion of the population of Quebec claiming French ancestry rises to over 90 per cent, and 77 per cent speak only French. In the rest of Canada, of course, the position is reversed: French is the mother tongue of only about 6.6 per cent of the people, and in British Columbia the proportion is only 1.7 per cent.

This geographical homogeneity of both the French and non-French groups is important, for without it, it is unlikely that French Canada would have persisted as a cultural entity. As it is, the day-to-day contacts of most French Canadians are with their ethnic confrères, and while there is an occasional requirement for English, especially in Montreal, it is quite possible for many French-speaking Quebeckers to get along without ever speaking English or seeing an English person. What is true for Quebeckers is true in reverse for many western Canadians; they have absolutely no need to use the French language.

While the coincidence of ethnic and geographic cleavage is probably the most important factor in maintaining the cultural duality of Canada, there are other important coincident cleavages. Of particular importance is the coincidence of religious and ethnic lines. In 1971, some 46 per cent of the population of Canada was Roman Catholic and 50 per cent Protestant—and virtually all French Canadians were Roman Catholic. Granted that there is a difference between being nominally a member of a particular denomination and being a practising member, it can still be argued that certain cultural characteristics are transmitted via religion. In any case French Canadians are much more likely to attend church than English Canadians. In 1965 eighty-five per cent of French-speaking Roman Catholics in Canada attended church at least weekly compared with 31 per cent of English-speaking Protestants.[73] The influence of the

[71]There are many small groups of "other" Canadians who prefer not to be assimilated but rather to maintain their distinct traditions. These may occasionally be significant in local politics, but unless they become violent, as did one fanatical sect of the Russian Doukhobors in the 1950s, they remain unnoticed in national politics. Even locally they are much less likely to be politically active (except within their own sect) than the original or "charter" ethnic groups.

[72]*Canada Year Book, 1972*, p. 1370, Table 4.

[73]Data from a 1965 public opinion survey directed by Professor J. Meisel of Queen's University.

Roman Catholic Church in Quebec has been directed towards the preservation of the cultural integrity of French Canadians, for the Church in Quebec has viewed assimilation as a threat to its position.[74] Furthermore, the churches form the social centres of small Quebec communities; they have traditionally provided the sort of gathering place which is essential to the establishment of that group cohesion which maintains cultural independence.

Through long periods of Canada's early history the French–English cleavage was actually overshadowed by the religious.[75] The Irish immigrants of the 1840s transplanted much of the Orange–Roman Catholic strife from Ireland, and for some 50 years afterwards the predominant cleavage in Canada was Protestant–Catholic rather than French–English. Schools were denominational, not ethnic, as were hospitals, welfare institutions, newspapers and many of the other institutions which connect citizens to society.

Still, nineteenth-century Canadians, no less than many of their descendents today, had a tendency to equate the religious and ethnic cleavages. Thus, Protestants in the nineteenth and early twentieth centuries often saw a close tie between "popery" and "knavery," and since the French Canadians were papist to a man, it followed that they must also be knaves to a man. In 1889 the Toronto *Mail* warned that in view of French migration into Eastern Ontario,

> Ontario will not be safe. . .our eastern gate has already been opened. . .Catholic invasion is already streaming through. . .to detach Eastern Ontario from the British and Protestant civilization of which it now forms a part and annex it to the territory of the French race which is also the dominion of the priest,

and, added Dalton McCarthy in speaking of the Jesuit Estates Bill:

> This is a British country and the sooner we take in hand our French Canadians and make them British in sentiment and teach them the English language the less trouble we shall have to prevent. Now is the time when the ballot box will decide this great question; and if it does not supply the remedy in this generation, bayonets will supply it in the next.[76]

Today there are still other cleavages than the religious and geographic which aggravate the ethnic dimension of the French–English cleavage. Undoubtedly the most important of these is the economic disparity that exists between Quebec and most of the provinces west of her, between French Canadians and English Canadians in general, and between French and English within Quebec.

[74]On the role of the church in French Canada, see Jean Charles Falardeau, "The Role and Importance of the Church in French Canada," translated from *Esprit*, Paris, août–septembre 1952, in Marcel Rioux and Yves Martin, *French Canadian Society*. (McClelland and Stewart, Toronto, 1964). A more passionately separatist statement of somewhat the same ideas can be found in Marcel Rioux, *Quebec in Question*, (James Lewis and Samuel, Toronto, 1971), Ch. 3, p. 27 ff and *passim*.

[75]K.D. McRae, "Consociationalism and the Canadian Political System," K.D. McRae (ed.), *Consociational Democracy: Political Accommodation in Segmented Societies*, (McClelland and Stewart, Carleton Library #79, 1974), pp. 242 ff.

[76]Both quoted in Joseph Schull, *Laurier*, (Macmillan, Toronto, 1965), p. 227.

In 1961 the income of French-Canadian male members of the labour force was 85.8 per cent of the national average, whereas that of men who were of British origin was 110 per cent of the average.[77] Even more important is the fact that within Quebec, French-Canadian incomes were 92 per cent of the provincial average while English Canadians received 140 per cent of the provincial average.[78] Among Canadian ethnic groups only Italians had lower income levels than French Canadians. In Quebec, per capita income in 1970 was 90 per cent of the national average and only 78 per cent of that of Ontario. Among French Canadians there is a larger proportion of poor families than there is among English Canadians, and there may also be a larger disparity in incomes, for in 1961 37 per cent of the French-Canadian labour force received less than $3,000 per year and fully 78 per cent were receiving less than $5,000, while the figures for English Canada were 31 and 70 per cent.

Unemployment figures by ethnic origin are not available but, aside from the Atlantic Provinces, Quebec consistently has the highest levels of unemployment in Canada, and it is a safe bet that it is not the high income British Quebeckers who appear in the jobless lines.[79] Moreover, aside from the one or two years before the Expo 67 World Fair, Quebec's unemployment picture has worsened relative to the rest of Canada through most of the years following World War II.[80] The causes of these high unemployment figures are many, and it is not our intention to speculate on them here; however, the effect has been a certain amount of discontent, frequently expressed in ethnic terms—fertile soil upon which further ethnic tensions may grow.

This dissatisfaction may be further fed by the fact that, both within and outside of Quebec, French Canadians hold jobs with lower status than those held by English Canadians. The "repatriation" of industry in Quebec (by which is meant the taking over of executive jobs by French Canadians) has been going on since the start of the 1960s, but a vastly disproportionate share of "boss" jobs, from foreman to company president, is still held by English Canadians. The causes of this problem are many, ranging from the lack of a French-Canadian entrepreneurial class, to straightforward ethnic discrimination by English managers, but a sense of resentment on both sides has often been the result. The resentment on the French side comes from a feeling that talents are going unrecognized; on the English side, it may result from the feeling of "we did all the risk-taking; we supplied all the capital; why shouldn't we hold the top jobs?"

Quebec is not primarily an agricultural economy and has not been

[77]Report of the Royal Commission on Bilingualism and Biculturalism, Book III, The Work World, vol. 3A, (Ottawa, 1969), pp. 18–19.
[78]Report of the Royal Commission on Bilingualism and Biculturalism, Book III, The Work World, vol. 3A, (Ottawa, 1969), pp. 18–19.
[79]For more extensive figures see Sheilagh Hodgins Milner and Henry Milner, The Decolonization of Quebec, (McClelland and Stewart, 1973), p. 53.
[80]In Quebec unemployment rates have risen from an average of 3.3 per cent in the five year period from 1946 to 1951 to 9.3 per cent in 1956–60. The corresponding figures for all of Canada are 2.9 and 5.6 per cent. In 1969 the relative rates were 6.9 and 4.7 per cent.

for many years. Notwithstanding English-Canadian misconceptions to the effect that most French Canadians are *habitants*, and in spite of the best efforts of the Roman Catholic church for most of a century, the base of Quebec's economy is today and has been for many years, industrial. Quebec, next to British Columbia, is the least agricultural province in Canada, with only 4.5 per cent of the labour force in agriculture versus 6.5 per cent for Canada as a whole.[81] What agriculture there is is generally not advanced. In 1963, a survey by the Agricultural and Rural Development Agency showed that over half of Quebec's farm units were not properly profitable and that Quebec had the lowest farm incomes, the lowest educational levels of farmers, the largest per capita debt among farmers, and the largest farm family size in Canada.

Quebec's industrialization was rapid, and the rapid depopulation of Quebec's countryside has had certain unsettling effects. The high rate of unemployment, for example, results partly from the migration of unskilled workers to cities and partly from the rapid population growth in the province in the past. Because of the lack of job opportunities, many of the most able workers leave Quebec and those who remain behind may make less productive employees.[82] Societies in such rapid transition have often undergone turmoil and expressed their discontent either internally or against some easily definable external force. Discontent may increase when rapid industrialization slows down and expected increases in living standards and job opportunities, particularly for youth with middle class aspirations, fail to materialize quickly.[83] This too has happened in Quebec since World War II, and the external force on which anger can be vented is close at hand in the person of *les maudits anglais*.

It is not correct to designate the Quebec economy as "backward." In fact, in the sense of being industrialized it is well advanced. Yet clearly, French Canadians have not shared fully in the fruits of this industrial society, and this fact has helped deepen the French-English cleavage in Canada. A number of conflicting theories have been advanced to explain the failure of French Canadians to share in industrial rewards. Probably the most venerable, but least accurate, is the theory that because of their cultural background French Canadians are simply unable to operate a modern economy. This view was stated at length at the turn of the century by a prominent French-Canadian intellectual, Sir John Bourinet:

> In commercial and financial enterprise the French Canadians cannot compete with their fellow citizens of British origin who practically control the great commercial undertakings and bank institutions of Lower Canada, especially in Montreal. Generally speaking the French Canadians cannot compare with the English population as agriculturalists. . . .It must be ad-

[81] *The Canada Year Book, 1972*, p. 834., Statistics Canada.
[82] A. Raynauld, *The Canadian Economic System*, p. 64 ff.
[83] See James C. Davies, "Toward a Theory of Revolution" *The American Sociological Review*, XXVII, No. 1 (February, 1962), pp. 5–19 for a full statement of the theory that revolution frequently results from a gap between expected economic rewards and the actual satisfaction of economic wants created when a society experiences a long period of improving circumstances followed by a sharp drop in economic well being.

mitted, too, that the French population has less enterprise and less disposition to adopt new machines and improved agricultural implements, than the people of the other provinces.

As a rule the habitant lives contentedly on very little. Give him a pipe of native tobacco, a chance for discussing politics, a gossip with his fellows at the church door after service, a visit now and then to the country town and he will be happy. It does not take much to amuse him, while he is quite satisfied that his spiritual safety is secured as long as he is within the sound of the church bells, goes regularly to confession and observes all the *fêtes d'obligation*. If he or one of his family can only get a little office in the municipality or the "government," then his happiness is nearly perfect.

Like the people from whom he is descended—many of whose characteristics he has never lost since his residence of centuries on the American continent—he is greatly influenced by matters of feeling and sentiment, and the skilful master of rhetoric, etc.[84]

One wonders whether this is a description of people or of old hound dogs. It is an expression, albeit an extreme one, of the point of view which saw French Canada as simply an isolated folk society. This view does not stand up to close examination. At the time the above quotation was written, Quebec was undergoing a rapid burst of industrialization, and by the end of World War I less than half the population of Quebec was rural: Quebec was ahead of Canada in this respect.[85] The annual rate of industrial growth in Quebec since then has been satisfactory, usually equalling that of Ontario, though the gap between the two provinces has not closed appreciably.

However, while Quebec's growth rate may have been satisfactory, the participation of French Canadians in that growth has not. If we do not accept the more extreme forms of the "cultural difference" hypothesis, we must suggest something in its place: a historical interpretation may be valuable here.[86]

It is generally agreed that prior to the British conquest, French Canada was a feudal society with a mercantile bourgeoisie capable of operating business and industry. The conquest destroyed the commercial

[84]Sir John Bourinet, *Canada* (G.P. Putman and Sons, New York, 1898), pp. 438–439.

[85]Raynauld, *The Canadian Economic System*, pp. 69–71.

[86]There has been for many years a great debate about the nature of French-Canadian society after the conquest and prior to industrialization, and the consequences of this structure for present day society in Quebec. On one side are the folk society analysts represented by Gerin, Miner, Hughes and, in an early extreme, Bourinet, and on the other are those who saw the Quebec of the nineteenth and early twentieth centuries as being much more than simply a folk culture. The most prominent member of this school is Philip Garigue. A synthesis produced by Herbert Guindon: "The Social Evolution of Quebec Reconsidered," *Canadian Journal of Economics and Political Science*, vol. 26, Nov. 1969, pp. 533–551 sums up the argument and produces a challenging synthesis. Parts of the debate are reproduced in Marcel Rioux and Yves Martin, *French Canadian Society*, vol. 1, (McClelland and Stewart, Toronto, 1964). An interpretation similar to the one given here but with a separatist slant may be found in Marcel Rioux, *Quebec in Question* (James Lewis and Samuel, Toronto, 1971).

structure of French-Canadian society, and the British presence, plus the impoverishment of the colony by the war, induced most of the bourgeoisie to return to France. The only elite then left in the colony was that of the Church, and it moved naturally, together with newly arrived English-speaking businessmen, to fill whatever power gap remained. The Church took care of the spiritual and social needs of Quebec, and the English businessmen took care of its business needs. The loss of the entrepreneurial French elite was followed initially by a movement of French workers and small businessmen back to the soil and later to employee positions in industry. The proper ambition for a bright young French Canadian was not to enter business, but rather to become a member of the clergy, a doctor or a lawyer, or failing that, a farmer or a worker.

Once a· cycle like this had started it was extremely difficult to break. The Church and.English business elites naturally moved to perpetuate themselves, and a new elite, the governmental, arose to join the other two. Each of these elites developed vast bureaucratic structures and these structures had their own "maintenance needs" which, among other things, led them to recruit the best minds from the population: the same people who in a less firmly structured society might have become entrepreneurs. In this situation the lack of French-Canadian entrepreneurs persisted. To this lack was added a shortage of technically trained people, for the Church, the largest of the hierarchies and the one which dominated education in the province, had no need for them. As a result, technical jobs were not defined as "appropriate" ambitions for young French Canadians.

For a cycle like this to be broken, one of the hierarchies (in this case the governmental) had to gain ascendancy over the others and then respond to the real needs of the environment. This has been happening in Quebec at an accelerated rate since 1960. The government has displaced the Church in such fields as education and social welfare. For example one of the results has been an increasing number of technically trained French Canadians capable of handling many of the developmental needs of Quebec society. But an English-dominated business elite cannot simply turf out its many settled English technocrats and managers, so there has arisen an underemployment of a large number of intelligent young French Canadians who can see that the English hold the jobs to which they aspire—and in their own province at that. Control of the Quebec economy hangs tantalizingly just beyond the grasp of this rising class of French Canadians. Understandably they grow impatient with "200 years of waiting." The characteristic turmoil of a society whose middle class is in transition goes on, and one more problem deepens the French–English cleavage.

To conclude, then, the cultural difference between French and English Canada runs very deep and would undoubtedly constitute a lasting cleavage in itself, but it is the coincidence of the ethnic dimension of this cleavage with economic, geographical and religious cleavages that has made it loom so important. Quebec is not Canada's poorest province, nor is she the only province in rapid transition, and all of Canada's five regions can make equal claims to unique geographic problems. It is the running together of so many lines of cleavage with that between French and English that has created Canada's most serious political problem.

In the course of Canadian political history, the French–English cleavage has found expression in a series of crises, usually focused on a concrete issue. Hence it has provided some of the most interesting case studies of how the Canadian political system handles competing demands.

Ethnic Crises in Canada The chronology of French-English relations in Canada since the conquest of Quebec has been one of a series of crises of varying proportions, interspersed with periods of relative calm. Those who are the witnesses of each separate crisis tend to see it, usually wrongly, as the ultimate threat to the Canadian political community. In some ways each crisis of French–English relations is unique, but there are many features common to all of them. Thus, for example, while the FLQ crisis of 1970 was unique in its use of kidnapping, it was similar to crises of the past in other ways and a good deal less violent than some, notably the conscription crisis of 1917. It is therefore important to examine briefly some of the crises which have occurred since 1867 in order to set things in historical perspective.[87]

The period immediately following Confederation could be called a honeymoon period in ethnic relationships in Canada. Upper Canadians had achieved their goal of "representation by population" and French Canadians had a government in Quebec which they felt they could call their own. The coalition of Macdonald and Cartier seemed to be working well at the federal level, and the two ethnic groups seemed more concerned with internal than external problems. There was a brief uprising of the Métis people in Manitoba in 1870, in which an Ontario Orangeman died, but Louis Riel, the leader of the rebellion, fled to the United States and little more was heard of the incident. Riel, however, returned to Canada in 1885, and Canada's first major ethnic quarrel since 1867 broke around him. On his return he regrouped his Métis and Indian forces and led them in a second rebellion. Troops were sent from eastern Canada to put down the rebellion and Riel himself was captured and sentenced to death for treason. He became a symbol for anti-Catholic Protestants in Ontario and also for anti-Protestant Catholics in Quebec who were disturbed that the originally Catholic and French-speaking communities of Manitoba were being swamped by English-speaking settlers. Mass rallies swept both provinces. In Montreal *La Presse* screamed, "Henceforward there are no more Liberals nor Conservatives nor Castors. There are only PATRIOTS and TRAITORS." For Quebec the issue was one of the execution or pardon of a patriot; for Ontario, one of the execution or pardon of a traitor. Riel was executed. But the bitter dispute did not end with his death. Even today, he is often presented in French Canada as a hero and in English Canada as an addled, misguided and vaguely dishonest mystic.

The Riel controversy illustrates a number of important aspects of ethnic conflict in Canada. The first of these is the role played by the incumbent political leaders and their difficulty in coping with this environmentally produced stress. In this case the conflict had originated in large

[87]We were assisted in the preparation of this section by unpublished material prepared by Professor Richard Simeon of Queen's University.

measure from various religious and ethnic organizations, and politicians of both major parties had tried to moderate it. Macdonald tried to delay Riel's execution but was forced to give in to pressure from Ontario and particularly from the Orange Lodge, that most potent of forces in early Ontario politics. The French-Canadian members of Macdonald's cabinet, while privately opposed to the execution, refused to break with Macdonald and urged calm in Quebec. Sir Wilfrid Laurier, then leader of the opposition, opposed the government's handling of the matter, but urged his countrymen to adopt a moderate approach. The higher leaders of the Catholic Church also played a moderating role, and Bishop Taché even urged French-Canadian Conservative MPs not to vote against their own party.

Another set of leaders, however, acted to foster and exacerbate the conflict. In Ontario, the Orange Lodge and other Protestant groups played an important role in condemning the French-Canadian "papists." The Ontario press also played on ethnic hostilities. For example, the *Toronto Mail* declared:

> As Britons, we believe that the conquest will have to be fought over again. Lower Canada may depend on it, there will be no new treaty of 1763. The victors will not capitulate the next time.

In Quebec, on the other hand, the "out" political leaders seized this opportunity to overthrow and virtually destroy the provincial Conservative party. Playing on the same sort of ethnic hostility as that used by Ontario's Orangemen, Honoré Mercier formed the *Parti National*, which was aimed at uniting all French Canadians in a single party. The Parti National was never successful at the federal level, but it did gain power provincially in spite of the fact that it was opposed both by the church hierarchy (though not necessarily the lower clergy) and by the incumbent political leaders.

A pattern can be discerned here which recurs frequently in Canadian politics. The incumbent leaders and some important community institutions acted to minimize inter-group conflict. Other potential leaders, currently out of power, built up the hostilities on either side. From another perspective, the "outs" were attempting to use the crisis to gain political power, while the entrenched "ins" tried to save the *status quo*.

The bitterness left by the Riel affair and the hostilities raised in English Canada by many of the actions of the Mercier government in Quebec inspired a general climate of distrust, especially among middle levels of the elites of both sides. It was against this background that the Manitoba schools crisis erupted. Conflicts over schools were to provide the focal point for ethnic disagreements for the next 20 years and are still important today. All the earlier ones involved attempts by provincial governments to abolish or limit French-Catholic educational rights. In 1890, Manitoba passed a law establishing a completely non-sectarian educational system; previously Catholic schools had received provincial aid. Similar issues arose in New Brunswick, in Alberta and Saskatchewan when they became provinces in 1905, and most ominously, in Ontario just before World War I.

The Manitoba school crisis placed the opponents of the legislation in an anomalous position, for most of them were French, Roman Catholic and from Quebec. To oppose Manitoba's school law was to demand that the federal government, under its power to disallow provincial legislation, kill the plan. This would obviously be a case of federal interference in provincial affairs, and on principle, Quebec was opposed to this idea. Provincial politicians in Quebec squirmed uncomfortably while the church pressured the federal government to disallow the legislation. Laurier, still leader of the opposition, took his stand on the side of provincial rights and spent much of his time in the next few years explaining his position. The courts finally declared the Manitoba legislation to be within provincial powers, but recommended that the federal government disallow it anyhow, and the Conservative government finally did introduce a bill to invalidate the law. An election intervened and the subsequent campaign was fought largely on the school issue.

For once ethnic and religious divisions did not coincide, since the church, demanding that the legislation be killed, supported its traditional ally, the Conservative party, while Laurier, the first French Canadian to lead a national majority party, appealed to the Quebec electorate on ethnic grounds. Quebeckers could vote either for their church or for their ethnic group. They voted for their ethnic group, and Ontarians split their votes. The result was a Liberal victory. In Quebec Laurier received 54 per cent of the vote; it was the first time since Confederation that the Liberals had gained over half the vote. They were not to drop below 50 per cent again until 1958.

It was pointed out earlier that conflicts may be made worse by coincident cleavage lines. Similarly they may be muted when cleavage lines do not coincide. The lack of coincidence of two major cleavages did much to reduce the bitterness of this particular issue. It was settled by negotiations between Laurier and the provincial government in 1897, with the substance of the legislation basically unchanged.

In the early part of the twentieth century, several nationalist movements appeared in French Canada. The most important of these was led by Henri Bourassa. The new movements posed a threat to Laurier, as the nationalist demands generally ran counter to the Laurier policy of moderation and compromise. The movements may have been partially a response to defeats on the questions of language and education; but, ironically, it was the defection of Bourassa and his followers from the Quebec Liberal party which led to the election of the English-Canadian-dominated and strongly pro-British Borden government in 1911. Bourassa and the other nationalists supported the Conservatives in that election campaign, and this led to a 6 per cent decline in Liberal votes in Quebec. The campaign was unscrupulous on both sides and left a further residue of bitterness as Canada approached one of the greatest ethnic crises of its national life.

That crisis came during World War I. Perhaps Canada came closer to civil war then than at any other time in its history, as two issues combined to bring ethnic tensions to the boiling point. The first was yet another school crisis, brought on by a 1913 Ontario regulation limiting the use of French in Ontario schools. The second was the battle over conscription for war service.

At a time when national unity was most vital, the agitation over schools made it impossible. For Quebec, traditionally inward-looking, the educational issue was far more important than fighting a foreign war. There were frequent mass rallies and demonstrations in the province. Quebec school children and school boards contributed money to maintain the French schools in Ontario, as did many municipal governments in Quebec. A petition signed by 600,000 people asking for disallowance of the Ontario regulation was presented to the federal government. Virtually all elements of the Quebec population supported the attack on Ontario's "Regulation Seventeen." As *Le Soleil*, a Quebec City newspaper, put it: "The hour of mobilization of the French-Canadian race has come." This agitation had its counterpart in Ontario. The Orange Lodge demanded an end to all teaching of French in Ontario schools. English-Canadian newspapers presented the issue as a question of papist domination and as a French-Canadian conspiracy to dominate English Canada. Said one overwrought member of parliament: "Never shall we let the French Canadians plant in Ontario the disgusting speech they use." How widespread such feelings were on either side will never be known, but it appears they were general.

It was in this already tense atmosphere that the conscription crisis arose. At first all elements of the population had enthusiastically supported Canadian participation in the war, though some nationalist leaders like Bourassa advocated only limited activity. As the war went on, however, enlistments from Quebec, which had never been high, dwindled. There were many reasons for this: the overwhelmingly English nature of the armed forces, the lack of French-speaking units and the failure to promote French Canadians, the hostility arising out of the school issue, and the contrast in outlook between Quebeckers, who had been cut off from Europe since 1759, and English Canadians, many of whom had only recently arrived from England. As Canadian casualties in Europe mounted, the need became more and more urgent for new recruits to maintain Canada's commitments. In efforts to stave off the possibility of conscription, political leaders like Laurier and even the Church hierarchy campaigned for French Canadians to volunteer. There was widespread resentment among English Canadians who felt that the *Québecois* were not "pulling their weight." Finally in 1917, after a visit to the troops in Europe, Borden became convinced that conscription was necessary.

In May, 1918, he announced that selective conscription would soon be introduced. The Quebec reaction included riots, attacks on progovernment newspapers, and mass demonstrations. Laurier, still playing the mediating role, warned that if the Liberals agreed to conscription, they would, in effect, be handing Quebec over to the nationalists. Conscription would, he said, ". . .create a line of cleavage within the population, the consequences of which I know too well, and for which I will not be responsible." But he also said if the English-Canadian majority passed a conscription law, he would devote his energy to securing Quebec's compliance. All but one French-Canadian cabinet minister resigned, as did the Deputy Speaker and the chief government whip from Quebec. The depth of feeling was revealed in speeches by French-Canadian members of parliament. Said Louis-Joseph Gauthier: "My people are willing to go to the limit if you impose on them such a piece of legislation." Another MP warned that conscription might mean civil war and the end of Confederation. When the vote on conscription came, most English-speaking Liberals supported it; virtually all French-speaking Conservatives voted against it.

After passage of the bill, and in the election campaign which followed, there was a serious threat of civil strife in Quebec. The extreme polarization of the electorate was revealed in the bitter election fight. English Liberals united with the Conservatives to form a Union government which ran Union candidates. The French-Canadian nationalists this time supported the Laurier Liberals. In Quebec, the Laurier followers won 84 per cent of the vote and 62 of the 65 Quebec seats; the Unionists won only three seats and 15 per cent of the vote. Outside Quebec, the split in popular votes was not so glaring, as the Laurier Liberals gained 35 per cent of the vote versus the Unionists' 65 per cent, but Laurier's Liberals won only 20 seats while the Union government won 150. In terms of parliamentary seats, a united Quebec faced a united English Canada. The split which Laurier had always feared, and which he had worked all his life to avoid, was at hand.

Fortunately the war ended. Few people were actually drafted and the conscription crisis blew over; but the bitterness remained and served to nourish a new movement which was distinctly provincialist and sometimes separatist in outlook. In the first postwar election, in 1921, the Unionist government broke up, and the Liberals again formed the government, winning all 65 Quebec seats and 53 seats elsewhere in Canada. In the first provincial election after the war, the Conservatives were so weak that they did not even bother to run candidates in 41 of the 83 Quebec constituencies and with the sole exception of the 1958 federal election they have never since been a strong force in Quebec politics.

During the 1920s and 1930s nationalist agitation grew in Quebec, partly as a result of the wartime hostility and partly in response to the economic factors which were discussed earlier. It gained strength under the impact of the depression and found expression in the rise of a new Quebec provincial party, *L'Union Nationale*, led by Maurice Duplessis. Duplessis was elected in 1936 on a program of provincial rights and opposition to the federal government and English-owned business. With the sole exception of 1939 this appeal led him to victory in every election until 1958. Under his government, conflict frequently took the form of friction between the Quebec and federal government, with the province protesting against alleged federal encroachments on provincial jurisdiction, especially in federal anti-depression measures. The conflict thus became more institutionalized. This institutionalization of French–English conflict was important in keeping some sort of restraint on French–English relations during most of the Duplessis period. With the exception of the 1944 conscription crisis, the most obvious expressions of the French–English cleavage were the arguments which broke out in federal–provincial conferences and the Ottawa-baiting speeches of Duplessis.

The only crisis in Canadian ethnic relations during that period came during World War II and again revolved around the issue of conscription. When Canada entered the war in 1939, the Mackenzie King government was understandably afraid of a recurrence of the 1917 crisis and hence promised not to institute conscription. But, just as in World War I, the demands of total war soon outran voluntary enlistment and the Conservative opposition as well as other elements in English Canada and the military began to demand conscription again. Mackenzie King, in the hope of avoiding a full-scale crisis, sought a national referendum to permit the government to back out of its promise to French Canada. The referendum was a disaster. French Canadian groups such as *La Ligue pour la défense du Canada*, supported by such groups as the lower clergy, campaigned for a *non* vote. In this they opposed the politicians and the upper hierarchy of the Catholic church. In the eight English speaking provinces the vote went 80 per cent in favour of the referendum; in Quebec it was 72 per cent against and among French Canadians in Quebec the *non* vote rose to 85 per cent. Opposition to the war in Quebec was polarized by the campaign and statements on each side grew more bitter. *La Ligue* grew stronger and became a political party, the *Bloc Populaire*.

The government avoided imposing conscription until 1944 when it finally appeared that King could no longer walk a tightrope between the English and French sections of his party and the country. In the final parliamentary vote on conscription, King lost the support of 34 French-Canadian Liberals, though they continued to support him as Prime Minister. His dismissal of his pro-conscription Defence Minister, J.L. Ralston, allayed some French-Canadian suspicion. Fortunately the war was by now near conclusion, and it did not become necessary to use any of the conscripts in battle. French-Canadian leaders appeared to realize that it was better to have limited conscription under King than full conscription under the English-dominated government which would replace him should he fall. King's political skill and the end of the war avoided a conscription crisis of anything like First War magnitude, but again a residue of mistrust was left.

The immediate postwar period and the 1950s was a time of apparent calm in Quebec, and except for the occasional forays of Maurice Duplessis against the federal government, there was relatively little activity across the lines of French-English cleavage in Canada. The calm was more apparent than real, however, for the rapid urbanization and industrialization of Quebec society, combined with the economic hegemony of the English population both within and outside of Quebec, were sowing the seeds for the crisis of the 1960s.

That crisis, more drawn-out than many of the earlier ones, really began with the death of Maurice Duplessis in 1959. His successors were unable to establish the tight control he had had over Quebec society. In 1960 the *Union Nationale* was finally defeated by the Liberals under Jean

Lesage, using the slogan of *maîtres chez nous*. It is difficult to know in retrospect just how seriously most of the Lesage Liberals took this slogan, but whether they did or not, it shortly became evident that some other groups in the population took it very seriously. Starting with a pamphlet called *Pourquoi je suis séparatiste* by Marcel Chaput, a disaffected scientist with the federal Defence Research Board, and carrying on with a wave of terrorism under the *Front de Libération du Québec* (FLQ), separatism gained strength in Quebec. The 1960s saw a steady growth in the separatist movement, culminating when one of Quebec's most popular politicians and public men, René Lévesque, joined the cause and unified the movement's various factions under the *Parti Québecois* label.

In the period since its formation in 1968 the *Parti Québecois* has gained considerable electoral success. In the 1966 Quebec election, 8 per cent of Quebec voters supported one of the P.Q.'s predecessors, the RIN (*Rassemblement pour l'indépendence nationale*). In 1970 some 23 per cent supported Lévesque's *Parti Québecois* and some 33 per cent of the French speaking population of the province voted for it. The P.Q. won seven seats in that election, but its representation in the National Assembly fell to six after the 1973 election in spite of the fact that it won 30 per cent of the popular vote in that election.

It is difficult to evaluate what proportion of P.Q. voters are actually *séparatistes* and what proportion are supporters of Lévesque the man or of the democratic socialism the party espouses. Surveys by the McGill sociologist, Maurice Pinard, suggest that only about half the P.Q. voters espouse the *séparatiste* ideal; P.Q. activists make higher claims. What is probably more significant is the steady increase in the number of voters for what is certainly known to be a separatist party and the tendency for P.Q. voters to be disproportionately concentrated among the young rising middle class in Quebec. The sporadic violence of the FLQ is perhaps just an unfortunate footnote to Quebec's history; the *Parti Québecois* and the *séparatiste* movement may be a great deal more than that.

Whether we concentrate wholly on its separatist aspects or not, the "crisis" of the 1960s and 1970s in Quebec differs in some important ways from earlier expressions of the French–English cleavage in Canada. It arose from demands for a revision of the constitution in the direction of greater provincial autonomy. The demands ran the gamut from those for the outright separation of Quebec, through recognition of a "special status" for Quebec, to relatively minor changes in the financial structure of Canadian federalism. Such differing ideas, said the Royal Commission on Bilingualism and Biculturalism, all had a common denominator:

> They expressed a wide and deep dissatisfaction with the present political position and a manifest will to conduct a search for many possible roads, which almost all went in the direction of more or less radical reforms.[88]

Strangely, the current situation evokes a different kind of ethnic hostility from that of past conflicts. Declarations such as those that accom-

[88]*The Preliminary Report of the Royal Commission on Bilingualism and Biculturalism*, (Queen's Printer, Ottawa, 1967).

panied the Riel, the Manitoba schools and conscription crises are notably absent, and the majority of concerned French Canadians avoids the recriminations of the past in seeking redress of current grievances. Nonetheless, the gravity of the present manifestation of ethnic cleavage is clear. First, separatism was not usually considered as a solution in the past; on these grounds alone the crisis of the 1970s is much more of a threat to the political system than were previous ones. Second, the problem was not a single issue but a broad principle, which presumably will not disappear so easily.

Religion is no longer such a major component of the English–French cleavage in Canada, and this in itself may dampen the conflict to some extent. The old nationalism of Quebec was inward looking, seeking to preserve French Canada by shutting out the world. The new nationalism, judging from its manifestations in the 1960s and early 1970s, is more outward looking, seeking to emphasize "Frenchness" as well as "Quebecness." The overall claims of the new Quebec nationalism can probably best be summed up in the old slogan *maîtres chez nous*, but now there appears to be considerable difference of opinion about what *chez nous* should be like.

Analytical Perspectives on French–English Relations

For most of the period since Confederation, the French–English division of Canadian society has been the country's single most visible cleavage. Hence it figures prominently in most analyses of politics in Canada. Different writers have brought widely differing analytical perspectives and personal values to bear on the problem. At one extreme are those analysts who have viewed the French–English cleavage as a red herring which obscures what should be the most important cleavage in Canada, that between the rich and the poor. At the other extreme are the separatist analysts who view the French–English cleavage as so predominant that until it is resolved and Quebec has achieved separate statehood, nothing can be done to redress other problems.[89]

Perhaps the most popular recent framework within which to cast French–English relations in Canada (and also the relationships formed across other cleavage lines) is that of consociational democracy.[90] In its barest form the theory suggests that democratic politics in highly pluralist

[89]The clearest example of the first type of analysis is John Porter's *The Vertical Mosaic*. Most of the separatist analysts also view the class cleavage as important but see the ethnic cleavage as logically prior. The clearest exposition of that point of view is Marcel Rioux, *Quebec in Question*, but see also Sheilagh Hodgins and Henry Milner, *The Decolonization of Quebec*.

[90]The framework was originally developed by A. Lijphart and other European analysts. For a brief description see A. Lijphart, "Consociational Democracy", *World Politics*, 21 (1969) 207–225, and "Cultural Diversity and Theories of Political Integration", *Canadian Journal of Political Science*, 4 (1971) pp. 1–14. For Canadian applications see S.J.R. Noel, "Consociational Democracy and Canadian Federalism" *CJPS*, 4 (1971) pp. 15–18, and especially K.D. McRae, *Consociational Democracy: Political Accommodation in Segmented Societies*, (Carleton Libary #79, McClelland & Stewart, 1974).

societies works best when its operating principles include at least partial segregation of the masses along whatever cleavage lines are most salient, together with a process of accommodation between the elites at the head of the various subsections of society.

> The essential characteristic of consociational democracy is not so much any particular institutional arrangement as overarching co-operation at the elite level with the deliberate aim of concentrating disintegrative tendencies in the system.[91]
>
> Deep, mutually re-inforcing social cleavages do not form an insuperable obstacle to viable democracy. The crucial factor in the establishment and preservation of democratic stability is the quality of leadership. The politics of accommodation opens up the possibility of viable democracy even when the social condition appears unpromising.[92]

It is not a formal requirement of consociationalism that the subcultures be separated in a physical sense, but most consociational theorists at least imply that the work of the elites is made easier if there is considerable separation. This will minimize tensions at the mass level and help maintain cohesion within each subculture, thus helping the elite to gain support for agreements they have made and to articulate adequately the interests of their subcultures.[93]

If we apply these ideas to the study of French–English relations in Canada some suggestions appear which have long been familiar to French-Canadian intellectuals, but which often startle English Canadians. In theory, according to the assumptions of most English-speaking Canadians, if the two solitudes which are French and English Canada could be thrust together and the masses of the two groups partiably integrated, then French–English tensions would disappear. In fact, the industrialization of Canada has partially achieved such a mixing of the two populations. Yet inter-ethnic relations have not necessarily been improving, and the scene of most unrest is Montreal, where the two groups come together most closely.

Consociational analysis suggests that this worsening of relations may be caused by the very integration that was supposed to ameliorate the problem. The integration of large numbers of people may simply make it harder for the elites to establish the accommodations which produce inter-ethnic harmony. The problem may be exacerbated by the fact that the French-Canadian elite sees its traditional clientele disappearing as more French people learn English and become part of the English-Canadian industrial tradition. Paradoxically, it is at least conceivable that the nearer a cleavage comes to disappearing at the mass level, the more desperately elites may fight to maintain it. For French-Canadian elites the alternatives may be painfully clear: separation of Quebec from Canada and the conse-

---

[91]A. Lijphart, "Typologies of Democratic Systems", *Comparative Political Studies*, 1 (1968) p. 21.

[92]A. Lijphart, *The Politics of Accommodation, Pluralism and Democracy in the Netherlands*, (Berkeley, 1968) p. 211. Both these quotations may be found in McRae, "The Concept of Consociationalism".

[93]McRae, "Introduction" in *Consociational Democracy*, pp. 1–28.

quent preservation of French-Canadian culture, or loss of the French-Canadian tradition and hence of a role for the French-Canadian elite.

K.D. McRae has pointed out that there are both ideological and structural factors in the Canadian political tradition which act to exacerbate the problem.[94] Structurally, Canada has lacked political parties which express and formulate the interests of English and French Canadians separately. In the politics of some ethnically plural European countries there are such parties and the accommodations which must be made between various ethnic groups are then made by the parties themselves—often in the process of forming a coalition to govern. In Canada some accommodations may be worked out within the parties, particularly the Liberal party, but most must be worked out on the federal–provincial stage. There the rigidities introduced by the categories of the BNA Act and by ponderous governmental structures with their own maintenance needs may impede the establishment of livable accommodations.

Perhaps equally important is one of the unstated premises of English-Canadian political ideology, that there is no particular need to accommodate minorities because it is the political right (and indeed duty) of minorities either to become a majority or be assimilated and disappear. This is a usable premise only if the minority is not a permanent one. It is hardly likely to be appealing to French Canadians, who clearly will not become a majority in Canada as a whole and who certainly do not want to assimilate and disappear. The implication for them is clear: to be a majority you must either separate or find some other way to maintain the kind of "Quebec Reserve" politics which characterized much of the period from 1867 to 1960. In that situation, French-Canadian politicians play a rather minor national role, while Quebec politics is viewed as their preserve. As long as Quebec life remained traditional the Quebec Reserve option was viable but under the impact of modernization its viability may have diminished to the point where, viewed from the perspective of at least some elements of the French-Canadian elite, the separatist option is the only one available. English Canadians do not seem to have grasped the point that special accommodating devices are needed in this sort of situation.

> . . .because they have not done so, French-Canadians have reacted in the only way open to them, by an instinctive attempt to build—either by themselves or in concert with others—stable majorities of their own. As long as English-Canadians remain majority minded, many French-Canadians will find their most effective response in an increasingly autonomous Quebec. . .any genuinely pluralist society must learn to do better.[95]

Actions like the Official Languages Act or the bilingualization of the federal public service may conceivably be steps in the right direction although from this analytical perspective that is doubtful. Rather, what may

[94]MacRae, "Consociationalism and the Canadian Political System," in *Consociational Democracy*, pp. 238–261.
[95]From *Consociational Democracy: Political Accommodation in Segmented Societies*, Carleton Library No. 79, p. 301, 1974; edited by K.D. MacRae. Reprinted by permission of The Canadian Publishers, McClelland and Stewart Limited, Toronto.

be required if the separatist option is not to prevail is a much more fundamental restructuring of Canadian politics and of attitudes on both sides.

For vast numbers of Canadians, French- and English-speaking alike, the tragedy of the situation may be that while English and French elites fight out the consequences of their earlier failures to develop adequate mechanisms of accommodation, the problems generated by other regional, class and economic cleavages are neglected.

Conclusion The reader may well wonder at this point whether the emphasis in this chapter is not misplaced. Have we, perhaps, by concentrating on cleavages and neglecting the sources of consensus in Canada, painted too bleak a picture of the problems with which the political system must deal?[96]

We think not. Our emphasis on cleavages and problems is intentional. Politics is a process of conflict resolution, and in the end much of that conflict is generated by cleavages in society. There is a very broad area of consensus in Canada concerning politics. But the things Canadians agree about do not become political issues. Our intention here has been to emphasize for our reader the many extremely difficult problems with which the political system must cope. Much of the rest of the book is concerned with the institutional and procedural manifestations of consensus which allow it to do so.

It is our conviction that, viewed in the context of other political systems, it does so extremely well.

[96]A. Cairns, "Alternative Styles in the Study of Canadian Politics", *Canadian Journal of Political Science*, VII, 1 (March, 1974), p. 115.

3
Canadian Political Culture: Values, Attitudes and Public Opinion

The determinants of political behaviour can logically be reduced to two significant groups of variables: those which are external to the individual and those which are internal or "of the mind". Having discussed many of the former in Chapter Two, we now seek to describe the latter, the basic values and attitudes which in the aggregrate compose the Canadian political culture, and to elaborate upon their consequences for the Canadian political system.

We use the term "political culture" with some reservations, for there are nearly as many definitions of the term as there are political scientists. Most would agree, however, that it is composed of the political values, attitudes, and empirical beliefs of the citizens of a political system and that it is a determinant of political action or behaviour.[1] We shall use the term in this descriptive and basically uncomplicated sense.

There are three major approaches to the study of political culture. The most obvious focus is the values and attitudes that make up that culture. It is possible to establish what these attitudes and values are simply by asking people through the technique of public opinion surveys. Another approach is to speculate about the predominant attitudes of a political culture by observing the patterns of political behaviour which are typical of the political system. The researcher works backwards, deducing the likely attitudinal causes from the observed behavioural patterns. Finally, it may be possible to understand a political culture by studying the institutional framework of the political system. Constitutions, legislation and the actual structure of government itself may prove to be fairly accurate indicators of the basic values of a political culture. All of these approaches are employed in cross-national comparisons of political systems.

There is also a fourth approach to the analysis of political culture, which is a hybrid strain of the direct attitudinal approach. It may be that important clues to a clear understanding of political culture lie in the nas-

[1]See especially: Sydney Verba, "Comparative Political Culture", in Lucien Pye and Sydney Verba (eds.), *Political Culture and Political Development*, (Princeton, 1965), p. 513, and Samuel C. Patterson, "The Political Cultures of American States", in N.R. Luttbeg, *Public Opinion and Public Policy*, (Dorsey, Homewood, 1968), p. 276.

cent political values and attitudes of children. This view assumes that the process whereby individuals acquire their attitudes toward politics has a significant effect on the substance and intensity of their attitudes, and thus on the political culture itself. Hence the focus in this approach is on political socialization.

In general, these chapters are concerned with the values, attitudes, opinions and patterns of political socialization and political participation of what, for want of a better term, we will call the "mass"—that large part of the Canadian population which is not engaged full-time in playing political roles. We are concerned here not so much with politicians, senior bureaucrats or the leaders of the largest interest groups as with the man on the street or the woman in the middle row of a community association meeting. However, it is important to assert at the outset that most of the values and attitudes described here are shared by the players of more highly politicized roles. Indeed it is this sharing of values which does a great deal to stabilize the Canadian political system and to ensure that, in spite of the barriers which the average person may encounter when trying to participate in politics, political decision makers do take account of many of his attitudes. Their attitudes are very often the same.[2]

In the first of this pair of chapters on the Canadian political culture we will discuss values, attitudes and public opinion. In the second we will examine political socialization and political participation.

POLITICAL VALUES IN CANADA

Political values underlie attitudes towards specific political objects and also set the broadest parameters of political behaviour in a society. Because they are basic they are seldom articulated; but they form the guiding principles for the operation of the political system. Hence, they are usually reflected in its institutions as well as in the behaviour of citizens and governmental officials alike.

The most basic values held by Canadians are rooted in the Western political tradition, in the Judaeo–Christian religious tradition and in eighteenth- and nineteenth-century democratic theory modified to some extent by the traditions and events of the twentieth century. These basic values include a commitment to popular sovereignty, political equality and majoritarianism. They form a set of unstated premises which underlie attitudes more directly related to the day-to-day workings of the political system.

Popular Sovereignty Canadian political values are traditionally broadly described as democratic. Democracy may be viewed as a set of ultimate values, but we prefer to view it primarily as a set of operational procedures for realizing certain broad societal goals. Stated as a theoretical abstraction, the democratic aim, or ultimate democratic value, is the

[2]On this point see Norman R. Luttbeg, *Public Opinion and Public Policy*, Part V, pp. 245–390.

"common good" or the common interest. Democracy as a means of realizing the common good is a system of government designed to reflect the will of the people as a whole rather than that of an individual or of a small elite. The limitations of democracy, as stated in such ethereal terms as these, follow from the fact that there is likely to be no agreement as to what the common good is. In many cases the "common good" will conflict directly with the particular short-run demands put forward by individuals and groups within the society. Therefore, democracy is perhaps best viewed as a form of government which attempts to maximize or "optimize" the common good by satisfying the needs of as many people as possible. This attempt is expressed in the principle of popular control or popular sovereignty.

Direct democracy, or the actual involvement of all of the members of a society in the policy process, is not possible in a large nation state. The complex and technical policies being dealt with by governments today do not encourage direct participation in government by all of the people. Indeed, the difficulty of passing even non-technical legislation in a legislature of 20 million would immensely slow an already tedious process. Some indirect means must be found, therefore, to give effect to popular sovereignty, and the most common method of achieving this in a modern democracy is through elected representatives. Thus, in a modern democracy, the people do not govern; rather they choose their governors.

Political Equality Popular sovereignty is usually institutionalized through a system of periodic elections, which in turn presumes certain secondary values. The secondary values have been referred to collectively as the principles of political equality: every adult should have the right to vote; each person should have one vote; no man's vote should be weighted differently from any other man's vote; and representation should be at least roughly proportional to population.[3]

Political equality, however, means more than "one man, one vote", for a further assumption behind democratic elections is that the voter has real alternatives from which to choose, and that he can make his choice freely. Thus, the political freedoms, such as freedom of assembly, association, conscience, and expression are fundamental values tied up inextricably with democracy as a governmental form. The institutional guarantees of these basic freedoms are to be found in devices such as the secret ballot, and in legal documents such as the Bill of Rights.

Majoritarianism Majority rule is a key operational principle of democratic government. The term means two things. First it applies to the electoral process itself, in that the candidate who gets the largest number of votes in an election becomes the representative for his societal unit. Sec-

[3]Note here that Robert Dahl views political equality as a goal of democracy, and majority rule as a guiding principle for attaining it. The socio-political process for attaining the democratic goal he calls "polyarchy". See R.A. Dahl and C.E. Lindblom, *Politics, Economics and Welfare*, (Harper and Row, New York, 1953), p. 41, chs. 10–11.

ond, it applies when the representatives make policy decisions. In cases where there is not unanimous agreement as to what should be done, the alternative preferred by the largest number of representatives is the one implemented. However, the majoritarian principle is not absolute; there are limits placed on the majority. For instance, if a majority decided to abolish one of the basic political freedoms, such as freedom of association, the system would cease to be democratic. Such tampering with democratic values, even by the majority, is normally considered to be unacceptable in democratic political systems. Thus, while majority rule is a very important principle of democracy, it is seldom if ever deemed to be absolute.

A corollary of the limitation on the principle of majority rule is that the minority will accept decisions of the majority as long as the majority does not violate other democratic values such as political equality. Should a dissident minority refuse to abide by a policy decision of the majority, or should the majority take an extreme measure to suppress the legitimate rights of the minority, the political system would be in danger either of breaking up or of ceasing to be democratic.

Liberal and Non-liberal Democracy Many Canadians have come to identify democratic values with the somewhat more specific principles embodied in the "semi-ideology" of liberal democracy. In its most extreme incarnation, liberalism includes a commitment to individualism and to individual liberties, a closely related commitment to the principles of private property and individual property rights, and a commitment to economic free enterprise and capitalism. These may very well be important values held by a majority of people in the Western democracies and particularly in the United States, but they are not necessary to a system of democratic politics. As Professor C.B. Macpherson has pointed out:

> . . .democracy is not properly to be equated with our unique Western liberal-democracy [for]. . .clearly non-liberal systems which prevail in the Soviet countries and the somewhat different non-liberal systems of most of the underdeveloped countries of Asia and Africa, have a genuine historical claim to the title democracies. . .[4]

In fact, it seems inarguable that liberal values in Canada are being diluted gradually by at least partial acceptance of such socialist principles as economic equality, social and economic planning, and increased intervention of government in our everyday lives. More importantly, there is a school of thought (which we will describe below) which posits that the Canadian value system differs significantly from the American on just this point of commitment to liberal ideals, and that the differences spring from long-standing historical causes. However, the conflict between liberalism and socialism as sets of political values is a very central aspect of political life, not only in Canada but in other Western democracies as well. To tie the fundamental principles of democracy, such as popular sovereignty, political equality and majoritarianism, to either liberal or non-liberal values is

[4]C.B. Macpherson, *The Real World of Democracy*, (The Canadian Broadcasting Corporation, Toronto, 1965), pp. 3–4.

endangering the value consensus on which democracy rests. The commitment to democracy is far more important than the commitment either to liberalism or to some non-liberal ideology such as socialism, for democracy can be made compatible with either.

The values we have described so far are basic not only to Canadian political culture but to the rest of the Anglo-Saxon democratic world as well. They do not serve to tell us how the Canadian political culture differs from that of Britain or the United States. One of the best known of the various approaches to identifying indigenous Canadian patterns of political culture is a comparative historical analysis first suggested by Louis Hartz and later developed by K.D. McRae and Gad Horowitz.[5] McRae and Horowitz differ substantially on several points concerning the differences between the Canadian and U.S. value systems, but they do agree that the Canadian system is more "small c" conservative. They also both conclude that collectivism, corporatism and an organic view of the state are more prominent in Canada, while "small l" liberalism and a belief in the individual are more prominent in the United States. Paradoxically, it is suggested that the conservatism of Canadian society supports collectivist tendencies in the nation since the state is viewed as responsible for its citizens and therefore obligated to provide some minimum level of subsistence for them. Thus, compared to the U.S., Canada, on the one hand, has been more amenable to the norms of economic egalitarianism and the use of state power to implement those norms. On the other hand, it is suggested that U.S. society is more highly committed to social and political egalitarianism.[6]

> Canadian political society has thus stressed order, loyalty and deference to government more than popular assent. Rather than 'life, liberty and the pursuit of happiness', the need has been peace, order and good government. Social equality is desired but with less fervour than in America. Hierarchy in all spheres of life is taken for granted.[7]

If these analysts are correct, there is then a somewhat paradoxical commitment on the one hand to some form of very rough economic equality, and on the other to the maintenance of a considerable amount of social inequality. This paradox is underscored by some of the speculations of Seymour Martin Lipset.[8] In a broader framework which includes Austra-

[5]In the writing of this section we are highly indebted to Prof. David Falcone of Duke University who synthesized much of the material in his Ph.D Dissertation. See *Legislative Change and Output Change: A Time Series Analysis of the Canadian System* (unpublished Ph.D. Dissertation, Duke University, 1974). See also Louis Hartz (ed.), *The Founding of New Societies*, Ch. 4, for Hartz's analysis and Ch. 7 for McRae's and Horowitz's, "Conservatism, Liberalism and Socialism in Canada: an Interpretation" *CJPS*, 32 (May 1966), 144–171.

[6]Kaspar Naegele, "Canadian Society, Some Reflections" in B. Blishen *et al.* (eds.), *Canadian Society*, (Macmillan, Toronto, 1961), pp. 27–29.

[7]Erwin Hargrove, "Popular Leadership in Anglo-American Democracies" in Lewis Edinger (ed.), *Popular Leadership in Industrialized Societies*, (John Wiley and Sons, New York, 1966), p. 147.

[8]See S.M. Lipset, *The First New Nation: The United States in Comparative Perspective*, (Basic Books, New York, 1963).

lia and Britain as well as Canada and the U.S., Lipset uses census data to show that Canadians generally evince more of a collective orientation than do Americans, albeit less than the British. Lipset also concludes on the basis of his data that Canadians are both more elitist and more ascriptive in their attitudes than Americans but, again, less so than the British.

The points that Lipset makes are corroborated by many Canadian historical scholars on the basis of more impressionistic material.[9] Moreover Lipset and those same Canadian historians are also in agreement that the major reasons for Canadian–American differences revolve around the relatively tame style of Canada's westward expansion, the relative dominance of Anglican and Roman Catholic rather than Calvinist and fundamentalist religious traditions in Canada, and the non-revolutionary nature of Canada's achievement of nationhood.

Studies such as Lipset's, W.L. Morton's, A.R.M. Lower's or George Grant's, based on interpretations of historical trends or elite ideologies, or on limited aggregate data, are also borne out by what empirical data we have. In the next section of this chapter we will use a national public opinion survey to indicate that the description "spectator–participant" most aptly describes the attitudes with which Canadians participate in electoral politics. Canadians are generally quite willing to leave actual political decision making to "the authorities". Kornberg, Smith and Bromley have interpreted data on Canadian–American differences in the recruitment of political elites as indicating "a generally less politicized Canadian social environment".[10] This suggestion is also corroborated by some of the studies of political socialization in Canada. Thus, Jon Pammett hypothesizes that "politics has less salience for. . .Canadians than it does for citizens of many other countries (the United States for example)".[11] And A.B. Hodgetts concludes that Canadian schools teach a ". . .bland consensus story. . .without the controversy that is an inherent part of history".[12] Hence, a picture begins to emerge of a set of Canadian political values which is at once more deferential and less politicized than that of the U.S. On the other hand, Canada, and particularly English Canada, is probably less deferential than the United Kingdom and about equally politicized.

[9]E.g., W.L. Morton, *The Canadian Identity*, (University of Wisconsin Press, Madison, 1961), pp. 84–87; S.D. Clark, "Canada and the American Value System", O. Kruhlak *et al*, pp. 39–46; Chester P. Martin, *The Foundation of Canadian Nationhood*, (University of Toronto Press, Toronto, 1955); A.R.M. Lower, *Colony to Nation: A History of Canada*, (Longmans Green, Toronto, 1946); J. Porter, *The Vertical Mosaic*, Erwin C. Hargrove, "Note on American and Canadian Political Culture," *CJEPS* 33 (February 1967), pp. 21–29; and George Grant, *Lament for a Nation*, (Van Nostrand, Princeton, N.J., 1967).

[10]A. Kornberg, Joel Smith and David Bromley, "Some Differences in the Political Socialization Patterns of Canadian and American Party Officials", *CJPS* (March 1969, V. 2), p. 73.

[11]Jon Pammett, "The Development of Political Orientations in Canadian School Children," *CJPS* 4 (March 1971), p. 140.

[12]A.B. Hodgetts, *What Culture, What Heritage*, (Ontario Institute of Studies in Education, Toronto, 1968), p. 24.

She may also be less committed to economic equality than the U.K. but more committed to that path than the U.S.

What these studies and a host of others are sometimes said to suggest is that Canadian political values support a sort of "noncreative", managerial or "apolitical" politics rather than a truly participatory and conflict-oriented politics on the American model. Thus one observer has noted that Canadians often display an ambivalence toward politics; a mixture of interest and affect towards the political system combined with a general lack of efficacy in dealing with it.[13] For the political decision makers, this may mean that they can go about their work without being overly concerned about the possibility of a surge of demands overwhelming them.[14]

This description of the values underlying Canadian political behaviour is supported by Robert Presthus' synthesis and interpretation of the same body of literature. His conclusions are summed up in the following quotation:

> The elements [of Canada's national political culture] include a pragmatic appreciation of government's role in the economy; an underlying corporatist theory of societal life; traditional and deferential patterns of authority; and a quasi-participative political culture insofar as the ordinary citizen is concerned.

Presthus mentions three features of the political value system of Canadians: corporatism, traditional or deferential patterns of authority and a quasi-participatory approach to political activism. We have already examined the concepts of traditionalism and deference and we will discuss political participation later in this chapter, but the corporatist feature requires more elaboration here. According to Presthus:

> Corporatism is essentially a conception of society in which government delegates many of its functions to private groups which in turn provide guidance regarding the social and economic legislation required in the modern national state. . .Corporatism rests upon an organic view of society in which collective aspirations are seen as prior to those of any discrete individual or group, including the state. . .In English-Canada, corporatism has been widely celebrated by both the church and many leading intellectuals.[15]

Hartz, Horowitz and McRae agree that corporatism was imported into Canada in part by the earliest French settlers, who brought with them a feudal conception of society not unlike modern corporatism, and in part

---

[13]Robert Presthus, *Elite Accommodation in Canadian Politics*, ©1973 Cambridge University Press, (published in Canada by Macmillan), p. 39.

[14]John Porter observes: "It is not that Canadian social structure is so static that it has no imminent potential for dynamic politics; it is rather that Canada's basically opportunistic parties have not harnessed this potential system. They have either ignored these basic social differences or covered them up in the pretence that they do not exist. (*The Vertical Mosaic*, p. 373.) Somewhat in contrast to this view, Hargrove seems to think that the quiescence of Canadian politics is due to the lack of political interest on the part of the middle class, ("Popular Leadership", p. 198).

[15]R. Presthus, *Elite Accommodation in Canadian Politics*, pp. 25–26.

as a component of the conservatism which the loyalist element brought from the thirteen colonies after the American Revolution.[16]

The corporatist component of the Canadian value system conceives of society as a collection of interest groups and hence it has an anti-individualistic bias. This means that unless an individual puts forward his claims on government as part of the claims of a larger group, his behaviour may be viewed as inappropriate, and political decision makers may define him as a "crank" or otherwise ignore him. Hence the corporate ideal may have major consequences for the way in which the Canadian political system operates. In fact Presthus goes on to conclude:

> These components of Canadian political culture culminate, in turn, in a national political process that may be called one of elite accommodation. Essentially,. . .this is a system in which the major decisions regarding national socio-economic policy are worked out through interactions between governmental (i.e. legislative and bureaucratic) elites and interest group elites.[17]

Our discussion of political participation in the final section of the next chapter will do much to corroborate this impression of Canadian political culture.

While we have attempted here to speculate on the political values which are generally accepted by Canadians, and to point to some of the basic ideas around which ideological cleavage may arise, we make no pretense that our list is exhaustive and the reader must be cautioned that much of this material is highly speculative. The overall picture of the component parts of the Canadian political culture will continue to emerge as we discuss attitudes to specific political objects and the fundamental principles implicit in the Canadian Constitution.

CANADIAN POLITICAL ATTITUDES

Less fundamental than the basic values discussed in the preceding section are the attitudes or patterns of thought towards specific objects in the political world. Because they are more specific, our political attitudes may not be as universally accepted within the political community as our political values. On the other hand, because they are related directly to real world objects, political attitudes are likely more important as immediate determinants of behaviour. Thus, for example, not only are individual attitudes to a particular political party likely to vary widely, but they are more likely to stimulate political action than a basic value such as popular sov-

[16]L. Hartz (ed.), *The Founding of New Societies*, Ch. 4; K.D. McRae, in *The Founding of New Societies*, Ch. 7; and G. Horowitz, "Conservatism, Liberalism and Socialism". It might be worthwhile to suggest a re-interpretation of their views of French-Canadian society as a "feudal fragment" to take account of the prevailing view of French-Canadian sociologists and historians that the earliest French society in North America had a predominantly mercantile value system, and that it was only after the Conquest that the mercantile elements of that value system disappeared leaving the corporatist feudal fragment.

[17]Presthus, *Elite Accommodation in Canadian Politics*, pp. 20–21.

ereignty. The latter is so widely accepted in Canada that most Canadians neither think about it nor have to act upon it.

The Subjective Dimension Political attitudes can be classified according to two main sets of criteria or dimensions: a subjective one and an objective one.[18] Using the subjective criteria we may classify an attitude as "cognitive", "affective", or "evaluative", according to its psychological significance for the individual who holds it. Objective criteria classify attitudes according to the phenomena on which they are based. They will be discussed in the next section.

Cognitive attitudes involve simple knowledge of, or empirical beliefs about, real world phenomena. The manner in which we acquire cognitive attitudes is empirical or objective, and we can communicate them by using "is" or "is not" statements. *Affective attitudes* on the other hand consist of the feelings and aesthetic preferences we have for things in the real world. While it is accepted that knowledge or awareness of a political object must logically precede any feelings towards it, in many cases we acquire positive or negative feelings simultaneously with simple awareness. Affective attitudes are a reflection of our likes and dislikes and the mood in which we acquire them tends to be more emotional and aesthetic than empirical. Finally, *evaluative attitudes* are moral and ethical, and involve the conscious application of preexisting values or standards to real-world phenomena. Evaluative attitudes are moral judgements about the goodness or badness of a political object and are expressed as "should" or "ought" statements. These three subjective dimensions are summarized in Figure 3-1.

Figure 3-1

THE SUBJECTIVE DIMENSION OF POLITICAL ATTITUDES[19]

Type	Form	Mood	Mode of Expression
Cognitive	knowledge, beliefs, information	empirical, objective	is/is not statements
Affective	feelings, preferences	emotional, aesthetic	like/love (not) statements
Evaluative	values, judgments	moral, ethical	should/ought (not) statements

[18]For an elaboration of this framework see the introductory article of Pammett and Whittington (eds.), *The Foundations of Political Culture; Political Socialization in Canada*, (Macmillan, Toronto, 1975).
[19]See Pammett and Whittington, (eds.), *op. cit.*

While it is helpful to make the analytical distinction among cognitive, affective and evaluative attitudes, the distinction blurs somewhat in reality. Our values and emotions will colour our perceptions of political objects, our feelings towards them will depend upon how we perceive them, and our political evaluations will often tend to be rationalizations of our aesthetic or emotional preferences. Moreover, the intensity with which an attitude is held will have an important influence upon the extent to which it can affect our behaviour. Thus, the certainty with which we hold our beliefs, the strength of our likes and dislikes, and the firmness of our value commitments may be as significant as the substance of those attitudes.

The Objective Dimension Using "objective criteria" we may classify political attitudes according to the phenomena upon which they are focused. Naturally, the primary objects of political attitudes are those related to the political system. However, attitudes towards political participation or abstention, for instance, involve perceptions of a "self to system" relationship. The attitudes to that relationship are, in the first instance, affected by the individual's perceptions of the system, but can also be affected by his perception of himself. Thus, "self" as a political object must be considered when evaluating complex and behaviourally significant attitudes such as efficacy and civic competence. Thus one's self esteem can be an important factor in the level and intensity of political participation.

However, despite the fact that our political attitudes involve perceptions of self, the basic foci for our political attitudes are still objects in the political system. We can therefore categorize political attitudes as being related to the political community, the regime, or the authorities. By adding a second dimension, which views all political objects as "structural", "symbolic", or "conceptual" in form, we can classify the range of political objects in a still more detailed framework. Figure 3-2 is a nine-cell table showing the resulting objective dimensions of political attitudes with examples from the Canadian political culture.

Figure 3-2 is fairly complex and some of the categories require a bit of elaboration. Our attitudes to authorities for instance, are based mainly on indirect contact; few of us know personally the people who "rule" us. What we know of them is based rather on our view of the roles they occupy classified in Figure 3-2 as "structural objects"; stereotypes with which we can categorize them, such as their party affiliations or the images of them which are imparted to us through the media, classified as "symbolic objects"; and finally our view of how they handle the specific issues of the day, classified as "conceptual objects". Furthermore, political values can themselves become political objects. To the extent that our political values are conceptualized or articulated as ideology it is possible for us to acquire attitudes towards them; thus, for example, Canadians learn cognitive, affective, and evaluative attitudes towards regime-related conceptual objects such as liberalism, capitalism, and welfare.

Finally, what we have classified here as conceptual objects related to the authorities are simply the political issues about which public opin-

Figure 3-2

THE OBJECTIVE DIMENSION OF POLITICAL ATTITUDES[20]

Level of System	Objective Types		
	STRUCTURAL	SYMBOLIC	CONCEPTUAL
POLITICAL COMMUNITY (Canada)	Views about territorial factors: the geography of Canada, etc.	Views about beavers, flags, maple leaves; also personalized symbols, such as national heroes	Views about nationhood or nationality—the Canadian way of life or the Canadian identity
REGIME (the framework of government, constitution of Canada)	Views about the BNA Act, Parliament, the federal system, the public service, etc.	Views about the Parliament Buildings, the Crown, etc.; also personalized symbols such as the Queen	Views about ideology: the principles of liberal democracy, socialism, etc.
AUTHORITIES (the government of the day; the people in the political system)	Views about specific roles and (rarely) the incumbents themselves	Views about symbols of the authorities, such as the political parties	Views about issues

[20] Adapted from Pammett and Whittington, *op. cit.*

ion is formed. The next step in our examination of the Canadian political culture, then, will be to focus upon the final cell of Figure 3-2 and discuss public opinion in Canada.

PUBLIC OPINION AND OPINION FORMATION

An individual's political behaviour is determined partly by his environment, which includes the institutional channels of participation provided by the system itself, and partly by his political attitudes. However, for this behaviour to be meaningful, it must be related to the specific political issues of the day. In other words the individual must formulate a personal opinion about the various issues. The collectivity of private opinions about political issues is often called *public opinion*. It is of course possible to have opinions about public affairs (such as sports or the sex lives of movie stars) which are certainly not political, but the term is to be used here in its explicitly political sense.[21]

It might logically be expected that public opinion would provide concrete guidance for the political system. However, considerable work by the Survey Research Center of the University of Michigan has shown that in the United States there is often relatively little correlation between public opinion and public policy. In some well established areas of controversy there is a reasonably close correlation between constituency opinions and the representative's stand in the legislature, but in an area such as foreign policy, there is frequently none at all.[22]

In Canada there is less empirical evidence, but at least one source suggests that there is little significant correlation between the attitudes of legislative policy makers and the opinions of their constituents.[23] On some issues, such as capital punishment, there has been an easily visible gulf between public opinion (which favours capital punishment) and legislative decision (which in 1973 was to continue the virtual ban on capital punishment for a further five years). In general, we might expect even less correspondence between the views of Canadian MPs and their constituents than between American congressmen and theirs; after all, MPs are restricted in their voting by a more rigid party discipline.

As far as political stability is concerned, the important question is whether the opinions of cabinet ministers, senior bureaucrats and interest

---

[21]The most convenient reference in this area is the excellent booklet by R.C. Lane and D.O. Sears, *Public Opinion*, (Prentice–Hall, Englewood Cliffs, 1964). On pages 117 and 118 there is an extensive bibliographical note. In addition, the student should be aware of V.O. Key Jr., *Public Opinion and American Democracy*, (Knopf, New York, 1961). An excellent collection of articles on the subject can be found in Norman R. Luttbeg (ed.), *Public Opinion and Public Policy*. Each of the sources cited in this footnote is American, but the nature of the generic concept, Public Opinion, does not vary greatly from one Western democracy to another.
[22]R.C. Lane and D.O. Sears, *Public Opinion*, pp. 3–4.
[23]See A. Kornberg, Wm. Mischler and Joel Smith, paper presented to the International Political Science Association, Montreal, August, 1973.

group leaders approximate public opinion. Here we are in territory where there is very little research available in Canada or anywhere else. We do know that many social values are shared by elite and mass, but as to opinion on specific issues we have little information.

For the individual, holding opinions about politics may fulfil certain psychic needs. These include the need to find meaningful contact with the world, or more simply, just to have something to talk about to other people. The opinions of most individuals about political matters are not usually sophisticated or complex, and they are often inconsistent with other views held by the same individual.[24] For the individual, the inconsistency is irrelevant but simplicity is important. To most people political questions are both difficult and of relatively low significance, and unless they can be simplified the individual may tend to ignore them. Therefore, the political opinions which most people hold simplify complex issues to the point where the individual, however mistaken he may be, can take a stand and at least feel that he is participating in politics. This sense of participation, in addition to its importance for the individual (who may have been filled to his ears with public school democratic ethics and his supposed obligations thereto) is vital to the system, for it is one of the bases of political legitimacy.

Opinion Formation and Change The formation of opinions is clearly affected by the political socialization process. The agents of opinion formation are the same as the agents of socialization in general, but in transmitting and helping to define opinions about issues and about the authorities who champion the issues, personal and group influences play perhaps the most significant role.

Group impact on opinions may occur through personal influence within the group, through mass persuasion by the group, or by the group's providing reference points for the individual. Direct personal influence within a group will depend on the nature of the group itself. The likelihood of such influence is increased if the group is a primary one—that is, one where relationships are close and "face to face". Influence is further enhanced if the group persists over long periods, if it meets frequently and if it is relatively homogeneous. If the individual has participated in decision making in the group, and if the norms have not been externally imposed, the group's influence is heightened still further. The influence of the group will also depend on the salience of current issues for the group and for the individual members. Of secondary importance is the setting in which the group finds itself—the status of the group in the larger society, the presence or absence of external opposition and the availability of alternative groups.

Between 50 and 60 per cent of Canadians belong to some form of secondary group, an organization such as a business association or trade union. Such organizations can be important in shaping an individual's opinions of public affairs.[25] Many of these organizations are used to repre-

[24]R. Lane, *Political Ideology*, (The Free Press, New York, 1962), *passim.*
[25]In a 1965 survey of 2,100 Canadians, 55.5 per cent belonged to some secondary

sent their members' interests in politics, and as part of their technique they may try to shape their members' opinions in the "right" direction to support group aims.

Tertiary or categoric groups are another type, and everyone is a member of a number of these. A person does not join such a group; he is in it because of his socio-economic class, his religion, his nationality, or his skin colour, or for any number of other reasons. Thus French-Canadians form a categoric or tertiary group as do Blacks or Roman Catholics. The influence of a categoric group in defining a Canadian's opinions may be very great or it may be negligible, depending on whether the group has taken a stand on a particular issue, and whether or not the individual actually identifies with the group in which he is categorized. For example, various segments of the Roman Catholic Church took a negative stance towards the 1969 Criminal Code amendments which legalized abortion and homosexuality. Whether an individual Catholic would agree with his church's stance would depend, among other things, on whether for the purposes of the issue he identified himself as a Catholic rather than as something else, such as a union member or a homosexual. Nevertheless, later on we will show that membership in particular tertiary groups is correlated with a person's political participation. Indeed, in practice there is virtually no difference between the limits of these categoric groups and some of the cleavages discussed in Chapter 2. It should hardly be surprising, then, that being a member of such a group influences one's political opinions.

We have not yet examined, except incidentally, the direct influence of one individual over another in the formation of political opinions. Under what circumstances will an individual—be he a close friend or a political leader—be able to influence another individual, and under what circumstances will the influence not occur? To examine this question we may use the theory of cognitive dissonance.[26]

In any situation where a person is being influenced he will have three sets of "cognitions":
1. his evaluation of the source seeking to influence him
2. his judgement of what the source's position is
3. his own opinion of the issue

Cognitive dissonance results if the three sets of cognitions are not consistent. It places a strain on the individual, the intensity of which will depend on the issue's salience for him. He will try to resolve the strain by rationalizing the conflicting positions. The dissonance can be resolved in many ways, but generally it will be the weakest of the three cognitions which will be changed. For example, if the person being influenced has great respect for the leader and if he perceives the leader's position to be widely different

organization. This particular definition excludes church membership since almost all Canadians are formally affiliated with some church. We have described churches as tertiary organizations.

[26]For a fuller treatment see R. Lane and D.O. Sears, *Public Opinion*, Ch. 5. The most authoritative treatment is in Leon Festinger, *A Theory of Cognitive Dissonance*, (Stanford University Press, Stanford, 1957).

from his own and if he does not hold the opinion strongly, then he will change his own opinion. From this it follows that a wide difference will exist between a present opinion and that to which it may change only when the opinion is the weakest link. Should the esteem for the leader be the weakest of these three links, the change will occur in the individual's evaluation of the leader. Change may also occur in the perception of the leader's position, for the distortion of perception to relieve dissonance is also a well-known phenomenon.[27] To take a concrete example, suppose that Prime Minister Trudeau found it necessary to go on nationwide television to attempt to justify a large increase in income tax. People who were not strongly against higher taxes and who were "Trudeau fans" would be convinced of the rightness of his point of view, whereas people who were great fans of the Prime Minister and strongly against higher taxes might well misinterpret what he had said to fit with their own policy predilections.

A change of opinion will be impeded if the opinion has been tested and found to fit reality, if it is anchored somehow in group membership, if it serves some social or economic function or some psychic function for its holder, or if the holder has some public stake in it.

Public Opinion—Informed and Uninformed Opinion may be expressed spontaneously or with little prompting, and directed to relevant authorities by knowledgeable groups or individuals. The vast majority of people do not express opinions in this way but, few though they may be, such informed opinions are important inputs into the policy-making process.

There is also a second type of opinion which is drawn from people by opinion-sampling techniques or by less sophisticated methods. Such opinion is likely to be, at best, poorly informed. For example, three months after the 1965 general election in Canada, 25 per cent of the population could not identify their member of parliament and 15 per cent could not name his party; only 58 per cent claimed ever to have heard or read anything about him. Yet 95 per cent of the people interviewed were willing to express an opinion about how good a job MPs from the major parties were doing, and only about 3.5 per cent did not have opinions on the major issues of that campaign. Opinions are thus often held and expressed by large numbers of people in the virtual absence of information. In fact, opinions are often formed before information is gained and then information is selected to fit the opinion already held. The French-Canadian separatist may simply not notice opinions that separatism would be detrimental to the Quebec economy, while the hater of all things French will not notice media reports of brilliant work by French-Canadian doctors.

The nature of public opinion also depends upon the type of issue involved. In their historic work on the influences behind electoral choice, Berelson, Lazarsfeld and McPhee divide issues into style issues and posi-

---

[27]S.E. Asch, "Effects of Group Pressure upon the Modification and Distortion of Judgements," in D. Cartwright and Alvin Zander (eds.), *Group Dynamics*, (Peterson, Evanston, Ill., 1953), also R. Lane and D.O. Sears, *Public Opinion*, pp. 34–39.

tion issues.[28] Position issues involve such questions as "should taxes be raised or lowered" or "should the anti-combines legislation be extended". They are more likely than style issues to evince a rational response, because they may be objectively rather than psychically important to the individual. Style issues such as linguistic rights issues or liquor laws typically concern matters of taste, or "style of life", and may serve the ends of self-expression. Style issues, therefore, often evoke an irrational response and engage the attention of large numbers of people. The information content of such opinions is typically very low, and information is used mainly to buttress pre-existent opinions.

The Measurement of Public Opinion There are some problems with the way in which much of what we take to be public opinion is measured. Public opinion as expressed in the many polls we see is usually measured in terms of its direction, that is, its position with respect to a particular policy or personality. This is, however, incomplete information, for in order to evaluate it properly, we must also know something of the intensity with which an opinion is held. For instance, suppose the issue is that of Quebec's status in Confederation. In Quebec we ask the simple question, "Do you think Quebec should leave Canada and establish a separate state?" The answer might appear as follows:

Yes—24.5%
No—55.2%
Undecided—20.3%

From this we might conclude that there is not much danger of Quebec's separating from Canada, at least if the majority has its way. Suppose, however, that this question which now measures only the direction of opinion were set up to measure its intensity also:

How to do you feel about the following statement:
"Quebec should leave Canada and establish a separate state."
Are you strongly in agreement, moderately in agreement, undecided, moderately against the idea or strongly against it?

Now consider two possible patterns of responses both of which could give the same overall results as we saw above:

	I	II
Agree Strongly	20.5%	3.1%
Agree Moderately	4.0%	21.4%
Undecided	20.3%	20.3%
Disagree Moderately	53.0%	50.0%
Disagree Strongly	2.2%	5.2%

In pattern I, a large minority (20.5%) feels very strongly in favour of separating. Some 53% favour staying in Canada but do not feel strongly about it, while only 2.2% strongly want to stay in Canada. Does one still feel that

[28]Bernard Berelson, P.F. Lazarsfeld, W.N. McPhee, *Voting*, (University of Chicago Press, Chicago, 1966), p. 184.

there is not much danger of Quebec's separating? Pattern II is probably the most common one for most issues in a democratic society, although possibly not on a highly charged issue like separatism. In this pattern, the vast majority of people do not feel strongly one way or the other and overt conflict is unlikely. In this situation the political decision maker has much more freedom of action than in the situation where a passionate minority opposes an indifferent majority. There are other patterns of intensity possible as well, but they are probably less common than these. The important point is that a public opinion poll which reports only the direction of opinion is a dangerous thing, for it may be more misleading than no information at all.

To make matters even more difficult, many of the public opinion polls which we see publicized are based on woefully inappropriate sampling procedures. For example, one Ottawa area MP mailed out some 50,000 questionnaires to his constituents in 1971 in an attempt to determine their opinion on several issues. He received 7000 replies, and the results were reported locally as being highly significant because of the large number of replies received. After all, Gallup polls, which *are* reliable, have only 1200 respondents and they are usually accurate to within plus or minus 2 or 3 per cent. But the 7000 replies in this case represented only 14 per cent of the original "sample" of 50,000, whereas Gallup polls regularly get 60 to 70 per cent response rates. What is worse, the 7000 respondents were self-selected, i.e. not chosen at random, so they were bound to overrepresent heavily the fringes of the population which hold strong enough opinions to bother to write back. This type of survey has almost no scientific utility unless we want to overrepresent that group which will select itself, and its results can in no way be taken as representative of public opinion at large. Large numbers of responses do not guarantee by themselves that the results will be valid. Thus, as guides to policy formulation, public opinion polls are very tricky devices indeed. One well done can be very valuable, but one which is poorly done—and many are—is worse than useless, for it may mislead policy makers as to the real nature of opinion.

There is little point in discussing the content of contemporary Canadian public opinion on specific issues.[29] Given the ephemeral nature of opinions and of many of the issues themselves, by the time a book can be set in type and published, the issues and the opinions are likely to have changed. What is more important for our concerns is the nature of the behaviour or political activity which results from the interaction of an individual's political values, attitudes, and opinions. And before we can discuss

[29]The most valuable source of opinion on particular issues is the periodic soundings of the Gallup poll conducted by the Canadian Institute of Public Opinion. Many universities maintain files of the raw data on which the newspaper reports are based, and there are also some valuable secondary analyses of the data. See in particular Mildred Schwartz, *Public Opinion and Canadian Identity*, (University of California Press, Berkeley, 1967) and F.C. Engelmann *Political Parties and The Canadian Social Structure*, (Prentice-Hall, Toronto, 1967), Ch. 10, "The Shaping of Public Opinion", pp. 204–221.

that we must also examine the way in which political attitudes and values are acquired—the process of political socialization. We will turn to both those questions in the next chapter.

4
Canadian Political Culture: Political Socialization and Political Participation

POLITICAL SOCIALIZATION: THE LEARNING OF POLITICAL ATTITUDES, VALUES AND OPINIONS[1]

Stated most generally, political socialization is the process whereby we acquire our political values, attitudes, and opinions. At root it is simply political learning and is the vehicle through which a political culture is transmitted from generation to generation. Political socialization is but one dimension of the total process of socialization. As political scientists we may tend to assume that "the political" is as central to the day-to-day concerns of the average Canadian as it is to us; in fact, however, politics may be but a minor and intermittent concern in an indivdual's life.[2]

Political socialization and the more general process of socialization are in no way discrete processes. Political learning and non-political learning are profoundly related. Our manifestly political attitudes and values can be affected by our general attitudes and by aspects of our overall personalities, and it is possible, too, that political attitudes have an impact on personality development in general.

In this section we will first discuss political socialization as an ongoing process; how do we learn about politics? We will then examine the agents which teach us about politics and finally we will develop a profile of the early values, attitudes and opinions of children as we discuss "who learns what, and when?"

[1]Some of the ideas for this section are reflected in M.S. Whittington, "The Concept of Political Socialization and the Canadian Political System", *Quarterly of Canadian Studies*, 2, no. 4; 1973, pp. 207-215. See also major U.S. works on the subject: F. Greenstein, *Children and Politics*, (Yale University Press, New Haven, 1965), *passim*; Kenneth P. Langton, *Political Socialization* (Oxford University Press, New York, 1969); Richard E. Dawson and Kenneth Prewitt, *Political Socialization*, (Little, Brown, Boston, 1969); Roberta S. Sigel (ed.), *Learning About Politics*, (Random House, New York, 1970); Robert Weissberg, *Political Learning, Political Choice and Democratic Citizenship*, (Prentice-Hall, Englewood Cliffs, 1974); Dean Jaros, *Socialization to Politics*, (Praeger, New York, 1973).

[2]See: Weissberg, R., *op. cit.*, pp. 20–23; also Pammett and Whittington, *op. cit.*

Political Socialization as a Continuing Process Political socialization is a lifelong process. While it is likely that the attitudes we acquire as children will have an important impact on our adult political attitudes, there is always the possibility that we can change our minds as we mature. We continue to learn new facts about politics, and such new information may either reinforce existing attitudes or cause us to revise our attitudes to various political objects.

That socialization is cumulative or developmental seems beyond dispute. Few would disagree that as we mature the amount of political information that we possess increases. (Table 4-1 illustrates this fact.)[3] Similarly, it is to be expected that the intensity with which we hold certain political facts to be true will vary as new information either reinforces or contradicts our existing beliefs.

TABLE 4-1: PERCENTAGE OF STUDENTS SCORING 50% OR BETTER ON TWELVE COGNITIVE QUESTIONS, BY GRADE

Score	Grade in School					
	4	5	6	7	8	9
50% or better	20.7	35.2	56.1	63.6	81.5	90.1
(6/12)	(169)	(306)	(496)	(537)	(567)	(155)
Total No. of Respondents	816	869	884	845	696	172

However, cognitive development is but one aspect of the cumulative nature of the political socialization process; in the same way as our cognitive awareness of political objects increases over time, the sophistica-

[3]Tables 4-1 to 4-16 are taken from data collected in a cross-regional survey of children's political attitudes in Canada. The study was administered with the assistance of school boards and teachers through a questionnaire filled out by the children themselves. There were two versions of the questionnaire. One was filled out by children in grades two and three as the teacher read out the questions. The second version of the questionnaire was more elaborate and was filled out by the students in grades four to eight and was also administered to a small group of ninth graders. The completed study included almost 6000 children in Halifax, Trois Rivières, Ottawa, Peterborough, St. Boniface, Lethbridge and Port Alberni. The principals in the survey were T.G. Carroll, of the University of Alberta, D.J. Higgins, of St. Mary's University, and M.S. Whittington of Carleton. The research was furthered through grants from the Canada Council and Carleton University and through the goodwill of the school boards and officials involved. The tables included in this chapter reflect but preliminary findings in the data analysis. The principals in the study are engaged currently in the preparation of a manuscript tentatively entitled, *Regionalism and Political Attitudes: Political Socialization in Canada.*

tion of our political attitudes can also be expected to increase. While our earliest attitudes to politics may be vague perceptions of political symbols and personalities and possibly diffuse affection or dislike for the objects of which we are aware, with some degree of political sophistication we become more capable of evaluating political objects with respect to our individual political value systems. Thus, while cognitive and affective attitudes dominate our political make-up in the earliest years, as we grow older, evaluative attitudes will come to take an ever larger place.

Tables 4-2 and 4-3 illustrate the development of sophistication in Canadian children's perceptions of political authority figures. In the early grades it appears that their affection for and objective assessment of the power of three "head of state" roles are closely interdependent. As they grow older, the children develop the ability to evaluate the power of an authority role in a more objective fashion. Thus, while relative affection for the PM declines slightly from grades 4 to 8, the likelihood that he will be judged the "most powerful" increases markedly; conversely, while affection for the Queen remains quite high, the likelihood that she will be judged "most powerful" declines significantly.

TABLE 4-2: CHILDREN'S EVALUATIONS OF MOST POWERFUL HEAD OF STATE ROLES (QUEEN, GOVERNOR GENERAL, PRIME MINISTER

Role Perceived as "Most Powerful"	Grade				
	4	5	6	7	8
Queen	60.5	55.6	46.6	42.9	35.3
Governor General	10.6	12.2	11.8	11.7	11.4
Prime Minister	29.0	32.2	41.7	45.4	53.2
Total No. of Respondents	100.1 (559)	100.0 (590)	100.0 (629)	100.0 (557)	99.9 (481)

A further feature of the process of political socialization is that the earliest awareness of political objects occurs in the absence of any behavioural requirements. A child, while he may acquire knowledge of and feelings about political objects, is seldom, if ever, called upon to act upon those feelings. Thus his perception of himself as an actor in the political process must be anticipatory or vicarious; his political attitudes are acquired in the anticipation that at some future time personal involvement will be permitted or even expected. An example of this anticipatory socialization is the development of partisan preferences in children, which follows a pattern similar to that of the acquisition of political knowledge. While there are significant regional variations and while the intensity of the preference

TABLE 4-3: CHILDREN'S "FAVORITE" OF HEAD OF STATE ROLES

Role "Liked" Best	Grade				
	4	5	6	7	8
Queen	74.0	73.3	69.3	65.9	59.4
Governor General	9.2	12.8	16.3	20.4	29.3
Prime Minister	16.8	13.9	14.4	13.7	11.3
Total No.	100.0	100.0	100.0	100.0	100.0
of Respondents	(596)	(619)	(655)	(583)	(505)

TABLE 4-4: CHILDREN HAVING A PARTY PREFERENCE, BY GRADE, IN EIGHT CANADIAN COMMUNITIES

Grade	4	5	6	7	8	Total
	(Percentage with party preference)					
Ottawa–Carleton	34.0	40.9	58.6	59.0	59.6	1163
Ottawa	49.1	42.2	42.9	42.9	53.7	289
Peterborough, Ont. Public	18.4	23.4	34.5	38.2	48.9	395
Peterborough, Ont. Separate	34.3	12.5	16.0	36.4	54.8	126
Lethbridge, Alta.	15.4	25.0	29.9	33.3	33.7	520
Three Rivers, Que.	40.3	51.7	54.8	48.0	*	232
St. Boniface, Man.	28.1	32.5	44.7	39.8	57.5	419
Port Alberni, B.C.	18.1	30.7	44.6	40.8	*	274
Halifax, N.S.	47.9	56.8	67.8	77.3	80.9	512

*Grades not present in schools studied.
Sources: Table from Pammett and Whittington, *op. cit*; data from Carroll, Higgins and Whittington, Survey of Canadian Children's Attitudes.

for a party may be very weak, children do begin to make such choices at an early stage in their personal development. Table 4-4 indicates that even in grade 4 a large minority of school children can express a partisan preference and that by grade 8 a majority have such preferences.

The implications of the non-behavioural context of early socialization is that the pattern of socialization may be altered when an individual does become active in politics. One's perception of the voter's role or his party preference, for instance, may be altered after some years of experience in the role. This *post-incumbency socialization* becomes particularly politically important with respect to highly political roles. The expectations that one might have of the role of MP for instance, will likely alter considerably after a few years of experience in the job. In sum, not only do our attitudes shape our political behaviour, but our experiences resulting from our behaviour shape our attitudes.

The Agents of Political Socialization The acquisition of attitudes to objects in the world of politics is usually thought of as taking place through intermediary agents or media, which transmit and interpret the "real world" to us. While it is clear that some of our information about political objects can be acquired directly through observation of a sitting of the House of Commons, attendance at an election meeting, or even a stroll around Parliament Hill, a far greater percentage of such information is transmitted to us through our parents, peers, schools and the mass media. These four agents of socialization not only function as lines of communication connecting us to a reality with which we cannot have direct personal contact, but they also interpret, consciously or unconsciously, the information for us. Because in our younger years almost all of our contact with political objects occurs through such agents or interpreters, particularly our parents, the agents of socialization can have a deep-seated impact on the substance and intensity of our political attitudes.

The family, since it gets to the child first, is virtually the only important socializing agency during his first few years. Tables 4-5 and 4-6 show the impact of parents' talking about politics on the cognitive awareness and partisanship of elementary school children in Canada. Like many learning processes, political socialization within the family does not usually proceed by direct parental teaching but rather by the child's picking up what is "in the air" in the family environment. If no discussion of politics occurs in the child's home, he may very early in life decide that political stimuli are not worth his attention, and he may never again pay much attention to politics. On the other hand, if the child is brought up in a home where politics are constantly under discussion, he will begin to look

TABLE 4-5: PARENTS "TALKING ABOUT POLITICS" AND COGNITIVE AWARENESS

Cognitive Score	"Talking"	
	little or no	a lot
75% or better	8.5	13.6
50–75%	40.4	49.9
less than 50%	51.2	36.5
Total	1568	2448
	100%	100%

TABLE 4-6: PARENTS "TALKING ABOUT POLITICS" AND PARTY IDENTIFICATION

Party Identification	"Talking"	
	little or no	a lot
No party identification	60.1	42.5
Some party identification	39.9	57.5
Total	100.0	100.0

for political information outside the home as well, so that he will be able to participate more actively in his home life.

The importance of the family in arousing political interest has results which can readily be observed. Of those children whose parents talked little about politics, only 8.5 per cent scored in the highest range on the test for cognitive awareness. Of those whose parents talked about politics a lot, 13.6 per cent scored in the highest range.

Time and again politicians reminisce about how politics was a constant topic of discussion in their childhood homes, or about how politically active their parents were. This process, of course, repeats itself, and leads to certain family names appearing over and over again in politics. This may, in effect, reduce the size of the population from which politicians are drawn.[4]

The school is another agent of political socialization. The child can pick up political information through the curriculum, particularly through formal instruction of government in "civics" type courses. However, preliminary data from a national survey of Canadian elementary school children's attitudes shown in Table 4-7, indicates that, while there is a relationship between formal instruction and cognitive awareness, it is fairly weak.

TABLE 4-7: FORMAL "CIVICS" INSTRUCTION IN SCHOOL, AND COGNITIVE AWARENESS

Cognitive Score	None	Some
75% or better	9.0	14.4
50 to 75%	44.3	45.7
Less than 50%	46.8	39.9
Totals	4286	1110
	100%	100%

[4]See for example: C.G. Power, *A Party Politician*, (Macmillan, Toronto, 1966), pp. 3–14.

Perhaps more important than the impact of the school curriculum on the child's perceptions of politics is the structure of the school itself. While on the one hand it may pass on general attitudes towards authority which are necessary to the stability of the political system, an overly authoritarian school may serve to discourage the mass participation which is likely an important component of a healthy democratic system. A school environment which is overly permissive may have equally unhappy results. Also within the context of the school, the child may be confronted with "significant others", authority figures to whom he can look for advice and for a personalized model on which to pattern his own political life. Not only the teachers, but also informal leaders among peers and cohorts may emerge as important agents in molding a child's attitudes to both authority in general and specific political objects.

The mass media can also be expected to have an impact during the period of transition from close adherence to the political views of parents to those of peer group opinion leaders, teachers, etc. Tables 4-8 and 4-9 illustrate the impact of reading the newspaper on political cognitive awareness and partisanship. Only 3.7 per cent of those children who seldom read newspapers achieve a high cognitive score, as opposed to 16.7 per cent of those who read newspapers a lot. Of those who read newspapers seldom, almost 65 per cent had not developed a party identification; the corresponding percentage of those reading newspapers a lot runs considerably lower, at 43.7 per cent.

TABLE 4-8: READING THE NEWSPAPER AND COGNITIVE AWARENESS

Cognitive Score	Reading		
	A Lot	Some	Seldom/Never
75% or better	16.7	8.8	3.7
50 to 75%	50.0	42.9	32.2
Less than 50%	33.3	48.3	64.1
Totals	1343	1784	1143
	100%	100%	100%

Perhaps surprisingly, no strong relationship appears to exist between exposure to TV and political awareness. This finding, illustrated in Table 4-10, possibly reflects the tendency of the child to select programs which have little or no political content. However, while children who watch a lot of TV are marginally more aware of politics than are those who watch little, the difference is so small that it may call into question the long-held assumption that there is a direct causal connection between television and political attitudes. These findings may also serve to reinforce the suggestion that the relationship between the mass media and attitudes

TABLE 4-9: READING THE NEWSPAPER AND PARTISAN IDENTIFICATION

Partisanship	Reading		
	A Lot	Some	Seldom/Never
No party identification	43.7	56.5	64.9
Party identification	56.3	43.5	35.1
Totals	1296	1305	1089
	100%	100%	100%

TABLE 4-10: HOURS OF TV WATCHING PER DAY AND COGNITIVE AWARENESS

Cognitive Score	2 hours or less	More than 2 hours
75% or better	12.21	12.19
50 to 75%	44.04	46.81
Less than 50%	43.76	41.00
Totals	(1065)	(3339)
	100.01	100.00

is a two- or multi-step process, involving not only the media as the primary source of the information but other secondary agents who interpret or translate the political data for us.[5]

Political information appears to be picked out of the media by a fairly small portion of the population whom we could call *political opinion leaders*. The majority of people pick relatively little political information directly out of the media. Instead they receive it second-hand from opinion leaders who can be found in almost every formal or informal group. The information is further processed by the recipient in accordance with his pre-existent beliefs and possibly even passed on to another group—perhaps his family—in which he himself functions as an opinion leader. One thing is certain: the role of the media as agents of socialization is a complex one.[6]

While most works on the subject of political socialization limit their discussion of agents to "family", "peers", "school", and "mass media", there are other socializing agents. Significantly, in a society that has come to be referred to as "organizational"[7] and in which most adults spend

[5]E. Katz, and P. Lazarsfeld, *Personal Influence.* (The Free Press, Glencoe, 1955), *passim.*
[6]See also Pammett and Proudfoot, in Pammett and Whittington (eds.), *op. cit.*
[7]Presthus, Robert, *The Organizational Society*, (Knopf, New York, 1962).

many of their waking hours occupying an organizationally defined role, the organizations or institutions themselves must have a significant impact on the substance and intensity of our attitudes. To a large extent people who operate within the context of organizations by necessity have to identify their personal best interests with those of the organization of which they are a part—"what's good for General Motors may in fact be good for me," if I happen to work for that organization. Hence some of the values of the organization either consciously or unconsciously will become internalized over time.

Voluntary associations, too, can come to influence our political attitudes through the use of "in-house" publications, by publicizing an organizational aim, and by providing an institutional vehicle through which opinion leaders can more efficiently reach a "ready-to-be-convinced" audience. Even children may feel the impact of such institutional socialization not only through the school system as mentioned above, but also through organizations such as the Boy Scouts, which foster and disseminate the values of worship, loyalty to Queen and country and good citizenship.

Finally, institutional or organizational agents of socialization come to play a very significant role in the process of post-incumbency socialization. As discussed above, our political elites are socialized in part through the process of incumbency. Membership in the House of Commons, cabinet, judicial system or bureaucracy cannot help but have an impact not only on the incumbent's perception of the institution of which he is a member, but on the importance of all related intitutions. Because post-incumbency socialization affects only the elites and not the masses, and because it is the socialization of our political elites which in the long run will have an effect on the kinds of policies that our system produces, future studies of political socialization should address themselves more seriously to this aspect of the process.

Who Learns What, and When? While it is not likely that politics have any great significance for very young children, we do know that they begin to learn about political objects at a fairly tender age. The first objects about which Canadian children become aware are ones which are primarily symbolic in content. The Canadian flag for instance is recognized by almost 90 per cent of children in grades 2 and 3, and even the American flag was recognized by over 70 per cent of the same sample of Canadian children. Next to symbolic objects, it would appear that the more highly personalized roles in the political system, such as that of the Prime Minister, are the most likely to be identified by children.

Thus it seems safe to conclude that the level of knowledge about political objects depends at least in part upon the nature of the object itself. Generally it is the symbolic objects which are learned about first, with awareness of the more personalized structural objects coming next, and with an awareness of the conceptual objects coming quite a bit later. But there are variables other than the nature of the political object which can also have an impact on the level of cognition. Studies consistently indicate that male children acquire more political information than do female children; in a similar fashion partisanship is higher and acquired sooner in boys than in girls. As might be expected, the socio-economic status of parents,[8] the region of the country in which the child is living[9] and even religion[10] are independent variables which correlate with the level and intensity of cognition and partisanship in Canadian children. Tables 4-11 and 4-14 provide several examples of the relationship between these variables and partisanship and cognition.

TABLE 4-11: SEX DIFFERENCES IN PARTISANSHIP

Party Identification	Male	Female
No Party Identification	46.3	62.9
Liberals	28.3	20.9
Progressive Conservatives	9.3	6.5
New Democratic Party	6.9	4.3
Others	9.2	5.4
Totals	100%	100%
	2023	2065

TABLE 4-12: SEX DIFFERENCES IN COGNITIVE SCORES

Cognitive score	Male	Female
75% or better	13.5	8.3
50 to 75%	47.2	43.4
50%	39.3	48.3
Totals	100%	100%
	2931	2882

While it is clear that some awareness of political objects occurs early in the child's life, it has also been found that one's earliest attitudes towards the political system reflect positive affect. Young Canadian children—like their American counterparts—have a basically benevolent view of politics. Since it was suggested that one of the primary functions of political socialization is the inculcation of attitudes of support for the political system, this is obviously a vital point. Looking at some actual figures, it was discovered in Kingston in 1966 that among Grade 4 children 52 per

[8]See: Richert, "Political Socialization in Quebec," *CJPS*, June 1973, p. 310.
[9]See: Pammett and Whittington, *op. cit.*
[10]Pammett, *op. cit.*

TABLE 4-13: FATHER'S OCCUPATION AND PARTY IDENTIFICATION

Party Identification	Professional	Executive, Managerial	Clerical, White Collar, Skilled	Manual
No party identification	47.2	45.7	50.5	61.4
Liberals	33.5	30.9	30.3	16.4
Progressive Conservatives	8.1	10.1	9.7	7.4
New Democratic Party	2.2	4.9	2.8	6.8
Others	9.0	8.4	6.7	8.0
Totals	100% (534)	100% (405)	100% (390)	100% (1224)

TABLE 4-14: FATHER'S OCCUPATION AND COGNITIVE SCORE

Cognitive Score	Professional	Executive, Managerial	Clerical, White Collar, Skilled Labour	Manual Labour
75% or better	14.9	14.1	12.4	7.6
50 to 75%	47.5	51.9	44.4	37.1
50%	37.6	34.0	43.2	55.3
Totals	(550)	(418)	(403)	(1277)

cent thought the Prime Minister was doing a "very good" or "fairly good" job and only 5.7 per cent thought he was "not very good" or "bad". By Grade 8 about 60 per cent of school children evaluated the Prime Minister's work positively, while only 9.5 per cent made a basically negative evaluation.[11]

This benevolent view of political life may be related to the subordinate and dependent position of the child in a multitude of life situations. With age and experience, the child becomes less dependent and less dominated and thus more prone to cynicism about those in positions of authority. While it would be nice to think that such optimism and faith in our system is stimulated by inherent qualities of the Canadian system, the fact that other political systems enjoy similar loyalty from their children would indicate that the phenomenon is a function of the nature of childhood and not of the nature of the political system. Canadian children are also gener-

[11]Pammett, *op. cit.*: See also Greenstein, *Children and Politics*, (New Haven, 1965).

ally conservative, a fact that, again, is probably related to the subordination and dependency of most childhood situations.[12]

The benevolence of school children, moreover, carries over from political personalities to issue areas. When children in both Colborne[13] and Kingston[14] were asked, in open-ended questions, about what they would do to change the world, the overwhelming majority of them mentioned things one would consider benevolent. Helping out the poor or hungry was frequently cited, and a substantial majority said in one way or another that they would end war.

More recent studies, however, particularly in the United States, have indicated that the children of the seventies are likely to be more cynical about politics. Politicians in the age of Vietnam war and Watergate do not look as trustworthy and as "parental" as they did in the previous decade. It would appear that American children are losing some of their idealism about politics[15] and the same seems to be the case in Canada. Stephen Ullman[16] writes about the low levels of support for the Canadian political community among the Micmac subculture in Cape Breton, Donald Forbes points to significant pro-separatist attitudes among French-Canadian high school students, and J.-P. Richert talks of the "non-idealistic conception of government" among both English- and French-speaking elementary school children.[17] Simple observation tells us tht the young of today are less benevolent and much more critical of and cynical about the political system than were their parents. The implications of this for our future political culture could be significant.

One idiosyncrasy of children's political attitudes in Canada is the fact that American political objects may be perceived as part of the Canadian child's political world. Table 4-15 indicates the relative awareness of Canadian children for selected Canadian and American political objects. They indicate that some Canadian children were more likely to recognize the U.S. flag than the Canadian after grade 4 and that their recognition of the U.S. president was nearly as high as that of the Prime Minister. There is any number of ways to interpret a table such as this, but one should probably avoid the temptation of inferring that Canadian children know more about the U.S. than they do about Canada. The differences in recognition of flags are very small and do not apply before grade 4. In these data, the Prime Minister is consistently better known than the President.[18] By grade 8, nearly 25 per cent of these Canadian school child-

[12]Taken from: Whittington, "Political Socialization and the Canadian Political System," Q.C.S., op. cit., p. 214.
[13]Hill, John, "Political Socialization of Children in a Rural Environment" (unpublished thesis, Queen's University, 1969).
[14]Pammett, op. cit.
[15]See particularly: H. Tolley, Children and War, (Teachers College Press, New York, 1973); Jaros, Hirsch, and Fleron, "The Malevolent Leader: Political Socialization in an American Subculture" APSR, 1968, p. 564.
[16]See articles by Ullman and Forbes in Pammett and Whittington (eds.), op. cit.
[17]J.-P. Richert, "Political Socialization in Quebec," CJPS, VI, no. 2 June 1973, p. 310.
[18]These results disagree to some extent with a survey of some 200 students in ten

ren could identify all four Canadian items in Table 4-15 whereas only 3.8 per cent could identify all the U.S. items.

TABLE 4-15: RECOGNITION OF CANADIAN AND AMERICAN POLITICAL OBJECTS, BY GRADE[20]

Grade	2	3	4	5	6	7	8
	(Per cent correct identification)						
Canadian flag	86.4	91.8	92.4	92.0	95.7	95.5	97.4
American flag	71.7	87.7	95.8	96.7	98.2	97.1	98.8
Prime Minister	68.3	74.1	79.8	88.2	95.7	98.4	99.4
Governor General	14.3	27.8	29.3	44.0	61.7	71.1	84.8
U.S. President	25.7	42.8	57.9	69.8	89.2	89.3	93.3
Canadian cabinet	NA	NA	14.1	21.9	28.6	38.5	51.1
American cabinet	NA	NA	4.1	3.2	6.2	6.0	10.1
Canadian MPs	NA	NA	9.5	13.6	18.0	22.9	32.0
U.S. Congressmen	NA	NA	3.3	5.2	5.2	6.0	6.8

NA—question not asked of children in grades two and three.

TABLE 4-16: AMERICAN POLITICAL ROLES VERSUS CANADIAN POLITICAL ROLES

Political Role	affect	confidence
Queen	78.8	70.1
President of the United States	15.8	22.0
don't know	5.4	7.9
President of the United States	28.8	34.3
Prime Minister of Canada	64.7	53.9
don't know	6.5	11.8
President of the United States	22.4	37.8
Governor General of Canada	70.6	50.7
don't know	6.9	11.5

schools in Kingston, Ontario, in December 1966. In it, 17 per cent of Grade 8 students could give a reasonably accurate description of the Prime Minister and 72 per cent could name him while over 26 could describe the role of the U.S. president and 94 per cent could name him. Jon Pammett, "Political Orientations in Public and Separate School Children," (unpublished M.A. thesis, Queen's University, 1967), pp. 41–2.

[19]The figures in Tables 4-15 and 4-16 are from Donald Higgins, "The Political

Table 4-16, which is taken from the same study as Table 4-15, indicates another facet of Canadian relations with the United States as seen through the eyes of school children. The term "affect" is used in that study to mean a positive feeling towards someone. Thus in the "affect" column of the Table, we see that 78.8 per cent of the children in this study chose the Queen over the president when asked "who is your favourite?" "Confidence" is used in the study to indicate who the respondent feels is more likely to be right if the leaders named disagreed. Thus in the "confidence" column of the Table we see that 53.9 per cent of these children felt that the Prime Minister was more likely to be right in a disagreement with the President. These are data gathered before the Watergate scandal of 1973, which severely damaged the credibility of the American President then in office, but they likely reflect the "normal" situation.

Again, the interpretation of Table 4-16 is to some extent up to the reader, but the consistently higher levels of affect for Canadian political leaders and the somewhat lower but still considerable edge that Canadian leaders hold in confidence seem to suggest that while significant, American cultural influence has not by any means obliterated the positive feelings Canadian children have for objects related to their political system. On the other hand it is perhaps alarming that such a sizable percentage (ranging from 15.8 per cent to 37.8 per cent) of Canadian children do have higher regard for the American President than they do for significant Canadian authorities.

This concludes our discussion of political socialization. In the final section of this examination of political culture, we will look at the logical culmination of the various aspects of our discussion of political culture, for it is through the overt channels of political participation that values, attitudes and opinions are fed into the political system. Thus, political participation is logically the last link in the chain leading from political values to actual action by the political system.

POLITICAL PARTICIPATION IN CANADA: FROM ATTITUDE TO ACTION

Political opinions are most significant for the political system if they are translated into some kind of action by the opinion holder. The action may be voting, writing to an MP, or just talking to people at the factory; if the action is concerned with politics, we call it political participation. Obviously the participatory behaviour of Canadians is a vital link—indeed it is *the* link between the environment of politics and the political system. As such it is a key part of the political process.[20] In addition, the ways in

Americanization of Canadian Children", in Pammett and Whittington (eds.), *op. cit.*

[20]As pointed out earlier, political participation can occur at the input side and at the output side of the political system. In this section, when we speak of political participation we will be referring specifically to input participation. Output-side participation will be dealt with in the context of policy making.

which Canadians participate in politics and the attitudes with which they do so provide a valuable additional indicator of the nature of the political culture.

There are three major questions to be asked about the participation of Canadians: first, how do people participate in politics?; second, who participates in politics?; and third, why do they participate? Different types of people are engaged in different types of political activity and with different motivations, and many people do not participate in politics at all.

The Hierarchy of Participation There are different levels of political participation, the highest of which is usually envisaged as the holding of a political office. People who participate at any particular level of activity will likely participate in all or most of the activities below that level in a *hierarchy of participation*. Thus, virtually every person who holds a political office has also engaged in a variety of other political activities, including voting, campaigning either on his own behalf or for someone else, and participating in political strategy meetings. Similarly, a person who participates in strategy meetings will certainly vote and be an active party member as well. The hierarchy of political participation, as it applies to the electoral process in Canada, is summarized in Figure 4-1.

Figure 4-1

A HIERARCHY OF ELECTORAL PARTICIPATION

	Holding a public office
	Being a political candidate
Gladiatorial	Holding an office within a party
Level	Soliciting party funds
	Attending a strategy meeting or planning a campaign
Transitional	Contributing money to a political party
Level	Being an active party member
	Contributing time in a campaign
	Attending a meeting or rally
	Contacting a public official or politician
Spectator	Attempting to convince people how to vote
Level	Initiating a political discussion
	Being interested in politics
	Exposing oneself to political stimuli
	Voting

Source: Adapted from Lester Milbrath, *Political Participation*, (Rand McNally, Chicago, 1965), p. 18.

The higher up the hierarchy, the fewer participants there are. At the most, 3 or 4 per cent of the Canadian people participate at the "gladiatorial" level while another 10 to 20 per cent participate in "transitional" level activities. Participation at the spectator level is considerably higher. About 22 per cent of Canadians tried to convince other people how to vote in the 1965 election campaign, and about 72 per cent of the people paid attention to the campaign in some way or other. In federal elections, about 70 to 75 per cent of eligible Canadians vote fairly regularly. In several provinces, however, levels of participation in provincial elections are considerably lower, and in many municipal electoral settings, levels of participation are so low that the hierarchy could hardly be applied at all.

The hierarchy as it appears in Figure 4-1 refers only to electoral participation. We will discuss the functions of elections in Chapter 9, but it is important to recognize here that the electoral process is neither the only nor necessarily the most important way in which people can participate in politics.[21] For many purposes, participation outside the electoral process may be more effective than participation within it, for it is difficult to determine the issue content of electoral participation. Some people may work for the Liberal party because they like the "style" of Pierre Elliott Trudeau. Others may participate because they believe that the welfare policies of the Liberals are superior to those of the Conservatives or NDP. But if a person marches in a demonstration against the treatment of Canadian Indians, his input to the political system is much less equivocal—he probably dislikes the way Canadian Indians have been treated. If a person is a leader of an interest group and presents a brief to a minister, a parliamentary committee, or the bureaucracy, there can be no doubt about the policy direction of his political input. Therefore simply looking at the hierarchy of electoral participation does not tell one much. It is necessary to look at another hierarchy of participation, this time for non-electoral behaviour.

Figure 4-2

A HIERARCHY OF NON-ELECTORAL PARTICIPATION

Attempting to brief or otherwise persuade politicians or bureaucrats
  on behalf of an organized group (lobbying)
Holding office within a politically active interest group
Planning strategy within a politically active interest group
Being an active member of a politically active interest group
Demonstrating on behalf of an issue or group
Being a passive member of an interest group

The use of the term "hierarchy" in Figure 4-2 may be somewhat misleading. Not all of the activities involved are of the same type, and it is difficult to know where to place an item like "demonstrating". The essen-

[21]L. Dion, "Participating in the Political Process," *Queen's Quarterly*, vol. 75, no. 3, pp. 432-447, Autumn, 1968.

tial problem here is lack of research. Political scientists have tended to concentrate on the processes of electoral participation to the exclusion of other types of input participation which, as we have seen, may very well be more important in the long-term political process.[22] This is unfortunate, but perhaps understandable in that most electoral activities are overt and relatively easy to examine compared to non-electoral activities. We shall return to what is known about non-electoral activities when we discuss interest groups in the Canadian political system, but for the moment we will confine ourselves to electoral activity.

In order to examine who participates in electoral activity and why they do so, an index called the campaign activity index (CAI) will be used. It is a summary of many of the components of the hierarchy of electoral participation.[23] Based on a 1965 national survey of 2,100 Canadians, the index shows that 4.4 per cent of Canadians had a high CAI rating, 21.8 per cent had a medium rating, and 73.3 per cent a low rating. Very roughly these would correspond to the gladiatorial transitional and spectator levels on the hierarchy of electoral participation shown in Figure 4.1.

Who Participates in Politics? It can be suggested that there are three basic determinants of a person's participation in politics. The first of these is the sum of the individual's socio-economic resources: the amount of time and money he can "invest" in political activity. How much he invests will depend upon his occupation and income, other activities which compete for his resources, and, of course, upon the nature of the political system itself. A second and vital determinant is the individual's personality resources. Political participation at most higher levels of the hierarchy is a sociable activity and consequently has social costs and requires social resources. People who have more social aplomb and who find interaction with other people to be easy are therefore more likely to participate in politics.[24] The third determinant is the political resources available to the citizen who wishes to participate in politics. If there are many institutions where he can participate, or if the existing institutions such as political parties encourage participation, then he is more likely to become involved in politics. This last point can be examined further in two ways. First, we can look at Canadian institutions such as parties to see whether they do, in fact, encourage participation. This we will do in Chapters 9 and 10. Second, we can determine whether or not Canadians feel that the political system responds to their efforts to influence it, and

[22]The most important exceptions to this generalization are John Porter, *The Vertical Mosaic* and more recently Robert Presthus, *Elite Accommodation in Canadian Politics*.
[23]For those who are interested in such things, the campaign activity index consists of voting and reading about politics each weighted singly; trying to convince someone of how to vote, doubly weighted; and belonging to a political party or working during an election campaign, triply weighted. The weight factors are arbitrarily chosen to express the "difficulty" of the activity.
[24]For an extensive bibliography comprising mainly American work in this area, see L. Milbrath, *Political Participation*.

then determine whether or not their feelings in this respect correlate with participation. An individual's feeling that he has a meaningful role in politics and his confidence that the system will respond to him are termed a sense of *political efficacy*. Its role in Canada is summarized later in this chapter using an efficacy index similar to the campaign activity index.

The next step, then, will be to outline who participates in the Canadian electoral process by examining the socio-economic correlates of participation. From there it is possible to proceed to an examination of the attitudes of participants in Canadian politics with a view to discovering the effect of these attitudes on the decision makers in the political system.

Socio-Economic Factors and Political Participation Table 4-17 indicates that a person's socio-economic class is correlated with his level of activity in a political campaign. The row showing "low" campaign activity is most instructive. In it one can see that 58 per cent of the upper middle-class respondents showed low campaign activity ("low" in this context means that the respondent may, at most, have voted and paid some attention to the campaign) and that the figure increases rapidly as we move down the class scale until some 84 per cent of lower-class respondents showed low activity levels. If income is used as a measure of social class a similar result appears, for the same survey indicates that 56 per cent of Canadians whose family incomes were over $10,000 per year in 1965 showed low levels of activity while 80 per cent of Canadians earning less than $3,000 per year had low ratings.[25]

TABLE 4-17: CAMPAIGN ACTIVITY IN DIFFERENT SOCIO-ECONOMIC CLASS GROUPS

Campaign Activity Level	Upper Middle	Middle	Working	Lower
	(Figures are percentages*)			
High	5.9	5.3	3.5	4.2
Medium	35.3	23.2	19.4	11.8
Low	57.9	70.9	76.7	84.0
Total No. of Respondents	226	1,034	1,223	96

*In all this and all succeeding tables in this chapter all figures are percentages expressed vertically, e.g. the upper left-hand cell of the table indicates that 5.9 per cent of the upper middle class showed high activity. Figures may not add vertically to 100 per cent because of rounding errors.

All data in this and succeeding tables in this chapter come from the 1965 national political survey carried out by Professors John Meisel, Philip Converse, Maurice Pinard, Peter Regenstreif and Mildred Schwartz. The project was supported by the Canada Council, the Laidlaw Foundation and the Federal Committee on Election Expenses.

[25]The reader may be surprised at the number of lower- or working-class people

If instead of the campaign activity index one simply uses voting as an indicator, a similar pattern emerges. In this case, some 77 per cent of lower-class respondents claim to vote in all or most federal elections while the same claim is made by over 90 per cent of upper middle-class respondents and 87 per cent of middle-class respondents. Table 4-18 indicates a similar situation with education used as the measure of class.

TABLE 4-18: VOTING FREQUENCY IN DIFFERENT EDUCATIONAL GROUPS

Voting		Education Years						
		0–5	6–8	9–11	12–13	14–16	more than 17	Total No. of Respondents in row
				(Figures are percentages)				
All	Federal	51	50	55	63	64	69	1447
	Provincial	50	46	46	48	52	38	1214
Most	Federal	36	26	29	25	26	16	712
	Provincial	35	26	31	26	22	29	734
Some	Federal	11	20	13	8	8	12	339
	Provincial	10	18	14	11	11	10	356
None	Federal	1	4	3	4	3	4	79
	Provincial	4	7	8	15	14	23	253
Total No. of Respondents		228	670	867	464	227	110	

An examination of Table 4-18 indicates what one might have expected, namely that voting turnout and education increase together. The reader can no doubt find the general patterns in the table for himself but there are some interesting details in it as well. For example, people with fewer than eight years of education make almost no differentiation, as far as voting is concerned, between federal and provincial politics. But as educational levels rise so does the differentiation in voting frequency between provincial and national elections. For example, in the "all", "most" and "some" rows of the table there is never more than 1 per cent difference between claimed turnout in federal and provincial elections for people with less than 5 years of education, whereas among those with more than 17 years' education the difference between federal and provincial politics in

with high CAI readings. This results from the fact that a significant number of lower- and working-class people work for parties during a campaign doing such work as envelope-stuffing or driving voters to the polls for pay. Middle-class workers tend to be volunteers who do jobs like canvassing, organizing, or strategy planning.

the "all" row is 31 per cent. The same pattern appears throughout the table. The reader is invited to speculate on two points here. First, what might be the causes of this finding, and second, what might be its consequences for Canadian politics?

There are, of course, many other cleavages in the Canadian environment which might be significantly connected with electoral participation. In Chapter 2 it was suggested that the ethnic cleavage is Canada's major one. Table 4-19 examines the effects of ethnic cleavage (expressed by language) on our campaign activity index.

TABLE 4-19: CAMPAIGN ACTIVITY BY LANGUAGE GROUPS

Campaign Activity Index	Language		
	English	French	Other
		(Figures are percentages)	
High	4.2	5.0	2.5
Medium	23.0	18.7	20.5
Low	72.2	76.0	77.0
Total No. of Respondents	1,860	740	117

If we expect a dramatic difference between ethnic groups with respect to campaign activity, Table 4-19 will be a disappointment. French Canadians showed slightly larger numbers of people whose activity was high but a considerably smaller number of people with a medium level of activity. Other ethnic groups showed a substantially lower number of highly active people, but the proportion of medium-activity people was not unlike the French and English groups. It is important to remember, however, that this table refers only to a federal election campaign. Data for provincial politics are lacking, but it might be hypothesized that French Canadians would show a substantially higher level of activity in this area than other ethnic groups. Data on voting itself tend to back up this contention. In each of the eight Quebec provincial elections from 1931 to 1965, voter turnout exceeded the turnout in Quebec in the preceding federal election.[26] Furthermore when people were asked which government handles the most important political problems, 57 per cent of English Canadians and only 24 per cent of French Canadians felt that the federal government did so.

With the exception of the Atlantic Provinces, which show consist-

[26]Howard A. Scarrow, "Patterns of Voter Turnout in Canada," in J.C. Courtney (ed.), *Voting in Canada*, (Prentice–Hall, Toronto, 1967), p. 111. A similar pattern, however, also appears in Alberta and Nova Scotia.

ently lower levels of participation than the rest of Canada, it is difficult to find large regional differences in electoral participation. Overall differences in levels of participation by province are more likely affected by particular local political conditions than by regional cleavages. Any consistent differences which can be found are quite readily attributable to differing levels of education or income, with poorer and less well-educated regions showing lower levels of most types of participation. The level of activity in a province, however, may be temporarily increased by a heightened level of political party competition in the province, by a particularly exciting political leader, or by the emergence of a new political movement.[27]

There are some sex and age differences in the Canadian population with respect to participation. In middle-class English Canada there is not much difference in levels of participation between men and women, but in French Canada and among people with less than a highschool level of education, men are much more likely to participate than women. The pattern in Canada in this respect is similar to that in other western democracies. In underdeveloped areas of a country, where educational levels are low, there are large differences between the sexes. Where educational levels are higher, sexual equality extends to political participation as well as to some other fields.

An age profile of participation shows a peak in the middle years with a tailing off at either end. Very old or very young voters appear particularly unlikely to be active participants in the electoral process, and this pattern prevails in Canada regardless of regional, cultural, or class differences.

Any of the above facts can be explained without too much difficulty by keeping in mind what was said earlier about the individual's resources. The explanation can be further sharpened to apply to particular types of campaign activity if it is suggested that all activities have specific requirements which will call more or less directly on specific resources.[28] For example, reading about a political campaign obviously requires the ability to read relatively easily. If reading about the campaign is correlated with level of education, it will be seen that as the level of education declines so does reading about politics. On the other hand, belonging to a party or working for one takes time and requires social interaction. Thus, people with more time (retired people, housewives whose children are grown up), or with flexible time requirements for their jobs (lawyers, professors, or other professional people), could be expected to and do participate in this way, more frequently than others.

Nonetheless, even a cursory glance at our tables is enough to indicate that socio-economic factors alone are not sufficient to explain why people participate in politics. There are still many people who have all the

[27]S.M. Lipset, *Agrarian Socialism*, (University of California Press, Berkeley, 1950), discusses in detail the effect of a new movement (the CCF) on patterns of participation in Saskatchewan.

[28]L. Milbrath in *Political Participation* calls these requirements "dimensions" See p. 22 ff.

necessary resources but pay no attention to politics. In some cases our predictions can be fairly clear. If the person in question is an older, poorly educated, rural French-Canadian woman we can assert with a considerable degree of confidence that voting is likely to be her only political act. But much of the Canadian voting-age public is middle-class or working-class with enough education to give it many of the necessary resources to participate; whether or not a member of this group will in fact participate must depend upon some other factors as well.

Table 4-20 reveals that the act of identifying with a party is a significant correlate of electoral participation. Among those with no party identification, 83 per cent showed low activity levels, whereas among the "committed", the figure fell to 69 per cent. In this case the figures shown corroborate the findings of many other surveys. The well-informed, active, independent voter is largely a myth. Active participation in the political process (whether during elections or at other times) is usually accompanied by partisan commitment. People may switch their allegiances from time to time—indeed, about 40 per cent of people who identify with a particular party in Canada have at some time switched allegiance—but the very fact of having some partisan commitment is an inducement to participation.

TABLE 4-20: PARTY IDENTIFICATION AND CAMPAIGN ACTIVITY*

Campaign Activity Index	Party					
	Progressive Conservative	Liberal	Social Credit	Créditiste	NDP	None
	(Figures are percentage)					
High	4.1	3.6	1.7	12.8	12.8	1.6
Medium	23.5	22.6	20.4	27.7	28.7	14.4
Low	72.3	73.3	77.1	59.6	58.4	82.6
Total No. of Respondents	677	1,011	118	47	288	461

*Party identification is based on the question, "Generally speaking do you usually think of yourself as Conservative, Liberal, Social Credit, Créditiste, NDP, or what?"

Party Identification and Political Participation Table 4-20 also indicates that, in 1965 at least, there was little to choose between Canada's two major parties with respect to the activities of their partisans. However, over three times as many NDP and Créditiste identifiers were highly active as were members of the old parties. A good-sized web of speculation could be built around this point, but it should be noted that the NDP and Créditistes in 1965 simply asked their partisans to help out more often than did the older parties and were suitably rewarded. Finally, the quiet death of the federal Social Credit party (as opposed to its Quebec wing) may be seen in the very low levels of participation of its partisans in 1965.

It is also possible, of course, that the strength of party attachment will be significant in determining a person's level of activity. Other findings in 1965 indicated that over three times as many people with strong partisan attachments worked for a party or candidate in 1965 as did people with weak party attachments, and twelve times as many strong identifiers worked as did people with no identification at all. Nearly three times as many strong identifiers tried to convince others of how to vote as did non-identifiers.

It is a truism that there is not very much difference between Canada's political parties. The public, however, seems to be rather ambivalent on this point. Some 24 per cent of the 2,100 respondents talked to in 1965 thought that, "considering everything the parties stand for," there was a "good deal" of difference between them, while 36 per cent thought there was "some difference" and 35 per cent that there was "not much". More interesting yet, the level of participation of people did not appear to be strongly connected with whether or not they perceived an ideological difference between the parties.[29] However, while people do not see much ideological difference between Canada's parties, they do think it matters which one is in power. When asked if they felt it made a "great deal of difference", "some difference" or "none" which political party runs the country, 44 per cent thought it made a great deal of difference and 34 per cent thought it made some. Only 18 per cent thought it made none. Furthermore, Canadians appear to back up their convictions with information and action. People who feel it makes a great deal of difference are much more likely to have paid some attention to the election campaign and are twice as likely to have attempted to convince others of how to vote.

This leads us to a rather important point. Canadians do not see much ideological difference between their parties but they do believe it matters who wins, and they participate partially on the strength of this conviction. It is possible, therefore, that they perceive party differences mainly in terms of personalities, and are not disturbed by the lack of ideological differences. When combined with the psychological factors which accompany participation in Canadian elections these points have some interesting and important implications for Canadian political leadership.[30] However, it must be emphasized again that because of the paucity of research in Canada, the results reported here are based on just one survey.

Psychological Correlates of Participation
There are a number of psychological factors which might be supposed to underlie political participation. In other countries it has been found that such things as an absence of anxiety or an absence of authoritarian outlook on life are correlated with political participation. These finds have been replicated in

[29]See Chapter 10.
[30]See p. 120.

enough different settings than we can probably expect that they are true for Canada as well, though unfortunately there has been no specific research in Canada. The 1965 national survey does permit us to look at three related factors: the level of interest a person shows in politics, his sense of political efficacy, and his sense of satisfaction with the way life is going for him generally.

Taking the last of these factors first, it is significant that a person's perception of his own financial and life situations does not tell us much about whether or not he will participate in politics. None of the forms of behaviour in our electoral hierarchy was significantly correlated with a person's satisfaction. People in Canada do not appear likely to participate in order to change an unsatisfactory status quo. This may be highly detrimental to the legitimacy of the system. It may mean that electoral politics is not perceived as a satisfactory way of expressing discontent, despite the fact that it is one of the ideological foundations of Canadian government that if people are not satisfied they can vote out the government.

We can investigate this point further by looking at Table 4-21, which shows the connection between the level of efficacy a person feels and his political participation. It can be seen there that those who feel a sense of efficacy are more likely to be participants in the electoral process. While only 19 per cent of people who felt low levels of efficacy were high or medium participants in the electoral process, 34 per cent of people feeling high levels of efficacy were such participants. This table indicates that if people feel that the political system will pay attention to their efforts they are considerably more likely to participate.[31] However, a problem arises when one asks "*who* feel efficacious?" It turns out that only 8 per cent of our lower-class respondents felt a high level of efficacy as compared with 18 per cent of the working class, 38 per cent of the middle class and 49 per cent of the upper middle class. Thus an extremely high proportion of the Canadians who have the most cause for discontent do not feel that they can have any influence over political allocations. This attitude, plus a lack of resources, leads them to abstain from participating in campaigns and their very abstention makes their low sense of efficacy a self-fulfilling prophecy.

Table 4-22 indicates something which at first glance probably

[31]The 4.6 per cent of people who scored "low" on the efficacy scale and who are also highly active participants appears to be an anomaly. Further analysis has shown that these people are not disproportionately drawn from the lower-class respondents who worked in the campaign for money. Most of them were middle-class people working voluntarily for parties. A partial explanation is suggested in N.H. Nie, C.B. Powell and K. Prewitt, "Social Structures and Political Participation: Developmental Relationships," *American Political Science Review*, vol. 63, June and September 1969. See especially p. 813 ff. They found in a comparative study that there are two underlying variables which are most likely to influence participation: socio-economic status and membership in voluntary organizations. People whose participation was based on relatively high status exhibited a relatively high correlation between participation and efficacy, whereas people who were led into participation through membership in a voluntary organization did not. The same may be true in Canada and, indeed, these figures suggest that it is.

TABLE 4-21: SENSE OF EFFICACY AND CAMPAIGN ACTIVITY

Campaign Activity Index	Sense of Efficacy		
	High	Medium	Low
		(Figures are percentages)	
High	5.0	3.8	4.6
Medium	29.1	21.3	14.6
Low	65.8	74.1	80.3
Total No. of Respondents in Column	778	1,243	700

TABLE 4-22: INTEREST IN POLITICS AND CAMPAIGN ACTIVITY

Campaign Activity Index	Level of Interest		
	High	Medium	Low
		(Figures are percentages)	
High	10.9	2.7	1.1
Medium	36.3	19.9	12.0
Low	52.6	77.0	85.8
Total No. of Respondents in Column	711	1,180	820

seems rather obvious, but which on closer examination will prove quite important. There is a high correlation between campaign activity and the level of interest in politics. The finding would be obvious except that no single factor or cluster of factors will entirely explain the level of interest a person shows. The better-educated upper socio-economic groups show much higher levels of interest than the lower, but there are highly interested people among all socio-economic groups, and such people, naturally, are most likely to participate. Moreover, no other variable has anything like the effect on campaign activity that interest does. A high level of interest in politics will completely screen the effect of another important variable. If interest were not a key variable it might be expected that people showing low levels of efficacy, for example, would be unlikely to participate, no matter what their level of interest. In fact, however, one discovers that 15 per cent of people having a low level of efficacy and a high level of interest will show a high CAI rating, while 11 per cent of people with a high efficacy rating and a high level of interest show a high CAI rating. A high level of interest thus effectively screens out the influence of efficacy. Similar results are seen if level of interest is considered together with such other important variables as socio-economic class or education.

Our earlier comments on political socialization indicated that interest in politics is stimulated early in life by the family, peer groups and the schools. This stimulation, it was pointed out, is much more likely to occur with middle-class children than with lower-class children. The vital point here, however, is that the stimulation of interest in politics can occur in virtually any environment and, one might hypothesize, at any time during a person's life. Most importantly, once that interest has been stimulated, participation in the electoral process, and probably in the non-electoral hierarchy of political participation as well, is much more likely to occur. Participation in politics in Canada can be induced even among people who would not normally be considered to have the resources or the necessary propensity to participate.

In general terms, the Canadian political culture, both French and English, and largely without regard for most of Canada's other major lines of cleavage, might be described by the catch phrase *spectator–participant*.[32] This seemingly self-contradictory phrase is used for a number of reasons. First, relative to most democratic countries, Canadians do have a very high level of political participation: only the United States shows one consistently higher.[33] It must therefore be described as a *participant* political culture. Not all Canadians, however, are participants. In particular it was seen that lower socio-economic groups do not participate except in the fairly infrequent cases where people have picked up a high level of interest in politics. Indeed, those 40 per cent or so of Canadians who are below or near the poverty line[34] are almost totally excluded from the input side of the political process and consequently have to accept the outputs of the system with very little control over them. They are truly the silent poor, although it might be a mistake to assume they will remain so. With increasing levels of education they may slowly become mobilized politically, and if they do not participate within the context of the "legitimate" political system, that is, in ways which have become traditional in Canadian politics, they may participate in "illegitimate" ways. Such a situation would create serious stress on the political system which, if not alleviated, could in the long run cause its disintegration.

The term "spectator" in the phrase spectator–participant is used to describe the predominant motivational factors of people who do participate. To some extent they may be motivated by efficacy—a feeling that their efforts will be rewarded by the political system—but for the most part

[32]Robert Presthus uses a similar term, *quasi-participative*, to describe the Canadian political culture. (*Elite Accommodation in Canadian Politics*, pp. 38 ff.)
[33]Comparative data can be found in L. Milbrath, *Political Participation*, R. Lane, *Political Life* and G. Almond and S. Verba, *The Civic Culture*, (Princeton University Press, Princeton, 1963).
[34]See Chapter 2.

they appear to be motivated by a sort of spectator interest in what is going on in politics. It was seen that they perceive little ideological difference between the parties, feeling simultaneously that it matters which leaders are in power. They will apparently participate in politics if they find the differences between these groups of men to be "interesting". Otherwise, aside from voting, they are unlikely to participate at all. Graphic illustration of this was provided during the 1968 election campaign when electoral participation was higher than it had been since the 1958 halcyon days of John Diefenbaker, largely because of the emergence of a new and interesting personality, Pierre Elliott Trudeau.

Canadians appear to approach politics much as they would a hockey game. If the game is good they will come out and cheer. On election day they may "go to the game" by voting and watching the returns on television, and if they are really interested they may participate at higher levels in the hierarchy. If their party wins they will be happy, and if it loses they may be sad, but not for long. Their involvement with "the event" has been motivated by interest and psychological identification with the principals, but not based on genuine objective concern.

All of this has significant implications for the political system and, in particular, for its decision makers. One famous Canadian historian has described cabinet government as a system where the citizen "gives full power of attorney to a small committee each four years or so, well knowing that virtually nothing he can do in the interval will have much effect on the groups to whom he has given his blank cheque."[35] This means that under normal circumstances, politics in Canada can be, if the authorities choose, about nothing. The system will appear to be retaining its legitimacy because the level of participation, by which we measure such things, can remain high as long as politics are interesting. The level of interest can be kept high as long as colourful personalities are presented. Occasional infusions of new and interesting personalities or of "style issues" will serve to retain support for the system.

A further consequence of the spectator–participant nature of Canadian politics is a reinforcement of tendencies favouring the status quo. The people who do participate in the process are disproportionately drawn from the middle and upper middle classes and from the elites which represent them. They have reason to be satisfied with the status quo and they are organized into the types of group structure which allow them to promote their own interests in consonance with governmental elites. Thus "government to some extent, is pushed into the anomalous position of defending the strong against the weak. While the governmental elite plays an equilibrating role in welfare areas, much of its energy is also spent in reinforcing the security and growth of interests that already enjoy the largest shares of net social product".[36] The spectator–participant orientation of the Canadian political culture may both allow and force political elites to behave in this way if they are to retain the public support they require.

[35] A.R.M. Lower, *Canadians in the Making*, (Longman's, Toronto, 1958), p. 281.
[36] R. Presthus, *Elite Accommodation in Canadian Politics*, p. 347.

The term *apolitical* is used by political scientists to denote a politics which is not concerned with genuine ideological or policy differences, but which is highly supportive of the status quo. It would occur, for example, if all the members of the political elite—this is, all the major actors inside the political system—were basically in agreement about policies and political objectives. The real difference between the actions of one group and those of another would be slight, and the real significance of elections or other changes of power would be small. Apolitical politics may or may not be dangerous; the reader can make his own judgments on this point. The main point here is that in such a system the decisions of those in authority might not and probably would not represent the real cleavages in the environment, yet popular support for the decision makers could still be made to appear high.[37]

This apparent legitimacy can be disadvantageous for a political system. The system will remain stable as long as the outputs are at least marginally effective in satisfying active members of the political community, and the marginal level may be considerably depressed by the distraction of people's attention from issues to personalities. However, if there is an infusion into the system of people who were formerly politically inactive, as may occur when educational levels of the lower socio-economic classes have been raised or when significant new issues arise, the system may become unstable unless it quickly changes its outputs to help satisfy the needs of these people.

All of this may read like a denunciation of the Canadian political system. However, all that has been said so far is that the Canadian political culture is such that it may permit apolitical politics. It is too early in this book for us to finalize such an assessment. It must first be determined whether Canadian political institutions and the authorities occupying them do in fact behave in such a way as to make politics issue-less. Not only is it too early in this book; it may be too early in the history of Canadian political science. Most of the results used in arriving at these conclusions came from just one public opinion survey.[38] One must ask different types of questions of different people at different times in order to verify what has been said here.

This concludes our discussion of the socio-cultural context of the Canadian political system. Every facet of the environment can be considered to influence the political system in some way, either actually or potentially, and one should always be alert for such influences when examining the system itself. In any finite amount of space only some of the

[37]Ulf Himmelstrand, "A Theoretical and Empirical Approach to Depolitization and Political Involvement," *Acta Sociologica*, vol. 6, pp. 83–111, fasc. 1–2, 1962, provides a similar analysis in the Swedish setting and arrives at similar conclusions.

[38]They are, however, supported by two subsequent surveys of comparably high quality, one conducted in 1968 by Professor John Meisel and one conducted for the Federal Government Task Force on information by The Survey Research Centre at York University. See also R. Presthus, *Elite Accommodation in Canadian Politics*, pp. 38–59, which utilizes the results of these surveys to arrive at substantially the same conclusions as are presented here.

relevant facets of the environment can be examined, but the student should watch for others which may have been neglected and should apply them to his analysis wherever necessary.

Part 2
The Constitutional and
Legal Environment

5
The Constitutional Context

From the point of view of a political scientist, the constitution of a political system is significant for two major reasons. First, the constitution can be viewed as a device which modifies human behaviour, for constitutional change is one of the *independent variables* which influences the political process. Secondly, the constitution can be viewed as a reflection of the political culture; in this sense it is a *dependent variable* which is itself but a product of societal forces. By studying the constitution therefore, we not only learn about the formal institutional parameters within which the policy process takes place, but we also find out more about the fundamental values of our political community as embodied in the Canadian constitution.

THE FUNCTIONS OF THE CANADIAN CONSTITUTION

Paradoxically, all institutions of a political system must be both rigid and flexible.[1] On the one hand, rigidity is necessary if the regime is to acquire legitimacy; for in order that the citizen may learn either positive or negative attitudes towards a political system, that system must to some extent be static. The process of political socialization takes time, and it would be impossible to learn about the nature of our political system and its implicit values and norms if all of its institutions were constantly in a state of violent flux. On the other hand, because environmental conditions are continually changing, there is a necessity for considerable flexibility in the regime. If the system is to persist, it must be able to adapt relatively quickly to meet new problems and to relieve related stresses. A system with only very rigid institutions would be fragile, given the ever-changing nature of modern society.

In the Canadian political system, flexibility is provided partly by political parties and pressure groups and partly by institutions such as the buneaucracy. All of these institutions have at least some ability to react directly and immediately to rapid environmental changes. The constitution,

[1]Talcott Parsons refers to these requisites as "pattern maintenance" and "adaptation", each of which must be achieved if the system is to persist.

because it cannot be changed as easily[2], provides the political system with some of its necessary rigidity. Thus in the widest sense, the function of a constitution is to provide the system with a "backbone"—to give it the rigidity which is necessary if it is to persist over time. But constitutions have more immediate and more specific functions to perform, which are often unique to the individual political system, and to the particular form of government in operation.

The Rule of Law The manifest function of any constitution is to define the relationship between the citizen and the state, and to the extent that the relationship can be defined at all, every country can be said to have some form of constitution. However this is too general an assertion to be of much value in the Canadian setting. What is implicit in the notion of constitutionalism, at least in the Western democracies, is the basic principle of *the rule of law*. To put it simply, for Canada and other Western nations, a constitution is one of the means of achieving the goal of a system where law is supreme.

The rule of law, in the British and Canadian tradition, means that all allocations of resources performed by the political system must, in the final analysis, be achieved by law. Every output of our political system to some extent affects the raw freedom of individuals in our society. The principle of the rule of law states that any such interference with the freedom of any individual must be performed only according to the legal process and carried out by legitimate authorities. No one is exempt from the law, and no one can affect the rights of any individual except through the legal process.

But if we grant that the constitution of Canada is a means to the end of rule of law, we must then ask why the rule of law is a norm of our political system in the first place; and, eventually, we must ask whether and how this value is really honoured in Canada. The function of the rule of law is, briefly, to protect us from the arbitrary interference of government, or of government officials, in our everyday lives. The law is knowable: in principle, one can become aware, through the law, of standards of behaviour which are expected of everyone. The relationship of the individual to the political system becomes, to some extent, fixed and impartial. Aristotle pointed out that even rule by a benevolent dictator could conceivably deteriorate to rule by whim and caprice, for even the most benevolent of dictators gets out of bed on the wrong side once in a while. The law, on the other hand, is presumed to be coldly impersonal, predictable, and rational rather than emotional.

Defining the Régime The rule of law is thus desirable in a society that values the principle of an impartial and predictable relationship between the citizen and the authorities of the political system. The principle of the rule of law, however, is not sufficient to secure in perpetuity such a set of values, for its inherent weakness is the fact that the law is made by men and applied and interpreted by men—and men are not always

[2]Constitutional change will be discussed in the next chapter.

impersonal, predictable and rational. Thus, in order to prevent unjust laws from being passed and to guard against the unjust or inequitable application of laws, a constitution must go beyond the mere recognition of the rule of law; it must also define the form of the regime. The Canadian constitution defines the operational structures of the political system, such as Parliament and the office of the Governor General, and it also defines the relationships between them. In Professor Corry's words, "The constitution is the frame or chassis in which the working engine of government is set. . ."[3]

Further, the Canadian constitution defines many of the "rules of the game" of politics. It broadly defines the tactics and the means that are acceptable within the Canadian political process, and describes formal procedures that must be followed in order to secure an allocative output. The Canadian constitution, in other words, sets formal parameters beyond which the authorities may not go in performing the basic function of the allocation of resources. It does not matter what the ends are, nor how popular the ends may be; the constitution sets limits on the means that can be legitimately employed to achieve them. An example of these "rules of the game" of politics in Canada is the principle that there should be ample time provided in the House of Commons for the opposition to criticize government policy. No matter how urgent the government policy may seem at the time, the opposition is always guaranteed at least some opportunity to debate the issue. Although the constitution does not specify exactly how much time, even in the cases where government has the power to limit debate, the opposition must still be given a substantial opportunity to make its views known in parliament.[4]

Defining the Legitimate Role of Government Not only does the Canadian constitution place limits on the means that can be employed in the political process, it also sets limits on the kinds of laws that can be made. Our constitution defines very broadly the area of legitimate law making by giving us an "unwritten" body of fundamental principles to which all laws must conform. These principles are the norms of the regime, and they are a part of the constitution inasmuch as the constitution is an embodiment of the basic values of Canadian society. For example, a law which made it a crime to go to church would not be acceptable in Canada, because religious tolerance has long been one of the basic values of Canadian society.[5] It must be noted here, however, that the strength of such a principle lies not in the fact that it is entrenched in a body of fundamental law which, whether unwritten or written, goes to make up the constitution, but rather because it reflects a consensus of political attitudes in our society. If the political attitudes in Canadian society were to

[3]J.A. Corry and J.E. Hodgetts, *Democratic Government and Politics*, (University of Toronto Press, Toronto, 1959), p. 85.
[4]See Chapter 18 for a discussion of measures such as closure and Standing Order 75 (c).
[5]See Chapter 2.

change, and if religious intolerance were perceived as desirable in our system, the fundamental law would change accordingly.[6]

Symbolic Functions Finally, a constitution is, or should be, a source of pride and a unifying influence within a political community. Professor Cheffins has described a constitution as ". . .a mirror reflecting the national soul. . . ."[7] Generally this is correct, and certainly it applies to the constitution of the U.S. and to the "unwritten" constitution of the U.K. In each of these systems the constitution, for widely differing reasons, has become a symbol of the society's particular brand of democracy and, indeed, an object of national pride. Canada, on the other hand, may or may not have a "national soul" and if we do have such a rare thing, it is arguable whether our much-maligned constitution can be dubbed a "mirror" that reflects it.[8]

COMPONENT PARTS OF THE CANADIAN CONSTITUTION

The British North America Act of 1867, as amended, forms the core of the Canadian constitution. Legally the Act is a statute of the British parliament, the contents of which are based on the resolutions drawn up at the Quebec and London conferences by the representatives of the original four provinces. The legal–historical significance of the Act is that it created the federal union out of Upper and Lower Canada and the Maritime provinces of New Brunswick and Nova Scotia. Because at the time of Confederation the Canadas were united, the BNA Act also created the provinces of Ontario and Quebec. The scope of the BNA Act is somewhat limited; it deals with certain broad topics like the federal distribution of powers, the general form of the central government, and the bilingual dimension of Canada. The farthest the BNA Act goes in defining the principles of government in Canada is in the preamble where it states that Canada shall have a form of government "similar in principle to that of the United Kingdom." In other words, as a constitution, the BNA Act is rather restricted. It does not pretend to be the omnicompetent document that the constitution of the United States is, or was intended to be, and in fact much of what is described as the constitution of Canada is not found even implicitly in the BNA Act.

A few British statutes other than the BNA Act and some British orders-in-council are usually considered to be part of the Canadian constitution. The most noteworthy of these are the Statute of Westminster, the Colonial Laws Validity Act, and the order-in-council ceding Rupert's Land to the Dominion. These British enactments all have to do with the gradual process of withdrawal of British authority over the Dominion and

[6]See also Chapter 3.
[7]R.I. Cheffins, *The Constitutional Process in Canada*, (McGraw–Hill, Toronto, 1969), p. 5.
[8]See Chapter 7.

its present territories, and were more significant at the time of their passage than they are now.

Some statutes passed by the Canadian parliament, such as the Alberta and Saskatchewan Acts of 1905, which created the provinces of Alberta and Saskatchewan out of the Northwest Territories, can also be included in this group of constitutional components. These particular Canadian Acts are unique, in that they are not amendable by the federal parliament. Since the Alberta and Saskatchewan Acts form the constitutions of the respective provinces, once passed, they can be amended only by the provincial legislature.

Other federal statutes that can be included in any inventory of the Canadian constitution, are classed by R.M. Dawson as "organic laws."[9] These are laws which, while legally amendable by a simple act of parliament, involve fundamental principles of a constitutional nature. The best example of such an organic law is the Supreme Court Act, although the Canadian Bill of Rights also may be taking on such a status. While parliament may from time to time change some of the provisions of such legislation, the fundamental principles remain, for practical purposes, entrenched.

Section 92(1) of the BNA Act gives the provinces the power to make laws in relation to "The Amendment from Time to Time notwithstanding anything in this Act, of the Constitution of the Province, except as regards the Office of the Lieutenant Governor." This means essentially that the provincial legislatures have the power to unilaterally amend the constitutions of their respective domains by an ordinary statute. Any provincial statutes which amend the provincial constitutions, therefore, must, like the British or Canadian federal statutes which originally set them up, be considered a part of the Canadian constitution.

It must be noted at this juncture that not all political scientists and constitutional experts would agree that provincial or state constitutions should be considered integral parts of the constitution of a particular federal political system. Perhaps there is some justification for separating the United States constitution from the constitutions of the various states, but in Canada such a separation would distort the realities of the Canadian political system. The provinces are given the power to legislate with regard to matters that directly affect the rights and freedoms of the individual in his relationship with the state. An example of this would be Section 92(13) of the BNA Act which gives the provinces the legislative competence to deal with "Property and Civil Rights in the Province." If the provinces possess the power to affect the property and civil rights of Canadian citizens, then surely the provincial constitution which regulates the exercise of this power within the province must be considered a part of the Canadian constitution.

It has been asserted that constitutions are basically formal rather than informal, and therefore, basically static. But constitutions consist in part of law or of collections of laws, which means that they are general

[9]R. MacGregor Dawson, *The Government of Canada*, fifth edition, revised by Norman Ward, (University of Toronto Press, Toronto, 1970), p. 63.

prescriptions which in practice must be applied to specific cases. The application of constitutional principles to specific cases involves the interpretation of the constitution, which, in our system, is performed by the judiciary.[10] As the courts apply the constitutional principles to many different cases, a body of judicial decisions is built up which elaborates and fills out the constitution. The judicial decisions which interpret the constitution are an integral part of that constitution. In the case of Canada, because our legal system is based on the English common law tradition, and because the BNA Act states in the preamble that we are to have a form of government similar in principle to that of the U.K., precedents established in British common law make up a part of our constitution. As well, the interpretation of the BNA Act itself by the Judicial Committee of the Privy Council, which was the final court of appeal for Canada until 1949, built a large body of decisions which elaborate and clarify the Act. These judicial decisions are a most important component of the constitution of Canada, especially as they have helped to fill out the federal dimension of our constitution.

In addition, the Canadian constitution includes a number of clearly defined principles such as the conventions of cabinet government and the firm, though unwritten, rule that the government must hold the support of a majority in the House of Commons or resign. These conventions are not found in the BNA Act, nor in any constitutional document, yet they are as much a part of the Canadian constitution as the BNA Act. Because they have no documentary manifestation, however, the exact definition of them and their legal enforceability defies analysis. The only sanction that effectively enforces the principle of responsible government is the weight of public opinion that places a value on it. A few of the customary and conventional parts of our constitution have been written down in some form and therefore have acquired the support of legal or quasi-legal sanction. For instance, the rules and privileges of parliament are implicitly if not explicitly entrenched in the Standing Orders and the Rules of Procedure. Generally, however, while conventions and customs involve some of the most important principles of the Canadian constitution, they exist in an unwritten form rather than as documentary and legally enforceable instruments.

Finally, a constitution can be considered to contain a number of principles or values which form the normative basis of the regime. These are difficult to pin down, for they exist largely as tacit assumptions in the minds of the members of the political community and they are passed on in very subtle ways through the process of political socialization. In Canada, they involve the whole complex of democratic political values. There is some argument whether such principles should be considered a part of the constitution itself or principles which underlie it. In this book they will be regarded as a part of the constitution.

Written and Unwritten Constitutions

It has become a tradition of political science, when making comparisons between the political

[10]This subject is covered more extensively in Chapter 6.

system of the United Kingdom and that of the United States, to state that the former has an unwritten constitution and the latter a written constitution. This distinction is a relative rather than a categoric one, which places constitutions, for the purposes of comparison, on a continuum ranging from the hypothetical extreme of "purely written" to that of "purely unwritten." Upon examination, it rapidly becomes apparent that the constitutions of the two largest English-speaking democracies are neither purely written nor purely unwritten. Nor could any constitution be completely written if we choose to define the political value structure of a society as part of the constitution. The American constitution, while starting with the impressive document of 1789, has been filled out by conventions, judicial decisions and statutes which express "fundamental" principles. Similarly, the constitution of the U.K., while consisting largely of principles embodied in the common law, has at its core written documents such as the Magna Carta and the Petition of Right. The Canadian constitution, consisting of a hodgepodge of written documents and unwritten conventions, falls on the continuum somewhere between the constitutions of the U.K. and the U.S.

A difficulty with the "written/unwritten" classification is that it is not clear what the criterion of evaluation is. Surely the exercise involves more than judging what proportion of a constitution is documentary and what proportion is customary. The relevant criterion seems to be whether or not an attempt has been made, at some point in history, to codify or list all the fundamental principles of a political system in a single document. This is the sense in which the constitution of the U.S. can be described as "written."

Perhaps the best method of clarifying the "written/unwritten" distinction is according to the formulae for changing the constitution.[11] The major difference between the documentary components of the British constitution and the U.S. constitution is that the former can be amended by a simple act of parliament, whereas the amendment of the U.S. constitution can only be achieved by a complicated, formal process that requires the participation of other institutions in addition to the federal Congress. The point of the distinction thus becomes not whether a constitutional principle is written or unwritten, but whether or not constitutional documents are entrenched behind a special amending formula. This gives the "written/unwritten" classification more meaning when making a comparison between the U.S. and British constitutions. Because of the confused and hybrid status of constitutional amendment in Canada, the classification can only complicate the issue here.

Finally, whatever the nature of this system of classification, it must be asked whether such a distinction has any inherent significance for the analysis of the Canadian constitution or, for that matter, any constitution. The ultimate strength or stability of a constitution does not depend on whether it is by any definition written or unwritten, but whether or not the principles it embodies are congruent with the values of the political com-

[11]See Chapter 6.

munity. If a constitution does not reflect the values of the society, it does not matter whether it is written or unwritten, it cannot last or be effective.

With that said, there may be some justification for discussing the relative merits of written and unwritten constitutions with respect to the function of political integration. Perhaps a written constitution may be more effective in creating a sense of national pride, but on the other hand, such a sense of national pride is not absent in the U.K., where the constitution, by any criterion, is basically unwritten. Also, a written constitution may be more effective in inculcating the norms of the regime to children and newcomers, for through a written constitution the values of the society are given visible manifestation.

In summary, the Canadian constitution is a conglomeration of British, Canadian, and provincial statutes, the British common law, Canadian judicial decisions, and a number of real but invisible conventions, customs, values and assumptions, all clustering rather loosely and haphazardly around the central kernel of the BNA Act. It is clearly not a written constitution, but it is not an unwritten one either—and for us the distinction is probably not very important.

THE OPERATIVE PRINCIPLES OF THE CANADIAN CONSTITUTION

It has already been established that all forms of constitutional government are rooted in the principle of the rule of law. But, if law is to "rule" us, it is going to need a lot of help from the people who occupy positions of authority in the political system. Laws must be made by somebody, they must be carried into effect by somebody, and disputes over the interpretation of the law must be settled by somebody. As a result, the substance of a constitution is fundamentally concerned with three political problems corresponding to the three functional classifications of allocative outputs of the political system: legislative outputs, executive outputs, and adjudicative outputs. In most political systems it is possible to make at least some functional distinction between these three types of outputs, and usually it is possible to distinguish between the organs or branches of the political system to which the constitution delegates the performance of each function.[12] However, the constitutional relationship among these branches can vary a great deal from one political system to another.

Finally it must be recognized that the three output functions of government are performed not by one but by several sovereign governments. The legislative, executive and, to a certain extent, the adjudicative functions of government are performed by both federal and provincial governments in Canada. This operative principle of the constitution is *divided sovereignty* which adds greatly to the complexity of the political process in Canada.

[12]Later, when discussing the policy process, it will be seen that it is very difficult to make realistic distinctions between different institutions such as parliament, the civil service, etc. on the basis of these particular types of functions.

The Supremacy of Parliament and the Rule of Law: the Legislative Function in Canada

The constitution of the U.S. explicitly states not only that there is to be a functional distinction among the three branches of government, but also that each of these functions should be vested in a separate man or body of men. This principle, which is known as the *separation of powers*, originated with the writings of Montesquieu, and it means in the American case that no individual is permitted to hold office in more than one branch of government at the same time. Hence for example, the president cannot be a member of the Senate or the House of Representatives during his term of office, nor can a congressman be a judge at the same time he is sitting in the House of Representatives. The logic behind the separation of powers is that the concentration of too much power in one man, or, for that matter, in one institution, is a corruptive influence. In an attempt to insure a "good" and "just" form of government, the drafters of the United States' constitution tried to ensure that no man would be tempted by the possession of too much governmental power. Just to make sure, the principle of the separation of powers was given an added twist in the United States' constitution. It was decided that, in order to prevent the abuse of any of the three powers by occupants of the respective branches, an elaborate system of *checks and balances* would be woven into the relationship among branches. Thus, for instance, the president can veto any legislation passed by Congress, the Supreme Court can declare acts of Congress unconstitutional, the president appoints all members of the Supreme Court with the consent of two-thirds of the Senate, and the Congress can impeach the president and can override his veto by a two-thirds majority.

Starkly contrasting with a constitutional commitment to the principle of the separation of powers is the basic principle of the British constitution, *the supremacy of parliament.* In the British parliamentary system, not only is there no real separation of powers, but the legislative branch directly controls the executive branch, and is itself beyond interference by either the executive or the judiciary. No act of the British parliament can be declared unconstitutional by the courts, and the executive branch (to all intents and purposes, the cabinet) is not only made up of members of parliament but also must resign if a majority in the House of Commons fails to endorse its policies. Furthermore, no parliament may bind a future parliament by stating in a piece of legislation that that legislation is unamendable. In such a case, the later parliament, which is supreme in its own time, merely passes another law which takes precedence over the earlier one. Therefore, the principle of the supremacy of parliament vests awesome formal power in the legislative branch.

But we have already described the political system of the U.K. as being a constitutional form of government, and it has been pointed out that at the roots of the principle of constitutionalism is the principle of the rule of law. How then can there be rule of law and parliamentary supremacy without contradiction? Is parliament bound by the principle of the rule of law, or is the rule of law subject to the supremacy of parliament? The only answer here is that the concept of the rule of law must have two meanings. In the first sense, the rule of law means that any authoritative output of the political system can only be achieved by law. If this is all that the concept of the rule of law means, then a contradiction does not exist between it and the supremacy of parliament, for any act of parliament is a law or has the effect of law. However, there is a second sense of the concept of the rule of law which implies such things as the right to have access to the courts and the right not to be imprisoned without a trial, etc. If this definition is accepted, the rule of law and the supremacy of parliament are mutually exclusive principles. Parliament in the U.K. can, by "act of parliament", abolish such revered rights as *habeas corpus*, which would mean that parliament could, in effect, "abolish" the rule of law[13] in the second sense of the term. There is no way of settling this confusion in the terminology. It would be pointless to say that "henceforth the term shall mean such and such," for the term is so widely used in both senses that the confusion would remain. It must be kept in mind that when speaking of constitutionalism generally, the first sense of the rule of law is usually what is intended, and when speaking specifically of the British constitution it is the broader sense that is intended. The significance of this distinction is that the narrower usage of the term is the purer form of the concept and the broader usage is the peculiarly British version of it.

As noted before, the preamble of the British North America Act (1867) states that Canada is to have "a Constitution similar in principle to that of the United Kingdom." This means, *prima facie*, that the supremacy of parliament is a substantive principle of the Canadian constitution. The BNA Act, however, goes beyond this broad statement of intent of the preamble, and the extent to which the Canadian parliament is really supreme must be examined in the light of the provisions of the Act which limit the power of parliament in Canada.

First of all, certain key sections of the BNA Act are not amendable by the Canadian parliament, but can be changed only by an act of the parliament of the U.K. An amendment to the Act secured in 1949[14] states that the Canadian parliament can, from time to time, amend the constitution of Canada except as regards matters assigned exclusively to the provinces, guarantees of minority education and language rights, the provision that parliament must meet at least once a year, and the provision that no parliament shall continue for more than five years. Hence, the supremacy of the Canadian parliament is legally limited by the fact that these sections of the BNA Act can be changed only by the action of the parliament of the U.K., although as will be seen later, the *de facto* limitation in this regard may not be very significant.[15]

The second and perhaps the most important limitation on the supremacy of the Canadian parliament is found in the federal distribution of

[13]See Corry and Hodgetts, *Democratic Government and Politics*, p. 96. Note also that we are speaking here only in strict legal terms, for in practice, because of the nature of the British political culture, there is a practical limitation on the extent to which parliament can restrict the rule of law even in the narrower sense.
[14]BNA Act, 1949 (2).
[15]See Chapter 6 for a more detailed discussion of this situation.

legislative powers set out mainly in Sections 91-95 of the BNA Act. Because of these sections of the Act, the courts in Canada, unlike the courts in the U.K., have the power to declare acts of the federal parliament unconstitutional because they are beyond the legislative jurisdiction assigned to the federal level by the BNA Act. Many pieces of legislation passed by the Canadian parliament have been declared invalid on these grounds, and in fact, the interpretation of the federal legislative competence by the judiciary has played a significant role in remodeling Canadian federalism since 1867.[16] The important point here is that the judicial branch in Canada has the power to declare laws passed by either the federal parliament or by the legislatures of the provinces to be *ultra vires* and therefore invalid. In sum, legislative authority in Canada is divided up among three separate types of legislative bodies: the parliament of the U.K., the parliament of Canada, and the legislatures of the ten provinces, with the judiciary deciding any jurisdictional disputes.

The final question concerning the extent to which the doctrine of the supremacy of parliament obtains in Canada is whether or not the combination of these three types of legislatures possesses legislative supremacy. In other words, is the legislative authority of ten provincial parliaments, one federal parliament and one imperial parliament *exhaustive*? In the United States, there are matters which are beyond the legislative competence of all levels and branches of government. These are principles which are considered to be so fundamental that no government should be able to interfere with them, and which are therefore entrenched in the constitution. Are any matters so entrenched in the Canadian constitution? Judicial opinion in this area has generally supported the doctrine of exhaustiveness, giving to the provinces and the federal parliament virtually complete authority.[17] While in a strictly legal sense this is not the case, practically speaking, the encroachment on the collective legislative authority of all eleven Canadian legislatures by the U.K. parliament's amending role is virtually nil.

There are some minor and technical restrictions on the doctrine of exhaustiveness in Canada which are directly related to the legal difficulties imposed by our unique method of formal constitutional amendment. One of these restrictions has come through a series of narrow judicial interpretations of the ability of the provinces and the federal parliament to delegate legislative authority to each other. The *Nova Scotia Interdelegation* case of 1951 is a landmark in this regard, the Supreme Court of Canada having found that interdelegation is incompatible with federalism.[18] While this imposes a *de jure* limitation on the doctrine of the supremacy of parliament

[16]See Chapter 7.
[17]See Bank of Toronto v. Lambe (1887), Olmsted, vol. 1; Attorney-General for Ontario v. Attorney-General for Canada ("Labour Conventions Case") (1937), Olmsted, vol. 3.
[18]Attorney-General for Nova Scotia v. Attorney-General for Canada, (1951) *SCR* 31. See also: Cheffins, *The Constitutional Process in Canada*, pp. 40–42 for an excellent analysis of the legal implications of this decision and its potential effect on the doctrine of the supremacy of parliament.

in Canada, in practical terms it would be possible for the federal government to secure an amendment to the BNA Act specifically permitting interdelegation. Finally, there are a few laws still in effect that were passed by the united legislature of Upper and Lower Canada before Confederation. Legislation such as this cannot be repealed or legally amended because it was the product of a legislative body that no longer exists. Practically, however, it is possible for the legislatures of the Provinces of Ontario and Quebec to pass complementary laws which would change the effect of a pre-Confederation statute without actually altering it in law. Certainly, limitations such as these on the legislative competence of Canadian legislatures are of minimal importance in the total picture.

To conclude, then, the principle of the supremacy of parliament is definitely an integral part of the constitution of Canada, and while the form it takes is not as unambiguous as it is in the U.K., the implications remain as significant here as there. Unlike the constitution of the U.S., which puts some matters beyond the grasp of all legislative bodies, the constitution of the Canadian political system vests total legislative authority for all practical purposes in the collectivity of federal and provincial legislatures.

The Crown and Cabinet Government: The Executive

Function The legislative function of a political system is to make laws. In Canada that function is performed, according to the constitution, by parliament. The executive function of a political system is to put the laws into effect, to carry out or to "execute" acts of parliament. In Canada, the executive power is defined by Section 9 of the BNA Act: "the Executive Government and Authority of and over Canada is hereby declared to continue and be vested in the Queen." Formally, therefore, the executive function in Canada is peformed by the Queen, and we can be said to have a monarchial form of government. The most significant implication of this fact is the consequent transferral of all prerogative rights of the Crown in the U.K. to the Crown in respect of Canada. This statement, however, requires some explanation, particularly the terms *the Crown* and *prerogative rights*.

The Crown is a term used to describe the collectivity of executive powers which, in a monarchy, are exercised by or in the name of the sovereign. There is nothing mystical about this term. It does not imply the existence of an authority greater than that possessed constitutionally by the reigning monarch. These executive powers vested in the Queen flow from the historic common law rights and privileges of the Crown in England which are referred to as the *royal prerogative*. Prerogative rights exist primarily because they always have, and not because they have been created at some point in time by statute. The prerogative rights and privileges of the Queen are the residue of authority left over from an age when the power of the reigning monarch was absolute. This absolute power has been whittled away bit by bit until today there are only a few remnants of it that are left to the Queen. It is important to note here that prerogative rights cannot be created by statute. If a statute formally increases the power of the Crown, the effect is to delegate some of the authority of parliament to the executive, but not to vest any new prerogative rights in the person of the monarch.

On the other hand, the prerogative can be limited by statute. An example of this is in the Crown Liability Act (1952), which takes away the prerogative right of the Crown not to be held liable in tort for damages resulting from acts done by public servants or for acts done by the monarch personally. This prerogative can never be returned as a prerogative right, although a future parliament could return it as a statutory right. Hence, the royal prerogative is slowly shrinking, and in Canada it is being replaced by statutory provisions that define the real limits of executive power.

While the royal prerogative is not what it used to be, there are still some significant executive powers that are based on it. Among these are the right of the monarch to all ownerless property (*Crown land*); the right to priority as a creditor in the settlement of bankruptcies, etc.; and the right to summon, prorogue and dissolve parliament. Because of the convention that these powers are all exercised "on the advice" of the Ministers of the Crown, in fact they are almost all possessed in reality by the Prime Minister and the government of the day.

In the U.K. the formal functions of the monarch are performed personally by the Queen. In Canada, while the Queen can still be called "Queen of Canada", most of the monarchial functions are performed in her name by the Governor General at the national level and the Lieutenant-Governors at the provincial level. The appointment of the Governor General was originally the responsibility of the Queen acting on the advice of the government of the U.K. This made the Governor General effectively independent of the Canadian cabinet. Since the Imperial Conferences of 1926 and 1930, however, the Governor General has been independent of the imperial government and is now removable by the Queen only on the advice of the government of Canada. While the appointment of the Governor General is, formally, a function of the Queen, in fact it is always made today with the advice of the Canadian cabinet. Also, while the normal term of office of the Canadian Governor General is five years, this can be shortened or stretched according to the wishes of the government of the day.

While the BNA Act defines many of the powers of the Governor General, the office itself is a creature of letters patent from the monarch. By the Letters Patent of 1947, the Governor General is empowered to exercise "all powers and authorities" that belong to the Queen in right of Canada. This means that the exercise of the royal prerogative in Canada is a function of the Governor General, to be carried out by him, at his discretion, with the advice of the Queen's Privy Council for Canada.[19] Among the powers specified by the Letters Patent of 1947 are the use of the Great Seal of Canada, the appointment of judges, commissioners, diplomats, Ministers of the Crown, etc., along with the power to dismiss or suspend them, and the power to summon, prorogue and dissolve parliament. In ad-

[19]See Chapter 14 for a discussion of the Privy Council Office.

dition to the prerogative powers that are bestowed upon the Governor General by the Letters Patent (1947), he has certain other powers that are ceded to him by the BNA Act of 1867. Among these are the authority to appoint Senators and the Speaker of the Senate; the exclusive right to recommend legislation involving the spending of public money or the imposition of a tax; and the right, formally, to prevent a bill from becoming law by withholding his assent, or by reserving the bill "for the signification of the Queen's pleasure."[20] The Governor General has the power, by Section 56 of the BNA Act, to "disallow" any provincial legislation of which he disapproves. The real significance of the disallowance power is that it gives to the federal government a potential veto power over all provincial acts. While it has not been used since 1943, the legal power to use it still remains as a reminder to the provinces that the Fathers of Confederation viewed the provincial legislatures as "second-class citizens."

The office of Lieutenant-Governor was created by Section 58 of the BNA Act. The holder of the office is appointed by the Governor General in Council, and his salary is set by the Canadian parliament. Furthermore, he is removable "for cause" by the Governor General in Council. This means that in some respects the Lieutenant-Governor is an officer of the federal government who is responsible to the Governor General. On the other hand, the courts have decided that, in fact, he is a representative of the Queen directly, despite the fact that his appointment and salary are controlled by the government of Canada. In an important constitutional case in 1892, the Judicial Committee of the Privy Council held that the Lieutenant-Governor was a representative of the Queen in right of the province and that therefore he could exercise all the prerogative powers that the monarch could.[21] The significance of this is that the Lieutenant-Governor, while in some respects the subordinate of the Governor General, is in other respects his equal and enjoys the same powers in right of the province that the Governor General enjoys in the right of Canada. In turn, this has the effect of making the provincial governments, who are personified in the Lieutenant-Governors, more important than they would otherwise be. The BNA Act provides that the Lieutenant-Governor of the province has the power to assent to or to refuse his assent to acts of the provincial legislature, and furthermore, he is given the power to reserve a bill for the signification of the Governor General's pleasure. In sum, the Lieutenant-Governor in his province has powers that are analogous to and commensurate with the powers of the Governor General at the level of the federal government.

Up until now we have been speaking in rather formal and legalistic terms about the powers of the Governor General and the Lieutenant-Governors. The intention has been to clarify the strict constitutional nature of the executive function in Canada. Now, however, it is necessary to bring the discussion of the executive function down from this rarefied atmos-

---

[20]BNA Act, s. 55.
[21]The Liquidators of the Maritime Bank v. the Receiver General of New Brunswick (1892), Olmsted, vol. 1.

phere and to deal with the constitutional realities of the executive function in Canada.

The BNA Act provides for a body of advisors to assist the Governor General in performing the onerous burden of executive responsibilities with which the same Act and the Letters Patent (1947) saddle him. Section 11 of the BNA Act states that:

> There shall be a Council to aid and advise in the Government of Canada, to be styled the Queen's Privy Council for Canada: and the Persons who are to be Members of that Council shall be from Time to Time chosen and summoned by the Governor General and sworn in as Privy Councillors, and Members thereof may be from time to time removed by the Governor General. . . .

The BNA Act states quite specifically that the Governor General does not have to listen to his advisors, but in fact even at the time of Confederation there was a well-established convention that the Governor of the colony would, in almost all cases, act purely on the advice of the government of the day. The Queen's Privy Council for Canada includes a great number of people such as ex-cabinet ministers who never function as advisors. The *cabinet*, which is not mentioned at all in the BNA Act, is really a committee of Privy Councillors, chosen by the leader of the majority party in the House of Commons from among his supporters in parliament. Formally all executive acts are performed by the Governor General in Council, but in reality, executive decisions are made by the Prime Minister and his cabinet, and are "rubber-stamped" by the Governor General.

There is still a body of opinion among prominent experts which argues that one should not dismiss the Governor General as merely a "rubber stamp" for the Prime Minister and his cabinet, for the simple reason that he still does possess a great deal of executive authority by virtue of the BNA Act. The argument is that if the government of the day attempted to violate a basic principle of our political culture, for instance by abolishing free speech, the Governor General could step in and refuse his assent to the bill, thus thwarting the culprits. In doing so, however, the Governor General would himself be violating a fundamental norm of our system of government, by claiming to represent the public interest better than the public's elected representatives. To say that a Governor General would never dare to oppose the will of his Prime Minister is pure speculation, but the fact remains that the norm of popular sovereignty which is at the core of the Canadian constitution imposes severe political limitations on the actual powers of the Queen's representative. The last time a Governor General went against the wishes of his Prime Minister was in 1926, when Lord Byng refused Prime Minister King a dissolution of parliament. The result was a general outcry led by Mackenzie King against the unilateral action of the Governor General, and a subsequent electoral disaster for the man who had immediately benefited from Byng's decision, Arthur Meighen.[22]

The relationship between the Lieutenant-Governor of a province and the provincial Premier is almost identical to that between the Prime

[22]See E.A. Forsey, *The Royal Power of Dissolution of Parliament in the British Commonwealth*, (Oxford University Press, Toronto, 1968), ch. 5.

Minister of Canada and the Governor General, and the BNA Act provides that the Lieutenant-Governor may act with the advice of the executive council of the province. The executive council is, in fact, the provincial cabinet, which is chosen by the Premier. All executive decisions are made by the Premier and his cabinet, and the Lieutenant-Governor, like his federal counterpart, more or less "rubber-stamps" them. The one time when a Lieutenant-Governor might be called upon to exercise some discretionary authority is in the case of the death in office of a Premier where the man's successor is not obvious. Clearly the Lieutenant-Governor must seek the advice of the cabinet ministers, but in some cases the advice tendered by these men might not be unanimous. In such a situation, the Lieutenant-Governor must decide whose advice to take, on the basis of his own discretion and political acumen, for above all else he must insure that there is a government. Such a situation appeared to develop at the death of Premier Maurice Duplessis of Quebec. Initially, the cabinet was by no means solidly united behind one candidate to succeed Duplessis. Apparently the cabinet managed eventually to achieve a consensus by itself, but the incident makes it clear that there is a potentially important political role to be played by the Lieutenant-Governor in such rare, but conceivable, circumstances.[23]

To conclude, the formal executive power in Canada is vested in the Crown and, in a very formal sense, we can be said to have a monarchial form of government. The Governor General exercises all of the prerogative rights and privileges of the Queen in right of Canada, according to the BNA Act and the Letters Patent that define his office. The constitutional doctrine of popular sovereignty has, however, reduced the *de facto* role of the Governor General to that of a figurehead. The real power is exercised by the Prime Minister and his cabinet who obtain their legitimacy from the fact that they possess a popular mandate.

The Judicial Function[24] The judicial function is the hardest to distinguish of the three basic output functions of the political system. In fact, it can be argued that there are only two basic output functions: making law and applying it—and both the judiciary and the executive can be perceived as applying the law to specific cases, each doing it in a slightly different fashion.[25] There are two reasons, however, for shying away in this text from that two-fold method of classification. First, the core document of our constitution, the BNA Act, makes very definite distinctions between the Executive Power, the Legislative Power, and the Judicature.[26] Sec-

[23]For a discussion of the role the Lieutenant-Governor plays in finding a successor to a Premier who dies in office, see J.R. Mallory, "The Royal Prerogative in Canada: The Selection of Successors to Mr. Duplessis and Mr. Sauvé," *The Canadian Journal of Economics and Political Science*, vol. 26, no. 2, pp. 314–319, May, 1960. See also G.F.G. Stanley, "A 'Constitutional Crisis' in British Columbia," *The Canadian Journal of Economics and Political Science*, vol. 21, no. 3, pp. 281–292, August, 1955.

[24]W.R. Lederman, "The Independence of the Judiciary," *Canadian Bar Review*, 1956, p. 769 ff.

[25]See also Chapter 16.

[26]BNA Act, part III, IV, VII.

ondly, even if a functional distinction is difficult, the judicial branch in Canada can be clearly distinguished through the principle of *judicial independence*, which insulates the judiciary from any direct responsibility to either of the other two branches. The independence of the judiciary is one of the essential principles of our system of government, and as such, it merits a longer look.

The constitutional source of judicial independence flows from Sections 96 to 101 of the BNA Act. Section 99 states that Superior Court judges shall hold office during "good behaviour" up to the age seventy five, implying that a judge cannot be dismissed for incompetence or laziness but only for a criminal offence. Section 99 also provides that a judge is removable only by the Governor General on address by the Senate and the House of Commons. This means that the executive can remove a judge only at the request of both Houses of the Canadian parliament, and the practice has evolved that even this is undertaken only after a judicial inquiry into the man's wrongdoings. The salary of a judge is set by statute, so that it is not possible for the judge to become involved in bargaining with the executive for salary increments, nor is it possible for the executive to "pressure" a judge through controlling his livelihood. In sum, every effort is made to insure that the judge is protected from influences that might affect his objectivity. As R.M. Dawson has said,

> The judge is placed in a position where he has nothing to lose by doing what is right, and little to gain by doing what is wrong, and there is, therefore, every reason to hope that his best efforts will be devoted to the conscientious performance of his duty.[27]

Further to the guarantees of the personal independence of the judge is the guarantee of jurisdictional integrity that is given to the Superior Courts in Canada. A common assumption is that any governmental official will attempt to widen the scope of his jurisdiction, a practice often referred to as "empire building." Limits must be placed on this sort of activity, usually by the intervention of other officials. However, the independence of the judiciary is perceived as such an important value in our system that the danger of judicial empire building is ignored. Instead, a remarkable faith in the honesty and level-headedness of our judges is indicated by allowing Superior Courts to decide not only their own jurisdiction, but the jurisdiction of other governmental offices as well.[28] In effect, this means that the legislative branch cannot vest Superior Court jurisdiction in other than a Superior Court without first securing amendments to the BNA Act (Sections 96 to 101)[29] and/or the Supreme Court Act. Granted, there is nothing in law to prevent parliament from amending

[27]R. McGregor Dawson, *The Government of Canada*, fifth edition, revised by Norman Ward, (University of Toronto Press, Toronto, 1970), p. 409.

[28]See Lederman, "The Independence of the Judiciary", p. 1175.

[29]Ss. 96-101 of the BNA Act can apparently be amended (per section 91 (1) of the Act). See E. Forsey, "Independence of the Judiciary," *Canadian Bar Review*, 1957, p. 240. He rejects Lederman's contention that 96–101 cannot be amended unilaterally by the federal government. See also B.L. Strayer, *Judicial Review of Legislation in Canada*, (University of Toronto Press, Toronto, 1968), p. 37.

Sections 96 to 101 or the Supreme Court Act, the latter being a federal statute to begin with, but the principle of judicial independence is a norm of our system with which even parliament cannot tamper lightly.

Judicial review has been cited already as a possible limitation on the supremacy of parliament in Canada. Now it is necessary to consider to what extent the principle of judicial review is itself a part of our constitution. The concept of judicial review can be looked at in two different ways: the narrow one limits the concept to the power of the courts to declare laws unconstitutional or *ultra vires*, and therefore void; the broader definition of judicial review includes, as well, the ability of the courts to slow up or "brake" the legislative branch by rigid interpretation of the law.[30] The former definition has it that judicial review does not exist in the U.K. because the courts there cannot declare acts of parliament void, but the latter definition suggests that because British courts interpret the law, there *is* a form of judicial review in the U.K. It is not necessary to make a choice between these two definitions, as long as it is recognized that they are both popularly in use, but for purposes of our discussion of the judicial function, it seems more helpful to use the broader one.

Keeping this in mind, we can now look at the two levels of judicial review that are implicit in the second definition. Professor J. E. McWhinney describes these two levels of judicial review as *direct* and *indirect* forms of judicial authority.[31] Direct judicial review is the kind exercised by, for example, the U.S. Supreme Court. The U.S. court has the power[32] to declare acts of Congress and acts of the state legislatures unconstitutional and therefore void. This judicial power exists in Canada to the extent that the judiciary here has the authority to interpret the federal distribution of powers as laid out by the BNA Act, Sections 91 and 92.

The constitutional status of direct judicial review in Canada, however, is confusing. The right to declare acts of parliament *ultra vires* certainly does not flow from the English common law, which recognizes the principle of parliamentary supremacy. On the other hand, this judicial right is not specifically vested in the courts by the BNA Act, either. The historical origins of the practice of direct judicial review can likely be traced to the fact that the Privy Council traditionally had that power with respect to the colonial legislatures which were subordinate to the imperial parliament. McWhinney argues that, although the Canadian parliament has long since ceased to be subordinate, the practice of judicial review has "ripened", through continued use, into a binding convention of our constitution.[33] Probably, too, the roots of direct judicial review in Canada can be traced to pragmatic considerations flowing implicitly from the principle of federalism which is one of the critical dimensions entrenched in the BNA Act. To back up this hypothesis, it can be noted that direct judi-

---

[30]See Edward McWhinney, *Judicial Review*, (University of Toronto Press, Toronto, 1969), p. 13.

[31]McWhinney, *Judicial Review*, p. 13.

[32]The predominant view, as set forth in *Marbury* v. *Madison* (1803), is that the power to review acts of Congress is "implicit" in the constitution.

[33]McWhinney, *Judicial Review*, p. 14.

cial review of legislation in Canada has occurred almost exclusively with respect to the distribution of powers between the federal parliament and the provincial legislatures, and never has it functioned to place matters beyond the competence of government generally.

Indirect judicial review, as described by McWhinney,

> . . .is where a court, either not having the power to annul or override enactments of the legislature as "unconstitutional" or else simply choosing not to exert that power in the instant case, says in effect in the process of interpretation of a statute, that the legislature may or may not have the claimed legislative power, but it has not in the language it has used in the enactment now in question employed that power. . . .[34]

This form of judicial review will naturally be more significant in countries like the U.K., where the constitution is extremely flexible and without clear boundaries, but such "judicial braking" will be used occasionally in countries like the U.S. and Canada, where direct judicial review is also an appropriate judicial alternative. The reason for a court's choosing indirect rather than direct review might be that the facts of the case are not clear enough to justify setting a precedent that may preclude legislative enactments in that area in the future. Or it may be the more practical reason that the court does not wish to become embroiled in the political hassle that could ensue if popular legislation were to be rendered void by a judicial decision.

The techniques of indirect judicial review will be dealt with further in Chapter 16, but generally the exercise of this type of constitutional control is achieved by a set of presumptions which the courts will make in the interpretation of a piece of legislation. For example, they will assume, unless the legislation states specifically to the contrary, that parliament does not intend laws to have retroactive effect; and they will not interpret any statute in such a way as to take away the citizen's right to a fair hearing. The effect is to slow up, or to "brake" the legislative branch when the judiciary feels it has overstepped the bounds of constitutional propriety, though perhaps keeping within the limits of de jure constitutionality.

The constitutional basis for the exercise of indirect judicial review in Canada is the English common law.[35] The limitation on this type of judicial review is that it is merely a "stalling" technique. Parliament can always, in theory, rework the legislation so that there is no ambiguity and in this way bypass even the most rigorous and stringent application of the judiciary's power of indirect judicial review. However, as Professor McWhinney points out, ". . .at best this is likely to involve time consuming delays and at worst, the corrective legislation may bog down comletely. . . ."[36]

A further limitation on the power of judicial review may be imposed by the principle of stare decisis.[37] Stare decisis means that the judiciary is bound by previous decisions in deciding current cases. While precedents

[34]McWhinney, Judicial Review, p. 13 (italics added).
[35]McWhinney, Judicial Review, p. 15 passim.
[36]McWhinney, Judicial Review, p. 15 passim.
[37]See Chapter 6.

established by earlier courts are usually adhered to by the Canadian judiciary, this is done by choice and not by constitutional prescription. Lower courts are bound by the decisions of higher courts, but this aspect of the principle of *stare decisis* does not affect the constitutional implications of judicial review.

Divided Sovereignty: The Federal Principle

Divided sovereignty means basically that the legislative powers of government in Canada are divided between the federal parliament and the legislatures of the ten provinces. While we often refer to the federal and provincial "levels" of government, within their specified spheres of jurisdiction there exists no superior–subordinate relationship. The legislatures of the provinces and the parliament of Canada have constitutionally distinct functions and neither can trench upon the constitutionally granted authority of the other.

The operative principle of divided sovereignty is ensconced in the British North America Act, and represents an intention on the part of the drafters of that act to establish a federal system of government in Canada. There have been many definitions of federalism and many approaches to its study, and while the evolution of the Canadian federal system will be discussed in subsequent chapters, a few words here on the concept itself will help to clarify the use of the term. The most important modern contribution to the study of federalism has been that of K.C. Wheare. Since the 1946 publication of Wheare's classic, *Federal Government*, theoretical writings on the concept of federalism have added relatively little except qualifications and interesting changes in emphasis.

Wheare's analysis is institutional in the sense that he views federalism as a *form of government* which embodies the "federal principle":

> . . .By the federal principle I mean the method of dividing powers so that the general and regional governments are each, within a sphere, coordinate and independent. . . .[38]

He then draws a distinction between federal governments and federal constitutions stating that:

> . . .it is not enough that the federal principle should be embodied predominantly in the written constitution of a country. . . .What determines the issue is the working of the system. . .[39]

The prerequisites of a federal system are two according to Wheare:

> . . .To begin with, the communities or states concerned must desire to be under a single independent government for some purposes. . . .They must desire at the same time to retain or establish independent regional governments in some matters at least. . .[40]

Thus in functional terms a federal system reconciles a desire for overall *unity* with a desire for local or regional *autonomy*. In structural terms, a federal system is seen as having independent national and regional governments, each operating in a hypothetically distinct jurisdictional com-

[38]K.C. Wheare, *Federal Government*, (Oxford University Press, 1961), p. 11.
[39]*Ibid.*, p. 33.
[40]*Ibid.*, pp. 35-36.

partment. The federal process, or in Wheare's terms, "How Federal Government Works", will vary from federation to federation, but so long as the federal function is being performed and as long as the basic structural characteristics of federalism are present, the system can be called federal. federal.

The major source of criticism of Wheare has come from people studying emerging nations, many of which claim to be federal, and few of which conform perfectly to Wheare's definition. The reaction to this discontinuity between the term and the real world has been to redefine the term. The crux of most of these attacks on Wheare has been that his concept of federal government is "institutional", and his analysis is "legalistic". The most prominent of his detractors has been W.S. Livingstone, who argues that a legalistic definition of federalism is too narrow, and counters with a sociological one:

> . . .the essence of federalism lies not in the institutional or constitutional structure, but in society itself. . .[41]

Livingstone goes on to state that a federal society is one whose diversity is reflected territorially, and that a federal government is merely a ". . .device by which the federal qualities of the society are articulated and protected. . . .[42]

The great weakness of Livingstone's concept of federalism is that it is so inclusive that it is virtually useless for analysing and categorizing real political systems. He defines a federal government as one that presides over a federal society, and he defines a federal society as one that has regional or territorial diversity. With such possible exceptions as Lichtenstein, Monaco or San Marino, all modern states have varying degrees of regional diversity and therefore all modern governments could be classed as federal. Thus, where K.C. Wheare is too restrictive in his concept of federalism, Livingstone is far too broad in his conception of the term.

Riker improves on Wheare without going as far as Livingstone. He describes federalism functionally as ". . .the main alternative to empire as a technique of aggregating large areas under one government. . . ."[43] and structurally as a system with a constitution having three basic characteristics:

> . . .1) two levels of government rule the same land and people, 2) each level has at least one area of action in which it is autonomous, and 3) there is some guarantee (even though merely a statement in the constitution) of the autonomy of each government in its own sphere. . . .[44]

Then Riker goes on to deal with the federal process as a continuous *bargaining relationship* that is carried on among the various leaders of the regional and national governments. Here, by viewing the origins and the operation of federal systems in terms of elite accommodation Professor Riker

[41]W.S. Livingstone, "A Note on the Nature of Federalism", in J. Peter Meekison, ed., *Canadian Federalism: Myth or Reality*, (Methuen, Toronto, 1971), p. 22.
[42]*Ibid.*, p. 22.
[43]W.H. Riker, *Federalism: Origin; Operation; Significance*, (Little, Brown, Boston, 1964), p. 5.
[44]*Ibid.*, p. 11.

has added significantly to Wheare's rather mechanistic and admittedly legalistic analysis of federalism.

While there are many tomes written on the subject of federalism, and most of them address themselves at some stage to the problem of definition, Riker, Livingstone and Wheare represent the general range of approaches, and likely form the foundations for most other authors' conceptions of federal government.[45] The basic characteristics common to all federal systems can be derived from these authors. First, the origins and persistence of federal forms of government depend upon continuing general agreement among the various national and regional leaders that some form of union is desirable, and that because of differences in priorities among the member states or provinces, there should be at least some degree of independence guaranteed to them. (R.L. Watts speaks of this in terms of social integration. . .in terms of an equilibrium between integrating and disintegrating pressures within society.)[46] Secondly, in structural terms, federal systems are composed of two levels of government each of which is permitted to function independently of the other in specified although probably changing areas of jurisdiction.

The conceptual and definitional problems have arisen, moreover, only where political systems calling themselves federal have lacked these basic characteristics. In fact, most real governments can be very quickly and easily classified as either federal or non-federal, and only a few stand on the effective borderline between the federal and the non-federal and hence challenge the governmental taxonomists' categories. Canada, although regionally diverse, has survived for more than one hundred years, and thus has the first basic federal characteristic. Also, the Canadian system does feature two levels of government, each of which is independent of the other in constitutionally specified juridictional bailiwicks, and hence must be classified as federal in structural terms as well. In sum, neither the Canadian political system nor the Canadian constitution is a borderline case and both can easily be classified as federal. The evolution of the Canadian federal system, and the idiosyncrasies of our particular brand of federalism will be discussed in later chapters. The fact that three separate chapters are to be devoted to federal aspects of the Canadian political system indicates the importance that must be attached to federalism as an operative principle of the constitution. However, to discuss it further at this point would serve to repeat information which is better understood within a historical context in Chapters 7 and 8 and within the context of the policy process in Chapter 15.

This concludes our discussion of the substance of the Canadian constitution. But this is only a snapshot at one point in time. In order to com-

[45]The other significant source of inspiration for the development of the federal concept has been international relations theory, and the theories dealing with international institutions and international political integration. For example, see: K.W. Deutsch, *et. al.*, *Political Community and the North Atlantic Area*, Princeton, 1957; Plischke, E., *Systems of Integrating the International Community*, (Van Nostrand, 1964), Haas, E.B., *The Uniting of Europe*, Stanford, 1958.

[46]R.L. Watts, *New Federations*, (Oxford University Press, 1966), p. 111.

plete the picture we must now proceed to an analysis of the dynamic element of the Canadian constitution; its propensities and techniques for change.

6
The Dynamics of Law and the Constitution in Canada

Having looked at the component parts and substantive principles of the Canadian constitution it is now necessary to put that essentially descriptive detail within a more dynamic setting. It is the function of this chapter to look at the Canadian legal system from the perspectives of three different processes. The first section takes the most macroscopic approach possible and looks at the process of constitutional change. This section analyses the state-to-individual relationship as reciprocal, for constitutional change not only reflects changes in the political culture, but also induces change in the individual behaviour patterns that characterize the political culture. The second section looks at the nature of the positive law and the judicial system in Canada. Here the analytical focus is narrower and the emphasis is on a process whereby the specific rules of behaviour set down in statutes are applied to individuals in society—the means by which the society protects itself from individual excesses. Finally, the third section of this chapter analyses the process whereby civil liberties are protected in Canada; here the analytical focus is on the means by which the individual is protected from the excesses of the state.

THE PROCESS OF CONSTITUTIONAL CHANGE

In the long run, the constitution of a political system must reflect societal values if that political system is to persist. Hence, while it is true that the constitution provides the regime with necessary rigidity, the constitution must also have the capacity for change; it must not be so rigid that it cannot be adjusted to meet new needs and priorities in the environment of the political system. There are several ways in which the Canadian constitution can be changed, each of which must be dealt with in some detail.

Revolution and Political Violence While it is likely that compared to other countries in the world the Canadian political culture is relatively non-violent, it must be recognized that violence as a tactic of political change is always a possibility. It takes but one deviant individual to assassinate a political leader or place an explosive device in a public place, so that, while the dominant values of a political system may be basically non-violent, isolated violent events may periodically occur.

Political revolution[1] is also not likely to occur in Canada for the simple reason that there would appear to be a fairly deep-seated consensus about the desired directions and urgency of political change in this country. Moreover, needed changes in the Canadian constitution have usually been attainable through legitimate and non-violent means. Generally speaking, the empirical evidence of our history has backed up this contention about the non-violent and non-revolutionary nature of our political culture, although the terrorist activities of the fall of 1970 may lend some credence to the idea that perhaps even in Canada there is a minority which is willing to engage in non-legitimate[2] tactics to induce political change.

At the present time in Canada, the most likely form of non-legitimate constitutional change would appear to be that of a non-violent but also extra-legal nature. A non-Canadian example of this form of constitutional change is the unilateral declaration of independence by the Smith regime in Rhodesia, where in an extra-legal but non-violent way, a colony broke with the mother country. In a similar vein, if an increasing number of French Canadians in the province of Quebec come to prefer the option of independence from Canada, the secession of that province is a definite possibility. Despite the tactics of the FLQ, it seems likely that such a radical alteration in the Canadian political community could be achieved without resort to violence, although there are no provisions in the constitution which would legally sanction such a move. Here the secession of Quebec would be likely to occur extra-legally and also, hopefully, non-violently.[3]

[1]The concept of revolution has two dimensions; one emphasizes the *means* of change which are extra-legal and normally violent, and the second emphasizes the *extent* of the changes that occur. Thus, on the one hand, extremely violent "revolutionary" upheavals may produce relatively minor changes in the regime or the political community; examples of this are *coups d'état* which occur frequently in some military dictatorships. On the other hand, change of "revolutionary" dimensions may occur in the regime or political community of a system through perfectly legal and non-violent means; an example of this might be the Indian Independence Act which created the modern states of India and Pakistan out of what was previously British India.

[2]See R.J. Jackson and M. Stein, *Issues in Comparative Politics*, (Macmillan, Toronto, 1971), ch. 5 for a definition of revolution which combines both means and ends. Note here that violence may be considered a legitimate tactic of political change in some political cultures. Our referent in this text is the Western democracies and specifically Canada. Legitimacy, in other words, must be viewed in terms of the values of the existing regime.

[3]Note that the legality of such a move is irrelevant in the long run, for if such a change is accepted as providing a needed alteration in the regime and/or the political community, then the new regime will probably be accepted as legitimate by its citizens. Similarly, to bring the discussion closer to home, if the Province of Quebec should unilaterally secede from the Canadian political system, the question as to

In sum, while we do not pretend that violence and revolution have ever been or are likely to be significant means of achieving constitutional change in Canada, such options do exist *de facto*. Their likelihood could be expected to increase only if the basic attitudes towards the legitimacy of violence and the perceived urgency of the need for change were to produce radical alterations in the fabric of our political culture.

Customary and Conventional Change Customs and conventions[4] of the constitution can be changed in the same manner in which they originated. As the continued use of some political device over a period of time can result in its becoming a constitutional convention, similarly, changes in customs and conventions occur due to the establishment of new precedents that alter the current constitutional practice. Conversely, through disuse, what was at one time a convention of the constitution may, in time, cease to be accepted as one. As a possible example of constitutional change by convention, one need look no further than a piece of Canadian federal financial legislation that was defeated on third reading in the spring of 1968. On this occasion the Liberal government of Lester Pearson was a minority government, which meant that on any division in the House of Commons the government had to scrape up some support from other parties in the House to gain a majority. Owing to a miscalculation by the party whip and the acting Prime Minister, the Liberals allowed a vote on third reading when there were not sufficient government supporters in the house, and the bill was defeated. Some constitutional experts (particularly in the Conservative party) cried "resign!" for, they said, it was a firm convention of the constitution that if a government were defeated on a piece of financial legislation it had to resign. The Liberals instead called for a vote of confidence the next day, and won it quite easily, because while no opposition party was very enthusiastic about the particular piece of legislation that had been defeated, the Créditistes, at least, did not want an election at that time. While, in the past, financial bills have been defeated without forcing resignations, the publicity given to this incident may cause it to be viewed as a precedent. A convention may evolve that a particular piece of legislation can be defeated in the House without

the legality of such a move will soon become irrelevant to the Québecois, who, by agreeing with the action in the first place, have tacitly accepted the new regime as legitimate. Furthermore, the mere fact that the breakaway province would have gained its independence illegally probably would be rapidly forgotten, even by Canadians, in the need to establish friendly diplomatic and economic relations with a neighbour. The distinction, therefore, between legal and illegal (or extralegal) revolutionary constitutional change is more important analytically than it is practically. The more important question concerns the internal legitimacy of the change.

[4]Dawson, *The Government of Canada*, p. 65n. ". . .no attempt has been made to distinguish between custom, usage and convention. A common distinction is to treat custom and usage as synonymous terms, and convention as a usage which has acquired obligatory force." See also D.V. Smiley, *Constitutional Adaptation and Canadian Federalism Since 1945*, Royal Commission on Bilingualism and Biculturalism Study No. 4, (Queen's Printer, Ottawa, 1970).

necessarily forcing the government's resignation and precipitating an immediate election. If this happens, the opposition in a minority situation will no longer be handicapped by having to "throw the baby out with the bath water" if they don't like a piece of legislation.

As mentioned, conventional change can also be brought about by the disuse of a given constitutional provision. The best example of this is the disallowance power of the federal government, which has not been used since 1943 and appears now to be a dead letter. The reason it has ceased to be a viable constitutional device is related to the actualities of power distribution in Canada today, which are in turn related to the "coming of age" of the provinces. However, it is also possible that if the federal government had continued to make a habit of disallowing provincial acts, the provinces might never have come of age. Desuetude, therefore, may indeed play a part in determining the fate of various constitutional devices in this country.

Customary and conventional change is occurring constantly, and incrementally, through the use and desuetude of various constitutional practices, and while it is a difficult form of constitutional change to control or even to pinpoint, it does constitute a significant measure of the total of constitutional change in Canada.

Judicial Change Judicial decisions fill out the bare bones of the constitution by interpreting it and by applying it to specific cases. Consider, for example, the way in which the federal power to regulate trade and commerce was interpreted by the Judicial Committee of the Privy Council. Many of the Fathers of Confederation seem to have viewed the Canadian federal system as a highly centralized arrangement, with the provinces having a secondary role to play. In keeping with this view, the BNA Act gives the federal government jurisdiction over several very important matters, among them the regulation of trade and commerce.[5] The Judicial Committee chose to interpret this to mean the regulation of interprovincial and international trade and commerce, but not the regulation of trade within a province. In other words, the judiciary effectively changed the meaning of one of the provisions of the BNA Act in the process of interpreting it.[6]

Constitutional change through judicial review has certain built-in limitations, particularly because the courts do not review all legislation automatically. It is important to recognize that the courts can only interpret a law when its interpretation becomes central to deciding a case. In other words, the courts have to wait until, in the normal course of litigation, some citizen brings a case before them and questions the validity of a given statute, before they can rule on its constitutionality. The only exception to this rule is an unusual device available to Canadian governments known as a *constitutional reference*. A reference case occurs when the federal government submits a piece of legislation to the Supreme Court of Canada for a judgment regarding its constitutionality. This device was created by a sec-

[5]BNA Act, s. 91 (2).
[6]See also Chapter 7.

tion of the Supreme Court Act, and has the effect of allowing the federal government to test the constitutionality of a law in the highest court of the land before attempting to implement it. The provinces also have the right to submit reference cases to the highest court in the province and, ultimately, the decision on such a reference can be appealed to the Supreme Court of Canada. The problem with the constitutional reference as a method of judicial change is that the judges are forced to judge the legislation not merely within the context of the facts of a single case, but within all conceivable contexts in which it can be employed. More will be said about constitutional reference in a later section, but in the meantime let it suffice to say that the reference case is one way in which the judiciary can be given the opportunity to change or shape the constitution through the interpretation of legislation.

Legislative Change The forms of constitutional change that have been discussed thus far are all rather haphazard and incidental methods of producing change. Their end product is very difficult to plan for or predict. This is not the case with legislative constitutional change, for the essence of this form of constitutional change is the fact that it is deliberate or consciously contrived, with existing regime mechanisms being employed to produce it. There are two broad types of legislative change in the Canadian political system, not including formal amendment, which will be discussed separately.

The first type of legislative constitutional change that is employed in Canada involves the alteration of *organic laws* through acts of parliament[7] and orders-in-council. An example of this kind of constitutional change would be the amendment from time to time of the Supreme Court Act; while the subject matter is constitutional, the method of altering it is by a simple act of parliament. In some cases, such as under the War Measures Act, the Governor General in Council is given the power to make substantial amendments by executive fiat. Some of the changes that were introduced by order-in-council during World War II significantly changed what can be considered the constitution of Canada, although the achievement of change through this method is rather arbitrary.

The second type of legislative change is the kind of amendment of the BNA Act which was authorized originally by the Act itself. Examples are provided by a whole class of clauses of the Act which are prefaced by "Until the Parliament of Canada otherwise provides. . ."[8] These provisions of the Act were intended to provide interim measures at the time of Confederation until parliament could get around to setting up more permanent ones. Many of these clauses are now defunct, having been replaced by statutes soon after Confederation.

Formal Amendment of The BNA Act Perhaps the most significant form of constitutional change in Canada is formal *amendment* of

---

[7]Until we discuss parliament and the policy process in Chapter 17, we will speak of parliament's performing the functions which are formally its responsibility.
[8]See, for instance, ss. 35, 40, 41 and 47 (BNA Act, 1867).

the BNA Act. The BNA Act had no general provision for its amendment when it was passed in 1867. Since it was a statute of the parliament of the U.K., it seemed obvious at the time that it could and would be amended by ordinary British legislation. At Confederation, Canada was subordinate to the supreme British parliament, and her evolution to the independent status that she enjoys today was not foreseen by the British parliament or even by the Fathers of Confederation. The inability of the Dominion of Canada to amend the BNA Act soon became a problem for a young country growing rapidly both in political autonomy and in population, which was faced with a growing number of responsibilities due to the increasing involvement of government generally in matters such as education, welfare and public works. In other words, the BNA Act soon was obsolescent as a vehicle for the allocation of resources in this country, and required changes. In response to these demands for formal change of the BNA Act, a method, involving various conventional procedures for amendment, was gradually developed.

Canada and The U.K. At the core of this procedure for amendment of the BNA Act are three conventions which define relatively the roles of the provinces, the federal parliament and the U.K. parliament. The earliest of these to evolve was that the parliament of the U.K. would not amend the BNA Act without an express request by Canada. This convention, recognized before the turn of the century, was explicitly recognized by the Statute of Wesminster in 1931:

> 4. No act of Parliament of the United Kingdom passed after the commencement of this act shall extend or be deemed to extend, to a Dominion as part of the law of that Dominion, unless it is expressly declared in that act that the Dominion has requested, and consented to, the enactment thereof. . . .

The standard means for requesting British legislative action has emerged as either a petition of the Canadian government or a "joint address" of the House of Commons and the Senate. Executive petition by the government of the day was used in 1875 and 1895 to secure amendments to the BNA Act, and in these cases, the petition was approved by the federal parliament either explicitly or tacitly. In all other instances of amendment, however, the request has been made by a joint address (i.e., a joint resolution) of both Houses of the Canadian parliament—and it has become a firm convention of the constitution that amendment today can only be requested by the Canadian parliament and not by the government of the day acting unilaterally.

The second convention is the positive aspect of the first: that is, the parliament of the U.K. *will always act* to amend the BNA Act if requested to do so by a joint address of the Canadian parliament. While this convention has never been given statutory expression, there has never been an occasion in Canadian constitutional history when the parliament of the U.K. has refused to meet the request of the Dominion with regard to amendment of the BNA Act, and there is virtually no chance of this ever happening in the future.

Canada and The Provinces The third convention is far more complicated than either of the first two, for it involved the extent to which the consultation and consent of the provinces should be sought by the federal government prior to petitioning the U.K. by a joint address. The rule here is complicated because the practice of amendment by joint address is itself based only on constitutional convention. Thus, it is the particular procedure that has been followed in the past which more or less defines the nature and limitations of this particular convention. First, the parliament of the U.K. has never amended the BNA Act on the request of a province or of any number of the provinces, unless the provinces' wishes are expressed in a joint address by both Houses of the Canadian parliament. Secondly, the U.K. parliament has never turned down a request for amendment by the federal government because the amendment was opposed by the provinces or any particular provinces. It is possible that the 1907 amendment that secured an adjustment of the provincial subsidies, which was opposed formally by British Columbia, was altered slightly in its wording as a result of the objections of that province, but it is not likely today that objections by a province would precipitate changes in even the wording of an amendment requested by the Canadian parliament. Hence, in practice, the convention that has emerged is that, as far as the U.K. is concerned, it will provide any amendment that is requested by the Canadian parliament, regardless of whether it might affect the rights of the provinces, and regardless of whether the provinces have consented. This is merely a recognition of the fact that Canada has come of age politically and should be given the power and responsibility to make the decisions and take the consequences that might flow from an unpopular constitutional amendment.

If the U.K. will not step in to protect the provinces when the federal government secures an amendment by joint address, the entire question of the extent to which the provinces have to be consulted on amendments involves the provinces and the federal government mutually. In order to understand the problems surrounding this convention it is necessary to consider the provincial point of view with respect to consultation and consent of the provinces at some stage before the actual joint address. The original argument for the participation of the provinces in the amendment of the BNA Act stems from a theory of Confederation that has become known as the *compact theory*. The compact theory of the Canadian federal system states that the Act of 1867 was in effect a treaty or a *compact* between equal participants and that, therefore, any changes made in the original agreement must be made only with consent of all of the participants. This would mean that for Canada to secure an amendment of the BNA Act, it would be necessary to canvass the views of the provinces, then prepare a draft amendment which took into account all of the provincial views and objections, and secure the unanimous consent of the provinces, before securing a joint address of the Canadian parliament. Not only would this procedure be time-consuming, but it could also mean that any one province might veto an amendment that was agreed to by the rest of the provinces. To be sure, this state of affairs would protect provincial autonomy, but only at great cost in terms of other principles of our constitution such as majority rule and representation by population. The compact theory, however, has seldom been taken very seriously even by those who favour a great deal of protection for the autonomy of the provinces. Aside from the fact that such a system of constitutional amendment might prove extremely costly in terms of time, as R.M. Dawson points out, "The theory, while plausible, is constructed on sheer invention. It has no legal foundation; it has no historical foundation, and the precedents to support it are few. . . ."[9] Thus, not only is the compact theory impractical; it is also not based on either historical or legal fact.

A modern version of the compact theory of Confederation has been espoused recently by politicians in the Province of Quebec. This version states that the original Confederation agreement was a compact between the two founding "races" or language groups. The argument here is that no amendment of the BNA Act can be carried out without the consent of both the English-speaking and the French-speaking partners in Confederation. This version of the compact theory would appear to have some historical justification, in that the Confederation agreement did, in some respects, recognize cultural duality in Canada. The BNA Act itself contains provisions such as the language and religion guarantees which are obviously intended to protect the rights of the French-Canadian minority. However, the argument that this should place any legal restrictions on the ability of the federal parliament to request amendments from the U.K. is unfounded in law. Thus, as a legal argument for the inclusion of the provinces in the amendment process of the BNA Act, the compact theory in either of its forms is not very persuasive.

But on the other hand, the custom of consulting the provinces whenever an amendment under contemplation involves their rights has slowly developed over the years. The reason for this, of course, lies in the nature of the political process in this country, for if a government were to heavy-handedly abrogate the autonomy of the provinces, it might suffer badly in the next federal election. Furthermore, our federal system works today because the provinces and the federal government have evolved a set of procedures and practices which function effectively only by federal–provincial co-operation. It could not operate if the federal government attempted to force BNA Act amendments down the throats of the provinces by taking unilateral action. Thus, where historical and legal argument fails, the exigencies of our political process and the ethos of co-operative federalism have justified in very practical terms the principle of participation by the provinces in decisions to amend the BNA Act.

91 (1) Amendments   In 1949, by a joint address of the Canadian parliament, an amendment to the BNA Act was secured which gave the federal parliament the power to amend, by simple act of parliament, the constitution of Canada with the exception of the parts of the BNA Act that deal with the guarantees of minority language and education rights, the

[9]Dawson, *The Government of Canada*, p. 124. See also N.M. Rogers, "The Compact Theory of Confederation," *Proceedings of the Canadian Political Science Association*, 1931, pp. 205–230, and G.F.G. Stanley, "Act or Pact? Another Look at Confederation," *C.H.A. Annual Report*, (Ottawa, 1956).

rights of the provinces, the provision regarding the five-year limit on the life of a parliament, and the requirement that the federal parliament meet at least once a year. This amendment itself was secured without the consent of the provinces, and although there was some opposition to the unilateral action of the federal government, it all came to nothing in the end. But, it is possible that in creating this amending power in Section 91(1) of the BNA Act, the federal government may have unintentionally limited its ability to amend federal legislation such as the Supreme Court Act because it is a part of "the constitution of Canada" and because it affects the rights of the provinces. Whether or not the courts will interpret 91(1) to apply to all of "the constitution of Canada" or whether they will choose to interpret its scope as limited to the BNA Act only, remains to be seen, but in any event it appears that this "amending power amendment" places an added moral onus on the federal government not to interfere with the rights of the provinces without their unanimous consent. Its effect, therefore, besides transferring the amending power for most of the BNA Act from the U.K. parliament to the parliament of Canada, is implicitly to preclude the federal government from ever tampering with minority rights and provincial rights without the consent of the provinces.

In Search of an Amending Formula The question of how we should deal with the amendment of those "entrenched" parts of the constitution of Canada which are expressly excepted in 91(1) has been the subject of much debate in Canada for some time, and therefore deserves more detailed attention. Since 1927, there have been several Federal-Provincial conferences which were devoted almost entirely to discussions of ways in which the procedure for the amendment of the BNA Act could be completely "Canadianized"; that is, changed so that the Canadian parliament would no longer have to petition the U.K. parliament in order to get the Act amended. The parliament of the U.K. does not particularly cherish the function that it is called upon from time to time to perform on our behalf, and in fact, at the time of passage of the Statute of Westminster, Britain attempted to give the parliament of Canada the unilateral power to amend the BNA Act in its entirety. Canada refused because of pressures from the provinces.

Hence, it is clear that the parliament of the U.K. does not stand in the way of handing over to authorities on this side of the Atlantic the power to amend the BNA Act. The problem in finding a satisfactory "all-Canadian" amending scheme is that we in Canada cannot decide which authorities should have the power to amend the parts of the BNA Act which are expected from the federal amendment power in Section 91(1). Several schemes have been proposed, the most promising of which have involved a detailed breakdown of the various clauses of the BNA Act into categories or "pigeon-holes",[10] according to the extent of federal and provincial participation. Thus, some clauses of the Act would be amendable by the federal parliament and the provinces directly concerned (e.g. interprovincial boundary adjustments), and some clauses would be amendable

---

[10]See D.C. Rowat, "The 1949 Amendment and the Pigeon-Hole Method," in Paul Fox (ed.), *Politics: Canada*, 1st ed., (McGraw–Hill, Toronto, 1962), pp. 82–87.

by the legislatures of two-thirds of the provinces representing at least fifty per cent of the population of Canada. (This latter classification was to insure that a certain class of amendment which while not so fundamental as to require unanimity, could not be passed without the support of either Ontario or Quebec.)

At the 1964 Federal–Provincial Conference, an agreement was finally reached on a formula:[11] all of the provinces indicated that they were content with what clauses had been included in what pigeon-holes. Suddenly, Jean Lesage, then Premier of the Province of Quebec, changed his mind and refused to give the proposal the support of his government. Quebec's sudden turnabout was probably in objection to the requirement for provincial unanimity for the amendment of matters such as language rights. If the government of the Province of Quebec were to accept this part of the amending formula, it would have meant, for example, that she could no longer bargain bilaterally with the federal government for concessions in areas such as French language rights in provinces other than Quebec. In order to pry out concessions in such areas it would have been necessary to gain the unanimous consent of the other provinces as well as that of the federal parliament. The Quebec government obviously felt, at that time, that its bargaining position *vis-à-vis* the federal parliament was so strong that there would not be any immediate threat to its position in Quebec that would require it to use the unanimity provision to protect itself. Furthermore, Quebec might stand to gain considerable advantage by continuing the bilateral Quebec–Canada bargaining relationship. The Province of Quebec, it seemed, had come full circle from the defensive and inward-looking nationalism of Duplessis to the aggressive and outward-looking nationalism of Jean Lesage, at precisely that period in Canadian constitutional history when we were attempting to write a defensive and rigid amending procedure into the constitution.

The successor to the Fulton–Favreau formula was the Victoria Charter of June 1971. This document, agreed to by all federal and provincial representatives at a constitutional conference in Victoria B.C., proposes that all amendments to the Canadian constitution require the consent of parliament and a majority of the provincial legislatures, provided that the concurring provinces include: 1) every province which at any time has ever contained 25% of the population of Canada. [The function of this provision is to give either Ontario or Quebec a veto power, in perpetuity, although given current trends in population growth, B.C. could also enter this elite circle in the foreseeable future]; 2) at least two Atlantic provinces [This gives some recognition of the fact that there are distinct regional interests in Canada that must be given a veto power over decisions as fundamental as constitutional amendment]; 3) at least two western provinces provided the two have a combined population equal to 50% of the total population of the West.

All in all, the Victoria Charter provides an amendment formula which is less rigid than the Fulton–Favreau, for it does not require the

[11]This version came to be known as the Fulton–Favreau formula after the two federal justice ministers who held office while it was being drafted.

unanimous consent of the provinces for any matters at all. It is simpler to understand and it provides protection for all major regional and ethnic interests in Canada. Unfortunately the Charter, as agreed to by the provincial representatives in Victoria, was never given the necessary ratification by the legislatures of the ten provinces and the federal parliament. As was the case with the Fulton–Favreau agreement, the legislature of Quebec was the major dissenter.

While the Victoria Charter is less rigid than its predecessor, it is still appropriate to ask whether any formal and rigid amending formula is necessary for our constitution. What are the relevant facts that have been collected in this regard? First, the U.K. always has amended, and probably always will amend, the BNA Act when requested to do so by the parliament of Canada. However, it is still relevant to ask "what if?" at some future date, the U.K. should refuse to amend the BNA Act as we requested, or "what if?" the U.K. ceased to exist, for instance through entering a European political union. Despite the common myth that there will always be an England, there is some possibility that the old song is dead wrong. "How could we amend our constitution then?", the critics of the *status quo* ask. This is a very valid point, but perhaps it can be answered by pointing to the ever-present possibility of extra-legal change of our constitution. If the U.K. ceased to exist, or if for some unimaginable reason she refused to heed a joint address by both houses of our parliament, we in Canada could still take matters into our own hands and unilaterally make the changes that we needed. Ian Smith did it successfully with Rhodesia under circumstance of unfavourable world opinion that we would not, presumably, be facing in Canada. To all intents and purposes we would merely be taking what was rightfully ours *de facto*, if not in the strict letter of the British constitution.

The second fact is that the federal parliament today cannot, in reality, ask the U.K. for an amendment that affects provincial or minority rights without the consent of the provinces. The restraint on the federal parliament in this regard may or may not be a legal one, but it is certainly a political one. One of the things most Canadians are thought to hold dear (besides motherhood, beer, and Laura Secord) is provincial autonomy. As long as this is so, no federal government that wishes to be re-elected can afford the risk of political damage it would do itself by unilaterally tampering with the rights of the provinces. If, however, the value structure of Canadian society changed so that it became politically acceptable for the federal parliament to abrogate the autonomy of the provinces, then the fact that the provinces lack legal protection under the present amending system might assume more importance than it has today. Let us consider this hypothetical situation for a moment. If the federal parliament had enough political support to unilaterally change the rights of the provinces, then perhaps it is fair to say that it should be able to do so. Even the Victoria Charter respects the will of a "qualified majority". In fact it could even be suggested that if parliament possessed the political support to change the Canadian constitution in the area of provincial rights, then under a formula such as the Victoria Charter, there would likely be sufficient support to secure the change anyway. The point here is that while an amending formula such as the one suggested in 1971 would perhaps defend established interests, it would not protect them if mass public opinion turned against those interests. Like any value of the political system, provincial autonomy is only as safe as Canadians want it to be, and the Fulton–Favreau formula or the Victoria Charter would not, nor should they, change that fact.

The conclusion, therefore, (albeit a tentative one), is that the adoption of an amending scheme such as the Victoria Charter would formalize the procedure for constitutional amendment in Canada, without substantively changing the present situation. In the long run, the real justification for "repatriating" the constitution lies in the fulfillment of psychic needs which would be satisfied by giving Canadians the right to amend their own constitution. If this is important to Canadians in their search for an identity and in the ongoing problem of cementing national unity, then that in itself is sufficient reason to keep trying to devise a mutually agreeable formula for constitutional amendment. It is likely, too, that people need certainty in their dealings with government, and if our amending formula is codified and formalized, or if, as is currently the rage, our constitution is rewritten in its entirety, greater constitutional certainty will, for better or for worse, be one of the effects. On the other side of the picture, however, one must consider that the Canadian constitution has worked as well as any other constitution man has devised for more than one hundred years, and constitutional change has been achieved through various means. Perhaps the real beauty of such an amorphous constitution is that it is not rigid. It can be changed without having to resort to formalized legal procedures, and changes that do not pan out can be revoked in the same informal and *ad hoc* manner. To expect to do better with a nation whose cleavages run as deeply as do Canada's may be a dangerous conceit.

The difference between formal constitutional change and the forms of change that have marked the development of the Canadian constitution is the difference between doing a crossword puzzle in ink, which is not erasable, and doing it in pencil, which is. If a mistake is made, it can be remedied quickly and easily with the constitutional style that we enjoy in this country. In this way, the constitution can more closely reflect the current values and needs of Canadian society, not the needs of society at the time the constitution was originally written. Our present method of changing the constitution does not require a cumbersome and potentially unjust procedure that serves the values of an earlier age. Canadians may well want to take another close look before they codify the constitution. Fortunately, the near impossibility of getting agreement for change from eleven different governments makes it likely that they will have ample time to do so.

THE ADMINISTRATION OF JUSTICE

In Chapter 5 the concept of the rule of law was introduced as a basic tenet of the Canadian constitution, but little was said there about the nature of law in general or about the origins and characteristics of the Canadian judicial system. In this section it is our intention to describe the structure of the Canadian judiciary and those aspects of the judicial process relevant to the political process as a whole. Because it is law which is the subject-matter of judicial decision making, and because, formally, it is law which constitutes, regulates, or authorizes all allocative outputs of the system, a brief discussion of the law, its nature and origins is an appropriate introduction to this section.[12]

The Nature of Law in Canada
The function of law is to regulate human behaviour. In it broadest context, the law can be viewed as including all rules of human behaviour, whether customary, moral, ethical, or religious, which have application in a given society. However, when one speaks of the law in a modern society, what is usually implied is the positive embodiment of the customary, ethical, moral, and religious values of a society in the form of statutes and judicial decisions. Law in this more formal and positive sense is concrete and explicit in a way that a code of behaviour implicit in customs or moral standards can never be. Furthermore, as Professor J.A. Corry points out, law in the more positive sense can be distinguished from custom and morality by the existence of explicit sanctions and positive means for enforcement:

> . . .what distinguishes law from custom and morality is the additional sanction of sheriffs, bailiffs, police, jails and armed forces to be called into operation if needed to coerce the stubborn. . .[13]

For the purposes of this analysis, a narrow rather than broad definition of law has been chosen.

To perform effectively the function of providing guidelines for human behaviour in a society, the law must be *knowable*. In other words, people must be able to discover the standards of behaviour their society is imposing on them in order to be able to comply with those standards. The law must also be applied in a way which is predictable for the citizen. If he is to be capable of adjusting his behaviour so that it conforms to the requirements of the law, not only must he be aware of the broad principles embodied in the law, but he must also be able to predict the way in which the law will apply to him personally.[14]

The law in Canada can be said to consist primarily of statutes and judicial decisions. The former are enactments of the lawmaking institutions of the political system. They are the products of legislatures—in the strictest sense of that word. But while there is a large annual output of legislation today, legislatures do no more than add to or make alterations in a vast body of law which is already in existence and which is derived largely from other sources.[15] The bulk of the law is to be found not primarily in legislation, but in myriad judicial decisions which reflect a society's moral,

[12]See Chapter 5 for a discussion of the principle of judicial independence and Chapter 7 for a discussion of the role of the Courts in interpreting the BNA Act.
[13]Corry and Hodgetts, *Democratic Government and Politics*, p. 424.
[14]See Chapter 5 for discussion of the principle of the rule of law.
[15]Corry and Hodgetts, *op. cit.*, p. 423.

ethical, religious, and customary foundations far better than the specific enactments of any legislature. In this sense, the law is incremental. It is a body of principles that have been accumulated over time and modified as the values of the society have changed—modified subtly through minute judicial reinterpretations, and from time to time modified more explicitly by legislation.

While the law is a growing thing, its growth is controlled rather than random. The element of control in Canada is injected through the *rule of precedent*, or the principle of *stare decisis*. The basic principle of the rule of precedent is that judges, when making a decision today, take into account the decisions of previous courts in similar cases in the past. Precedents can be of two types: *binding* or *persuasive*. Professor Lederman points out that the former type of precedent exists where:

> . . .within any particular system of judicature the lower courts in the hierarchy are bound to follow the rules previously used to decide sufficiently similar cases in the higher court or courts of the hierarchy. . .[16]

Thus, in the Canadian system, decisions by higher courts are binding on lower courts in the same judicial hierarchy. However, the question as to whether a court is bound by its own precedents is dependent mainly on the court itself; a court can choose to consider itself bound by its own precedents or it can choose not to be so bound. The Supreme Court of Canada and, before 1949, the Judicial Committee of the Privy Council have chosen not to be strictly bound by their own precedents. The practice of both these courts of final appeal, however, indicates that a previous decision has a great deal of persuasive force in helping them to decide current cases, and it is seldom indeed that the Supreme Court of Canada reverses the stand it took in a previous case:

> . . .even though a court regards its own previous decisions as persuasive only, they turn out to be so highly persuasive that the distinction from a binding precedent becomes rather dim. . . .[17]

The Canadian legal system stems from two quite distinct legal traditions: one is rooted in the Roman law and the other in the English common law. Roman law is codified in the form of general rules and principles which must be applied to each case individually. It is Roman law which was adopted in varying forms throughout Western Europe at the time of the Renaissance. The settlers of New France naturally brought with them the laws of their mother country, so it is in the Province of Quebec that the Roman legal tradition is still to some extent reflected. The English common law is based on "the common custom of the realm"[18] as interpreted by judges. In other words, the common law is derived from judicial precedents that build on earlier precedents, and so on. It is not codified;[19] rather

[16]W.R. Lederman, "The Common Law System in Canada," in E. McWhinney (ed.), *Canadian Jurisprudence: The Civil Law and Common Law in Canada*, (Carswell, Toronto, 1958), p. 36.
[17]Lederman, "The Common Law System in Canada," p. 37.
[18]Corry and Hodgetts, *op. cit.*, p. 428.
[19]Note that parts of the common law are codified from time to time in various statutes such as the Criminal Code, the Landlord and Tenant Act, etc.

it is a set of principles merely implicit in the judicial decisions of England. The common law came to Canada via the early English settlers and was even partially introduced into Quebec through the Conquest. Today in Quebec, *private law* (or *civil law*) is based on the *Code civil du Québec* which is derived from the French *Code Napoléon*, whereas in the other Canadian provinces private law is based on the English common law. Criminal law in Canada is uniform across the country, being based on the Canadian Criminal Code which in turn is derived almost exclusively from the principles of English criminal jurisprudence. The main reason for establishing a uniform criminal code for all of Canada was the belief, rightly or wrongly, that English criminal procedures with their guarantees of innocence until proven guilty, etc., were superior to the French system. From the foregoing, it will be seen that the Canadian legal system is a unique reflection of the duality of the Canadian political culture.

The Judicial System[20] Because Canada is a federal political system, it is only natural that the Canadian judicial system should reflect federalism in its basic structure. By contrast to the U.S., however, where the federal and state courts exist separately from each other in vertically parallel hierarchies each with its distinct jurisdiction, the Canadian system of courts divides provincial and federal court jurisdictions horizontally.[21] The course of litigation in the United States may begin in either a federal or a state court and can normally be appealed only to the top of the particular hierarchy. For example, in the United States criminal law is primarily a state matter, and most criminal cases are tried only in state courts.[22] For such cases the final court of appeal is normally the supreme court of the state. There is no appeal from the supreme court of the state to the Supreme Court of the U.S. in state criminal matters, except where the issue can be couched in constitutional terms. In Canada, by contrast, while there are separate provincial and federal courts, the eventual course of litigation may move from provincial courts to a final appeal at the level of the Supreme Court of Canada. However, this statement cannot be made without qualification, for certain matters are not considered important enough to be appealable to the Supreme Court of Canada as of right. The appellate jurisdiction of the Supreme Court of Canada will be discussed in more detail below.

Not only are the various provincial and federal courts integrated in terms of jurisdiction but they are also integrated to some extent through the process of appointment set down in the BNA Act. Sections 96 to 100 provide for the appointment, removal and salaries of all superior, county and district court judges in the provinces. The judges of these provincial courts are all appointed and paid by the federal government. Federal court judges, naturally, are also appointed by the federal government, and

[20]Our research in this area was made simpler by the kind assistance of Professors Dick Abbott, Don Fraser, and King McShane, of the Department of Law at Carleton University. All errors and omissions are the responsibility of the authors alone.
[21]See ss. 92(14), 96–101 of the BNA Act, 1867.
[22]There are as well in the U.S., "federal crimes," which are tried in federal courts.

it is only the lesser provincial court judges who are appointed and remunerated by the provincial governments. In describing the jurisdiction and functions of the various provincial courts, the discussion will be limited to the Province of Ontario. While other provinces differ from Ontario in various ways, the judicial systems of all the Canadian provinces are similar and there is not sufficient room to discuss each individually.

The Provincial Judicial System[23] The lowest level of the judicial hierarchy in Ontario is the *Justice of the Peace*. A Justice of the Peace is appointed by the province—formally by the Lieutenant-Governor in Council—and holds office "at pleasure." There are no specific qualifications for the office and no retirement age is set.[24] The jurisdiction of a Justice of the Peace is usually territorially limited to the municipality or judicial district for which he is appointed. Within that territory, he is permitted to administer oaths, take affirmations and declarations, and try prosecutions under municipal by-laws. Under the direction of a Provincial Judge, a Justice of the Peace may also try summary conviction criminal offences. Other powers of a Justice of the Peace include the performing of civil marriages, the quelling of riots, and various procedural powers such as issuing warrants. Appeal from a decision of a Justice of the Peace goes to a Justice of the Supreme Court of Ontario sitting alone. Justices of the Peace in Ontario are currently being phased out and probably all of their functions will ultimately come to be performed by the more highly qualified Provincial Judges who possess the power of Justices of the Peace *ex officio*.

Provincial Judges have taken over the functions previously performed by Justices of the Peace, Magistrates, and Juvenile and Family Court Judges. In fact most Magistrates and Juvenile and Family Court Judges and many Justices of the Peace became Provincial Judges as a matter of course at the passage of the Provincial Courts and Judges Act in 1968.[25]

While there are no specific qualifications for appointment as a Provincial Judge, in order to exercise the criminal jurisdiction conferred upon Magistrates by Part XVI of the Canadian Criminal Code, he must be a member of the bar of one of the provinces, and he must have been acting as a Provincial Judge for at least five years, or he must have been acting as a full-time Magistrate or a Judge of the Juvenile and Family Court before the 1968 legislation was passed.

The Provincial Judges are appointed by the Lieutenant-Governor in Council, although provision is made for consultation with the Judicial Council for Provincial Judges. The Judicial Council was established by the 1968 legislation and is usually composed of representatives of the bench and of the bar. Its functions include consideration of the proposed appointment of Provincial Judges, advising the government, and conducting inquiries respecting complaints brought against judges in respect to their judicial capacity. A judge holds office during good behaviour until age 65,

[23]See Fig. 6–1. We were assisted in the collection of data for this section by William Janzen, a Ph.D. student in the Department of Political Science at Carleton.

[24]The Justices of the Peace Act, *Revised Statutes of S.O. Ontario*, (*RSO*), 1970, c.231; S.O., 1971, c.6.

[25]Provincial Courts Act, *RSO*, 1970, c.269.

with possible reappointment to age 75. He can be removed by the Lieutenant-Governor in Council, but only for misbehaviour or for inability to perform his duties, and then only after a judicial inquiry. The jurisdiction of
Provincial Judges extends throughout Ontario and includes presiding over
either the criminal[26] or the family[27] divisions of the Provincial Courts.

The criminal jurisdiction of Provincial Judges includes summary
conviction trials under certain Ontario statutes and under certain federal
statutes such as the Criminal Code and the Narcotics Control Act, as well
as trial of indictable offences where the accused specifically selects trial by
Provincial Judge. Provincial Judges may also conduct preliminary hearings for indictable offences in which the accused has chosen a jury trial or
trial by Superior Court Judge. Appeal from decisions of the Provincial
Judge is to a County Court Judge or a single judge of the Supreme Court
of the Province. Juvenile and family court jurisdiction of Provincial Judges
extends to both civil and criminal matters where families and/or juveniles
are involved. Appeal is as for a Provincial Court (criminal division) in
criminal matters, and to a County Court Judge or to the Court of Appeal
in civil matters.

Small Claims Courts, formerly known as *Division Courts*,[28] have been established under the Small Claims Court Act[29] in various counties and districts in the province. The judges of these courts are frequently *County Court
Judges* who act in an additional capacity, but in other cases they are judges
appointed by the Lieutenant-Governor in Council specifically as *Small
Claims Court Judges*. The jurisdiction of Small Claims Court Judges is territorially limited to the county or the division for which they were appointed, and is limited in subject matter to civil issues only. Procedure in
these courts is intended to be speedy, inexpensive and informal, and
specifically excludes certain tort actions such as libel, slander, breach of
promise and actions concerning estates of deceased persons. Appeal from a
decision of a Small Claims Court lies with a single judge of the Court of
Appeal, but only if the matter involves a sum of money greater than $200.

There is also a *Surrogate Court*[30] for each county and district of the
Province of Ontario, whose jurisdiction includes most testamentary matters, determination of claims against an estate amounting to less than
$800, the appointment of guardians for the children of the deceased and,
generally, all such matters except interpretation of wills, administration of
estates, and determination of actions for legacies. In all cases in Ontario
the judge acting as *Surrogate Court Judge* is the County or District Court
Judge, although the Lieutenant-Governor in Council is not legally restricted in this regard. Appeal from the Surrogate Court lies to the Court
of Appeal if the property affected amounts to more than $200, and if not,
to a single judge of the High Court of Justice.[31]

[26]Has replaced Magistrates' Courts.
[27]Has replaced Juvenile and Family Courts.
[28]*RSO*, 1970, c.107.
[29]*RSO*, 1970, c.439; S.O. 1972, c.107.
[30]See Surrogate Courts Act, *RSO*, 1970, c.451.
[31]*Ibid.*

County Court Judges[32] are appointed by the Governor General in Council, as provided for by Section 96 of the BNA Act. The courts on which these judges sit, however, are set up by the provinces who are empowered constitutionally to do so through Section 92(14) of the BNA Act which states that the provincial legislature can pass laws regarding:

> The administration of justice in the province, including the constitution, maintenance and organization of provincial courts both of civil and criminal jurisdiction and including procedure in civil matters in those courts. . . .

Thus, while the *County Courts* are provincially administered, the judges themselves are federally appointed and paid. The qualification of a County Court Judge is that he must be a barrister of at least ten years' standing, and his tenure is during good behaviour until age 75. He is removable by the Governor General in Council for various statutory reasons, but only after a commission of inquiry.

The jurisdiction of the County Court Judge includes presiding over the County Court[33] in civil matters, with or without a jury. Basically, the jurisdiction of the County Court includes contract actions and most tort actions when the claim does not exceed $7,500, actions regarding land if the value of the land does not exceed $7,500, partnership actions if the partnership capital does not exceed $50,000, certain actions for legacies and equitable actions if the subject matter involved does not exceed $7,500. It is important to recognize here, however, that the jurisdiction of the County Court is held concurrently with the *Supreme Court of Ontario*, and as a result actions may be commenced above the level of the County Court.

The County Court Judge also sits with a jury in the *Court of General Sessions of the Peace*. This court sits twice yearly in the county seat to hear most indictable criminal offences. *The County Court Judge's Criminal Court*[34] is composed of the County Court Judge sitting alone, and hears cases involving indictable offences where the accused has chosen trial by judge, or "speedy trial". This court also hears appeals from summary convictions by Provincial Judges. Appeals from decisions of the County Court Judge lie generally to the Ontario Court of Appeal with the exception of procedural appeals which can be heard by a single judge of the Supreme Court of the Province.

The Supreme Court of Ontario has two divisions, the *High Court of Justice of Ontario*, which includes the Chief Justice of the High Court and 31 puisne justices,[35] and the *Court of Appeal for Ontario* which includes the Chief Justice of Ontario and nine other justices of appeal. The appointment of all judges of the Supreme Court of Ontario is by the federal government, and while appointment is explicitly to either the High Court or to the Appeals Division, judges may serve in the other division if required. Appointment, as with all superior court judges, is during good behaviour until age

[32]County Court Judges Act, *RSO*, 1970, c.95.
[33]County Courts Act, *RSO*, 1970, c.94, S.O.1971 v.2, c.60.
[34]County Court Judge's Criminal Courts Act, *RSO*, 1970, c.93.
[35]Judicature Act, *RSO*, 1970, c.228.

Figure 6-1

THE CANADIAN JUDICIAL SYSTEM

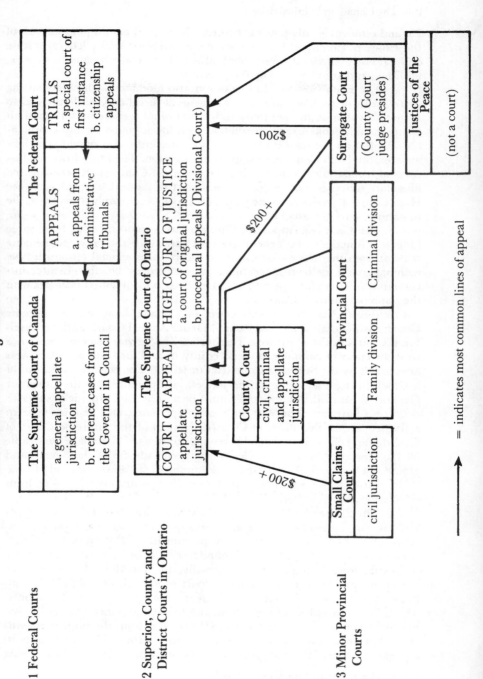

1 Federal Courts

The Federal Court

APPEALS	TRIALS
a. appeals from administrative tribunals	a. special court of first instance
	b. citizenship appeals

The Supreme Court of Canada

a. general appellate jurisdiction

b. reference cases from the Governor in Council

2 Superior, County and District Courts in Ontario

The Supreme Court of Ontario

COURT OF APPEAL	HIGH COURT OF JUSTICE
appellate jurisdiction	a. court of original jurisdiction
	b. procedural appeals (Divisional Court)

County Court

civil, criminal and appellate jurisdiction

Small Claims Court

civil jurisdiction

$200 +

Surrogate Court

(County Court judge presides)

-$200

$200 +

3 Minor Provincial Courts

Provincial Court

Family division	Criminal division

Justices of the Peace

(not a court)

⟶ = indicates most common lines of appeal

75, and removal is only possible by order-in-council after a joint address of the House of Commons and the Senate. Salaries are set by federal statute and paid by the federal government, although the courts themselves are established and administered by the province.

The High Court of Justice of Ontario functions with judges sitting singly, with or without jury, and has general jurisdiction unlimited as to monetary value in all civil matters. The criminal jurisdiction of the High Court includes concurrent jurisdiction with lower courts for most indictable offences, and in the case of the most serious indictable offences, such as murder, the High Court has exclusive jurisdiction. The High Court of Justice has a separate division called the *Divisional Court* which performs the appellate functions not vested in the Court of Appeal. Appeal from the High Court of Justice is to the Court of Appeal and, rarely, directly to the Supreme Court of Canada.[36]

The Court of Appeal of Ontario has a quorum of at least three judges. It functions as a general court of appeal for the province, hearing appeals from the lower courts and from certain provincial administrative tribunals, and delivering opinions on references by the Lieutenant-Governor in Council. Appeal from the Ontario Court of Appeal lies with the Supreme Court of Canada.

Federal Courts[37] Federal courts in Canada include the Supreme Court, the Federal Court, the Court Martial Appeal Court, and the Territorial Courts in the Northwest Territories. *The Supreme Court of Canada* is a superior court of common law and equity in and for Canada, which was established by the Supreme Court Act in 1875.[38] The court is composed of a Chief Justice and eight puisne judges, all appointed by the Governor General in Council. An appointee must be a judge of a provincial superior court or a barrister of at least ten years' experience, and he must take up residence within five miles of Ottawa. Justices of the Supreme Court of Canada hold office during good behaviour until age 75, and are removable by the Governor General in Council on joint address of the Senate and House of Commons. An additional requirement set down explicitly in the Supreme Court Act is that three of the nine judges must be appointed from the Quebec bench or bar.

The Supreme Court sits only in Ottawa and has three sessions per annum. Five judges normally constitute a quorum, except that on applications for leave to appeal, three is a quorum in civil matters. On appeal from the Province of Quebec it is mandatory that at least two of the sitting judges be from that province. Generally, the function of the Supreme Court of Canada is to be a general court of appeal, but usually the Supreme Court hears criminal appeals in the case of a capital offence only. There is an appeal as of right from the highest provincial court in civil matters where the amount exceeds $10,000 and from the highest provincial court on a constitutional reference where provincial law permits it. Appeal by leave of the highest provincial court from decisions of that court

[36]This is known as an "appeal *per saltum.*"
[37]See Fig. 6-1.
[38]*Revised Statutes of Canada*, 1970, c.259 as amended.

in most civil matters is permitted, and appeal by leave of the Supreme Court itself is permitted from final judgments of the highest court of the province, except in criminal matters.[39] The Supreme Court of Canada is also required to give opinions on matters referred to it by the Governor General in Council. In sum, the Supreme Court of Canada has all the powers of a superior court and also, since the abolition of appeals to the Judicial Committee of the Privy Council in 1949, it functions as the final court of appeal for Canada.

The Federal Court, which has replaced the Exchequer Court, was set up by the Federal Court Act, 1970.[40] The Federal Court consists of a court of original jurisdiction, known as the Trial Division, and a court of appeal known as the Appeals Division. The court is composed of a Chief Justice who functions as the president of the Appeals Division, an Associate Chief Justice who functions as the president of the Appeals Division, an Associate Chief Justice who functions as the president of the Trial Division, and up to ten puisne judges. At least three of the ten must be appeal judges and the rest trial judges, and there is an additional requirement that at least four of the Federal Court Judges must be appointed from among members of the bar or bench of the Province of Quebec.

The basic requirements for appointment to the Federal Court are the same as for the Supreme Court of Canada, and tenure is during good behaviour until age 70. While appointments are specifically to either the Trial or the Appeal Division, all judges are ex officio members of the division to which they were not appointed.

The original jurisdiction of the Federal Court includes matters involving claims against the Crown, intergovernmental actions involving interprovincial or federal–provincial disputes, citizenship appeals, and specific jurisdiction vested in the old Exchequer Court by federal statutes such as the Excise Act, Customs Act, Income Tax Act, National Defence Act, Patent Act, and Shipping Act.

The jurisdiction of the Federal Court of Appeal includes hearing appeals from the Trial Division of the Federal Court, and review of decisions of federal boards, commissions and tribunals. This latter appellate jurisdiction of the Federal Court is limited, however, to cases where administrative decisions are required by law to be judicial or quasi-judicial, or where the federal board or tribunal has failed to observe the principles of natural justice, has gone beyond its jurisdiction, has made an error in law, or has based its decision on an erroneous finding of fact. Futhermore, the Act provides that there will be no such appeal if other legislation already provides for a statutory appeal to the Treasury Board, the Governor General in Council, or the Supreme Court of Canada; nor are decisions of the Governor in Council or the Treasury Board reviewable by the Federal Court. These particular limitations on the appellate jurisdiction of the Federal Court Act have been subjected to some criticism from the legal profession as being regressive and contrary to the generally liberalizing effect of the legislation as a whole. Whether these so-called "privitive

[39]See Revised Statutes of Canada, 1970, c.259, ibid.
[40]Revised Statutes of Canada, 1970, c.10.

clauses" in the Act will actually prove to be detrimental to the overall operation of the court remains to be seen. It will probably depend as much on the attitude that the courts, the boards and the tribunals take to the privitive clauses as it will on the wording of the legislation itself.

Decisions of the Federal Court of Appeal are appealable to the Supreme Court of Canada as of right where the matter in controversy exceeds $10,000. Other than this general provision, an appeal to the Supreme Court of Canada lies by leave of the Supreme Court itself, or by the leave of the Federal Court of Appeal. Finally, an appeal lies automatically to the Supreme Court where the dispute is interprovincial or federal–provincial in nature.

Reform of the Supreme Court of Canada   The Supreme Court of Canada has been subject to much criticism since its creation in 1875, and has narrowly escaped abolition at several periods in its history. However, since the abolition of appeals to the Judicial Committee of the Privy Council in 1949, when the Supreme Court of Canada became the final court of appeal for Canada, its position in the Canadian political system has been secure. The question now is not whether Canada needs a Supreme Court, but rather how the existing one can be improved. Much of the criticism of the Supreme Court (which applies equally to the higher provincial courts) has been levelled at the method of appointment of the judges, which is based, quite frankly, on partisan considerations. This does not usually mean that a Liberal government will appoint a bad lawyer to the bench just because he is a Liberal, but rather that the government will find a good lawyer who is also a Liberal and give him the appointment.

Basically, the argument against appointments to the bench which take into account party affiliation is that such a method of appointment goes contrary to the principle of an independent judiciary which is so crucial to our legal system.[41] A few exploratory studies of judicial behaviour indicate that judges usually take characteristic and predictable stands when particular issues are involved,[42] and further, that no judge is ever really independent in an absolute way, for he is influenced making his decisions by all sorts of personal biases, so that he tends to interpret the law in such a way that his decision is congruent with his own set of values. However, none of these studies have indicated that there is a positive correlation in Canada between the stand a judge takes on issues and the tenets of the political party which appointed him to the bench.

Suggestions for reform of the method of appointment of judges are twofold. In the first place, most legal experts feel that judges should be selected with some participation on the part of the existing bench, the Canadian Bar Association, or both. In other words, in order to get the best judges, the selection should be made not so much by a non-partisan body, as by a body of experts which has some knowledge about the requirements

[41]See Chapter 5.
[42]D.E. Fouts, "Policy Making in the Supreme Court of Canada, 1950–60," and S.R. Peck, "A Scalogram Analysis of the Supreme Court of Canada, 1958–67," in G. Schubert and D.J. Danelski (eds.), *Comparative Judicial Behaviour*, (Oxford University Press, Toronto, 1969), pp. 257–334.

and qualifications of a good judge.[43] Secondly, because most courts of first instance in our legal system are provincial, some critics argue that vacancies in provincial Superior, District and County Courts should be filled by the province and not by the federal government. The former of these suggestions for reform could be achieved informally, by simply co-opting the Canadian Bar Association into the selection process while continuing to make the formal appointment as provided in Sections 96 to 101 of the BNA Act. In order to implement the latter type of reform, however, an amendment to Sections 96 to 100 of the BNA Act would be required. Amendment to the BNA Act, as we have seen, is a difficult business at best, and before altering these critical sections of the Act, it would be wise to consider more carefully how switching the locus of such appointments from the federal level to the provincial would affect the principle of judicial independence.

Other than the appointment procedure, the major criticism of the Canadian judicial system has focused on the jurisdiction of the Supreme Court of Canada. Particularly in the Province of Quebec it is felt that appeals from the highest court in the province to the Supreme Court in matters involving the *Code Civil du Québec* are unjust. The Supreme Court of Canada, although it includes three civil code judges, functions predominantly as a common law court, and as such it is felt that it should not have the power to overturn decisions of the highest court of Quebec in civil matters.

Finally, it is argued that the Supreme Court of Canada should not have both general appeal jurisdiction and jurisdiction to settle constitutional matters. The feeling is that the Supreme Court of Canada should become a final Court of Appeal only in constitutional matters, and that either another court should be vested with final appeal jurisdiction in non-constitutional matters or the final appeal in such matters should rest with the provinces. The argument against this latter suggestion is that if there is to be uniformity of law throughout Canada there should be a system whereby provincial supreme courts are all subjected to a common source of precedent flowing from a higher court. If the current government makes good its long-standing promise to rewrite the Canadian constitution in its entirety, all of these matters will have to be considered in very great detail.

CIVIL LIBERTIES IN CANADA

Unlike the United States, Canada does not have an "entrenched" Bill of Rights, although Canadians enjoy basically the same fundamental rights and freedoms as Americans. The primary constitutional source of Canadian civil liberties is the preamble to the BNA Act which states that we are to have a constitution similar in principle to that of the U.K. Consequently, because the U.K. has no entrenched Bill of Rights, the actual extent of the rights and freedoms of Canadians is enshrined only in the many

---

[43]Note that the Judicial Council in Ontario to some extent performs this function with respect to the appointment of Provincial Judges.

centuries of British legal tradition—a fact which, while not a restriction on our liberties, makes them difficult to define precisely. Before proceeding to attempt to describe the basic rights and freedoms of Canadians, it is necessary to add a note to explain the terms involved.

Rights, Freedoms, and Liberties[44]   For the purposes of this discussion it will be assumed that the terms *liberties* and *freedoms* are synonymous. However, it is not as easy to dismiss distinctions between the terms *right* and *liberty*. In their broadest sense, *civil rights* and *civil liberties* can be viewed as meaning basically the same thing, the former term being more common in the U.S. and the latter being more popular in the U.K. and Canada. In Canada, however, the term "civil rights", as used in Section 92(13) of the BNA Act and throughout extensive judicial interpretation, is closely connected not only with individuals' rights, but also with rights that accrue through property and through contract. It is better therefore to avoid the term "civil rights" when referring to fundamental political freedoms.

In 1953, while delivering a judgement on a case involving the principle of religious freedom, Mr. Justice Ivan C. Rand attempted to clarify the distinction between civil rights and civil liberties. He assumed that every man, simply by virtue of being a man, has a total area of freedom, the limits of which are defined only by his physical strength, mental capacity, etc. However, by virtue of being a member of a community which makes rules to which he must adhere, a man gives up a certain percentage of his absolute, or original, freedom. Each piece of positive law, therefore, limits the individual's freedom by creating some sort of obligation to obey that law. For example, a law prohibiting patricide creates an obligation in all sons not to kill their fathers, thus restricting the absolute freedom of sons. Conversely, however, such a law creates a right in all fathers not to be killed by their sons. The positive law therefore creates rights and obligations out of the existing area of absolute freedom.[45]

To return to our definitions, civil rights, in the purest sense of the term, are created through the enactment of positive laws, while civil liberties are the residual area of freedom left to an individual after the totality of the positive law is subtracted from it. However, as Professor Tarnopolsky has pointed out, most fundamental freedoms are in fact "beefed up" by the positive law.[46] By way of example, he cites religious freedom:

> In those terms, then, we speak of 'freedom of worship,' but only as defined

[44]See W.S. Tarnopolsky, *The Canadian Bill of Rights*, (Carswell, Toronto, 1966), pp. 1–3.
[45]See Saumur v. City of Quebec, (1953) 2 *Supreme Court Reports*, (*SCR*), p. 329.
[46]Note here that an entrenched and comprehensive Bill of Rights might be conceived of as replacing all residual freedoms with positive rights. Whatever the semantic difficulties with such a formulation of the terms, the effect would still be essentially to entrench certain freedoms once and for all behind a set of positive law barriers. In fact the effect is to create a "right to a set of freedoms," whereby the existing residue of individual freedom is protected from any further encroachment by the positive law.

by law, and not including such practices as human sacrifice, for example. Such a freedom can also be protected by law, for instance, by forbidding unlawful interference with the conduct of a religious service. . . .[47]

Another more current example of the evolution or development of a positive right out of an area of residual freedom might be occurring in the area of *privacy*. The foundation of a "right to privacy" likely lies in tradition and in the common law (a man's home is his castle). Violations of privacy on the part of private individuals are viewed as trespassing, and encroachments even by governmental officials such as the police require significant justification and some level of judicial involvement such as a warrant. However, most of the original tenets of a common law right to privacy involve only the physical or *territorial* dimension of privacy, which is related to the law of property.

Modern electronic technology has created a situation where *information* concerning an individual can be gathered, collated and retrieved with frightening efficiency. It has been recognized that the common law protections of the right to territorial privacy have to be backed up by legislation to protect the informational privacy of individuals from unscrupulous business enterprises and governmental agencies as well. The positive law response to this new threat to individual freedom has been legislation limiting the operation of consumer credit "ratings", and imposing strict limits on the use of electronic surveillance devices, by both public and private organizations. The result is that a previously unrecognized and unnecessary "right to privacy" is being defined incrementally, through a series of positive law enactments.

Finally, the point should be made here that an empirical distinction can be made between civil rights and civil liberties. The former tend to be concerned primarily with individual-to-individual relationships, whereas the latter tend to be concerned with individual-to-state relationships. Civil liberties are thus more frequently viewed as freedom from interference or restriction by the political system, and civil rights are viewed as protecting an individual from being discriminated against by another individual (as in the Civil Rights Bill in the U.S.).

Civil Liberties: What Are They? There are several implications which derive from the fact that the BNA Act gives Canada a constitution similar in principle to that of the U.K. Because the constitution of the U.K. reflects, or did reflect in 1867, primarily liberal democratic values, Canada also has a constitution which is democratic and predominantly liberal. Fundamental freedoms or civil liberties in Canada, therefore, can be related to either liberal values or democratic values.[48]

Democratic Freedoms These include both substantive freedoms and procedural rights, and are implicit in and necessary to a democratic system of government. The democratic freedoms are instrumental in realizing

---

[47]W.S. Tarnopolsky, *The Canadian Bill of Rights*, (Carswell, Toronto, 1966), p.2.
[48]Note here that the constitution of the U.K. is also parliamentary in form. The implications of this in terms of the supremacy of parliament are discussed in the following chapter.

the basic democratic value of political equality, and they function by setting limits on governmental interference with the individual. The substantive democratic freedoms in Canada include freedom of association, freedom of assembly, freedom of expression, freedom of conscience and freedom of the press.

The procedural rights include freedom from arbitrary arrest, right to a fair hearing, right to counsel and the right of *habeas corpus*. Moreover, they have come to include the rules of evidence which, in judicial proceedings, determine the admissability of evidence and the determination of privileged information. As a "right to privacy" becomes more clearly articulated, the procedural right will likely be expanded to include protection from invasions of informational privacy through electronic eavesdropping etc. These procedural rights institutionalize the rule of law, insure "equality before the law" for all individuals, and prevent arbitrariness and discrimination on the part of governmental officials.

Liberal Freedoms   These are implicit in the values of liberalism, but not necessarily in the values of democracy. Where the democratic freedoms are negative, being freedom *from* government interference or hindrance, the liberal freedoms are positive, giving individuals freedom *to* do many things. In large part these liberal freedoms deal with the individual's rights in regard to property and contract, including the right to own property, the right not to be deprived thereof except through due process of law, and the freedom of contract. While it is difficult to separate liberal freedoms from democratic freedoms in a country whose values are "liberal–democratic", a possible distinction is that the former are very closely tied up with the economic system of capitalism. The liberal freedoms are therefore more important in achieving the liberal goal of a free economy than they are in achieving the democratic goals of popular sovereignty and political equality.

Egalitarian Freedoms   These are the so called "human rights" which are instrumental in achieving the goals of social and economic equality. Stated in the extreme, liberal and egalitarian freedoms tend to conflict with each other, although in fact in Canada, there is gradual acceptance of limitations on the liberal freedoms to promote human rights. While the egalitarian freedoms would certainly restrict governmental discrimination against classes of individuals, they also involve individual-to-individual relationships, and include freedom from discrimination in employment, accommodation, transportation, etc., by reason of race, religion, ethnic origin, or nationality.

To an extent that has never been clearly defined, basic economic egalitarian rights also exist in Canada. These are defined in the Universal Declaration of Human Rights of the United Nations:

> Every one has the right to rest and leisure, including reasonable limitation of working hours and periodic holidays with pay. . . .
>
> Everyone has the right to a standard of living adequate for the health and wellbeing of himself and of his family, including food, clothing, housing and medical care, and necessary social services and the right to security in the event of unemployment, sickness, disability, widowhood, old age, or other lack of livelihood in circumstance beyond his control.

Motherhood and childhood are entitled to special care and assistance. All children, whether born in or out of wedlock, shall enjoy the same social protection. . . .Everyone had the right to education. . . .[49]

Most Canadians would agree that these are indeed basic human rights, and there are many legislative enactments in this country that reflect a willingness on the part of the authorities to recognize that such human rights are fundamental. However, while the egalitarian freedoms are becoming more and more important values in Canadian society, the written parts of the Canadian constitution and even the Bill of Rights (which recognizes the freedom from discrimination) nowhere states the principles of economic equality found in the U.N. *Universal Declaration of Human Rights*.

Civil Liberties: How Are They Protected? Before speaking of the specific legal guarantees of civil liberties in Canada, it is necessary to point out that such enactments may provide merely illusory protection. If the values reflected in the statutory and common law statements defining our civil liberties are not congruent with the prevalent modes of thought and attitudes in the society at large, such laws will have little real effect on our substantive freedom. The best guarantee of fundamental freedoms in society, therefore, is a consensus in the society as to what they are.

Distribution of Legislative Jurisdiction Over Civil Liberties The principle of the supremacy of parliament, which is discussed in some detail in Chapter 5, means that nothing is beyond the legislative competence of parliament. A majority of the members of parliament can abrogate or abolish any civil liberties they wish to, at least in strict legal terms. Naturally, the normative limitations on this sort of legislative behaviour are very real, and because Canada is a federal system,[50] there are further limitations as well. The BNA Act ostensibly divides up all legislative power between the federal and provincial levels. The power to alter or to clarify the substance or extent of civil liberties is therefore also divided between the federal parliament and the provincial legislatures.

Section 92(13) gives the provincial legislature the power to legislate upon matters dealing with "property and civil rights in the province," but because the exact scope of civil rights and liberties in this country is not clear to begin with, the exact parameters of this "civil rights power" have had to be defined in piecemeal fashion as various civil liberties cases arose. Some of the earliest of these involved the discriminatory treatment of orientals by certain laws in the province of British Columbia. In *Union Colliery Company of B.C.* v. *Bryden* (1899),[51] provincial legislation which prohibited orientals from working in underground mines was declared invalid, not on the grounds that it was discriminatory, but because it interfered with the federal government's exclusive power to pass laws regarding "naturaliza-

---

[49]*The Universal Declaration of Human Rights*, Articles 24, 25, 26.
[50]See Chapters 7 and 8.
[51]R.A. Olmsted (ed.), *Judicial Committee Decisions Relating to the British North America Act, 1867*, vol. 1, (Queen's Printer, Ottawa, 1954), p. 443.

tion and aliens."[52] Four years later, British Columbia legislation denying naturalized Canadians of Japanese extraction the right to vote in provincial elections was upheld. The Judicial Committee of the Privy Council decided that it was quite within the rights of the B.C. legislature, through Section 92(1) "amendment of the provincial constitution," to pass laws, even discriminatory ones, relating to the provincial franchise:

> . . .the policy or impolicy of such an enactment as that which excludes a particular race from the franchise is not a topic which their lordships are entitled to consider. . . .[53]

Thus, early decisions relating to civil liberties were viewed entirely in terms of deciding which level of government had the power to interfere with them and never whether *any* government should in fact have such power. This passive or literal approach to judicial interpretation has plagued Canadian constitutional development throughout history,[54] and it has been particularly restrictive in the area of civil liberties.

An initial breakthrough in this area was made by Chief Justice Duff in the *Alberta Press Bill* case (1938). The "Press Bill" was declared to be *ultra vires* of the province because it was dependent upon the Alberta Social Credit Act which had already been invalidated by Duff. However, the bold law making that emerged from this case was the byproduct of a judicial "aside" (*obiter dictum*) which was not central to deciding the case and so could not become established as binding precedent until reinforced by further decisions. The substance of the "Duff Doctrine" established in this aside is based on the preamble to the BNA Act, which states that Canada shall have a system similar in principle to that of Great Britain. This in turn implies parliamentary democracy which ". . .contemplates a parliament working under the influence of public opinion, and public discussion. . . ."[55] and in effect accepts as axiomatic that ". . .the right of free public discussion of public affairs, notwithstanding its incidental mischiefs, is the breath of life for parliamentary institutions. . . ."[56] Consequently, Chief Justice Duff held that:

> . . .the parliament of Canada possesses authority to legislate for the protection of this right. . . .That authority rests upon the principle that the powers requisite for the protection of the constitution itself are by necessity implications from the BNA Act as a whole [Fort Frances Case (1923) A.C.695] and since the subject matter in relation to which the power is exercised is not exclusively a provincial matter, it is necessarily vested in Parliament. . . .[57]

Thus, while Duff did not say that such interference with a fundamental democratic freedom was beyond the competence of all legislatures, in stating that it was beyond the power of the province he definitely left the door

[52]BNA Act, Section 91(25).
[53]Cunningham v. Tomey Homma, (1903), Olmsted, *op. cit.*, vol. 1, p. 484. See also Quong Wing v. King, (1916) 49 *SCR*, 440.
[54]See Chapter 7.
[55]"Reference Re Alberta Statutes," (1939) *SCR*, 100 at p. 133.
[56]*Ibid.*, p. 133.
[57]*Ibid.*, p. 134.

open for future judges to view such matters as beyond the competence of the federal parliament as well. Perhaps more important, Duff stated once and for all that any limitation on the democratic freedoms should not be applied unequally in different provinces.

The federal–provincial distribution of the legislative power to limit the extent of civil liberties was further developed in two important cases in the fifties. In the earlier of these, *Saumur* v. *City of Quebec*,[58] the validity of a city by-law which prohibited the distribution of religious pamphlets on the streets without a special permit was challenged. The legislation was declared to be valid in lower courts and in the Supreme Court of the province, but the decision was finally overturned by a narrow 5 to 4 margin on appeal to the Supreme Court of Canada. In the judgment, four of the justices of the Supreme Court held that the Quebec by-law dealt merely with regulation and control of city streets, and therefore was valid. One judge, who had the deciding vote as it turned out, held that the city by-law conflicted with existing provincial legislation (the Freedom of Worship Act) and was therefore invalid. He went on to declare, however, that the power to restrict freedom of religion was quite within the jurisdiction of the provincial government. The remaining four justices, among them Mr. Justice Ivan C. Rand, held that the city by-law was invalid because it interfered with the freedom of religious expression. Utilizing the preamble of the BNA Act and the "Duff Doctrine" to varying degrees in their judgments, these four judges went on to declare that legislation interfering with a freedom as fundamental as freedom of religion was beyond the competence of a provincial legislature.

In the second important civil liberties case in the fifties, *Switzman* v. *Elbling*, the *Padlock* case,[59] legislation of the Province of Quebec which banned the propagation of "Communism and Bolshevism" by closing up and padlocking any premises used for those purposes, was declared invalid. While the province claimed that it was legislation dealing with "property and civil rights in the province" and therefore within its jurisdiction by section 92(13) of the BNA Act, the majority of the Supreme Court of Canada declared that the subject matter of the impugned legislation involved primarily criminal law which is an exclusive federal area [Section 91(27)]. However, in a minority but concurring judgment, Rand, Abbott and Kellock, three of our more "liberal" judges, held the act to be invalid because the provinces were not empowered to restrict the basic democratic freedom, freedom of opinion, which is implicit in the preamble to the BNA Act and in the "Duff Doctrine." They argued that such legislation could only be enacted by the federal parliament. Mr. Justice Abbott even went further than this in an *obiter dictum*, stating that such fundamental freedoms were possibly even beyond encroachment by the federal parliament, although there is little indication that subsequent courts have had any intention of following his lead.[60]

Thus, through a number of cases dealing with restrictive provincial

---

[58](1953) 2 *SCR*, 299.
[59](1957) *SCR* 356.
[60]Note, however that Mr. Justice Abbott reiterated his stand in a dissenting judg-

laws, the courts have begun to sort out the federal–provincial distribution of legislative power with regard to civil liberties. Through the federal power in the area of naturalization and aliens,[61] the criminal law power,[62] and the preamble to the BNA Act, the federal parliament has been declared to have jurisdiction over many aspects of civil liberties. However, in the *Tomey Homma* case, the provinces were declared to have the power to discriminate against people on the basis of their racial origins, with respect to the right to vote; and in the *Saumur* case, a majority of the Supreme Court of Canada admitted that the provinces have the right to restrict freedom of religion. Thus, today the protection of these civil liberties lies entirely with the individual provinces. British Columbia has long since abolished its discriminatory practices and has guaranteed fundamental freedoms,[63] and while there is by no means uniformity from province to province, there seems to be a general agreement in all provinces that certain rights and freedoms are too fundamental to be tampered with by any government.

Because of this vague consensus, legislative abrogation of substantive democratic freedoms by the provinces has been rare in recent years. However, the record in terms of procedural rights and freedoms has not been as clean. There have been many specific cases, particularly in the Province of Quebec, of violation of basic procedural rights such as *habeas corpus* and freedom from arbitrary arrest,[64] and many provincial laws exist which provide for rather arbitrary search and seizure at the discretion of the police.[65] Nevertheless, with the press and the public ever more aware of their rights and freedoms, it seems likely that such abuses will occur less and less frequently, except when governments can manage to convince their citizens that special circumstances prevail. The sanction against repressive laws is a public opinion which is opposed to them. The danger lies either in the public's ceasing to pay much attention to the government, thus letting repressive legislation slip by unnoticed, or in the majority's coming to approve of laws which suppress the democratic freedoms of minorities.

  The Canadian Bill of Rights The focus of the discussion up until now has been on the distribution of legislative jurisdiction in the area of civil liberties, and on the civil liberties record of the provinces. Now it is time to consider a specific federal statute which purports to protect many of our fundamental freedoms, the Canadian Bill of Rights, passed in 1960.

  The Canadian Bill of Rights is divided into two parts. Part I begins

ment in Oil, Chemical and Atomic Workers International Ltd. v. Imperial Oil Ltd. and A–G for B.C. (1963) *SCR*, 584.

[61]See also Winner v. SMT, (1951) *SCR*, 887

[62]See also Birks and Sons v. City of Montreal, (1955) *SCR*, 799.

[63]For a list of federal and provincial legislation protecting human rights, see P.E. Trudeau, *A Canadian Charter of Human Rights*, (Queen's Printer, Ottawa, 1968), appendix IX.

[64]Ontario, Royal Commission Inquiry into Civil Rights, *Report*, vol. 1, (Queen's Printer, Toronto, 1968), passim.

[65]See for instance, Chaput v. Romain, (1955) *SCR*, 834; Lamb v. Benoit, (1959) *SCR*, 321.

with a list of "the human rights and fundamental freedoms" that exist in Canada, "without discrimination by reason of race, national origin, colour, religion, or sex," and includes such things as property rights, equality before the law, freedom of religion, freedom of speech, freedom of assembly and association, and freedom of the press. The second section of Part I provides that "no law shall be construed or applied so as to" infringe certain basic procedural rights such as freedom from arbitrary arrest, freedom from cruel punishment, right to a fair trial, right to an interpreter, the right to be presumed innocent until proven guilty in criminal proceedings, the right to *habeas corpus* and to counsel, and the right to choose not to testify against oneself. The third section of Part I provides that the Minister of Justice must certify that each piece of draft legislation is consistent with the provisions of the Bill of Rights before it is introduced in the House of Commons.

Part II of the Bill states some limitations on the effect of the provisions in Part I. First, nothing in Part I can be interpreted so as to limit a right or freedom that existed before the Bill of Rights was passed. Secondly, Part I of the Bill is to apply to federal legislation only. It has no effect on legislation passed by the provinces which is within the competence of their legislatures according to the BNA Act. Thirdly, Part II provides explicitly that:

> Any act or thing done or authorized or any order or regulation made under the authority of [the War Measures Act] shall be deemed not to be an abrogation, abridgement, or infringement of any right or freedom recognized by the Canadian Bill of Rights. . . .

The effect of this last is that the "human rights and fundamental freedoms" enumerated in the Bill of Rights become inoperative when the federal government decides that a state of national emergency exists and invokes the War Measures Act.

Whether such emergency procedures can ever be justified in a democratic political system is a question that can only be answered on a trial and error basis. Great injustices were done to Canadians of Japanese origin during World War II simply because Canada was at war with Japan.[66] In retrospect, this seems a shameful blot on the civil liberties record of Canada, although at the time the government's action under the War Measures Act was probably condoned by nearly everyone except the Japanese Canadians themselves.[67] A similar situation may be developing with respect to the proclamation of the War Measures Act in the fall of 1970 because of unusual circumstances in the Province of Quebec. While there was by no means unanimous agreement that the Quebec situation required such drastic measures, it would appear that a sizeable proportion of the Canadian population was at the time in agreement with the government's move. It seems likely, however, that after the "crisis" has faded, many Canadians will look back on the FLQ emergency with something of the same sense of sheepishness with which we now regard the treatment of the Japanese Canadians in 1942.

[66]See (1946) *SCR*, 248 ("The Japanese Canadians Case").
[67]While many Canadians, particularly the CCF party, consistently opposed the

The only conclusion to which one can come in this regard is that if a comprehensive emergency power is to be vested in the government and if that emergency power is to be exercised unilaterally at the discretion of the government, the public must be aware of the anti-democratic potential in such procedures.

The more fundamental question here, however, is whether a political system can permit legislation such as the War Measures Act and remain "democratic." If it is possible to conceive of circumstances when fundamental freedoms may be abrogated, then perhaps those freedoms are not so fundamental after all. Possibly, even in so-called democratic systems, the stability and survival of the system becomes a more fundamental value than the substantive values implicit in the specific regime. Democratic systems are thus caught in a dilemma: on the one hand, if they do not take severe and arbitrary measures under certain circumstances they might be taken over and replaced by an undemocratic regime; on the other hand, by taking such measures they will be *ipso facto* less democratic themselves. There is no easy answer to this problem, but it is critical to an appraisal of the protection of civil liberties in Canada to ask the question.

Another restriction on the effectiveness of the Bill of Rights is the implication in Section 2 that the Bill can be bypassed if parliament states explicitly that a law "shall operate notwithstanding the Bill of Rights." While it is likely that parliament will seldom, if ever, actually use this power, the fact that it is written into the Bill of Rights significantly weakens its total impact.

Finally, perhaps the greatest weakness of the Bill of Rights has been the inconsistency of the Supreme Court's interpretation of it. Up until 1970, that Court has taken the general stand that legislation which existed prior to the Bill of Rights and which might on the surface appear to conflict with it must have been intended by Parliament to operate notwithstanding the Bill, or the offending legislation would have been repealed. In 1963, Mr. Justice Ritchie, in delivering the majority opinion of the Supreme Court, stated that the Bill of Rights

> . . .is not concerned with 'human rights and fundamental freedoms' in any abstract sense, but rather with such 'rights and freedoms' as they existed in Canada immediately before the statute was enacted. . .[68]

Furthermore, because the Bill of Rights is in form but another statute of the federal parliament, and because it is stated in very general terms, it is easy for the Courts to interpret it in such a way that other more specific statutes are not repugnant to it.[69]

A single case in 1969 may have altered this conservative trend in interpretation to some extent. In *The Queen* v. *Drybones*,[70] the Supreme Court of Canada declared a section of the *Indian Act* invalid because it de-

treatment of the Japanese Canadians, they were definitely in the minority.
[68]Robertson and Rossetani v. The Queen, (1963) *SCR*, 651, at p.654. Note that Mr. Justice Cartwright dissented in this case and argued that all legislation of the Parliament of Canada was meant to conform to the Bill of Rights.
[69]See: Tarnopolsky, *The Canadian Bill of Rights*, ch.24.
[70]The Queen v. Drybones, (1970) *SCR*, 282.

nied Indians the "equality before the law" which is guaranteed to all Canadians by the Bill of Rights. The rather timid interpretation of the Bill of Rights that the majority of the Court subscribed to in *Robertson and Rossetani* was qualified, and the Court agreed to view the Bill of Rights as having application to laws that existed before 1960. Mr. Ritchie, in delivering the majority judgment, modified his very conservative position in the earlier case and argued that:

> if a law of Canada cannot be sensibly construed and applied, so that it does not abrogate, abridge or infringe one of the rights and freedoms, recognized and declared by the Bill, *then such law is inoperative* 'unless it is expressly declared by an Act of the Parliament of Canada that it shall operate notwithstanding the *Canadian Bill of Rights*'. (p. 294)

The impugned section of the Indian Act was therefore declared to be inoperative because it created an offence which applied only to Indians and not to other classes of Canadian citizens.

However, some of the optimism about the applicability of the Bill of Rights which was generated by the *Drybones* decision has been tempered by a more recent decision of the Supreme Court. In *A-G Canada* v. *Lavell*, the issue involved a section of the Indian Act which provides that an Indian woman who marries a white loses her status as an Indian, whereas an Indian male can marry a white woman and not only is his status unaffected but his wife acquires Indian status. Counsel for the respondent in the appeal held that the relevant sections of the Indian Act were invalid because they constituted discrimination by virtue of sex.

A majority of the Court held that the particular section of the Indian Act was indeed valid because it involved only "the internal regulation of the lives of Indians *on* reserves." The Indian Act in this case does not discriminate between Indians and whites or between men and women, but between Indian men and Indian women, and therefore does not infringe upon the Bill of Rights.[71]

In sum, it would appear that the Supreme Court is ambivalent about the extent to which the Bill of Rights should be interpreted as rendering invalid existing federal legislation. The dilemma faced by the Court would seem to be a product of the various judges' perceptions of the legitimate role of the court rather than their perceptions of the Bill of Rights itself. As Mr. Justice Abbott stated in a dissenting opinion, because the Bill must have been intended as more than ". . .rhetorical window dressing",

> . . .the *Canadian Bill of Rights* has substantially affected the doctrine of the supremacy of Parliament. Like any other statute it can of course be repealed or amended, or a particular law declared to be applicable notwithstanding the provisions of the *Bill*. In form the supremacy of Parliament is maintained but in practice I think that it has been substantially curtailed. In my opinion that result is undesirable, but that is a matter for considera-

[71]For those interested in the detailed arguments presented in this case, both the majority judgment delivered by Mr. Justice Ritchie and a lengthy dissent delivered by Mr. Justice Laskin bear careful reading. The full implications of this case will only be discernable in the way it is applied to future decisions. Unfortunately at the time of this writing, the judgments are available only in mimeo and hence no citation is possible.

tion by Parliament, not the courts. . . .Of one thing I am certain, the *Bill* will continue to supply ample grist to the judicial mills for some time to come.[72]

Thus in the years to come, the impact of the Bill of Rights on existing federal statutes will depend as much upon the conservative/activist balance of the judges on the court as upon the construction and interpretation of the statutes themselves. Whatever the outcome of this ongoing debate, the overall effect of the Bill of Rights and corresponding provincial enactments has been beneficial in that such fundamental statements of our political values serve as symbolic objects of political socialization. Their function is as much to educate as it is to provide binding *de jure* protection of our civil liberties. Finally, the provision in the Bill of Rights that all federal legislation must be screened by the Minister of Justice before being introduced in parliament is a sort of "pre-audit" that may deter the passage of new laws which are contrary to the basic values of the Canadian political culture.

[72]Lavell Case (1974), *SCR*.

Part 3
The Historical
Environment

7

The Historical Context: Constitutional Development and Canadian Federalism

The Dominion of Canada came into existence with the passage of the British North America Act in 1867. Although this historic document is an Act of the parliament of the U.K., it was passed at the request of the British North American colonies themselves. The details of this remarkable piece of legislation were largely based on resolutions that had been put forward jointly by the colonies, and which had been worked out over a number of years of bargaining and compromise at several colonial conferences.[1] Originally, the deliberations had included all of the British North American colonies,[2] but Newfoundland and Prince Edward Island had soon lost their enthusiasm, and it was left to the remaining colonies, Upper and Lower Canada, New Brunswick and Nova Scotia, to come to an agreement on the terms of the union. Once the agreement had been thrashed out, it was a relatively simple matter for the U.K. parliament to put it into the form of a statute, which came into effect on July 1, 1867.

THE HISTORICAL ROOTS OF BRITISH NORTH AMERICAN UNION

In the mid-nineteenth century, as today, the most significant factor of the environment of our political system was the proximity of the United States. In the 1860s, the awareness of this fact was heightened by a number of events which gave people in the British North American colonies cause to fear direct military invasion from the south. At the conclusion of the American Civil War, the Union Army was the most powerful and advanced fighting machine in the world.[3] Furthermore, incidents during the war such as the St. Alban's raid in 1864[4] and the activities of the Brit-

[1]For an account of these see G.P. Browne (ed.), *Documents on the Confederation of British North America*, (Carleton Library, McClelland and Stewart, Toronto, 1969), p. 40.
[2]With the exception of British Columbia.
[3]D. Creighton, *John A. Macdonald*, vol. 1, *The Young Politician*, (Macmillan, Toronto, 1952), pp. 409–410.
[4]See Creighton, *John A. Macdonald*, vol. 1, pp. 385–430 (*passim*); D. Creighton, *The Road to Confederation*, (Macmillan, Toronto, 1964), pp. 194–195.

ish-built Confederate cruiser, the Alabama,[5] had incurred the displeasure of the United States. The American press was advocating the invasion of Canada at the conclusion of the war,[6] and there was a great fear in Canada that the newspapers would arouse sufficient public pressure to convince Congress and the President that it was, indeed, a good idea.

The sense of danger was given concrete justification by the militant activities of an American-based Irish nationalist organization, called the Fenian Brotherhood. The Fenians attracted large numbers of Irish veterans of the Civil War who were happy to re-enlist in this unofficial army in order to free Ireland from "English tyranny".[7] One of the ways in which they hoped to achieve this was by conquering Canada as a base for fighting the Irish Revolution, and their sundry pronouncements and the publicity that they gained were received with trepidation in Canada. The subsequent "invasions" of British North America by the Fenians were, in retrospect, more comic-opera than genuine threats, and all were repulsed by the Canadians without serious difficulty. But while the menace that the Fenians presented to Canada was exaggerated, when it was added to the existing "evidence" of an American predisposition to continental imperialism it did reinforce Canadian perceptions of a military threat from the south.[8]

While Canadians grew increasingly alarmed at the sabre-rattling in the United States, the British, who had the responsibility for defending their North American colonies, began to give every indication that they were no longer willing to go very far in the enterprise. Politicians in the U.K. began to speak of the necessity of shifting the responsibility for colonial defence to the colonies, and the U.K. cabinet was not overly generous in its budgeting for such things as the fortifications of Quebec. Thus, while the Canadians were looking apprehensively at the military might of the U.S., "There was remarkably little evidence of a sense of acute peril, of desperate urgency, in Great Britain;. . . ."[9]

Economic factors also helped in setting the stage for Confederation. Again, the United States played a starring role. The economic problems of the British North American colonies actually date back to 1846 when the Navigation Laws that gave preferential treatment to colonial trade were repealed by the U.K. However, the negative effects of this had been offset somewhat at the time by a reciprocity agreement with the U.S. which allowed Canadian primary products duty-free access to the U.S. markets. In the 1860s, partly because of generally bad Anglo-American relations and

[5]See Creighton, *John A. Macdonald*, vol. 1, p. 421; W.L. Morton, *The Critical Years*, (McClelland and Stewart, Toronto, 1964), p. 185.
[6]Creighton, *John A. Macdonald*, vol. 1, *passim*; and Dawson, *The Government of Canada*, p. 21.
[7]Creighton, *John A. Macdonald*, vol. 1, pp. 405–406.
[8]The best source of information on this period in Canadian history is an article by C.P. Storey, "Fenianism and the Rise of National Feeling in Canada at the Time of Confederation," *Canadian Historical Review*, vol. 12, pp. 238–261, September, 1931, and Morton, *The Critical Years*, pp. 195–196.
[9]Creighton, *John A. Macdonald*, vol. 1, pp. 405–406.

partly because of economic pressures at home, the United States served notice of its intention to terminate the reciprocity agreement. Reciprocity finally was terminated in 1866, at a time when the U.K. seemed more committed than ever to a policy of free trade. Thus, excluded from the American market and forced to compete with more advanced economies in the open British market, the British North American colonies looked at last to each other:

> If preferences in Britain and the United States were not to be had, the colonies could at least give preference to each other. Commercial union of the British American provinces would weld them into a single vast trading area within which products might be freely exchanged. If the markets of all the provinces could be opened to the industries of each, an economic system would be created which, by lessening dependence on external markets, would offer greater stability than the economies of the separate provinces could hope for, and which, because of the diversity and complementarity of its resources, would have a greater potential for growth. . . .[10]

Technological changes probably also helped to accelerate the movement towards Confederation, because the colonial economies were strained by the costs of taking full advantage of this technology. The shift from sail to steam and from canals to railways, for instance, forced the colonies, especially the Maritimes, to incur large provincial debts:

> By incurring debts to build the railways which they so earnestly desired, the Maritime provinces had, as it were, given hostages to fortune. By increasing the burden of fixed charges on their revenues, they had curtailed their ability to withstand adversity. . . .[11]

Thus, union offered Nova Scotia and New Brunswick not merely the hope of new markets in the Canadas, but also the promise of a share of national revenues that would ease the burden of their debts. To ensure that the Maritimes did, in fact, gain markets in central Canada, a very specific provision for the construction of the Intercolonial Railway was written into the BNA Act itself:

> It shall be the duty of the Parliament of Canada to provide for the commencement within six months after the Union, of a railway connecting the River St. Lawrence with the city of Halifax in Nova Scotia and for the construction thereof without intermission, and the completion thereof with all practicable speed. . . .[12]

While the promise of the Intercolonial Railway looks very much like a simple "bribe" to entice the Maritimes into the Union, it can be argued that the Canadas also could anticipate certain advantages from the railway. As well as facilitating interprovincial trade, the Intercolonial Railway would provide exporters in Ontario and Quebec with an ice-free port in the winter months when Quebec City and Montreal were normally

---

[10]W.T. Easterbrook and H.G.J. Aitken, *Canadian Economic History*, (Macmillan, Toronto, 1965), p. 251; D. Creighton, *British North America at Confederation*, (Queen's Printer, Ottawa, 1963).

[11]Easterbrook and Aitken, *Canadian Economic History*, p. 250.

[12]BNA Act, 1867, part X, section 145. This section was deleted from the Act in 1893.

closed.[13] This was an important consideration, for Canadian businessmen feared that the abrogation of the reciprocity agreement by the U.S. might close the winter ports on the U.S. eastern seaboard to Canadian exporters. The Martimers themselves certainly welcomed the opportunity to handle the transhipment of Canadian goods in the winter months through the ports of Halifax and Saint John.

Political factors also pushed the colonies toward Confederation. The union of 1841, which had tied Upper and Lower Canada in an uneasy political marriage, was no longer tolerable. The Act of Union had guaranteed equal representation in the colonial legislature to Canada East and Canada West, and by the 1860s, the population of Canada West (now Ontario) which was originally smaller than the population of Canada East (now Quebec) had been greatly increased by an influx of immigrants. Once the people of Canada West realized that the guarantee of equal representation was working against them, they began to agitate for "rep. by pop." The French Canadians of Canada East countered with demands for guarantees of their rights as a linguistic, religious and ethnic minority. The colonial government was left in a virtually permanent stalemate. Impetus to the demand for Confederation was added by the deadlock in the legislature of the United Canadas, for Confederation, whatever its faults, offered a viable solution by providing the separation of the Canadas into two provinces within the larger union.

When we view the history of the Confederation period in Canada, it becomes clear that the section of North America that was to become the Province of Ontario had more to gain from union than any other section. In fact, as Professor D.V. Smiley points out:

> The complicated compromise which was finally embodied in the British North America Act reflected in large part the aspirations and interests of that populous, prosperous and dynamic region, with such concessions to Lower Canada and the Maritimes as were necessary to gain the support of their leaders for union. . . .[14]

The Maritimes saw certain economic advantages in Confederation, but a large proportion of the people living in New Brunswick and Nova Scotia were fervently opposed to any agreement that tied them to Canada. It can even be argued that the Maritimes were never really in favour of Confederation, and were "railroaded" in by complicated political manoeuvering, the silver tongue of Sir John A. Macdonald, and the promise of a railway. French-Canadian politicians saw Confederation as a way of safeguarding their language and religious rights and, on the whole, as a lesser evil than the Union of 1841.

Generally, it can be concluded that there were no common purposes, no visions of greatness and no noble causes which united Canada initially. Perhaps, as Professor Smiley points out:

> The underlying agreement among colonial politicians which made Confederation possible was that the continuance of monarchial and

---

[13]Easterbrook and Aitken, *Canadian Economic History*, p. 249.
[14]D.V. Smiley, *The Canadian Political Nationality*, (Methuen, Toronto, 1967), pp. 13–14.

parliamentary institutions and of the British connection was infinitely preferable to absorption into the U.S.....[15]

But this is a very negative motivation for national unity, and it must be asked whether fear of invasion can ever produce any lasting unity among men. P.B. Waite makes this point with reference to the Fenian raids:

> Fenianism could not itself create a British American national identity. . . .The effects of the Fenian invasion were direct and immediate, but like all negative effects, once removed, the elements in North America tended to revert to their original state.[16]

Thus, to return to the original query as to what motivated the British colonies in North America to seek a union of some kind, one finds a generally negative and unstable set of attitudes towards Confederation in 1867. Apparently abandoned by the mother country, and left prey to the military and economic might of the war-torn but brawny U.S., the British North American colonies turned in desperation to each other.

Canadian Unity Today While many of the circumstances of the past no longer prevail, the question of national unity and national identity remains a burning issue even today. What factors create the sense of national unity among Canadians? How strong is this feeling? This section provides a very brief discussion of this complex question, though there are no real answers; we can only speculate.

In Canada, as we know, there are deep cleavages. The French–English conflict cuts far into any unity which might be achieved. Economic regionalism, too, has created wide divergence of opinion as to where Canada should be heading, and how to get there. Nevertheless, despite the ever present and often bitter clashes between French and English and despite other less visible areas of political conflict, Canada is still hanging together after more than 100 years. Given this startling fact, let us look further for some of the possible bases for this continued association.[17]

First of all, Canadians have one of the few frontiers left in the world today. If a Canadian becomes exasperated with his neighbour, he always has the choice of opting out and going "up north." Very few ever really do, but perhaps the fact that this option is perceived as being open to Canadians makes them psychologically better able to cope with internal political conflict and to resolve it.

The North—"the true North strong and free"—has figured periodically as a symbol of the Canadian nationality. The self-image of rugged northern people, able to cope with extremes of climate and physical hardship, which is exemplified in fact by only native northerners, a few white trappers, Mounties, bush pilots and similarly hardy types has possibly been a factor in stimulating national pride.[18] Interest in the North, and

[15]Smiley, *The Canadian Political Nationality*, p. 2.
[16]P.B. Waite, *The Life and Times of Confederation*, (University of Toronto Press, Toronto, 1962), p. 281.
[17]See P. Russell, *Nationalism in Canada*, (McGraw–Hill, Toronto, 1966), *passim*; also Canadian Dimension, *Kit No. 3: Canadian Nationalism*.
[18]See W.L. Morton, *The Canadian Identity*, (University of Wisconsin, Madison,

more specifically, in the goal of "opening up the North" is stimulated from time to time by politicans, but for most people the enthusiasm is quick to fade when they are faced with the realities of the Arctic winter—or even the Arctic summer.

The proximity of the United States, and the perception of a threat to our independence from that quarter has, since the time of Confederation, played a significant role in keeping Canada united. The self-image that buttresses this factor of consensus is that of a "non-American North American". While anti-Americanism periodically produces a wave of nationalist sentiment in Canada, it is normally a short-lived phenomenon, for while the United States is the greatest single threat to our cultural integrity, Canadians are ambivalent towards their giant neighbour. As do many other countries in the world, Canada views the United States as a sort of model upon which to pattern parts of her own society. Canadians do not want to *be* Americans, but in some respects they want to be *like* Americans. However, there does not seem to be a great deal of consensus in Canada about how much like Americans we want to be.

The British and Commonwealth connections of Canada are perceived by some Canadians as an important factor in distinguishing us from Americans. To them, the Crown, the British form of parliamentary democracy and constitutional government, and the direct genealogical connections of many Canadians to the British Isles are perceived as making us patently non-American. In other words, some Canadians take pride in the self-image of "British North Americans." The disadvantage of the British connection as a unifying factor in Canada, however, is that the French and the "other" Canadians cannot share it. It is not realistic to expect French Canadians to identify with a set of symbols alien to their own cultural traditions and which were actually the symbols of a conquest. In fact, undue attention to the Queen, the Union Jack, or the Commonwealth in Canada today is likely to foster dissension between French and English Canadians, leaving "other" Canadians cold.

In international affairs, Canada has variously attempted to create the image of a "cool-headed middle power," of a "linchpin" in the "North Atlantic Triangle" or of a United Nations "peace-keeper." It is difficult to say whether these attempts at creating an international identity for Canada function to stimulate nationalism at home, but if they do, their unifying effect is probably marginal, since the salience of international politics for most people is very low.

Finally, more than a century of settling or putting off internal squabbles in a peaceful manner may give Canadians in all parts of the country and of all cultural groups some grounds for national pride. In this sense we are defined by our conflicts and by the uniquely Canadian way of settling or avoiding them; we are a "mosaic" and not a "melting pot"; we

1961). Evidence of this can be found in an almost incessant progression of television series such as the 1970-71 CBC series, "This Land", which imply that all true Canadians live in and love the wilderness. The average Canadian would be no more likely to survive in the wilderness than the average Briton or Italian, yet the assumption that we are somehow a wilderness people persists.

are a multitude of competing interests and not a single-minded, unidirectional "nationality."

THE GENESIS OF FEDERAL UNION

Having described the hesitant and uncertain way in which the colonies finally reached an agreement that some form of union was desirable for British North America, let us deal with the forces and events that influenced the decision that the union should be federal in form. The social, economic and ethnic diversity of the colonies made a unitary form of government, or a legislative union as it was then called, completely unacceptable to the Maritimes and Quebec, although evidence indicates that Macdonald and many of his Upper Canadian colleagues preferred this alternative.[19] Quebec wished to preserve its unique linguistic, religious and cultural character, and the Maritimes wished to ensure that the peculiar economic needs of their region be provided for. All provinces wished to retain control over matters that would allow them to preserve their local character and institutions. Provincial autonomy, therefore, had to be protected within any form of British North American Union before the Maritimes and Quebec would agree to it.

Given the obvious differences that existed between the founding provinces, the Fathers of Confederation realized that a legislative union was not a viable alternative for British North America. Furthermore, it was hoped that Prince Edward Island, British Columbia, Newfoundland, and the Northwest could subsequently be lured into the union of 1867, in which case the regional and economic diversity of Canada would increase rather than diminish. Even Sir John A. Macdonald recognized that there could be no union *a mare usque ad mare* unless the provinces were left some degree of local autonomy. It was therefore incumbent upon the Fathers of Confederation to work out the distribution of powers between the provinces and the federal government.

The alternative of an economic and military *alliance* of the British North American colonies was initially considered as a form of union which would go a long way to solving the immediate problems of the 1860s. At both the Charlottetown and Quebec Conferences, a British North American customs union, or *Zollverein*, was suggested—an innocuous form of union which would leave the sovereignty of the members intact. Neither a *Zollverein* nor a military alliance, however, would have provided a permanent central decision-making body or a central enforcement mechanism. In other words, since there would be no derogation of the sovereignty of the signatories of the treaty of alliance, the alliance itself would be powerless to enforce its own provisions. *Furthermore,* such a weak form of union would have been inefficient in financing the joint defence and/or economic programs of the union. A project such as the Intercolonial Railway, for instance, would have been out of the question. Sir John A. Macdonald recognized the inadvisability of a customs union, and suggested that be-

[19]Creighton, *John A. Macdonald*, vol. 1, chs. 13, 14 and 15 (*passim*).

cause of the potential economic conflicts between the colonies it would not be congenial to all its members: "It is impossible to have a *Zollverein*. We must continue to have hostile tariffs unless we have a political union."[20]

A second major disadvantage of any form of union less than political union is that it would lack permanence. Members would have the right to withdraw from it at any time if they felt that its terms were no longer advantageous. It was obvious that if the economic and military problems of British North America were to be solved, they would have to be dealt with continuously over a long period of time. It was not possible to find immediate cures for the ills of the colonies, and therefore a form of union that was not "for keeps" would not be acceptable.

The third drawback of a simple alliance of the British North American colonies was that an alliance is *functionally specific*. In other words, the terms of reference or functions of the alliance are set very specifically at the outset in such a way that new needs of the members of the alliance cannot be dealt with without renegotiating the original agreement. In a rapidly changing world, a form of union that could adapt itself quickly to the performance of new functions was viewed as imperative.

There were other objections to a non-political union, such as the fact that a mere alliance would not satisfy the need for Canada East and Canada West to be separated, and the legalistic point that colonies within the British Empire were not sovereign and therefore could not enter into alliance unilaterally, even with sister colonies. These objections were secondary, however, and could have been overcome had the notion of an economic and military alliance been acceptable otherwise.

A confederal union was also an alternative for the British North American colonies, but when this form of union was subjected to scrutiny it was recognized that a *confederation*[21] would provide only a slightly higher level of political integration than an alliance. In fact, a confederation is a union of sovereign states which features a permanent central decision-making body, or congress, to which the members of the confederation send delegates. Functionally, a confederation is more diffuse than an alliance, for the central congress is empowered to make decisions concerning a very wide range of subjects. The weakness of a confederation is that, as with an alliance, there is no transfer of sovereignty from the member states to the central congress. While empowered to make decisions, the congress is given no power to enforce them, and the members of the confederation can, if they choose, refuse to comply with any decision with which they disagree. The parties to a confederation agreement also have the right to secede from the union if they feel that its terms of reference no longer provide any benefits. Thus, while the confederal form of union is functionally more diffuse than an alliance, it suffers from many of the same faults. Furthermore, the example of the United States under the Articles of Confederation in the 1780s, with the chaotic condition of government during that

[20]Browne, *Documents on the Confederation of British North America*, p. 96.
[21]The term *Confederation* when applied to the Canadian union of 1867 is a misnomer, for the form of government set up by the BNA Act is definitely not confederal.

period, gave the Fathers of Confederation ample cause for avoiding that particular form of union.

A federal form of union was ultimately decided upon by the Fathers of Confederation because, unlike either an alliance or a confederal union, it vested real powers in the hands of a central decision-making body, the federal parliament. In a federal system, sovereignty is divided between the provinces and the federal parliament, and the exercise of legislative and executive powers of each is limited to subject matters allotted to them by the constitution. A federal system is also permanent in the sense that the member states or provinces do not have the constitutional right to withdraw unilaterally from the union. This prohibition might, of course, be swept aside very quickly if the people of a member state or province were determined to secede from the union. In law, however, a federal union is indivisible.

The constitution of the federal system distributes the power and the responsibility for the authoritative allocation of resources between the provinces and the federal government, and that constitutional distribution of powers is exhaustive (with the possible exception of certain basic rights and freedoms which may be entrenched in the constitution.)[22] In a confederal union, on the other hand, it is simply assumed that the state or provincial governments have the responsibility for everything except a few matters that are specifically the responsibility of the confederation. In other words, in the case of a confederation, the *residual power* is always left with the states and constitutes a very large area of jurisdiction, whereas in the case of a federal system, the residual power can be left with either the provinces of the federal government and the residual area of jurisdiction is, in fact, very small. The advantage of such a comprehensive definition of the powers and the responsibilities of government is that the element of uncertainty is eliminated. The federal government and the provincial or state governments are each in possession of exclusive and sovereign powers which cannot be encroached upon by the other level of government. Unlike the central congress in a confederal union, the national government in a federal union has the authority to make some decisions which are binding on the citizens of the member states, and furthermore, it is granted the power to enforce them.

Finally, a federal form of government was adopted by the Fathers of Confederation because they hoped to create a union that would eventually become more than a marriage of economic expedience and military convenience. People like Sir John A. Macdonald wished to create a new political community in North America, and it is largely to their credit that Canada has evolved as more than merely a temporary association of friendly but independent neighbours.

> That Canada exists today is probably the result of the effort and determination of Sir John A. Macdonald more than any other man. . . .It was he who provided the most determined leadership and who went on after the political framework of federation was accomplished to endow Canada with. . .Nationhood.[23]

[22]See Chapter 5.
[23]Paul Martin, *Hansard*, Wednesday, January 11, 1967, p. 11651.

Thus, the fact that the form of union ultimately selected by the Fathers of Confederation was federal and not confederal was to a large part due to the political genius, vision, and ambition of Macdonald. The actual shape of our federal system and the idiosyncrasies that make Canadian Federalism a genre apart also bear the stamp of Macdonald's personality and his view of the ideal relationship that should exist between the provinces and the national government in a federal system.

Having in mind the then recent and tragic experiences of the Civil War in the United States, Macdonald wanted to see as centralized a federal system as the provinces would accept: "We should concentrate the power in the federal government and not adopt the decentralization of the United States. . . ."[24] In fact, there is some evidence that Macdonald viewed federalism as a temporary arrangement to secure initial unity, and that he fully expected the provinces to wither away from lack of exercise, leaving a basically unitary system in Canada. Some aspects of the BNA Act, 1867, do indeed indicate that the intention of the drafters of the Act was to leave the preponderance of legislative power with Ottawa. But in spite of these biases, the British North America Act does vest some significant legislative power with the provinces. One eminent political scientist has asserted:

> . . .the provinces are of equal constitutional power and status, and they operate without any serious interference from the Dominion. . .Provincial powers are as full and complete as those of the Dominion within the areas allotted by the BNA Act. . . .[25]

It is now necessary to turn our attention to a consideration of the federal distribution of powers in 1867 as a base point for a subsequent analysis of the evolution of the Canadian federal system.

The Distribution of Powers: Canadian Federalism in 1867

The legislative powers of the federal parliament are, for the most part, defined in Section 91 of the BNA Act, 1867. Section 91 is in two parts. The first part of the section is a broad and general grant of power, giving parliament the authority to make laws for ". . .the Peace, Order, and Good Government of Canada in relation to all Matters not coming within the Classes of Subjects by this Act assigned exclusively to the Legislatures of the Provinces. . . ." The second part of the section included 29 (now 31) enumerated matters such as "the Public Debt and Property," "the Regulation of Trade and Commerce," "the Raising of Money by any Mode or System of Taxation," etc. which were intended ". . .for greater Certainty, but not so as to restrict the Generality of the foregoing Terms of this Section,. . ."

The legislative powers of the provinces are for the most part set out in Section 92 of the Act, which has the appearance of being a far less complicated section than is 91. Section 92 does not begin with any comprehensive grant of power to the provinces, but simply states that, "In each Prov-

[24]Browne, *Documents on the Confederation of British North America*, p. 124.
[25]Dawson, *The Government of Canada*, p. 78.

ince, the Legislature may exclusively make Laws in relation to Matters coming within the Classes of Subjects next herein-after enumerated. . . ." and then proceeds to list 16 matters such as "Direct Taxation within the Province in order to the raising of a Revenue for Provincial Purposes," "the Solemnization of Marriage in the Province," "Property and Civil Rights in the Province," and "Generally all Matters of a merely local or private Nature in the Province." Thus, when Sections 91 and 92 are read together, it is clear that the intention is to give the federal government a comprehensive power to make law and then to except from this general grant certain carefully specified powers which are to be retained by the provincial legislatures.[26]

Section 95 establishes concurrent federal–provincial powers in matters of agriculture and immigration, and an amendment to the Act in 1951 added a third concurrent power in the area of old age pensions. While establishing the right of both levels of government to make laws with regards to the specified subjects, the section establishes federal *paramountcy* in the case of conflicting legislation:

> . . .any Law of the Legislature of a Province relative to Agriculture or to Immigration shall have effect in and for the Province as long and as far only as it is not repugnant to any Act of the Parliament of Canada. . . .[27]

The subject of education is normally considered to rest within the exclusive jurisdiction of the provincial legislatures as is stated in Section 92 of the Act. However, Section 93 places certain limitations and conditions on the exercise of this power by the provinces. First, it states that no provincial law shall "prejudicially affect any right or privilege with respect to denominational schools" that existed at the time of union. Secondly, it states that the rights of separate schools in Upper Canada shall continue after the union and shall apply equally to Protestant separate schools in Lower Canada. The third clause of Section 93 establishes a right of appeal to the Governor General in Council if the education rights of a Protestant or Catholic minority are abrogated by a provincial legislature. Finally, in the event that the province does not respond positively to an appeal which is allowed by the Governor General in Council, provision is made for the parliament of Canada to ". . .make remedial Laws for the due Execution of the Provisions of this section and of any Decision of the Governor General in Council under this Section. . . ."[28] The significance of this section of the BNA Act is that it makes the federal government a "policeman" with the power and the responsibility to protect the education rights of religious minorities from encroachments by the provinces. This has proved an awk-

---

[26]The manner in which the Judicial Committee of the Privy Council interpreted these sections will be discussed in the next part of this chapter.

[27]Note that the 1951 amendment to Section 95, which established old age pensions as a concurrent power, specified that provincial laws be paramount in the case of repugnancy: ". . .but no law made by the parliament of Canada in relation to old age pensions shall affect the operation of any law present or future of a provincial legislature in relation to old age pensions. . . ." BNA Act, 1951, 14–15 George VI, C. 32, U.K.

[28]BNA Act, S. 93 (4).

ward burden for the federal government to bear, from time to time, for in protecting the rights of a minority, the federal government is forced to interfere with the autonomy of the provinces. If the federal government doesn't act it is damned by the minority concerned, and if it does, it is damned by the province concerned. One such dilemma, commonly referred to as the *Manitoba Schools Question*, played a significant role in the downfall of the Conservative government in the election of 1896.[29]

A further grant of legislative competence is specified by Section 132, which states that the parliament of Canada

> ". . .shall have all Powers necessary or proper for performing the Obligations of Canada or of any Province thereof as Part of the British Empire towards Foreign Countries arising under Treaties between the Empire and such Foreign Countries."

This particular clause and the manner in which the courts have interpreted it will be discussed at greater length below.

Finally, to round out this "snapshot" of Canadian federalism at the time of Confederation, the federal government's power over the legislatures of the provinces contained in the *reservation* and *disallowance* provisions of the BNA Act must be mentioned. These provisions, which are unique for a federal system, have been dealt with briefly in Chapter 5. The power they vest in the central government amounts to a federal veto that may be applied to any act of the provincial legislatures. Through the Lieutenant-Governor of the province, who was to function relative to the Governor General as the pre-Confederation colonial governor functioned relative to the British government, it was intended that the federal government would be enabled to keep a tight reign on all provincial legislation. The Lieutenant-Governor has the power to reserve a bill for the pleasure of the Governor General in Council after which, if no positive action is taken by the federal official, the bill is dead. In the case of the disallowance power, the federal government can unilaterally invalidate any provincial law within a year of its passage. These powers, the reservation and disallowance, were used extensively before the turn of the century and then intermittently until 1941 when the last disallowance was recorded. Today, they have become vestigial appendages in a federal system that has evolved past the stage where such heavy-handed devices are politically feasible.

Thus, the Canadian federal system at Confederation gave the lion's share of the legislative power to the federal government, established the principle of federal paramountcy in areas of concurrent jurisdiction, set up the federal government as a policeman in the area of the educational rights of religious minorities, and, just to make sure nothing had been forgotten, gave the federal government a veto power over all provincial enactments. Had the spirit of the BNA Act of 1867 been upheld in subsequent judicial decisions, our federal system would look very different than it does today. Now let us trace the development of Canadian federalism from its beginning as a highly centralized form of union to the form it takes today.

[29]See Chapter 11.

THE EVOLUTION OF CANADIAN FEDERALISM

The literature of Canadian constitutional law is replete with articles on the interpretation of Sections 91 and 92 of the BNA Act by the Judicial Committee of the Privy Council. Some commentators approve and others strongly disapprove,[30] but virtually all are agreed that, in the process of interpreting the Act, the Judicial Committee significantly altered its effect. From the ultra-centralist document of 1867, the British North America Act was transformed by the incremental process of judicial review into a more truly federal constitution which vested extensive legislative authority in the hands of the provinces. All of this was accomplished by a succession of British "law lords" who took upon themselves the task of defending provincial autonomy, perhaps at the expense of the English language, which had to be tortured until it met their requirements. In order to "beef up" the legislative competence of the provinces, the Judicial Committee developed certain principles of interpretation which explain the often puzzling construction placed on the crucial sections, 91 and 92.

The Erosion of the Federal Power The thin edge of the wedge that opened the way for a provincial rights interpretation of Sections 91 and 92 was the series of Privy Council opinions which separated the "Peace, Order, and Good Government" clause of Section 91 from the twenty-nine enumerated sub-headings of that section. This principle was initially conceived by Sir Montague Smith in the *Parsons* case in 1881,[31] and re-emphasized by Lord Watson in the *Local Prohibition* case (1896).[32] Lord Watson went a step further, placing the general part of Section 91 in a position secondary and subordinate to the enumerated subheads of both Sections 91 and 92:

> . . .the exercise of legislative power by the parliament of Canada, in regard to all matters not enumerated in s. 91, ought to be strictly confined to such matters as are unquestionably of Canadian interest and importance, and ought not to trench upon provincial legislation with respect to any of the classes of subjects enumerated in s. 92. To attach any other construction to the general power which in supplement of its enumerated powers is conferred upon the parliament of Canada by s. 91 would, in their Lordships' opinion, not only be contrary to the intendment of the act but would practically destroy the autonomy of the provinces. If it were once conceded that the parliament of Canada has authority to make laws applicable to the

[30]See, for instance, Kennedy, "Interpretation of the BNA Act," *Cambridge Law Journal*, vol. 8, p. 146, 1963; Macdonald, "The Constitution in a Changing World," *Canadian Bar Review*, vol. 26, p. 21, 1948; O'Connor, *Report to the Senate of Canada on the BNA Act*, annex 1, p. 25, 1939; Bora Laskin, "Peace, Order, and Good Government Reexamined," in Lederman, *The Courts and the Canadian Constitution*, (Carleton Library, McClelland and Stewart, Toronto, 1964), p. 66n. The best single article on the subject for political scientists is Alan Cairns's "The Judicial Committee and Its Critics," *Canadian Journal of Political Science*, IV, Sept. 1971, pp. 301–345.

[31]Citizens Insurance Company of Canada v. Parsons, 7 *Appeal Cases (A.C.)* 96.

[32]Attorney-General for Ontario v. Attorney-General for Canada, (1896) *A.C.* 348.

whole Dominion in relation to matters which in each province are substantially of local or private interest, upon the assumption that these matters also concern the peace, order and good government of the Dominion, there is hardly a subject enumerated in s. 92 upon which it might not legislate to the exclusion of the provincial legislatures.[33]

Thus, by 1896 Section 91 had been interpreted by the Judicial Committee of the Privy Council in such a way that the once proud Peace, Order, and Good Government clause gave no exclusive legislative jurisdiction to the federal parliament, but rather only a residual power that permitted federal legislation with regard to a few matters that could be found neither in the enumerated subheads of Section 91 nor in Section 92. The federal parliament now enjoyed exclusive jurisdiction only with regard to matters that came under the enumerated subheads of Section 91,[34] despite the fact that the drafters of the BNA Act had anticipated that the general grant of authority at the beginning of Section 91 would put the largest part of the responsibilities of government in the hands of the central parliament.

This narrow construction of the Peace, Order, and Good Government clause evolved in spite of the fact that there were earlier decisions which upheld the more generous view of this clause. In the *Russell* v. *the Queen* decision in 1882, federal legislation that provided for local prohibition subject to local option was upheld by the Judicial Committee on the grounds that liquor control was a subject matter not enumerated in Section 92 and therefore the federal parliament had jurisdiction through the Peace, Order, and Good Government clause. Had the principles of interpretation that were employed in this case been followed in subsequent cases, the federal power to pass laws for the peace, order, and good government of Canada might have developed along the lines anticipated by the Fathers of Confederation. However, this was not to be.

In 1883, in a decision that involved the power of the provinces to regulate the liquor trade,[35] their lordships invented another canon of interpretation which has come to be known as the *aspect doctrine*. In the case in point, the appellant was fined for an offence under an Ontario Act which regulated liquor traffic in the province. He argued that the conviction was invalid because the regulation of the traffic of liquor was a federal matter that concerned the peace, order, and good government of Canada, and he cited the *Russell* case as a precedent. In delivering the judgment of the Judicial Committee, Lord Fitzgerald held that the Ontario act was *intra vires* because it involved matters which are clearly enumerated in Section 92. He went on to state that the *Russell* case did not apply because the federal

---

[33]Attorney-General for Ontario v. Attorney-General for Canada, (1896) *A.C.* 360.
[34]The argument here is very complicated and it hinges on the way in which one construes the closing words of Section 91: ". . .and any matter coming within any of the classes of subjects enumerated in this section shall not be deemed to come within the class of matters of a local or private matter comprised in the enumeration of the classes of subjects by this act assigned exclusively to the legislatures of the Provinces. . . ." The best discussion can be found in Bora Laskin, *Canadian Constitutional Law*, second edition, (Carswell, Toronto, 1960), PP. 65–75.
[35]Hodge v. the Queen (1883), 9 *A.C.* 117.

legislation that was validated in that decision involved another aspect of the regulation of the liquor traffic:

> ". . .subjects which in one aspect and for one purpose fall within section 92, may in another aspect and for another purpose fall within section 91. . . ."[36]

In this way, with the birth of the aspect doctrine, the tide was turned, and the decision in the *Russell* case never did gain the respectability as a precedent that would have ensured expansion of the federal power through the Peace, Order, and Good Government clause.

The Judicial Committee of the Privy Council continued to whittle away at the introductory words of Section 91 and to reduce further the significance of the *Russell* decision. In a 1916 case, Viscount Haldane, who was to become renowned for his championing of provincial rights, and for his imaginative interpretation of Section 91, attempted to summarize the relevance of the Peace, Order, and Good Government clause at that time:

> It must be taken to be now settled that the general authority to make laws for the peace, order and good government of Canada, which the initial part of section 91 of the BNA Act confers, does not, unless the subject matter of legislation falls within some one of the enumerated heads which follow, enable the Dominion Parliament to trench on the subject matters entrusted to the provincial legislatures by the enumeration in s. 92. There is only one case outside the heads enumerated in s. 91 in which the Dominion Parliament can legislate effectively as regards a province and that is where the subject matter lies outside all of the subject.matters enumeratively entrusted to the province under s. 92. *Russell* v. *the Queen* is an instance of such a case.[37]

Not yet satisfied that peace, order, and good government and the *Russell* case were dead issues, Viscount Haldane continued to attack them in a series of cases in the 1920s. In the *Board of Commerce* case in 1922, he admitted that the Peace, Order, and Good Government clause might be used as a justification for federal encroachments on matters enumerated in Section 92, but only in extreme circumstances such as war or famine:

> . . .circumstances are conceivable, such as those of war or famine, when the peace, order and good government of the Dominion might be imperilled. . . .[38]

A year later, Haldane reinterpreted the Peace, Order, and Good Government clause as purely an emergency power, to be used in times of national crisis:

> . . .in a sufficiently great emergency such as that arising out of war, there is implied the power to deal adequately with that emergency for the safety of the Dominion as a whole. . . .[39]

---

[36]Hodge v. the Queen. See also Laskin, *Canadian Constitutional Law*, second edition, p. 79.

[37]Attorney-General for Canada v. Attorney-General for Alberta (1916), I.A.C. 588; 26 *DLR* 288.

[38]In *Re the Board of Commerce Act and the Combines and Fair Prices Act*, 1919, (1922) *DLR* 513.

[39]Fort Frances Pulp and Power Co. Ltd. v. Manitoba Free Press Co. Ltd., (1923) 3 *DLR* 629.

Utilizing this fully developed interpretation of the Peace, Order, and Good Government clause as an emergency power, Viscount Haldane went on to dispatch the decision of the *Russell* case once and for all, in what is perhaps the most unusual judicial dictum in the history of Canadian constitutional law:

> Their Lordships think that the decision in *Russell* v. *the Queen* can only be supported today. . .on the assumption of the Board, apparently made at the time of deciding the case of *Russell* v. *the Queen*, that the evil of intemperance at that time amounted to one so great and so general that at least for the period, it was a menace to the national life of Canada, so serious and pressing that the Parliament of Canada was called upon to intervene to protect the nation from disaster. An epidemic of pestilence might conceivably have been regarded as analogous.[40]

To summarize, having virtually emasculated the Peace, Order, and Good Government clause in cases before the 1920s, the Judicial Committee then reinterpreted it as an emergency power. According to three decisions in the 1920s, the *Board of Commerce* case, the *Fort Frances* case, and the *Snider* case, the federal government could make laws for the peace, order, and good government of Canada with regard to matters that would come *prima facie* within the powers of the provincial legislatures, but only if a national emergency required it.

In the *Fort Frances* case,[41] the Judicial Committee of the Privy Council allowed that the federal government should be given the full benefit of the doubt in determining when a national emergency existed and when the state of emergency had ceased to exist. This power was extended to the federal government during both world wars when parliament vested significant powers in the federal executive through the War Measures Act. The Privy Council was not so generous, however, when the federal government parliament attempted to implement a series of welfare measures, usually referred to as the "Bennett New Deal". In the reference case that tested the validity of these measures, their Lordships refused to agree that the economic hardships of the depression constituted a national emergency, and the entire legislative package was declared *ultra vires* the federal parliament.[42] Thus, after approximately fifty years of interpretation by the Judicial Committee of the Privy Council, the opening words of Section 91 had been transformed from a general and comprehensive grant of legislative competence to the federal parliament, to a grant of tempo-

[40]Toronto Electric Commissioners v. Snider (1925) 2 D.L.R. 5; also in Laskin, *Canadian Constitutional Law*, second edition, p. 241. In defense of Haldane it is possible that Canadian consumption of firewater in the 1870s was alarmingly high; O.J. Firestone, *Canadian Economic Development 1867–1953*, (Bowes and Bowes London, 1958) cites the per capita consumption of spirits as 1.58 gals. in 1871 and only .59 gal. in abstemious 1951.
See also, Robinson J. "Lord Haldane" and the BNA Act *U. of T. Law Journal*, XX, 1970; pp. 55–69; XXI 1971, pp. 175–251.
[41](1923) 3 *DLR* 1629.
[42]Attorney-General for Canada v. Attorney-General for Ontario, (Reference Re Unemployment and Social Insurance Act), (1937) A.C. 355; (1937) 1 *DLR* 684; Olmsted, vol. 3, p. 207.

rary federal power in times of national emergency. Furthermore, in fifty years of judicial review their Lordships had construed only two events as national emergencies—the First World War and an "epidemic of intemperance" in the 1870s.

At a very early point in the evolution of Canadian federalism, it became clear that the Judicial Committee of the Privy Council was willing to admit exclusive federal powers with regard only to subject matters enumerated in Section 91. Accepting this setback, the federal authorities proceeded to try to find justification for federal legislation within the various subheads of that section. The one which seemed most comprehensive and which the federal authorities hoped would replace the legislative competence lost with the narrowing of the Peace, Order, and Good Government clause, was 91(2), "the Regulation of Trade and Commerce." In two early judgments in the Supreme Court of Canada,[43] Section 91(2) was interpreted not only as a very broad but also as an exclusive power of the Dominion. The Canadian judges, at least at the outset, seemed willing to view the regulation of trade and commerce as a comprehensive grant of power that might extend even to the regulation of trade that was carried on within the boundaries of one province. In *Citizen's Insurance Co.* v. *Parsons*, however, both the Supreme Court of Canada and the Judicial Committee of the Privy Council placed a far more limited construction on the federal trade and commerce power:

> The words "regulation of trade and commerce" in their unlimited sense are sufficiently wide, if uncontrolled by the context and other parts of the act, to include every regulation of trade ranging from political arrangements in regard to trade with foreign governments, requiring the sanction of Parliament, down to minute rules for regulating particular trades. But a consideration of the act shows that the words were not used in this unlimited sense. In the first place the collocation of No. 2 with classes of subjects of national and general concern affords an indication that regulations relating to general trade and commerce were in the mind of the legislature when conferring this power on the Dominion Parliament. If the words had been intended to have the full scope of which in their literal meaning they are susceptible, the specific mention of several of the other classes of subjects enumerated in section 91 would have been unnecessary; as, 15, banking; 17, weights and measures; 18, bills of exchange and promissory notes; 19, interest; and even 21, bankruptcy and insolvency. . . .[44]

Briefly, therefore, the federal trade and commerce power was construed so as not to interfere with the provinces' power to "regulate contracts of a particular business or trade such as the business of fire insurance in a single province."[45]

In *Montreal* v. *Montreal Street Railway* (1912), Lord Atkinson argued against broader interpretation of the federal trade and commerce power on the grounds that:

[43]Severn v. the Queen, (1878), *SCR* 70; Fredericton v. the Queen, (1880), 3 *SCR* 505.
[44]Bora Laskin, *Canadian Constitutional Law*, third edition, (Carswell, Toronto, 1969), p. 303.
[45]Laskin, *Canadian Constitutional Law*, second edition, p. 302.

taken in their widest sense, these words would authorize legislation by the Parliament of Canada in respect of several of the matters specifically enumerated in s. 92 and would seriously encroach upon the autonomy of the province.[46]

This is notable partly because it is the same argument used by Lord Watson to justify his restrictive interpretation of the Peace, Order, and Good Government clause in the *Local Prohibition* case. While both the "collocation argument" and the "provincial autonomy argument" produced inflexibility in determining the scope of the federal trade and commerce power,[47] it took the imagination of Viscount Haldane in the *Board of Commerce* case and the *Snider* case to defuse completely the federal power. In the former decision, Haldane queried:

Must not it be taken that since the 1896 case, at all events, perhaps earlier, subs. 2 of s. 91 must be taken as containing merely ancillary powers? A power that can be exercised so as to interfere with a provincial right only if there is some paramount Dominion purpose as to which they are applicable.[48]

and in the latter, he summed up the position of the trade and commerce power, concluding that:

. . .it must now be taken that the authority to legislate for the regulation of trade and commerce does not extend to the regulation for instance, by a licensing system, of a particular trade in which Canadians would otherwise be free to engage in the provinces. It is, in their Lordships' opinion, now clear that, excepting so far as the power can be invoked in aid of capacity conferred independently under other words in s. 91, the power to regulate trade and commerce cannot be relied on as enabling the Dominion Parliament to regulate civil rights in the province. . . .[49]

In this fashion, Viscount Haldane reduced the federal trade and commerce power to a "merely ancillary" power that was only relevant "in aid of" some other subhead of Section 91. Furthermore, it seems that the only aspect of trade and commerce that could be regulated by the federal government was international and/or interprovincial trade. As with the federal peace, order, and good government power, the trade and commerce power had, courtesy of Viscount Haldane, been reduced to a mere shadow of what the Fathers of Confederation had intended it to be.

Since the *Snider* case, there has been a partial retreat from the restrictive Haldane view of both these parts of Section 91. In *Proprietary Articles Trade Association* v. *Attorney-General for Canada* (the *P.A.T.A.* case), Lord Atkin gave back some respectability to the Trade and Commerce clause by dissociating their Lordships from the decision in the *Board of Commerce* case:

---

[46]Montreal v. Montreal Street Railway (1912), 1 *DLR* 681, at p. 687. See also Laskin, *Canadian Constitutional Law*, second edition, p. 306.

[47]Laskin, *Canadian Constitutional Law*, second edition, p. 314.

[48]Quoted in Laskin, *Canadian Constitutional Law*, second edition, pp. 312–313; [(1922) 1 A.C. 191.].

[49]Laskin, *Canadian Constitutional Law*, second edition, pp. 313–314.

Their Lordships merely propose to disassociate themselves from the construction suggested in argument from a passage in the judgement of the *Board of Commerce* case, (1922) 1 A.C. 191, 198, under which it was contended that the power to regulate trade and commerce could be invoked only in furtherance of a general power which Parliament possessed independently of it. No such restriction is properly to be inferred from that judgement. . . .[50]

In a similar fashion, when called upon by the appellant in a 1946 case to find that the *Russell* case had been wrongly decided, Viscount Simon held that the decision in the *Russell* case should stand, and he was furthermore severely critical of the emergency power interpretation of the Peace, Order, and Good Government clause in the *Board of Commerce, Fort Frances* and *Snider* cases.[51] Despite these more recent decisions, however, the damage has already been done, and while other cases, particularly since the abolition of appeals to the Judicial Committee of the Privy Council in 1942,[52] indicate the possibility of a slightly less restrictive interpretation of the federal power in the future,[53] the constitutional ground rules of Canadian federalism will likely remain much the same as they have been since 1925. If, therefore, all the power that the Fathers of Confederation conceived as federal has been taken away from the federal parliament, it is time to consider where that power now rests.

Section 92(13) reads, "Property and Civil Rights in the Province" and it was intended as merely one of the sixteen subheads of Section 92. The Judicial Committee of the Privy Council, however, chose to interpret the words of this subhead in their widest connotation. They were deemed to include such things as contracts, contractual rights, and civil rights in its broadest interpretation, that is, including almost every aspect of all subject matters that are not specifically inter-provincial and/or international in their scope. By construing Section 92(13) in its widest sense and by strictly limiting the interpretation of the more general sections of Section 91, the Judicial Committee transformed the Property and Civil Rights clause into the *de facto* residual clause of the BNA Act.[54] Thus the general grant of power in the opening words of Section 91 was transferred from the federal parliament to the provincial legislatures, with the result that, fifty years after Confederation, the face of Canadian federalism would have been unrecognizable to the men who created it.

One enumerated federal power that was permitted to encroach upon subject matters that are *prima facie* covered by this wide interpretation of Section 92(13) is Section 91(27), the Dominion *criminal law power*. The competence of the federal parliament to encroach upon the area of

---

[50]Laskin, *Canadian Constitutional Law*, second edition, p. 314; [(1931) 2 *DLR* 1.].

[51]Attorney-General for Ontario v. Canada Temperance Federation, (1946) 2 *DLR* 1.

[52]Attorney-General for Ontario v. Attorney-General for Canada, (1947) A.C. 127 (Re abolition of appeals to the J.C.P.C.).

[53]*E.g.* Pronto Uranium Mine v. O.L.R.B., et al. (1956), 5 *DLR* 342.

[54]Royal Commission on Dominion–Provincial Relations, *Report* (*Rowell–Sirois Report*), (Queen's Printer, Ottawa, 1954), Book I, p. 247.

"Property and Civil Rights in the Province" when legislating with regard to criminal law was at first questioned, particularly by Viscount Haldane, who argued that the Dominion could not create a crime where the subject matter did not by its very nature belong to "the domain of criminal jurisprudence."[55] In the *P.A.T.A.* case, mentioned above, the Judicial Committee of the Privy Council dissociated itself from the restrictive Haldane interpretation and admitted that the federal government could, in fact, declare an act to be criminal even if it has not in the past been considered so.[56] The only limitation on this federal power to declare a certain act or category of acts criminal is

> . . .the condition that parliament shall not in the guise of enacting criminal legislation in truth and in substance encroach on any of the classes of subjects enumerated in section 92.[57]

Thus, the criminal law power of the federal parliament, while not to be used merely to secure entry into a field of legislation that is in pith and substance provincial, can properly encroach upon the powers of the provincial legislatures if such an encroachment is truly incidental to the achievement of a genuine federal purpose.

Before concluding this section of the chapter, mention should be made of one section of the BNA Act which affects the federal–provincial distribution of powers and which became a bone of contention in the 1930s. Section 132 reads as follows:

> The Parliament and Government of Canada shall have all Powers necessary or proper for performing the Obligations of Canada or any Province thereof as Part of the British Empire, towards Foreign Countries, arising under Treaties between the Empire and such Foreign Countries.

Essentially, this section means that in the implementation of British Empire treaties to which Canada is a signatory, the distribution of powers in Sections 91 and 92 is inoperative, and the federal parliament possesses exclusive authority over all subject matters. The interpretation of this federal power did not come into question until after World War I, when Canada gained the right to enter into treaties with foreign countries, not as a member of the Empire but as an independent signatory. The federal authorities felt that the evolution of Canada's independent role in foreign relations could not have been foreseen by the Fathers of Confederation, and that, as a result, the full power that the federal parliament had possessed with regard to the implementation of Empire treaties should continue with regard to the implementation of treaties signed by Canada in her new international role.

The Judicial Committee of the Privy Council, however, did not agree with the view of the federal authorities. That the federal executive possessed the full power to make treaties with foreign countries was never

[55]The "Board of Commerce Case," in Laskin, *Canadian Constitutional Law*, p. 282.
[56]Proprietary Articles Trade Association v. Attorney-General for Canada, (1931) 2 *DLR* 1; A.C. 310.
[57]Attorney-General for British Columbia v. Attorney-General for Canada, (1937) 1 *DLR* 688, as quoted in Laskin, *Canadian Constitutional Law*, second edition, p. 284.

seriously questioned. However, their Lordships held that the power to sign them does not give the federal parliament the unfettered right to pass laws implementing them in Canada:

> There is no existing constitutional ground for stretching the competence of the Dominion Parliament so that it becomes enlarged to keep pace with enlarged functions of the Dominion executive. . . .the Dominion cannot, merely by making promises to foreign countries, clothe itself with legislative authority inconsistent with the constitution which gave it birth.[58]

The Judicial Committee went on to point out that "in totality of legislative powers", the provincial legislatures and the federal parliament can, together, pass laws implementing any treaty signed by the federal executive. The fact, however, that the legislation happens to be necessary to implement a treaty does not alter the constitutional distribution of powers in Sections 91 and 92:

> While the ship of state now sails on larger ventures and into foreign waters she still retains the watertight compartments which are an essential part of her original structure.[59]

It can be seen from what has been said in the past several pages that the interpretation of the BNA Act, specifically the interpretation of Sections 91 and 92, achieved a major alteration in the relationship of the provinces to the federal parliament. The clear intention of the Fathers of Confederation had been to leave the provinces as relatively insignificant entities in the possession of relatively modest legislative powers. The Judicial Committee of the Privy Council, however, according to the tradition of the British legal system, took a passive attitude to the interpretation of the BNA Act. In short, they sought to construe the terms of the Act literally, with little regard for either the intentions of the men who had drafted it or current political opinion. Based on this principle of a literal construction of the BNA Act, a specific pattern of interpretation emerged with respect to Sections 91 and 92. If the subject matter of a particular piece of legislation came *prima facie* under one of the subheads of Section 91, then without question it was within the exclusive jurisdiction of the Dominion parliament. If the subject matter came under one of the subheads of Section 92, the federal parliament was still the paramount authority as long as the subject was also covered by one of the enumerated subheads in Section 91. The provincial authority to make laws with respect of "property and civil rights in the province",[60] was construed very broadly and the federal enumerated powers were, for the most part, construed narrowly, with the result that in the case of any doubt as to the proper location of a particular subject matter, it was given to the provinces. The only exception to this rule was deemed to exist in times of national emergency, when the federal power to make laws for the peace, order and good government of Canada might permit federal encroachments in normally provincial matters.

---

[58]"Labour Conventions Case," 1937, as quoted in Laskin, *Canadian Constitutional Law*, second edition, p. 286.
[59]*Ibid.*
[60]BNA Act, S. 92 (13).

Finally, if a subject matter could not be located either among the enumerated subheads of Section 91 or within Section 92, then it came within the jurisdiction of the federal parliament through the Peace, Order, and Good Government clause as a *residuary power*.[61]

It is tempting, at this point in our analysis of the evolution of the federal–provincial distribution of powers, to pass judgment on the manner in which the Judicial Committee of the Privy Council "rewrote our constitution." However, in order to come to any verdict as to the culpability of their Lordships, it would be necessary to assume that the BNA Act as drafted in 1867 was itself beyond criticism. Clearly this is not the case, for Sections 91 and 92 contain especially ambiguous phrases which lend themselves to various and often conflicting constructions. Questions which come to mind are: if the Fathers of Confederation saw the Peace, Order, and Good Government clause as a truly comprehensive grant of power, why did they confuse the issue by adding twenty-nine "examples"?; if they viewed the trade and commerce power as a broad grant of authority to the federal parliament, why did they proceed to "collocate" other subheads which related to trade and commerce?; and if they wanted the provinces to have a modest role in the government of Canada why did they give them the ambiguous power over property and civil rights in the province? Certainly, one can maintain that many of Viscount Haldane's judgments are puzzling, but it also must be admitted that the Act itself is not exactly airtight. The purpose of this analysis is not to praise or blame the Judicial Committee of the Privy Council for altering the intention of the BNA Act, but to describe the shape into which our federal system has been moulded.

[61]Cases such as this have been few and far between. The only example that comes to mind is the *Radio Reference* case in 1932, when the J.C.P.C. granted the federal parliament the power to make laws with regard to radio communication because it involved a subject matter not enumerated in either 91 or 92. It is necessary to note, however, that even in this case there were other reasons cited for the decision. See in *Re Regulation and Control of Radio Communications*. (1932), 2 *DLR* 81; Laskin, *Canadian Constitutional Law*, second edition, pp. 267–269.

8
The Historical Context: Federal–Provincial Finance from 1867 to 1974

THE FEDERAL–PROVINCIAL REVENUE STRUCTURE: THE NINETEENTH CENTURY

The character of any system of public finance depends largely upon the nature and extent of the role government is expected to play in the lives of its citizens. In 1867, the role of government was perceived in terms of "rugged individualism"; this was the heyday of the philosophy of *laissez-faire*, and the best government was judged to be the one that governed least. The bare minimum of governmental intervention in the life of the private citizen in this period included primarily the provision of national security, including defence and the administration of justice, and the promotion of national economic development through a few essential public works.

At Confederation, these primary governmental functions were placed in the hands of the federal parliament, along with the burden of the provincial debts existing at that time. In this way, the federal government was given responsibility for the major areas of public expenditure, and the provinces were given the responsibility for matters of a local or provincial nature. Among these provincial responsibilities were education, public welfare, and transportation within the province, all of which involved relatively modest expenditures when contrasted with the federal share in 1867. Expenditures for education and welfare, for example, amounted to a paltry 14 per cent of total governmental outlay in 1866.[1]

The largest revenue sources at Confederation were customs and excise duties, which accounted for approximately 80 per cent of the revenues of the colonies of Nova Scotia and New Brunswick, and 66 per cent of the revenue of Canada.[2] Provincial revenue at Confederation came from real property taxes, various types of fees and permits, and provincial licensing systems. Because the BNA Act vested the responsibility for the "great functions of government" in the federal parliament, and because the Dominion was to assume responsibility for the existing debts, the major sources of rev-

[1] *Rowell–Sirois Report*, Book I, p. 39.
[2] *Ibid.*, p. 41.

enue at that time were given to the Dominion. The federal tax power, as specified in Section 91(3), gives the parliament of Canada the authority over "the Raising of Money by any Mode or System of Taxation". The provinces, on the other hand, were limited by Section 92(2) to direct taxation within the province, for raising revenue for provincial purposes.

It was felt by the Fathers of Confederation that the provinces' control over the public domain,[3] with its incidental revenues and the power to impose systems of licensing, would provide adequate provincial revenues to meet what were expected to be modest needs.[4] Provincial deficits which might occur from time to time were to be met by federal subsidies. The area of direct taxation was viewed as a sort of residual source of provincial revenue, which it was not intended should be used extensively:

> . . .direct taxes were extremely unpopular: they had never been levied by the provinces and. . .the nature of the economy made the administration of direct taxation, except by the municipalities, very difficult. . .[5]

Before continuing, let us say a few words about the terms *direct* and *indirect* taxation. Sections 91 and 92 do not make any clear distinction between these two terms, and it was not until a decision of the Judicial Committee in 1887 that a working definition was set down. The distinction made then has pretty well withstood the ravages of time, and remains even today the basic rule for determining the validity of provincial tax measures. The Judicial Committee took a definition from the writing of John Stuart Mill and stated:

> Taxes are either direct or indirect. A direct tax is one that is demanded from the very persons who it is *intended* or desired should pay it. Indirect taxes are those that are demanded from one person in the expectation and *intention* that he shall indemnify himself at the expense of another. Such are the excise or customs. . . .He shall recover the amount by means of an advance in price.[6]

Thus, direct taxes include such things as personal income tax, corporate income tax, real property tax, and succession duty and indirect taxes include customs duties, excise taxes, etc.

The courts have tended to emphasize the intention of a provincial tax measure as the crucial determinant of its validity, and have not too seriously limited the power of the provincial legislature to tax, merely because one of the effects of a measure may be indirect. In the case of corporation income taxes, for instance, it is quite likely that corporations do attempt to indemnify themselves at the expense of the consumer, but the courts have judged such a provincial tax valid because the intention is that it shall be paid directly by the corporation. In the case of retail sales tax, the provinces have been enabled to collect from the retailer a tax which is levied on the customer because the retailer is assumed to be the "agent" of the government for the purposes of administering this tax. When the store

---

[3]BNA Act, S. 109.
[4]*Rowell–Sirois Report*, Book 1, p. 44.
[5]*Rowell–Sirois Report*, Book I, p. 44.
[6]*Bank of Toronto v. Lambe*, 1887, as cited in Olmsted, vol. 1, p. 222. See also *Rowell–Sirois Report*, Book I, p. 59.

clerk punches up the cost of one's purchase, he is functioning on behalf of the store, and when he calculates the sales tax and adds it to the total, he is functioning as an agent of the province. By naming each retailer a sort of "tax collector," and by requiring that he calculate the tax separately, the province ensures that the sales tax can pass as direct. If the sales tax were included in the price of retail goods, and collected from the store, it would be indirect, because the retailer would be "indemnifying himself at the expense of the customer" by a rise in the retail price of the goods.

While the province is given the power to levy direct taxes, and the interpretation of the scope of "direct taxation within the province" has been very broad, this tax power has not been deemed to be exclusive. It has been felt by the courts that the terms of 91(3) are general and that they therefore give the federal parliament the power to impose both indirect and direct tax measures. Conversely, Section 92(2) is very specific and it therefore must be construed only to limit the provincial legislatures to the raising of revenues by direct taxation, and not to reserve the direct tax fields to the exclusive use of the province. In other words, the constitutional authority to levy indirect taxes rests exclusively with the parliament of Canada, and the authority to levy direct taxes is shared by the provinces and the federal government.

In retrospect, the way in which sources of revenue were distributed between the provinces and the federal government seems naive and short-sighted. The drafters of the BNA Act assumed that there would be no change in the percentage of the total costs of government that each would bear. Furthermore, they assumed that the major revenue sources would remain the same after 1867. Both of these assumptions were to be proven incorrect. It would be unfair, however, to criticize the Fathers of Confederation for lack of foresight because the changes in the environment of the Canadian political system which have taken place since 1867 could not have been foreseen except through the gift of clairvoyance. One of the effects of these environmental changes was the enormous expansion of the revenue needs of the provinces. The federal share of the costs of government fell from more than two-thirds of the total in 1867 to less than one-half of the total seventy years later.[7] The tax base also changed, so that customs duties, for instance, which accounted for 63 per cent of the total federal revenue in 1867–68, accounted for a mere nine per cent of the total in 1967–68.[8]

THE FEDERAL–PROVINCIAL REVENUE STRUCTURE: THE EARLY TWENTIETH CENTURY

By the turn of the century, the federal–provincial financial structure had begun a startling metamorphosis. Following a period of economic stagnation when provincial expenditures did not increase remarkably, the so-

[7] *Rowell–Sirois Report*, Book I, p. 63.
[8] Canadian Tax Foundation, *The National Finances 1967–68*, (Toronto, 1969), p. 51.

called "wheat boom" produced an immense growth of overall government expenditures. All sectors of government, federal, provincial and municipal, were spending large sums of money on urban development and economic expansion, and from 1896 to 1913 total expenditures by all governments quadrupled.[9] The costs of this rapid expansion of the role and responsibilities of government were met by corresponding increases in revenue. Customs and excise receipts accounted for over 90 per cent of federal revenues and produced surpluses during most of the years between 1900 and World War I.[10] Provincial revenues from standard tax sources also increased, but provincial expenditures grew more rapidly, so that the traditional tax bases of the provinces began to be squeezed dry. The inelasticity of federal subsidies and the inability of existing revenue sources to cope with the rising costs of government services forced the provinces to venture into the field of direct taxation, despite the current unpopularity of such measures.[11]

From 1914 to 1920, the federal government had been forced to impose special taxes in order to meet the uniquely high costs of the war effort. During this period, under the provisions of the War Measures Act, the federal government virtually took over the control of the economy, and the question of federal–provincial financial relations was left in a state of suspended animation until the end of the war. During the immediate postwar period and through most of the 1920s, ". . .in its whole fiscal policy, the Dominion was labouring for a return to pre-war 'normalcy'."[12] In pursuit of this goal, the federal government tried to reduce or withdraw the special taxes that had been imposed at the time of the war, but the economy had changed so much that it was difficult—or indeed impossible—to go back. Prewar normalcy and postwar normalcy were completely different economic species.

Between 1921 and 1930, welfare expenditures increased by 130 per cent, and three-quarters of this increase was taken over by the provincial governments and the municipalities.[13] Federal outlays in this period were limited largely to grants to the provinces in support of provincial old-age pension schemes and unemployment relief. Meanwhile, the costs of the traditional provincial and municipal responsibilities for roads and highways grew rapidly. The coming of the automobile increased the need not only for interurban highways but for better roads and road systems within the cities and in the suburban areas.[14] Fortunately, during the 1920s, while the cost of roads and relief soared, provincial revenues increased rapidly as well. The automobile, for instance, brought in large additional revenues through taxes on gasoline and motor vehicle licences. Indeed, provincial revenues doubled from 1921 to 1930, and two-thirds of this increase was due to additional tax yields in the three fields of motor vehicle licences,

[9]*Rowell–Sirois Report*, Book I, p. 80.
[10]*Rowell–Sirois Report*, Book I, p. 81.
[11]*Rowell–Sirois Report*, Book I, p. 87.
[12]*Rowell–Sirois Report*, Book I, p. 127.
[13]*Rowell–Sirois Report*, Book I, p. 128.
[14]*Rowell–Sirois Report*, Book I, p. 129.

gasoline taxes and liquor control. Thus, the growing responsibilities of the provinces and the fiscal instability of the provincial financial structure were disguised to some extent by a growing economy which brought a high yield from direct taxation.

Revenues from the public domain, which had been expected to meet a large part of the costs of provincial programs, dropped to a mere 10 per cent of the total provincial revenues in 1930. Succession duties and corporation taxes increased as sources of revenue during this period, but in 1930, of the total provincial revenue from these sources, 87 per cent was collected in the Provinces of Ontario and Quebec, who together accounted for only 60 per cent of the population of Canada. The reason for this disparity was the growing number of national companies with head offices in Toronto or Montreal. The imposition of provincial corporation taxes occurs at the head office of a corporation, with the result that profits which the corporation makes elsewhere in Canada are taxed by the governments of Ontario or Quebec. This was to prove an important factor in producing serious regional disparities in per capita revenues, as corporation taxes and succession duties came to play a larger and larger role in provincial finance during the 1930s.[15]

The Canadian federal system thus entered the hard years of the depression with a very vulnerable revenue structure. The provinces relied heavily on revenue from tax fields such as liquor control and automobile licences, which tended to vary with economic fluctuations of a general nature. Similarly, the municipalities relied entirely on real property revenues which declined when the value of real estate dropped during the depression.

Constitutional and practical considerations prevented the provinces from diversifying their tax base. Indirect tax measures were constitutionally beyond the competence of the provincial legislatures, and direct tax measures such as personal income tax would have produced a low yield except in the central provinces. Moreover, the federal government had already occupied the field of personal income tax, and any extra tax on the already hard-pressed individual income would have produced further economic problems.

Total government expenditures on relief grew from 18.4 million dollars in 1930 to a peak of 172.9 million dollars in 1935, and since responsibility for such matters lies with the provinces, the federal government transferred large portions of national revenue to the provinces to help pay for them. Provincial and regional disparities were enhanced by the incidence of the depression, for

> . . .the larger the decline in the income and the larger the consequent rise in government expenditures in the most unfavourably situated provinces, the more rapidly did local revenues and credit become hopelessly inadequate and the larger was the support which had to be obtained from the Dominion.[16]

[15]*Rowell–Sirois Report*, Book I, p. 131.
[16]*Rowell–Sirois Report*, Book I, p. 160. Reproduced with the permission of Information Canada.

Thus, by the mid-thirties Canadian federalism was faced with a financial crisis which was the product of several factors. First, traditional functions of government had grown far beyond the expectations of the Fathers of Confederation, and the bulk of this growth involved great increases in provincial expenditures. Secondly, new responsibilities of government had emerged which had not even been conceived of in 1867, and the interpretation of the BNA Act by the Judicial Committee of the Privy Council had vested only the provincial legislatures with the constitutional power to deal with them. Thirdly, the revenue structure of the Canadian federal system provided the provincial governments with inadequate tax fields to meet both the new responsibilities and the inflated traditional responsibilities. Finally, the incidence of a world-wide depression exaggerated the already serious disparities in wealth between the various regions of Canada, and produced startling inequalities in the standard of governmental service from one province to the next.

The Dominion government's immediate response to this crisis was to engage in extensive programs of intergovernmental and interregional transfers of revenue in the form of conditional and unconditional grants to the provinces. Before entering a discussion of these grants, however, let us look briefly at the evolution of the system of federal payments to the provinces from Confederation to the 1930s.

FEDERAL GRANTS TO THE PROVINCES

The Statutory Subsidies It was clear even to the Fathers of Confederation that the provincial revenue sources provided in 1867 were not going to meet the expenditures of the provincial legislatures, at least for a transitional period. In recognition of this, provisions for federal subsidies to the provinces were written directly into the BNA Act. Section 118, which was subsequently repealed and replaced, gave the provinces three broad types of federal grants: 1) annual grants to support provincial governments and legislatures; 2) per capita grants; and 3) payments on debt allowances. The first of these was a subsidy based on the population of the province at the 1861 census, which was to be paid to the province to assist in the initial setting up and operation of the government and legislature in the first few years. This grant was to be given to the provinces annually and in perpetuity, and was not to be adjusted with population increase. When a general revision of the federal subsidies to the provinces took place in 1907, however, this grant was raised for all the provinces. Despite this, the grants to support the provincial governments and legislatures amount to a mere pittance (rânging from $100,000 for Prince Edward Island to $240,000 for Ontario) by comparison with the total federal subsidies. The second subsidy, the per capita grant, was intended to be the major assistance that the federal government would render to the provinces. Based on the 1861 census, the provinces were to be given 80 cents per capita per annum in perpetuity, although the per capita grants to New Brunswick and Nova Scotia were to increase with population up to 400,000 people.

The per capita grant was manipulated from time to time in order to entice new provinces into the federation and meet the special needs of one province or another. The manner in which this was achieved was through the device of estimating the population of the province generously. For instance, when British Columbia came into Confederation in 1871, her population was estimated at 60,000 when in fact it was only 34,-000; and Manitoba was given the fictitious population of 17,000 when it had only 12,200.[17] While these grants were to be fixed at the figure established at the time of Confederation, the 1907 revisions of the subsidies saw the 80 cents per capita grant permitted to increase up to 2½ million people and 60 cents a head was provided for any number over that figure.

Finally, while the federal government had accepted the responsibility for all of the debts of the provinces at Confederation, it was felt that the provinces which had smaller debts should be rewarded in order to equalize the benefits that each would reap from the union. Each province was allowed a certain debt based on approximately $25 a head[18] according to the 1861 census. If the actual debt of a province amounted to less than this figure, that province was to receive 5 per cent of the difference as a grant from the federal government, annually and in perpetuity. According to this scheme, while New Brunswick and Nova Scotia either broke even or gained a little from the Dominion, Ontario and Quebec had debts that were far in excess of the debt allowance. It was arranged that these provinces would pay the federal goverment a figure equal to 5 per cent of the difference between their actual debt and the amount allowed by the Confederation agreement. This arrangement was never implemented, partly because of the difficulty of assessing how much each of Ontario and Quebec should pay on a debt that they incurred jointly as the colony of Canada. To get around this difficulty, and to further appease the Province of Nova Scotia, the debt allowance was raised so that Ontario and Quebec broke even and New Brunswick and Nova Scotia got an even larger payment from the Dominion. As the other provinces came into the federation, they also were given generous debt allowances. Even the Provinces of Alberta and Saskatchewan, which had been federal territories before their coming of age and so obviously had no debt, received an annual payment based on the difference between their debt allowance and their nonexistent debt.

In addition to these three basic kinds of subsidies, ever since Confederation there have been a number of special federal grants to various provinces and regions in order to meet special needs. New Brunswick, for example, received a grant for ten years after Confederation, and the Province of Newfoundland received a healthy subsidy on entering Confederation in 1949. Special grants were given to the Prairie Provinces on entering Confederation in 1905, as compensation for the Dominion's retaining its rights to their natural resources. Even after the Dominion gave the natural resources of the Prairies back to Saskatchewan and Alberta, the compensation grant was continued. Thus, while it was assumed that the arrange-

[17]Dawson, *The Government of Canada*, p. 102.
[18]Dawson, *The Government of Canada*, p. 100.

ments concluded at Confederation would be permanent and inalterable, in fact the federal subsidies to the provinces have undergone almost constant revision. Faced with the pressures of economic circumstances and the remarkable inadequacies of the federal–provincial revenue structure, the Dominion has been forced by political exigency to adjust and supplement the original arrangements. Despite these constant adjustments of the subsidies, the statutory subsidies today form a very small part of the total which is transferred from the federal to the provincial governments.[19]

Conditional Grants The statutory subsidies discussed above have "no strings attached." In other words, when a province receives such a grant from the federal government, it may spend the money in any way that it deems suitable. Such grants to the provinces are usually referred to as *unconditional grants*. Since 1913, federal transfer payments to the provinces have more frequently taken the form of *conditional grants*, or *grants-in-aid*. The conditional grant is offered to the province only so long as it is spent for the purposes specified by the Dominion. The first conditional grants were for agricultural instruction and were offered for a ten-year period. The province got the money from the Dominion on the condition that it be spent for agricultural instruction which met certain standards. Most conditional grants work this way, and furthermore, most require that the province itself contribute some proportion of the costs of the program.

In the early period, such shared-cost programs were viewed as either ". . .experimental or. . .given under extraordinary circumstances. . . ."[20] and as such they were usually intended to terminate after a specified time period. At the close of World War I, federal grants-in-aid were provided for such things as assistance for highways, technical education, the control of venereal disease and the maintenance of employment offices.[21] It was at that time that two schools of thought regarding the utility and the advisability of conditional grants first evolved. One group felt that the conditional grant was a handy device for pursuing vigorous policies of federal leadership in spite of the strait jacket of the BNA Act. The opponents of this particular form of subsidy agreed that it permitted the federal government to take vigorous initiatives, but they did not think that this was a good thing.

The clearest argument against the conditional grants is that they permit the federal government to set spending priorities for the provinces even in fields that are constitutionally beyond its legislative competence. The basic source of power which is possessed by the federal sector in this regard is the so-called "spending power," by which the central government is free to spend its tax dollars in any way it sees fit. By offering to pay one-half of the cost of a particular welfare program, the federal government

---

[19]Total federal payments to the provinces in 1973 amounted to $4773.1 million, and of that only $33.7 million was accounted for by statutory subsidies. Canadian Tax Foundation, *The National Finances, 1972–73* p. 145.

[20]*Rowell–Sirois Report*, Book I, p. 131.

[21]*Rowell–Sirois Report*, Book I, p. 131.

can usually "bribe" the provinces to implement programs which it could not constitutionally undertake itself. The province, although it may feel that a different program should have priority, will usually be forced by economic expediency to commit its limited resources to programs partially funded by the federal government. By allowing the federal government to prejudice provincial priorities in predominantly provincial fields, shared-cost grants place the autonomy of the provinces in some jeopardy.[22]

The second criticism of conditional grants is based on the old maxim of the English constitution that the government which spends public funds should be accountable for them.[23] With conditional grants, once the money has been transferred to the province, there is no sure procedure by which the federal authorities can ensure that all of the funds transferred have been spent for the purposes specified. Hence it would be possible for a province to accept money for a shared-cost program in higher education and then turn around and spend it on highways. Even if it was discovered that the money had been used for purposes other than those specified, it would be very difficult for the federal government to take any action in retaliation. The only recourse for the federal government would be to refuse to support the province in future joint projects, which might be politically unwise, since the people of the provinces also vote in federal elections. Hence, it is likely that the provinces, from time to time, will spend a bit of their conditional grant money for programs other than the federally sanctioned ones. The federal authorities, on the other hand, minimize this possibility by supporting basically popular programs, the neglect of which could prove costly at the next election for the delinquent provincial government.

The final objection, especially pertinent for the smaller provinces, is that the federal grants-in-aid can tend to pressure the provincial government into undertaking shared-cost programs which cannot be easily supported by the limited financial resources of the province. If the federal government offers to pay 90 per cent of the cost of building a stretch of the Trans-Canada Highway between two cities in New Brunswick, it is difficult for the province to refuse, although it may well be that the 10 per cent which constitutes the provincial share is beyond the means of the province at that time. As a result, shared-cost programs encourage the provinces to borrow so that they can take advantage of federal conditional subsidies, even though they are living beyond their means.

THE FINANCIAL STRUCTURE IN CRISIS: THE ROWELL-SIROIS COMMISSION

As pointed out in earlier sections of this chapter, the 1930s saw the Cana-

---

[22]*Rowell–Sirois Report*, Book I, p. 131. See also Dawson, *The Government of Canada*, p. 105; D. Smiley, "Conditional Grants and Canadian Federalism: The Issues," in Meekison, *Canadian Federalism*, pp. 256–268.

[23]*Rowell–Sirois Report*, Book I, p. 131.

dian federal system faced with a number of apparently insoluble problems. The federal financial structure was totally inappropriate for an era which called for massive expenditures on unemployment relief. The provincial governments were saddled with the responsibility for not only relief, but highways and education as well, all of which were among the most costly governmental programs being financed in the thirties. The federal government, on the other hand, had been denied any role at all in the performance of these functions because of the construction placed on the terms of Sections 91 and 92 by the courts. Denied the legislative competence to deal with the problems of the thirties, the Dominion, however, possessed the revenues which were needed to pay for programs such as relief and education. The result was an enormous increase in transfer payments, in the form of both conditional and unconditional grants to the provinces. The federal government collected the taxes and the provinces spent them, an unhappy situation for federal politicians.

Besides increasing the financial difficulties of the provinces *vis-à-vis* the Dominion, the depression accentuated the problem of regional disparities. Some provinces suffered more than others from the hardships of the depression, with the result that the standard of services offered to Canadians in some parts of the country was poorer than the standard of services in others. Regional economic disparities became a major variable in Canadian politics, and it soon became obvious to the government of the day that action had to be taken to remedy the situation before it led to serious disharmony within the federation. One major response to the financial crisis of the thirties was to appoint a Royal Commission in 1937 which was directed to undertake:

> a reexaminaticn of the economic and financial basis of confederation and of the distribution of legislative powers in the light of the social and economic developments of the last seventy years.[24]

The research by the commission was extensive, as the commissioners travelled from one end of the country to the other several times, hearing the recommendations of provincial governments, various pressure groups, and interested individuals. The findings and recommendations were finally reported in May of 1940.

The focus of the *Rowell–Sirois Report* was on the two basic problems of federal provincial finance in Canada: 1) the distribution of responsibilities and revenues between the provinces and the Dominion, and 2) the economic disparities existing among the various provinces and regions of Canada. As a solution for the former, the Commission recommended an extensive shift of both governmental functions and tax powers, and as a solution for the latter, the Commission recommended "equalization payments" from the federal treasury to the needy provinces.[25]

Specifically, the *Report* stated in its recommendations that the Dominion should take over the debts of all of the provinces, take over the responsibility for unemployment relief, and pay a National Adjustment

[24]*Rowell–Sirois Report*, Book I, p. 9.
[25]Dawson, *The Government of Canada*, pp. 107–108.

Grant to the less fortunate regions of Canada in order to bring the standard of services there up to the national average. In return for this, however, the report recommended that the provinces give up all claim to the fields of income tax, corporation taxes, corporate income taxes and succession duties, and that the original statutory subsidies be abolished.

The recommendations of the *Rowell–Sirois Report* were discussed in Federal–Provincial Conferences in 1940–41, and were not met with any great enthusiasm by the provinces. The "have" provinces, especially, were not willing to give up their taxing powers in return for an "allowance" from the federal government, and even the "have-not" provinces were not very happy with being raised merely to "the national average" by the national adjustment grants. By 1940, too, Canada was involved in World War II, and the focus of the national attention had shifted to matters other than federal–provincial relations. Besides, prosperity had returned. The economic hardships of the 1930s were quickly forgotten during the inflationary wartime period, and it was easy for the provinces and the Dominion to postpone any serious consideration of the Rowell–Sirois recommendations until after the war.

THE POSTWAR PERIOD

The outbreak of war had given the federal authorities the moral justification and the legal authority (under the "emergency power" in Section 91) to usurp all of the remaining governmental spending initiatives from the provinces. The Dominion occupied, among other things, much of the field of direct taxation to the exclusion of the provinces, and paid the provinces a *rent* in lieu of the revenue that was lost to them. The result of this was that the federal government controlled the entire revenue structure of the federation and the provinces were reduced to the state of receiving an "allowance" from the Dominion. In terms of the expectations and perceptions of the public, the federal government had become *the* government; the provinces were of secondary importance. Governmental initiative appeared to rest solely in the hands of the Dominion, and the provinces, particularly the "have-not" provinces, humbled as they were by the financial catastrophe of the depression, seemed willing to accept the leadership of the Dominion.

Despite this apparent acceptance of the postwar leadership of the federal government, neither the "have" nor the "have-not" provinces were eager to adopt the terms of the *Rowell–Sirois Report* which would have permanently centralized both public finance and the responsibility for all major policy initiatives. The federal government countered with a new set of proposals for federal–provincial relations, which were produced in the so-called "Green Book" of 1945. These proposals, in accord with the *Rowell–Sirois Report*, would have handed over to the federal government the exclusive power to levy income taxes, corporate income taxes, and succession duties. Unlike the Commission's report, the Green Book did not provide for unconditional equalization payments to the poor provinces. Instead, the federal government preferred to subsidize the provinces through a series of shared-cost programs funded jointly by provincial revenues and federal conditional grants.[26] This alternative had been specifically singled out by the Royal Commission as undesirable:

> . . .the conditional grant as it works under Canadian conditions is an inherently unsatisfactory device. . . .We believe it to be more costly than if the service in question were financed by a single government. It unquestionably leads to delay and to periodic friction between Dominion and provincial governments.[27]

Because the Green Book proposals were presented as a package deal and because the provinces would not give up their share of the key direct taxes, the Dominion–Provincial Conference of 1945 was unsuccessful in its attempts to secure a permanent arrangement. But as Professor Smiley points out:

> . . .almost from the day the conference was finished, federal authorities began to seek limited and piecemeal agreements with the provinces in particular matters.[28]

It seems that although provincial politicians were not willing to sell their birthright, they were willing to allow the federal government to continue setting the major policy priorities, at least for the time being. The political pressure to equalize the standards of services in the various economic regions of Canada played a large part in securing this cooperation between the provinces and the Dominion. A faint blush of nationalism, the result of a common cause and shared hardships during the war, was perceptible on the face of Canada at this time. Although there was some residual bitterness in Quebec as a result of the conscription issue, for a while at least, Canadians of all regions and walks of life became accustomed to thinking in national terms, rather than provincially or regionally. The goal of raising the standard of living of the less fortunate regions of Canada was politically popular in all provinces, and the natural vehicle for programs which would achieve this goal was the federal government. The keystone of postwar federal–provincial relations was formed by a series of federal–provincial fiscal agreements, to which we must now address ourselves.

FEDERAL–PROVINCIAL FISCAL ARRANGEMENTS 1945–1977

Through the Wartime Tax Agreements of 1941, the provinces had ceased to levy personal income taxes, corporation income taxes, and all other cor-

---

[26]Smiley, "Public Administration and Canadian Federalism," *Canadian Public Administration*, Vol. VII, No. 3, Sept. 1964, pp. 371–388.

[27]*Report of the Royal Commission on Federal–Provincial Relations*, (*Rowell–Sirois Report*), (King's Printer, Ottawa, 1940), p. 259. Reproduced with permission of Information Canada.

[28]Smiley, "Public Administration and Canadian Federalism," *op. cit.*, p. 277.

poration taxes. While these fiscal arrangements are euphemistically referred to as "agreements," the fact was that in 1941, because of the emergency conditions of wartime, the federal government possessed the
constitutional power to unilaterally exclude the provinces from the field of
direct taxation and, for that matter, to interfere with any of the matters reserved exclusively to the provinces by Section 92 of the BNA Act.[29] Under
the circumstances, all the provinces entered into tax agreements with the
federal government for the period 1941–1946. In return for the revenue
that would be lost to them by giving up these fields of taxation to the Dominion, the provinces were to be paid a rent or a *tax rental payment* based either on the revenue yields in the vacated fields in the year 1941, or on the
total cost of servicing the provincial debt. The choice between these alternative formulae of compensation for lost revenue was left to the provinces
themselves, and as it turned out, Quebec, Ontario, Manitoba, and British
Columbia opted for the former and the rest of the provinces opted for the
latter.

In order to discourage the provinces from increasing their succession duties, provincial succession duty collections were subtracted from the
federal rental payment to those provinces which elected the formula based
on the cost of servicing the provincial debt (i.e., New Brunswick, Nova
Scotia, Prince Edward Island, Alberta and Saskatchewan). Another provision that was unique to these wartime agreements was that which guaranteed the existing level of provincial revenue from liquor and gasoline taxes,
regardless of the rental payment formula selected by the province.[30]

1947–1957

By the time the 1941 tax rental agreement had expired, the war
was over, and it was no longer within the jurisdiction of the Dominion to
compel the provinces to enter into fiscal agreements. A second tax rental
agreement which covered the period 1947–1952 was signed by most provinces, but the federal government could not convince Quebec and Ontario
that it would be to their advantage to rent any of their tax fields. These
provinces, therefore, did not enter the tax rental agreements of
1947–1952, although the rest did. Upon entering Confederation in 1949,
Newfoundland also agreed to the existing tax rental arrangements, which
meant that eight provinces participated for most of the 1947–1952 period.
During this period, the eight provinces agreed not to levy income taxes,
corporation taxes, and succession duties; and in return, the federal government paid them a rent based on either a per capita payment, or on the
revenue yield in the province from the vacated tax fields—except in the

[29]See Fort Frances Pulp and Paper Company v. Winnipeg Free Press, (1923) 3
D.L.R. 629; Cooperative Committee on Japanese-Canadians v. Attorney General
for Canada, (1947) 1 D.L.R. 577; *Reference Re Validity of Wartime Leasehold
Regulations*, (1950) 2 D.L.R. 1.
[30]This was in part to compensate the provinces for revenue lost as a result of wartime rationing.

case of Prince Edward Island which was given a specified lump sum. The 1947—1952 tax agreements also permitted the participating provinces to levy their own five per cent tax on corporation income in the province.

The real benefit that the provinces gained by entering the rental agreements of this period was that the federal government, which had set up the machinery for collection of direct taxation on a national basis during the war years, could collect the taxes more cheaply than the provinces. Most of the provinces could not afford to duplicate the federal machinery, and those which could afford it could see that the extensive administrative machinery required for the collection of personal income tax particularly would render separate federal and provincial systems extremely inefficient. Partly for this reason, Ontario reconsidered its position during the negotiations for the next tax rental agreements.

The Province of Quebec alone refused to enter the federal–provincial tax agreements for the period 1952–1957. These agreements were generally similar to the preceding ones. The participating provinces refrained from imposing personal income taxes, corporation taxes and succession duties, with the exception of Ontario which continued to levy its own succession duties.

The most significant difference in the 1952–1957 arrangements was that the payments to the provinces were guaranteed at a certain minimum for each province, and the actual rent paid to each province was adjusted upwards according to a formula which related per capita GNP and provincial population.[31] In other words, the "have" provinces received larger payments than the "have not" provinces, but at the same time, the less fortunate provinces were guaranteed a certain amount regardless of the actual revenue yield of the vacated tax fields of that province. This particular provision of the 1952—1957 tax rental agreements contained the germ of the principle of the unconditional equalization payments to the "have–not" provinces which today form so significant a part of the federal–provincial fiscal arrangements.

1957–1962

The Tax Sharing Arrangements Act of 1956 set out the terms of the federal–provincial tax agreements for the period of 1957–1962. According to this act, the participating provinces agreed to vacate the *standard tax* fields of personal income tax, corporation taxes and succession duties, as before. The federal government, in return, agreed to pay the provinces a rent based on the revenue yield in the vacated fields. The basic federal payment to the provinces according to this agreement amounted to 10 per cent of federal personal income tax collections in the province, 9 per cent of corporation profits in the province, and 50 per cent of the revenues of federal succession duties in the province, based on a three-year average of collections.

[31]Canadian Tax Foundation, *The National Finances*, 1965–66, (Toronto, 1966), p. 126.

The 1957–1962 arrangements, however, also provided an un-conditional *equalization payment* to the poorer provinces. The federal government agreed to pay those provinces an amount sufficient to bring the per capita yield of each province in the three standard taxes up to the average per capita yield from those three taxes in the two wealthiest provinces. Finally, the Tax Sharing Arrangements Act also provided for a *stabilization grant* which was calculated to raise the total yield for a province up to a. set minimum. That minimum was based on either the previous financial arrangements extended into current years; or the last payments under the previous arrangements but adjusted for population growth; or, 95 per cent of the average payments for the previous two years under the 1957–1962 arrangements.[32] The aim of the stabilization payment was to prevent the revenue yield of the various provinces from fluctuating a great deal from one year to the next.

All of the provinces entered into these agreements to some extent. However, Quebec opted to accept only the unconditional equalization payment, and Ontario chose not to vacate the fields of corporation tax and succession duties. For those provinces which did not fully participate, a *tax abatement* was granted. The federal government, in order to prevent the taxpayer from being doubly taxed, agreed to withdraw partially from any of the fields of income tax, corporation tax, or succession duties if a province continued to levy its own taxes. Thus, as the Province of Ontario did not vacate corporation income tax fields, the federal government abated its own corporation income tax by 9 per cent of the corporation profits (an amount equal to what the province would have received as a rental payment had it chosen to rent that particular tax field). The Province of Quebec was granted, in lieu of rental payments, a tax abatement in each of the three standard tax fields which was equal to the amount the province would have been paid by the federal government had she entered the agreement (10 per cent of federal personal income tax, 9 per cent of the federal corporation tax, and 50 per cent of the federal estate taxes).

In 1958 in response to demands by the provinces, the federal government raised the rental payment for personal income tax to 13 per cent of the federal revenues collected, and provided an equivalent raise in the abatement in that tax field for the Province of Quebec. In 1960, a new twist was added to the already confusing structure of federal–provincial relations, by permitting any province which wishes to do so, to "opt out" of the federal program of conditional per capita grants to the provinces in aid of university education. If a province chose to opt out of this program it would receive, in lieu of the conditional grant, 1 per cent more of corporation profits in the province. It was provided that if the revenue from 1 per cent of corporation profits was less than the province would have received in the form of per capita conditional grants, the federal government would make good the difference. Conversely, if the 1 per cent happened to be greater than the per capita grant would have been, the province had to refund some revenue to the federal government. Only the Province of Que-

[32]See Canadian Tax Foundation, *The National Finances, 1965–66*, p. 127.

bec opted out of the university grants program, but the significance of this provision is that it set a precedent which led to a proliferation of "opting-out" formulae in a great many joint federal–provincial programs.

Other provisions were included in the 1957–1962 agreements to meet the specific needs of the Atlantic provinces. Special Atlantic Provinces Adjustment Grants were added to the agreement in 1958, in order to meet specific economic problems which that region of Canada faced at that time. These grants are unconditional, and they amount to an extension of the principle of equalization to secure added assistance for a region which cannot make ends meet with the standard equalized federal payments. The Province of Newfoundland was also given additional annual grants by special legislation that was passed in 1959.

1962–1967

Until 1962, the federal–provincial tax agreements had been based on the principle that the federal government should levy the taxes and collect the revenue, and then pass over a percentage of the "take" to the provinces participating in the agreement. The attitude of the federal government was that the ability to tax is an important power and that if the federal government could convince the provinces to give up at least some of this authority, it would enhance its own role in the economy. However, the unfortunate consequence of this situation from Ottawa's point of view was that the federal government was getting a "black eye" from the public which perceived it as the *taxing government*, while the provinces were getting credit as the *spending governments*. If the provinces were to receive the praise from the public for spending money on popular social welfare programs, roads, etc., the federal authorities felt that the provinces should also take some of the blame for high taxes. Therefore, the Federal–Provincial Fiscal Arrangements Act (1961), which was to apply to the period of 1962–1967, set out a tax-sharing plan which was different in form from anything which had existed before. According to this act, the federal government would undertake to withdraw partially from the taxes which it had previously shared with the provinces, in much the same way that the federal government had agreed to grant tax abatements to nonparticipating provinces in the previous agreements. Thus, the federal government would actually withdraw from the corporation income tax field to the extent of 9 per cent of corporate profits and from the personal income tax field by 16 per cent of the federal tax. The percentage withdrawal or abatement of the personal income tax field was to increase from 16 per cent in 1962 at a rate of 1 per cent per annum, until it reached 20 per cent by 1966. This arrangement was subsequently altered as a result of demands from the provinces so that the total withdrawal from the field of personal income tax was 24 per cent in 1966. In the field of succession duties, the federal government agreed either to pay the province 50 per cent of revenues from the federal tax or to grant an abatement to the extent of 50 per cent of the federal tax in the provinces that wished to levy their own succession duties. In

1963, the federal payment/abatement of succession duties was increased to 75 per cent of the federal tax.

Under the 1962–1967 arrangements, the equalization payment was based on the per capita revenues from the three standard taxes as before, but the equalization base was modified to include, as well, 50 per cent of the three-year average yield from taxes on natural resources in the province. This provision was added because some provinces, particularly Alberta with its vast revenues from oil and gas taxes, were receiving healthy equalization payments under the old formula, and did not really need them. What Alberta lacked in income and corporation tax revenues, she could easily make up with resource tax revenue, whereas provinces like New Brunswick suffered from low revenue yields in all tax fields. A further change in the equalization formula was to base the calculation on the national average yield in the standard taxes rather than the average yield in the two wealthiest provinces. However, in 1963, this was changed so that the equalization payment was calculated on the three standard taxes only and based on the average per capita yield in the two wealthiest provinces, as it had been in 1957–1962. While natural resources revenues thus no longer figured in the equalization formula, it was provided that any province whose revenues from this field of taxation exceeded the national average would be faced with a deduction from its equalization grant.[33]

While the intention of the federal government in undertaking to withdraw from the shared tax fields was to distribute the political responsibility for taxes among the governments that were spending the revenues, it did not wish to penalize the provinces financially. Hence, under the Fiscal Arrangements Act, the federal government offered to continue to collect the provincial share of income tax and corporation income tax, free of charge, provided the province utilized the same tax base. As a result of this, the provinces all began levying their own income taxes and corporation income taxes in 1962, and all except the Province of Quebec, which had previously set up its own collection machinery, signed collection agreements with the federal government. In the field of corporation income tax, Ontario, like Quebec, chose to look after its own collections. During the 1962–1967 period, six of the provinces set their tax rates at the same level as the federal government's, with Saskatchewan and Manitoba adopting higher rates, Quebec continuing the rates which were already in existence in that province, and Ontario raising the corporation income tax rate.

The stabilization grants continued during 1962–1967 much as they had in the previous period, with the federal government guaranteeing the provinces' yield from the standard taxes and equalization payments at a level equal to 95 per cent of the average yield for the preceding two years. The Atlantic Provinces Adjustment Grants and the special grants to Newfoundland were continued for the 1962–1967 period with only slight changes. The 1 per cent abatement of corporation income tax in lieu of

---

[33]For a further explanation of this arrangement, see Canadian Tax Foundation, *The National Finances, 1965–66*, p. 128.

grants in aid of universities was continued as before, and the Province of Quebec alone continued to exercise this option.

In 1965, the federal government passed the Established Programs (Interim Arrangements) Act by which provinces so desiring were permitted to opt out of certain federal–provincial shared-cost programs without any financial penalty. For each program that the province chose to opt out of, the federal government allowed either an additional abatement in the field of personal income tax, or a direct cash payment in lieu of the federal share of the cost of the program. Provinces wishing to take advantage of the opting-out provisions were compelled by the federal legislation to continue the program along the same lines as the federal program for a certain specified interim period, during which they had to submit to a sort of audit by the federal authorities to insure provincial compliance with the terms. It was furthermore provided in the act that the additional percentage points of income tax given up by the federal government would be equalized:

> . . .an equalization payment was made to bring the per capita yield from the abatement points specified for each program up to the average per capita yield of the same number of points in the top two provinces. If the equalized abatement provided more than what the federal contribution to the program would have been, had the province not opted out, a recovery was made; conversely, if the equalized abatement fell short, an additional payment from the federal government was forthcoming. . . .[34]

The programs to which the Established Programs (Interim Arrangements) Act applied are separated into two categories: those for which the province opting out would receive a certain number of equalized abatement points in personal income tax, and those for which the opting-out province would receive a straight cash compensation. The provinces were given until October, 1965 to decide whether or not they wanted to exercise the option set down in this legislation. When the time limit expired, only the Province of Quebec had accepted the opting-out formula, and that provincial government exercised the privilege in all of the Category I programs, and in the forestry program of Category II. The effect was to give the Province of Quebec an additional 20 per cent of the personal income tax. When this is added to the 24 per cent abatement of personal income tax which applied to all of the provinces by 1966, Quebec got a total abatement of 44 per cent of personal income tax, 10 per cent of the profits of corporations in the province, and 75 per cent of succession duties; the balance of provincial revenue comes from federal grants to finance the joint programs. The choice made by Quebec at this time was probably determined by the high level of nationalist feeling within the province, and by the desire of the provincial authorities to focus the loyalties of the Québecois on Quebec rather than on Canada. The rest of the provinces decided to stay in the joint programs for reasons of economic efficiency: it was cheaper for them to continue to use the machinery and procedures which existed at the time rather than try to create completely new provincial ones.

[34]Canadian Tax Foundation, *The National Finances, 1967–68*, p. 132.

1967-1977

The Federal–Provincial Fiscal Arrangements Act of 1966 defined the tax agreements and the various unconditional intergovernmental transfers for the period 1967–1972. Under this act, the federal government increased its basic abatement of personal income tax from 24 per cent to 28 per cent of the federal tax payable in the provinces. The corporate income tax abatement, which had been 9 per cent of corporate profits in the provinces other than Quebec, was raised to 10 per cent in all provinces for the 1967 tax year. The abatement of succession duties remained substantially the same as it had been under the previous arrangement; i.e., the abatement for provinces that levy their own estate taxes or the federal payment for provinces that do not levy their own tax was 75 per cent of the federal tax due in the provinces.

The formula for calculating equalization payments was altered radically by the 1967 arrangement. Instead of being calculated on the per capita yield of the three standard taxes, the payment was figured on the revenue yield of sixteen different provincial revenue sources. Although the actual mathematical calculations are rather intricate, the principle is that a national average per capita provincial revenue is calculated for each of the sixteen revenue sources, and the per capita yield in each of the revenue sources is figured for a particular province. Where the province's per capita yield is lower than the national average for a given revenue source, the province is given a *positive entitlement* and where the province's per capita yield is more than the national average for that field, the province is given a *negative entitlement*. If the total of all the entitlements for all of the revenue sources comes to a positive figure, the province receives that much in the form of a per capita equalization payment. If, on the other hand, the total of all the entitlements of one province comes to a minus figure, the province does not get any equalization payment. This equalization formula is felt to be more equitable than older formulae in the long run because, being based on all major provincial revenue sources, it gives a more accurate reflection of provincial need.

In order to prevent hardship being suffered by the provinces which were to receive smaller equalization payments under the new formula, the federal government agreed to make special interim equalization payments to such provinces. Saskatchewan was the only province that would have suffered under the new formula, so the federal government granted that province a five-year transitional equalization payment based on the province's equalization entitlement during the last year of the 1962–1967 arrangements. An additional equalization payment was also granted to the Atlantic provinces to compensate them for revenue lost through the termination of the Atlantic Provinces Additional Grants. The amount of this additional equalization payment was exactly the same amount that they had been paid under the Additional Grants Act, so that the change here was only in the title given the specific unconditional transfer payment.

The stabilization grants were continued for the 1967–1972 period, and the formula used to calculate the actual payment was based on the same principle as the equalization formula; that is, the base was the per capita yield from the sixteen provincial revenue sources in the previous year. If the revenues of a province for the current year fell below 95 per cent of the yield from the previous year, the province would get a stabilization grant. Partly because of growing provincial revenues, and partly because of the generosity of the federal government to Saskatchewan and the Atlantic provinces, no payments were ever made.

The 1972 Federal–Provincial Fiscal Arrangements Act established the basic tax agreements for the five year period 1972–1977. Under this agreement the equalization formula remains basically the same as for the previous five years, although the revenue sources on which the payment is calculated have been expanded from sixteen to nineteen. Stabilization grants are also provided for in the new act but to the time of writing no province had actually received any payments. The federal government has withdrawn completely from the estate and gift tax fields as a result of the 1971 federal income tax reforms, and in most cases the provinces have stepped in to occupy the vacated fields. The basic collection agreements which applied in the previous five years apply to the 1972–1977 period as well. Other minor changes have been incorporated in the legislation but the system remains virtually identical in principle to its predecessor.

TABLE 8-1: PROVINCIAL INCOME TAX RATES: 1971–1972

Province	1972 Specific Converted Rates % of Federal Tax	1971 Rates % of Basic Federal Tax
Newfoundland	36.0	33
Prince Edward Island	36.0	30
Nova Scotia	30.5	28
New Brunswick	41.5	38
Ontario	30.5	29
Manitoba	42.5	39
Saskatchewan	37.0	34
Alberta	36.0	33
British Columbia	30.5	28
Quebec (not specified in Act)	34.0	31
	+ 24 abatement	+ 22 abatement

Source: Canadian Tax Foundation, *The National Finances*, 1972–73, p. 144.

The opting-out provisions were increased to provide an additional abatement of up to 24 per cent of federal income tax. The percentage of the total income tax field left to the provinces varies from province to province under an arrangement whereby the revenues of the provinces are guaranteed not to fall below their 1971 level if they adopt income tax acts modelled on the new federal legislation. As shown in Table 8-1, provincial income taxes as a percentage of income taxes at federal rates range from 30.5 per cent for Ontario, B.C., and Nova Scotia to 42.5 per cent for Manitoba. The Province of Quebec, whose rates are not specified in the new legislation, taxes at a level equivalent to 34 per cent of the federal rate and gets an additional 24 per cent abatement for opting out of shared-cost programs. This means that if one is a resident of the Province of Quebec, a full 58 per cent of one's income taxes go to the provincial coffers.

The arrangements by which the provinces and the federal government share the tax revenues gleaned from the taxpayer are at least as complicated in 1975 as they were in 1941. However, since the war years Canada has moved a long way in making the system more equitable between regions. Many of the goals set by the Rowell–Sirois Commission have been adopted piecemeal through a gradual process of federal–provincial bargaining and compromise, although in some cases the means employed would not have met the stringent prescriptions of the Commission. The goal of reducing regional disparities in the standards of services provided has been at least partly achieved, through unconditional equalization and stabilization grants and through federal participation in various shared-cost programs. The fact that Quebec is not a province *comme les autres* has been recognized *de facto* in the opting-out arrangements for various joint programs, while at the same time, the basic equality of all the provinces has been asserted by extending the privilege of opting out without financial penalty to any province that so desires. The basis on which equalization payments are calculated has been elaborated and made more equitable between regions. And having set up many needed services either by itself or through joint programs, the federal government is now moving in the direction of handing back to the provinces the responsibility for maintaining many of them, along with the additional revenue sources to meet the costs.

TABLE 8-2: ESTIMATED EQUALIZATION ENTITLEMENTS BY REVENUE SOURCE, 1972–73

Equalization Entitlements	Nfld.	P.E.I.	N.S.	N.B.	Que.	Ont.	Man.	Sask.	Alta.	B.C.	Total 7 recipient provinces
					($000)						
Personal income taxes	41,302	9,341	38,480	42,457	117,219	-305,566	21,988	56,354	11,657	-38,616	327,141
Corporation income taxes	10,126	2,275	12,866	11,807	30,221	-74,296	3,924	17,441	-9,912	-4,452	88,660
General and miscellaneous sales taxes	14,416	3,764	11,661	9,902	114,039	-106,739	5,336	24,910	-28,751	-52,164	184,028
Motive fuel taxes	12,656	528	5,833	3,120	18,216	-31,893	4,081	222	-13,660	322	44,656
Motor vehicle licensing revenues	4,586	191	2,114	1,131	6,601	-11,557	1,479	80	-4,950	117	16,182
Alcoholic beverage revenues	7,216	153	1,842	5,374	40,237	-28,054	-2,637	3,048	-4,740	-23,483	55,283
Hospital and medical care insurance premiums	6,571	1,423	4,622	5,158	15,807	-38,432	1,434	7,136	2,020	-6,466	42,151
Succession duties and gift taxes	4,163	722	2,776	3,576	1,504	-23,950	3,267	3,754	5,160	-972	19,762
Race track taxes	1,048	47	911	943	-527	-6,948	976	1,582	-96	1,855	4,980
Forestry revenues	-1,126	749	4,548	-132	10,856	33,688	4,901	2,763	4,885	-61,132	22,559
Oil royalties	4,879	1,029	7,296	5,902	55,557	71,773	8,407	-18,832	-143,558	7,547	64,238
Natural gas royalties	1,226	258	1,833	1,483	13,958	17,731	2,279	1,208	-41,143	1,167	22,245
Sales of Crown leases and reservations on oil and natural gas lands	1,487	314	2,224	1,800	16,936	21,514	2,765	1,465	-49,920	1,415	26,991
Other oil and gas revenues	2,093	17	3,130	2,532	23,832	30,388	3,891	-5,169	-59,090	-1,624	30,326
Metallic and non-metallic mineral revenues	-5,790	348	1,940	978	3,500	-1,806	-3,398	-973	5,037	165	-3,395
Water power rentals	-295	282	1,790	683	-10,857	5,976	-234	1,380	3,730	-2,455	-7,251
Other provincial taxes	4,470	860	4,376	4,372	12,127	-27,948	900	5,095	-2,238	-2,014	32,200
Miscellaneous provincial revenues	5,757	1,108	5,636	5,630	15,618	-35,993	1,159	6,562	-2,883	-2,594	41,470
Federal government revenues shared with the province	-1,604	-263	-1,212	794	4,466	-1,955	620	1,117	-3,827	1,864	3,918
Total equalization entitlements	113,181	23,146	112,666	107,510	489,310	-514,067	61,138	109,143	-332,279	-181,520	1,016,694

Note: A negative total indicates no equalization payable.
Source: Canadian Tax Foundation, *The National Finances*, 1972–73, p. 144.

TABLE 8-3: BREAKDOWN OF FEDERAL CONTRIBUTIONS TO THE PROVINCES AND MUNICIPALITIES FISCAL YEAR 1970–71

	Nfld.	P.E.I.	N.S.	N.B.	Que.	Ont.	Man.	Sask.	Alta.	B.C.	Total
					($000)						
A. Payments to Provinces											
Total unconditional grants	107,321	36,847	97,155	89,276	668,002	186,991	70,006	62,984	70,175	17,649	1,406,406
Conditional Grants											
Hospital Insurance	24,002	4,829	37,498	28,077	305,784[b]	368,931	46,894	43,982	82,521	95,476	1,037,994
Medicare	12,281	809	17,754	3,426	56,126[b]	174,452	23,194	22,470	38,074	51,935	400,521
Other Health	691	249	1,352	810	14,785[b]	26,101	2,186	3,085	6,428	3,505	59,192
Welfare	22,219	3,812	17,294	16,480	221,994[b]	176,650	28,588	20,690	40,111	69,607	617,445
Education—other than post-secondary	8,672	2,252	9,723	11,193	76,709	11,730	18,929	15,384	2,057	20,197	176,846
Transportation	9,608	88	1,461	4,207	17,970	6,859	947	1,388	1,399	2,553	46,480
Resource development	37,759	277	16,072	36,625	27,077	5,815	3,873	3,729	5,305	3,870	140,402
Agriculture	17	28	27	30	981	561	907	358	1,087	262	4,258
Emergency Measures Organization	82	21	112	33	843	1,077	144	127	234	309	2,982
Recreation and Culture	29	26	35	33	121	133	34	39	65	69	584
Other	124	112	107	4,457	29,987	14,330	824	680	931	948	52,500
Total	115,484	12,503	101,435	105,371	752,377	786,639	126,520	111,932	178,212	248,731	2,539,204
B. Payments to Municipalities											
Grants in lieu of taxes	253	204	4,770	469	10,266	25,729	3,058	1,454	2,792	3,935	52,930
Conditional Grants[c]	—	—	966	841	460	19,597	1,050	278	2,016	5,252	30,460
Total	253	204	5,736	1,310	10,726	45,326	4,108	1,732	4,808	9,187	83,390
TOTAL FEDERAL PAYMENTS	223,058	49,554	204,326	195,957	1,431,105	1,018,956	200,634	176,648	253,195	275,567	4,029,000

[a]Includes cash transfers with respect to post-secondary education but excludes payments of provincial property tax.
[b]Represents equivalent received through opting out. [c]From Statistics Canada. *Local Government Finance* (Estimates)
Sources: Department of Finance, Statistics Canada (as above) and Public Accounts. Reprinted from *The National Finances*, 1972–73, Canadian Tax Foundation.

Part 4
System–Environment Linkages

9
Political Parties in the Canadian System

For many Canadians, to think of politics is to think of political parties. Media reports on politics concentrate on party reactions to issues of the day. Millions of Canadians simplify the complexities of politics by viewing politics almost exclusively through the focus of "their" party, and, to almost all politically interested Canadians, the most obvious part of political life is the activities of these large, distinctive and highly entertaining social organizations. Yet this very visibility makes it all too easy to view the functions of parties in an inappropriate light. We may easily attribute to parties a false importance in the policy process while failing to recognize their vital importance in the electoral process. This chapter is intended to clarify the role of political parties in the Canadian political system.

THE FUNCTIONS OF CANADIAN POLITICAL PARTIES

Perhaps the most reasonable way to begin the examination of Canadian political parties is to look at their main goal. That goal is, quite simply, to get people elected—preferably enough of them so that the party can formally control the government. That is not to deny that the people in political parties have other, perhaps more basic, goals. They may be very eager to institute certain policies and they may even aim at the restructuring of Canadian society. But whatever their ultimate purpose, they have chosen the political party as the organizational device with which to gain the power to realize their ideas; the immediate goal of the party is to gain and hold power, and in Canada that implies the use of the electoral system.[1]

---

[1]We refrain from giving a lengthy definition of a political party in this introduction, if only to avoid time-consuming and not very productive debates about whether organizations like the Créditistes are "really" political parties. We prefer to adopt the same loose definition used by Leon D. Epstein in *Political Parties in Western Democracies* (Praeger, New York, 1967) who suggests, "almost everything that is called a party in any Western democracy can be so regarded for the present purpose. This means any group, however loosely organized, seeking to elect governmental office holders under a given label." (pp. 9–10).

As a by-product of their effort to achieve this goal, political parties perform for the Canadian political system a number of other important functions which are discussed below. All these functions are vital to the survival of the system, but all can be performed more or less efficiently by other institutions. In fact, most are carried out simultaneously in various parts of the political system, so that if parties fail to perform a function thought to be within their realm, the system need not necessarily suffer; another institution such as the bureaucracy or an interest group may be performing it adequately.

First, political parties in Canada provide managers and decision makers for the political system and organize them in keeping with the requirements of a parliamentary form of government.[2] In a parliamentary system, priority decisions are made primarily by the cabinet, and parties not only recruit but help to organize the men who make up the cabinet. The party system ensures that whatever the backgrounds of cabinet ministers they do have one common loyalty—to the electoral machine which got them into power and must be used to keep them there. Equally important, in a parliamentary system where the cabinet can lose its right to govern if defeated on a major issue in the House of Commons, parties provide a framework within which legislative support is made predictable. Provided that a cabinet does not through arrogance and complacency abuse the loyalty of its supporters, it can count on a secure enough tenure to be able to plan for the future.

The management and operation of a political system requires that men and women be properly trained for the job, and political parties play an important role in the training of political decision makers. In this respect parties function as agents of political socialization, establishing campus political clubs, propagandizing the public and, most importantly, establishing electoral machinery within which people may advance up the hierarchy of electoral participation. In addition to socializing people to hold electoral office, this process may be effective in recruiting people to fill appointive offices in the system by arousing their interest in the political process.

Even if a person does not participate actively in politics, political parties may be important in his political socialization. At election time (and to a lesser extent between elections), political parties provide stimuli to which people can respond. They provide publicity for the issues around which political attitudes can be shaped, and symbols with which people can identify. It would be extremely difficult for the average citizen to make his voting decisions on the basis of personal knowledge of all issues. Because most people are only dimly aware of the issues, and because their views are often highly inconsistent over time,[3] they require relatively per-

[2] J.R. Mallory, "The Structure of Canadian Politics," in H.G. Thorburn, *Party Politics in Canada*, (Prentice–Hall, Toronto, 1967), p. 24.
[3] See Philip Converse, "The Nature of Belief Systems in Mass Publics," in D. Apter (ed.), *Ideology and Discontent*, (The Free Press, New York, 1964), pp. 206–262. Converse found that the reproducibility of opinions over time was often *less* than would have been expected had people merely guessed at their previous opinions. See also Chapters 3 and 4, above.

manent symbols to which they can attach their allegiance, and with which they can simplify the realities of politics.

Political parties in Canada have often been called the "broker-mediators" of society; they mediate conflict between society's competing interests. To a large extent, of course, the performance of this mediating role depends on the nature of the particular party. It would hardly be appropriate for instance, to call the Canadian Communist Party a broker or a mediator, for its aim is the complete remaking of Canadian society, and the overthrowing in the process, of most of the interests among whom the other parties mediate. Similarly, the early CCF could hardly have been called a broker-mediator for it, too, considered capitalists to be the fount of all evil. The two major parties in Canada, on the other hand, have epitomized the brokerage pattern of politics, and the traditional analysis of Canadian political parties has tended to revolve around this fact.

> Canadian politics, it is emphasized, are politics of moderation, or broker-age politics, which minimize differences, restrain fissiparous tendencies and thus, over time, help knit together the diverse interests of a polity weak in integration.[4]

The argument is that, in order to get elected nationally, a party must appeal to a broad cross-section of Canadians with all sorts of different opinions on all sorts of different issues. The party must *aggregate* a wide spectrum of interests into a voting coalition, and in so doing, it performs an integrative function for the political system as a whole.

At the provincial level, such aggregative behaviour may not be as necessary as at the national. In some cases there is sufficient consensus within a province to allow a party with a single overriding principle to at-

[4]A. Cairns, "The Electoral System and the Party System in Canada 1921–1965," *Canadian Journal of Political Science*, vol. 1, no. 1, p. 63, March 1968. See also F. Englemann and M. Schwartz, *Political Parties and the Canadian Social Structure*, (Prentice–Hall, Toronto, 1967), pp. 222–239. The original expressions of this "broker-mediator" function are found in H. McClokie, *Canadian Government and Politics*, (Longmans Green, Toronto, 1944), pp. 81–83; J.T. McLeod, "Party Structure and Party Reform" in A. Rotstein (ed.), *The Prospect of Change*, (McGraw–Hill, Toronto, 1965) pp. 4–5, 9, 14; Alexander Brady, *Democracy in the Dominions*, R.M. Dawson and N. Ward, *The Government of Canada*, 4th ed., (University of Toronto Press, Toronto, 1963), pp. 468–470; J.A. Corry and J.E. Hodgetts, *Democratic Government and Politics*, 3rd ed., (University of Toronto Press, Toronto, 1963), chs. 8–9; F.H. Underhill, *Canadian Political Parties*, Canadian Historical Association pamphlet, (Ottawa, 1957), pp. 4–5. For critiques of this theory, see Cairns, "The Electoral System and the Party System in Canada 1921–1965" and John Porter, *The Vertical Mosaic*, (University of Toronto Press, Toronto, 1965), pp. 373–377. Cairns points out that "...the necessity for inter-group collaboration in any on-going political system makes it possible to claim of any party system compatible with the survival of the policy that it acts as a nationalizing agency." (p. 63). He is thus, perhaps, suggesting that the brokerage theory of Canadian politics has limited utility since it is really tautological. We would not go so far as that since different political systems have different amounts of cleavage to reconcile and can use different institutions to do so. In Canada, political parties may have been more important in this reconciliation than in many other systems.

tain power. For example, C.B. Macpherson has argued that Alberta in the
1920s and 1930s was a single-class society with a dominant interest in re-
lieving the burdens of its "quasi-colonial" status *vis-à-vis* eastern Canada.
It was therefore possible for dogmatic parties which were not broker-
mediators to succeed in provincial elections. Both the United Farmers of
Alberta and the Social Credit Party in that province were a far cry from
the older national parties with their "omnibus nature".[5]

In general, the larger and more diversified the province, the more
difficult it becomes for a "party of principle" rather than a broker-
mediator type of party to get into power. In Ontario, for example, only
once did a party of principle gain power: The United Farmers of Ontario
won office in 1919, although they were defeated at the next election and
shortly disappeared from the political scene. In Quebec the experience has
been similar, the early Union National being the only party of principle to
have gained power. It, however, adopted rather quickly the typical brokerage position.

At the national level, the Progressives of the 1920s were a party of
principle.[6] They won 65 seats in the 1921 federal election, but soon fell
prey to internal dissension and were ultimately absorbed by the brokerage-
oriented Liberals. The CCF was, of course, the most persistent of the non-
brokerage parties at the national level. But while the CCF competed electorally for some 29 years, except for a brief period in 1944 and 1945 when
its Gallup poll popularity equalled that of the two older parties, it never
seriously threatened the preeminence of the Liberals and Conservatives.
Since the formation of the NDP in 1961 from elements of the old CCF, a
conscious attempt on the part of most of its leaders has led that party in
the direction of creating a more broadly based coalition with what they
hope to be correspondingly greater chances for electoral success.[7]

In addition to the function of aggregation, Canadian political parties perform the function of interest *articulation*. Once again, this function
derives from the electoral goal of parties in Canada. Since a party wants
power, it must maximize electoral support, and the simplest way of doing
this, as has been suggested above, is to attempt to aggregate the interests of
groups in society. In Chapter 4, however, it was seen that there are millions of Canadians who are eligible to participate in the electoral process
but do not do so: by virtue of their apathy and lack of political resources,
however caused, these people are functionally disfranchised. If a party
could mobilize them by articulating their interests in such a way as to gain
their electoral support, that party could possibly gain power even if it pays
less attention to the interests of more highly politicized groups.

Canadian parties, therefore, make *some* attempts to articulate the
needs and opinions of the politically weak. They frame appeals to gain the

---

[5]C.B. Macpherson, *Democracy in Alberta*, (University of Toronto Press, Toronto,
1953). See also S.M. Lipset, *Agrarian Socialism*, (University of California Press,
Berkeley, 1950) for an analysis of the rise of the CCF in Saskatchewan.
[6]W.L. Morton, *The Progressive Party in Canada*, (University of Toronto Press, Toronto, 1950).
[7]W. Baker and T. Price, "The New Democratic Party and Canadian Politics," in

support of the poor, immigrants, and other voters who might not otherwise be heard. But they do it rather badly. The voters they hope to reach are often so unaware of politics that they do not listen, and the political parties themselves are largely dominated by the middle and upper classes. It is still, then, evidently simpler and safer to gain power by the "tried and true" technique of aggregating the interests of the politically conscious groups.

In addition to transmitting information from the environment to political decision makers, parties also communicate decisions from the system back to the environment. Generally, the final stage in the communication of such information is handled by the media or by interest groups, but these structures often work with the assistance of political parties. Chapter 3 pointed out that people see information through a perceptual screen which colours that information according to their pre-existing set of attitudes. Thus, if a person has a strong or fairly strong party identification (and approximately two-thirds of Canadians claim such identification) he will pick up information which conforms to and reinforces his partisan preference. Hence the fact that parties take positions on political issues, combined with the fact that people pick up information associated with the position of "their" party, leads the parties to perform the function of communicating political information to society.

Closely connected with the communication of political decisions and information to society is the feedback of information to decision makers regarding the effectiveness of their policy decisions. Parties form an important link in this evaluation process. A party in power must have accurate information in order to assess public attitudes to its "record". Similarly, the opposition parties must know the weaknesses of the party in power in order to launch a credible attack at the time of the next election. Like most of the functions described so far, the feedback function is not particularly well performed by Canada's parties. The low level of political activity of many Canadians, and a number of features of the party structure (to be discussed below) result in parties not performing as effectively as they might in this role.

Parties also have a series of interconnected functions which could probably best be described as *support functions*. *Specific support*, derived from satisfaction with specific allocative decisions of the system, is often channelled through a political party because it provides one of the frameworks within which the citizen can express his attitudes to the authorities. There are, of course, parties in Canada which have sought to overthrow not only the existing authorities, but the regime or the political community as well. For example, the Communist Party, whose specific goal is the overthrow of the liberal democratic regime, and the Parti Québecois, which seeks to break up the existing political community, are certainly not functioning as channels of specific support for the Canadian political system. Most Cana-

Thorburn, *Party Politics in Canada*, 2nd ed., pp. 168–179. A more complete analysis of the difficulty the NDP has faced in creating a broader coalition is found in Desmond Morton, *NDP: Dream of Power*, Hakkert, Toronto, 1974.

dian parties, however, do help to channel support for the system in which they exist.

It was established in Chapter 4 that people participate in electoral politics primarily because they find it interesting. It is parties that provide much of the campaign pyrotechnics which, around election time, attract attention to politics. The party attempts to create support for its candidates by selling people on its policies, its leaders and, perhaps, its ideology. By creating support for itself, the party also incidentally creates support for the regime of which it is a part.

This *diffuse support*, derived from general confidence and faith in the system, is important for the stability of the regime. It may be created partially through the continued satisfaction of specific needs by appropriate policy outputs. Thus, as political parties channel and create specific support, they are also helping to add to the residual capital of diffuse support which will assist the system to survive in difficult times. Finally, diffuse support can also be created directly through the processes of political education, socialization, and what is often referred to as propaganda: people can be convinced that the system is good and deserving of their support through symbolic outputs as well as through allocative ones. In the attempt to get their candidates elected, parties try to identify themselves with such values of the regime as justice, freedom, equality, and democracy. An important incidental effect of this process is to make people aware of the values of the Canadian political system and to create in them a basically positive or supportive orientation towards the regime embodying those values.

Even dissident parties such as the Communists or the Parti Québecois may be functional for the existing system in that they provide a legitimate channel for the expression of dissent. Were this dissent expressed entirely through rioting, bombing and kidnapping, the total effect would be exceedingly disruptive and harmful to society. These extreme political parties, however, encourage dissident factions in society to express their grievances legitimately through the electoral process. Furthermore, by providing focal points for dissent, parties like the Parti Québecois make the system's authorities aware of the fact that certain segments of society have serious grievances with which the political system must deal. Thus, oddly enough, even parties whose major goal is the overthrow of the existing regime or community may unintentionally perform useful functions for the system to which they are opposed.

While political parties in Canada, like those in other Anglo-Saxon democracies, confine themselves almost entirely to electoral functions, in many other Western democracies—Israel, Austria and Sweden are examples—parties perform an array of tasks for their members, including the provision of cooperative buying services, leisure-time activities, special educational programs and even burial societies.[8] Since nations where at least some political parties perform these functions outnumber those where

[8]Leon D. Epstein, *Political Parties in Western Democracies*, (Praeger, New York, 1969) pp. 119–120.

they do not, Canada must be considered a sort of anomaly with respect to the rather limited social services performed by its parties.

So far we have considered the functions performed for the system by the individual party. But the aggregate of those individual organizations, the *party system*, also has important effects. The fact that in the Canadian party system several parties are competing for political office at election time means that the voter is presented with a choice. It matters little whether that choice is made according to perceived differences in the parties' leadership, policies, or campaign "style"; as long as the voter has some real choice, one basic requirement for the persistence of a democratic system is fulfilled.[9] A second result of party competition is that political leaders can be kept accountable. We can vote to "throw the rascals out" because we can draw a line between "rascals" and "non-rascals"; the party labels and party discipline provide us with this line. As we shall see when we discuss the policy process, this accountability is of a very general nature only; yet it remains important to the workings of the Canadian system that the voter have this vehicle for expressing his disaffection, secure in the knowledge that another team is waiting to take over political leadership.

Up to this point we have painted an essentially rosy picture of the activities of political parties and the party system in Canada. It will be suggested in what follows that Canadian parties do not necessarily perform even their electoral activities very well. The combination of the structural features of our parties and the nature of the electoral process may often produce significant problems for the political system. These dysfunctions of parties and the party system may be viewed as a price we pay for the positive aspects of party activity, but we should also be aware of much in the nature of Canada's parties which could stand reform.

CANADIAN PARTY STRUCTURES

Typologies of Party Structures The most durable typology of party structures is that first suggested by the French political scientist, Maurice Duverger.[10] He suggested that political parties could be broadly typified as being *mass parties, cadre parties,* or *militia parties.*[11] *Mass parties* are

[9]How "real" are the alternatives with which we are presented at election time is a matter for discussion. The fact remains, though, that the Canadian's choice is still greater than the simple "yes" or "no" offered to the citizen of a one-party state.
[10]M. Duverger, *Political Parties*, (John Wiley and Son, New York, 1963).
[11]Englemann and Schwartz have modified this typology to fit Canada. See *Political Parties and the Canadian Social Structure.* Other authorities posit different classifications. For example, Leon D. Epstein (*Political Parties in Western Democracies*) suggests a four-fold classification as follows:
Rural—with a bare skeletal organization
Urban—patronage based
Urban—middle class mass membership
Urban—socialist working class
This classification seems to mix incentive and structural bases of classifications. Moreover, it is difficult to envisage just how to accurately classify Canadian parties

characterized by extra-parliamentary origins and by the fact that the mass party organization has power over the legislative branch of the party in policy making. The British Labour Party, continental Social Democratic parties and, perhaps, the NDP or Parti Québecois could be adduced as examples of mass parties. However, an important qualification must be entered. Roberto Michels, writing early in the twentieth century, noticed that the Social Democratic parties in Europe showed a discouraging tendency to be controlled by small cliques within either the legislature or the party executive.[12] His "iron law of oligarchy," which posits that large organizations—no matter how democratic their origins and ideology—will be controlled by a relatively small group of men at the top, limits the extent to which any political party can be controlled by its mass membership. At a certain point the requirements of efficiency appear to override the requirements of democracy.

Cadre parties are characterized by the fact that a relatively small group of leaders overtly holds power in the party. The small, well-organized elite which controls the party itself is usually to be found in the legislature. With the possible exception of the NDP, traditional Canadian parties are of this type. Here it will be argued that even the NDP should be considered basically a cadre party.

Militia parties are parties which have a tightly organized central core with highly dedicated supporters. In mass and cadre parties, the party is a relatively minor part of the life of most members, but in a militia party the party is virtually everything. The militia party is essentially an organizational weapon to be used to overthrow an existing political system or to maintain a totalitarian one. The Canadian Communist Party would like to be a militia party but is too weak to be properly categorized as such. The *Front de Libération du Québec* is the closest recent Canadian example. The Communist Party of the Soviet Union and the Chinese Communist Party are the classic examples of militia parties. In Canada, then, our concern is mainly with cadre parties. There are exceptions such as the early CCF, the early Social Credit, the United Farmers parties and the FLQ, but these are relatively rare.

Structural Types Within cadre parties, however, a further structural differentiation can be suggested. A cadre party may take the form of a hierarchy, a stratarchy, an alliance of sub-coalitions, or an open accordion.[13] A *hierarchical* party structure is pyramidal with a single leader at the top and direct and clear lines of authority running through successive levels to the bottom. A traditionally organized bureaucracy is typical of this organizational form. However, Canadian political parties, and indeed virtually all large western political parties, do not operate with this

in it. They are not patronage based in the U.S. sense, yet it would be difficult to categorize the older parties as middle class mass membership and they are certainly not urban socialist or rural. We have hence returned to the standard Duverger typology with an elaboration of the cadre classification as suggested below.

[12] Roberto Michels, *Political Parties*, (Free Press, Glencoe, Ill., 1949).
[13] S. Eldersveld, *Political Parties*, (Rand McNally, Chicago, 1964), pp. 47–178.

structure, for the lines of communication from top to bottom within a political party are generally very weak. Party members often do not know what the leaders are doing, and even when they do they may not necessarily follow. The leaders of Canadian political parties have very limited coercive powers over party members, and followers may consequently make statements and act in ways which are not at all what party leaders might like.

In recognition of this, it has been suggested that most large political parties, especially in North America, more closely approximate a *stratarchy*.[14] A stratarchy is basically a hierarchical structure in which the lines of communication between and within levels are rather weak, and in which the lines of authority are not clearly drawn. In Canada, constituency association executives often have only the faintest idea of what the "higher" level is doing, and even when they do know they may take actions or suggest policies which actually run counter to national party policy. More important yet, the provincial structures of Canadian parties can in no way be viewed as subordinate to the national structures as we might expect in a classical hierarchical structure.

Parties may take on a structure which could be described as an *alliance of sub-coalitions*.[15] In this type of structure, the party consists of a miscellany of groups, each fairly cohesive in itself and bound loosely to others in the party. Party members are there by virtue of their attachment to the sub-coalitions rather than to the party itself. For example, this type of structure could occur if several religious groups, unions, trade associations and community organizations came together in an attempt to gain power. Within Canadian parties this kind of structure occasionally occurs at the local level. In some local organizations of the NDP, for instance, union locals and labour councils may be allied with community associations. In Canada, however, an alliance of sub-coalitions is rare. Canadians usually join and work for political parties *per se* rather than joining them as a result of belonging to some other organization.

Finally, a party structure may be described as an *open accordion*.[16] This term means that the party structure is extremely loose and flexible with respect to membership, that it will accept virtually anyone as a member, and that it can be used as an avenue of upward mobility. In Canada it appears to be a fairly accurate description of every party. No Canadian political party is likely to deny membership to anyone except the most notorious criminal—and sometimes not even him. And, in a survey of delegates to the 1968 Liberal party leadership convention and the 1967 Conservative convention, some 13 per cent of respondents asserted that they had found membership in the party to be helpful to them financially, and 37 per cent felt that membership had been helpful in their social lives.[17]

---

[14]*Ibid.*, pp. 98–117.
[15]*Ibid.*, pp. 73–97.
[16]*Ibid.*, pp. 47–72.
[17]The data are derived from a mail survey of the delegates to the 1968 Liberal party convention. Over half the delegates to the conventions replied to the survey

Canadian Party Structure: Generalizations[18] Figure 9-1 shows, in very general form, an organizational chart for Canadian political parties. Arrowheads have purposely been left off the connecting lines because in a stratarchical structure it is not always possible to say in what direction influence flows. At levels below national or provincial offices, the

Figure 9-1

CANADIAN POLITICAL PARTIES: GENERAL PICTURE

Strong line of communication or influence ——————

Moderate line of communication or influence - — — —

Weak line of communication or influence ....

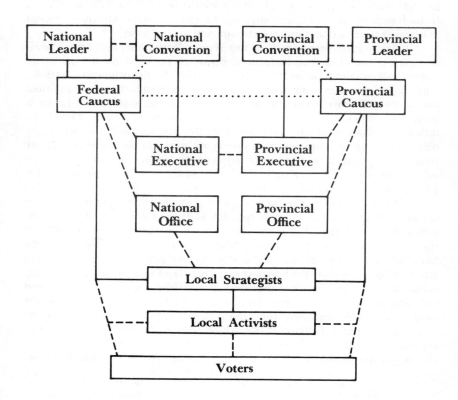

questionnaire. For this data we are grateful to Professors H.G. Thorburn, G. Perlin and J. Lele of Queen's University.
[18]Detailed information on specific party organizations is also provided in Chapter 10.

party structures virtually cease to exist between elections. The local strategists retire to their Kiwanis Club, neighbourhood committees or union halls, the local workers retreat to their households, and the local voters return to whatever they were doing before the election campaign started. Except for the local MP, a small office, and a few hyper-active local strategists, the party disappears.

This disappearance has many ramifications for Canadian politics. It means, first, that between elections, it is difficult to communicate with parties through channels other than the federal or provincial executive, or caucus. It is the well-organized representatives of middle-class or business Canada who are most able to do that. Although since 1973, MPs have been provided with a small budget to maintain local offices, and although virtually all of them try to be in their ridings frequently, the local machinery is not appropriate to effectively articulate the interests of the poverty-stricken, the poorly educated and the unemployed. Because these people are, generally, loath to approach an organization as "middle-class" as a Canadian political party, the party must approach them. However, except at election time, it does not have enough activists to do so.

As we have mentioned, in this respect both Canadian and American parties stand in considerable contrast to political parties in many other western democracies.[19] In Britain, Israel, the Scandinavian nations, Austria and to a somewhat lesser extent other western nations, the political party is much more a continuing living presence in society and hence is more able to act as an intermediary between citizen and state. The temptation is to draw from this the conclusion that the Canadian political system is deficient in some way that others are not; but one must remember that even if political parties do not perform this linkage function very well, other institutions—for example, the bureaucracy or interest groups—may perform quite adequately.

Perhaps one of the most curious features of the general picture shown in Figure 9-1 is the general lack of communication between federal and provincial party organizations down at least to the level of local strategists. Federal and provincial leaders frequently disagree or simply fail to communicate, the national and provincial executives and offices are often formally unconnected, and the national and provincial conventions, except for their having some members in common, are quite separate and independent. Since there are only a limited number of local strategists and activists available, and since their motivation may well be simply to be involved in the political "game" (for which purpose a provincial game is as good as a federal) there is a great deal of overlap between federal and provincial parties at that level. At the very bottom of the picture, however,

[19]A more detailed account of the structure and activities of western political parties between elections can be found in Leon D. Epstein, *Political Parties in Western Democracies*, pp. 98–166. Political parties in developing countries typically play a much larger role between elections. For a summary see Joseph Lapalombara and Myron Weiner, "The Origin and Development of Political Parties" in Lapalombara and Weiner (eds.), *Political Parties and Political Development* (Princeton University Press, Princeton, N.J., 1966).

there may again be considerable differentiation between federal and provincial parties. We will see in the next chapter that Canadian voters frequently vote for different parties at the federal and provincial levels.

Before concluding that the structural differentiation between federal and provincial parties is a dysfunctional aspect of Canadian politics, we should note that the provincial parties prefer it that way because it leaves them free to disagree with the federal government even if the parties in power are the same at the federal and provincial levels. Thus, while this structural feature may be disadvantageous for the creation of unified national policies, it may be quite appropriate in a federal society where intergovernmental bargaining is a critical dimension of policy making.

The independent status of provincial parties, long a feature of the Canadian party system, has stubbornly resisted sporadic efforts by federal-level parties to change it. Attempts to impose federal control over provincial parties have usually caused a furor in the provinces, with the result that the federal party must either retreat or watch the provincial party sever its ties with the national party.[20]

Paradoxically, this situation may not undermine the electoral success of the party, either federally or provincially. The most extreme example of the independence of a provincial party is the Liberal party in Quebec. Here, the federal and provincial organizations are formally completely separate, and informally, very nearly so. There is frequent disagreement on fundamental issues between the federal and provincial Liberals, yet the electoral success of the Liberal party in Quebec at both levels seems to indicate that this is a perfectly appropriate structure, given the main goal of Canadian parties.[21]

While the national and provincial executives and party head offices continue to exist between elections, the lines of communication between them and the parliamentary parties are often weak. The national executive committees meet at least annually, and MPs are often also members of the executive; but the feeling persists, especially in the caucus, that the executive exists to administer the party electoral machinery, and the caucus to determine party policy. Since members of legislatures are the most visible part of the party between elections, what they say or do is what the press reports and what the public picks up about the party. Thus, since the party organization is not important between elections, the extraparliamentary executives are relegated to second place in policy making.

Attached to the executive of most provincial and national parties is a permanent party office under the direction of a National or Provincial Director. The staff of this office is never very large. Until very recently, a typical national party office might contain—between elections,—a chief party organizer, an executive secretary for the party, two or three party re-

---

[20]For an example of this type of battle, see E.R. Black, "Federal Strains Within a Canadian Party," *Dalhousie Review*, Vol. 45, no. 3, 1965.

[21]Paul André Comeau, "La Transformation du parti libéral québecois," *Canadian Journal of Economics and Political Science*, vol. 31, no. 3, pp. 358–368, Aug., 1965. See also V. Lemieux, "Heaven is Blue, Hell is Red" in M. Robin (ed.), *Canadian Provincial Politics*, (Prentice–Hall, Scarborough, 1972), pp. 280–284.

searchers or administrative assistants, a public relations man, and a typist or two. Since 1966 there has been some expansion, but it has been slow. The national Liberal party office (the largest of the party offices) has traditionally been forced between elections, to scramble for money with all other party offices. This problem may partly account for the fact that Canadian party offices have not grown into large, well-organized institutions such as exist in Britain.[22]

Another location in Figure 9-1 where lines of communication are weak where they might be expected to be strong, is between the national and provincial offices, and the local strategists and workers. The problem again derives partly from the lack of work to do in a party organization between elections, and partly from the lack of finances for the permanent party organization. More surprising, however, is the fact that these lines of communication do not always become strong even during election campaigns. The torrent of directives, literature and information which issues from provincial or national headquarters at election time is sometimes ignored by the local organizations which feel that on the local issues they are better informed than the party bureaucrats in the capital.

The parliamentary structure of virtually all Canadian parties at either federal or provincial level revolves around the *caucus*. The parliamentary caucus is really just a regular meeting of the elected legislators in the party. While the legislature is in session, caucus meets at least once a week in plenary session. As well, there may be meetings of regional caucuses consisting of all the members from a particular region. In an opposition party, caucus meetings can often be quite lively; since very few men are clearly recognized as party leaders, almost all MPs feel free to have their say, and consequently policy debates can become heated. In the caucus of a governing party, the situation is different. There are clearly recognized party leaders—the PM and the cabinet. The government backbenchers have the clearly defined role of supporting the policies put forward by the leaders. The cabinet has access to considerable expertise from the civil service, and it is more likely to listen to the experts than to its own non-expert backbenchers on matters of policy. By the time caucus sees the policies, they have usually been approved by cabinet and are often in their final legislative form. This is not to assert that the government caucus has *no* influence on priority determination or policy formulation, but rather that its influence is often marginal. In reaction to this relegation to a minor role in government policy making, periodic "backbench revolts" occur in caucus, during which the backbenchers demand more policy influence. The upshot of these minor revolts, which seem to occur once in the life of every government, is nearly always the same: a few minor concessions by the cabinet, which disappear gradually over a few years until another backbench revolt occurs.[23]

The general picture of Canadian political parties shown in Figure 9-1 places the *convention* near the top of the party structure. Formally, this

[22]The structure of each party's national headquarters is discussed in greater detail in Chapter 10.
[23]More detailed material on caucus is presented in Chapter 17.

seems to be the most appropriate place to locate the convention, but in reality it is rather difficult to fit into the picture. Until recently conventions were not a regular feature of Canadian politics. In the two older parties they were held whenever there was a need to elect a new leader and only sporadically at other times.[24] Currently the Liberals, Conservatives and New Democrats are all committed to holding a mass gathering of the party faithful every two years.

For all three parties the convention performs similar functions, and is related more to the maintenance of group solidarity than to the establishment of party policy. The NDP convention may have slightly more influence over party policy than those of the Liberals and Conservatives. The November 1969 NDP conference in Winnipeg, however, was more or less typical of all Canadian conventions, the only major difference being that the backbenchers' policy proposals "talked out" by the party leaders were somewhat more radical than those regularly handled with disdain by the leaders of the older parties. That particular convention was preceeded by a great build-up of publicity surrounding the nationalistic "Waffle manifesto" drafted by a left-wing group of the extra-parliamentary party. The parliamentary wing of the party countered with a much less radical policy statement, which, supported by the rhetoric of the parliamentary party and the conservatism of the labour unions, was easily pushed through the convention. To no one's surprise the party leader, Tommy Douglas, was given an overwhelming vote of confidence—something his own constituents had denied him in the preceding election—and potential leaders, hoping desperately that Douglas would step down before too long, vowed undying support for their leader. The convention adjourned, the faithful went home, and the party carried on with little change in policy. Some NDP MPs, even remained in Ottawa throughout the convention because, after all, parliament was sitting.

A similar fate awaits many of the policy resolutions put forward at Liberal and Conservative conventions. Should the policy proposal accord with what the parliamentary leaders want, its chance of acceptance is good. Should it go contrary to the leaders' thinking, then even if the convention accepts the policy it will not appear in any legislative program proposed by the parliamentary wing until the leaders are convinced its time has come. Medicare, for example, was adopted by a Liberal convention in 1919 but not enacted by the parliamentary party until almost half a century later.[25] According to Joseph Wearing:

[24]While there is considerable material available on leadership conventions in Canada, there is very little on regular policy conventions. For a more detailed discussion of the nature and role of leadership conventions see D.V. Smiley, "The National Party Leadership Convention in Canada: A Preliminary Analysis," *Canadian Journal of Political Science*, vol. 1, no. 4, pp. 373–397, Dec., 1968. See also J. Wearing, "Party Leadership and the 1966 Conventions," *Journal of Canadian Studies*, vol. 2, no. 1, Feb., 1967; "A Convention for Professionals: The P.C.'s in Toronto," *Journal of Canadian Studies*, vol. 2, no. 4, Nov., 1967; "The Liberal Choice," *Journal of Canadian Studies*, vol. 3, no. 2, May 1968; and John Courtney, *The Selection of National Party Leaders in Canada*, (Prentice–Hall, Toronto, 1974).

[25]After the 1966 convention Prime Minister Pearson said in the House of Commons

The Liberals define accountability to mean that the convention determines policy (according to its amended constitution), which can be repudiated (according to Mr. Pearson). But it nonetheless exerts a strong moral force on the leadership.[26]

To call the moral force "strong" may be a bit of an overstatement in this case.

The above type of convention functions to create group solidarity. By bringing party members together it renews acquaintances and rekindles identity with the cause; in so doing, it improves party morale and the chances of success in the next election. A convention may conceivably also make MPs and leaders aware of changes in the environment which they might otherwise miss in their preoccupation with parliament. While policy changes may not be immediate, they may eventually result from the seeds sown at such conventions.

Even a leadership convention, held to elect a new party leader, is not entirely different.[27] It is bigger, noisier and more exciting than a policy convention and it gets the party vast amounts of free publicity which help in its attempts to get elected. And since leadership may be more important than ideology in determining party policy, the provision of a new leader may send a party off in a new policy direction. However, given the complex and aggregative nature of Canadian parties, even the shifts in direction produced by a change in leadership have usually been small. The election of Pierre Trudeau as Liberal leader in 1968 made little long-term difference to the direction of the Liberal Party, and the same can be said for the election of David Lewis as leader of the NDP and of Robert Stanfield as Conservative leader.

For the party activist and the public alike, leadership races within parties may be very much like elections. They focus attention on the party just as elections focus attention on the political system, and they provide a game which activists can play and the public can watch—not unlike a spectator sport. While everyone would like to see the leader of his choice win, the contest has "fun-value" in itself. Although there is little published data on the attitudes accompanying activity in leadership races, there is no reason to suppose that attitudes towards politics within parties should be any different from those towards the struggle between parties. There are occasional "sore losers" at conventions, but they are the exception rather than the rule.

Another type of party structure used increasingly throughout the 1960s was the *thinkers' policy conference*. These were small conferences in out-of-the-way locations or at out-of-season vacation resorts, attended by those MPs and MLAs who like to see themselves as "thinkers"; those party members who can afford to pay for their own transportation, accommoda-

---

that convention resolutions would be "taken very seriously as a guide to policy," but that they "did not establish policy." Even this was perhaps too generous an assessment of their significance. Joseph Wearing, "Party Leadership and the 1966 Convention", *Journal of Canadian Studies*, vol. 2, no. 1, p. 24.

[26]*Ibid.*, p. 25.

[27]See John Courtney, *The Selection of National Party Leaders in Canada.*

tion and registration fees; and a fair number of "resource people" or academics who lend or rent themselves out for such occasions. The purpose of these conventions was to keep the party in touch with current trends in the intellectual community and to provide policy initiatives. Conferences such as those at Niagara Falls (Conservative) and Harrison Hot Springs (Liberals) in the autumn of 1969 may indeed have had some influence over party policy. Earlier thinkers' conferences—such as that of the Liberals at Kingston in 1960 and that of the Conservatives at Montmorency Falls in August 1967—did produce discernible changes in party policy. The conference at Kingston helped push the Liberal party some distance to the left in the early and mid-1960s, and laid the groundwork for the rapid growth in government spending in the late 1960s; while that at Montmorency Falls produced the Conservative party's not overly successful flirtation with the *deux nations* theory.[28] The Niagara Falls Conference in 1969 kept the Progressive Conservatives from moving fully in support of a guaranteed annual income, even though the leader espoused the concept. Such conferences were the scene of much bitter argument and often elicited party-aimed tongue-lashings from the resource people, so they can hardly be viewed solely as a bid for favourable publicity.

It is difficult to know whether we should write about thinker's conferences in the present or the past tense. Although they were generally regarded favourably when they occurred, none have taken place since 1969—a fact which suggests that they have passed from the scene. Perhaps they are now just another memory of the high tide of "participatory democracy".

The party structures discussed up to this point have been primarily at the national or the provincial level. In 1969 parties entered municipal politics in Toronto and it is possible that the next few years will see further efforts by political parties in large urban areas.[29] So far the success of national parties in Toronto has been limited. Both the Liberals and the NDP, after a fairly intensive effort in 1970, agreed to keep a low profile in 1972 and abstained from conducting city-wide campaigns.[30] Even the specifically municipal "Civac" party which had considerable success in Toronto in 1970 disintegrated in 1972 as three of its leaders all decided to run for mayor. In Montreal, Mayor Jean Drapeau leads a political party of sorts but it is probable that his eventual disappearance from the political scene will see the end of the organization he now leads.

In summary, there is very little we can say yet about municipal political parties in Canada, whether they be offshoots of the national parties or purely local phenomena. Perhaps the question is of little overall significance; the national party allegiance of most local politicians is well

[28]Dalton Camp, "Reflections on the Montmorency Conference", *Queen's Quarterly*, vol. 76, no. 2, pp. 185–199, Summer, 1969.
[29]James Lightbody, "Party Politics and Local Elections", *Journal of Canadian Studies*, Vol. 6, no. 1, pp. 39–44, February, 1971.
[30]Stephen Clarkson, "Barriers to the Entry of Parties in Toronto Area Politics", in L. Axworthy and James M. Gillies (eds.) *The City: Canada's Prospects, Canada's Problems*, (Butterworth, Toronto, 1973).

known anyhow, and there is nothing to suggest that they would behave much differently in office if they were elected under national labels than if they were not.

In concluding our discussion of party structures and functions, we must resist the temptation to evaluate Canadian parties wholly according to preconceived notions of what parties *should do* in the political system. Unless it can be shown that the political system suffers thereby, Canadian parties should perhaps not be attacked for failure to perform functions which they have no intention of carrying out. What they are trying to do is to get elected; other functions are, for them, just incidental by-products of that effort. While we may note that parties have little success in standing for principles or in presenting the needs of the inarticulate, the fact that these functions are vital to the continued health of the political system does not mean that parties must perform them. On the other hand it may be that the political system would be healthier if parties did perform some of these functions. Perhaps readers can make up their own minds on this issue but they should not do so until they have obtained a picture of the entire Canadian political system.

10
The Bases of Party Support in Canada:
An Historical Perspective

Having discussed the overall role of political parties and the party structure in the Canadian political system, we turn in this chapter to a more detailed examination. First we will consider the early history of Canada's party system, examining the two older parties in some detail, and then we will discuss the more recent arrivals on the Canadian party scene.

THE CONSERVATIVES AND LIBERALS: THE RISE AND FALL OF THE TWO-PARTY SYSTEM, 1867–1917

While it is often assumed that Canada's two "old parties" have existed more or less unchanged in form since Confederation, this is far from true. Like any social structures which manage to survive, the Liberals and Conservatives have undergone a continuous process of adaptation in response to changes in their environment. In fact, in the Canada of the late 1860s and early 1870s there were no firm party lines at all.[1] Between 1867 and 1873 the Canadian government consisted of a loose coalition of many of the Liberal and Conservative elements which had initially favoured Confederation. Their unity, such as it was, arose out of a common desire to build a nation and to keep it together. Macdonald may have been the leader, but each of his ministers had his own personal following in both the House of Commons and the country. Building a government consisted of keeping enough of these men together to form a voting bloc in parliament.

Within the House of Commons there were "Tory" and "Grit" factions, but there were, as well, other kinds of groupings. On the government side sat cabinet members, their personal supporters, and assorted "loose fish" or "ministerialists" who had been elected by their constituents for the express purpose of supporting the government in hopes of gaining patron-

[1] E.M. Reid, "The Rise of National Parties in Canada", *Papers and Proceedings of the Canadian Political Science Association*, vol 4, 1932. See Also G.M. Hougham, "The Background and Development of National Parties", in H.G. Thorburn, *Party Politics in Canada*, (Prentice–Hall, Scarborough, 1972) pp. 2–14.

age prizes. The existence of ministerialists was made possible by a system of non-simultaneous elections whereby the party in power could call an election in safe seats first and gradually work out to more unfavourable ridings. In addition to giving the party in power a tremendous advantage, this system removed any uncertainty on the part of ridings which wanted to elect loose fish, by telling the local candidate which way to lean.

Sitting opposite the motley array on the government benches was an equally odd group. It consisted of members who, for a variety of reasons, did not like the governing coalition, together with a group of anti-Confederation Nova Scotia MPs who wanted out of the union and were not about to cooperate with anyone.

By 1872, however, the amorphous coalition of the Confederation period was beginning to break up and to be replaced by groupings of a slightly more coherent ideological cast. The group in power, which could now legitimately claim to be called the Conservatives, made the mistake of accepting rather large kickbacks (under the guise of "election fund contributions") from the promoters of the Canadian Pacific Railway, and although they won the election of 1872, they were forced to resign shortly thereafter when the dimensions of the scandal became known.[2] Nowadays it is expected that if one party is brought down, another coherent group will be available to take its place. Such was not the case in 1873. The Liberals who ruled Canada under Alexander Mackenzie from 1873 to 1878 had little to offer in the way of policy and lacked any cohesive party organization. In 1873 it was not absolutely certain who their leader was; Mackenzie, who emerged as titular leader and Prime Minister, had to fight a continual battle with Edward Blake, who was apparently unable to decide whether he wanted to lead the party, but who nonetheless retained great personal popularity. After five years in power, the Liberals had developed virtually none of the organizational attributes of a modern political party, and in 1878 they were defeated by the much better organized Conservatives.

The first ten years of Confederation, then, were characterized mainly by non-party government. Party structures had not yet had time to develop, and it is by no means certain that the relatively simple problems of government in the mid-nineteenth century really required strong party lines. There was not nearly so much need for a carefully integrated and coordinated set of policies. In addition, the lack of simultaneous elections and of the secret ballot made rigorous party organization less important in the years before 1878. Further, the process of functional differentiation of institutions—which accompanies industrialization and modernization in any society—takes time, and in political parties no less than in other Canadian institutions, the process was just beginning in the last third of the nineteenth century.

By 1878 there were simultaneous elections by secret ballot in eastern Canada, so that it was necessary for candidates to choose party lines before, not during, an election. This fact alone produced much firmer

[2]The "Pacific Scandal", as it was called, is covered thoroughly in Pierre Berton, *The National Dream*, (McClelland and Stewart, Toronto, 1970), ch. 3, pp. 90–134.

party lines in Canada. From 1878 to 1891 there was a consolidation of Conservative party lines under Macdonald, and in the Liberal party a period of aimlessness followed by a reformulation and regrouping under Laurier.

In the West, those were years of non-partisan and ministerialist politics. The primary concern of the West was to ensure that the railway went through and it would have supported any ministry that would build the railroad. In practice, that meant Macdonald's Conservatives—and the "kindly" Conservative government made it easy for westerners to support the government party by delaying the introduction of simultaneous elections in the West. This may account for the fact that strong two-party traditions never developed in the West. Provincial governments in Manitoba and British Columbia, and later in Saskatchewan and Alberta, sometimes went under standard party labels, but the lack of strong bipartisan competition led to an administrative form of government which later lent itself to easy capture by third-party movements.

The years from 1896 to 1917 could perhaps be characterized as "the golden age" of two-party politics in Canada. That period featured Robert Borden versus Wilfrid Laurier, both backed by well-organized electoral machines and well-disciplined parliamentary parties, in a genuine clash of ideas. No other party movements of any significance existed. Sectional discontent had not yet made a strong impression on the Canadian scene, ethnic cleavage was dormant for the time being, and the rural–urban cleavage which was to spawn the Progressive movement of the 1920s had not yet become important. The two major parties appeared able to aggregate the dominant interests in Canada successfully. Economic prosperity minimized dissent, and those who were discontented could move to the West to start again. In other words, the two-party system was able to successfully accommodate interests because the job was, for once, not particularly difficult.

Although Laurier was defeated in 1911, the years between 1911 and 1917 did little to disturb the equilibrium of the two-party system. But World War I, the "Conscription Crisis" of 1917, and the formation of the Union Government ended those days. Some three years after the outbreak of World War I, it became necessary, in Prime Minister Borden's view, to institute conscription in order to keep up the size of Canada's forces in Europe. French Canadians felt that the war had little relevance to their lives, and when this attitude was combined with evidence of inhospitable treatment received by any French Canadians who did join the armed forces, the opposition of French Canada to conscription was ensured. In an effort to unite Canadian opinion, Borden formed a Union Government with most English-speaking Liberals supporting him; but practically all French-speaking Liberals opposed him. The election which followed all but isolated French Canada, and temporarily destroyed the Liberal coalition which Laurier had so carefully constructed. In addition, it spelled the end of any strong support for the Conservative party in Quebec. The end of the war found the Canadian two-party system in a state of disarray from which it never recovered.

Although the immediate cause of the collapse of the two-party system was the conscription crisis and the formation of the Union Government, a number of more fundamental causes lay in the background. The Conservative party structure had become overcentralized in eastern Canada and particularly in Ontario, while the Liberals had become too strongly identified with their French-Canadian leader and with French Canada. The lack of any strong party tradition in the West was shortly to result in the election there of many Progressive MPs. Moreover, the parties had stopped trying to win elections by creating a consensus and had turned to the tactic of playing on ethnic cleavages while virtually ignoring rural–urban problems and the East–West cleavage. An excessive emphasis on ethnic cleavage was dangerous, as was an excessive concentration on fulfilling the demands of war. By failing to take account of other demands, the party system moved out of touch with its environment and the old parties lost the broadly based support they needed to maintain a two-party system. Finally, both parties were entering periods of instability in leadership. The Liberals recovered quickly and were able once again to build enough of a national coalition to win elections, but the Conservatives have been in a more or less perpetual leadership crisis since 1921.

MODERN PARTY POLITICS: 1921–1974

The period from 1921 to 1974 has seen tremendous changes in the environment of Canadian politics, but relatively few changes in the structure of the two older parties. One of the consequences of the perhaps inevitable failure of the major Canadian political parties to adapt completely to environmental changes has been the rapid rise of a host of minor parties. This section will look first at the two older parties from 1921 to the present, and then at the many newer parties that have sprung up in the same period.

The Liberals In 1921 the Liberal party of Canada elected as its leader a most unlikely man, W.L. Mackenzie King. History has not treated King kindly, and his biographers—even his official biographer—have made of him a less than heroic figure.[3] Yet in some ways King can be viewed as a hero albeit an unprepossessing one. He took over a party decimated by the events of the previous five years and rebuilt it into an organization which, in the subsequent half-century, dominated Canadian electoral politics. That he did so by equivocation, occasional deceit, large doses of compromise, and with the help of a medium, his departed

---

[3]There are a number of biographies of King. The best is undoubtedly the series of volumes begun by R. MacGregor Dawson and continued by Blair Neatby, *William Lyon Mackenzie King: A Political Biography*, (University of Toronto Press, Toronto, 1958 and 1963). See also J.W. Pickersgill, *The Mackenzie King Record*, vol. 1, *1939–1944*, and vol. 2, *1944–1948*, (University of Toronto Press, Toronto, 1960 and 1970). Many of King's diaries became available in 1975, and they provide fascinating pictures of the man and his view of Canadian politics in his era. The Diaries are in the National Archives, Ottawa.

mother, a dead dog, and the position of the hands on a clock is perhaps as much a measure of policy making in Canada as of the man himself.

The party that King and his helpers constructed has several features of at least two of the basic structural types discussed earlier. First, it was and remains a stratarchy. There were some nominal lines of authority from the leader down to the provincial and constituency levels, but in practice these lines of authority were weak. In contrast to the highly centralized nature of the Conservative party under Bennett, the Liberals showed considerable decentralization both in financial structure—which King claimed not even to know about—and in policy matters.

Second, the national Liberal party since 1921 has been an "open accordion". It has had to be in order to swallow up, first, most of the agrarian discontent of the West in the 1920s, and later, a portion of the unrest which characterized Quebec in the 1960s. King and his party were able to accommodate much of the western agrarian protest because they were primarily oriented towards electoral success and, unlike the somewhat more dogmatic Conservatives under Meighen and Bennett, they were willing to make room in their party leadership and on their platform for this discontent. The Liberal party under Pearson was also able to accommodate at least some of the Quebec unrest by allowing the Quebec provincial Liberal party to become an almost completely separate entity.

The structure of the Liberal party has changed slowly and surprisingly little since the days of King. The parliamentary organization and the cabinet are undoubtedly the centre of power in the federal party, yet their control over provincial organizations is minimal. In British Columbia, Alberta and Manitoba, the provincial structure is a negligible political force. The Ontario Liberal party has fairly close organizational ties with the federal party, but the relative electoral successes of the two parties would seem to indicate that in the voter's mind there is little connection. The Quebec Liberal party is essentially a separate entity, yet at the level of campaign workers and local strategists, many of the same people work for both the federal and the provincial Liberals. In the Maritimes, on the other hand, the ties between federal and provincial parties appear to be closer than in the rest of Canada.

There is some problem here in separating organizational myth from political reality. Except in Quebec, there is no separation, in the Liberal party constitution, between the federal and the provincial parties—one provincial organization is supposed to subsume both federal and provincial constituency organizations. However, the concentration of real power within the federal and provincial cabinets or legislative caucuses, which are totally separate organizations, ensures that there is a considerable split between the effective federal party and the effective provincial parties.

The national office of the Liberal party has a National Director acting as the full-time head of the party structure. Under the National Director are a number of divisions concerned with such functions as Communications, Policy and Research, Administration, Organization, Finance, Youth, and Printing. The largest of these divisions is Communications, which includes information officers, the editor of the national Liberal party magazine, and a speakers' bureau. The full-time staff between elections numbers about 26, 14 of them professional and 12 clerical and stenographic staff. This is large by past standards of Canadian parties, but during the past few years when almost every office in the Public Service has been expanding, the National Office has not grown much. This might suggest something either about the importance of its role or about the financial state of the Liberal party. Compared with the large and elaborate research establishments of British political parties, the office is small indeed.

Both of the older parties have experienced innumerable problems keeping the executive wing of the party—which does much of the work in election campaigns—in touch with the elected politicians. This has been more of a problem for the Liberals than for the Conservatives, perhaps because the Liberals have been in power more often. The cabinet ministers, who are at the centre of power both in government and in the party are notoriously busy men, and getting them to hold still long enough to communicate even with their own power base in the party has been difficult.

The Liberals have tried several structural innovations to ensure contact between the cabinet and the executive of the party. The most important of these has been the *political cabinet*. While it has not been an unqualified success, the persistence of this structure suggests that it has been of some use to the party. It consists of the real cabinet, the regional caucus chairmen and the President and the National Director of the Liberal Party of Canada. It meets (with varying degrees of regularity—depending partly on the nearness of an election) at intervals of about one month. Its agenda, set by the party executive rather than by the Prime Minister, is designed to keep the executive in touch with cabinet thinking and, to a lesser extent, to keep the cabinet in touch with party executive thinking. The party also has *provincial advisory* groups consisting of the provincial president, one cabinet minister from the province and one caucus member from the province. Nominally, they report directly to the party leader.

During election campaigns the Liberal party's structures expand, as the skeleton of full-time workers is fleshed out with hundreds of volunteers. The key national structure during a campaign is the National Campaign Committee, which has traditionally consisted of the National Campaign Chairman, the National Organizer, the National Treasurer (all appointed by the party leader) and representatives of each of the 10 provincial campaign committees, chosen in consultation with the provincial Liberal associations.[4] For the 1974 campaign the Liberals had two cochairmen. Senator Keith Davey, formerly the National Director of the party, and Transport Minister Jean Marchand.

The National Campaign Committee plans and directs the general strategy of the campaign. It consults with advertising experts and pollsters and draws up the national advertising campaign. In 1974, instead of hir-

[4]The main source used for general information on the Liberals' campaign organization is the *Report of the Committee on Election Expenses* (Ottawa: Queen's Printer, 1966) pp. 237–249. Information concerning the 1974 election machinery is drawn from the *Globe and Mail* (May 9, 1974) pp. 1–2.

ing one advertising agency, the Liberals drew together advertising experts from several agencies to form a "communications group" attached to the National Campaign Committee. This group not only advised the national committee on its advertising program, but also sent one of its members as an ex-officio member to each provincial campaign executive to help adapt the national advertising campaign to that province's needs.

The National Treasurer heads the standing finance committee of the party. This informal committee swings into action early in the campaign to provide the wherewithal for all of the other activities. The party's sources are mainly large corporations and wealthy individuals, and the fund-raising structure reflects this fact. Many of these donors hedge their bets by giving to both of the older parties, 60% to the one in power, 40% to the one in opposition. The "bag-men", as the fund raisers have come to be known, are generally well-to-do businessmen or lawyers who have good connections with others of their kind. The "first string bag-men"—to whom the many other collectors report—are located in the major cities of Canada, where business interests are concentrated. In 1974 the party's chief bag-man was Senator John Godfrey, a Toronto Rosedale lawyer.

It has been traditional for Liberal party leaders to disclaim all knowledge of the sources of their party's campaign funds and hence to deny any temptation to reward the benevolent for their generosity.[5] To suspicious minds such ignorance has always seemed unlikely. Soon, however, we should all know the identities of the party's benefactors, since the election expense legislation passed in 1974 requires public disclosure of the names of all donors of more than $100.[6]

Even while the funds are being raised, the campaign is under way. Indeed, payments for campaign costs are usually made on the instalment plan as donations are received. The National Campaign Committee arranges for national advertising, which includes radio and TV production, plans the leader's tour and big special events, and arranges for the extra staff needed at national headquarters. The provincial committees take charge of the leader's tour in their province, supplement the national advertising if necessary, distribute nationally-gathered funds for use at the constituency level, and provide advice and information to candidates. In most provinces, the national party simply takes over the provincial party office for the duration of the campaign. In Quebec things have traditionally been different. The Quebec Campaign Committee of the federal wing of the party has exercised considerable autonomy in both planning and fund-raising and has run its own campaign virtually coordinate with the national committee. The appointment of Jean Marchand, at that time the federal leader in Quebec, as co-chairman of the National Campaign Committee in 1974 probably indicates that this pattern has been formalized.

[5]K.Z. Paltiel, *Financing Political Parties in Canada*, (McGraw–Hill, Toronto, 1970) is the best account of the process of election finance in Canada.
[6]K.Z. Paltiel, "Some Aspects of Campaign Finance in Canada", paper presented to the International Political Science Association, Montreal, August 1973.

At the constituency level, the party's structures and activities vary greatly from one constituency to another and often reflect the local candidate's own idiosyncrasies. Chapter 12, which deals with elections in Canada, gives a general description of campaign activity at this level.

No picture of a political party would be complete without some view of its supporters.[7] The Liberal base of support shown in Table 10-1 is frequently viewed as paradoxically both broad and narrow. It is broad in the sense that no other Canadian party can claim to draw support from such a broad social spectrum; yet it is narrow in some of its regional aspects and its electoral dependency on the French-Canadian vote. Even here, however, the basis of the Liberal party's popular vote is not so narrow as it is sometimes perceived to be. The party nationally draws about 33 per cent of its popular vote from French Canadians (a figure very close to that group's overall representation in the population). Within Quebec, the heavy support of the Liberals by English Quebeckers ensures that the Liberals are actually less French than the population, and there is some evidence that much of the Liberal-French connection in Quebec is actually a Trudeau–French connection.[8] Moreover, in 1968 and 1972 the party appealed more to older than to younger French voters, so there is some evidence that whatever French–Liberal connection there is may very slowly be dissipating. There does not appear to be a similar danger with respect to the Liberal appeal to French minorities outside of Quebec. Franco-Ontarians and Acadians support the federal (and provincial) Liberals in overwhelming proportions and there is no evidence at all that this support is evaporating.

The Liberals, over the last 40 years, have traditionally drawn support from a broader class spectrum than other parties, but there are also some moderate deviations from this broad spectrum of support.

High-socio-economic-status voters have tended to support the Liberal party more than have others, and western farmers have tended to avoid it like the plague. Yet eastern farmers have given a larger portion of their vote to the Liberals than to other parties. The general lack of enthusiasm of western voters for the Liberal party is well known and is reflected in the figures which show that overall rural, small town and farmer support is somewhat lower than the proportion of those groups in the population.

In spite of strong efforts by all the other parties, the Liberals have consistently had greater appeal to minority groups ranging from the large English and French minorities in Quebec and Ontario respectively to "new Canadians"—immigrants who have arrived since 1945. The party also has been better supported by younger voters than older ones. Liberal voters in 1965 and 1968 (no comparable survey was done in 1972) also

---

[7]We have not footnoted in detail this or subsequent sections on the basis of party support. They rely particularly on two sources: John Miesel, *Working Papers on Canadian Politics* (McGill–Queen's Press, Montreal, 1972), pp. 34–51 and Mildred Schwartz, "Canadian Voting Behaviour", prepared for R. Rose (ed.), *Electorial Behaviour, A Comparative Handbook*, (New York, Free Press, 1973).

[8]J. Meisel, *op. cit.* p. 35.

TABLE 10-11: PERSONAL ATTRIBUTES: PROPORTION OF EACH PARTY'S VOTE PROVIDED BY VARIOUS GROUPS (Vertical Percentages, in *Italics*)

	CANADA					Atlantic				Quebec					Ontario				Prairies					British Columbia				
Group	T	Lib	PC	NDP+SC	RC	T	Lib	PC	NDP	T	Lib	PC	NDP	RC	T	Lib	PC	NDP	T	Lib	PC	NDP	SC	T	Lib	PC	NDP	SC
Religion (N)	2212	1241	632	255	84	228	102	122	4	581	394	107	29	51	804	456	222	126	418	185	158	64	11	181	104	23	32	22
Catholic	*43*	*53*	*26*	*30*	*68*	*30*	*45*	*18*	*25*	*90*	*88*	*94*	*97*	*100*	*30*	*42*	*8*	*25*	*22*	*28*	*15*	*19*	*36*	*14*	*18*	.	*13*	*9*
Other	*57*	*47*	*74*	*70*	*32*	*70*	*55*	*82*	*75*	*10*	*12*	*6*	*3*	.	*70*	*58*	*92*	*75*	*78*	*72*	*85*	*81*	*64*	*86*	*82*	*100*	*87*	*91*
Occupation (N)	2127	1197	588	260	82	204	92	109	3	543	371	96	26	50	791	452	212	127	402	178	149	65	10	187	104	22	39	22
Professional, etc.	*16*	*22*	*18*	*13*	*7*	*18*	*9*	*9*	–	*22*	*25*	*18*	*35*	*6*	*19*	*19*	*23*	*12*	*19*	*25*	*16*	*11*	*10*	*21*	*22*	*27*	*8*	*4*
Sales, clerical	*16*	*19*	*14*	*12*	*9*	*18*	*9*	*7*	–	*15*	*18*	*8*	*15*	*10*	*20*	*22*	*20*	*10*	*14*	*17*	*13*	*13*	.	*13*	*16*	*23*	*5*	*5*
Skilled labour	*35*	*35*	*29*	*45*	*45*	*39*	*40*	*37*	*67*	*36*	*36*	*34*	*31*	*44*	*35*	*33*	*28*	*53*	*30*	*34*	*26*	*31*	*20*	*39*	*35*	*9*	*54*	*59*
Unskilled labour	*13*	*12*	*14*	*14*	*16*	*26*	*28*	*24*	–	*13*	*11*	*11*	*15*	*18*	*12*	*12*	*10*	*14*	*8*	*8*	*5*	*12*	*20*	*13*	*12*	*5*	*15*	*9*
Farmer	*9*	*6*	*15*	*7*	*17*	*10*	*9*	*11*	–	*6*	*4*	*7*	.	*16*	*6*	*4*	*9*	.	*21*	*10*	*30*	*25*	*20*	*4*	*5*	*5*	.	*5*
Pensioner, retired	*8*	*7*	*10*	*9*	*6*	*7*	*5*	*12*	*33*	*7*	*6*	*10*	.	*6*	*8*	*6*	*10*	.	*8*	*5*	*11*	.	*50*	*10*	*7*	*14*	*18*	*9*
Class (N)	2172	1228	597	264	83	199	92	103	4	577	392	106	28	51	800	457	214	129	402	179	149	65	9	194	108	38	23	23
Upper	*8*	*10*	*7*	*4*	*4*	*4*	*3*	*5*	–	*12*	*12*	*11*	*11*	*4*	*8*	*10*	*8*	*4*	*6*	*10*	*2*	*2*	*9*	*8*	*11*	*12*	*4*	*4*
Middle	*48*	*51*	*48*	*34*	*47*	*32*	*33*	*30*	*50*	*53*	*56*	*46*	*43*	*47*	*48*	*50*	*53*	*33*	*47*	*46*	*55*	*29*	*44*	*49*	*55*	*52*	*34*	*44*
Lower	*44*	*39*	*45*	*62*	*49*	*64*	*64*	*65*	*50*	*35*	*32*	*43*	*29*	*49*	*44*	*40*	*39*	*65*	*48*	*44*	*43*	*69*	*56*	*43*	*34*	*36*	*66*	*52*
Education (N)	2272	1282	633	273	84	229	104	121	4	588	403	106	29	50	830	474	224	132	425	190	157	67	11	200	111	25	41	23
0 - 8 yrs.	*32*	*30*	*34*	*32*	*56*	*45*	*43*	*46*	*75*	*45*	*43*	*49*	*41*	*66*	*25*	*25*	*25*	*30*	*30*	*22*	*30*	*46*	*55*	*18*	*11*	*25*	*29*	*35*
9 - 13 yrs.	*54*	*54*	*55*	*55*	*39*	*53*	*55*	*52*	*25*	*39*	*40*	*40*	*48*	*30*	*60*	*58*	*59*	*66*	*57*	*61*	*59*	*42*	*46*	*67*	*69*	*76*	*61*	*57*
14 yrs. or more	*14*	*16*	*11*	*13*	*5*	*2*	*2*	*2*	–	*16*	*17*	*11*	*11*	*4*	*15*	*17*	*16*	*9*	*14*	*17*	*12*	*12*	.	*15*	*20*	*8*	*10*	*9*
Residence in Canada (N)	2280	1286	636	273	85	229	104	121	4	590	404	107	29	50	834	477	224	133	426	189	159	67	11	201	112	25	41	23
Born in Canada	*82*	*81*	*85*	*80*	*92*	*97*	*96*	*98*	*100*	*93*	*90*	*98*	*96*	*100*	*76*	*73*	*81*	*75*	*78*	*77*	*76*	*81*	*91*	*67*	*67*	*60*	*81*	*74*
Arrived before 1946	*8*	*7*	*7*	*11*	*4*	*1*	*1*	*2*	–	*2*	*2*	*2*	*4*	.	*8*	*8*	*10*	*16*	*16*	*18*	*18*	*16*	*9*	*16*	*14*	*36*	*12*	*13*
Arrived 1946 or after	*10*	*13*	*9*	*10*	*4*	*2*	*2*	*2*	–	*6*	*8*	.	.	.	*16*	*19*	*9*	*16*	*14*	*8*	*6*	*3*	.	*14*	*19*	*4*	*7*	*13*
Origin (N)	2284	1288	637	274	85	231	105	122	4	591	404	107	29	51	834	477	224	133	427	190	159	67	11	201	112	25	41	23
British	*44*	*38*	*58*	*41*	*8*	*64*	*56*	*72*	*50*	*7*	*7*	*9*	*6*	.	*62*	*54*	*79*	*65*	*42*	*40*	*51*	*30*	*18*	*63*	*58*	*84*	*61*	*70*
French	*28*	*33*	*18*	*15*	*85*	*13*	*21*	*6*	–	*84*	*79*	*93*	*93*	*98*	*9*	*12*	*8*	*5*	*6*	*10*	*5*	*5*	.	*3*	*5*	.	*10*	*4*
Other	*28*	*29*	*24*	*44*	*7*	*23*	*23*	*32*	*25*	*8*	*12*	*2*	*2*	*2*	*28*	*34*	*19*	*30*	*52*	*50*	*47*	*66*	*82*	*33*	*39*	*16*	*29*	*26*
Language (N)	2284	1288	637	274	85	231	105	122	4	591	404	107	29	51	834	477	224	133	427	190	159	67	11	201	112	25	41	23
Pure French	*19*	*22*	*14*	*6*	*84*	*10*	*16*	*3*	–	*69*	*64*	*78*	*72*	*84*	*1*	*2*	*1*	.	*1*	*1*	.	.	.	*1*	*1*	.	*2*	.
Part French	*5*	*5*	*3*	*3*	*8*	*2*	*2*	*1*	–	*12*	*11*	*12*	*21*	*16*	*2*	*2*	*1*	.	*5*	*6*	*6*	*10*	*9*	*3*	*4*	.	*2*	*4*
Mixed	*5*	*7*	*3*	*8*	*2*	.	*1*	.	–	*6*	*5*	*3*	.	.	*6*	*6*	*6*	*2*	*8*	*10*	*6*	*6*	.	*3*	*4*	.	.	*3*
Part English	*5*	*6*	*8*	*10*	*2*	*3*	*4*	*3*	–	*4*	*5*	*1*	.	.	*5*	*5*	*2*	*10*	*5*	*8*	*6*	*10*	.	*4*	*2*	.	*10*	.
Pure English	*67*	*60*	*79*	*73*	*0*	*86*	*77*	*94*	*75*	*9*	*11*	*7*	*7*	.	*87*	*82*	*96*	*87*	*85*	*81*	*88*	*90*	*91*	*94*	*92*	*100*	*93*	*96*
Community Size (N)	2284	1288	637	274	85	231	105	122	4	591	404	107	29	51	834	477	224	133	427	190	159	67	11	201	112	25	41	23
Metropolitan	*30*	*36*	*17*	*37*	*11*	.	.	.	–	*45*	*50*	*30*	*30*	*12*	*29*	*32*	*24*	*32*	*16*	*22*	*9*	*22*	*11*	*64*	*56*	*2*	*17*	*9*
100,000 - 500,000	*18*	*18*	*18*	*18*	*15*	*6*	*6*	*7*	–	*7*	*5*	*8*	*6*	*10*	*21*	*24*	*17*	*19*	*36*	*37*	*33*	*36*	*55*	*10*	*11*	*16*	*2*	*9*
1,000 - 99,999	*27*	*26*	*28*	*26*	*35*	*27*	*27*	*32*	*25*	*30*	*28*	*40*	*41*	*45*	*31*	*31*	*29*	*35*	*15*	*17*	*15*	*27*	.	*11*	*13*	*16*	*29*	*39*
Rural	*26*	*21*	*37*	*19*	*46*	*65*	*68*	*62*	*75*	*18*	*14*	*24*	*17*	*33*	*19*	*16*	*28*	*15*	*34*	*29*	*41*	*27*	*46*	*13*	*18*	*20*	*12*	*35*
Age (N)	2284	1288	637	274	85	231	105	122	4	591	404	107	29	51	834	477	224	133	427	190	159	67	11	201	112	25	41	23
21 - 30 yrs.	*22*	*23*	*20*	*20*	*11*	*18*	*21*	*18*	–	*27*	*28*	*28*	*38*	*33*	*21*	*21*	*23*	*20*	*21*	*21*	*18*	*18*	*36*	*25*	*25*	*8*	*15*	*17*
31 - 50 yrs.	*44*	*46*	*39*	*47*	*36*	*42*	*44*	*41*	*25*	*42*	*43*	*37*	*41*	*51*	*47*	*48*	*42*	*52*	*42*	*37*	*42*	*40*	*46*	*49*	*49*	*32*	*46*	*48*
51 yrs. or more	*34*	*31*	*41*	*33*	*46*	*40*	*35*	*43*	*75*	*31*	*29*	*35*	*17*	*16*	*32*	*32*	*28*	*28*	*38*	*41*	*40*	*40*	*18*	*29*	*28*	*60*	*39*	*35*
Sex (N)	2284	1288	637	274	85	231	105	122	4	591	404	107	29	51	834	477	224	133	427	190	159	67	11	201	112	25	41	23
Male	*51*	*50*	*49*	*60*	*48*	*50*	*47*	*52*	*75*	*50*	*50*	*49*	*66*	*47*	*53*	*50*	*52*	*62*	*50*	*52*	*47*	*51*	*55*	*51*	*53*	*28*	*61*	*48*
Female	*49*	*50*	*51*	*40*	*52*	*50*	*53*	*48*	*25*	*50*	*50*	*51*	*34*	*53*	*47*	*50*	*48*	*38*	*50*	*48*	*53*	*49*	*45*	*49*	*47*	*72*	*39*	*52*

Source: John Meisel, *Working Papers in Canadian Politics*, Appendix.

tended to be more satisfied with their economic situation, and more opti-
mistic than Conservative, NDP or Créditiste supporters. Professor John
Meisel has summed up this picture by asserting that:

> . . .the Liberal party can be thought of as being most progressive or "mod-
> ern", in the sense of appealing most to those elements in society which feel
> at home in the so-called "advanced", urbanized and highly technological
> world usually associated with urban North America. This is not to say, of
> course, that the supporters of the other parties were all, or even pre-
> dominantly, antique rustics dwelling in some sort of retarded psychological
> middle age but rather that the Liberals, on the whole, contained a larger
> proportion of "modern" electors. . .than the others.[9]

The Conservatives While Mackenzie King set the tone of party
structure for the Liberals from 1921 on, it was nearly a decade before anyone set the tone for the Conservative party. Arthur Meighen, Borden's successor as party leader, seemed unable to develop the "common touch" and
this, combined with his total lack of support in Quebec (in 1921 he won
only 18 per cent of the vote there, and no seats), ensured that he was a failure as a leader in that most vital of tasks—getting elected.[10] R.B. Bennett,
who succeeded him, did win an election, and from 1930 to 1935 definitely
did set the tone of the party. This was made all the easier for Bennett since
he also "owned" the party in that he was its largest financial backer. He
thus completely dominated the party organization, "a benefit which his
party scarcely survived."[11] The Conservative party's misfortune in getting
elected just when the depression was really starting to roll, ensured that it
would fail electorally in 1935. It seems doubtful that any government or
party could have successfully spanned the deep cleavages and crises caused
by the depression, but the Conservatives had developed an overcentralized
structure that was singularly inappropriate for attempting the feat.

Bennett's departure from the leadership was followed by another of
those periods in Conservative party history which can most charitably be
called "interregnums". One leader after another failed to lead the party
out of the electoral wilderness. Between 1940 and 1956, the Conservative
party went through four leaders, and even supported an abortive comeback attempt by Arthur Meighen.[12] Finally, in 1957 and 1958 the perpetual leadership crisis seemed to be resolved when John Diefenbaker led the
party to electoral victory, but by the mid-1960s, the party leadership again
came under violent attack and the party's leadership problems have continued since then.

The party structure of the Conservative party in the last half-
century has been, like that of the Liberals, highly stratarchical; but unlike
the Liberal structure, there have been few aspects of the open accordion
about the Conservative party. Only very recently has any very concerted

[9]*Ibid.*, (second edition, 1973), p. 38.
[10]Roger Graham, *Arthur Meighen*, (Clarke, Irwin & Co., Toronto, 1960).
[11]K.Z. Paltiel, *Political Party Financing in Canada*, p. 17.
[12]See J. Granatstein, *The Politics of Survival 1939–1945*, (University of Toronto Press,
Toronto, 1967).

effort been made by Conservatives to woo the Quebec voter or to understand the peculiarities of French-Canadian culture, and it is by no means certain that the party is unanimously committed to this effort. The Conservatives have occasionally tried to form alliances of subcoalitions with other groups. In the 1940s they attempted to gain Progressive support from the West by choosing as their leader the former Progressive Premier of Manitoba, John Bracken, and adding the name "Progressive" to their party masthead. Apparently they had not noticed that Mackenzie King had beaten them by nearly twenty years in gaining western Progressive support. Under Diefenbaker, the Conservatives tried to become the party of the "other" ethnic groups of Canada, but in attempting this they alienated as many new Canadians as they attracted by an overemphasis on the "differences" in their cultural backgrounds. At any rate they were not successful in attracting much permanent support from such groups since only about 15 per cent of recent immigrants supported the Conservatives in 1968 as opposed to the 72 per cent who supported the Liberals.[13] Perhaps Conservative party structure over the last fifty years could best be described as a broken concertina, rather than an open accordion.

The formal structure of the Conservative party is rather similar to that of the Liberals, and there are also many similarities in the two parties' informal structure. Like the Liberals, the Conservatives have a permanent staff at a national party headquarters, and several regional offices with permanent staffs. Like the Liberals, the more important component of Conservative party structure is the voluntary part which appears, magically, just before each election.

The permanent party organization consists of a national organizer and his staff (which is also part of the election campaign staff) and, when the party can afford it, sundry public relations and clerical help in the Ottawa headquarters. The Progressive Conservative National Headquarters has traditionally been slightly smaller than the Liberal party headquarters, and in 1974 totalled about 20 people. An equally important part of the present structure of the Progressive Conservatives is the leader's headquarters staff. The executive and special assistants and advisors in the opposition leader's office, while formally on the House of Commons staff and payroll, are actually engaged in the overall direction and development of strategy for the party. In this they are performing functions which are analagous to some of those performed in the Prime Minister's office for the party in power. Were the Liberals the official opposition, there is little doubt that they would use the office of the leader of the opposition in the same way.

In 1969 Parliament voted funds for the establishment of parliamentary research offices for the caucuses of the opposition parties, and in 1970 similar funds were provided for the government caucus. The amount provided for each party is proportional to its strength in the House of Commons. In 1973–74 the Liberal research office was granted $182,000, the

[13]M. Schwartz, "Political Behaviour and Ethnic Origin", in J. Meisel (ed.), Papers on the 1962 Election, pp. 253–272, John Meisel, *Working Papers on Canadian Politics*, pp. 37–8.

PCs $180,000, the NDP $62,000 and the Créditistes $40,000. The money is formally used to provide research services for MPs and most of the duties of the eight or nine researchers and the Director and his assistant in the older parties' offices do involve the provision of research material for MPs. However, the research offices also provide broader policy research for the party as a whole, help out during annual meetings and conventions, and may provide some auxiliary headquarters support during campaigns.

At election time the National President and National Secretary of the party, both of whom hold part-time positions and are elected at party meetings, are augmented by a National Campaign Chairman and a group of fund raisers who start about the job of collecting money. The regional and provincial organizers (some of whom may be permanent employees of the party), suddenly spring to life and constituency organizations, generally consisting of a Campaign Chairman and many helpers, together with poll captains who work at the individual poll level, appear where nothing was before. Candidates are nominated and the contest goes on.

With regard to popular support, "it is generally safe to assume that for practically every statement made about the Liberal party the reverse holds for the Conservative voters'."[14] A glance at Table 10-1 will suffice to indicate the contrasts in support between Liberals and Conservatives. Thus in 1968, 53 per cent of Liberal support came from Catholics versus 26 per cent of Conservative support. While only 6 per cent of Liberal voters were farmers, 15 per cent of Conservatives were. Eleven per cent of Conservative support came from the highly educated (14 or more years of schooling) whereas 16 per cent of Liberal support came from these groups. Thirty eight per cent of Liberal voters were of British origin whereas 58 per cent of Conservative voters were British.

Conservative voters also were more likely than Liberals to be English speaking, to be middle aged or older, and to come from small towns or rural areas. Only in the Atlantic provinces were these tendencies reversed—there the PCs draw more heavily than the Liberals from upper class urban voters. This pattern is perhaps attributable to the personal appeal of Mr. Stanfield in his home-base Atlantic region, and the heavy rural and western appeal is at least partially attributable to the residual appeal of the ex-leader John Diefenbaker on his home grounds. Such patterns of personal appeal can be remarkably stable in Canada politics, often persisting for decades; the suggestion has sometimes been made that this pattern is the Canadian counterpart of the strongly persistent party identification of United States voters.[15]

Perhaps the most important overall point which emerges from an examination of Conservative party supporters is related to their lack of homogeneity relative to the Liberals. Liberal support was, with the partial exception of the west, more evenly distributed across the country and, as John Miesel has noted in all of his election studies since the late 1950s,

---

[14]J. Meisel, *Working Papers on Canadian Politics*, p. 40. The material in the following paragraphs is derived largely from that source.

[15]*Ibid.*, pp. 41–43. The instability of party identification is explored further in Peter Regenstreif, *The Diefenbaker Interlude*, (Longmans, Toronto, 1965).

shows less regional variation in the way supporters look at the party and the leader. This may produce problems and strains in the Conservative party when it attempts to develop policies which will appeal to its supporters and also broaden the base of party support. If the supporters themselves are a highly "mixed bag" with highly divergent views of the world, reconciliation becomes difficult.

> . . .the task of reconciling the demands of the most active members from the Atlantic and Prairie regions and from Ontario, (or, to put it slightly differently, those of the vestigial Drew men, the Stanfield admirers and the Diefenbakerites) imposes extremely awkward tensions on the leadership which, as a consequence, makes it difficult for the national party to appear forceful and consistent both inside and outside the House of Commons.[16]

The task of the Conservative leader is indeed a difficult one.

THE MINOR PARTIES

Major studies of the two older parties are very scarce, and those that have been done have, for the most part, been left to blush unseen in university libraries in the form of doctoral theses. With minor parties, however, the situation is far different. Canada's minor parties have existed over limited time spans, they have usually been small, and they have been "different" enough to stimulate the scholar's interest. They have, in short, formed ideal material for academic studies. A great deal is known about rise and fall of the Progressive movement, for example, and it may not be an exaggeration to suggest that more is known about it than about the Liberal Party of Canada. It must be remembered, however, that except in certain provinces, the newer parties have been relatively less important than the older ones in any overall picture of party politics; one can hope that students of Canadian political parties will begin to pay more attention to our major parties.[17]

The Progressive Movement In November of 1919 there was a provincial election in Ontario and, when the smoke had cleared, a coalition of two parties (which had scarcely existed ten months earlier) was in power. A minor part of the coalition was provided by the Independent Labour Party, but the largest single group in the legislature was the United Farmers of Ontario—the Ontario version of a movement whose political arm came to be known nationally as the Progressive Party.[18] The

[16] *Working Papers*, p. 46.
[17] Some well-balanced accounts are available. The party chapters in Dawson and Ward, *The Government of Canada*; Engelmann and Schwartz, *Political Parties and the Canadian Social Structure*; and Thorburn, *Party Politics in Canada* have all attempted to provide a balanced statement though all these writers appear to have run into the same problem as we—a dearth of well-researched material on the older parties.
[18] The words "movement" and "party" are both used in political science literature to describe the Progressives. There are a number of excellent studies of the group. Two are: W.L. Morton, *The Progressive Party in Canada*, (University of Toronto Press, Toronto, 1950), and P.F. Sharp, *The Agrarian Revolt in Western Canada*, (Uni-

movement grew in strength in the ensuing years, and in the 1921 federal election, any notion that Canada actually had a two-party system was rudely shattered when 65 Progressive MPs were elected, making them the second largest group in the House of Commons with 15 more seats than the Conservative party. For our purposes, two questions arise with respect to the Progressives: where did they come from, and what was the structure of this brand-new force in Canadian politics?

Unlike other Canadian parties, the Progressive movement was, at least on the surface, a relatively homogeneous aggregation. Aside from a few small businessmen from Manitoba, the group consisted entirely of agrarians. They gained 28 per cent of the vote in the federal election in Ontario in 1921 and won 24 seats, with virtually all their support coming from rural areas. In Manitoba they gained 44 per cent of the vote and 12 seats, in Saskatchewan 61 per cent and 15 seats, and in Alberta 57 per cent and 11 seats. In general, the more agricultural the economy of a province, the more likely it was to return Progressives. Even New Brunswick, which virtually never breaks with older party lines, returned a Progressive MP in 1921, and Nova Scotia gave the Progressives 15 per cent of the vote although they won no seats there.

What can explain this sudden outpouring of support for a new rural political movement? The first part of the answer to this question is that the rise of agrarian political consciousness was not quite as sudden as it appears. Party lines were always weak in the West. In Ontario there had been previous sporadic bursts of support for agrarian movements with, for instance, the Patrons of Industry, an agrarian protest party, winning 17 seats in the Ontario provincial election of 1894. However, the agrarian movement had relatively little force before 1919, at which time a number of factors had coalesced to provide a real impetus for agrarian protest movements. The government in Ottawa really was dominated by eastern urban and big-business interests, and these interests did use the traditional political parties as their means of control. Rural Ontario was being rapidly depopulated, as farm families moved to the city, and the insecurity of farm life combined with the feeling that the farmer was a dying species led to cooperative action. Tariff structures had been hurting the farmers for years by keeping produce prices down and farm equipment prices up. The problem was brought to a head by an over-supply of agricultural produce after World War I and by a recession following the war. The conscription of farmers' sons in 1917 after the government had specifically promised to exempt them, and the Union Government's ignoring of farmers' protest marches helped to convince farmers that the older parties were not responsive to their inputs.

The farmers were right. It has been seen above that there are reasons why the older parties were not then, and are not now, structurally adequate to articulate genuine protest movements or to accommodate them when they arise. Instead they responded in 1921 much as they do now:

only after the agrarian interests become politically mobilized and formed new social and political structures did the older parties adjust and attempt to assimilate them.

The farmers concentrated much of their criticism on the caucus-dominated structure of older parties because, as they pointed out, the agrarian-dominated Western regional caucuses were inevitably outvoted by the parties' Eastern interests. They therefore correctly surmised that the only way to make themselves heard in parliament was to get outside of caucus altogether and form a new movement; where conflict resolution within the older parties failed, they attempted to achieve their ends through the interparty process. The problem with their theories was that they had to be applied within a parliamentary system. And since the farmers had rejected the idea of a legislative caucus, there were no structural mechanisms for achieving the integration of the Progressive MPs. Within four years, the movement had lost much of its impetus as the lack of internal cohesion produced a series of warring factions. No unified program could be agreed upon, and it became relatively easy for Mackenzie King to absorb some of the leaders and most of the followers into the Liberal party.

Structurally, the Progressives were truly an alliance of sub-coalitions. Each of the sub-coalitions was a regionally-based collection of farm organizations; overall national cohesion was provided by adherence to a few common principles expressed in "The Farmers' Platform". The most important of these ideas was simply opposition to the old party system and to Eastern business interests. There was considerable emphasis among Progressives on grassroots democracy, but the means of achieving it varied from one regional sub-coalition to another. Thus, the Manitoba farmers' government experimented with legislation to provide for the recall of MPs to face their constituents in a by-election if a specified proportion of the voters in a riding requested it, and other wings of the Progressive party toyed with various forms of the referendum.

In the Progressive party, conventions were considerably more important in policy making than they had been in the older parties, although by 1923 a split was developing within the movement between elected representatives, who were beginning to resent excessive interference in "their" affairs by conventions, and the mass membership of the movement, which wanted to maintain its influential position. Most of the structural decentralization of the movement and its emphasis on constituency control derived from its anti-party ideology. This ideology was extended into a form of syndicalism or corporatism, with a call for representation by occupational group rather than geographic constituency. This was combined with a call for cabinets which would not be overthrown if they lost a vote in parliament. This general plan had considerable appeal to the farmers, who felt that their underrepresentation in legislatures over the years had been prejudicial against them. The plan was, however, simply unworkable in the existing parliamentary system, and the farmers were not radical enough to want to overthrow the entire system to satisfy their needs.

The Progressive movement perished of its own structural deficiencies, for the militant Alberta caucus could not work with the more traditional Manitoban and eastern wings of the party. By the mid-1920s the Progressive party had ceased to be an institution in Canadian national politics, although it continued to be important in provincial governments in the West, remaining in power in Alberta until the Social Credit sweep in 1935, and in Manitoba in one form or another for some 30 years.

The Social Credit By the end of the third decade of this century, the Progressive movement no longer acted as an effective vehicle for protest in the West. Yet the depression and the prolonged drought on the prairies in the early 1930s served, if anything, to emphasize the differences between eastern and western Canada. By 1935 a new protest movement, led by a man who was possibly Canadian politics' most charismatic leader, had established itself in Alberta provincial politics. On August 22, 1935, Alberta voters eliminated all members of the United Farmers of Alberta (the Alberta wing of the Progressives) and filled 56 of the 63 seats in their legislature with followers of Social Credit.[19]

Strictly speaking, Social Credit is a financial theory introduced by Major C.H. Douglas, a retired British army engineer, although it contains other elements as well. The root of the theory is the "A plus B theorem" where A is the flow of purchasing power to the masses (i.e., wages, salaries and dividends) and B is bank charges, overhead costs, taxes, and the cost of raw materials. The discrepancy between purchasing power (A) and the costs of production (A and B) was thought to be a permanent feature of modern capitalism and would always result in the masses' getting less than their share.[20] The solution offered by Social Credit theory was to give them more purchasing power in the form of a bonus.

> A functional financial system should be concerned with the issue of credit to the consumer up to the limit of the productive capacity of the producer, so that the consumer's real demands may be satisfied and the productive capacity of the industrial system may be capitalized and developed to the fullest extent.[21]

As with the Progressive movement, Social Credit also featured a critique of parliamentary democracy, pointing out that control over representatives had got away from the little man and escaped to large financial interests.

The theoretical aspects of the Douglas theory are not, however, particularly important to an understanding of the rise of the Social Credit movement. In Alberta that rise was due to the coincidence of the depression of the 1930s and the organizational and histrionic abilities of William Aberhart, who used the new medium of radio to great advantage in presenting his case. Aberhart began his working life as a school teacher and

---

[19]There are three major accounts of the Social Credit Movement in Alberta. These are C.B. Macpherson, *Democracy in Alberta*; J.A. Irving, *The Social Credit Movement in Alberta*, (University of Toronto Press, Toronto, 1959); and J.R. Mallory, *Social Credit and the Federal Power in Canada*, (University of Toronto Press, Toronto, 1954).
[20]Irving, *op. cit.*, p. 5.
[21]*Ibid.*, p. 6.

preacher. After moving to Alberta as a young man he founded the Prophetic Bible Institute and, given Aberhart's abilities and the limited range of alternative Sunday afternoon activities in Alberta in the early 1930s, his religious radio broadcasts enjoyed tremendous popularity. He began to use these broadcasts to present the ideas of Social Credit in 1932, and the broadcasts, together with an excellent grassroots political organization, swept him into power in 1935. After a few attempts to apply Social Credit principles through legislation, the Alberta Social Credit movement, thwarted by the realities of the constitution and the economic system, became a political party of more or less standard form. The prosperity of the province following the oil boom ensured the re-election of Social Credit governments in the province for 36 years until 1971, when resurgent Alberta Conservatives captured the province.

The other mutations of Social Credit in Canada have been born and have either prospered or died quite independently of the Alberta movement. Most similar to the Alberta party has been the *Ralliement des Créditistes*, the Quebec-based wing of the party.[22] In spite of the purely French nature of the Créditistes and the fact that they chose at first to compete federally rather than provincially, there are more similarities between them and their Alberta counterparts than there are differences. The Créditistes, too, started life as a protest movement, and they have been successful in Quebec largely because rural Quebeckers did not find the federal Conservative party a credible alternative to the Liberals, and because the Liberals had ceased to look after their interests. It has been suggested that in situations where one party is dominant for long periods of time as the Liberals in Quebec have been, the regular opposition party (in this case the Conservatives) will lose its credibility and be replaced by a third party—in this case the Créditistes. The same situation may well account for the rise of Social Credit in Alberta.[23]

The void left by the failure of the Conservatives in Quebec was filled by Réal Caouette, who exploited the new medium of television as effectively as Aberhart had exploited radio. In the 1962 federal election, to almost everyone's amazement, the Créditistes won 26 seats in rural Quebec; since that time they have not had less than 18 per cent of the federal vote in Quebec nor won fewer than 9 seats. Whether the party will become a permanent fixture of Canadian politics remains to be seen; the movement does have solid organizational strength and it does seem to fulfill a real need in Quebec politics, but it is heavily dependent upon Réal Caouette's leadership and would be vulnerable were he to disappear. In addition, it is uncertain how much longer Quebec voters will be willing to support a party apparently doomed to perpetual opposition.

[22]Le Ralliement des Créditistes has also been extensively studied. See particularly Maurice Pinard, *The Rise of a Third Party*, (Prentice–Hall, Engelwood Cliffs), 1971, and Michael Stein, *The Dynamics of Right Wing Protest: a Political Analysis of Social Credit in Quebec*, (Toronto, 1973), Graham White, "One Party Dominance and Third Parties", André Blais, "Third Parties in Canadian Provincial Politics" and Maurice Pinard, "Third Parties in Canada Re-Visited", all in *Canadian Journal of Political Science*, September 1973.

[23]M. Pinard, *The Rise of a Third Party*. This is one basic theme of Pinard's book.

Early in 1970 the Créditiste party entered provincial politics. They entered hurriedly and were forced into action before they were ready, when the Union Nationale government called a snap election, but nonetheless, they did achieve considerable success. The region of Quebec which voted Créditiste in federal elections showed itself willing to support the party provincially, and the result was 13 seats in the National Assembly elected in April, 1970. These seats were taken largely from the Union Nationale and were important in the overthrow of that government. However the Créditistes were unable to build their provincial strength into a permanent power base. In the 1973 provincial election the party's support declined and they were able to capture only 2 seats. Their support would appear to be too narrowly based to enable them to win an election, and it is questionable whether they can continue to hold support once this becomes apparent. On the other hand, because they do represent a right-wing point of view which is traditionally strong in Quebec and which none of the other parties adequately represents, their disappearance—which may be inevitable—is unlikely to be immediate.

In British Columbia, the Social Credit party won a minority victory in the provincial election of 1952. Here again the roots of the movement had some things in common with the roots in Quebec and Alberta.[24] Economic conditions in B.C. were not nearly as bad as they were in Alberta in 1935 or in rural Quebec in 1962, but the B.C. government in 1952 was a tired coalition of Conservatives and Liberals in the process of disintegration. Neither of the older parties had much in the way of provincial organization, the CCF was too militant and too small to gain broad support, and the only credible alternative that emerged was the Social Credit party. The 1952 campaign was run with considerable help from Alberta, but without a leader, for W.A.C. Bennett, a dissident former Conservative, did not become leader until after the election. Social Credit was helped in the election by the two older parties who enacted an "alternative vote" electoral scheme which rebounded to their disadvantage. Bennett, recognizing that proportional representation systems rarely work to the advantage of majority parties in power, which Social Credit then was, promptly eliminated it after the election. The party is virtually non-ideological, although Bennett once defined Social Credit simply as "the opposite of socialism". In British Columbia, Social Credit fell rather than charged into power, but a prosperous economy and ebullient, if not overly polished, party image kept it there for some 20 years until its defeat by the NDP in 1972.

In two of the three cases, then, Social Credit caught on because a charismatic leader, skilled in using a new medium, arrived at a time when there were no other effective vehicles of protest. In all three cases effective political alternatives were lacking because the politics of the area were dominated by one party. The ideology of Social Credit had its uses because it was easy to understand and it blamed troubles on those convenient bugbears, the absentee financial interests. Finally, like many Cana-

[24]Martin Robin, "The Politics of Class Conflict", in M. Robin (ed.), *Canadian Provincial Politics*, (Prentice–Hall, Scarborough, 1972).

dian protest or minor parties, Social Credit has generally done well in provincial politics and poorly in federal politics, with the Créditiste wing being the exception to the rule.

There is a good explanation for the relative success of Social Credit provincially. The impossibility of gaining national power with a regionally-based protest group has doubtless made all protest movements conscious that their only real chance to gain power is in provincial elections. Thus, if they want to see any of their policies implemented they must concentrate on provincial politics. This has led to a concentration of the best party leaders and workers at the provincial level. In fact, the Alberta Social Credit party has taken only sporadic interest in federal politics, and the British Columbia wing of the party little more. Indeed, if one were to look for the national structure of the Social Credit party, one would find it to be virtually absent. Even when there was a national Social Credit party (up to 1965), it was really just a collection of provincial organizations which were more interested in provincial than federal politics. Social Credit was and is essentially a provincial and regional movement which, with the exception of the diehard Créditistes, can be expected to remain outside federal politics.

The CCF-NDP: Socialism in Canada

We aim to replace the present capitalistic system, with its inherent injustice and inhumanity, by a social order from which the domination and exploitation of one class by another will be eliminated, in which economic planning will supersede unregulated private enterprise and competition and in which genuine democratic self-government based upon economic equality will be possible.

These words are from the "Regina Manifesto", a declaration of principles passed at the first annual convention of the Cooperative Commonwealth Federation, in Regina in 1933. Since 1921, J.S. Woodsworth had led a tiny group of Socialist MPs in the federal parliament, and by 1932, the depression, Woodworth's own leadership, and the intense interest of many Canadian farm and labour leaders and academics led to the formation of a formal party structure oriented towards the principles outlined in the Regina Manifesto.

The CCF was militantly socialistic for the first twenty years of its life, but by 1956 it had begun to change its ideological face.[25] While it continued to favour an egalitarian and classless society, the party began to shift towards the ideological centre in Canadian politics, in response to the fact that its electoral support appeared to have peaked in 1944–45 without producing a political victory. No longer did the CCF consider it necessary to nationalize all industry, and no longer did it call for the eradication of all capitalism. Support for the party, however, continued to run at only 14 to 16 per cent of the popular vote.

Meanwhile, organized labour in Canada—particularly the Canadian Labour Congress—began to take an interest in openly supporting a

[25]Leo Zakuta, *A Protest Movement Becalmed: A Study of Change in the CCF*, (University of Toronto Press, Toronto, 1964), pp. 169–173.

political party, particularly a party with ideas such as those of the CCF. A change of name, however, seemed desirable, in order to expunge the western rural image that went with the title CCF. The result was a dissolution of the old Cooperative Commonwealth Federation and the formation of the New Democratic Party in 1961.[26] The NDP contained many of the same people as had the CCF, but by now these leaders were chastened into a willingness to modify their principles somewhat in order to gain power. The years of watching policy making and trying to woo recalcitrant voters had left some marks. Although these changes, plus the influx of labour influences into the party machinery have added a dash of pragmatism to the NDP, the party remains a democratic–socialist party in the tradition of English rather than Marxian socialism. And like most democratic–socialist parties, it has drifted to the right even as the structure of capitalist society has drifted to the left.

What has been said about ideological drift in the CCF-NDP, however, should not be interpreted to mean that the party is identical to the older parties. For example, the CCF-NDP has been more pacifist and is less likely to support the Canadian military establishment and defense expenditures than are those parties. The party itself has never been as extremely pacifist as its first leader, J.S. Woodsworth, who voted against Canada's entry into World War II, but it stood some distance from the older parties in this regard—particularly in the past, when the military aspect of foreign policy received much more attention than it does today. As well, the CCF-NDP remains more committed to economic equality than the older parties. The Liberals and Progressive Conservatives have occasionally sought to institute some rough notion of "equality of opportunity", but the NDP has tended to favour a more substantive equality here and now.

The NDP has also tended to be more nationalistic than the Liberals vis-à-vis the United States and more so than the Conservatives vis-à-vis Britain. It has been suggested that its position on questions of Canadian nationalism is really much closer to that of the Conservatives than to that of Liberals, and that in particular there are close parallels between the Conservative position under John Diefenbaker and the NDP position.[27]

The various nationalist tendencies in the party have led to some severe organizational stresses and strains. The most recent of these was caused by the strongly nationalistic "Waffle" group which sought much

[26]The best study of the CCF is W.D. Young, *The Anatomy of a Party: The National CCF 1932-61*. (University of Toronto Press, Toronto, 1969). For the post-1961 period, see: Desmond Morton, *NDP: The Dream of Power*, (Hakkert, Toronto, 1974), and N.H. Chi and George Perlin, "The NDP: A Party in Transition" in H.G. Thorburn (ed.), *Party Politics in Canada* (3rd edition) pp. 176–187. See also W. Baker and T. Price, "The New Democratic Party and Canadian Politics", in *Party Politics in Canada* (2nd edition) pp. 168–179.

[27]See George Grant, *Lament for a Nation: The Defeat of Canadian Nationalism*, (McClelland and Stewart, Toronto, 1965), for a provocative re-evaluation of the Diefenbaker position on Canadian–U.S. relationships. Grant sees many similarities between NDP and Conservative positions.

greater Canadian control of Canadian industry. The group became sufficiently strong that in the 1971 leadership convention, their candidate ran a fairly close second to the winner, David Lewis. However, the conservative trade union wing of the party and the almost equally conservative (for a socialist party) parliamentary caucuses—both provincial and national—were able to force the explusion of the group as an entity from the Ontario party in 1973 and their overall influence has declined since then.

It has often been suggested that the CCF and NDP have been the parties of innovation in Canadian politics. The Liberals, especially, have often been accused of (or praised for) continually moving to adopt ideas which have been developed and popularized by the NDP or the CCF and gaining the credit for putting them into play. It could be suggested, however, that the NDP has fallen into the role of innovator virtually by accident. The CCF started with a left-wing position just at the time when a leftward drift in the politics of all western democracies was beginning. This made it inevitable that any party in power would at least appear to be adopting some of their positions.

Structurally, the NDP is not so different from the older parties as its origins and ideology might lead one to expect. Its leader, like the leader of the two older parties, is elected at a convention and is subjected to a vote of confidence at party conventions held at least biennially. In fact no CCF or NDP leader once elected has ever been seriously challenged by the convention. The party is not formally a federation, but like its older party counterparts it is informally very nearly so with its provincial party organizations being fully autonomous but represented both at the national convention and on the National Council. The latter body is formally responsible for the operation of the party between elections and meets at least twice yearly at the call of the party Executive. However the Council has more than 100 members and such large groups generally rule more in form than in substance. The real operation of the party machinery is directed by the Executive and by the party caucus. The NDP national office is smaller than that of the other two parties, as is the leader's office establishment, but this is partially compensated for by the somewhat higher level of activity of constituency and provincial associations between elections. In sum, however, the locus of control for most matters in the NDP is not much different than for the older parties, residing primarily in the leader and parliamentary caucus, the national Executive and the permanent offices of the party.

Table 10-1 indicates that there are some substantial differences in the bases of support of the NDP and the older parties. The religious distribution of NDP votes is similar to that of the Conservatives, but some 59 per cent of NDP votes come from either the skilled or unskilled labour versus 47 per cent for the Liberals and 43 for the PCs. Sixty-two per cent of NDP votes come from "lower" classes compared to just 39 per cent for the Liberals, and the NDP have a higher proportion of "other" ethnic voters than either older party. NDP votes are more heavily concentrated in metropolitan areas than those of either older party (in spite of the signal weakness in Montreal), but, perhaps surprisingly, the age distribution of its voters is not different from that of the others. The NDP draws disproportionately from union voters; in 1968, 31 per cent of them voted NDP compared to 16 per cent of the population as a whole.[28]

The profile of NDP supporters suggests that while Canadian politics in general is not class based, support for the NDP is. Thus we have the phenomenon of a class-based party in what is not a class-voting system. But there is also a strong regional bias to NDP support. The CCF was born in Saskatchewan, had its first substantial victory there, and both the CCF and its successor, the NDP, have been strong—both federally and provincially—there ever since. Another area of consistent support has been Winnipeg, and lately support has apparently spread out across the province, producing an NDP victory in the 1969 Manitoba provincial election. There is also sufficient support centred in the powerful west-coast trade union movement to enable the party to capture British Columbia's provincial government. Urban support in eastern Canada has also been growing, particularly in heavily unionized areas such as Toronto and Hamilton. However, the NDP remains totally without support in Quebec, the Maritimes, and large sections of Ontario. It is conceivable that these holes may eventually be filled in, but current progress in this direction is very slow. Until these "holes" are filled, it is highly improbable that the NDP will be serious contender for national office.

As a socialist movement which has had some electoral successes, the CCF-NDP is unique on this side of the Atlantic. Why has this been possible in Canada and not in the United States? Gad Horowitz, developing the ideas of Louis Hartz, suggests one important reason.[29] Using a dialectical analysis, he posits that socialism, as an acceptable ideology in a society, can only grow out of confrontation of Toryism with nineteenth-century liberalism. If only one of the two ingredients is present, the essential dialogue is lacking and socialism cannot develop. The United States can be looked at, ideologically, as a fragment thrown off from Europe— particularly from Britain—at a time when liberalism was ascendent. Most Tories who were in the United States at the time of the American Revolution left and came to Canada. Ideological dialogue is therefore less likely in the U.S. than in Canada and nineteenth-century liberalism remains the predominant ideology of that nation. Other ideologies are simply not tolerated by American society. In Canada there is a predominance of the same liberal tradition, but it is tempered with a "Tory touch" which has allowed Canadians both to see the state as something greater than the sum

[28]N.H. Chi and G. Perlin, "The NDP: A Party in Transition", p. 179. This source provides graphical pictures of many of figures shown in Table 10-1.
[29]These ideas are expressed in Gad Horowitz, "Conversatism, Liberalism and Socialism in Canada: An Interpretation", in *Canadian Journal of Economics and Political Science*, vol. 32, no. 2, May, 1966. Hartz's are expounded in several places, most notably Louis Hartz, *The Liberal Tradition in America*, (Harcourt, Brace and World, New York, 1955) and *The Founding of New Societies*, (Harcourt, Brace and World, New York, 1964). See also K.D. McRae, "The Structure of Canadian History", in Hartz, *The Founding of New Societies*.

of its parts and to tolerate the socialist ideology which is the dialectical synthesis of the two older ideologies.

Horowitz's ideas are highly interesting but there is no way of testing them for validity. The reader may lose little analytical power by ignoring the ideological content of the CCF-NDP movement and analyzing it as the largest and most persistent example of the general group of newer and relatively smaller political parties in Canada.[30]

Interpretation of Third-party Movements in Canada

By now it may very well be obvious to the reader that there is much in common among various third-party movements in Canadian politics, even when they have such sidely disparate ideological stances as the Social Credit and the NDP. Virtually all of them originate either in Quebec or in western Canada; with the exception of the United Farmers of Ontario no important third party has ever originated elsewhere. Virtually all of them have expressed discontent with Canada's central political institutions, particularly her political parties. None of them has yet grown to be a major party, yet with the exception of the Progressives, all have persevered in political action, resisting absorption by the older parties and continuing to exist today.

These common features have led several political scientists to suggest reasons why third parties have been such a persistent feature of the Canadian party system. The most frequently used and probably the most convincing explanation revolves around the parliamentary system itself and the demands it makes on political parties. Professor Hugh Thorburn sums up this point of view when he writes:

> Canadian parties, although vague in their policies, are disciplined parliamentary groups requiring of their members a high degree of conformity. The leader has great authority and there is little room for dissidence. Protest, then, must occur outside the old parties, and if it is to be effective must itself assume the form of a political party.[31]

Because of the necessity of maintaining cohesive parliamentary voting blocs, party discipline must be high. In the United States, very loose party discipline allows protest to occur within parties, so the formation of third-party groups is seldom necessary. In Canada, by contrast, if radical dissent is to be heard at all, it must be heard outside the confines of the older parties.

The Canadian federal system may also have provided some incen-

---

[30]We have ended this section of the chapter without discussing those political parties which operate exclusively on the Quebec stage, the Union Nationale and the Parti Québecois. It is our feeling that we cannot do justice to the details of the party system within any province, particularly Quebec without going into more detail than we have space for here. In effect, each of the ten separate party systems deserves several pages of treatment and since this text is not intended to cover provincial politics in detail we have not done so here. The interested reader is referred to M. Robin (ed.), *Canadian Provincial Politics*, (Prentice–Hall, Scarborough, 1972). 1972).

[31]*Party Politics in Canada*, (3rd edition), p. 159.

tive to the formation of third parties, for even if a minor party cannot win a national election, it does have a fair chance of winning power in a province. Every province west of New Brunswick has, at some time, had a third-party government, and in 1972 three provinces possessed them. Provincial third-party governments have been remarkably stable, sharing in the proclivity of all Canadian provincial governments towards longevity.

At first glance, a similar potential for third-party power might appear to exist in the American states, but there are important differences between the Canadian and U.S. situations. First, state elections in the United States are held in conjunction with national elections. The ability of the national parties to dominate the media makes it very difficult for a smaller party to compete. Secondly, winning power in an American state is not necessarily the plum that winning power in a Canadian province is. American federalism, in spite of the constitutional niceties, is far more centralized than Canadian federalism, with correspondingly less power left to the states. As a power base, an American state is not nearly so attractive as a Canadian province. And, of course, the special case of Quebec has made third-party activity more likely there. Power in Quebec politics is, for many French-Canadian politicians, the summit of their ambitions. The reason is relatively simple: while 57 per cent of English Canadians think that the federal government "handles the most important problems", only 24 percent of French Canadians think so.[32] This raises the status of provincial political office in Quebec and makes political power there much more worth winning than in the other provinces. Indeed, two Quebec parties, the Union Nationale and the Parti Québecois, are the only major third-party movements in Canada which have not had any federal ambitions.

The coincidence of social cleavage with provincial or sectional boundaries, and the relative homogeneity of the provinces have also been important in fostering third-party movements. It would be difficult to imagine much success for the Union Nationale or the Parti Québecois in a Quebec which was 50 per cent English. C.B. Macpherson attributes much the early success of third-party movements in Alberta to the relative social homogeneity of that province. The CCF may have succeeded in Saskatchewan partially because of a similar homogeneity.[33]

Another theory to account for the rise of third parties in Canada has been suggested by Professor Maurice Pinard.[34] Canadian electoral politics is characterized by long periods and large areas of one-party dominance. Looking specifically at the rise of the Créditistes in Quebec, Pinard hypothesized that the long period of Liberal party dominance in federal politics in rural Quebec led to a perception on the part of Quebeckers that the Conservative party was not a legitimate alternative. They voted Progressive Conservative in 1958 so as not to be cut off politically from the party in power, but they shortly discovered that the Conservatives under

---

[32]This data is taken from the 1965 National Political Survey carried out by John Meisel et al.

[33]C.B. Macpherson, *Democracy in Alberta*, and S.M. Lipset, *Agrarian Socialism, passim*.

[34]Maurice Pinard, "The Rise of a Third Party". See also the discussion of this theory in the *Canadian Journal of Political Science* (vol. VI, no. 3) Sept. 1973.

Diefenbaker did not pay any attention to them. If they were still not satisfied (and rural Quebec has had a great deal to be dissatisfied about), their only legitimate outlet for protest was through a third party, and the Ralliement des Créditistes provided this. A similar situation prevailed in Alberta in 1935—there was no effective opposition to the United Farmers government and hence no place for voters to express their discontent, until Social Credit came along. One could apply this type of analysis fruitfully to many of Canada's third-party movements.

Special reasons for the success of third-party movements in Quebec have been mentioned, and there were also special reasons for their success on the prairies. C.B. Macpherson has suggested that the Prairies constituted a quasi-colonial economy with respect to the East, that they had effectively only one class of citizens, and that the result of this was a quasi-party system.[35] The one-crop economy and lack of social cleavage on the prairies may well have made possible the type of mass party political action represented by the CCF in Saskatchewan and the Social Credit and United Farmers in Alberta.

Finally, a suggestion about the genesis of the CCF victory in Saskatchewan in 1944 has been made by S.M. Lipset.[36] Given the one-crop economy of that province and the antipathy which western farmers felt for eastern grain-marketing organizations, the Saskatchewan farmers early organized a series of wheat pools and cooperatives. These organizations produced many active citizens who later used the wheat pool cooperative structure to organize party opposition to the Liberal government then in power. Such a widespread social structure was not available in other provinces, and it did much to aid the organization of the CCF in Saskatchewan as a strong political force.

Undoubtedly all of these explanations have some validity. It is in the coincidence of two or more such factors that one finds the most fertile ground for third-party activity. Whatever the explanation, however, the fact remains that third-party politics have done much to give the Canadian political system its present distinctive complexion.

CONCLUSION:
THE PARTY SYSTEM: 1921–1974

One of the favourite traditional exercises of political scientists has been the attempt to characterize the party systems of various nations. The most widely accepted descriptive parameter has been the number of parties in that system. Thus the United States is usually characterized as a "two-party" system, as are Britain and Germany. Scandinavian nations are usually described as "multi-party" as are France and Israel. There are obvious difficulties with this classification scheme; lumping the party systems of France, Israel and Norway together in one cell of a table does relatively little to help us to understand the political systems of those countries. The

[35]Macpherson, *op. cit.* See especially pp. 215–250.
[36]Lipset, *op. cit.* This is a general theme running through this book.

classical two-party system—Britain—found itself with a minority government in 1974 and the "third-party" contender for the presidency of the U.S. in 1968 gathered 13.9 per cent of the popular vote.

The numerical typing of party systems breaks down almost completely when applied to Canada. Does Canada have a "one-party dominant" system because the Liberals have held power in Ottawa for 42 of the last 54 years? Do we have a 2-party system because the Conservatives have proven capable of defeating the Liberals? Do we have a 3-party system because the CCF-NDP has shown considerable consistency in its bases of support and has, in every federal election for 40 years, won at least a few seats? Or it is a multi-party system? After all, the Créditistes have shown considerable staying power, and several provinces have had minor-party governments. These difficulties lead us to have grave reservations about hanging any particular label on the party system and we have tried to resist doing so in this chapter.

The structures of Canada's major political parties have been rather slow to change over the last half-century. The locus of power, the sources of finance and the backgrounds of the leaders are remarkably similar to what they were even before the First World War. The society has changed greatly in that period, and if the parties as individual structures have not changed much in relation to social change, it may be that the party system has. If the Liberal and Conservative parties themselves have ceased to be omnibus vehicles for aggregating the country's vast array of political interests, it may be that the political system is none the worse off. For if the party system as a whole articulates and aggregates interests, it matters little that individual parties fail to do so. Thus the frequently recurring minority government situation, which Canadians seem so reluctant to face, may be—and indeed, probably is—quite functional as the vehicle whereby the party system (however characterized) aggregates the interest that were once aggregated within the older parties themselves.[37]

[37]This point is elaborated and examined from several angles in John Meisel, *Working Papers on Canadian Politics*, pp. 51–60. The election of majority governments such as happened in July 1974 may well be the exception rather than the rule.

11
The Electoral Process

THE FUNCTIONS OF THE ELECTORAL PROCESS

To most Canadians, elections are the most visible and most interesting of political events, and voting is the most common form of political participation. Between 70 and 80 per cent of the eligible population will show up at the polls on the day of a federal election. The election campaign is the most widely covered and closely watched of political events in Canada.

The primary purpose of elections in Western democracies is to provide a process whereby the highest political authorities can be selected or changed peacefully. What seems like an obvious point to citizens of Western democracies is not so obvious viewed in world context, for many political systems do not have formalized and peaceful processes for changing authorities. Even in many of the systems with formal election mechanisms, the possibility of changing political authorities via the polls is non-existent. When a society becomes deeply dissatisfied with its political system and the system does not provide for a peaceful expression of discontent through the electoral process, change can only be accomplished in an unstructured and, very often, a violent manner.

In a non-electoral system, it is possible for a group of leaders to retain power long after they have lost the support of the majority of the society. By controlling the armed forces, for instance, a "banana republic" *presidente* can continue to rule without any reference to the interests of the public. The authorities in the Canadian system, on the other hand, know that they must put their jobs on the line at least every five years, and they know that they must satisfy at least a plurality of the people if they are to be re-elected.

Perhaps the most important latent function of elections is the generation of support for both the authorities and the regime. The generation of support for authorities is a rather obvious function—after all, in order to get elected, a set of authorities must convince a majority of the electors that they are worthy of support. Support for the whole system is produced by elections because the campaigns arouse people's interest in politics and give them a sense of participation in the system's operations.

While it is true that elections focus the people's attention on the system and the authorities, it has often been asserted that election campaigns do not do much to change people's minds. While this hypothesis has not yet been completely verified, it does appear that socio-economic factors and pre-existing attitudes may have considerably more to do with Canadian voting patterns than do election campaigns. One analyst of Canadian election campaigns has estimated that in only 7 (or possibly 8) of the 28 national elections since Confederation have campaigns altered the final outcome, and 4 of these were Diefenbaker elections, which were probably atypical.[1] This point finds some corroboration in analyses of American elections. For example, in 1948, a year in which the election campaign itself was generally considered to have won the day for President Truman, one study found that 64 per cent of voters had made up their minds before the nominating conventions and that only 21 per cent decided during the campaign itself.[2] On the other side of the argument, in 1965 a national survey in Canada indicated that some 36 per cent of voters had made up their minds at some point during the election campaign, and 18 per cent said they had decided during the last few days of the battle.[3] This argument, however, may lead us aside from the major point: even if election campaigns do little to change most people's minds, they do, at least, cause people to pay attention to the political system, and perhaps make them realize that it is in some ways relevant to them. The actors in an election campaign do not set out consciously to achieve this purpose, but the attention they create as a by-product of their attempt to gain power may do it automatically.

In addition to the functions enumerated above, elections may perform an input function for the political system. Achieving a maximum of electoral support requires that parties search high and low for votes, and this search can often lead them to articulate the interests of groups in the population which might otherwise remain in the background. The elections force the parties to initiate new policy issues, particularly those which are relevant to people who normally do not vote, for if enough non-voters can be motivated to cast a ballot, the outcome of the election might possibly be altered. And the fact that approximately half a million Canadians are working for the political parties during a national election campaign means that if a relevant issue exists, it will likely be discovered by someone.

Similarly, parties are forced by elections to be considerably more responsive to new ideas than they might otherwise be. Is this a policy idea that will catch the imagination of the voters? Is that a policy that will get the economy back on the rails and insure the kind of distribution of wealth which will satisfy the mass of voters who can keep the party in power? If parties and leaders did not periodically have to stand the test of public satisfaction, they might well sink even further into the conservative cast of

[1]J.M. Beck, *The Pendulum of Power*, (Prentice–Hall, Scarborough, 1968), p. 424.
[2]B.R. Berelson, P.F. Lazarsfeld, and W.N. McPhee, *Voting*, (University of Chicago Press, Chicago, 1954), pp. 14–24.
[3]Data from a survey conducted by J. Meisel *et al.*, 1965 and 1966.

mind that characterizes most elites. In addition to stimulating policy input processes, it has often been suggested that elections cause parties to "step up" their aggregative activities. During an election campaign, parties try to find widely acceptable sets of policies which will maximize voter support.

These imputed input functions have a nice ring to them, for they suggest a picture of political parties, ever vigilant for the vote, forming a vital link between the citizen and the policy making apparatus of the modern state. There are, however, a number of flaws. The most important is that this paradigm ignores the fact that, as pointed out in Chapter 9, most political decisions in Canada are made with relatively little input from the party organization. Thus, even if the articulation of our policy needs does occur, it is to some extent ineffectual; once in power, parties seem to pay little attention to their election platforms. Politics in New Brunswick are not entirely typical of Canadian politics, but the following words will ring true to most people who have carefully observed parties in office:

> It is not unusual to find an item (expressed in different words) appearing on four election platforms of the same party in a row. The fact that the party was in power throughout the entire period and might presumably have enacted the required legislation during this time does not seem to occur to those who draw up the platform.[4]

Moreover, party platforms and the policies that parties suggest during elections are extremely nebulous things. They usually contain a little bit for everyone but almost no detail which could facilitate their conversion to specific policy outputs. For example, the Liberal program for the 1963 election contained such exciting and specific items as:

PROSPERITY FOR CANADIANS
Fundamentals for a Sound Economy
Cure unemployment. . .
Manage the nation's finances well. . .
Expand Canada's foreign trade
A new Liberal government will act positively. It will have a constructive plan for free trade with Britain, the United States and the European Common Market, as a step towards the establishment of an Atlantic Community. Commonwealth nations, Japan and other interested countries will be invited to join in progressively reducing the barriers to World trade.
Planning and Finance
Make monetary policy an instrument for steady economic growth. A new Liberal government will take clear responsibility for the money supply, credit policies and the exchange rate of the Canadian dollar. It will improve the country's financial machinery, to make more Canadian capital available for industry and to safeguard the consumer against credit abuses. . .

It would be difficult to find people anywhere in Canada who would not espouse these policies. They have appeared in virtually every Liberal and Conservative party platform since at least 1945.

[4]H.G. Thorburn, *Politics in New Brunswick*, (University of Toronto Press, Toronto, 1961), p. 107.

This is not to deny that Canadian parties frequently work out programs in considerable detail before they take office. The background papers for party annual meetings or biennial conventions attest to this. However, once a party takes power in Ottawa, this type of discussion paper usually recedes in importance and is superseded in the cabinet's eyes by inputs from the large bureaucratic departments headed by ministers. In fact, as will be suggested when the policy process is examined in more detail, policy initiation is carried out to a large extent by the bureaucracy.

In spite of all this, one can assert that in some ways elections are important vehicles for the aggregation and articulation of interests in Canadian politics; the threat of future elections forces cabinet ministers to ensure at least some minimal level of performance by their departments and it also forces them to hold new policies up to the litmus of broad public acceptability. While that may not always be the most propitious measure of a policy's advisability it certainly keeps our policy makers broadly accountable.

There are three other latent functions of the electoral process in Canada which have particular importance. First, elections have a "sociability function". Party workers work hard for little or no monetary reward, so many participants in the electoral process must be there because it is fun.

Secondly, elections provide "spectator interest" which was discussed at length in Chapter 4.[5] Whatever effect election campaigns have on the final outcome, they do make a fine national show with leaders dashing to and fro trying to establish their images, followed by retinues of weary newsmen who daily fill the newspapers with all manner of fact, fancy and comment on the race. Then there is the thrill of the race itself, with Gallup polls and assorted pundits giving us a week-by-week picture of the positions of the various parties. At the local level, Stephen Leacock's description is not so far from the mark:

> . . .the whole town and country is a hive of politics, and people who have only witnessed gatherings such as the House of Commons at Westminster and the Senate at Washington and never seen a Conservative convention at Tecumseh Corners or a Liberal Rally at the Concession Schoolhouse, don't know what politics means.
>
> So you may imagine the excitement in Mariposa when it became known that King George had dissolved the Parliament of Canada and had sent out a writ or command for Missinaba County to elect for him some other person than John Henry Bagshaw because he no longer had confidence in him.[6]

Third, in some parts of Canada elections are still a minor means of redistributing income. Middle-class metropolitan ridings see relatively little of this and it is, perhaps, a dying tradition even in much of the countryside, but votes can still be bought and public works can still be built. The

---

[5]It may be argued with some justification that this function is merely a manifestation of the support-building function which was mentioned earlier.

[6]From *Sunshine Sketches of a Little Town* by Stephen Leacock, reprinted by permission of The Canadian Publishers, McClelland and Stewart Limited, Toronto.

votes of local opinion leaders—not necessarily the upper class of a community—are particularly valuable. Although many party workers are volunteers, some are paid something for their efforts and these are usually the lower-class workers. In Quebec the "good old days" are now disappearing, but there, until recently, a provincial election in a marginal riding was always good for at least one road paving and a considerable number of farm electric installations, usually carried out by a local contractor who, incidentally, supported the governing party. Even today, in Newfoundland each election sees some extension of the pavement in small towns and outports. Electoral patronage was not necessarily the most efficient redistribution system on earth, but then neither are the bureaucratic redistribution systems we have today. Indeed, Hubert Guindon has pointed out that:

> The possibly unanticipated effect of the crackdown on patronage funds [by the Lesage government in Quebec], in actual fact, was to halt or substantially reduce the flow of provincial funds to the lower social strata. Holding up the new "bureaucratic" public morality was a hidden net reorienting public expenditures to the other social classes.[7]

In short, elections carry out many functions in Canadian politics. They do not necessarily do what might be expected at first glance, and their role in the actual policy-making process has often been overstated, but they are still in a very real sense the foundation upon which the present "rules of the game" in Canadian politics are based.

THE STRUCTURE OF THE CANADIAN ELECTORAL PROCESS

The Formal Structure[8] Barring the defeat of a government in the Commons, the timing of an election in Canada is wholly the prerogative of the Prime Minister, who decides, with more or less advice from his cabinet, on the exact date. This has not always been the case. From 1867 to 1926 it seemed generally conceded that it was the right of the Prime Minister to decide the occurrence and the timing of elections; at least they always did so. In 1926, however, Lord Byng refused Mackenzie King a dissolution and asked Arthur Meighen to attempt to form a government in the existing House. Meighen did so but was almost immediately defeated on a vote of confidence. King campaigned in the ensuing election mainly on this issue and won a clear majority of seats. In spite of some subsequent debate, King's victory may have finally established the principle that the Prime Minister has the right to control the timing of elections and, incidentally, removed any illusions about the real power of a Governor General.[9]

[7]Hubert Guindon, "Social Unrest Social Class and Quebec's Bureaucratic Revolution," *Queen's Quarterly*, vol. 71, no. 2, 1964, and in Thorburn, *Party Politics in Canada*, p. 188.
[8]The formal electoral machinery is described in greater detail in T. Qualter, *The Election Process in Canada*, (McGraw–Hill, Toronto, 1970).
[9]The events of 1926 are analyzed in detail in Eugene Forsey, *The Royal Power of Dis-*

The issue could have arisen again after the 1972 federal election, when the Liberals were returned with only two more seats than the Conservatives, the NDP holding the balance of power with 31 seats. If the Liberals had been defeated in a vote of confidence when they met parliament, would it have been Prime Minister Trudeau's right to ask for another election, or would he have been obliged by constitutional convention to merely resign and let the Governor General call upon the leader of the opposition to form a government? If the principal enunciated above stands, then the Governor General would have had to do whatever the Prime Minister suggested, but some constitutional experts did assert that even if the Prime Minister had requested dissolution, the Governor General could have denied him that privilege and called instead on Mr. Stanfield.

As it turned out, the issue blew over leaving nothing more than residual deposits in the bank accounts of sundry academic constitutional experts who appeared on radio and television in the days following the election, and it is likely that if Mr. Trudeau had done anything, he would simply have resigned, leaving the options open for the Governor General. The constitutional experts did seem to agree that once the Liberals had won one or two votes of confidence in the House and had their Throne Speech accepted, the normal rules would then apply, i.e., dissolution would be a Prime Ministerial prerogative or else would follow automatically from a major government defeat. One and one-half years later the government was in fact, defeated and dissolution did follow virtually automatically.

Customarily, if the government in power is in a majority, elections will occur at about four-year intervals, although the maximum allowable term under the BNA Act is five years. A government will not wait out the full five years unless it is in trouble, and then the results, as found by R.B. Bennett in 1935 and Joey Smallwood in 1972, are not likely to be propitious. A Prime Minister will usually make his decision about precise election timing on the basis of information from his party about its state of preparedness, from his cabinet about how any policy initiatives undertaken by the party are progressing, and particularly from information obtained fnom public opinion polls about the party standing across the country. Depending on his temperament, the Prime Minister may also feel moved to look at horoscopes or tea leaves, or to consult his long-dead mother, for the timing of an election can be a tricky business.

Once a decision on timing has been made, the Prime Minister visits the Governor General, who has the formal power to dissolve parliament and call an election. In the provinces the Premier visits the Lieutenant-Governor, who has a similar formal power with regard to provincial elections. The Governor General or Lieutenant-Governor then issues a writ in the name of Her Majesty declaring the election, and the electoral machinery goes into motion.

By the time electoral writs are issued, the official electoral machinery under the direction of the *Chief Electoral Officer* is ready to begin moving.

solution of Parliament in the British Commonwealth, (Oxford University Press, Toronto, 1945).

Indeed, the apparatus is ready a considerable time before the usual four years have passed, since there is always the possibility of a "snap election", particularly in a time of minority government. Even the rapid succession of federal elections beginning in 1962 did not catch the Electoral Office unprepared, although the huge job of preparing for an election must have subjected it to considerable strain.

As soon as the Governor General or Lieutenant-Governor has signed the electoral writs, instructions go out to the *Returning Officers*—the official heads of the electoral apparatus in each riding—and *enumerators* begin to knock on doors to list the eligible voters. The job of enumerator is a minor . patronage position which, in urban areas, goes to supporters of the two parties which led the polls in the previous election. Enumerators travel in pairs—generally one pair for each poll—with one member of the pair coming from each party. Polls are sometimes located in the houses of supporters of the "right" party, but in more affluent areas where the remuneration is hardly worth the inconvenience of a stampede through one's house, churches and schools are more usual polling locations.

The enumeration process must start on the 49th day before polling day and it must finish by the 44th day. Since some time is required to get out the writs calling for the whole process to begin, this means that an election cannot usually take place in less than 60 days.[10]

A preliminary list of voters is compiled, distributed to those whose names appear on the list, and posted on neighbourhood telephone poles so that people may see if their names are on the list (and can determine the occupations of their neighbours!) Copies of the preliminary list are also sent to the Chief Electoral Officer. Potential voters whose names do not appear on the list then have 5 to 8 days in which to challenge their omission before an appeal court—a simple procedure which normally requires only a declaration on the voter's part. Final lists are then prepared and the polls set up. *Advance polls* are established for those who must be out of town on voting day and these are run on the ninth and seventh days before the election. The votes from advance polls are not counted until after the close of regular polls.

After the regular polls close on voting day the *Deputy Returning Officers*, who are in charge of each poll, count the ballots under the watchful eyes of the party *scrutineers*. This is an entirely unofficial count although it is usually accurate. The results of this unofficial count, tabulated in newsrooms and party headquarters, are what produce the excitement on election night. The ballot boxes are delivered to the Returning Officer after the unofficial count, and he then has the responsibility of keeping them until the official count which may not be sooner than 7 days after the election. By this time, of course, the excitement is over in all but ridings which were very close and where the armed service vote, which is added at this time, may be decisive.

The Informal Structure So far, in discussing preparation for

[10]T. Qualter, *The Election Process in Canada*, pp. 163–4. His diary of a federal election pp. 162–166 provides a valuable summary of the whole process.

elections, the parties have not been mentioned, but parallel to the official activity during an election campaign, there is a great deal of unofficial activity. Indeed, by the time the Prime Minister visits the Governor General to ask for a dissolution, political parties will already have undergone the long process of waking up from their deep sleep of the previous few years, oiling and polishing their local machines, nominating candidates, reactivating their national organizations, and generally acting like the textbook pictures we have always had of parties. The actual setting of the election date is rather like the firing of the starter's gun. Unfortunately, as we will see, sometimes the "runners" trip over the starting blocks.

At national campaign headquarters a number of things will be happening. Schedules for speaking tours by the leaders will be set up for the whole campaign. An avalanche of party literature, speaker's handbooks, etc. will descend on the local constituency associations. Party "bagmen" will redouble their efforts, and budgetary priorities will be set by a small, sometimes informal, campaign committee under the National Chairman. New staff and volunteers will be taken on, and press releases and speeches ground out by the yard. National polls will be commissioned in order to divine the "major issues"—which are invariably inflation, unemployment and the high cost of living.

At the local level, events will be much more variable. Some local election machines are highly efficient, and some are comedies of errors. Nominations of candidates will usually have taken place some time before the campaign begins, but in some ridings the announcement of the election date will find one or more parties so ill-prepared that no candidate is available. Nomination procedures vary from party to party and from riding to riding. At the one extreme are completely open conventions where anyone who has paid his nominal party membership dues may vote, while at the other extreme are carefully controlled nominating conventions where all the delegates are handpicked by the party executive to avoid any unfortunate "errors". In practice most nominating conventions lie somewhere between the two extremes, with the delegates representing poll organizations or other small units in the riding. In truth, parties are as often embarrassed by a lack of potential nominees as by an excess, and at every election some constituency executives face the unpleasant task of searching frantically for someone to run as the party candidate. If all else fails, a member of the party executive will himself accept a "draft" and carry the party's colours into the local campaign.

Ideally, the earliest stages of an election campaign will see the establishment of a careful schedule of activities peaking on election day. Local workers will be recruited and fund raising will be attempted in earnest. Poll captains will be appointed to coordinate party efforts in a given neighbourhood. Some tentative door-to-door canvassing will begin, rising in intensity as the great day approaches, and mail and telephone campaigns will be conducted to reach as many voters as the party workers can find. On voting day the poll captain will arrange for the transportation of any known supporters who could not otherwise make it to the polls, and scrutineers will sit in the polling station to ensure that irregularities do not occur, and equally important, to chat with friends and neighbours.

In practice it may be difficult to find willing party workers. Canvassing itself is often a hit-and-miss affair, with large sections of the city, especially in lower class areas, left untouched, and phone campaigns are also usually rather spotty. In most homes the candidates' literature is usually "filed" in the garbage can. Meanwhile, communication is flowing back and forth between the constituencies and local, provincial, and national headquarters and, as befits a stratarchical structure, much of it gets lost or is grossly misinterpreted along the way. Yet the whole structure does lumber ahead towards election day. Leaders criss-cross the country, leaving enthusiasm or despair in their wakes. Money flows into close ridings and out of safe or hopeless ones. The media give millions of dollars of free publicity to the parties and the parties spend millions of dollars doing things for the electorate to watch and the media to report.

All this activity costs money, and the spending is often regarded with a jaundiced eye by the public. It is true that the total amounts spent are high. Professor Norman Ward has estimated that the total real costs of running the electoral machinery amount to about $47,000,000 per year, an estimate made as "a trial run at the job by a political scientist who, it must be conceded, is not convinced that it can be done".[11] Lest this amount be regarded as excessive, Professor Ward goes on to conclude:

> A sum rounded upward to $47,000,000 for the annual costs of democracy... may seem enormous, but it is barely $2.40 a head ...Even taking the most extravagant view of the costs of the electoral and parliamentary process and the supporting activities, it would be difficult to argue that the democratic parts of Canada's governmental machinery are an expensive indulgence.

Another leading authority, Professor K.Z. Paltiel, has estimated that the total expenditure by parties in the 1972 election campaign was at least 31 million dollars, up at least 30 per cent from 1968.[12] Expenditures by individual candidates ranged from $92,100 declared by mining magnate Stephen Roman (who was defeated) down to nothing but the $250, the required deposit from all candidates. The average reported expenditure per candidate was $18,700 for the Liberals, $16,500 for the PCs, $5,400 for the NDP and $1,885 for the Social Credit.

At the national level alone the Liberals raised over $6.5 million dollars and spent at least $5.9 million, with the largest amounts being disbursed by provincial party organizations either for their own expenses or as partial reimbursement to candidates for local expenses. The national office itself spent nearly $1.3 million, mainly on the leader's tours, the me-

[11]Norman Ward, "Money and Politics", *Canadian Journal of Political Science*, Vol. 5 no. 3, (Sept. 1972), pp. 335–347. This article also gives a brief description of efforts at reform in the area of electoral finance.

[12]The following descriptive material on election expenses is from K.Z. Paltiel, "Some Aspects of Campaign Finance in Canada," paper presented to the International Political Science Association, Montreal, August 1973. For historical material see K.Z. Paltiel, *Political Party Financing in Canada* and the Committee on Election Expenses, *Studies in Canadian Party Finance*, (Queen's Printer, Ottawa, 1966). Professor Paltiel's estimate does not include the cost of operating the formal electoral machinery, whereas Professor Ward's does.

dia and printing. The money was raised largely in Ontario and Quebec with at least 50 bagmen prowling Ontario, ever watchful for corporate or individual donors. The National Campaign chairman himself canvassed the 90 largest firms in the province. It is important, in view of what we said earlier about the small size of the national headquarters between elections, that $600,000 of the money raised in 1972 had to be allocated to paying off the accumulated deficit of the national office, whose approximately $350,000 annual operating costs are not easily covered by the party in non-election years.

By comparison with the Liberals, the PCs raised almost $4 million at the national level in 1972 and managed to spend nearly $200,000 more than they raised. Their donors are also concentrated in Ontario and to a much lesser extent in Quebec, but they also received substantial amounts of money from Alberta. Like the Liberals, they receive the bulk of their money from large (over $1000) donors and—even more than the Liberals—they tend to spend it in areas where their support is greatest, or in marginal areas rather than on lost causes in safe Liberal or NDP seats.

By contrast with the older parties, the NDP in 1972 raised and spent at the national level only $370,000, but the straight comparison of this figure with the Liberals' $6.5 million is misleading. The NDP provincial organizations provide support for the national headquarters whereas the situation is reversed in the older parties, so the appropriate comparison should be between the NDP's $370,000 and the Liberal headquarters expenditure on the national campaign of $1.3 million. Even so, the contrast is obvious. The NDP headquarters costs about $250,000 to operate between elections but because of the constancy of the NDP's union support, it does not operate at a deficit between elections as do the older parties.

The financing of the electoral activities of Canadian parties has depended heavily on donations from corporations or, in the case of the NDP, large labour unions. Party bagmen have lists of corporations which have given in the past and can be expected to do so again, and the calling of an election will see them knocking discreetly on the doors of company presidents or treasurers. It has already been noted that many corporations follow a 60–40 policy, dividing their donations 60 per cent to the party in power and 40 per cent to the major opposition party as an "insurance" gesture.[13] In many cases, corporate giving is regularized and counted as a regular budgetary expenditure, although in other cases company donations may be highly personalized. In one such case a rookie bagman was sent by the Ontario Provincial Liberal Association to a medium-sized southern Ontario firm and was firmly rebuffed by the president, who insisted that his company had never given money to the Liberal party. A veteran bagman was then called back into action and sent around to jog the president's memory. The happy ending for the Liberal party was that the

[13]It might be argued that the "insurance" is against an NDP victory. Corporations likely do not care much whether there is a Tory or Liberal government in power, but they normally prefer to keep the more "threatening" socialists in the political wilderness.

appearance of a familiar face was enough to revive the president's memory, and the party coffers were enriched by a tidy sum.

In addition to money, corporations often make substantial gifts of services. This is particularly true of public relations and advertising agencies, which may donate the services of large staffs together with supporting supplies and advertising time. Corporations that give money may often do so for relatively non-immediate reasons having to do with the preservation of "the system" or "a good business climate". Advertising agencies, however, hope to benefit immediately from large governmental contracts for tourist advertising, the publicizing of new programs and other governmental work, and if they have picked the winning party they are often suitably rewarded.

In addition to these sources of funds, there are assorted semi-institutionalized sources which come under the general heading of "kickbacks" or "rake-offs". For example, it is rumoured that in some provinces distilleries are assessed a regular percentage of gross sales which goes to the coffers of the party in power as an informal "tax" for listing their brands in liquor outlets. In another province, rumour has it that there are specialized lawyers who are very good at getting liquor licenses. Their fees are high, but they don't get to keep quite all of them. A certain percentage goes to make the gears of the administrative machinery run more smoothly and, incidentally, tends to help the fortunes of the party in power.

These methods of party finance are obviously open to the grossest abuses, and the whole question of campaign finance in Canada has been a constant target for reformers. Early in 1974 parliament passed a series of sweeping reforms which will do much to change the face of campaign financing in Canada.[14] The legislation requires disclosure of the names and amounts given by any donor who provides over $100 to a party while also allowing tax deductions to the donors on a sliding scale depending on the amount given. It requires that the government pay half the cost of television time for parties and provides for the allocation among parties of a total of 6½ hours of time on all TV stations according to a complex formula related to seats in the Commons and to popular vote. It limits total spending by national parties to 30 cents per voter (about what the Conservatives and Liberals did spend in 1972) and also limits the amounts which can be spent by individual candidates. Any candidate who gets 15 per cent of the vote will be reimbursed for part of his expenses—about one-third of them in an average riding. Parties and candidates, through their official agents, must provide full accounting of all money spent and received.

While the legislation may go a long way in reducing abuses of the electoral system, there are still some problems. The ceilings on expenditures are very high while the total that would be paid out of the public purse is still quite low. Professor K.Z. Paltiel estimates that in 1972 the leg-

[14]A detailed account is available in K.Z. Paltiel, "Some Aspects of Campaign Finance in Canada", and a more general account is available in the *Globe and Mail*, January 4, 1974, p. 1.

islation, had it been in force, would have permitted expenditures of $36 million and reimbursement from the government coffers to the tune of $7.7 million. Those parties able to raise large sums of money (and in practice that means from corporate donors) will still have a huge advantage. It is also too early to say just how rigorously the legislation might be enforced—in the past electoral law has been honoured more in the breach than in the observance because of lack of adequate enforcement provisions.

However the legislation does constitute a potential major reform in the electoral system in Canada. Together with such legislation as the Redistribution Act, which provides for the setting of constituency boundaries by an independent commission, and a political culture which demands comparatively high standards of electoral morality, Canada is better served than most countries by the standards of morality in her electoral process.

DYSFUNCTIONS OF THE ELECTORAL SYSTEM

In spite of all the functional attributes of the Canadian electoral system, it is quite possible that its basic structural feature, *the single member plurality system* of electing MPs, is highly dysfunctional when viewed in the overall context of the political system.

One of the basic defences of the present electoral system in Canada is that it provides the Canadian political system with electoral majorities and consequently with governmental stability. However, the occurrence of three different minority governments in Canada between 1957 and 1968 set some scholars wondering about just how valid this assertion was, and whether the present Canadian electoral system might not have some dysfunctional aspects. In particular, Alan C. Cairns has noticed a number of anomalies and pointed out some questionable features of the electoral system.[15]

Aside from the elections of 1940 and 1958, when a majority of voters actually supported one party, the present system has consistently given the party gaining a plurality of votes more seats than its share of votes.[16] However, it has transformed a minority of votes into a stable majority of seats on only 7 of 14 occasions and it has occasionally reduced an opposition with a fair amount of public support to numerical ineffectiveness in

---

[15]A.C. Cairns, "The Electoral and the Party System in Canada, 1921–65", *Canadian Journal of Political Science*, vol. L, no. 1, March, 1968. See also the critique of Cairns' ideas in J.A.A. Lovink, "On Analyzing the Impact of the Party System in Canada" *Canadian Journal of Political Science*, vol. 3, no. 4, pp. 497–516, and Cairns's reply, pp. 517–521.

[16]The 1972 election constitutes a minor exception to this rule since it provided a better balance than usual between popular vote and seats won. We have updated some of the numbers in this section to take account of the 1972 and 1974 elections even though they occurred after Cairns published his article.

the Commons. In 11 of the last 17 elections the electoral system has either not produced a majority government or has left the opposition ineffectually small. Moreover, the system encourages minor parties, such as the Social Credit or the Créditistes, with sectional bases of support. Such parties can concentrate their resources in one area. The system damages minor parties such as the NDP, with a broad base of support not focused in one region. For example, in 1935 the Reconstruction Party got 9 per cent of the vote and exactly 1 seat, while Social Credit with less than half as many votes got 17 seats. In 1963, 13 per cent of the vote garnered 17 seats for the NDP, while 12 per cent of the vote gained 24 seats for Social Credit and the Créditistes.

Cairns goes on to point out that, within a given party, representation in the House of Commons by region is not proportional to the party's votes by region. For example, in 1945 the CCF gained 260,000 votes in Ontario (32 per cent of its total) yet won no seats, while the 167,000 votes the party received in Saskatchewan (21 per cent of its total) resulted in 64 per cent of its federal seats.[17] From 1921 to 1965 the Liberals had 752 electoral victories in Quebec, to the Conservatives' 135. Cairns continues, "The ratio of 5.6 Liberals to each Conservative in the House of Commons contrasts sharply with the 1.9 to 1 ratio of Liberals and Conservatives at the level of voters.[18]

All of this, Cairns suggests, exaggerates the already deep sectional cleavages in Canadian society by ensuring that any partisan discrepancy will be magnified mightily by the electoral process. Such a system has made adequate representation from Quebec almost impossible in the Progressive Conservative party, and has ensured that whenever that party does get into power it will lack inputs from Quebec. Thus, part of John Diefenbaker's celebrated inability to get along with French Canada may have resulted from the fact that he had never had an opportunity to work with French Canadians in his party.

There are still more disadvantages to this electoral system. We have already mentioned that the present electoral system, or at least the two major parties, are often posited as being great unifying or nationalizing agencies. Cairns suggests a rather different interpretation:

> Sectionalism has been rendered highly visible because the electoral system makes it a fruitful basis on which to organize electoral support. Divisions cutting through sections, particularly those based on the class system have been much less salient because the possibility of payoffs in terms of representation has been minimal.[19]

There are several instances in Canadian history where parties have emphasized regional and, more particularly, ethnic differences in order to get elected. In Quebec in the 1920s and 1930s, Liberal campaigns were often directed towards stirring up the fears and animosities of French Canada in order to maximize electoral support in specific sections and thus

[17]Cairns, "The Electoral and the Party System in Canada, 1921–65," p. 61.
[18]*Ibid.*, p. 62.
[19]*Ibid.*, p. 64.

maximize the number of seats held. The "Gordon Churchill strategy" in 1957 was another example of the effects of sectionalism. Over the years it had become clear to the Conservatives that money spent in Quebec was money lost, even though a substantial minority of Quebec voters might support them, for they would get very few seats. The decision was consequently made in 1957 to forget about Quebec and concentrate on the rest of the country. The result was a handsome pay-off in terms of seats. Perhaps, however, this analysis should not be pushed too far. Until 1957 and since 1965 the Conservatives, whether strategically correct or not, consistently spent a large proportion of their campaign funds in Quebec, and all regions of the country have shown a propensity to swing their votes one way or another together.[20]

Nonetheless it can at least be suggested that the electoral system in use in Canada has a detrimental effect on national unity:

> This is essentially because sectional politics has an inherent tendency to call into question the very nature of the political system and its legitimacy. Classes, unlike sections, cannot secede from the political system and are consequently more prone to accept its legitimacy.[21]

We need not agree entirely with Cairn's analysis, but it does force us to ask a very important question: is Canadian party politics, characterized primarily by its brokerage nature, impeded only slightly by the counterforces from the electoral system, as Dawson, Corry, and most of the political scientists of the 40s, 50s, and early 60s have suggested; or, as Cairns and S.M. Lipset have postulated, does Canadian politics suffer mightily from the divisive effects of an inappropriate electoral system only slightly counterbalanced by the brokerage activities of some of its political actors?[22]

There are additional dysfunctions of the party–electoral system, less directly connected with the "single member plurality system". There are frequent delays and inaction in the priority stage of the policy process because of partisan manoeuvering for electoral advantage by cabinets and opposition parties. There may be an inefficient national distribution of program funds because of attempts to hold power in certain constituencies. There may be deliberate distortions and confusion in political communication in the attempt to maximize support in one region or another, and the uncertainty of a political career is a major deterrent to many excellent people who might seek office under conditions of greater certainty.

PARTIES AND ELECTIONS: AN OVERVIEW

Is the Canadian party system breaking down? Does the prevalence of minority governments over the last 15 years indicate a bleak and disheartening collapse of the ability of our parties to perform their functions ade-

---

[20]Beck, *Pendulum of Power*, pp. 422–423.
[21]Cairns, *op. cit.*, p. 75. Cairns has failed here to note that classes may question the legitimacy of the regime without questioning the political community.
[22]Beck, *op. cit.*, p. 423.

quately? Can Canadian party politics be viewed as results of the failure of the British party system to operate properly in a society with complex internal divisions? Is our electoral system inappropriate for a country like Canada with a complex social and physical environment? This gloomy litany of questions—more appropriate perhaps to the end of a daily episode of a soap opera than to a chapter on Canadian elections—might conceivably be the overall impression left by our discussion of Canada's political parties. If so, we would hasten to dispel it. There may be much that is wrong with Canada's party system and much than can be done to improve it, but viewed from a comparative perspective it looks very good indeed.

There are still reforms that need to be made. For example, the 1974 election finance legislation still does not provide funding for the ongoing costs of operating a party between elections, and the corporate donors who provide so much of the older Canadian parties' money have been notable for their lack of consideration of this fact. Thus parties are much less effective articulating and aggregating agencies than they could be. This leaves the field of policy initiation and priority determination open to the bureaucracy, the cabinets and to the federal–provincial bargaining process. But all of these agencies are secretive at the best of times, and the federal–provincial process is occasionally also fissiparous, so that some counterbalance is needed. Parties and parliament could provide that counterbalance, but there is not yet much evidence they are doing so.

One must tread lightly if making predictions in this area, especially since much of Canada's history has been written over a background of increasing bureaucratic and decreasing parliamentary and party power, but there are straws in the wind that suggest the possibility of a hand-in-hand comeback by parliament and party structures. Over the last 7 years we have seen the establishment of parliamentary research offices (which are really party appendages), the provision of modest public funding to MPs for constituency offices between campaigns, the regularization of at least biennial conventions, the publication of much more sophisticated policy documents from the parties and an increasing recognition of backbench MPs of their relative powerlessness in the policy process coupled with their increasing desire to do something about it. There are thus many more pieces in place than there were just a few years ago. If properly manipulated and augmented, they could increase the relative power of both parties and parliament in the determination of policy in Canada. Coupled with the possibilities inherent in frequent minority government situations, the conditions might even be ripe for such a development. Despite this the electoral functions of parties are and will continue to be the most important of their roles, and it would be unrealistic to expect them ever to wrest vast amounts of decision making power from the bureaucracy, the cabinet and the federal–provincial arena. But some minor steps in that direction may well have been taken in this past decade.

12
Interest Groups in Canada

Interest groups are active everywhere in Canadian politics. The industry-financed Canadian Tax Foundation criticizes and examines the whole financial structure of government in Canada. The Canadian Bar Association often works closely with the Federal Department of Justice and various provincial attorneys-general. Nationality associations are vital to the operation of the Department of Manpower and Immigration. The commercial banks work hand in hand with the Bank of Canada. At times, the Canadian Federation of Agriculture appears to be almost an extension of various departments of agriculture. Federal and provincial Departments of Labour work very closely with labour unions. The tie-in between the Canadian Medical Association (and its provincial constituents) and the various departments of health hardly requires highlighting. The list could be multiplied endlessly. Wherever government turns its hand, there it will find some kind of organized group operating—and wherever groups operate they find that government activities overlap their own.

SOME THEORETICAL CONSIDERATIONS

Gabriel Almond has suggested something of the importance of interest groups in modern society:

> Interest groups articulate political demands in the society, seek support for these demands among other groups by advocacy and bargaining and attempt to transform these demands into authoritative public policy by influencing the choice of political personnel and the various processes of public policy making and enforcement.[1]

Another perspective on the role of interest groups is provided by Harry Eckstein, who suggests:

> In democratic systems parties must perform simultaneously two functions which are on the evidence, irreconcilable: to furnish effective decision makers and to represent, accurately, opinions. The best way to reconcile

[1]Gabriel Almond, "Interest Groups and the Political Process", in R.C. Macridis and B.E. Brown, *Comparative Politics*, (Dorsey Press, Homewood, Ill., 1964), pp. 132–3.

these functions in practice is to supplement the parties with an alternative set of representative organizations which can affect decisions without affecting the position of the decision makers. This is the pre-eminent function of pressure groups in effective democratic systems, as the competition for power is the pre-eminent function of parties.[2]

Eckstein, then, helps to differentiate the manifest function of political parties—furnishing decision makers—from the manifest political function of interest groups—influencing political decisions.

Interest groups may also perform other functions in Canadian society. The vast majority of Canadian groups make their demands through legitimate channels and by legitimate means. They thus tend to buttress the political system in its present form and to provide, at least implicitly, support for that system. There is perhaps an even more important way in which the interest-group structure of Canadian society provides support for the political system, and that is by providing an integrating force in society which can "connect" the individual to the political system. As the sociologist Emile Durkheim put it,

> Collective activity is always too complex to be able to be expressed through the single and unique organ of the state. Moreover, the state is too remote from individuals, its relations with them too external and intermittent to penetrate deeply within individual consciences and socialize them within. When the state is the only environment in which men can live communal lives, they inevitably lose contact, become detached and society disintegrates. A nation can be maintained only if, between the state and the individual, there is intercalated a whole series of secondary groups near enough to the individuals to attract them strongly to their sphere of action and drag them, in this way, into the general torrent of social life.[3]

In this sense, interest groups are key instruments of policy initiation.

However, not only do interest groups perform functions on the input side of the political system; they also aid the system in the implementation of policy. Thus groups often act as the agents of the state in the application of rules to individuals and in the dissemination of information about new policies. Clearly, interest groups are ubiquitous in the politics of

[2]Harry Eckstein, *Pressure Group Politics*, (George Allen and Unwin, London. 1960; published in United States by Stanford University Press), p. 163. There is no agreement in the literature on whether the term *pressure group* is more appropriate than *interest group*. We have chosen the term interest group since we wish to emphasize the multiple functions of these groups, of which the application of political pressure is only one. In general, however, the two terms can be read interchangeably. Both of the preceding quotations are also cited in Engelmann and Schwartz, *Political Parties and the Canadian Social Structure*, pp. 92–114. Their chapter on interest groups provides a good coverage of the subject.

[3]Emile Durkheim, *The Division of Labour*, (The Free Press, Glencoe, 1947), cited in R. Presthus, *Elite Accommodation in Canadian Politics*, (Macmillan, Toronto, 1973). While we have alluded to Presthus at some length in this chapter and in Chapter 2, his work has not found universal acceptance among Canadian scholars. See, for example, R.E.B. Simeon's review (in *Canadian Journal of Political Science*, Sept. 1974, pp. 567–71) and that by John Meisel (in *Canadian Forum*, May–June 1974, p. 44). Critics such as Simeon have more to criticize in Presthus' research and presentation than in the conclusions which we have quoted in this text.

western democracies. This ubiquity has led some political scientists—most notably, Arthur Bentley—to adopt a *group approach* to the entire study of politics. In his book *The Process of Government*, Bentley wrote:

> When the groups are stated, everything is stated. When I say everything I mean everything. . . The whole of social life in all its phases can be stated in. . . .groups of active man.[4]

Bentley was writing in 1908, when hyperbole was more popular in academic writing than it is today, but there are some modern disciples of the Bentley approach, among them David Truman, author of *The Governmental Process*. Eckstein has summarized the modern group approach (typified by Truman) as asserting that:

> Politics is the process by which social values are authoritatively allocated; this is done by decisions; the decisions are produced by activities; each activity is not separate from every other, but masses of activity have common tendencies in regard to decisions; these masses of activities are groups; so the struggle between groups (or interests) determines what decisions are taken.[5]

This, as Eckstein states, is a truism and has very limited analytical value. What is more, as a tool of analysis it puts an impossible load on the researcher because it insists that he delineate the entire galaxy of interests which could even indirectly affect any decision he wants to investigate. Moreover, it denies the individuality of decision makers.[6] It leads political science into a sort of fatalism which eulogizes the effects of organized interests because they are there, and leads political scientists (and the decision makers whose activities they legitimate) to ignore all those who are not organized into interest groups.[7]

We are merely touching here on a very deep and important argument in the study of politics. In true Canadian fashion, however, we can reconcile it for our purposes by coming down firmly astride the fence. In the first place, most political scientists do not fit neatly under the heading of group theorists and, if the relative paucity of information on interest groups in Canada is any indication, Canadian political scientists seem to

[4]Quoted in Harry Eckstein, "Group Theory and the Comparative Study of Pressure Groups," in H. Eckstein and D. Apter (eds.), *Comparative Politics* (The Free Press, Glencoe, 1963), p. 390.

[5]Eckstein, "Group Theory and the Comparative Study of Pressure Groups", p. 391.

[6]Roy Macridis, "Groups and Group Theory", in Macridis and Brown, *Comparative Politics*, p. 140. Another cogent criticism of group theory is found in Stanley Rothman, "Systematic Political Theory: Observations on the Group Approach", *American Political Science Review*, XLIV, No. 1 (March 1960). pp. 15–33.

[7]This is the central theme of T. Lowi, *The End of Liberalism* (W.W. Norton and Co., New York, 1969). Lowi is probably flogging a dead horse in that the halcyon days of group theory are past, and the pluralists, whom he includes in his indictment, seem to be declining in popularity as the consensus politics of the 1950s and early 1960s in the United States declines.

The analysis of the underlying assumptions of political science is not really within the terms of reference of this chapter, but the interested reader will find a vast array of introspective literature on political science with very little searching in the analytical political theory section of the library.

lean too far the other way. In the second place, what information there is about Canadian groups and Canadian government indicates that the influence of organized interests in Canada may be less than it is in Britain or the United States. The overwhelming importance of Canada's federal structure and her deep environmental cleavages suggest that factors other than interest group activity may be more important in the minds of Canadian decision makers.[8]

A Typology of Groups To make sense out of the activities of the great number of interest groups in Canada, it may be useful to classify them in some way. One can then anticipate that groups which fall in the same classification or category will tend to behave in similar ways. There are a number of bases on which such a typology could be constructed. The structure of groups could be used, or their origin, or their activity, or their goals. One typology divides interest groups into economic and non-economic groups. The economic groups are, in turn, subdivided into agriculture, labour, and business groups; and the non-economic into nine sub-types.[9] Such a scheme however, tells us relatively little about the activity of groups or of their orientation towards government.

Another, more useful, taxonomy involves classifying groups according to a number of paired opposite categories. The paired opposites suggested by Robert Presthus are:

Compulsory	vs.	Voluntary
Temporary	vs.	Permanent
Economic	vs.	Instrumental
Mass	vs.	Selective
Producer	vs.	Consumer
Local–Provincial	vs.	Federal
Federated	vs.	Unitary
Oligarchical	vs.	Participative
Private	vs.	Public[10]

While these categories are fairly complete and useful, and while we hesitate to add yet another classificatory scheme to a field which already has too many, we prefer to categorize interest groups in Canada along three more-or-less independent dichotomies, one referring to *activity*, one to *origin*, and one to *structure*. Any particular interest group can be located on one side or the other of each of these three dichotomies.

[8]This is an assertion which must be made with considerable caution. Robert Presthus, in his study of the role and activities of interest groups in Canada, seems to be leaning towards the opposite conclusion. See also Presthus' *Elites in the Policy Process*, (Macmillan, Toronto, 1974), for a further comparative perspective.
[9]Engelmann and Schwartz, *Political Parties and the Canadian Social Structure*, pp. 95–96.
[10]*Elite Accommodation in Canadian Politics*, p. 67.

The first dichotomy refers to activity. It can be suggested that the activities of interest groups can be either *self-interested* or *promotional*.[11] Self-interested groups are usually economic in their orientation, whereas promotional groups are usually interested in doing things for some "selfless" reason, perhaps pertaining to the good of the community. For example, the Canadian Manufacturers Association is usually concerned with securing an economic, political and social environment which will be advantageous to its own members. It is thus a self-interested group, as is the Canadian Federation of Agriculture which, when it approaches government, is concerned basically with securing outputs advantageous to the interests of Canadian farmers. On the other hand, members of the John Howard Society, which is interested in penal reform and prisoner rehabilitation, do not themselves expect ever to become prisoners. Thus, the John Howard Society is a promotional interest group.

A second dichotomy is between groups which have been primarily responsible for their own creation and maintenance, and groups which have been either created or strongly encouraged by government itself. The latter type we call *reverse* pressure groups, while the former are *autonomous*. Reverse pressure groups come about because political decision makers are usually anxious to have all the inputs they can get before they set out to make policy. If there is no existing organized interest to which they can turn, policy makers will often try to create an interest group which they can then use in the input process. Alternatively, they may attempt to reinforce existing groups. At one time or another, close to one-half of all federal government departments have created such groups.[12]

It is often difficult to decide whether a particular interest group fits into the reverse category. For example, although the John Howard Society was not created by the government, the Departments of Justice and the Solicitor General provide support for the organization—speakers for meetings, information and other services—and many members of the society are employees of those departments. This has occurred because reform-minded members of the bureaucracy realize that in order to get their ideas across to their political superiors they must have public support. In addition, many groups which could not be defined as reverse pressure groups do receive a certain measure of financial and other support from government. For example, the Consumers' Association of Canada has been given government grants to continue expressing the viewpoint of the consumer.[13]

Finally, groups may be dichotomized according to their structure, dividing them into *active* and *categoric* groups. This dichotomy assumes that there are latent interest groups in society which may become active only if a pressing issue presents itself. For example, practising Christians can hardly be viewed as a single cohesive interest group, yet if the political system were to threaten to outlaw religious practices, this categoric group would soon become active. A categoric group, then, is one to which people

[11]S.E. Finer, *Anonymous Empire*, (Pall Mall, London, 1958) p. 3.
[12]*Elite Accommodation*, p. 79.
[13]Helen Jones Dawson, "The Consumers' Association of Canada", *Canadian Public Administration*, Vol. 4, No. 1, p. 96, March 1963.

belong by virtue of some classification into which they fall and one which could conceivably coalesce if the right issue presented itself. An active group, on the other hand, is just that: one which has ongoing activities.[14]

A Cautionary Note We have focused on the role of interest groups in representing interests before government. This, however, is not necessarily their primary activity. Most interest groups do not spend the majority of their efforts on political activity. Rather they concentrate mostly on performing a number of other functions necessary to their own members and to society.[15] Thus, for example, the primary activity of the Canadian Construction Association—one of the most active interests in Ottawa—is the dissemination of information and the maintenance of communication among the various members of the Association; and the most important activities of the Alcoholism and Drug Addiction Research Foundation—in some ways a reverse interest group—relate less to the activities of government than to research and publicity about drug problems.

One of the major non-political functions of any ongoing organization is, of course, self-maintenance. Many Canadian interest groups today are bureaucracies, and the bureaucrats in them, in addition to "doing their job" are interested in maintaining a job to do and an organization to do it.[16] This occasionally leads to the situation where the greatest enemy of an interest group is another interest group pursuing the same goal, for both are competing for the same clientele and for the recognition of the same governmental agencies.[17] For example, the Consumers' Association of Canada and the Canadian Home Economics Association do not always get along well and may compete with each other even though their goals are the same.[18] The Canadian Federation of Agriculture and the National Farmers Union often find themselves implacably opposed, even though one would expect their goals to be similar. The classic cases of this type of behaviour are to be found in the annals of labour union relations. For example, David Kwavnick has hypothesized that one of the major incidents of labour unrest in Quebec in the 70s—the Lapalme mail truck drivers' strike—was exacerbated because it became the focal point for strife between the Quebec-based Confederation of National Trade Unions and the nationally-based Canadian Labour Congress. Kwavnick goes on to con-

[14]See D. Truman, *The Governmental Process*, (Alfred A. Knopf, New York, 1965), pp. 23–26. A distinction similar to our own is made here between *categoric* and *institutionalized* groups.

[15]Lowi, *The End of Liberalism*, pp. 36–38. On page 38, Lowi points out that "all such interest groups possess political power but only occasionally are they politicized. The rest of the time they administer".

[16]For a series of examples, see David Kwavnick, "Pressure Group Demands and the Struggle for Organizational Status: The Case of Organized Labour in Canada", *Canadian Journal of Political Science*, Vol. 3, No. 1, pp. 56–72, March, 1970.

[17]Kwavnick, "Pressure Group Demands and the Struggle for Organizational Status", p. 58.

[18]Dawson, "The Consumers' Association of Canada," p. 113. Elsewhere, however, the author points out that one of the most successful tactics of the CAC is harnessing other interest groups to pressure government. See pp. 111, 112.

tend that "the CNTU leadership risked, and ultimately sacrificed, the most vital interests of the Lapalme drivers in a dispute which ultimately concerned only those leaders' ambitions for organizational aggrandizement."[19] Thus, for interest groups, no less than for other large organizations, the welfare of the organization may become the goal even to the detriment of the membership.

THE INPUT ACTIVITIES OF INTEREST GROUPS

The input activities of interest groups involve attempts to either initiate policy or influence the process of priority determination. No matter what type of interest group is being discussed or at what stage of the policy process the interest group intervention occurs, three basic questions can be asked. First, where must the group apply pressure in order to have its demands recognized; towards what specific *regime focus* must the group's activity be directed? Secondly, what methods and channels of access to the system are to be employed by the group; how may the group "get the ear" of appropriate authorities in the system? Thirdly, what are the sources of policy influence or the determinants of strength of a group; what makes its activities effective?

The Focus of Activity Both the location at which pressure is applied and the channels of communication on which a group concentrates are related to the structure of the government and its decision-making processes, and to the structure of the pressure group itself.

The Structure of Government[20] Interest groups in Canada face two essential facts about the structure of Canadian government: its federal nature and its parliamentary nature, which contribute to the fact that the system's effective power is widely dispersed.

[19]Kwavnick, "Pressure Group Demands and Organizational Objectives: The CNTU, the Lapalme affair and national bargaining units", *Canadian Journal of Political Science*, VI, No. 4, December 1973, p. 583. See also Kwavnick, *Organized Labour and Pressure Group Politics: The Canadian Labour Congress: 1956–1968*, (McGill–Queen's University Press, Montreal, 1972).

[20]The reader is referred, for general information, to the articles by Gabriel Almond and Harry Eckstein cited above, to Eckstein's *Pressure Group Politics*, and to Presthus' *Elite Accommodation in Canadian Politics*. Specifically Canadian examples are also drawn from the articles by Helen Jones Dawson (in addition to those cited above, see "Relations Between Farm Organizations and the Civil Service in Canada and Great Britain", *Canadian Public Administration*, Vol. 10, no. 4, Dec. 1967, p. 460); from M.G. Taylor, "The Role of the Medical Profession in the Formulation and Execution of Public Policy", *Canadian Public Administration*, Vol. 3, 1960, pp. 223–225; from Englemann and Schwartz, *Political Parties and the Canadian Social Structure*; from some valuable journalistic accounts in "Pressure Groups in Canada", *Parliamentarian*, Jan. 1970, prepared by the Research Branch of the Library of Parliament in Ottawa; from Hugh Winsor, "Lobbying: A Comprehensive Report on the Art and its Practitioners", *The Globe Magazine*, Feb. 27, 1971, pp. 2–7;

Divided jurisdiction in the Canadian federal system sometimes makes it necessary for a group to exert influence at both federal and provincial levels of government. For example, when the insurance companies were trying to block government-sponsored medical care insurance, they were forced to operate at both governmental levels. At the federal level they attempted to block enabling legislation which permitted the federal government to enter into cost-sharing arrangements with the provinces, and at the provincial level they attempted to prevent the actual implementation of the plan. On the other hand, when insurance companies have tried to block compulsory, government-sponsored auto insurance, they have had to operate exclusively at the provincial level where the jurisdiction in such matters lies. Under the existing system of federalism, decisions are often taken at both levels of governments simultaneously, giving an interest group more points upon which to focus its activity, but forcing it at the same time, to spread its resources rather thinly.

Modern government in Canada concentrates the bulk of power in the cabinet and the bureaucracy. Parliament, therefore, is not likely to provide interest groups with a successful arena. As one experienced lobbyist said, "When I see members of Parliament being lobbied, it's a sure sign to me that the lobby lost its fight in the civil service and the cabinet."[21] He might have added that while the group lobbying MPs may occasionally win some temporary victory, its chances of success in the longer run are slight unless they can convince some cabinet ministers as well. Most interest groups and their agents in Ottawa acknowledge this fact, yet it is surprising how much effort occasionally goes into a pressure campaign when legislation is before Parliament.

One of the most spectacular examples of a group's failure to recognize the futility of struggling once a bill has reached parliament was provided by the Pharmaceutical Manufacturers Association of Canada (PMAC) and its president Dr. William Wigle.[22] The PMAC began to exert pressure in December of 1967 when the government introduced Bill C-190 which would allow the importation of drugs with the consequent lowering of drug prices in Canada. The PMAC organized many witnesses to go before the parliamentary committee studying the bill, besieged reporters with propaganda, attempted to get suppliers of the pharmaceutical industry to write MPs, urged drug company presidents to contact the 100 top

and from "Inside the Ottawa Lobby", *Monetary Times*, July 1968, pp. 14–17. The reader may also want to refer to S.D. Clarke, *The Canadian Manufacturers' Association*, (University of Toronto Press, Toronto, 1939), and to H.G. Thorburn, "Pressure Groups in Canadian Politics: Recent Revisions in the Anti-Combines Legislation", *Canadian Journal of Economics and Political Science*, Vol. 30, no. 2, pp. 157–174, May 1964. In general, the same sources have been used throughout succeeding sections unless otherwise cited.

[21]Quoted in Engelmann and Schwartz, *Political Parties and the Canadian Social Structure*, p. 105.

[22]Described in "Pressure Groups in Canada", *Parliamentarian* Jan. 1970, pp. 15, 16. Dr. Wigle also headed the Canadian Medical Association's fight against Medicare so he has been more conspicuous by his presence than his success.

industrialists in Canada and request them to write cabinet ministers and the Prime Minister; in general, they applied pressure whenever they could. The PMAC won an apparent victory, for the bill died on the order papers before the Liberal leadership convention. But the victory was short-lived. In the following session, the bill was re-introduced and, notwithstanding the PMAC's earlier efforts, it passed in March 1969. No doubt the PMAC was successful in delaying the legislation somewhat, but if a government is really committed to a piece of legislation, it will be a rare pressure campaign that will stop its passage. In fact, Dr. Wigle and the PMAC had lost the fight long before the bill was approved in parliament: once the cabinet had approved the establishment of a bureaucratic interdepartmental committee to investigate drug prices, it had already signalled an intention to do something about high drug prices. Had the PMAC learned of this committee in time, then contacted and worked with the bureaucrats, and had it reached the cabinet ministers before the cabinet ever decided to present legislation, its chances of success would have been much greater.

There are, of course, exceptions to the rule that the parliamentary arena is a bad one for interest groups to play in, and sometimes simply delaying a piece of legislation is worthwhile to a group. But the exceptions may well be evidence of limited government commitment or of successful behind-the-scenes lobbying directed at the cabinet.

The cabinet is a somewhat more fruitful pressure point. Each year several large national groups, such as the Canadian Labour Congress, the Canadian Chamber of Commerce, and the Canadian Manufacturers' Association, present an annual brief to the whole cabinet, with much attendant fanfare. While such briefs are generally filled with pious generalizations, they do let the cabinet know something about the "mood of the country". They also provide us with an opportunity to see ministers at their most human: being forced to sit in the midst of a busy day and listen to generalizations or badly researched policy proposals often brings out the testier side of the ministerial character.

More important, the relationship between individual ministers and interest groups may be quite close. For instance, when they entered the cabinet during the Pearson years, both C.M. Drury and Mitchell Sharp were members of the Canadian Manufacturers' Association. James Gardiner, Minister of Agriculture for many years under Mackenzie King, developed a close personal relationship with the Canadian Federation of Agriculture dating, oddly enough, from the time in 1941 when the delegates to a London convention of that association held him a virtual prisoner for several hours until he agreed to some concessions. C.D. Howe, of all people, seems to have got along particularly well with the Consumers' Association of Canada.

Sometimes, however, organized interests will lobby a minister over a particular issue when they could more productively concentrate their activities on senior bureaucrats. In the winter of 1969–70, there was a parade of soap company presidents through the office of J.J. Greene, then Minister of Energy, Mines and Resources, whose department was in the process of formulating a policy to limit the phosphate content of detergents. Their efforts were wasted, partly because of the minister's strong, publicly-stated position on this issue and the prominence of pollution as an area of government concern, and partly because the minister would do little, when technical matters were being discussed, except reiterate the position of his departmental advisors who interpreted all such information for him.

The main focus for input activities of interest groups is neither parliament nor cabinet but the bureaucracy. The close ties between the Canadian Federation of Agriculture and the Department of Agriculture, between veterans' groups and the Department of Veterans Affairs, between consumers' group and several departments, between the medical associations and the various departments of health, have already been noted. To these one could add the close relationships of industry and trade associations with various branches of Industry, Trade and Commerce, Supply and Services, and so on. The specific techniques used by groups will be examined later in this chapter, but we can state that in general, the main contact between government and interest groups is at the middle and upper levels of the bureaucracy.

For the sake of completeness, the relatively unimportant role that political parties play in this process should be mentioned. Much has been made of the interrelationship between parties and interest groups in other political systems. In Britain most labour unions are directly affiliated with the Labour party. In the United States it has sometimes been suggested that the Democratic party is little more than a coalition of interest groups. However, in both Britain and the United States, the groups which have been most successful—at least with respect to their political activities—tend to shy away from formal party affiliations. After all, the party might lose the election and even if it wins, as many British unions have found to their chagrin, it may be easier to affect policy from outside the party hierarchy than from within.

Except for the affiliation of some union locals with the NDP, Canadian interest groups have generally avoided formal connections with political parties. At election time, the parties themselves will attempt to incorporate the most important demands of the main groups in their platforms; but these platforms mean very little except at election time and the more active members of interest groups know it. Between elections the interest group which wishes to approach a political party faces exactly the same problems as anyone else—it is nearly impossible to find a Canadian political party between elections. Even if a group succeeds in that enterprise, the party structures are of practically no value in directly influencing an output of the political system.

Interest Group Structure Most large Canadian interest groups are federations, and the provincial bodies which make up these federations are often, in turn, coalitions of local groups. Frequently the local and provincial organizations are more powerful than the national structure. In some cases, such as the National Farmers Union, there is no effective central structure at all. Obviously this feature has some influence on the way in which groups will make contact with government. While the Canadian

Federation of Agriculture is closely tied in with the federal government, in many ways it exerts a stronger influence on provincial governments. The National Farmers Union has almost no influence on national policy, but in the Prairie Provinces it is a most important group. Similarly, it would be difficult to suggest federal legislation on which the Canadian Chambers of Commerce have had much influence, but at the local level their power is often very great. When the Alberta government was amending the Alberta Labour Act, both the provincial chamber and some local chambers were frequently consulted. The Calgary Chamber of Commerce presented its views in Edmonton, and when the legislation was drafted the ministers of Labour and Industry and Development arrived in Calgary to discuss the draft legislation with the local chamber.[23] That the national organization does not wield such power in Ottawa is partly a reflection of the decentralized structure of the group.

On the other hand, a few interested groups, whether or not they are formal federations, have become, in fact, highly centralized. The Consumers' Association of Canada does most of its governmental work from Ottawa, as does the Canadian Manufacturers Association. In such cases, of course, contact between the federal government and the national organization is much stronger than that between the provincial government and provincial organizations.

The Methods of Influence The methods or types of access, used by interest groups approaching government, may be broken down into several categories. Direct and continuous contact is probably the most effective technique, but the presentation of briefs and other sporadic contact may be equally effective. The numerous advisory committees of the Canadian government may provide a convenient channel of access, and the use of interlocking membership between the bureaucracy and the interest groups may be even more effective. Indirect access, or influencing public opinion in order to enlist allies in the press, general public and other groups is sometimes used, although this is not a favourite technique in Canada.

Direct Contact and Briefing　One analyst—perhaps slightly biased, for he had served on the ill-fated Housing Task Force of 1969—has suggested that:

> The Ottawa based lobby and the pressure group organizations which had an interest in urban matters such as the Canada Welfare Council and the Federation of Mayors and Municipalities were closely linked to CMHC and the ruling structure of the federal government, and contented themselves with making an annual plea for more money or more public housing, goals also shared by CMHC. So in effect there was a closed system of policy making populated by a small number of men who, over the years, had become well acquainted with each other and each other's views.[24]

[23]Engelmann and Schwartz, *Canadian Political Parties*, p. 104.
[24]Lloyd Axworthy, "The Housing Task Force–A New Policy Instrument", unpublished paper read at the Canadian Political Science Association, Winnipeg, June 4, 1970.

Whether for good or evil, the same situation prevails in many vital areas of government policy. In the field of agricultural policy making, the executives of the Canadian Federation of Agriculture tend to retain their positions over long periods and thus build up close and continuing contacts with the Minister of Agriculture and his departmental officials. Over the years the relationship has become very close and rather informal and has led to the situation, also common in other interest group-government relationships, where the group will never publicly name or criticize a departmental official.[25] The Consumers' Association of Canada has spent much time and effort establishing a liaison with senior civil servants in many departments and has succeeded to the extent that it is now often consulted informally before action is taken. For example, the Dominion Bureau of Statistics informally consulted the association before revising its consumer price index.[26]

Continuing contacts may also be made at the cabinet level, but it is likely that they are less common than contacts between the bureaucracy and interest groups. In the first place, a minister does not usually remain in one portfolio long enough to become truly close to interest-group representatives. In the second, groups realize that since the most decisions of interest to them are made in the bureaucracy where most of the detail is thrashed out, that is where influence can be most effective.

Direct contact between groups and government may also be of a more sporadic nature, and when this is the case the general membership as well as the executive members of the group may be involved. Sporadic contact at the executive level will occur when a group which normally is not politically active becomes so because of a particular issue. Thus, before 1970, detergent manufacturers had not been noted for political activity and were quite unknown at the Department of Energy, Mines and Resources, but the formation of policy to limit the phosphate content of detergents brought them banging on the door of the minister. Contact between groups and political decision makers may occur when an issue of interest to a group is being considered by parliament: write-in campaigns or deluges of telegrams may be organized and groups of delegates may attempt to see MPs or cabinet ministers. As was suggested earlier, these campaigns are usually misdirected since they are directed at MPs, who have relatively little to do with priority determination and policy formulation.

Contact between groups and the political system frequently involves the presentation of briefs to the standing committees of the House of Commons. This tactic, like the mass write-in campaign, is seldom very effective. When legislation is before a House Standing Committee, it is expected that all interested groups will present briefs, but presentations made at that stage do not usually alter legislation in significant ways. Indeed, they could not do so, since the committee stage follows second reading of a bill, which constitutes approval in principle of its major measures.

[25]Dawson, "Relations Between Farm Organizations and Civil Service in Canada and Great Britain", p. 452. The Federation may occasionally complain in private to the minister about an official with whom they are having trouble.
[26]Dawson, "The Consumers' Association of Canada", p. 109.

Instead, the real policy makers tend to seize upon briefs favourable to their position as tangible evidence of wide support for their policies, and to ignore briefs which are against them. The presentation of annual briefs to the cabinet is probably effective in putting across the general views of certain interests. However, these briefs are so general that one can hardly draw any cause–effect relationship between them and subsequent government outputs. Indeed the effectiveness of such briefs, which frequently are also presented to opposition caucuses, probably depends directly upon the closeness of the personal relationship which has been cultivated between group executives and the real decision-makers in the area of concern.[27]

The contact men in Ottawa, whose job it is to provide continuing representation of interests before government, form an interesting group of actors on the governmental scene. They range from local lawyers and relatively unheralded officers of small trade associations on up to the "superstars" of the lobbying game. Some of the latter, such as Ross Tolmie of the Ottawa law firm bearing his name, act as representatives of just one company (in Tolmie's case, Trans-Canada Pipelines). Others such as Mel Jack and David Golden (of the Brewers Association and the Air Industries Association, respectively), represent large industrial groups. Still others, such as William Lee and William Neville, represent different clients at different times.

The best lobbyists have in common excellent connections with politicians and senior bureaucrats. Mel Jack was formerly executive assistant to George Hees and a moving force behind Mr. Hees' success as Minister of Transport and, later, Trade and Commerce. Bill Lee was executive assistant to Paul Hellyer in the latter's sojourn as Minister of National Defense, and managed the 1968 Liberal election campaign for Mr. Trudeau. David Golden was Deputy Minister of Defence Production, then became head of the Air Industries Association, and then helped set up the Department of Industry before returning to private industry, from whence he has recently emerged as president of the government's communications satellite corporation, Telesat. In addition, many of the Senators in Ottawa double as lobbyists and industry representatives. The easy access which men such as these could have to government policy makers makes them important "mouthpieces" for organized interests.

The lesser lights of the direct contact business are certainly more numerous. Well over 200 national associations have Ottawa offices. It is not always necessary to retain a big-name lobbyist for an organization to have an input to the policy process. Bureaucrats often welcome contact with interest groups as alternative sources of information and for alternative perspectives on the policy-related or administrative issues with which they may be concerned.

In summary, the most effective presentations of interest-group views are the kind that the public never hears about: they involve direct and informal contact between the bureaucracy and interest groups during the process of policy formulation and, occasionally, between group leaders

[27]Helen Jones Dawson, "An Interest Group: The Canadian Federation of Agriculture", *Canadian Public Administration*, Vol. 3, No. 2, June 1960, p. 146.

and cabinet ministers. A formal brief is probably rare in these circumstances, although the fortunate group that learns from friendly insiders that policy related to its interests is being drafted, and then manages to get a brief to the officials and ministers concerned may be in a good position to influence the formulation process. This is more likely to occur if informal and continuing contacts are religiously maintained.

The Advisory Committee Advisory committees are committees of outside experts, or representatives of various interest groups concerned with a particular issue area. They are formed to advise the bureaucracy on its policies, and virtually every federal department can boast several. As long ago as 1957, one analyst was able to name more than twenty such committees active in the province of Saskatchewan alone, and there is certainly no reason to suspect that their numbers have since diminished.[28] At the federal level, for example, the main advisory committee to the "Health" side of the Department of National Health and Welfare is also a standing committee of the Canadian Medical Association. Organizations like the Canadian Tax Foundation and the Canadian Bar Association act in many ways as advisory committees to the departments concerned with their areas of expertise. Similarly, the Canadian Federation of Agriculture is asked to appoint representatives to advisory boards in the field of agricultural policy, and the head of the Alberta Wheat Pool holds a seat on the Canadian Wheat Board. At one time or another, the Canadian Manufacturing Association has held positions on at least 35 different advisory boards and committees.[29]

The importance of such committees in the policy process varies a great deal from department to department and from time to time. Helen Jones Dawson concludes that in the field of agricultural policy making, such groups are more important in Britain than in Canada.[30] On the other hand, Malcolm Taylor concludes that in the field of Canadian medical policy making they are extremely powerful.[31] Taylor, however, was writing before the fight over government-sponsored health insurance came to a head in the mid 1960s. The members of the Canadian Medical Association lost this fight even though they put all their resources into it and their representatives on advisory committees consistently spoke out against the plan.

Not all interest groups are anxious to serve on advisory committees. For one thing, they may realize that such committees are often set up by government not to consult but rather to explain policies on which the government has already settled, and to co-opt potential opponents. Interest groups may also feel that if they are consulted about a policy they then lose their right to criticize it, or at least their credibility when they do so.

[28]T.K. Shoyama, "Advisory Committees in Administration", in Hodgetts and Corbett, *Canadian Public Administration*, p. 465. See also Corbett, "The Pressure Groups and the Public Interest", p. 454–462.
[29]"Pressure Groups in Canada", *Parliamentarian*, Jan. 1970, p. 19.
[30]Dawson, "An Interest Group: The Canadian Federation of Agriculture", p. 147.
[31]Taylor, "The Role of the Medical Profession in the Formulation and Execution of Public Policy", pp. 245 ff.

This reasoning is in part responsible for the Canadian Federation of Agriculture's reluctance to get too deeply involved in advisory committees established by various departments of agriculture. Thus, while advisory committees have become a ubiquitous feature of the Canadian bureaucracy it is safe to assert only that the amount of influence that interest groups exert through them varies widely.

Interlocking Memberships   One of the most effective routes of access to decision makers is the very direct one provided by the fact that political decision makers themselves are often members of the interest groups which seek to influence decisions. The membership of some cabinet ministers in the Canadian Manufacturers Association has already been mentioned, and a search through the biographies in the *Parliamentary Guide* will provide many similar examples. Many of the doctors who have been health ministers or officials in federal and provincial departments of health have also been medical association members. Indeed, it has been suggested that the Canadian Medical Association is consulted whenever medical personnel are appointed to government advisory committees or similar positions, although this may be an exaggeration.[32] Along similar lines, many of Ottawa's higher-level bureaucrats or their spouses are members of the Consumers' Association of Canada—a fact which can hardly hurt that organization's political activities.

On occasion, an interest group will succeed in getting one of its members on a Royal Commission in which it is interested. The Hall Royal Commission on Health Services included some members who had been nominated by the Canadian Medical Association.[33] In this case, however, it is interesting to note that the Commissioners were true to their task rather than to the Medical Association, and were instrumental in the preparation of a report which the medical association itself roundly condemned.

An even more important type of influence on political decisions occurs as men move from a private industry into a government department concerned with regulating that same industry. It becomes an even more complex situation when the same individual later moves back again to the private sector. For example, when the Department of Industry, Trade and Commerce is recruiting employees to regulate the iron and steel industry, it naturally looks to people from that industry for, after all, their experience is relevant. Later these same men may move back to a more-or-less grateful corporation. Such influence is not necessarily harmful but the close web of contact and friendship which can be woven between those who regulate and those who are regulated, and between groups demanding certain policies and those who have the power to make the policies does bear close watching.

Public Relations   Because of the importance of Congress in the decision-making process in the United States, groups in that country attempt to bolster their position by conducting large-scale public relations cam-

[32]Engelmann and Schwartz, *Political Parties and the Canadian Social Structure*, p. 100.
[33]*Ibid.*, p. 100.

paigns which will, they hope, add general public support for their cause to the primary support of their own members. This, they hope, will convince influential congressmen of the wisdom of supporting their cause. By contrast, because of the relatively minor policy role played by back-bench members of parliament, Canadian groups depend more on their access to bureaucratic decision makers and on the expertise they possess than on demonstrated public support. Public relations campaigns are thus less important in Canada. Nevertheless, because public support, or the appearance of it, can never be totally ignored by decision makers, groups will from time to time launch large-scale public relations offensives to supplement their other sources of influence.

Often it is groups which have been unsuccessful in establishing good lines of access to the decision makers, or groups which do not control a certain area of expertise, which are forced to utilize the public relations campaigns as a tactic of political influence. The Canadian Mining Association, which has very little demonstrated expertise in the area of tax reform, but which nevertheless stood to be directly affected by the changes outlined in the 1969 White Paper on Taxation, turned to a series of radio commercials to gain support for its position. Similarly, the Ontario Farmers Union, which has had difficulty in developing good channels of access to the decision makers, has organized several marches and tractor parades in an attempt to gain public sympathy for the plight of the farmer. Such instances, however, are not as common in Canada as they are in the U.S., and are looked upon here with some disdain—not only by the authorities in the system, but by other interest groups as well—for the recourse to these tactics is often indicative of weakness or of failure in more traditional tactics.

Successful groups seldom employ only one tactic at a time. A full-scale campaign will involve several techniques used simultaneously to back up continuing close contact with decision makers. For example, when the Consumers' Association of Canada began its campaign against trading stamps, it requested that all its members write to MPs and ministers, it made submissions to local authorities and to federal and provincial attorneys-general, it made submissions to the Prime Minister and Minister of Justice, it obtained the full support of many other groups including the Retail Merchants Federation, the Canadian Federation of Agriculture, the Canadian Labour Congress and various women's groups, and simultaneously it provided material for the media so that they too could become involved in the issue. In spite of this impressive effort, the Association was not totally successful. Speculation as to why leads directly to the next consideration of this chapter, namely, what determines the effectiveness of interest groups in influencing the policy process?

The Determinants of Success

Organized medicine influences legislative policy with respect to the timing and design of public programs, guides the choice and structure of administrative procedures, participates in the continuing decisions of administrators and, in four provinces actually serves as the governmental agency in the administration of major programs.[34]

Some groups, such as the Canadian Medical Association, are much more successful in influencing governmental processes than are others. The reasons for the success or failure of a group relate to its own structure and to that of government, to the existing government's policy orientations, and to the extent of conformity of the group's interest to the needs of the environment.[35]

The Structure and Resources of the Group　Plainly enough, one of the most important resources any group can have is money, and most interest groups are chronically short of it. The Canadian Federation of Agriculture is probably fairly typical as it receives widely varying amounts of money from year to year, as farm fortunes rise and fall. And promotional interest groups seem to suffer even more difficulty in finding money than groups like the CFA. What money is found is used by both types of interest group to hire executive and clerical help, to research briefs, and to operate offices in capital cities.

Not all interest groups are perpetually short of funds; indeed some of the most powerful are very well financed. The Canadian Manufacturers' Association has an annual budget of nearly one million dollars—larger than that of any of the national political parties.[36] It also carries a contingency fund of over half a million dollars. Its main source of funds is membership dues from over 6,000 firms representing more than three-quarters of Canada's manufacturing capacity. For its money, the CMA is able to buy, among other things, a permanent staff of well over 100, with at least 70 experts in various fields related to the promotion of interests of Canadian industry. Thus CMA briefs to governments are invariably well prepared and often influence the bureaucracy in the formulation of regulations or the creation of new legislation.

With its budget, the CMA is able to carry on a wide array of activities.[37] In addition to briefing the bureaucracy and the cabinet, it sends an annual "delegation" to Ottawa to interview most of the cabinet ministers and many deputy ministers. However, its most effective activities are almost certainly related to its efforts to influence the implementation of legislation. The CMA studies all regulations made under the Customs Act, the Excise Tax Act, the Income Tax Act and the various Sales Tax Acts, and makes representations to the bureaucracy in those areas where the departments have wide discretionary power. It is very concerned with the formulation and application of all regulations dealing with restrictive trade practices, monopolies, combines and mergers. It cooperates with provincial departments of education and with federal manpower authorities to provide information about what employee skills are required and what training programs would be useful. Such pervasive contacts with govern-

[34]Taylor, "The Role of the Medical Profession in the Formulation and Execution of Public Policy", p. 253.
[35]For a similar formulation, see Eckstein, *Pressure Group Politics*, pp. 15–39.
[36]"Pressure Groups in Canada", *Parliamentarian*, January, 1970, pp. 13–14.
[37]*Ibid.*, p. 18.

ment are made possible by the large financial resources available to the CMA.

The number of members an interest group can boast is a less important determinant of success than one might expect. Decision makers know that a person's membership in a group does not guarantee agreement with the group's views on a particular issue. If sheer numbers were the determining factor, labour organizations would be Canada's most important interest groups. In fact, a more important attribute of a group may be its organizational cohesiveness. If an organization's executive really does speak for its members and if the members might be mobilized *en masse* in support of the group's ideas, any threats which the group makes or implies will have considerable credibility.

The prestige of a group is important. Decision makers may be impressed by the group's ideas in direct proportion to how impressed they are by its members as individuals. Almost everyone will at least listen to the medical associations, but the Amalgamated Association of Apprentice Septic-Tank Pumpers or the Canadian Institute of Motorcycle Buffs might have more difficulty getting a hearing.

Monopoly over a certain area of expertise is a potent factor in determining the prestige of a group. The Canadian Bar Association, for instance, is always listened to with respect by authorities both because it is the only national spokesman for the legal profession in Canada and because it has established a reputation for reason in its recommendations. Prestige may depend on how much the government needs the expert resources of the group, on the past record of the group in its relationship with the government, or on the socioeconomic status of group members. No matter what its source, prestige will play an important role in determining the effectiveness of the group in influencing policy.

The Structure of Government There is a great deal of disagreement between those who write about interest groups concerning just what influence the structure of government has on group effectiveness. It is often suggested that interest groups are more active in the U.S. than in Canada because the congressional system with its many centres of decision making is much more open to group activity than the parliamentary system. In the U.S., if a group is not successful at the presidential level it may still influence Congress or the bureaucracy, each of which is a separate centre of power: in Canada, if a group fails with the bureaucracy and cabinet, which are closely tied together, it has failed entirely.

Such suggestions may oversimplify the situation. Britain, with a system more centralized than Canada's, has a very high level of interest-group activity—perhaps due to the division of British society vertically (by class) rather than horizontally (by region). Further, the decentralization of the Canadian system is regional rather than administrative and political. Perhaps Canadian scholars have merely looked in the wrong place for group activity: there is some possibility that it centres mainly in the provincial capitals rather than in Ottawa. Or perhaps they have simply underestimated the influence of groups in Ottawa.

It is difficult to determine whether Canada's federal system aids or hinders interest group activity. On the one hand, it does provide more sites at which undesirable change can be blocked. On the other, it imposes on groups, most of which are perpetually short of money, the necessity to cover several capital cities simultaneously if they are to be truly effective. Thus most groups, unlike the Canadian Manufacturers Association, are forced to concentrate on only a few issues which affect them and on immediate goals.

About all that can be said with certainty is that to be effective, groups must have channels of access to the system, and the more channels of access the system provides, the more definite their influence will be. But, in the absence of considerably more comparative study of government structure and group success, it is difficult to go much beyond this nearly tautological statement.

Overall Government Policy   Sometimes external factors, such as the state of the economy, may force the government into a position where interest groups' demands can have very little effect. For example, in 1969–70, the federal government decided that to ease innflation it would be necessary to cut back government expenditures. A major expenditure in the past had been a $50 million annual loan fund for municipal sewage treatment plants. In 1970 the demand for such loans increased greatly, and The Canadian Federation of Mayors and Municipalities, together with many promotional groups interested in pollution control, asked for a large increase in the size of the fund. Their request was viewed sympathetically by most government officials, yet the fund was raised to only $75 million when at least $150 million could have been profitably spent. What had happened was a simple clash of priorities, which had to be resolved by Treasury Board officials who, in the prevailing fiscal climate, could not possibly have agreed to the entire appropriation demanded by interest groups and bureaucrats in the Department of the Environment. Welfare groups, whose demands usually involve an increase in government expenditures, also fare badly in times of austerity, while in times of government expansion even the most poorly organized group can succeed.

Party fortunes may have an effect on interest-group success by altering the prevailing policy climate. An NDP government, for example, would be sympathetic to some demands that a Liberal government might ignc re because the general direction of policies in each case might be quite different.

The Nature of the Environment   An interest group will succeed best if its overall aims are in keeping with the prevailing values of the society in which it operates. For example, an interest group whose main goal is to have Buddhism established as the state church in Canada has relatively little probability of success, for the dual reasons that the establishment of any state religion is antithetical to prevailing Canadian ideas, and that in Canada the public is little acquainted with Buddhism and not particularly sympathetic to its ideals.

Equally important is the fact that the nature of the social environment will define the role and even the prevalence of interest groups. Premodern societies lack a significant interest-group structure, so it is hardly conceivable that groups there can play a major role in government. But even among developed western cultures there are subtle differences. Interest groups may be more significant in American government than in Canadian simply because they are considered to be a proper way of influencing government in the U.S. and not in Canada.

Another important variable may be the level of efficacy and of political activity in a society. Citizens of the United States are the most politically active in the world, and their high level of activity, together with a relatively high level of political efficacy, may provide part of the explanation for the high level of interest-group activity in the United States.[38] Canadians show slightly lower levels of efficacy and political activity than Americans, and this may be related to the lower level of visible interest-group activity in Canada.

Summary: Group Impact on Government Policy Much
of what has been said in this section has been speculative: it has been so not just because facts concerning interest-group activity in Canada are few, but also because there has been relatively little comparative work done on which to base generalizations.

In sum *access* to the decision makers of government is the *sine qua non* of interest group influence on public policy, but in a way, that is all it is. Access is a necessary but not a sufficient condition for political influence in Canada for, having attracted the attention of the decision-maker and having convinced him he should listen to the group's "case", the group must still convince him that the case is, indeed, a good one. Because the minister must ultimately seek reelection, he will not always meet the demands of big business for example, at the cost of broader if less articulate or organized interests. Similarly, because the bureaucrat must ultimately sell a policy idea to his minister, he must not automatically accede to the demands of a close friend or client unless those demands have at least some broad support in Canadian society.

By way of illustration, we can return to the example of the Canadian Medical Association in the late 1950s and early 1960s. Having analysed that group's activities, one writer attributed its relatively high degree of success not only to its privileged access to the focal point of decision making in its field, but also to:

a) the Association's prestige
b) the identification of the medical profession with the public interest
c) the cohesiveness of membership
d) the lack of articulation of an opposing point of view
e) general agreement among key policy makers on the group's high level of responsibility and public interest.[39]

---

[38]See G. Almond and S. Verba, *The Civic Culture*, (Princeton University Press, Princeton, 1963).
[39]Taylor, "The Role of the Medical Profession in the Formulation and Execution of Public Policy", p. 254.

When a group has this much on its side, in combination with ready access, the probability of its success is high indeed.

THE OUTPUT ACTIVITIES OF INTEREST GROUPS

Some organizations are deeply involved in the administration of government policy. For example, even though they might shudder to think so, doctors are acting as public employees when they make out birth and death certificates, hospital admissions, or insurance claims. When they sit on hospital boards or workmen's compensation boards and when they administer public health programs, they are acting as agents for important executive outputs of the political system. The Canadian Medical Association has been vital in organizing their activities along these lines. The Canadian Legion is vital in the administration of veterans' pensions through close cooperation with the Department of Veterans Affairs. Similarly, when a regulation is promulgated, the government publishes the regulation in the Canada (or provincial) *Gazette*, but no one seriously expects everyone who is affected to read about it there. The expectation is that the various associations who are concerned with the regulation will, through their agents or headquarters in Ottawa disseminate the appropriate information to those concerned.

The output activities of interest groups can be divided into those of an administrative nature, where the group or its members are actually a part of the output process, and those of an informational nature, where the group is acting as an indirect agent of the system.

Administrative Functions One of the most important administrative functions of many groups is self-regulation. For example, society makes the assumption that it would be undesirable to have a large number of unqualified people claiming to be doctors or dentists or lawyers or perhaps even teachers. Accordingly, governments delegate self-policing powers to medical associations, bar associations and some teachers' groups, which allow them to define who is a doctor, dentist, lawyer, or teacher. This self-regulatory mechanism extends far in Canadian society, for not only are professions controlled in this way, but so also are trades and crafts. The function extends beyond the mere definition of who is allowed to call himself what, to include a definition of ethical or fair practices and appropriate fee structures. In this form it extends into the business community through Better Business Bureaus and other business associations. Were it not for the self-regulatory functions of many interest groups in society, the governmental structure in Canada would have to be considerably larger than it is now.

Another activity is the actual administration of government programs. The administrative tasks which many doctors carry out under government medical insurance programs have already been mentioned. Elevator cooperatives and farmers' associations also administer many aspects of government programs. Groups interested in fighting pollution provide inspection services and warn government agencies of sources of pollution. Universities administer some aspects of student aid programs subject to advice, in some cases, by faculty associations and by government. These activities cannot be viewed as anything but an integral part of government activity; the interest groups in such cases become part of the output side of the political system.

Information Dissemination Probably the most important output activity of interest groups, however, is the dissemination of information about government policies. It is a simple truism, often overlooked, that people cannot obey the law unless they know what it is, and they cannot take advantage of government programs unless they know about them. Interest groups often provide the required information. Here endless examples can be provided. Virtually every trade association, union, or promotional group publishes at least a newsletter, and much of the work of the head offices of interest groups consists of first determining which government activities are pertinent to the group's interests and then informing members about them. The Consumers' Association feels that one of its most effective techniques is the dissemination of full information to its members and to anyone else who will listen. The same is true of nearly every self-interested group in Canada and many of the promotional ones as well.

The factors which affect the usefulness of interest groups as output institutions for the political system are broadly similar to those which affect their value as input devices. Of particular importance are group cohesiveness or dedication to a single set of aims and the possession of good internal communications. Obviously, the effectiveness of the offices in the capital cities is important—especially the effectiveness of their communication with the governmental structures with which they are concerned.

Scholars who have studied interest groups have tended to concentrate almost exclusively on the input side of their activities. While this aspect is vital, failure to look at the output activities of groups seriously understates their importance in modern government. The political system in Canada and in other developed countries has become highly dependent on these activities.

CONCLUSIONS

One of the greatest difficulties in writing about interest groups in Canada—indeed in any industrialized Western society—is the problem of determining where to place them in any conceptual schema of the political system. They are traditionally placed on the input side of the process and at the boundary of the political system; but we have seen examples in this chapter of their participation not only in the very core of the policy process, in priority determination and policy formulation, but in policy implementation as well. In short, interest groups pervade the whole of the policy process in Canada, so much so that at least one analyst has been led to characterize the Canadian political process as a process of elite accommodation between interest group and governmental elites,[40] and a whole school of analysis—consociationalism—has been erected on a very similar foundation and applied widely in Canadian political science.[41]

Interest groups provide undoubted benefits in Canadian society. Since there are far more Canadians who participate in interest group activities than in political parties we might be tempted to define such groups as the pre-eminent representative structures in Canadian society. There is no doubt that if one wishes to influence the political system in the periods between elections, the channels afforded by interest groups are more effective than those provided by parties. We have seen, too, that groups provide information to government and to their own members, that they are prominent in the administration of government policy and that they create a support structure for the political system upon which much of its legitimacy depends.

However one must be careful not to go too far in eulogizing the interest group system. We pointed out in an earlier chapter that about 40 per cent of Canadians are not integrated in any way into the interest group structure of Canada, and that this 40 per cent is generally the lower stratum of society. Thus, if the influence of interest groups is as significant as we have suggested, such groups may act to reinforce the disparity of power.

There are of course, limits to the power of interest groups.[42] The cabinet has a collective policy role which may effectively counter the pressure on individual ministers, and the requirements of party unity in the parliamentary system limits the legislature as an arena for lobbyists. The Public Service is by no means always sympathetic to interest group demands. Even the largest and wealthiest interest group can in no way approach the research resources available to the smallest federal department, so that the independent capabilities of the Public Service can and often do provide an effective counterweight to group activity. One should not underestimate the tenacity of the public servant in pursuing either the public good as he sees it or the aggrandizement of his own activities, and both of these may be inimical to interest group desires. Moreover, strong lobbies tend to create strong counterlobbies, and the more clearly a group's position can be made to appear against the public interest the less its chance of success. Thus counterlobbies may be able to overcome even the best financed interest group.

Proposals for reform of the political system to limit the power of interest groups are much less common in Canada than in the U.S. or Britain. Whether this reflects the rather belated "discovery" of interest groups by the Canadian academic world, press and public, or the greater acceptability of interest groups in Canada, or whether it is due to the belief that

[40]Robert Presthus, *Elite Accommodation in Canadian Politics.*
[41]Consociationalism is described in detail in Chapter 2.
[42]Similar limitations have been described for Britain by R.M. Punnett, *British Government and Politics*, 2nd. ed., W.W. Norton, New York, 1971, pp. 152–156.

such groups are less important here than elsewhere is irrelevant. Slight reforms of the political system or tinkering with the rules that govern interest group activity will not change the structure of modern society, and it is in that structure that the real strength of the interest groups lies.

Part 5
Inside the System

13
Authorities and Elites in the Canadian Political System

Not everyone shares equally in the making of political decisions; time after time in this book and elsewhere we have been confronted with the fact that effective political power rests in the hands of relatively few people in Canadian society. These people are the political decision-makers, the authorities, or the political elite. This chapter looks at them in more detail.

THE PROBLEMS OF DEFINITION

There are nearly as many definitions of the term "political elite" as there are people who have studied the subject. Political elites may be defined *positionally*—that is by taking a number of positions such as cabinet portfolios, bureaucratic positions and leadership positions in larger interest groups and defining the occupants of those positions as members of the elite.[1] Or elites may be defined *functionally*—by what they do rather than by the positions they hold. In those terms, a political elite would be the small group of people who share the most power over political decisions in Canada.[2]

Our own definition of the Canadian political elite derives primarily from the first of these approaches. While we will define "elite" as the relatively small group of people who make the important decisions about the authoritative allocation of resources for Canada, for practical purposes we will supplement this functional defintion with a positional one; the political elite will be defined as consisting of upper-level bureaucrats and cabinet ministers and the leaders of some of the largest and most important

[1] John Porter, in *The Vertical Mosaic*, adopts this approach. He attempts to differentiate between the political and the bureaucratic elite, but we suggest that in terms of the actual making of decisions, such a differentiation is not necessarily appropriate. Porter's work has recently been extended and updated by Wallace Clement in *The Canadian Corporate Elite*, (Carleton Library, McClelland and Stewart, Toronto, 1975).

[2] Suzanne Keller, *Beyond the Ruling Class*, (Random House, New York, 1963), p. 4., describes elites in general as ". . .a minority of individuals designated to serve a collectivity in a socially valued way. . .Socially significant elites are ultimately responsible for the realization of major social goals and for the continuity of the social order".

interest groups with whom they routinely interact. We will also consider members of parliament.[3] This positional definition includes by no means all of the positions that are significant in the making of authoritative decisions for our society. However, it does provide a manageable number of actors with whom to deal. Furthermore, as will become evident during the description of the policy-making process throughout the rest of the book, these positions do bestow on their holders a disproportionate amount of control over policy making.[4]

Elite Studies and Approaches Unless it is purely anarchistic, any approach to politics is an elite approach; but it has been conventional in recent years to differentiate between *elite* and *pluralist* approaches to the study of politics. The elite theorists assert that the political and economic systems of a nation are controlled by a coherent industrial-military-political elite which attempts to ensure that its own interests are foremost in any situation where a decision is being taken.[5] The pluralist analysts find evidence of a multiplicity of competing elites, which become active in different combinations over different issues.[6] In the middle stand analysts such

[3]The description of the elite which follows refers almost exclusively to the federal level of government. Our positional definition would not change for provincial elites, but the socio-economic composition of the elite could be expected to vary slightly from province to province.

[4]The reader is cautioned that this might be considered too restrictive a definition. Every government has advisors who are important in the decision-making process and who are not covered in this sort of definition. Sometimes it might be the wife of the premier, sometimes a trusted friend of top cabinet members or bureaucrats. Different advisors may be influential on different topics and it will often be found that on a specific topic a particular lobbyist was more influential than anyone else. We cannot include all such people in our definition nor can we hope to describe them, for the members of an elite who are not there by right of a formal position may move in and out considerably faster than those who are. The influence of such people may be great, but in ideas and socio-economic background, they are not likely to differ much from the positional elite through whom they must communicate their ideas. Very few of the upper-middle class professional men who make up most of the Canadian political elite for example, would choose unskilled labourers for their confidants.

[5]The writer most usually cited as the ultimate proponent of this view is C. Wright Mills, *The Power Elite*, (Oxford University Press, New York, 1959). There are many others who use this perspective—for example, most of the community power studies of the 1950s do so. It is also a common component of popular or semi-popular writings on politics. See, for example, David Halberstam, *The Best and the Brightest*, (Random House, New York, 1972), who constantly demonstrates the plurality of elites in U.S. politics while frequently referring to a mysterious, unidentified THEY, who control all the vital decisions. In general, the pure elite model has been more the province of sociologists than political scientists. There is rather little pure elite theory in Canadian political science.

[6]See for example, Robert Dahl, *Who Governs?*, (Yale University Press, New Haven, 1961), Edward Banfield, *Political Influence*, (University of Chicago Press, Chicago, 1961), or Nelson Polsby, *Community Power Studies* (Yale University Press, 1964). The

as John Porter and Robert Presthus, who assert that—while there may indeed be some competition between elites and some differentiation of elites depending upon the issue involved—all of those elites have been drawn disproportionately from a fairly narrow portion of society, mainly the upper middle class. They thus bring a set of common biases to bear upon their decisions.[7]

The position taken in this study is on the middle ground with Presthus and Porter. It is not assumed that there is a single cohesive elite which controls the Canadian political system—either nationally or in any of the larger provincial jurisdictions. But it is assumed that there is a good deal of cohesiveness and agreement among the many sub-elites which are active over various issues. Thus, Robert Presthus asserts that, for Canada,

> we assume that these three elites [interest group leaders, M.P.s and high level bureaucrats] play the major role in shaping and carrying out public policy, through a sustained process of mutual accommodation encouraged by a battery of compatible social, experiential and ideological ties.[8]

This does not imply that there is complete harmony among the elites. While evidence of serious schisms appears in the newspapers every day, some form of accommodation is usually worked out among them. This leads Presthus to characterize Canadian politics primarily in terms of a system of elite accommodation, and Porter's position is not much different.

The small size of the Canadian national elite compared to what might be found in the United States or Britain, the low proportion of Canadians with university education in the elite age groups of 45–60, and the southward migration which has reduced the elite to a relatively small group have made possible a situation where considerable interaction is probable, and where a high degree of self-consciousness of elite status could be expected to develop.[9]

> Interaction between the governmental elite and the one-quarter of interest groups who are most active politically, the shared socio-economic properties, their strategic political roles and. . .the pervasive cohesion among them on selected ideological and cognitive dimensions all tend to provide behavioural and effective commonalities that enable them to interact effectively.[10]

If this is so, then it is vital for an understanding of how the Canadian political system works that we understand the nature of these elites. In the remainder of this chapter we will look at the socio-economic backgrounds of these decision makers and at some of the attitudes with which they will approach the allocation of resources in Canada. We can then

pluralist approach is more often utilized by political scientists than by sociologists. It is probably the most commonly accepted approach in Canadian political science.

[7]Robert Presthus, *Elite Accommodation in Canadian Politics*, John Porter, *The Vertical Mosaic*. Most academic analysts do stand on the middle ground in this controversy.
[8]*Elite Accommodation in Canadian Politics*, p. 268.
[9]*Ibid.*, p. 274.
[10]*Ibid.*, p. 332.

attempt to determine whether there is a common set of attitudes among these elites and what this might mean to Canadian politics.

THE CABINET IN CANADA

In describing the men who make up the cabinet in Canada, there are two possible approaches. One can examine the process through which a Prime Minister constructs a cabinet, in order to see what constraints are placed upon him, and what groups he seeks to represent in his cabinet structure; or alternatively, one can examine the results of cabinet formation—the types of men who end up in the cabinet when the selection process has been completed. This section will concentrate on the latter method; but it would be artificial to merely discuss the results of "cabinet making" without saying something about the actual process of selecting a cabinet, so the latter will be looked at very briefly as well.

One can look at the men who have become Canadian ministers from a number of perspectives: the geographical distribution of cabinet members, their ethnic and social backgrounds, and their career patterns can all be examined. When that is done, one can take a fresh look at the well-worn question of how Canada's various social cleavages are represented in the cabinet for, as will be seen, this highest level of decision making in Canada is consciously designed to be representative of some of the country's major cleavages.

The Provincial and Ethnic Distribution of Cabinet Ministers

> I think I may defy them to show that the cabinet can be formed on any other principle than that of a representation of the several provinces in that cabinet. Your federal problem will have to be worked out around the table of the Executive Council.[11]

This prediction was made in 1865 by Christopher Dunkin, one of the most perceptive critics of Confederation. From the very first days of Confederation, it was obvious that the Senate, which was intended to represent regions or provinces in Ottawa, would not suffice as an arbiter of the regional cleavages of the federation. The Senate itself had little real power and the basis of its representation was only very approximately based on federal principles. Yet four distinctive colonies had been brought together and each was anxious to retain some substantial degree of control over federal political decision making. In the first cabinet, Cartier would accept no fewer than four positions for Quebec, of which three were to be held by French Canadians. Larger than Quebec, Ontario had to demand one more seat, and if Nova Scotia and New Brunswick were to have any say in the councils of Confederation, they should have two posts apiece. The federal principle of cabinet composition was thus immediately established as the most important determinant of cabinet structure.

[11]Christopher Dunkin, *Confederation Debates*, (Queen's Printer, Ottawa, 1951), pp. 497, 513.

There has been no substantial change since. In 1966 Lester Pearson's cabinet had at least one minister from each province in which the Liberals could muster a seat. The Prime Minister would no doubt have been happy to represent Saskatchewan and Alberta in his cabinet as well, but those provinces were not kind enough to give him the chance. The one prairie Liberal who was elected was immediately put in the cabinet and given the Veteran's Affairs portfolio.

Table 13-1 compares the 1966 Pearson cabinet with the early 1974 Trudeau model. While attrition and the fortunes of political war had worked some subtle changes, the basic principle remained the same. As far as possible, and with the temporary exception of New Brunswick, each province had at least one minister, although once again the prairie provinces made the Prime Minister's task of selection very simple by returning so few Liberals.[12] The first edition of the Trudeau cabinet, in 1968, was the only one in history to have more Quebeckers than Ontarians, but since that time the distribution of portfolios has returned to normal, with more Ontario than Quebec ministers.

Historically, much the same pattern has been evident. Between Confederation and 1965, the provincial distribution of cabinet ministers was as shown in Table 13-2. The reader should concentrate on the cor-

TABLE 13-1: PROVINCIAL REPRESENTATION IN THE CABINET UNDER TRUDEAU AND PEARSON

	Pearson (Dec. 1966)		Trudeau (Feb. 1974)	
Province	Cabinet	Liberal MPs elected 1972	Cabinet	Liberal MPs elected 1972
Newfoundland	1	7	1	3
Prince Edward Island	0	0	1	1
Nova Scotia	2	2	1	1
New Brunswick	3	6	0	5
Quebec	7	56	11	56
Ontario	10	51	12	36
Manitoba	1	1	1	2
Saskatchewan	0	0	1	1
Alberta	0	0	0	0
British Columbia	2	7	2	4

[12]The omission of New Brunswick was rectified immediately after the 1974 election. Alberta again failed to give the Prime Minister a chance to represent it in the cabinet but a Senator from Alberta was appointed to the ministry, in a partial attempt to compensate for Alberta's unrepentant Conservatism.

TABLE 13-2: THE DISTRIBUTION OF CABINET MINISTERS BY PROVINCE, 1867–1965

Province	Per Cent of Ministers	Corrected Per Cent*	Per Cent of National Population, 1971
Newfoundland	0.9	4.6	2.4
Prince Edward Island	2.4	2.4	0.5
Nova Scotia	8.9	8.4	3.7
New Brunswick	8.0	7.6	3.0
Quebec	32.0	30.4	27.9
Ontario	30.8	29.2	35.7
Manitoba	5.3	5.2	4.6
Saskatchewan	2.4	3.7	4.3
Alberta	2.7	4.2	7.5
British Columbia	4.4	4.3	10.1

*To take account of the fact that different provinces have been in Confederation for different lengths of time, a column called "corrected per cent" has been included. The figures in that column are derived by multiplying figures in the first column by the number of years between when that province joined Confederation and 1965. The figures so derived were totalled and a new percentage distribution within that total was calculated.

rected per cent column rather than the simple per cent column. For comparative purposes the provincial distribution of population by provinces for 1971 is also shown in the table. It can be seen readily that the distribution of cabinet ministers and of population by province has been very roughly similar. However, the provinces of Saskatchewan and Alberta appear to have had rather fewer than their share of ministers, and the Maritimes rather more than their share. Perhaps some explanation of this can be found in the fact that Western provinces have often returned MPs from minor parties who could not be considered for the cabinet, whereas the Maritimes have consistently returned MPs from the two major parties. The number of ministers shown from Quebec may be somewhat misleading, for, relative to English Canadians, French Canadians have tended to stay in the cabinet for shorter periods. When the distribution is examined by "man-years", the parallel with provincial populations in every period since Confederation is almost exact. However, the shorter period of service of French Canadians in the cabinet may well have acted to diminish their real power.

The ethnic distribution of cabinet ministers shows similar patterns. In 1966, the Pearson cabinet contained 9 French-Canadian ministers and 18 English-Canadian, while in 1974 the Trudeau cabinet contained 9 French-Canadian ministers, including the Prime Minister, in a cabinet of 30 members. The 1974 composition of 30 per cent French ministers is very close to the average since Confederation and, once again, the proportion of French-Canadian ministers very closely parallels the proportion of French Canadians in the population.

As with provincial representation, the attempt to provide proportional representation by ethnic group, at least between the French and English segments of the population, has been intentional. On the other hand, "other" Canadians have not been well represented in the cabinet. Occasionally someone such as J.T. Thorson, a man of Icelandic descent who was minister of National War Services in 1941 and 1942, does enter the cabinet, and Trudeau's short-lived appointment of Stanley Haidasz as Minister of State in charge of "multiculturalism" could certainly have been construed as an attempt at representing "other" ethnic groups. However, there has been no clear pattern set in this respect, and it is too soon to begin looking for precedents.

In the nineteenth and early twentieth centuries there was also an attempt to provide balanced representation of sub-groups within the English-speaking portion of the cabinet. Thus, under Macdonald or Laurier, the well-balanced cabinet would have perhaps one-quarter of its members of English descent, one-quarter Scottish and about twenty per cent Irish. Each of these nationalities formed a powerful and cohesive voting group in Canada, and a Prime Minister could offend them only at his peril.

Another interesting pattern becomes evident if we look at the distribution of ministers in the Pearson and Trudeau cabinets by the rural or urban location of their riding. In the Pearson cabinet, 12 of 26 cabinet ministers came from the three metropolitan areas of Toronto, Montreal, and Vancouver, which, together, had only about 26 per cent of the Canadian population at that time. There were 9 ministers from smaller urban centres and 5 from ridings where there was no town with more than 25,000 residents. In the 1970 cabinet, 14 of the 28 ministers came from metropolitan areas and only 4 from rural ridings. This is partly a reflection of the fact that there are very few Liberals elected from rural ridings, the more-or-less exclusive property of the Conservatives. But it is also a reflection of the realities of the present Canadian economic and social structure.

It should be clear by now that although the cabinet is not representative of rural-urban cleavages, it is intended to be an ethnically and provincially representative institution. However, there is a type of hidden under-representation in the French–English distribution in the cabinet, which becomes apparent when one examines the distribution of portfolios by ethnic groups. Until 1968, no French Canadian had ever led the ministry of Industry, Trade and Commerce (or its predecessors), and up to the time of this writing in 1975, none has ever been Minister of Finance. These are two of the most powerful portfolios in Canadian government, and the lack of French-Canadian ministers in them may have seriously weakened French-Canadian representation in the cabinet. Furthermore, until the appointment of Marc Lalonde in 1973, there had never been a French-Canadian Minister of Health and Welfare. There has never been a French-Canadian Minister of Labour, and French-Canadian Ministers of Defence are rare creatures.

There may be some objective reasons for these facts. French Canada does not have a long history of sympathy towards governmental social welfare measures or labour unions. The great majority of cabinet ministers from Quebec have been lawyers; most of them have known relatively little about business or finance and were unknown to Bay or St. James Streets. Consequently, French-Canadian ministers were usually not considered for the portfolios mentioned above. But whatever the reason, the tendency, until recently, to assign French Canadians to portfolios such as Public Works, Postmaster General or Veterans Affairs, with the hope that at cabinet meetings they would not speak unless spoken to, did lead to an under-representation of French Canadians in the decision-making process.

Two caveats must be entered. First, by 1970 this pattern appears to have changed. There have been French-Canadian ministers of Industry, Trade and Commerce, of Transport, of Communications and of Health and Welfare, and these constitute some of the most important portfolios in the present cabinet. Naturally, a French-Canadian Prime Minister adds a certain amount of clout to the French representation. Second, one must not too hastily draw a parallel between portfolio and power. Sometimes portfolios which have very little departmental responsibility can be very powerful, depending upon the person who occupies the portfolio. Occasionally, light or less visible portfolios are given to vital ministers in order to free them to consider broader questions of national policy. Thus some of the less visible portfolios such as Treasury Board (occupied in 1974 by C.M. Drury and subsequently by Jean Chrétien) or Communications (occupied by Gérard Pelletier) may be held by ministers with a considerable amount of real power.

The Socio-Economic Background of Cabinet Ministers

The cabinet is clearly intended to be representative of provincial and ethnic cleavages in Canada, but is it really a representative institution? If the answer is affirmative one would expect to find in it a socially representative cross-section of Canadians. A reader who has even a passing knowledge of Canadian politics will realize that this is simply not the case. The poor are not represented in the cabinet by one of their number, nor are the Indian or Eskimo people, nor are unskilled labourers. Women are vastly under-represented. But how far does the discrepancy go? How socially unrepresentative is the cabinet?

Both by education and by occupation, cabinet ministers have been extremely unrepresentative of the general population. Between 1867 and 1965, fully 52 per cent of Canada's cabinet ministers were lawyers, whereas the proportion of lawyers in the population is far less than one per cent. Lately the preponderance of lawyers has perhaps grown slightly less. Table 13-3 indicates that in the 1966 Pearson cabinet only 9 of 27 members were lawyers, but in the Trudeau cabinet of 1974 the proportion was up again to 15 out of 30. Some 22 per cent of ministers since Confederation have been from the business world, 6.5 per cent have been farmers, and 4 per cent have come from the public service. Only 5 ministers since Confederation have had a labour background or a close connection with labour.

A similar bias pertains if one looks at the educational backgrounds of Canada's ministers. Only two of some 376 since Confederation have had no formal education, and only 18 per cent stopped at elementary school.

TABLE 13-3: OCCUPATIONS OF CABINET MINISTERS

Occupation Before Entering Politics	Pearson Cabinet (1966)	Trudeau Cabinet (1974)
Law	9	15
Other Professions	7	6
Civil Service	5	2
Business	5	4
Farm	0	2
Labourer	0	0
	1	1

Only one since World War II has not had at least high-school education. In the 1970 cabinet, there were two members with only high school education, one who had attended technical college, seven who stopped after one university degree, ten lawyers, and nine members with a postgraduate degree or some post-graduate studies. In terms of education the cabinet has been far from a microcosm of the Canadian social structure.

Religion and the Cabinet One more aspect of the "representative" nature of the Canadian cabinet should be mentioned, and that is its religious composition. In the 1970 cabinet there were fourteen Roman Catholics, four members each from the United Church and the Anglican Church, one Baptist, two Presbyterians, and three "others". Between Confederation and 1965, there were almost equal numbers of Anglican, Presbyterians and United Church or Methodist cabinet ministers while about 35 per cent of cabinet ministers were Catholics. In an age when religious differences no longer stir people's deepest passions in this country, the religious affiliation of cabinet ministers is of no great consequence. Yet, as Chapter 2 demonstrated, there was a time when religious differences in Canada were taken more seriously, and in that era, a proper balance of religions within the cabinet was vital.

The evidence does not suggest that religion has been a great factor in the selection of cabinet ministers in Canada over the last 50 years. It is more probable that the distribution of cabinet posts on the basis of religion is, in fact, a by-product of other factors. The geographical and ethnic basis of cabinet distribution dictate that a reasonably constant Catholic/Protestant ratio will prevail. Other fluctuations in the religious distribution of cabinet members probably reflect the random fluctuations characteristic of any small population. It seems ludicrous to think of a modern Prime Minister saying, as Alexander Mackenzie once did,

> I may, with feelings of pride, refer to the standing of the members of the Cabinet. . .In the matter of religious faith there are five Catholics, three members of the Church of England, three Presbyterians, two Methodists, one Congregationalist and one Baptist.[14]

It is possible that if a Prime Minister discovered that he had appointed 27 Roman Catholics he might feel a bit embarrassed, but much beyond that the question of religious distribution does not go.[14]

Aside from geographical and ethnic cleavages then, the cabinet is anything but representative. In part, this is a reflection of what cleavages are the most important in Canadian politics, but it is also a reflection of other factors. The vast preponderance of male lawyers, especially in our earlier cabinets, was partly due to the fact that a law career was considered the appropriate one for a young man to follow if he wanted to go into politics. The elite nature of present cabinets may result to some extent from the facts that middle- and upper-middle-class socialization patterns are more likely to give a person the skills and attitudes essential to the performance of political roles, and that upper-middle-class occupations are more likely to provide the flexibility of hours necessary to politicians.

Nonetheless, there may be some dangers inherent in the heavily middle-class male bias of this highest decision-making body in the country. It is difficult to make equitable and sympathetic decisions affecting welfare, poverty, abortion or discrimination if few of the decision makers have ever been welfare cases, or poor, or pregnant, or have suffered discrimination. However, one must also remember that it is not necessary for a person to be the mirror image of the people he represents to be a good representative. It is at least possible that ministers can represent people quite unlike themselves, because "being a good representative" is a learned skill which, in theory at least, may be unconnected with social background.

The Career Patterns of Cabinet Ministers
What do people do in order to point their careers towards a cabinet post? There is a wide variety of possible ways into the cabinet but some career paths are more common than others. Many ministers, particularly in Liberal cabinets since World War II, have been welcomed into the cabinet more or less directly from outside parliament, especially from the public service. The most prominent example was Lester Pearson, but others such as Marc Lalonde have also been taken directly into the cabinet from government posts. A similar attempt was made in 1975 with Pierre Juneau who was appointed Minister of Communications, after serving as head of the Canadian Radio-Television Commission. He was, however, defeated in his attempt to get elected in Hochelaga, and resigned from the cabinet. It is not uncommon to arrange beforehand that a political candidate will join the cabinet if both he and his party are successful in a general election.

In the early years of Confederation, it was usual for ministers to

---

[13]William Buckingham and George W. Ross, *The Honourable Alexander Mackenzie: His Life and Times*, (reissued by Greenwood, New York, 1969), p. 354.
[14]But see Paul Fox, "The Representative Nature of the Canadian Cabinet," in Fox, *Politics: Canada*, 3rd ed., (McGraw-Hill Ryerson, Toronto, 1970), especially p. 341. Later in his career, even Mackenzie asserted "I have no sympathy personally with the feeling that appears to be growing. . .that every available place should be filled in accordance with the religious views of certain portions of our population," Mackenzie, *Papers*, Vol. I, p. 121.

serve a fairly long apprenticeship in parliament before being appointed to the cabinet. The relative importance of parliament in a minister's activities has decreased steadily over the years, while the importance of administrative, departmental, federal–provincial, and general priority-setting duties has steadily increased. For this reason it has become increasingly conventional to choose ministers not on the basis of parliamentary experience but rather on the basis of policy-making skills, administrative capabilities or, occasionally, tactical skills in electioneering. This has occasionally led to the spectacle of a cabinet which was administratively quite competent but which could not defend its activities before parliament.[15] Cabinets have also been tending to get younger in the post-World War II era. Prior to 1945, the average age of a man on entering the cabinet was 50 years. Pearson's 1965 cabinet had an average age of 47.7 years at appointment, and Trudeau's 1970 cabinet ministers had an average age of only 44.4 years at the time of their appointment.

It has occasionally been suggested that in Canadian politics there is no place for a man to go after he has left the cabinet, so that when a minister loses an election he must go back to private industry in order to earn a living. The result of this, it is alleged, is that ministers are never free of the necessity to look over their shoulder to be certain that they are not offending industry, with the result that they are psychologically limited as creative spokesmen for other interests in society.[16]

Evidence does not really support this suggestion. Only 26 per cent of the cabinet ministers who left their portfolios for any reason from 1867 to 1965 returned to private life. There are far more jobs in politics or public life for former cabinet members than is popularly supposed. The Senate, which has little direct role in the policy process has at least one vital indirect role: since Confederation, it has provided a good "pasture" for over 20 per cent of retired cabinet ministers. Provided that his party does not go out of power before he leaves office, a minister can be fairly assured that he will, if he wants, be appointed to the Senate. The importance of this role of the Senate must not be underestimated, for it means that ministers need not depend on the good will of the private sector for employment when they retire from office. An increase in pensions would not necessarily be a functional alternative to the Senate in this respect, since many ex-ministers wish to remain active. A further 20 per cent of ex-ministers went back to being ordinary MPs before eventually retiring. This happens most commonly when a government is defeated, but Pierre Trudeau did demote several of his former cabinet ministers to the backbenches in 1974, perhaps

[15]This point requires some qualification. The Pearson cabinets of 1963–1968 seemed particularly prone to parliamentary pratfalls caused by legislative inexperience. However, in 1975 a great many members of those early Pearson cabinets still hold office and they are by now well experienced in the parliamentary game, and hence, less liable to make the spectacular goofs which characterized Liberal cabinets in the 1960s. Given the rapid turnover of Canadian MPs, almost any new cabinet could be expected to face problems in defending its program before parliament.

[16]Porter, *The Vertical Mosaic*, Chapter 12, especially pp. 405–411. See also Chapter 16, below.

establishing for Canada a precedent often followed in Great Britain. Another 12 per cent went into the judiciary, 10 per cent became Lieutenant-Governors, and 10 per cent went into some form of public service, usually on a board or commission. Thus, contrary to some analyses, the ex-cabinet minister does have places in politics where he can go when his day in power is over.

The Business Connections of Cabinet Ministers[17] There have frequently been close connections between cabinet ministers and the Canadian business community. The politics of the immediate post-Confederation era were largely concerned with railways, and cabinet ministers were deeply involved. Thus, six of the original directors of the Grand Trunk Railway were cabinet ministers, and in 1885, a cabinet minister, Sir Charles Tupper, had no qualms about accepting $100,000 of CPR stock—a gift given in grateful appreciation of his help in selling CPR bonds. Earlier, while acting as Secretary of State, Sir Charles had simultaneously held three paid directorships; yet none of these activities precluded him from serving as Prime Minister for a brief stretch in 1896, nor were they held against him in the election of that year.

Laurier continued to be a director of Mutual Life Assurance during his term as Prime Minister,[18] and one of his Ministers of Justice—Allen Bristol Aylesworth—carried on a private law practice at the same time as he held that portfolio. Sir Robert Borden refused to permit his ministers to maintain outside business connections, but Mackenzie King had no such compunctions. His Minister of Justice—Lomer Gouin—was simultaneously a director of the Bank of Montreal, the Cockshutt Plough Co., Montreal City and District Savings Bank, Royal Trust, and the Mount Royal and Mutual Life Assurance Companies.

In 1922 King stated, "In the long run we will gain more in virility in our public life by leaving some matters to conscience and honour rather than by seeking to enforce prohibitions that may be too severe and too drastic".[19] One of the major sources of strength in King's and St Laurent's cabinets was C.D. Howe who had been, prior to his appointment in 1935, a highly successful construction engineer. The C.D. Howe Co. which he "disposed of" before taking office, continued to receive government business and to employ Howe's son and son-in-law.

Mr. St. Laurent's cabinets contained two ministers who retained private business practices after entering the cabinet. George Prudham was one, and the other was J.J. McCann, who retained a directorship in Guaranty Trust even though his department, National Revenue, often engaged in negotiation with that company. Mr. St. Laurent may have been embarrassed, but the ministers remained unrepentant even under an opposition barrage.

In recent years, convention has required ministers to divest them-

[17]See also William A. Matheson, *The Canadian Cabinet and the Prime Minister: A Structural Study*, unpublished Ph.D. dissertation, Carleton University, April, 1973, pp. 249–258.

[18]*Ibid.*, p. 252.

[19]*Ibid.*, p. 253.

selves of directorships and holdings before taking office, a practice followed, for example, by Eric Kierans and Robert Winters in recent Liberal cabinets. The management of their concerns is turned over to a "blind" trust which manages them without any consultation with the minister. Whether such a divestiture of interests really constitutes a complete surrender of concern for what may have been a person's life work is at best debatable. But perhaps the price of having such men as Winters, Kierans, Drury, Sharp or Gordon in the cabinet must include trusting that they can in some way divorce themselves from past concerns. Ironically, Eric Kierans and Walter Gordon, who came to the cabinet directly from the business community, proved to be two of the most "leftward leaning" of recent Liberal cabinet ministers.

In 1973 the question of conflict of interest in cabinet ministers was broached directly by the Prime Minister in the House of Commons, but no legislation was introduced. Instead, Mr. Trudeau said that

> guidelines are preferable to additional legislation. . .an element of discretion, to be exercised by a minister on the basis of discussion with the Prime Minister of the day, seems the best solution.
> . . .A minister will be expected in the future, as is the policy today, to resign any directorships in commercial or other profit-making corporations that he may hold before becoming a minister".[20]

Cabinet ministers would also be covered by the provisions of a proposed "independence of Parliament Act", which would require disclosure of any pecuniary interest or benefit which the member might have in any matter upon which he wished to speak in parliament.[21]

These provisions are rather informal and far from stringent, but it may be impossible to make them any stronger than that. Cabinet ministers are, and always have been, drawn from the upper socio-economic levels, and they are bound to have accumulated certain attitudes and interests along their road to the top. While no legislation can ever erase the attitudes which a person may have accumulated during a lifetime, we might hope that ministers and senior public servants will openly disclose all relevant present and former interests. A truly vigilant press would be of great value here.

THE BUREAUCRACY IN CANADA

We have made the point frequently in this book that the public service is a vital link in the policy-making process in Canada. Together with the cabinet and the various constellations of interest groups which revolve around any given issue, Canada's senior bureaucrats must be viewed as largely responsible for the shape of public policy in Canada. What are these people like? Who are they and where do they come from? What are their career patterns and their socio-economic backgrounds?

The Ethnic Distribution of Bureaucrats

No one will disagree, I am sure, with the notion that the execution of pub-

[20]Statement on Conflict of Interest, House of Commons, July 18, 1973
[21]*Members of Parliament and Conflict of Interest*, Information Canada, July 1973, p. 34.

lic policy in Canada deserves the best minds and the highest executive, administrative and professional skills available in the land. The Civil Service Act recognizes this requirement and makes provision for its fulfillment. However it is an unfortunate fact that the Public Service of Canada has, up to now, been unable to attract and retain its fair share of competent persons reflecting the two cultures of Canada. We have not succeeded in recruiting, particularly for intermediate and senior positions, a sufficient number of well qualified citizens from French-Canada, and it is the Commission's view that this vacuum is detrimental to the public interest.[22]

This statement, made by the chairman of the Public Service Commission, is a reflection of the concern which federal leaders felt, and feel, at the small number of French Canadians in senior positions in the federal bureaucracy. The situation has undergone some rather violent fluctuations in the past. For example, the proportion of French Canadians in highly responsible positions in the Public Service declined steadily from some 25 per cent in 1918 to 8.1 per cent in 1949.[23] Paradoxically, the cause of the decline during this period, and hence of many subsequent problems, was a rationalization of recruiting methods and the introduction of a merit system of recruitment and promotion in 1918. Under the old patronage system, French-Canadian cabinet ministers and members of parliament were allowed to appoint their ethnic *confrères* to civil-service positions. Under the "merit" system, largely English-speaking boards tended to equate merit with facility in the English language, and French representation in the federal bureaucracy fell drastically. Nathan Keyfitz has pointed out:

> There is a tendency for the English to judge the French not by the breadth of their vision, nor by their ability to communicate, but by their mastery of the intricacies of English usage and vocabulary and even by their pronunciation of English. Since the French, in judging one another attach very little weight to speaking English at all and none whatsoever to whether it is spoken with a good accent, they will, as far as this element is concerned, arrange one another in a different order of merit from that in which English speakers make the choices. [The English] not only choose too few French but they also do not choose the right ones.[24]

The general response of the federal government has been to redefine the concept of merit somewhat to make ability in both of Canada's official languages a component of merit in a way it has not been in the past. Thus many of the lower- and middle-rank jobs in the public service, and all of the upper rank jobs have been classified as requiring some level

[22]J.J. Carson, "The New Role of the Civil Service Commission" an outline of remarks to the Federal Institute of Management, Ottawa, Feb., 1966. Quoted in V.S. Wilson, *Staffing in the Canadian Federal Bureaucracy*, unpublished Ph.D. dissertation. Queen's University, 1970.
[23]Chambre de commerce du District de Montréal, *Mémoire soumis à la commission royal d'enquête sur le service civil fédéral*, avril, 1946.
[24]Nathan Keyfitz, "Canadians and Canadiens", *Queen's Quarterly*, vol. 77, 1963, no. 2, p. 174.
The presence of Francophones on the selection boards has improved the situation somewhat since 1963, but there is still some tendency for the English to rate the French by the ability of the latter to speak English.

of bilingual capability. The level of capability varies according to the job itself but no one can be brought in or moved to fill any of the 1000 or so top jobs unless he is either already bilingual or willing to undergo continuous training to become so.

The question now is: has this policy been succeeding? The Public Service Commission has been rather quiet on this subject. Naturally the numbers of officially bilingual public servants have increased, but departments have found various ways to circumvent some of the more rigorous requirements of the policy, and the level of knowledge of the second language required for most of the positions is not very high. Moreover the proportion of Francophones in the upper- and middle-level positions in the public service (the senior executive officer category) has not increased greatly since the inception of the policy although it is considerably greater than the 8.1 per cent of 1946. In the highest-level positions, the situation seems somewhat better. In 1975 about 26 per cent of deputy ministers and 21 per cent of assistant deputies were Francophones.

The Socio-Economic Background of Bureaucrats While there have been few cabinet ministers with less than middle-class background, a significant proportion of the middle levels of the federal bureaucracy has either a farming or a working-class background. Indeed, the public service appears to be an important path of upward mobility in Canada—provided that somewhere along the way our potential Horatio Alger manages to obtain a university degree. In both French- and English-speaking groups in the public service the proportion of middle- and upper-level decision makers with working-class or farming backgrounds is close to 50 per cent. Thirty per cent of English and 20 per cent of French middle-level public servants had upper- and upper-middle-class backgrounds.[25] About 15 per cent of present public servants had fathers in the public service, a figure which indicates a substantial degree of occupational succession, considering that the service has been expanded rapidly in the post-war era.

A university education is extremely important in climbing to higher decision-making levels in the federal service. In 1967, some 81 per cent of the people at "Senior Officer" levels (director, director general and assistant deputy minister) had obtained at least one degree. Only one of those under 40 years of age lacked a degree. Many of them had more than one.[26] The particular university one has attended is not of much significance. Some 18 per cent of top-level public servants attended the University of Toronto, 8 per cent McGill, and 7 per cent Queen's University; but these figures are close to the proportional size of these universities in the 1940s, when such men were students.

There has been a great deal of discussion about whether the Cana-

[25]C. Beattie, J. Désy and S. Longstaff, "Bureaucratic Careers: Anglophones and Francophones in the Canadian Public Service", Internal Report for the Royal Commission on Bilingualism and Biculturalism, p. 211.
[26]P.J. Chartrand and K.L. Pond, "A Study of Executive Career Paths in the Public Service of Canada", (Public Personnel Association, Chicago, 1970).

dian public service, like the cabinet, should mirror fairly accurately the regional cleavages in Canada. Whatever the theoretical merits of representative bureaucracy, the fact is that the federal bureaucracy exhibits a strong bias, in its middle levels, towards those who were born in Ontario, particularly those born in Ottawa. Thirty-six per cent of Canadians lived in Ontario in 1971; yet 48.5 per cent of the middle- and upper-rank civil servants in 1965 were born in Ontario, and 23 per cent grew up in Ottawa–Hull region which has only 2 per cent of the nation's population. Among French-Canadian middle-rank civil servants, fully 43 per cent grew up in Ottawa–Hull. This bias is explicable. People tend to stay where they are brought up. Moreover, in the Ottawa–Hull area a civil service job is looked upon as a highly legitimate form of work, whereas this is not always true in other areas of the country. Nonetheless, this heavy centralist bias is regrettable and may in fact lead to a lack of sympathy towards "peripheral" Canadians when decisions are being made. It is perhaps difficult to create policies appropriate for the West or the Maritimes if the policy-maker knows these regions only from an airplane window.

One of the most important biases in the makeup of the senior levels of the public service is the under-representation of women. Table 13-4 indicates that the proportion of women diminishes drastically as one moves up the salary (and responsibility) scale in the federal public service. Thus, while women make up over 60 per cent of the lowest-paid workers in the public service, they make up only 2 per cent of the highest. Since the educational level of women in the public service is not vastly different from that of men, one would have to suggest a conscious or unconscious bias against the recruitment of women into the most important bureaucratic positions. The suspicion is increased when one notes that in 1975, among the most senior positions in the federal bureaucracy (at the deputy-ministerial level), there are just two women—far less than even the 2 per cent in the highest salary range in Table 13-4.

TABLE 13-4: SEX DISTRIBUTION OF FEDERAL PUBLIC SERVICE POSITIONS BY SALARY (1972)*

Salary ($/year)	Men	Women	Percentage of Group Who are Women
under 4,000	1,735	3,927	69.4
4,000 to 5,999	14,295	21,775	60.4
6,000 to 8,499	70,990	33,419	31.2
8,500 to 11,999	40,866	6,784	14.2
12,000 to 16,999	23,768	2,068	8.0
17,000 to 21,999	7,209	229	3.1
22,000 and over	3,617	74	2.0

*Only regular departmental positions are covered in these figures.

The Career Patterns of Bureaucrats There is a great deal of switching between private and public careers among top-level bureaucrats. Among public servants at the deputy-minister level, a full 80 per cent followed a private–public career pattern, working first outside the public service.[27]

The overall picture which emerges of the typical senior executive in the federal government is one of a thoroughly upper-middle-class male. In 1974 his salary was likely about $32,000. He was 51 years old and had at least a B.A., most likely in a social or management science. He was bilingual—at least by the standards of the federal government, which is to say that if he was Anglophone he likely read French very well, understood most of what was said in French and could, at the cost of some offense to his listeners' ears and French syntax, make himself understood. There was about one chance in five that he was Francophone and this chance increased the higher his rank. He was more likely to have come from Central Canada than from the periphery.

What motivates a person to go into a civil service career? At the middle levels, such a career can be very attractive. Salaries are kept competitive with salaries in industry. The work is certainly varied, and there are many opportunities for advancement in many different types of work. At the top decision-making level, however, motivations may well be different. Salaries, while hardly at starvation level, are considerably lower than those of top executives in the private sector.[28] The responsibilities are often huge and the work load crushing. At such levels, other compensations—such as the opportunity to actually do something for the public welfare, the chance to work on huge programs of nation-wide importance, and love of the power that derives from this opportunity may well be the primary motivations. In addition, there may simply be a desire to see how things "really work".

The epithet "mandarin" no longer fits the senior civil servant so well as it once did. There is considerable heterogeneity in the early career patterns and socio-economic status at birth of Canada's senior bureaucrats.[29] The situation has changed somewhat since 1953, when Porter found senior civil servants to be a rather collegial group with enough in common that each one knew all the others and decisions were transmitted by a sort of osmosis.[30] Still, one could not say, nor could one expect, that senior bureaucrats are in any real sense representative of the spectrum of the socio-economic interests which they serve.

[27]V.S. Wilson, "Staffing in the Canadian Federal Bureaucracy". Ch. 8 of Professor Wilson's thesis has been very helpful in writing this section. See also P.J. Chartrand and K.L. Pond, *op. cit.*, pp. 47–75.
[28]It may seem strange to rate the salaries of deputy ministers, who in 1975 could earn up to $66,000 per year as relatively low. However, when compared with corporation presidents, who usually head organizations which are smaller than government departments but who frequently earn six-figure salaries, they are low. The comparison with the salaries paid professional athletes is even more discrepant.
[29]Wilson, "Staffing in the Canadian Federal Bureaucracy", Ch. 8.
[30]Porter, *The Vertical Mosaic*, Ch. 14, pp. 417–457.

There are no comprehensive data on provincial public servants. In the larger provinces, public-service posts are well paid, and the higher-level civil servants in Quebec, Ontario and perhaps B.C. and Alberta are no less important as factors in national decision making than their federal counterparts. On the other hand, holding a deputy-minister post in a Maritime province may give relatively little real power to the incumbent, at least when viewed in national perspective, and the financial rewards may be commensurately smaller. Provincial civil services differ quite markedly from one another in their makeup, and as yet, research has not gone much farther than to point out that these differences exist. It is unlikely that their socio-economic makeup would differ very greatly from that of the federal bureaucracy.

MEMBERS OF PARLIAMENT

Among the most visible of Canada's political elites are the members of parliament. While their role in deciding what policies the government will promulgate is sometimes marginal, they are nonetheless the most visible link between the public and the rest of Canada's political elites. Because they have important symbolic significance in addition to whatever policy role they may play, it is important to ask ourselves what they "look like" with respect to ethnicity, socio-economic status, career patterns and the like.

The Socio-Economic Background of MPs[31] Since Canadian MPs are elected from geographically-based constituencies which are apportioned among the provinces roughly in accordance with population, there is no point in describing the provincial distribution of MPs. Nor is there as much point now as there once was in discussing the rural–urban distribution of federal MPs, since periodic redistributions of seats by an impartial board of commissioners has at least partially rectified the huge rural overrepresentation of MPs which persisted until the late 1950s.

The ethnic distribution of MPs shows a heavy bias towards the two charter ethnic groups. Thus 94 per cent of all MPs since 1940 have been of either British or French descent while only 78 per cent of the general population is of either British or French. The distribution between the English and French groups has been quite equitable since French MPs normally represent French ridings. However, it is unfortunate that there have not been included within the ranks of MPs more "other" Canadians. In a body which is symbolically important (i.e. the House of Commons), that sort of representation might be quite valuable.

The religious, distribution of MPs parallels fairly closely that of the general public. Thus, since 1940, some 56 per cent of MPs were Protestant, 41 per cent Catholic and 3 per cent "other". The corresponding population percentages were 50, 45 and 5.

It is when we turn to the class backgrounds of MPs that we find the greatest discrepancies between the public and their representatives. Table 13-5 indicates that the occupational status of MPs, though not as high as

TABLE 13-5: OCCUPATIONAL STATUS OF MINISTERS, BACKBENCHERS AND THE PUBLIC[31]

	Percentage of each group in "high status" occupations		
Period	Cabinet Ministers	MPs	Public
		(Figures are percentages)	
1867–1904	80.4	71.8	8.6
1905–1939	83.0	73.8	11.0
1940–1968	81.1	61.9	14.0

that of cabinet ministers, is nonetheless quite high. In 1961, while only 14 per cent of the general public held occupations which could be classified "high-status", 62 per cent of MPs and 81 per cent of cabinet ministers did so before entering politics. Although lawyers make up much less than 1 per cent of the Canadian population, 41 per cent of all new MPs elected between World War II and the 1965 election were lawyers. Since Confederation the proportion of lawyers in the House of Commons has risen steadily from 19 per cent before 1895 to 25 per cent between 1895 and 1945, and to nearly 40 per cent, since then.[33] Lawyers appear especially likely to be election winners—the proportion of winners who are lawyers normally exceeds the proportion of candidates who are lawyers.[34]

As one might expect, the educational level of MPs is correspondingly much higher than that of the public at large. Since 1940 some 73 per cent of MPs have been to university, compared with a general population figure of less than 10 per cent.[35] Moreover, MPs have tended to come disproportionately from homes with a relatively high socio-economic status. Some 16 per cent of MPs elected in 1962 had fathers who were professionals, whereas in 1921 (when most of these fathers would have been working), only 6 per cent of the labour force could have been classified as professional. Thus, Canadian MPs, like their legislative counterparts elsewhere in the western world, are territorially representative, but they are not socially representative. Table 13-6 summarizes the occupational

[31]We have drawn heavily on this section on D.J. Falcone, unpublished Ph.D. dissertation, Duke University, 1974. See also D. Hoffman and N. Ward, *Bilingualism and Biculturalism in the Canadian House of Commons*, Royal Commission on Bilingualism and Biculturalism, Document No. 3, (Queen's Printer, Ottawa, 1970), especially Ch. 2.

[32]D.J. Falcone, *op. cit.*

[33]Norman Ward, *The Canadian House of Commons: Representation*, (University of Toronto Press, Toronto, 1950), p. 132. A. Kornberg, *Canadian Legislative Behaviour*, (Holt, Rinehart and Winston, New York, 1967), p. 43, and data supplied by Professor R.R. March.

[34]Kornberg, *Canadian Legislative Behaviour*, p. 44.

[35]D.J. Falcone, *op. cit.*

and educational backgrounds of MPs in 1962 and compares them to American Senators and candidates for the British House of Commons.

TABLE 13-6: OCCUPATION AND LEVEL OF EDUCATION OF CANADIAN MPs, AMERICAN SENATORS, AND CANDIDATES FOR THE BRITISH HOUSE OF COMMONS (1962)

	Canadian MPs	American Senators	Candidates for British Commons
Occupation	(Figures are percentages)		
Professional	51	64	45
Proprietor-Manager	25	29	20
Farmer	12	7	4
Low Status	12	—	22
Blue Collar or Clerical	—	—	9
Education			
College or University	72	85	52
Less than College	28	15	48

Source: Data adapted from Table 3.1, p. 45, from *Canadian Legislative Behaviour: A Study of the 25th Parliament*, by Allan Kornberg. Copyright 1967 by Holt, Rinehart and Winston, Inc. Used by permission of Holt, Rinehart and Winston, Inc.

The Career Patterns of MPs Aside from what has already been said about the occupational backgrounds of MPs, what can one assert about their political careers? Are most of them rank amateurs in politics or do they, in general, have significant amounts of political experience before coming to the House of Commons?

Both Kornberg and Ward have found that a large proportion of MPs did have considerable political experience before they were elected to the House of Commons: in the period between 1921 and 1945, 31 per cent had been members of various provincial legislative assemblies, and 5 per cent had been in a provincial cabinet. However, since Confederation the proportion of MPs with prior experience in provincial or municipal politics has been steadily declining. In the parliament elected in 1887, which was fairly typical of other parliaments of that time, only 34 per cent of MPs had no prior experience in provincial or municipal politics. By 1945, the proportion of MPs without prior experience had risen to 60 per cent, and by 1974 it had become the exception rather than the rule for MPs to have experience in other legislative bodies.[36] Fewer than 30 per cent of

[36]Ward, *The Canadian House of Commons: Representation*, p. 123.

MPs in the 28th Parliament had been candidates for public office and fewer than one-tenth of current MPs have ever sat in provincial legislatures.[37] However, a lack of experience in other legislative bodies cannot necessarily be equated with a complete lack of political experience. Many Canadian MPs have served a political apprenticeship in their own party organizations and have held some kind of elected office in the party itself.[38]

As might be expected, the post-parliamentary careers of MPs were much less political than those of cabinet ministers.[39] A few MPs trickle into the Senate, the judiciary or the various commissions and boards of the public service. For the most part, however, defeated MPs return to private life or retire.

In 1962, members of the 25th Parliament were found to have a relatively high level of satisfaction with their jobs:

> 75 per cent said there were no other public offices in which they were interested; 9 per cent were interested in judgeships or appointments to the Senate; 7 per cent wanted to return to provincial politics; 6 per cent said they would like to be the mayors of cities in which they resided and an additional 3 per cent said they were interested in other public offices but they would not reveal what these were.[40]

Kornberg attributes this satisfaction to a number of factors, but it is possible that the major one was that he was interviewing just after an election. Whether legislators would feel the same way half-way through a parliament is more problematical. Backbench MPs are frequently quoted as expressing considerable dissatisfaction with their jobs.

It is perhaps paradoxical, in view of the highly public nature of their jobs and the need to gain support from a broad spectrum of voters, that MPs can be so unlike the people they represent. They are representative of the French and English divisions in Canadian society and they are quite representative with respect to religion and geography, but there the resemblance ends. MPs are not at all representative of whatever class differences exist in Canadian society. Some writers have suggested that this may be caused by the deferential nature of Canadian society compared to, for example, the United States or Australia.[41] However, the "deferential" British regularly elect at least 100 union leaders and working class people to their parliament, while, as Table 13-6 indicates, our allegedly non-deferential southern neighbours elect Senators almost exclusively from upper socio-economic groups. Perhaps the easiest explanation of the non-representative nature of our parliamentary elite is simply the lack of a work-

---

[37]D.J. Falcone, *op. cit.*
[38]Kornberg, *Canadian Legislative Behaviour*, pp. 54–55.
[39]Ward, *The Canadian House of Commons: Representation*, p. 145, has a tabulation of the careers of ex-MPs up to 1935. His data, however, must be interpreted carefully for he has apparently not separated ex-ministers from other MPs. The ex-ministers, of course, get a disproportionate share of the "plums".
[40]Kornberg, *Canadian Legislative Behaviour*, p. 35. Used by permission of Holt, Rinehart and Winston, Inc.
[41]R. Alford, *Party and Society, passim.*

ing-class party in Canada comparable in size to the British or Australian Labour parties. The reasons for this lack were explored in earlier chapters, but the reader will perhaps share our feeling that we are far from a satisfactory understanding of this problem.

CONCLUSIONS

There is no such thing as a "politically irrelevant" elite, for elites are normally defined as those who have a disproportionate share of power in society, and such people will naturally be vitally interested in the authoritative allocation of a society's resources. Porter has suggested that many of Canada's elites are interconnected. Many men are members of more than one elite and they cannot help but carry ideas from one to another. Thus, for example, the late Robert Winters, who finished a fairly close second to Pierre Trudeau in the Liberal party leadership race, moved back and forth freely between the political work and the business world, where he was president of such corporations as Rio Algom and Brascan. In a different vein, Jean Marchand moved from being president of the Confederation of National Trade Unions, Quebec's largest grouping of labour unions, to being a powerful member of the federal cabinet. Prime Minister Trudeau provides an excellent example of inter-elite connections. His father was a millionaire, which by most reckoning puts him in the economic elite; he edited the small but very influential periodical, *Cité Libre*, which puts him in the communications elite; he lectured at the University of Montreal law school, edited a successful book entitled *La Grève de l'amiante*, and wrote many articles, which qualify him as part of the intellectual elite; and he has certainly managed to get into the political elite.

In *The Vertical Mosaic*, Professor Porter identified not only political and bureaucratic elites, which were approximately the same ones as those discussed here, but also labour, communications and religious elites. Porter was able to show that the political and economic elites, and to a lesser extent the religious and communications elites, shared common backgrounds like those described in this chapter. His material did not show, although it implied, that those common backgrounds led to common attitudes and values which would lead to similar policy predilections. Thus Porter was not able to show directly whether or not the elites at the top of each segment of Canadian society were likely to agree among themselves because they were elite, or were likely to disagree because they "represented" different segments of Canadian society which might easily have differing interests.

The evidence suggests at least the possibility of a shared overall attitude towards issues among elites combined with a certain amount of inter-elite conflict over specific issues. Robert Presthus has shown in his recent book, *Elite Accommodation in Canadian Politics*, that the common factors in the social backgrounds of various elites have led at least the political, bureaucratic and industrial elites to have many common attitudes.[12]

---

[12]Presthus, *Elite Accommodation*, Ch. 11.

Presthus' elites were hardly intensely ideological creatures, indeed their most cherished common ethic was perhaps best characterized as "managerial" or pragmatic. Their process of accommodation was lubricated more by agreement on this managerial ethic than by any strong commitment to, for example, maintain the capitalist system.[43] But commitment to the managerial ethic—that the problem is not to provide sweeping social changes but rather to maintain and operate more efficiently the system we already have—was enough to provide a basis for interaction. When that interaction is further facilitated by common backgrounds and overlapping membership in clubs, on boards of directors, boards of governors, or whatever, we find in Canada no less than in any other developed nation the framework for the politics which Presthus characterizes as "elite accommodation".

There are elements of both heterogeneity and homogeneity among Canada's politically relevant elites. Regional, French–English, and religious cleavages are, on the whole, quite faithfully reflected in the composition of elites; occupational, educational and general class differences are not. The upper socio-economic class bias is most marked in the backgrounds of cabinet ministers and perhaps least marked among bureaucrats, although even there the educational requirements eliminate the vast majority of Canadians from contention.

The temptation is to conclude from this analysis that the political process in Canada is bound to favour middle- and upper-class Canadians. When one adds the evidence presented in Chapter 3 concerning political participation and political socialization to that adduced here, it begins to appear overwhelming. A very large body of Canadians may be placed by the combination of these circumstances and the nature of the political system in a "subject" orientation towards the outputs they receive. Cut off by their lack of education, money, membership in interest groups or representation among decision makers, they may feel they have no real control at all over what emerges from "their" political system.

This does not mean that the political decision makers will always act against the interests of the working or lower classes. There is ample evidence that they often provide redistributive policies in spite of considerable middle- and upper-class opposition. Nor does it mean that the outputs of the political system with respect to welfare policy, for example, would necessarily be much more equitable if there were more representation of lower socio-economic groups in our political elite. We would need many more case studies of actual decisions than we now have to determine whether these things are so. But it does mean that the way the 40 per cent or so of Canadians at the lower end of the socio-economic scale perceive our politi-

[43]*Ibid.*, p. 344.

cal system might be considerably different given the presence of 50 or 60 working-class MPs.[44] The symbols as well as the reality of power are important for the stability and legitimacy of a political system.

[44]While Canadian data are lacking here, it is interesting to compare Britain and the U.S. in this respect. The British feel more efficacious than Americans with respect to getting their political point of view across, and they feel it especially likely that politicians would listen to them. This *might* be attributed to the fact that the Labour party in Britain does have a substantial proportion (usually one-half) of working class MPs, whereas the working-class U.S. politician is practically unknown. See G. Almond and S. Verba, *The Civic Culture*, (Little, Brown, Boston, 1963) Ch. III.

14
Cabinet, Bureaucracy and Executive Support Agencies: Priority Determination[1]

Society today expects governmental solutions to so many of its problems that it is practically impossible for the political decision makers to consider more than a few of the demands impinging on them at any point in time. Moreover, even if they had infinite amounts of time, government officials could never meet all of the demands of the public, for the needs of one group of individuals often will conflict directly with the needs of others; to satisfy one interest will frequently mean thwarting or actively prejudicing others. Given both multiple and conflicting demands, it is not surprising that the central concern of modern political decision makers is often less with *solving* societal problems than it is with determining *which problems* deserve most to be solved. The process of deciding which problems a government should face, and which it should face first, we refer to as *priority determination.*

Before describing this very complex "stage" in the policy process it is necessary to point out that priority determination involves two broad levels of policy making. The one which is perhaps the central concern of this text is distinguishable by the fact that it normally culminates in a legislative output of the political system or a *law*. At this macro-level of policy making, the concern is with producing totally new policies, or with expressing new priorities in already established policy areas. The second level of priority determination is concerned with the process of establishing administrative and financial priorities for the allocation of resources among ongoing programs and among the departments and agencies which implement those programs. This level of priority determination occurs primarily within the bureaucracy, and is achieved through two related but

[1]In the revision of this chapter we have been assisted by the comments of Mr. Ivo Krupka of the Government of Canada and Carleton University, and by tape-recorded interviews with Jean-Luc Pépin, a former Liberal cabinet minister, and James Wilson, Ottawa editor of the *Montreal Star*. The interviews were prepared by Professor Jane Jenson of Carleton University. A.W. Johnson, "Management Theory and Cabinet Government", *Canadian Public Administration*, Vol. 14, no. 1, Spring 1971, and for provincial perspectives, Hon. W.D. McKeough, "The Relations of Ministers and Civil Servants", *Canadian Public Administration*, Vol. 12, no. 1, pp. 1–8, Spring 1969 are valuable sources as well.

distinct sets of mechanisms: the budgetary process and the interdepartmental coordinative process. These will be discussed in some detail in the second half of this chapter and in the following chapter.

POLICY INITIATION AND PRIORITY DETERMINATION

As we stated in Chapter 1, the cabinet is the "core" institution for priority determination. By this we mean that while no one part of the political system possesses a monopoly over the determination of priorities, *where new policies are concerned* the cabinet is by far the most important institution involved. But it must also be recognized that the determination of policy priorities in fact begins in the environment of the political system during the initiation stage. The various agencies of policy initiation such as political parties and pressure groups reduce and combine their policy demands in such a way as to maximize both the substantive benefits to their members and the likelihood of success. Thus, by determining which policy options to ask for and when, the policy initiators themselves help to define the broad parameters within which cabinet-level priority decisions ultimately occur.

In a similar manner, the executive support agencies of the government, most notably the Prime Minister's Office (PMO), the Privy Council Office (PCO) and the executive assistants and special assistants who work for individual ministers, often begin the process of priority determination long before their political masters are forced to take action. As we have mentioned already, the major problem in establishing policy priorities is "information overload" and not lack of data. It is humanly impossible for cabinet ministers to deal intelligently with all of the policy ideas and supporting information generated by the bureaucracy, provincial governments, the press, interest groups and individuals. Consequently, it is incumbent upon the executive support agencies to act as information "gatekeepers" who can filter or help to rationalize and organize the deluge of inflowing information.

Some of the most important of the "information filtering" functions are performed by the PM's appointments secretary, by the ministers' receptionists and private secretaries, and by the many untitled young gentlemen in dark suits and paisley ties who bar access to the busy cabinet ministers. These persons stalk the corridors and antechambers adjacent to ministerial "lairs", politely fending off most would-be visitors and quietly ushering in those deemed worthy of audience. Simply by determining who is important enough to get a personal hearing from one of the priority setters, these gate-keepers can have a significant impact on what policy options ultimately get to the cabinet level.

In a similar way, *correspondence secretaries* must filter the tons of incoming mail, bringing the most important correspondence (as they see it) to the ministers' attention, and drafting appropriate replies. Press secretaries also must help to organize and interpret the opinions expressed by daily newspapers all across Canada, and must inform the cabinet of trends in public opinion as reflected by the press. In monitoring and interpreting the press in this way, these officials of government can have an influence on what issues are brought to the attention of the cabinet and PM, and when. While there is no doubt that priority decisions must ultimately be made by the political executive, the nature and number of the policy options from which they choose, are to a large extent defined by the non-elected gate-keepers who "choreograph" the political tattoo of ministerial appointments, correspondence and daily media exposure.

Finally, it must be pointed out that the actual decision-making phase of priority determination involves two distinct but closely related choices. First, there is the question of what policy options should be acted upon, and which of those should be acted upon first; and second, there is the question of who will be given the responsibility for formulating and ultimately implementing the policy. The first question will depend upon the nature of the demand input itself, and upon the political, technical and financial feasibility of an appropriate policy response. The second set of choices, depends upon the availability of personnel with suitable expertise in the various departments and agencies of the government, and upon the outcome of a complex and competitive intrabureaucratic "sorting out" process.

The next section of this chapter will comprise a more detailed consideration of the priority-determining activities of the Canadian cabinet, with particular attention to the institutional mechanisms which have evolved to cope with the complexity of the modern policy process. Here we will not only describe the structure of the cabinet itself, but also look at key political and financial advisory bodies operating in the federal executive arena.

MACRO PRIORITY DETERMINATION: THE CABINET AND NEW POLICIES[2]

The cabinet is formally a committee of the Queen's Privy Council for Canada, but since that august body has met only twice since 1867, it has no consequence beyond providing its members with the prefix "the Honourable". The cabinet, which is the *de facto* executive instrument in Canada, in turn delegates the responsibility for priority determination among a number of committees of its own. (See Figure 14-1.) The cabinet has, at the time of this writing, nine standing committees, each of which meets regularly, usually once a week. The members of these committees are cabinet ministers, who sit on two or three committees apiece, and all committees have a small but permanent secretariat which is provided by the PCO. In addition to performing the duties described below, these secretariats assist the ministers with their paperwork, help to set committee

[2]See also the description and historical analysis in Fred Schindeler, "The Prime Minister and Cabinet: History and Development", in Thomas Hockin (ed.), *Apex of Power*, (Prentice–Hall, Scarborough, 1971), particularly pp. 43 ff.

agendas, and generally facilitate the flow of information from the line departments of government to the cabinet.

Figure 14-1

THE COMMITTEE STRUCTURE OF THE CABINET

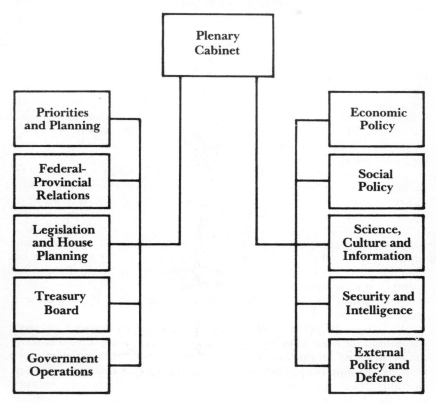

The Standing Committee Structure of The Cabinet

Items which are to go to the whole cabinet, are usually approved first by the appropriate standing committee. However, there are also special committees of the cabinet established from time to time to deal with specific policy problems. For example, there is a semi-permanent Labour Relations Committee, which deals with particularly serious national strikes, and there have been special committees on Western grain and on tax reform—the latter working on the White Paper on Taxation and its implementation in 1969 and the early 1970s.[3]

[3]*Ibid.*, p. 44.

The most common type of input to a cabinet committee is a "cabinet document" or "memorandum to the cabinet". By far the largest number of these documents are written within the bureaucracy, and are channelled through the appropriate minister to the Operations Secretariat in the Privy Council Office and thence to the appropriate cabinet committee. Such documents may express demands arising within the bureaucracy (for example, when officials ask for changes in departmental terms of reference or programs) or they may result from demand inputs which have been communicated through bureaucratic channels. Items appearing before cabinet committees may also be written by individual ministers or by the Privy Council Office itself, but this is relatively rare. Such memoranda may appear when ministers pick up demand inputs from the press, their personal acquaintances, members of their parties, or interest groups. Or they may appear when officials in the PCO feel that they have seen policy needs that departments, because of the fragmented nature of their reponsibilities, have missed, or when the subject is a major reorganization of departments. All memoranda to cabinet bear the signature of a minister or a group of ministers, who then become responsible for piloting the document through cabinet with the aid of their departmental officials.

The nine cabinet committees are not all of equal importance. In particular, the Cabinet Committee on Planning and Priorities, which is chaired by the Prime Minister, has occasionally been likened to a sort of "inner cabinet". Its smaller size, the eminence of its chairman, and the fact that the most powerful cabinet ministers are its members make it a better forum for important discussions than a full-scale cabinet meeting where 25 to 30 ministers may be present. Relative to the Committee on Planning and Priorities, the Cabinet Committee on Social Policy, for example, is considerably more restricted dealing only with matters arising from the policy concerns of departments falling within its own subject area.

It must be noted here that the complexity of provincial cabinets varies from province to province. In some of the larger ones, cabinet committee structure and procedures rival or surpass those of the federal government in complexity, while in the smaller provinces there may be considerably fewer ministers and not much need for a complex cabinet structure.[4] While we do not intend to deal with the structure of provincial cabinets in any detail, some additional light will be thrown on this subject in the next chapter.

Individually, cabinet ministers are busy men requiring considerable administrative and advisory support. In addition to his departmental staff, a minister has a personal staff consisting of one or more executive assistants who serve to ease part of his general work-load, to run his office and to assist him in his constituency work. As well, he will have a number

---

[4]See, for instance F.F. Schindeler, "Responsible Government in Ontario", (University of Toronto Press, Toronto, 1969), ch.3. The Ontario structure is at least as complex as that of the federal government. See G.B. Doern, "Horizontal and Vertical Portfolios in Government", in G.B. Doern and V.S. Wilson, *Issues in Canadian Public Policy*, (Macmillan, Toronto, 1974).

of special assistants responsible for fairly closely-defined areas of the ministerial responsibility. These assistants are concerned mainly with the departmental work of the minister—that is, with his administrative duties rather than his activities relating to priority determination.

But it must be kept in mind that the ultimate priority-determining function is performed—in our political system—not by individual ministers, but by the cabinet as a whole. It is as a part of a collectivity that the individual minister is a priority setter. While as an individual, and particularly as the formal administrative "head" of a department, the cabinet member will have an input in the determination of policy alternatives, in the *formulation* of specific policies and perhaps even in the decision as to the best options for implementation, when it comes to governmental policy priorities, the responsibility for the decision lies with the cabinet as a collective unit. One of Canada's senior public servants has summarized the situation:

> . . .who is it that develops and decides upon government programs—the individual minister or the cabinet as a whole? To most of us the answer will be self-evident: it is the individual minister and his officials who develop program alternatives but it is the cabinet as a whole which chooses the programs[5].

Inside The Cabinet: Prime Ministerial Power and Collective Responsibility

Up until now, our emphasis has been upon the role of the cabinet acting as a collectivity. However, before considering the executive support agencies which assist the cabinet in the collective determination of governmental priorities, it is necessary to say something about the distribution of power within that collectivity.

In Canadian politics, the Prime Minister is much more than "first among equals"; he sets the tone and style of the government and can establish the broad outlines of its most important policies. A Diefenbaker, a Pearson, or a Trudeau stamps his era of Canadian politics unmistakably with his style and ideas. However there are many checks on what a Prime Minister can do to influence priority determination.[6]

Undoubtedly the most important of these checks is simply the environment of the political system—both domestically and internationally. By this we mean only that the Prime Minister is subject to the same limitations as other politicians, but this is a vital point. For example, no matter how much he might personally want to do so, there is no way that a Prime Minister could institute a guaranteed annual income of $20,000 per capita. The environment of the political system is simply not productive enough to provide the goods and services involved.

Cabinet colleagues also place restraints on the Prime Minister's power to set priorities. While he can likely force them to accept any single

---

[5]A.W. Johnson, "Management Theory and Cabinet Government", *op. cit.*, p. 75.-
[6]See also the discussion in Thomas Hockin, "The Prime Minister and Political Leadership: An Introduction to Some Restraints and Imperatives", in Hockin (ed.), *Apex of Power*, pp. 1–22, and "Two Canadian Prime Ministers Discuss the Office", *ibid.*, pp. 184–199.

policy initiative he chooses, if it is not impossible given the state of the environment, he may choose not to force the issue. The reason is that, like any man, the Prime Minister only has so much power; and, in many ways, his power may be very much like currency—it can be spent, but it should be spent judiciously. Unless an item has a very high priority in the mind of the Prime Minister, he may not wish to spend his personal "power currency" on it. Thus, except on a few questions to which a Prime Minister is personally vitally attached, he is always somewhat amenable to being convinced by his colleagues. No one would resign from his cabinet in a huff if the Prime Minister pushed a few small items down its collective throat; but a cabinet must, in the parliamentary system, at least appear to work as a team, and too many such incidents could be damaging to the image of cabinet solidarity. A Prime Minister must walk a narrow line between allowing his ministers too much leeway—creating consequent disarray, disunity, and bickering on his team, and allowing them too little leeway—thus bringing himself to ruin through defections. The problems of the Pearson cabinets are amply illustrative of the former fault, while the breakup of the Diefenbaker cabinet in 1963 is illustrative of the latter.[7]

In addition, the cabinet has some control over the Prime Minister by virtue of its numbers, the personal strengths of its members, the access and contact which ministers have to information and input sources in the bureaucracy, and the personal followings which some ministers have managed to establish. On the other hand, the Prime Minister has their jobs in his hands. He can reorganize his cabinet at any time and remove troublesome ministers to lower-status portfolios, to the backbenches, to the Senate, or to the Judiciary.

Almost every Prime Minister and provincial Premier has completed at least one major governmental and cabinet reorganization during his stay in office. Usually these do not come at the first of his term in office for he will have inherited a cabinet with all kinds of vested interests that he dare not disturb until he is sure of himself in his new role. As well, he will usually be genuinely indebted to some of his ministers for helping to get him into power. However, after two or three years in office, he will usually have consolidated his personal position and will have some idea of the

[7]The last days of the Diefenbaker cabinet are particularly well covered in Patrick Nicholson, *Vision and Indecision*, (Longman Canada, Toronto, 1968), particularly pp. 227–266. On the assorted fiascos of the Pearson era, see Peter C. Newman, *The Distemper of Our Times*, (McClelland and Stewart, Toronto, 1969), and Judy La-March, *Memoirs of a Bird in a Gilded Cage*, (McClelland and Stewart, Toronto, 1969). Peter C. Newman *Renegade in Power: The Diefenbaker Years*, (McClelland and Stewart, Toronto, 1963) is also highly instructive and useful. See also the volumes of the Mackenzie King biography, *William Lyon Mackenzie King*, by R.M. Dawson and Blair Neatby. The first four books mentioned are examples of "inside" books so popular in the late 1960s. These books provide insight into the workings of politics in Ottawa; however, when reading them the reader should try to maintain a broader perspective. Politics is not the activities of a few people in Ottawa or provincial capitals. It is an extremely complex process set in an extremely complex environment. Its actors in capital cities are only transient figures who shape some events, and are, in turn, shaped by them.

sort of government organization he would like. At this point a major reorganization may occur, and ministers in anticipation will usually avoid incurring the sort of prime-ministerial disfavour that could land them out of their jobs.

It is sometimes suggested that one of the major ways in which a cabinet and Prime Minister can control parliament is through the threat of dissolution. The same thing could be considered applicable to a particularly recalcitrant cabinet, but one should not overemphasize this point because a dissolution carries risks for the Prime Minister as well as for his cabinet. Moreover, the thought of fighting an election with a cabinet in disarray, as Diefenbaker had to in 1963, can hardly be appealing to a Prime Minister.

Perhaps the greatest source of control that a Prime Minister has over his cabinet is simply his personal popularity. Highly popular or freshly elected Prime Ministers, or those who have established a solid tradition of getting themselves and their parties re-elected have rarely had much trouble with their cabinets. This Prime Ministerial asset will, of course, vary a great deal from PM to PM, as well as from cabinet to cabinet, and from time to time. The Pierre Elliott Trudeau of July 1974, fresh from a major electoral victory was more powerful *vis à vis* his cabinet colleagues than was the electorally chastized Pierre Elliott Trudeau of November 1972.

Political Advisors: The Privy Council Office and The Prime Minister's Office[8] Important assistance in the determination of priorities is provided to the cabinet by the Privy Council Office (PCO) and the Prime Minister's Office (PMO). Within the former, the three deputy secretaries to the Cabinet, for Plans, for Operations and for Federal–Provincial Relations each head up secretariats staffed with Ottawa's bright young men as well as special advisors, seconded from other parts of the bureaucracy or from the provincial governments. The PMO is staffed at the senior levels by personal appointees of the Prime Minister, and occupies offices in the East Block of the Parliament Buildings contiguous with those of the PCO.

[8]Valuable descriptions of the PMO and the PCO have been written by their former heads, Marc Lalonde and Gordon Robertson. See Gordon Robertson, "The Changing Role of the Privy Council Office" and Marc Lalonde, "The Changing Role of the Prime Minister's Office", both in *Canadian Public Administration*, Vol. 14, no. 4, Winter 1971, pp. 487–537. For a much more controversial point of view see Denis Smith, "President and Parliament: The Transformation of Parliamentary Government in Canada", and the different point of view expressed by Joseph Wearing in "President or Prime Minister", both in Thomas Hockin (ed.), *Apex of Power*. Events over the five years since Smith's article was written would seem to negate many of his arguments, perhaps largely because the now retired head of the PCO, Gordon Robertson, seems to have been determined to keep the office relatively small and its powers somewhat limited. More recently, see Thomas D'Acquino, "The Prime Minister's Office: Catalyst or Cabal" and Denis Smith, "Comments on the Prime Minister's Office: Catalyst or Cabal", both in *Canadian Public Administration*, Vol. 17, no. 1, Spring 1974.

Figure 14-2 THE PRIVY COUNCIL OFFICE *

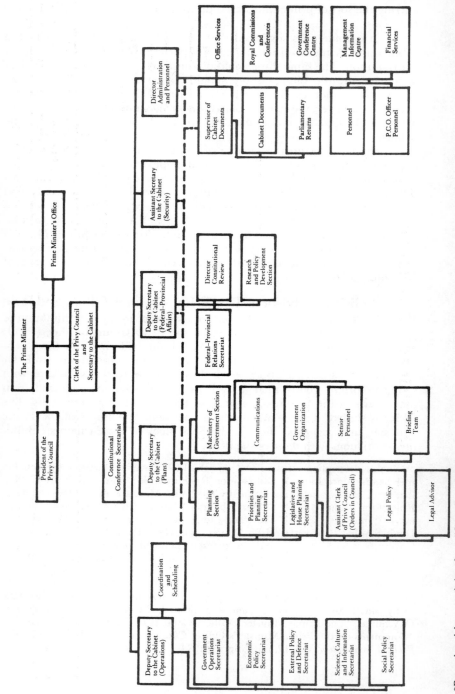

*Reproduced by permission from "Canadian Government Programs and Services," published by CCH Canadian Limited, Don Mills, Ontario.

Figure 14-3

THE PRIME MINISTER'S OFFICE *

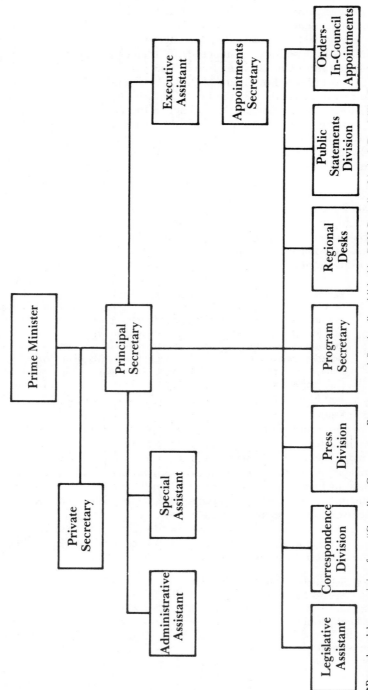

*Reproduced by permission from "Canadian Government Programs and Services," published by CCH Canadian Limited, Don Mills, Ontario.

The PMO reports directly to the Prime Minister and its task is essentially to provide the government leader with political advice. Where the line departments are called upon to inform and advise the cabinet as to the relative technical feasibility of competing policy alternatives, the PMO functions as a political technocracy to advise the leader as to the political losses and gains to be expected from various policy options.

As indicated in Figure 14-2, the President of the Privy Council has no direct responsibility for the Privy Council Office. That post is presently used to give a position in the cabinet to the Government House Leader and ensure that he has no particular departmental responsibilities to impede his efforts in manoeuvering the government's program through the House of Commons. Instead the Privy Council Office directly serves the Prime Minister and the cabinet.

Since 1968 there have been great changes in the structure and functions of the Privy Council Office, reflecting an attempt to make a rather fundamental change in the locus of power within the federal government. In the years prior to 1968 (with the possible exception of the Diefenbaker era) not only did the bureaucratic establishment dominate the process of policy formulation, but the senior bureaucratic "mandarins" played a major role in the process of priority determination as well.[9]

> . . .The pre-eminent position that senior bureaucrats occupied for a number of years in Ottawa is humourously illustrated in the story of the ambitious young man who wrote the Prime Minister asking that he be given a position in the cabinet. The Prime Minister replied to the effect that he did not feel that the member had the depth of experience, the breadth of knowledge and the intellectual vigour required for such an exalted position. Undaunted, the young M.P. wrote back: "My dear Prime Minister, I believe you misunderstood the nature of my request: high as my ambition can aspire, I do not expect to become a *Deputy* Minister; I merely want to be a Minister."[10]

The influence of the mandarins over the determination of priorities was based on a number of factors, some related to structural features of the system and others related to the personal characteristics of the individuals involved. The most important of the structural factors was the Deputy Ministers' control over the flow of information upwards from the departmental technocracy and downwards from the cabinet. In other words, one of the mandarin's sources of strength was related to his place in a complex system of communications, and in fact a large vestige of this particular source of policy influence still resides with the senior bureaucrats.

The most important personal factor contributing to the hegemony of the mandarin was his combination of expertise in a substantive field and

[9]See F. Schindeler, "The Prime Minister and Cabinet: History and Development", pp. 27–8, and Maurice Lamontagne, "The Influence of the Politician", *Canadian Public Administration*, Vol. XL, no. 3, Fall 1968, p. 265.
[10]By kind permission of Professor Thomas Hockin, Senator Maurice Lamontagne and Mr. Fred Schindeler, from "The Prime Minister and Cabinet: History and Development" in Thomas Hockin (ed.), *Apex of Power*, (Prentice–Hall, Toronto, 1971).

long experience as a participant in the policy process. Because his experience extended over a number of years and, frequently, through a series of different ministries, the senior bureaucrat possessed a perspective that was much broader than that of his political boss. The result was that the deputy minister could have a profound influence on his minister not only because he possessed a much higher level of technical competence in the field, but often because over the years he had acquired a "feel" for the political marketplace; he had political acumen which made him significant as a political as well as a technical advisor. While the influence of the mandarins would naturally also be related to the willingness of the individual ministers and the current government to take their advice, for the most part they either become "trusted" and therefore influential, or they simply ceased to be "mandarins".

It was apparently the intention of the 1968 Trudeau government to alleviate this situation via the obvious solution of providing alternative sources of policy advice. During the Diefenbaker era, alternative information had been derived from the Conservative party, from the personal acquaintances of the Prime Minister and the cabinet, from the press, and from the mind of the leader himself. The somewhat strained relations between the leader and the bureaucracy during those years ensured that there was less chance of priorities being determined by the bureaucracy, and that more than "normal" attention was paid to these alternative sources. Similar alternative sources had been available during the Liberal years prior to 1957, but Liberal Prime Ministers had shown relatively little propensity to use them. Prime Minister Trudeau and his advisors, on the other hand, appear to have recognized that the most effective counter for one bureaucratic institution is another bureaucratic institution with parallel responsibilities. The political advisory power of the mandarins was to be attenuated through the increase in size and influence of the PMO, and their technical advice was to be placed in competition with that coming from a revamped PCO.

The final verdict on the effectiveness of these two executive support agencies in altering the locus of power in priority determination must be postponed until their actual place in the system has crystallized. But some trends may be emerging. In the first place, because the PMO is composed of "political" rather than "bureaucratic" personnel, it seems likely that it has indeed assumed many of the political advisory functions of the mandarins. However, this may also relate to the increased size of the departments and the fact that the modern deputy minister is sometimes too busy being a "manager"of a large organization to have the time to develop much political acumen.

The PCO, while composed of bureaucratic personnel, has been viewed by old-style senior bureaucrats as an organization of "upstarts" and "outsiders". They have often perceived the PCO as a competitor for the government's "ear", although this is possibly a misconception. The cabinet's percieved unwillingness to listen to the deputy minister's personal technical advice may be due less to competing advice from the PCO than to the vastly increased levels of technical specialization among his subordinates. The decline in the deputy minister's power as a technical advisor, in other words, may be as a result of his inability to "add much" to the aggregated technical wisdom of his many highly specialized subordinates. He no longer *initiates* technical advice—he simply transmits it, and in this sense, his real power stems from his ability to affect the flow of information.

Thus, while it seems likely that the influence of the mandarins has indeed declined since their heyday in the 1950s, we must be careful in attributing this decline to an increase in the power of the PCO. There is no question that individuals in the PCO and the PMO appeared to have an influence on the timing and even the substance of some of the policies of the first Trudeau government; but this is more easily attributable to the personalities involved than it is to structural features. With the departures of some of the more forceful personalities who were originally placed in the PCO in 1968, there has been an apparent eclipse of the PCO as a source of substantive policy advice. The role that is evolving for the PCO would appear to grant them significant influence as gate-keepers who can filter the deluge of technical information being generated by the technocracy. By setting cabinet committee agenda, by "ordering" the line-up of documents awaiting cabinet attention, and by "briefing" or summarizing such documents before they are looked at by the busy ministers, the officials in the PCO can have a big impact on the "timing" of policies; but most of the time, the substantive information they are dealing with originates elsewhere, either "above" them in the political world or "below" them in the technical one.[11]

Financial Advisors: The Department of Finance and The Treasury Board[12]

The Privy Council Office, as we have seen, is strictly speaking a part of the bureaucracy, but it is a part unlike most others. A similar stricture could be applied to the Department of Finance and the Treasury Board Secretariat, for they too occupy rather distinct places in advising the cabinet on priority determination. Having determined the political and technical feasibility of a policy option, the next question that must be asked is "Do we have enough money to do it?" It is one of the jobs of the Treasury Board Secretariat, the Department of Finance, and their provincial counterparts to advise the priority setters as to the relative financial feasibility of policy alternatives.

For example, if the federal cabinet were considering making a major priority decision in the area of income support for the working poor, there are a number of steps it would have to take. First, it would attempt to assess the demand for such a policy in the country; and indeed, as was

[11]As this edition was being prepared, Michael Pitfield, perhaps the most dynamic of the cast of characters in the PCO in the late 1960s and early 1970s, was appointed Clerk of the Privy Council and Secretary to the Cabinet. His return to the PCO from the comparative limbo of the Department of Communications may presage a new era of activism in the East Block.

[12]For detailed structure description of the Department of Finance and the Treasury Board Secretariat, see *Organization of the Government of Canada*, Information Canada. Updates of this manual are published bi-annually.

pointed out earlier, the matter would not normally come to the cabinet's attention at all unless there were some public pressure. Since the inputs would normally have been channelled at least partially through relevant departments, (particularly, in this example, National Health and Welfare), those departments themselves would be pushing for a priority decision. And since most major policy areas, including the one in this example, are in areas of divided jurisdiction, discussions with provincial governments at both the ministerial and bureaucratic levels will also be going forward simultaneously.

However, some of the most important questions in approaching a priority decision on a matter such as income supplementation concern the financial feasibility and the macro-economic effects of such a step. The Department of Finance has as one of its duties the responsibility for preparing economic forecasts and projections for the whole economy and for government revenues. This information will become a vital part of the data required to make a priority decision on such issues. If the Department of Finance is forecasting declining government revenues, then the cabinet will be extremely reluctant to take on a big new program however desirable it may otherwise be. Similarly, if the Department of Finance opines that an income supplementation program will create critical economic problems in the country, the cabinet may well be reluctant to assign a high priority to such an item.

Closely connected to the foregoing questions are the problems of how such a program could be fitted in with current government activity in other fields, and whether the federal budget could stand the strain. The Treasury Board Secretariat must determine whether the current budget will stand the potential increase in expenditure or whether the adoption of a new policy will necessitate the deletion of one which is ongoing. While the Secretariat can—through the budgetary process—have a more direct impact on alterations in the spending priorities of ongoing policies, the financial advice of this agency's officials, because of their grasp of the entire budgetary picture, can have a significant impact on the establishment of priorities for new policies as well.

Unlike the Department of Finance, which is structurally the same as any other department, the Treasury Board is a statutory committee of the cabinet. The Board itself is composed of five cabinet members whose responsibilities affect the financial affairs of the government of Canada, the Minister of Finance *ex officio*, and the President of the Treasury Board who is its Chairman and is also the minister in charge of the Secretariat. The Treasury Board has two broad sets of responsibilities. The first of these relates to the "management" of the public service. In this regard it attempts to improve the public service as an administrative system, offers advice to the line managers of government as to how they might improve their individual operations, and acts as the "Employer" for purposes of collective bargaining.

Its second set of responsibilities relates to the budgetary process. Here the Treasury Board must act as an overseer of the budgetary process, helping to determine which departments and programs of government get how much of the estimated total annual expenditure of the federal government. It is as a committee on the expenditure budget, and not as a committee of management, that the Treasury Board plays the most significant role in determination of priorities among ongoing policies or programs. The role of the Treasury Board and, more importantly, the role of the Treasury Board Secretariat, in the determining of priorities among existing programs will be discussed at length when we come to consider the budgetary process. For the moment it is sufficient to conclude that, because of its pre-eminence within the budgetary process, the officials of the Treasury Board will inevitably play an influential role as advisors in the determination of new policy.

Ad Hoc Executive Support Agencies: Royal Commissions and Task Forces Frequently, areas of special concern to the cabinet, and about which it is particularly anxious to gain information, are covered by special task forces or Royal Commissions set up by cabinet decree. The use of task forces and, to a lesser extent, Royal Commissions has in recent years become increasingly popular at both federal and provincial levels of government as a way of combining external and governmental expertise in a particular area.[13] Royal Commissions of Inquiry have a long history in Canadian politics.[14] At first they were usually set up to investigate particularly sensitive areas where some wrong-doing in the governmental structure was suspected, and were usually headed by a justice. They had little real importance in the policy-making process. By the mid 1960s, however, they were used increasingly to investigate areas of policy concern, such as taxation, health services, and of course, bilingualism and biculturalism. Today's typical royal commission is small—with one, two or three commissioners and a staff of some ten or twelve; but the Carter Commission on Taxation and the Hall Commission on Health Services both had considerably larger staffs of experts, and the Royal Commission on Bilingualism and Biculturalism featured nine commissioners with a staff of hundreds and managed, for a few brief years, to almost completely eliminate unemployment among Canadian social scientists. A government is not formally bound by a royal commission report, but by the very act of appointing the commission, it indicates substantial concern about a problem. Since most commissions publish most of their findings, and since there has, presumably, been considerable public interest in this process, governments usually move to implement at least a part of what the commissions suggest.

The task force is a structure much less formal than the royal commission, but it is coming into increasing use at both federal and provincial

[13]Lamontagne, "The Influence of the Politician", pp. 271—366, especially p. 266 ff.
[14]John C. Courtney, "In Defense of Royal Commissions", *Canadian Public Administration*, Vol. 12, no. 2, pp. 198–212, Summer, 1969. See also H.R. Hanson, "Inside Royal Commissions", *Canadian Public Administration*, Vol. 2, no. 3, pp. 356–364, Fall, 1969 and C.E.S. Walls, "Royal Commissions: Their Influence on Public Policy", *Canadian Public Administration*, Vol. 12, no. 3, pp. 365–371, Fall, 1969.

levels. Task forces vary widely in size and structure, but frequently have one overall director and a small staff of professionals, and typically, they farm out much of their research responsibilities in the form of contracts. Many of them, including the ones that are most important at the priority setting stage of the policy process, report directly to the cabinet through some responsible minister, but the term "task force" is also increasingly used to describe lower-level working groups set up to investigate some area of concern within a department. As far as governments are concerned, the great advantage of the task force is that its work can usually be kept secret. Consequently, if a government does not like what it is told, it simply fails to publish the task force's report and makes its priority determination in favour of the status quo.

Constraints on Cabinet and Prime Minister in Priority Determination

If there are constraints acting on the Prime Minister when he is dealing with his cabinet, there are equal constraints on the cabinet and Prime Minister when they are acting together to determine priorities. In the first place, there are the environmental constraints which one should by now expect. However, an equally great constraint on the actions of both federal and provincial governments derives from the division of powers under the British North America Act. It will do the federal government little good to establish elementary education as a high priority area unless the provinces can somehow be induced to go along. Nor will it be very useful for the provinces to establish the revision of the criminal code as a high priority area unless the federal government cooperates and leads in the venture. The role of the federal–provincial process in the determination of priorities as well as in the more detailed formulation of policies is so vital that we devote the whole of the next chapter to it. For the moment, it is necessary only to keep in mind that it forms the greatest of the formal constraints on priority determination in Canada.

Another important constraint on the cabinet and Prime Minister is imposed by the difficulty involved in obtaining and digesting information. Task forces, Royal Commissions and the expansion of the PMO and PCO can all be viewed as attempts by the cabinet to alleviate the effects of the overload and frequent disorganization of the information which often impinges upon its members.

Paradoxically, the bureaucracy—by far the largest source of information for the cabinet—can also be viewed as one of its greatest constraints. The bureaucracy's near monopoly over many types of information ensures that the cabinet is highly dependent upon it when many priority decisions are made. Despite attempts to alleviate this dependency somewhat—via task forces (themselves usually composed of bureaucrats), Royal Commissions and the expansion of the PMO and PCO—Canadian governments are still perhaps more dependent on their bureaucracies than are most other Western governments. Interest groups, which in other polities sometimes form a counterbalance to the power of the bureaucracy, work through and with it in Canada. Canadian party structures are not really adequate as alternative information sources—unlike their counterparts in places like Britain and the Scandinavian countries. Nor do Canadian legislatures form an effective counterweight to bureaucratic power. The reader might well speculate on the seriousness of this problem to the Canadian political system; the authors think it very serious indeed.

INTERDEPARTMENTAL PRIORITY DETERMINATION: THE BUREAUCRACY AND ONGOING POLICIES

While cabinets determine the highest-order priorities within the Canadian political system, they cannot be expected to consider all of the administrative and financial priorities in programs already in existence. Therefore, priority decisions concerning the administration of ongoing programs are constantly being made throughout the bureaucracy. Once again, two basic decisions must be taken: which existing programs will be expanded or combined with similar ones, and who or which governmental agencies will be given the responsibility and necessary funds for carrying them into effect. Although the formal approval of even relatively minor changes of this type is the responsibility either of individual ministers or of the whole cabinet, the core of this part of the policy process is to be found in mechanisms for interdepartmental coordination and in the budgetary process.

Interdepartmental Coordination One major system for establishing priorities among the various departments and agencies of the Canadian government is the voluntary interdepartmental coordinating structure which includes several formal institutions and a vast interpersonal network of coordination and control.

The most common institutional embodiment of the interdepartmental coordination process is the interdepartmental committee. Typically, an interdepartmental committee will be created wherever more than one department is responsible for a single subject area. For example, because many departments within the federal government have responsibility for programs which bear upon water and water quality, there is an Interdepartmental Committee on Water, on which the departments of Transport, Environment, National Health and Welfare, Regional Economic Expansion, Energy, Mines and Resources, (and others) are each represented.[15] Similarly, there have been interdepartmental committees within the federal government on Resources, on Pesticides, on "Innovation", and on many other subjects. Frequently the formal membership of one of these committees will consist of deputy ministers or assistant deputies, but the meetings are generally attended by the middle-ranking delegates of the formal members. This is perhaps fortunate since the bulk of professional expertise is concentrated at these middle levels, and if any

---

[15]The Interdepartmental Committee on Water is actually a subcommittee of the larger Interdepartmental Committee on the Environment.

detailed policy work is to be done, these delegates are perhaps the most appropriate people to do it.

The manifest function of interdepartmental committees is to ensure the coordination of policies in some issue area. However, their effectiveness is often negated by a latent function—the pursuance of departmental interests. Interdepartmental "coordination" often becomes a competitive process through which departments bargain for aggrandizement or defence of their own spheres of authority.[16] This is a necessary reflection of the fact that the members of these committees spend most of their time taking care of their own departmental responsibilities and only a relatively small part of their time in interdepartmental coordination. Moreover, it may be inevitable, given the segregated hierarchical structures of the Canadian bureaucracy. People naturally tend to view matters in the light of the interests of the department in which they spend so much of their working day, and on whose growth and prosperity their own careers may depend.

This defensive posture of committee members may have severe repercussions for the policy-making process, as it tends to preclude a truly problem-oriented approach to issues. For example, if both the Department of Environment and the Department of Energy, Mines and Resources are eager to expand their influence over the uses of energy resources, it means that each may view the other's quite legitimate actions as a "power grab" and act either to block them, or to provide a counter-offensive of its own. The institutional devices of interdepartmental coordination often become the arena for these battles, and the result may be committee deadlock, or much bureaucratic redundancy with no clear policy decision. The problem is compounded by the fact that the cabinet may often choose to delay its own decisions if there is lack of consensus among its bureaucratic advisors. In cases like this, the cabinet may simply wait until one group or the other has gained ascendancy and a clear-cut policy alternative has been articulated.

There are partial solutions to such blockages. First, the Prime Minister can move to break up such deadlocks by a pre-emptive re-allocation of departmental responsibility. Second and more important, perhaps, is the fact that the interdepartmental priority-setting process is not purely a conflict situation: in fact, not all departments are "imperialistic" and indeed most individual bureaucrats are genuinely interested in solving substantive problems even if they sometimes get in one another's way. Because many of the middle-level specialists in a given subject area get to know

---

[16]This is not to assert, as is occasionally done, that departments must expand at the expense of others or die. However, the people who are involved in interdepartmental coordination are frequently fairly ambitious and this leads to expansion being thought desirable. The whole question of interdepartmental and interagency conflict and cooperation has been classified by one analyst under the heading "subsystem politics." See E.S. Redford, *Democracy in the Administrative State*, (Oxford University Press, New York, 1969), pp. 96–106. Redford's analysis applies to the American system where the process is much more complex than in Canada, and hence we have not made extensive use of his terminology.

each other personally,[17] there are many channels of informal communication which can help to ease the process of interdepartmental coordination. Furthermore, department heads are not always anxious to expand their own departmental work-loads and are often willing to share the burden. This tendency may be reinforced because many senior bureaucrats seem to have difficulty delegating authority; they quickly find themselves in a position where they cannot imagine their organization undertaking greater responsibilities, even when there may be considerable spare capacity lower down in the department.

A third partial solution is to be found in another aspect of the activities of the central agencies. Together with the Treasury Board, the Privy Council Office and the Department of Finance are represented on virtually all of the formal interdepartmental coordinating committees, subcommittees, working groups and so on. They are there not because they have programs in these particular areas but rather because of their coordinative and supervisory responsibilities. Thus, attached to the Department of Finance, to the Privy Council Office, and to the Treasury Board are people whose job it is to stay on top of interdepartmental coordination mainly by attending an endless round of meetings. These people then report back to the appropriate division of their own agency, producing a check on all facets of interdepartmental activity. While the interdepartmental coordinating system still does not work very well, perhaps it is less a failure because of the watchdog activities of these departments and agencies.

The Budgetary Process and Financial Priorities Because of the obvious relationships between interdepartmental coordination and the budgetary process, the workings of this dimension of priority determination and the relative roles of the Department of Finance and Treasury Board can best be clarified by a more detailed consideration of the budgetary cycle.

The cycle begins with the establishment of the "fiscal framework", i.e., the proposed or estimated total revenues and expenditures of government for the coming fiscal year.[18] The framework is established in discussions of the cabinet committees on Economic Policy and on Priorities and Planning, and is based upon proposals submitted by the Department of Finance. These proposals suggest to the cabinet what the government's overall fiscal policy should be for the year. They are based on the Department's projections of Canada's economic outlook in that year and on its consequent predictions of what government revenues will be. Such propos-

---

[17]We are, here, back to Professor Porter's concept of a bureaucratic elite, but at a lower level in the bureaucracy. One of the less nefarious features of the older elite system which Porter describes is that it makes slicing of the priority pie considerably simpler. See *The Vertical Mosaic*, Ch. 14, pp. 417–456.

[18]This description of the budget cycle follows closely that of A.W. Johnson, "The Treasury Board of Canada and the Machinery of Government in the 1970's," *Canadian Journal of Political Science*, Vol. IV, no. 3, September 1971, pp. 354–356. When Mr. Johnson wrote that article he was Secretary of the Treasury Board, a position in some ways analogous to the deputy minister of a regular department.

als also include the Department of Finance's recommendation as to whether the economy need be stimulated or dampened, and suggestions as to how the government might go about achieving this.

On the basis of these proposals and their own feelings about the political climate, the cabinet committees decide what macro-economic posture the federal government should assume, whether it should aim for a budget deficit or surplus, and what total amount of revenues the government should aim for. One should note that in making these decisions, ministers are very much at the mercy of the Department of Finance, for it is really the cabinet's only major source of information on these subjects. The Economic Council of Canada occasionally provides information which differs from that of the Department, but it lacks direct access to cabinet and does not have as large a staff as the Department. Advice is also freely available from the press and from interest groups, but the busy ministers will rarely have the time or the expertise to consider very much beyond what their resident experts tell them.

Once the cabinet has approved the expenditure guidelines for the next year, the Department of Finance relinquishes centre stage to the Treasury Board, whose job it is to effect spending priorities by allocating revenues among competing bureaucratic claimants. The Board works with the total level of expenditures established by the Cabinet Committee on Economic Policy, and with a list of priorities established by the Cabinet Committee on Planning and Priorities. To do its job, the Planning and Priorities Committee must already have developed a list of policy objectives which it can put together with the expenditure guidelines to identify what policy areas ought to have first call on any increases in revenue. The result is a set of broad policy directives which is forwarded to the Treasury Board to guide it in the supervision of the preparation of the departmental estimates.

The range of choices open to the Treasury Board at this stage is large, for there are many competing claims for any new available resources. To help it cope with this problem, the Board has developed a "three-budget system." The "A" budget specifies the cost of continuing present programs at current levels, given linear increases in expenditures necessitated by inflation, population growth, etc. Because the "A" budget is essentially an incremental one, there is little real choice involved in dealing with it; for unless a program has been marked explicitly for extinction, and this is extremely rare, it will be maintained. Thus, the "A" budget which consumes the great bulk of available resources in any given year, is inflexible, and as a result most of the expenditure decisions are tied up at an early stage in the process, leaving a limited range of decisions for the Treasury Board to make.

The "B" budget is essentially the list of new programs or major expansions of existing ones proposed by the departments. The items on the "B" budget have normally already been considered at least tentatively by the cabinet committees, have been assigned an order of political priority, and are, in a sense, "waiting in the wings" for some funds to become available. The likelihood that a "B" item will be accepted, however, is very low—unless there has been an explicit directive from the cabinet. It is significant that the "B" budget proposals are submitted at a much later date than the "A" proposals, with the result that the former get considered only after all linear expenditure increases in the "A" items have been provided for. Thus, while the Treasury Board may have a lot of leeway in allocating *residual* resources to "B" budget proposals, they must do so according to cabinet's stated priorities, and then only if some residual funds are left over when the "A" budget proposals have received the lion's share of the resources.

The "X" budget, originally an integral part of the "three-budget system", was intended to provide for the selective elimination of non-operative, redundant, or grossly inefficient programs on a government-wide scale. According to this scheme, each department was expected to prepare a list of "negative priorities" to indicate which of its programs could or should be dropped. The problem with this system is that if a department faithfully recommends the discontinuance of an existing program, there is no guarantee that the resultant residual resources will be allocated to the "B" proposals of the same department. In other words, if an "X" budget proposal is accepted, the moneys thereby freed may be lost to the department for good. Given the "defensive imperialism" so conspicuous in interdepartmental affairs, very few departments are selfless enough to give up any resources in the interests of government-wide benefits. The Treasury Board, as a result, has realistically dropped the "X" budget device from its repertoire, and it normally takes a cabinet decision to axe (or "X") any existing program.

By now it should be clear that, while cabinet and Treasury Board decisions involving the "B" budget proposals of a department can be an important dimension of interdepartmental priority determination, the "A" proposals are the "guts" of the budgetary process. There are a vast number of problems of interdepartmental coordination which result from minor changes in existing programs or from disclosures of redundancy, inefficiency, or even impropriety in long-standing programs. One of the ways in which some coordination can be affected among existing programs and the departments that implement them is the continual supervision[19] and annual review of departmental expenditure proposals.

At the federal level, the key institutional actor in the process of annual program review is the Program Branch of the Treasury Board. This body is formally responsible for both *inter*departmental and *intra*departmental[20] coordination of financial matters. While it is, in practice, utterly impossible for this branch to keep up with much interdepartmental coordination through its five program divisions, each of which is responsible for monitoring interdepartmental (and, formally, intradepartmental) activities within a particular area. Thus, for example, if the Program Branch discovers that both the Department of National Health and Wel-

[19]This is normally referred to as the *pre-audit* or *operational audit* function and is discussed in Chapter 16.
[20]The process of internal coordination will be dealt with in Chapter 16, as will the details of the traditional process of preparing the estimates.

fare and the Department of Environment are concerned with the leakage of sewage into shellfish beds in Nova Scotia, it will attempt to ensure that they coordinate their efforts. If they do not, then the Board can, at least in theory, move to cut off appropriations to one or the other of these programs, thus effectively settling the "who" part of the priority-determination process.

Perhaps the major tool available to the Planning and Programs Branches of the Treasury Board for ensuring the coordination and rationalization of ongoing programs is the Planning, Programming, Budgeting System (PPBS). PPBS can also be vital in assisting departments themselves to maintain internal control and coordination of priority decisions and of ongoing programs. Thus it requires some discussion here.[21]

The new budgeting system has been hailed as the ultimate saviour of rational government, and damned as nothing but a minor change dressed in very flashy clothing. The truth is, doubtless, somewhere between the extremities. PPBS was first introduced into the budgeting system of the U.S. Department of Defense as a way of controlling cost allowances for weapons systems and providing for the rational planning of other departmental activities. Since the U.S. Department of Defense has managed to become infamous for some of the largest cost overruns in history, and since this system was being used as the U.S. was getting steadily deeper into the Vietnam War, one might wonder just how effective the system is. Ironically, at a time when the U.S. has begun to seriously reconsider its commitment to this particular "rationalist" budgeting technique, it has become firmly ensconced here in Canada as a part of the priority determining apparatus of the federal government.

One of the great problems about PPBS is that it is almost impossible to say what it is—two different practitioners will tell you two different things. In the federal government in Canada, the process is defined by the Treasury Board manual as involving the following concepts:

(a) the setting of specific objectives;
(b) systematic analysis to clarify objectives and to assess alternative ways of meeting them;

---

[21]Much has been written about PPBS. On the general system, see F.J. Lyden and E.G. Miller (eds.), *Planning, Programming, Budgeting: A Systems Approach to Management,* (Markham, Chicago, 1965) or David Novich, *Program Budgeting,* (Harvard University Press, Cambridge, 1965), or J. Burkehead, *Government Budgeting,* (John Wiley and Son, New York, 1966), or H.A. Hovey, *The Planning-Programming-Budgeting Approach to Government Decision-Making,* (Praeger, New York, 1968). On Canadian applications, see Canada, Treasury Board, *Planning, Programming, Budgeting Guide,* (Queen's Printer, Ottawa, 1968), Canada, Treasury Board, *Statement to the Senate Committee on Science Policy,* by S.S. Reisman, Feb.2, 1969); G. Guruprasad, "Planning for Tax Administration in Canada: The PPB System in National Revenue and Taxation", *Canadian Public Administration* , Vol. 16, no. 3, Autumn, 1973, pp. 399–421; A.W. Johnson, "The Treasury Board and the Machinery of Government in the 1970's", and Michael Hicks, "The Treasury Board of Canada and its Clients, Five Years of Administrative Reform 1966–1971", *Canadian Public Administration,* Vol. 16, no. 2, Summer 1973.

(c) the framing of budgetary proposals in terms of programs directed towards the achievement of the objectives;

(d) the projection of the costs of these programs a number of years in the future;

(e) the formulation of plans of achievement year by year for each program; and

(f) an information system for each program to supply data for the monitoring of achievement of program goals and to supply data for the reassessment of the program objectives and the appropriateness of the program itself.[22]

The manual goes on to emphasize that this is a process for determining priorities through resource allocation by asserting:

> The elements of the Canadian government PPB system have been developed. . .within the context of total resource allocation. By the latter phrase is meant that there is an explicit recognition that the total resources are limited in terms of the individual and collective demands of departments and there has to be a setting of priorities by the government itself in light of which departments can plan and budget. . .Program budgeting is primarily concerned with resource allocation within the department.[23]

Briefly, the process requires that forecasts of spending needs for departments be made three years ahead (although a department is not necessarily bound irrevocably to its spending forecasts), and that such forecasts must be made on a program and activity basis rather than on the basis of "standard objects" of expenditure. Under older budgetary systems, departments would simply submit budgets consisting of such items as "salaries and wages, Operations Branch, $3,238,000" to the Treasury Board, and thence to parliament. The Treasury Board and parliament could either accept or reject these, but they would have little idea of how personnel activities were distributed within the Operations Branch or how they related to the various programs in the department. Under PPBS however, estimated expenditures list not only the standard objects such as "salaries and wages" or "repair and upkeep" but also account for the distribution of those expenditures among the programs and activities of the department. Two of the obvious values of this technique are that it facilitates more effective control by the Treasury Board, and it makes it easier for the MPs and Cabinet Ministers to see the potential impact of their appropriations on the society. Moreover, even within the department, it likely has the effect of forcing the line administrators to rationalize their own activities. By forcing the "managers" of the government to justify their estimated expenditures in terms of objectives, sub-objectives, etc., the PPB system may potentially assist them in understanding the relevance of their day-to-day activities in relation to the overall goals of the government and thus make them better managers. Whether its practitioners will succeed, in the near future, in bringing PPBS up to its full potential is another question.

Finally, while PPBS has important uses as a tool of management

[22]Canada, Treasury Board, *Planning, Programming, Budgeting Guide*, p. 1. Reproduced by permission of Information Canada.
[23]*Ibid., loc. cit.*

and as a device facilitating more rational allocation of limited financial resources, it has also been touted as a mechanism of policy *planning*. It is here
that the critics of the system have had their field day, for, as a planning
system, PPBS has never lived up to its press releases. The reason lies not so
much in a failure of PPBS as in the somewhat naive optimism of its cre-
ators who failed to comprehend the complexity of the modern world. It is
impossible, given current technology, to take into account all future contingencies or even to state with reasonable accuracy the probability that a
future event will occur. Thus, most policy making in government (and particularly budgetary decisions) cannot be based on long term "plans".
Rather, they will continue to be incremental extensions of ongoing policies, and responses to crises. The best we can hope for from techniques
such as PPBS is some rationalization of the basically incremental patterns
of priority determination, and the provision of contingency funds or some
"budgetary slack" that will permit necessary adjustments to unforeseen
crises. While these expectations are not as grandiose as those originally
held for PPBS, they are more likely to be "lived up to". By understanding
the limits of the system, government will be able to use it more effectively.

Because PPBS is first and foremost a budgetary system, it can obviously be applied anywhere budgeting is conducted—in private corporations or in government. It can therefore, also be, applied to provincial and
municipal governments as well. The problem is that the application of
PPBS is an art which is not widely practised in Canada, and thus the
problem for all levels of government becomes one of finding enough practitioners to carry it out. For this reason, its diffusion into provincial and municipal governments may be somewhat delayed.

CONCLUSIONS

As can be seen, the ways in which priorities are established in Canada are highly complex. Moreover, if the provincial and municipal levels
are added to the process, it becomes extremely complicated indeed. How,
then, can any overall sense be made of this part of the policy process?

There is, perhaps, one framework which may be more useful than
others: the whole priority process might be viewed as a set of bargaining
relationships. Since resources are scarce they must be rationed, and as soon
as people begin to feel any sort of shortage they will begin to bargain to
maximize their satisfactions.[24] Thus, when decision makers discover that
not all of the demands they consider important can be satisfied, they will
begin to trade off one project against another in an attempt to ensure that
those which they consider to be most important can be satisfied. The
official who is well down the line is concerned with only one or two pro-

---

[24]See, for example, Thomas C. Schelling, "An Essay on Bargaining", *The American
Economic Review*, Vol. 66, no. 3, pp. 281–306, June, 1956. The classic statement of
this approach, developed in the United States but, we suggest also applicable to
Canada, is Aaron Wildavsky, *The Politics of the Budgetary Process*, (Little, Brown, Boston, 1964).

grams or parts of programs that directly affect him, and it is usually up to him to administer these projects, not bargain for them in the first instance. The higher officials in departments and agencies bargain within their own departments to ensure that their own spheres of influence survive and expand. In the game of interdepartmental politics, departments themselves are engaged in a continuous process of bargaining and building coalitions to maximize their own departmental power and to "optimize" their own "program mix."

At the cabinet and intergovernmental levels, this bargaining process is particularly evident. Cabinet ministers must frequently trade their support on one issue for the support of a colleague on another, and federal–provincial conferences tend to be the arenas for a great deal of inter-governmental bargaining. Thus, while the structures for priority determination tend to look somewhat different at various levels within the political system, there do tend to be underlying similarities of process which shape the nature of priority determination.

Before leaving the subject of priority determination, there are two particularly important points which need to be emphasized, especially since they draw attention to dangers and problems in the Canadian political system. The less important of these is the problem of blockages caused by breakdown in the bargaining process among bureaucratic agencies. These blockages are caused by the normal desire of departments or agencies to expand, and the necessity—in view of the scarcity of resources—of doing so partially at the expense of other departments and agencies. Blockages developed in this way introduce major inefficiencies into priority determination.

There is, however, a larger problem revolving around the establishment of *new* priorities for Canada. In the end, such priorities are normally set by political people. No matter how important the bureaucracy may be in priority determination, the final gate-keepers are still the cabinet ministers. Their motivation is, at least partially, to get votes for what is being done. Thus, the determination of new priorities may be largely induced by *immediate* demands, for only if a politician is acting directly in response to a demand is he likely to get much immediate recognition for his actions. No one gets much political credit for planning ahead and thus solving a problem if the problem has not yet become serious enough to be perceived by the public. Hence, political systems often tend to respond to crises rather than to anticipate them in advance. Those who must formulate new policies are often thrust into the middle of a problem with no time to even attempt to develop long-range strategy, rational goals, or activities and processes which will get them to those goals.

This analysis, however, cannot be taken too far, for a politician has to do two things to keep himself in power. He must, of course win elections, but at an even more fundamental level, he must maintain support for the system of government within which he works. A regime which is constantly faced with crises may eventually lose public support and collapse. Therefore, in addition to responding to demand inputs, a cabinet must plan ahead to some extent in order to avoid critical crises, and to avoid giving the appearance of merely stumbling from one crisis to another.

15
Federalism and the Policy Process: Intergovernmental Priorities

Having concluded that priority determination is a complex process of political and bureaucratic bargaining, occuring not only among competing agencies within government but also between government and various extra-governmental actors, it is now necessary to escalate our analysis to the level of *intergovernmental* relations. We have seen in Chapters 7 and 8 that the responsibility for policy making in Canada is distributed among the various provinces and the federal government, each of which is sovereign in its own jursidictional sphere and each of which possesses at least some of the financial resources necessary for carrying into effect its own policies. While the problem of interjurisdictional conflict has long been recognized by academics and practitioners alike, it is perhaps because of the complexity of the problem that only recently we have begun to probe the subject in depth through the research device of the case study.[1] It is the intention of this chapter to attempt to an overview of intergovernmental relations in Canada and to attempt some generalizations about the impact of divided jurisdiction on the policy process.[2]

THE PROBLEM: INTERJURISDICTIONAL POLICY COORDINATION

That there is a need for intergovernmental coordination in Canada is not difficult to establish. The very existence of a federal system is predicated on the existence of regional diversity. The cultural and economic variance among the regions of our federation produces wide differences in

[1]See especially: Simeon, R., *Federal Provincial Diplomacy*, (University of Toronto Press, Toronto, 1971); S. Dupré, *et al.*, *Federalism and Policy Development*, (University of Toronto Press, 1974).
[2]The influence of the writings of Donald Smiley on our basic approach to Canadian federalism will quickly become obvious to the reader. However, since his influence has been so broad it is easier to acknowledge our debt in a single comprehensive footnote: Of the many works by Professor Smiley, see especially: *Canada in Question: Federalism in the Seventies*, (McGraw–Hill Ryerson, Toronto, 1972); *Conditional Grants and Canadian Federalism*, (Canadian Tax Foundation, Toronto, 1963); *The Canadian Political Nationality*, (Methuen, Toronto, 1967); "The Two

policy priorities not only among the provinces, but between the provinces and the federation as a whole. If all policy issues docilely conformed to the rigid jurisdictional boundaries established by the BNA Act and its judicial interpreters, the conflicting priorities of the various governments in Canada would not be a serious problem. However, there are, in fact, very few subject areas of public policy today which do not in some way fall into the jurisdictional bailiwicks of more than one government. Thus, if government in Canada is to meet the problems of a modern society with policies which are both appropriate and effective, there must be coordination of the efforts of eleven governments. Such coordination of federal and provincial policies can only be achieved if there is agreement on basic social goals, and a willingness to seek, through compromise, some mutually acceptable policy priorities which will maximize the achievement of those goals. The agreement on basic goals is reflected in our political culture—such a value consensus is either already present, or there is nothing that can be done about it. The necessary compromises on governmental priorities, however, can be achieved only through a process of intergovernmental bargaining.

But interjurisdictional bargaining is substantially different from interdepartmental bargaining for the simple reason that the latter occurs among legally *subordinate* agencies. While the *de facto* decision-making power usually rests within the complex maze of interdepartmental coordination, any "logjams" that might crop up in the negotiations can ultimately be settled by cabinet-level intervention. This not only encourages the bureaucrats to compromise in the interest of avoiding an imposed settlement which might please nobody, but it also means that stalemates will not be permitted to stand in the way of needed action to solve pressing problems. While we cannot underestimate the primacy of the bureaucratic-level bargaining process, in the final analysis, hierarchical processes of control do exist and these can be utilized where interdepartmental bargaining has broken down.

By contrast to interdepartmental bargaining within a single government, intergovernmental bargaining occurs between legally equal, and sovereign entities. There is no superior authority which is empowered to intervene and force a settlement when the negotiations have broken down. The judicial system can to some extent play the role of arbitrator in intergovernmental disputes, but only if the stalemate involves jurisdictional issues, and then only if the courts are asked to do so. As was seen in Chapter 6, the Canadian judiciary cannot initiate litigation; it can act only when legal action is initiated by parties to a real dispute, or when a government "refers" a piece of legislation for judicial opinion.

Thus in the arena of federal–provincial relations, the basic sociopolitical medium of control known as hierarchy is absent, and in most cases,

Themes of Canadian Federalism", *Canadian Journal of Economics and Political Science*, Vol. 31, no. 1, 1965; "Federalism and the Public Policy Process", and "Cooperative Federalism: An Evaluation", in J.P. Meekison (ed.), *Canadian Federalism: Myth or Reality*, (Methuen, Toronto, 1971); and "Public Administration and Canadian Federalism", *Canadian Public Administration*, Vol. VII, no. 3, 1964, pp. 371–388.

intergovernmental conflict can be resolved only through a combination of good will, a natural value consensus, and an active process of self-interested "horse trading". The federal–provincial dimension of policymaking is therefore a "purer" form of bargaining than either the process of interdepartmental bargaining which occurs within a single government, or the process of intergroup and group–system bargaining which was discussed in Chapter 12.

THE EVOLUTION OF INTERJURISDICTIONAL COORDINATION

In the earliest days of the federation, the dominant medium of federal–provincial coordination was the political and bureaucratic hegemony of the Dominion rather than any true process of bargaining. Despite the anti-federal sentiments in the Maritimes, the leadership of the federal government in matters of public policy was virtually unchallenged by the then confused and demoralized provinces. This is likely a partial reflection of the ultimate "capture" by the Dominion of the most prominent political figures of the colonial era, in the 1860s and 1870s. Canadian politicians expected that the major functions of government would be performed by the Dominion, and for a brief time the provincial politicians were either convinced as well, or too timid and insecure to complain. While this "quasi-hierarchical" process of coordination never became firmly established, an analogous situation does occur even today when the War Measures Act is proclaimed; during such times, the federal distribution of powers is effectively suspended and the federal government can achieve the necessary policy coordination by fiat. Needless to say, this is rare and need be considered only in passing.

It did not take long for the provinces to begin to assert their sovereign right to establish their own priorities in public policy. They quickly matured during the 1870s and 1880s and became capable of recruiting committed and capable politicians and public servants. The provinces very rapidly acquired the confidence and the political legitimacy to challenge the policy priorities of the federal government when those touched upon matters within the legislative jurisdiction of the provinces. The dominant mechanism of interjurisdictional coordination during this period of classical federalism was the arbitration of jurisdictional disputes by the judiciary. In fact, it can be argued that this period was characterized by an almost total lack of interest in coordination. Both the federal government and the provinces seemed willing to presume that all matters of concern to policy makers could be parcelled out "once and for all" to one or other of the various governments in Canada, and that any apparent overlap in jurisdiction was simply a cue to ask the courts to refine their interpretations with a new pronouncement.

That this combative attitude to federal–provincial relations continued well into the twentieth century was due to the essentially uncomplicated nature of the issues facing the policy makers of the day. That the sovereign governments in Canada had different policy priorities was beyond question, but the kinds of policy alternatives being considered likely lent themselves more readily to being introduced and administered unilaterally, by either the federal government or one of the provinces.

While the settlement of jurisdictional disputes through judicial arbitration occurs even today, it is used somewhat less now than it was in the first fifty years of the federation. The demise of this mode of conflict resolution in Canada was precipitated in large part by social and economic forces. In the first place, where power to make policy had once depended primarily upon the constitutional jurisdiction to do so, the expanding scope and the complexity of the problems facing government in the twenties and thirties dictated that the costs of implementing the programs would become an even more serious constraint. Often it was the case that the provinces, while possessing the full jurisdiction to initiate policies, lacked the money to finish the job. The federal government, on the other hand, seemed to possess the necessary resources, but all too often it lacked the jurisdiction.

The second factor precipitating the decline of the combative style of federal–provincial relations was the untidyness of contemporary problems. Policy makers began to recognize that most issues facing them were interrelated, and that it was impossible for a single level of government to produce a policy which would deal comprehensively with major social problems which crossed jurisdictional boundaries. It was a combination of the growing financial crisis facing the provinces and the realization that one government acting alone lacked the full jurisdiction to deal adequately with most contemporary policy matters which led to the adoption of a coordinative mechanism based on true interjurisdictional bargaining.

Through the thirties, the mood of federal–provincial relations remained basically combative; however, the desperate circumstances of the period forced genuine federal–provincial coordination. Differences in priorities among the various governments were resolved through the negotiation of piecemeal agreements to meet specific problems. The emphasis was on specific problem solving and not on the consummation of a new style of federalism. The attitude was that federal–provincial cooperation and the coordination of federal and provincial programs were only necessary evils, and the most common policy manifestations of these bargains were shared-cost programs or federal conditional grants to the nearly bankrupt provinces. While not a highly integrated system of conflict resolution, the piecemeal coordinative efforts of the thirties flowed from a genuine bargaining situation; the bargaining "capital" (or "currency") used in the negotiations was jurisdiction and tax revenues. The provinces, for the most part, could promise to implement necessary social legislation which met federally established standards, in return for which the federal government would pay all or a percentage of the operating costs of the programs. While naturally some provinces were financially better off than others and hence could afford to "hold out" for better offers from the "feds", by and large, because the provinces possessed equal jurisdictional clout, all of nine could take an active part in periodic negotiations.

But the process of Canadian federalism changed somewhat during the war years. At the termination of hostilities the provinces were resigned to the fact that for a while at least the federal government would be in the driver's seat; having provided both substantive and psychic leadership during the war, the federal government would continue to assume that role in the public eye for the period of postwar reconstruction. The federal government maintained some initiative in policymaking into the 50s setting many of the priorities for the provinces through the traditional instrument of conditional grants and subsidies which the provinces could not politically affort to reject. The provincial role in the meantime was to act as a brake on the activities of Ottawa.

However, as the war became merely tragic history, and as the Canadian economy continued to grow despite minor setbacks, the federal government began to fade in the eyes of the public as the government that necessarily could and should set our political goals. The initiative began to shift again to the provinces, as the public focus and public expectations turned to welfare programs and highway construction, both of which lie in provincial spheres of jurisdiction. Also, towards the end of this period, Quebec was involved in what has loosely been referred to as the "Quiet Revolution", with the result that the erstwhile passive and defensive nationalism that has characterized the province's posture towards federalism became an aggressive and assertive nationalism. The government of the Province of Quebec began to demand a sufficient share of the tax dollar to be economically *maître chez lui* and to run its own programs, instead of merely sharing the cost and administrative responsibility for those which were federally sponsored. Taking the lead from Quebec, the other provinces also began to assert themselves, reflecting the new confidence inspired by an economic and administrative "coming of age" and a patent dissatisfaction with "the inherent paternalism of the grant-in-aid device".

But the rejuvenated political muscles of the provinces did not precipitate a return to the federalism of the thirties. Not only had the mood of federal–provincial relations become more "cooperative" and less combative, but the interjurisdictional bargaining ceased to be purely piecemeal and problem-oriented. There was by now a tendency to seek more completely integrated programs such as the comprehensive tax-sharing system. Moreover, the provinces were growing very important with respect to their contributions to and effects on the Canadian economy as a whole, and it was becoming clear that any meaningful control over economic fluctuations would have to be exercised through joint federal and provincial action. An example of this is the effort to stem the tide of inflation in Canada through a policy of fiscal restraint. In order to regulate the Canadian economy, it is no longer sufficient for the federal government to undertake an austerity program or to grant tax incentives to certain industries. Unilateral action by the federal government will only make a "dent" in the economic status quo; the provinces themselves are in a position to strongly affect the working of the economy through fiscal measures that are constitutionally within their exclusive jurisdiction. The regulation of the Canadian economy, which has traditionally been considered one of the prerogatives of the central government, must now be achieved through federal–provincial cooperation. Thus, where cooperative federalism was characterized at one time by the federal government's sharing the responsibility for provincial matters with the provinces, the tables have been turned, and cooperative federalism today includes the additional sharing of federal matters with the provinces.

As intergovernmental policy coordination became more holistic in its focus, the bargaining process became a regular, if not constant, activity for the eleven governments. It is obvious that this would tax the resources of the smaller provinces more than those of the big ones, but the introduction of unconditional federal subsidies for the poorer provinces in the form of equalization grants helped to cover some of the administrative costs of maintaining constant intergovernmental liaison. Despite the new administrative burdens of cooperative federalism, therefore, possession of the basic bargaining capital of jurisdiction over social welfare permitted all of the provinces to participate actively in the negotiations. Coordination was ultimately achieved where it was necessary to integrate federal and provincial programs, and mutual compromise in the interest of solving Canada's problems was made easier by the basic mood of cooperation. However, before moving to a consideration of the current trends in cooperative federalism in Canada, it is necessary to describe the institutional devices which have evolved to facilitate the almost constant process of interjurisdictional bargaining.

THE STRUCTURES OF INTERJURISDICTIONAL COORDINATION

In the early years of federal–provincial relations, meetings of federal and provincial officials occured in an *ad hoc* manner, and at fairly senior levels in the governmental hierarchies. Meetings of the Premiers and the Prime Minister would be called at irregular intervals, usually at the initiative of the federal government, to discuss specific problems of concern to all jurisdictions. In recent times however, these conferences have become institutionalized to the extent that they now meet on a fairly regular basis and include bureaucratic as well as political decision makers. While *ad hoc* meetings still occur, the necessity for such informal talks is reduced by the existence of many formal bodies which meet at least annually if not more often.

In an article published in 1965, Edgar Gallant (then a Deputy Secretary to the Cabinet remarked that "...the number of [federal–provincial] conferences and committees doubled over eight years."[3] In absolute terms the number of such committees had risen from 64 in 1957 to 125 in 1965, which by most standards is indeed a remarkable rate of growth. However, based on information sifted from an unedited and as yet unpublished *Inventory of Federal Provincial Committees* (2 vols.), compiled by the PCO in 1972, the number of interjurisdictional institu-

¹E. Gallant, "The Machinery of Federal Provincial Relations", *C.P.A.*, December, 1965, p. 515.

tions in existence today can fairly safely be established at more than 400.[4] It is safe to conclude even from the imperfect data available to us that more is happening in the federal–provincial arena every day, although one could probably have made such an assertion without any numerical information about interjurisdictional committees. What is more interesting than numbers, however, is the distribution of these institutions among various policy areas and governmental decision-making levels, and their internal structure.

The Distribution of Interjurisdictional Bodies by Policy Area Because the inventory which is the source of these data was compiled from submissions by federal departments listing their own interjurisdictional affiliations, it is possible to make some rough generalizations as to the distribution of these bodies among broad policy areas. All federal–provincial committees can likely be categorized in this manner with the exception of the Plenary first minister's conference which concerns itself with macro-priority determination in all policy areas of concern to both the federal government and the provinces.

TABLE 15-1: DISTRIBUTION OF INTER-JURISDICTIONAL BODIES BY POLICY AREA

Portfolio	Number	Percentage
Environment	117	24.27
Health and Welfare	90	18.67
Indian Affairs and Northern Development	43	8.92
Regional Economic Expansion	39	8.09
Transport and Immigration	36	7.46
Manpower	32	6.63
Agriculture	26	5.39
Statistics	24	4.97
Others	75	15.60
Totals	482	100.00

As indicated by Table 15-1, the largest number of committees is to be found in the policy areas of the environment and health and welfare. The reasons for this concentration of federal–provincial institutions in these two broad areas is related in part to the political relevance of such is-

[4]The inventory lists about 400 committees, but there is considerable duplication in the list owing to the fact that committees attended by more than one federal department were sometimes listed twice. On the other hand, there are many subcommittees which went completely unlisted, so that while no exact figures can be stated, the general trends indicated by this inventory can still be very helpful in making some generalizations about the nature of such committees in Canada.

sues in contemporary Canadian society, and related in part to the degree of jurisdictional "untidiness", or overlap which characterizes the fields. The corollary of the latter point, that where the jurisdiction is clear and settled there will be less intergovernmental contact, is, however, only partly true. In fact, where the matter is clearly within the legislative juris-diction of the federal government such as Veterans Affairs, or National Defence, it holds true that there is little federal–provincial interaction. On the other hand, in areas such as housing, highways, education and urban affairs, which are fairly clearly provincial matters, it is not unusual to see a number of interjurisdictional bodies in existence. Thus, it would not seem incautious to hypothesize that the federal government's "spending power"[5] combined with its relative wealth gives it a potential bargaining lever even in policy areas totally within the jurisdiction of the provinces. The bargaining process which is at the root of cooperative federalism is thus perhaps more one-sided than it might appear at first glance.

The Distribution of Interjurisdictional Bodies by Decision-Making Level
Another important dimension in the analysis of interjurisdictional institutions is the decision-making level of government at which they operate. The level is determined first by whether the person-nel on the committee are political or bureaucratic, and second, if they are bureaucrats, by their organizational "rank" or position in a governmental hierarchy. For clarity and ease of discussion we have defined four decision-making levels at which interjurisdictional committees operate in Canada: the *political*, the *senior bureaucratic* (including Deputy ministers and Assistant Deputy Ministers), the *technical* or professional, and the *operational*. It must be noted that operational and technical committees (while functionally quite distinct) may in fact include personnel at approximately the same level or rank. The former tend to be involved directly in the implementa-tion of joint federal–provincial programs, while the latter tend to act more as policy-analysis and research groups. Finally, in attempting to distin-guish between operational and technical committees, we will discover, in fact, that implementation and policy advice frequently flow from the same committee.

The actual distribution of committees among these four decision-making levels in Canada is uneven. For the most part, there will be but one political-level committee in each policy area, composed of appropriate federal and provincial cabinet ministers. On the other hand, more than two-thirds of the total committees in any given policy area will be at the technical and operational levels. In the most active policy area, the envi-ronment, in fact almost three quarters of the interjurisdictional committees are at these levels. One can thus conclude that the most common form of federal–provincial interaction occurs below the ministerial level meetings which we read about in the papers.

The problem with analysing federal–provincial committees in the

[5]Simply, the power of the federal government to spend money on any matter it chooses, provided it does not pass legislation which is *ultra vires*.

context of their numerical distribution by decision-making level is that this does not take into account comparative measures of their impact on policy outputs. For instance, perhaps the most important interjurisdictional committee in operation in Canada today (with the possible exception of the First Ministers' Conference) is the Continuing Committee on Fiscal and Economic Matters. This is a senior bureaucratic-level committee composed mainly of the Deputy Ministers of Finance or the Deputy Provincial Treasurers. Its responsibility is to provide technical support for the Conference of the Ministers of Finance and, to a large extent, for the Conference of the First Ministers. The fact that this body meets more frequently than its political-level "parent" committees, the fact that it is composed of highly skilled professionals in key administrative roles, and the fact that the committee membership is more constant than that of the political-level bodies, mean that this committee is in a position of great potential influence over the country's broad fiscal priorities.

The Distribution of Interjurisdictional Committees by Inclusiveness

Federal–provincial committees can also be classified according to the number of governments included. Because of the amount of attention paid to the political-level conferences by the media, one might get the impression that interjurisdictional committees are for the most part "omnilateral", or composed of representatives of all eleven governments. This is far from the case, for in fact, far more than half of the bodies listed in the PCO inventory are "bilateral", composed of representatives of the federal government and one province only. Less exclusive than the bilateral committees, and yet more inclusive than the omnilateral committees, are the multilateral committees composed of the federal government and some but not all of the provinces. In most policy areas, multilateral committees are more numerous than the omnilateral ones and less numerous than the bilateral ones. A major exception to the general rule about the predominance of bilateral committees is in the area of finance and fiscal relations where almost all of the active committees are omnilateral. Regional Economic Expansion offers the opposite extreme where almost all of the committees are bilateral.

The overall distribution of interjurisdictional committees by decision-making level and by inclusiveness is illustrated graphically (but not quantitatively) in Table 15-2 with examples where appropriate. As illustrated by this chart, the political-level committees tend to be omnilateral almost exclusively. The reason for this is three-fold: first the ministers are less likely than their bureaucratic and technical staff to be able to deal with the "nitty gritty" type of bargaining that often occurs at the bilateral level; second, it is at the political level that the final agreement on priorities affecting the federation as a whole must be agreed upon—perhaps the political level meetings are only confirming agreements hacked out by lower-level officials, but formal agreement must ultimately come at the ministerial level; and finally, the Ministers at the federal level tend to be too busy to devote the time needed to haggle individually with the provinces. They prefer to meet only after some general agreement has been worked out at lower levels through bilateral and multilateral talks.

TABLE 15-2: INCLUSIVENESS OF COMMITTEES

Decision-making Level of Committees	Omnilateral	Multilateral	Bilateral
Technical and Operational	Few—e.g., Some technical level financial committees	Some—e.g., Prairie Provinces Water Board, Atlantic Tidal Power Programming Board	Most—e.g., Coordinating Committee on Northern Ontario Water Resources
Senior Bureaucratic	Most—e.g., Continuing Committee on Fiscal and Economic Matters	Some—e.g., Federal–Provincial Atlantic Fisheries Conference	Few—e.g., Joint Planning Committees of DREE, Consultative Committees under Canada Water Act
Political	Most—e.g., Plenary Conference of First Ministers, Conference of Ministers of Finance	Very Few—e.g., Forestry Ministers' Conference, (because PEI has very little forestry)	None—Ministers are too busy for the most part —some *ad hoc* meetings

By contrast, almost all of the technical and operational level committees are either bilateral or multilateral. Some of the technical level committees in the area of finance, in fact, involve representatives of all of the provinces and the federal government, but for the most part the role of the technical people is more specific—not only in terms of subject matter but in terms of geography as well.

Structural Variations Up until now we have spoken only of federal–provincial committees. While such committees make up by far the largest percentage of interjurisdictional bodies in Canada, it must be pointed out that there are other organizational forms. The interprovincial committees are bodies which exclude the federal government, although in most cases the "feds" are permitted to send an observer.

As with the federal–provincial bodies, the interprovincial ones can be classified as omnilateral, (including all provinces), multilateral, or bilateral, (including two provinces). They also vary as to the decision-making level in the same way that the federal–provincial committees do, and for the most part the generalizations about the distribution of such bodies by level and inclusiveness apply to interprovincial arena as well. While it has been suggested that some political-level multilateral interprovincial committees—such as the Council of the Maritime Premiers and the Prairie Provinces Economic Council—are "proto-coalitions" which will ultimately strengthen the federal–provincial bargaining power of individual regions, there has been little hard evidence that this trend is developing. For the most part, the provinces will squabble among themselves as much as or more than they currently do with the federal government, and moreover, informal and *ad hoc* collusion among groups of provinces tends to be a better way of maximizing the provincial bargaining position on any particular issue.

A third possible structural variation in intergovernmental bodies is the "Tri-Level Conference". This type of committee features representatives not only of the federal government and the provinces, but of municipalities as well. While the federal government has very little constitutional authority in the area of urban affairs, its vast financial resources and its access to the multitude of experts in federal agencies such as the Ministry of Urban Affairs, ensure that there will inevitably be a federal presence in policy decisions affecting the cities. The provinces are very jealous of their primacy in the urban area but they have agreed to permit the federal government to invest its money in urban projects which have the joint approval of the provinces and the municipalities concerned. Such federal contributions to municipal development are negotiated in conferences where all three governments are represented, but where the municipal officials attend formally as part of the provincial delegation. While it is still difficult to assess the impact of tri-level conferences on intergovernmental relations in Canada, it seems fairly certain, given the growing importance of urban problems as a policy concern, that this institutional form will become more common.

Another organizational form often included in compilations of intergovernmental institutions, is the *federal advisory council*. While organizations of this sort are formally unilateral, being established under federal statute to advise a federal minister, and usually located within the organizational labyrinth of a federal department, they often feature representatives from provincial governments. Edgar Gallant points out that "their composition, with representation from all provincial governments, is such that they do, in effect, function as federal–provincial committees to a large extent. . . ."[6] Gallant, however, goes on to cite examples of these advisory committees, most of which seem to have disappeared since his article was first published in 1965. On the basis of this admittedly flimsy evidence of the attrition of such federal advisory councils, and with the knowledge that "true" federal–provincial committees have proliferated in the same period of time, it seems reasonable to hypothesize that the unilateral advisory council is declining in relative importance in federal–provincial relations.

While up until now our focus has been upon interjurisdictional co-ordinative bodies which are purely governmental in composition, we must note that there are some committees which operate in the intergovernmental arena but which have non-governmental members as well. Perhaps the best example of this genre of interjurisdictional body is the *Green River Work Committee* which is composed of representatives of the federal government, the province of New Brunswick and the Fraser Lumber Company; similarly, subcommittees of the Atlantic Fisheries Committee which deal with sport fish are composed of relevant governmental representatives as well as local anglers' associations and commercial fishermen. While this "mixed composition" type of committee is not yet common, it could become more conventional with increasing emphasis on public participation. There are advantages to such organizational forms. On one hand, intergovernmental bargaining must occur with the public looking on, thus "keeping government honest". On the other hand, by including members of the public in the early stages of policy development, policy ideas can be "presold" or legitimized before they enter the political arena through cooptation of ordinary citizens.

Support Staff: Intergovernmental Bureaucracy While we have indicated that interjurisdictional coordination has become institutionalized and less *ad hoc* than it once was, the same is not true of the support staff for the committees. Generally the provision of secretariat services to intergovernmental committees even today is still *ad hoc*, worked out informally by the members of the committee. The most common arrangement seems to be for the necessary support staff to be provided by the government whose representative chairs the particular committee. This means, in effect, that federal departments often provide support services for federal–provincial committees for the simple reason that it is the federal government which has the financial and manpower resources to be able to afford it. In the case of interprovincial committees, the secretariat is normally part-time, composed of temporarily seconded officials of the government which chairs the meetings. As the chairmanship of interprovin-

[6]Gallant. *op. cit.*, p. 515.

cial committees often rotates, this means that the secretariat to the committee is located in a different provincial capital in each year.

While permanent support staff is the exception rather than the rule for interjurisdictional committees in Canada, there are significant exceptions, and the current trend is if anything away from *ad hoc* or rotating secretariats. The commonest form of permanent secretariat is a staff paid by and located in Ottawa. This is the case with the important Continuing Committee on Fiscal and Economic Matters whose secretariat is a division of the Department of Finance, and with the First Ministers' Plenary Conference, whose secretariat is provided within the PCO.

The strengths of permanent secretariats are that they provide continuity and a level of expert advice which the committee could not achieve with rotating secondments from year to year. However, the great potential weakness of this organizational form is obviously that one government will come to dominate the setting of committee agenda, the briefing of conferees, and to an extent, the conduct of the meetings themselves. While the provincial members have the opportunity to bring their own advisors to meetings, some smaller provinces can either ill afford the expense or do not have expert advisors in the same numbers and quality as the "feds". In addition to the fairly obvious advantage to the federal government of having the committee "on its payroll", the legitimacy of the secretariat may be doubted by provincial officials who, quite rightly, come to feel that the support staff is "in Ottawa's pocket".

An experiment aimed at overcoming the weakness of the federally domiciled style of permanent secretariat in intergovernmental affairs was tried with the Canadian Council of Resource and Environment Ministers (CCREM). This interjurisdictional body has been given the status of a private corporation, although its members and its Board of Directors consist of federal and provincial cabinet ministers. The presidency of the Council rotates annually among the member governments, and the secretariat is permanent, composed of staff who are employees of the corporation but not of any of the member governments. The effectiveness of the CCREM in the ten years from 1963 to 1973 has been related largely to its secretariat which operates as a clearing house for information, as a direct non-governmental link with the public through its publications, and as the administrative and support component of a number of major omnilateral conferences at political, senior bureaucratic and technical levels. Perhaps the greatest strength of this secretariat is that it has not carried the brand of any government; its explicit mandate is to serve all eleven governments equally. The obvious problem of such a body is the difficulty in exercising political control over it. The fact that it is permanent and independent of any single government gives it the potential to become an "intergovernmental bureaucracy" within the federation, analogous, perhaps, to the permanent staff of international organizations. The fear of "losing control" of the secretariat has caused some of the CCREM's member governments to become increasingly suspicious of it. Some of the provincial ministers on the council have come to view the CCREM and particularly its permanent secretariat as dangerous competitors in the process of wooing public support for environmental policy reforms. Consequently, we will likely see a significantly reduced role for the Council and for either a very small permanent staff or an *ad hoc* secretariat. Whatever its ultimate fate, the secretariat of the CCREM is an organizational form which could be used as a prototype for future forays into interjurisdictional coordination.

TRENDS IN CANADIAN FEDERALISM

Executive Federalism: Neo-Centralization As the need for continual federal–provincial consultation and cooperation increases in response to the growing interdependence of all social and economic problems, the institutions of interjurisdictional cooperation which have been described above will grow in terms of their political significance. These bodies will increasingly be entrusted with the responsibility for making policy decisions which affect the allocation of resources in Canada, and it is probable that we will see a continuing decline in the importance of the federal parliament and the provincial legislatures. The critical political decisions will more and more frequently be referred to the federal and provincial representatives who meet at federal–provincial conferences, and there is little to indicate that existing institutions are capable of countering the trend. There is a startling lack of attention paid to federal–provincial relations in either parliament or the provincial legislatures. There is virtually no contract between legislators of the eleven senior governments, and the party system itself has failed as an alternative mechanism of interjurisdictional coordination. While it could be suggested that the representatives at intergovernmental conferences continue to feel a responsibility to their home governments, that responsibility is not direct. The legislature "back home" does not exercise day-to-day control on its delegates; rather, it functions as an "electoral college" which goes no further than making the initial choice of who will represent the government in the particular interjurisdictional arena.

The irony of this trend is that in a period when many would see the increased power and automony of the provinces as a *decentralizing* or centrifugal force, "executive federalism"[7] may, in fact, be far more centralized than a federal system where the central government sets the broad national goals, and perhaps even more centralized than a unitary system. For where the key priority decisions are made by committees of eleven men at federal–provincial conferences, democratic control is certainly more difficult than in a system where such decisions are approved by a parliament of 264 men from all parts of Canada and by provincial legislatures comprising hundreds more. It may be that we are entering a period of *neo-centralization* where any apparent decentralization in the federal system may be offset by more fundamental centripetal tendencies in the political system as a whole.

[7]See Smiley, *Canada in Question, op. cit.*, p. 56.

Bureaucratic Federalism As we have seen, executive federalism may have helped to precipitate a new trend towards centralization in the Canadian system. Moreover, in earlier chapters, we have spoken of the general tendency for policy making to depend upon technical inputs from various non-elected officers of government residing in the federal and provincial bureaucracies. When these two trends are viewed in light of the increasing number of interjurisdictional committees operating at the senior bureaucratic, technical and operational levels of government, one cannot avoid the conclusion that it is bureaucratic and not political executives who dominate "executive federalism".

Undoubtedly, the non-elected personnel play an increasingly dominant role in interjurisdictional coordination at the stages of policy *formulation* and *implementation*. However, it is more difficult to maintain that bureaucratic committees dominate interjurisdictional *priority* determination, for the policies under consideration must ultimately be justified to eleven electorates by the Ministers concerned. Nevertheless, given that there is more constant interaction among the non-elected officials, and given that politically successful programs will often be contingent upon technical feasibility, it is likely that ideas of coordination will often be generated by senior bureaucratic and technical committees and adopted as priority items by the ministerial committees. In the extreme, this could mean that the first ministers' conferences, and ministerial conferences might become purely symbolic in significance. It is possible that in future our political leaders will spend their time at conferences either posturing for the TV cameras or mouthing the carefully prepared "positions" of their high-priced "top hands" who, as always, remain faithfully and discreetly off camera. While it is impossible to conclusively show that this tendency is a significant one, we do know from even the most casual observation that little real bargaining goes on in the public portions of ministerial meetings; to the extent that intergovernmental priorities are determined by the politicians, therefore, the process is *in camera* and not "in front of camera".

We can likely come to the cautious conclusion that *bureaucratic federalism* exists to the extent that the macro-level bargaining positions of the political officials at conferences are often worked out by their bureaucratic advisors, and that any interjurisdictional deals involving the formulation or implementation of joint policies are worked out mainly in bureaucratic, technical or operational bodies. The overall significance of bureaucratic federalism is that intergovernmental coordination is probably improved. In the first place, as the frequency of interaction has increased at the non-elected levels of government, the people involved in the bargaining process actually come to know each other. They often supplement formal exchanges at committee meetings with informal contact through telephone calls and correspondence.[8]

[8]Note that the basic evidence for the hypothesis was uncovered in a series of thirty-four interviews with members of federal–provincial committees from all ten provinces and the federal government which were conducted in the summer of

Secondly, because the personnel involved are not constrained directly by a critical and partisan public back home, the non-elected committees can bargain more honestly. Bureaucrats may be able to assume a problem-orientation partly because they do not have to be as concerned as the politician with faithfully advocating the interests of a particular region; there is greater freedom for compromise. But a problem-orientation is also more likely because of shared *professional* concerns of the bureaucrats; for instance, if forestry officials are meeting to set up a program for combatting a spruce budworm epidemic, they are usually more concerned with solving the real world problem in forestry than they are with defending provincial priorities. The combination of shared professional interests, personal ties such as friendships which grow through longstanding formal and informal contact, and a non-partisan milieu, thus tends to facilitate coordination at the bureaucratic level. As advisors to the ministers, the bureaucrats can in turn help to ease the more public and political dimension of federal–provincial bargaining, and contribute to an overall environment within which macro-level interjurisdictional compromise and cooperation is possible.

One must be careful, however, not to take these speculations too far. Anything more than the most trivial detail must eventually be at least tacily ratified at the ministerial level, and most ministers are far from being only automatons manipulated by their bureaucratic establishments. Sometimes the right to ministerial control is honoured more in the breach than the observance, but it would be a foolish bureaucrat who ignored his minister's wishes—expressed or implied—on a major policy question.

Bilateral Federalism: "Divide and Conquer" Coupled with the related trends of bureaucratization and neo-centralization is the apparent tendency for intergovernmental relations in Canada to be carried on in bilateral rather than multilateral or omnilateral committees. This tendency towards bilateral committees can be explained in part by the need for federal–provincial coordination in the implementation of many joint programs; a large percentage of the bilateral committees are in fact at the operational level, and are exclusive in their composition simply because the particular program being administered involves only two governments.

However, this tendency towards bilateral rather than multi- or omnilateral interaction may reflect more complex trends in the nature of federal–provincial bargaining. The multilateral meetings, particularly at the ministerial level, do not appear to be particularly effective as forums for intergovernmental bargaining; at the First Ministers' Conference, for instance, it is not uncommon for eleven separate sets of policy priorities to be presented as bargaining "positions". The number of combinations of positions possible as compromise solutions in an eleven-person situation is

1972. While most of the interviewed were in the resources field, it does not seem unlikely that they were fairly typical of the sorts of people involved in interjurisdictional coordinative activities, and in fact, they represented a good mix of senior bureaucrats and technical personnel.

so great that negotiation becomes very difficult. The individuals doing the bargaining have difficulty recognizing all options open to them, let alone choosing the one that maximizes the benefits to their government. The result is that the provincial representatives are often hesitant about making a deal in a multilateral or omnilateral situation for fear of "missing something"; they instead do what is safest, and simply state and restate the position that they started with.

Given the difficulty of bargaining in a highly complex omnilateral conference, and given the evidence of much bilateral interaction in operational and technical committees, one might hypothesize that there is, in fact, a lot of bilateral interaction at the more senior levels as well. This will not be manifested by the existence of many formal or permanent bilateral committees; the ministers and senior bureaucrats are simply too busy to be involved in regular meetings. However, it seems reasonable that informal bilateral meetings between a federal minister and his provincial counterpart may occur frequently to discuss specific policy questions. In such a meeting, with only two governments present, and only two sets of priorities to deal with, bargaining is a much simpler process. Moreover, as such meetings are informal and *ad hoc*, they will not be publicized to any great extent. The "horse-trading" can go on in fairly honest manner, with little need for the governmental representatives to make symbolic representations or to posture for television cameras.

But not only is compromise facilitated through informal bilateral bargaining; it may also be that the federal government can use this type of negotiation to control the bargaining process at omnilateral meetings. On a one-to-one basis, the federal government can usually dominate a bargaining situation, where in a one-to-ten basis the provinces hold sway. By consummating deals in several bilateral situations before going to the multilateral conferences, the federal government may be able to "divide and conquer". The only counter to this trend may result from an increased amount of bilateral interaction among the provinces. By making deals among themselves, the provinces can establish united bargaining positions before facing the "feds" in a bilateral situation; such temporary coalitions may offset the potential domination by the senior government, but to be truly effective, the tactic will have to be used more frequently than it is at present.

Rationalist Federalism In the first part of this chapter we determined that federal–provincial coordination was essentially a process of bargaining. In the *trends* discussed thus far, we have simply presumed that the traditional "capital" goods used for bargaining in the Canadian system have remained unchanged; that the provinces, for the most part, will bargain from their position of *jurisdictional* strength in key policy areas such as welfare and education, and that the federal government will bargain with its large revenues and almost unlimited spending power. It may be however, that the bargaining levers of the federal partners have changed.

A general trend in policy making which we have noted before is the increasing use of *policy planning*. No longer is it considered adequate for policy makers to make decisions about what we should do in future on the basis of what we are doing now. In rejecting this erstwhile acceptable "incremental" mode of setting new policies, the advocates of planning argue that decisions today should be more than linear extensions of past ones. Instead, policy decision should be made on the basis of full knowledge of present public demands, projections identifying future needs, a full awareness of all present policy options, and a careful analysis of the relative costs and benefits of each policy option. The determination of the policies which should be implemented must then be made with a view to maximizing long-range benfits, and minimizing political and financial costs. This approach is normally referred to as *rationalist* (as opposed to *incrementalist*), and rests on two "pillars of analysis"—systems analysis and cost benefit analysis. The former pillar assumes the interrelationship of all policies and posits the necessity to consider all options before coming to a decision; the latter pillar assumes that relative costs and benefits of policy options can be measured quantitatively, and that choices among alternatives should be based on such information. While the success of such techniques in real decision-making situations may be limited, the principles of policy planning have been adopted to some extent by almost all governments in Canada. As evidence of this tendency, it can be pointed out that the federal government and all of the provinces are busy creating "policy analysis" units in their bureaucratic and executive support agencies.

The impact of this new emphasis on policy planning, and that of relationalist policy analysis on interjurisdictional relations are still not clear. However, one apparent change is that the ability to bargain effectively in the intergovernmental arena is linked to whether a government's policy priorities are articulated in rationalist terms. The ability to bargain in this fashion is in turn linked to the number and quality of manpower resources available to the particular government. That the federal government and the wealthier provinces such as Ontario, Alberta, and British Columbia can afford to buy the commitment of high-priced policy planners is beyond question. However, the poorer provinces are less able to pay for sufficient high-priced help and may be reduced to accepting on faith the kinds of policy alternatives articulated by the "have" provinces and the federal government. In this sense, a new lever or "capital" with which to bargain successfully in the interjurisdictional sphere is the possession of expert manpower resources; governments lacking this resource may be functionally disfranchised from taking a full part in federal–provincial relations.

One possible way to offset the tendency in interjurisdictional relations towards a virtually permanent oligarchy of the "have" provinces and the federal government is for the federal government to increase unconditional grants to the poor provinces in absolute rather than per capita terms. Although it is unlikely that the larger provinces would ever accept this measure, it would, if adopted, perhaps increase the financial ability of the "have-not" provinces to hire the necessary manpower. A perhaps more feasible solution (although one which has never been tried) is to establish an intergovernmental secretariat patterned after the secretariat of the

CCREM but composed of planners and policy analysts. This would provide the provinces with access to a bank of experts responsible to all governments equally, and while it would only partially offset the advantage of the bigger governments, it might be a step in the right direction.

This concludes the discussion of possible trends in modern federal–provincial relations in Canada, and also concludes our chapter on federalism and public policy. Much of what has been said in this final section has been speculative and was intended to generate hypotheses about the directions of change in intergovernmental relations, rather than to present timeless truths. All that can be said in conclusion is that Canadian federalism is today, and always has been, in a state of flux; it has evolved from what it was in 1867 to what it is today through constant adaptation to new environmental circumstances. It is today a very tightly integrated network of federal–provincial consultative bodies at various governmental levels. There is a constantly changing relationship among the actors in the federal system, as each of the provinces and the federal government attempt to maximize their bargaining advantages *vis-à-vis* the others. There remains, however, under this coverlet of constant conflict, a willingness to seek agreement, to compromise and to continue to bargain.

16
The Bureaucratic Process and Policy Formulation

Before proceeding further with our analysis of the policy process and the role of the bureaucracy in it, it is necessary—even though we have already used the term often—to say a few words of clarification about *bureaucracy*. Long regarded as a term of contempt, its adjectival form, bureaucratic, has come to be associated with qualities such as inefficiency, "red tape", depersonalization, and slowness of execution. There is, however, a purer use of the term which is derived from the literature of organization theory and which has implications relating only to the objective structural characteristics of a certain type of organization. In this sense, bureaucracy is a purely descriptive rather than a pejorative term. We are here applying the latter connotation of the term, and do not mean to imply inefficiency, red tape, or depersonalization, all of which result, in fact, from perversions of bureaucratic structures.

The classic description of the pure bureaucracy derives from the work of Max Weber, but R.K. Merton has provided us with what is perhaps the most complete brief description:

> . . .there is integrated a series of offices, of hierarchized statuses, in which inhere a number of obligations and privileges closely defined by limited and specific rules. Each of these offices contains an area of imputed competence and responsibility. Authority, the power of control which derives from an acknowledged status, inheres in the office and not in the particular person who performs the official role. Official action ordinarily occurs within the framework of preexisting rules of the organization. The system of prescribed relations between the various offices involves a considerable degree of formality and clearly defined social distance between the occupants of these positions. Formality is manifested by means of a more or less complicated social ritual which symbolizes and supports the "pecking order" of the various offices. Such formality, which is integrated with the distribution of authority within the system, serves to minimize friction by largely restricting (official) contact to modes which are previously defined by the rules of the organization. Ready calculability of others' behaviour and a stable set of mutual expectations is thus built up. Moreover, formality facilitates the interaction of the occupants of offices despite their (possibly hostile) private attitudes toward one another. In this way, the subordinate is protected from the arbitrary action of his superior, since the actions of both are constrained by a mutually recognized set of rules. Specific pro-

cedural devices foster objectivity and restrain the "quick passage of impulse into action."[1]

Thus, a bureaucracy is simply a certain kind of organization. While bureaucracy can be used to apply to governmental and non-governmental organizations alike, in common usage in the discipline of political science the term refers specifically to the *public service* or to the *administrative branch* of government. The focus of this chapter is on the role of the non-elective officials of government, the bureaucrats, who work within both the Canadian Public Service and the public services of the various provinces, municipalities and territorial governments.

We will see that Canadian bureaucratic structures, like their counterparts elsewhere in the world, do not perfectly mirror the ideal type as set out in the statements of Weber and Merton. There is considerably more flexibility in bureaucratic structures than is implied in the classical descriptions of bureaucracy. This is a desireable attribute of real-world bureaucracies since it enables them to react more effectively to the multifaceted strains imposed on them by the modern world. However, the "ideal-type" presented here provides us with a bench-mark against which to measure real bureaucracies and is, as a first approximation, still a reliable guide to much of the internal structure of the Canadian Public Service. We will return to a more detailed and more realistic description of bureaucratic structures after we have examined the functions of the Canadian bureaucracy.

THE FUNCTIONS OF THE CANADIAN BUREAUCRACY

The public service and, more specifically, public servants were once viewed as mere instruments to be used by the politicians for carrying out or implementing public policy. The bureaucracy was viewed as a mere passive servant of political masters, performing no decision making of its own and incapable of independent influence in the political process. More recently, however, students of politics and administration have come to the realization that the bureaucracy is indeed involved in much more than the simple application of laws to specific cases. A description of its many functions in present-day Canadian government follows.

The Policy Function That the bureaucracy in Canada has a significant and positive role in the policy process is now accepted as fact. This role is based largely on the concentration of expertise within the public service, making the bureaucracy the major source of information concerning the technical and financial feasibility of policy alternatives faced by the politicians. Control over such information is the critical source of

[1]R.K. Merton, "Bureaucratic Structure and Personality", *Social Forces*, 18(1940), 561–568. Weber's classic statement is in H.H. Gerth and C. Wright Mills (eds.), From *Max Weber: Essays in Sociology*, (Oxford University Press, New York, 1946), pp. 196–244.

bureaucratic policy influence; and, as the complexity of our society increases, the reliance of political decision makers on bureaucratic specialists tends to increase commensurately.

It has already been mentioned that the bureaucracy performs important functions as an initiator of policy and a channel of policy initiation to be used by other institutions in the political system. Beyond this first-stage policy role, the bureaucracy becomes more and more deeply involved in the business of policy making. When priorities are being established, bureaucratic institutions such as the Treasury Board Secretariat and the Department of Finance have a great deal of control over policy planning because of their expertise in the area of public finance. It is in this particular area that the increasing application of the rationalist principles of Planning Programming Budgeting tends to regularize, and perhaps to further aggrandize the position of the bureaucrat in the Canadian policy process. The general adoption of this system of budgeting may tend to further enhance the priority-setting role of some agencies of the Canadian bureaucracy.

Federal–provincial committees at the bureaucratic level also play an important role in the setting of policy priorities in Canada. Specifically, these intergovernmental bodies are usually concerned with coordination of federal–provincial programs; but, for example in the process of researching the problems of fiscal relations, the Coordinating Committee on Fiscal and Economic Matters has great influence on the spending priorities of both levels of government. The same is true of the Continuing Committee of Federal and Provincial Deputy Ministers of Welfare which, from 1973 to 1975, formed the focal point of a major review and revision of the social security system in Canada—a review with major implications for government expenditures for years to come. However, while intergovernmental bureaucratic committees can and do affect the setting of governmental priorities in Canada, their greatest impact is felt at the formulation stage of policy making.

As was pointed out in Chapter 1, the bureaucracy is the core institution at the formulation stage of policy making in Canada. Although it is often interdepartmental committees or the cabinet that decides which department will be responsible for policy formulation in a certain area, and although several departments (under the aegis of the interdepartmental committee) look at most major policy decisions, the actual detailed formulation of specific policies is normally accomplished by the individual departments of the public service. Often, through the medium of white (or "coloured") papers, the departments set out the few policy alternatives which are most feasible in technical, administrative, financial, and even political terms. Most departments in very active fields of governmental activity have policy and planning branches or directorates. It is through this constant information gathering and compilation, the preparation of governmental white or coloured papers and memoranda to cabinet, that the Canadian bureaucracy is most effective in influencing public policy.

While policy formulation has been described here as a stage in the policy process which follows priority determination, it is, in fact, often the case that the bureaucracy's formulation activity has begun long before any clear priority has been established. Indeed, the cabinet often finds it impossible to make a clear priority decision in the absence of a good deal of detailed advice on policy formulation. The bureaucratic institutions are ever alert to indicators of future priority decisions, and the officials within the various government departments attempt to anticipate cabinet-level decisions and begin working on policy areas which are likely to be given priority or which they feel should be pushed forward to cabinet. One reason for this anticipatory activity by the institutions of the Canadian bureaucracy is that a department which has already prepared some proposals is more likely to be given the responsibility for policy formulation and ultimate implementation than one which is unprepared. Another reason is that the department may have already been asked to comment on the feasibility of the proposal at the earliest priority stage. And, of course, the department may have played a role in the initiation of the policy in the first place. Thus, bureaucratic involvement at the initiation and priority-determination stages of the process may not only determine which department gets the jobs of formulation and implementation, but may also result in many of the formulation decisions having been made early in the process.

While in terms of time and of the number of people directly involved, policy formulation is not the largest role played by the Canadian bureaucracy, it is certainly the largest *policy* role. And because policy formulation involves greater utilization of technical expertise than do other stages of policy making, it is this function of the bureaucracy which is the most difficult to control. By the time a large team of highly specialized economists has spent seven hours a day for 18 months putting together material such as might be found in a white paper on taxation, it is unlikely that their political "masters" in the cabinet will be able to mount an effective criticism of the detailed substance of their recommendations. To weaken any potential criticism in advance, it is a completely feasible tactic for the team of experts to cook up and include a few "throwaway" items in their proposals. Obvious "red herrings" can be carefully integrated into the policy paper to draw the fire of the opposition, whether it be the parliamentary opposition or potential dissenters in cabinet. Then, after a period of debate, the technical advisors can graciously accede to the wishes of their political critics and excise the troublesome proposals. In this way, it is possible to retain intact the basic structure of a policy option (as recommended by the technical people) while giving the political critics a feeling of efficacy. While the actual use of this tactic is difficult to document and while it is clearly devious on the part of the technical advisors, its use is sometimes apparent in the formulation process—sometimes by the technical experts *vis-à-vis* the cabinet, and sometimes by the cabinet against the political opposition. Perhaps the greatest safeguard against this type of behaviour, particularly when bureaucrats attempt to use it in dealing with the cabinet, is that the technical experts themselves, in various departments, are rarely sufficiently agreed to mount this sort of "attack" on the cabinet's supremacy.

The Output Functions   *Rule Making*   While the policy role of the Canadian bureaucracy may seem to place significant power in the hands of the bureaucrats and technocrats, this power is merely advisory and subject to the ultimate approval of the elected officials of our government. In other words, while the ability of cabinet and parliament to accept or reject the expert advice of the bureaucracy may be limited by the lack of expertise in the elected bodies themselves, the legal power to convert policies to legislative outputs of the political system remains formally superior to the power to tender technical advice. However, in many areas, even the power to directly convert policy to legislative output has been delegated to various administrative agencies of the government of Canada.

The delegation of legislative power to the executive is not a particularly new phenomenon in Canada; for instance, in time of national emergency, Canadian legislation has, for many years, granted very broad powers to the executive to make law by order-in-council. While this delegation of legislative power achieves a "short-circuiting" of the normal procedures of lawmaking by the sovereign parliament, the concerned citizen might take some solace in the fact that the *de facto* executive in this country is the cabinet, which is ultimately responsible to the public. However, two factors must be taken into account when assessing the total affect of such legislation on the governmental process. First, since the cabinet is not an expert body, it must *redelegate* the power to make law by order-in-council to non-elected officials from the bureaucracy, in police forces, and elsewhere. As legislation becomes more technical and more complex, this function of executive lawmaking will tend to rest increasingly with non-elected officials. Second, legislation today requires such detail that the elected officials of the political system do not have time to go much beyond debating the broad principles of the policy either before or after the non-elected officials made their decisions. Hence, the legislation setting up the Canadian Transportation Commission for instance, sets down certain broad objectives, creates the commission and then delegates to it the power to make detailed regulations as to air traffic, etc. To take another example, the post office makes regulations regarding postal rates, contents of packages, the use of the mails, etc., which directly affect our postal privileges and the quality of service we receive. In each case, elected officials may discuss broad policy issues, but they seldom discuss the details of regulations made by bureaucrats pursuant to the legislation. The point is that the power to actually *make* regulations which have the effect of law and which must directly affect the citizens frequently rests with non-elected officials in the bureaucracy, and not with the constitutionally-supreme lawmaker, parliament, or with even the formal executive, the cabinet. A most important bureaucratic function, therefore, is the power to make decisions which themselves constitute legislative outputs of the political system.[2]

Another important rule-making function of the bureaucracy is the

[2]See E.A. Driedger, "Subordinate Legislation," *Canadian Bar Review*, Vol. 38, no. 1, pp. 1–34, (March, 1960). See also: "Delegated Legislation in Canada" in Kernaghan and Willms, *Public Administration in Canada: Selected Readings*, (Methuen, Toronto, 1971), p. 406.

internalized making of regulations regarding the administrative process itself. For instance, an agency such as the Public Service Commission is concerned directly and constantly with problems of staffing. The Public Service Commission was created in the first place precisely to take matters of promotion, recruitment, and discipline out of the hands of the politicians. It was felt that public service appointments should be based not on patronage but rather on the merits of the individual job applicant and the requirements of the position to be filled; the logical way of doing this was to create a central agency that was independent of political control and to give it the power to make regulations necessary for bringing into effect a career public service based on the *merit principle*. Similarly, each department or agency must produce sets of rules outlining internal procedures and practices. The decisions as to what these rules should be are all made directly by administrative officials and are subject to little practical control by politicians. Although it is perhaps difficult to characterize these rules as outputs of the political system, such administrative regulations are very important through their potential effect on the administration side of the administrator-to-public relationship.

Rule Application It has been seen that the Canadian constitution distinguishes between executive and judicial functions. However, under closer scrutiny, one finds that the executive function and the judicial function are broadly similar in that they both require the application of general rules to specific cases. Viewed in this way, the rule-application function of the bureaucracy includes both executive and judicial decision making, and with respect to time, resources and immediate impact on the public, it constitutes the most important function of the Canadian bureaucracy.

In the process of administering the law, it is necessary to employ a great deal of discretion. Laws are stated very generally, and inevitably they do not take into account the infinite number of circumstances in which they might apply. Hence, to use an example from Corry and Hodgetts' *Democratic Government and Politics*, the administration of the Pure Food and Drug Act requires inspectors to make discretionary decisions as to whether permits should be issued or revoked.[3] Obviously, such a decision is not only administrative, but judicial and legislative as well. Indeed, so great is the discretionary power granted to the bureaucrat entrusted with administering the act that the distinction between legislative, executive, and judicial functions becomes illusory. Part of this blurring of the distinctions between the three functions of government occurs because the role of government generally has become positive. Thus, as government moved from a "thou-shalt-not" or punitive orientation to a more positive or preventive orientation, much of the responsibility for applying the law has moved from the judiciary to the administrative branch of government.

Rule application by the bureaucracy, however, involves more than

[3]Corry and Hodgetts, *Democratic Government and Politics*, p. 528. In this and similar cases, the law usually states that the ultimate decision rests with the responsible minister, but in fact the vast majority of cases never reach his notice, so the real power resides in the inspector.

taking purely preventive measures as cited in the example above. Rather, the bureaucracy today is vested with judicial or quasijudicial functions as well, requiring bureaucratic officials to make decisions which have punitive and compensatory effects on individuals. In other words, there are administrative agencies in Canada which function in much the same way as a court except that the members of such administrative tribunals are not judges but bureaucrats. The Canadian Pension Commission and the Canada Labour Relations Board are examples of quasijudicial bodies functioning within the framework of the bureaucracy. These administrative boards are empowered to make decisions which for example, could grant a pension to one man and not to another, or certify one bargaining agent and not another. In making such decisions, which are administrative in form, a board determines rights and privileges of individuals in the same way a court does; and, by establishing procedures for dealing with various types of cases, the same board makes law. An administrative body can thus exercise administrative, judicial, and legislative functions in the course of administrative decision making.

Symbolic Outputs There is a class of governmental outputs which cannot be called legislative, executive, or judicial.[4] More frequently today one can see the political system producing outputs which take the form of information, and the basic agencies for the dissemination of information from the political system are found predominantly within the bureaucracy[5] For example, it is necessary to inform the public of changes in the law. Some years ago, amendments to the Criminal Code made it an offence to drive while one's blood alcohol is in excess of .08 per cent. In order to insure that the public is aware of this new legislation, the Department of Justice publicized the changes widely on radio, TV, and in the newspapers. All new legislation is in fact published in the *Canada Gazette*, and the onus in law is on the individual citizen to find out what the law is and to obey it. However, it is also recognized by the government that a piece of legislation such as the "breathalizer" law is designed to act as a deterrent and will only be effective if everyone is aware of it. Furthermore, laws such as this affect so many people that it pays the government politically to widely publicize the fact that they are in effect.

Information outputs—such as the campaign to inform the public about the "breathalizer" law—are produced by the bureaucracy, possibly at the urging and certainly with the acquiescence of the cabinet. Outputs of such information are purely informative; what they say is, in effect: "Here is a new law. You must, as with all laws, obey it." However, other outputs of information are not so neutral as this one. Consider, for example, campaigns by the Department of Manpower and Immigration to increase the number of summer jobs for students. Here a bureaucratic agency was not stating that there was any law in existence; instead, it was actively campaigning to convince businessmen to hire a certain class of worker. What was implicit in this piece of government advertising is the

---

[4]See Chapter 1 re "symbolic outputs".
[5]See also Chapter 12. There it is pointed out that interest groups also may play an important part in the dissemination of information.

proposition that students should be hired instead of other classes of workers in the society. Perhaps this is not purely the brainchild of a group of public servants in a government department, but rather of some political advisor to the cabinet who feels that university and college students and/or their parents are politically a more important force than are other types of unemployed. That is not really important to our discussion; the point is that somebody has decided that an output of information should be made which appears to be completely neutral and yet which is very definitely favourable to one class of person and not another.

Whether, in the examples cited above, the decision to disseminate information was bureaucratic or political does not matter as much as the fact that the bureaucracy *can* do this almost unilaterally, subject to only the most cursory ministerial supervision. Most government departments publish information in the form of brochures, pamphlets, and even quarterly magazines, all aimed at simply informing a segment of the public; and yet most of these publications impart sets of values and points of view. This is not necessarily a result of public servants consciously attempting to propagandize, but rather it is often simply a function of the nature of information. It is impossible to publish information without some editing; and in the process of editing, the values of the editor are served, either consciously or unconsciously.

Most departments have information services branches[6] and some agencies, such as Statistics Canada, are concerned primarily with the collection, compilation, and publication of information. While the people in these bureaucratic roles likely try very hard to be impartial, they are only human, with biases, prejudices, and misconceptions of reality. Hence, when one reads the section of the *Canada Year Book* that deals with the Government of Canada, it is sometimes difficult to accommodate what is written there with the account given in this and other texts on the same subject; both pieces are likely correct, but the emphasis in each gives different impressions to the reader.[7] Both the authors of this text and the authors of the *Canada Year Book* have biases; the major difference is that we are not an

[6]See Royal Commission on Government Organization, *Report, vol.* 3, (Queen's Printer, Ottawa, 1962), pp. 63–72

[7]See for example, Statistics Canada, *Canada Year Book*, 1973, pp. 69–172. The year book tends to give a picture biased in favour of a more literal interpretation of the constitution, and of the written rules of administrative behaviour, although there has been a considerable improvement in its account of Canadian government in the last three or four years. This book, if anything, leans in the opposite direction. As an example of an even stronger bias in information published by the federal government, see *Canada, 1970*, (subtitled *The Official Handbook of Present Conditions and Recent Progress*,) (Queen's Printer, Ottawa, 1969) which asserts, "The House of Commons is the cornerstone of Canadian political life. It is the instrument through which the will of the Canadian people may be expressed by their elected representatives." p. 77. Like the *Canada Year Book*, subsequent editions have improved greatly in their description of Canadian government, and no statement such as that just cited appears in *Canada 1974*. Judged by this yard-stick, the quality of government publications is improving.

"official" source of information, and hence do not make any pretense of being impartial disseminators of neutral "facts".

The logical extension of the educative function of the Canadian bureaucracy has already occured in the creation of a semi-independent administrative agency known as Information Canada. The role of this agency is to provide information about the policies of the government, and its goal is to create a more informed public which will be subsequently more capable of participating in the policy process. Whether or not it is possible to inform the public to that extent is another question, but what concerns us here is the nature of Information Canada, *per se*. Most critical comment originally zeroed in on the potential for political propaganda from such an agency. Fear was expressed that the government in power would be enabled to promote its own particular programs at the expense of the Canadian taxpayer. This does not seem to have happened. What is virtually unavoidable, however, is that the bureaucrats who are charged with the responsibility for producing information packages will inevitably colour the outputs with their own values. It can be hoped that the values that are pushed will be congruent with those of the society at large; but more important, if the reader recognizes that the potential for bias, intentional or not, is very real, he will be able to evaluate all outputs in a critical light.

Hence, the symbolic educative or informative function of the Canadian bureaucracy is a rapidly expanding and important one. While this type of output is not strictly an allocation, it is, nonetheless, a vital ancillary to the allocation process, for it ensures that citizens know what rules have been made, and it supplies active citizens with information through which they can interact with the political system. The constant output of information from within the bureaucracy will be a beneficial development if the public can avoid being brainwashed by seemingly neutral (but in reality coloured) facts emanating from "impartial" bureaucratic editors. Since most of the public will pay no attention to these outputs, and since those who do will be among the better-educated or more actively concerned citizens, it seems at least plausible to hope that such "brainwashing" will be minimized.

This concludes our discussion of the functions of the Canadian bureaucracy. Far from being the passive instrument of the era of the negative state, the modern bureaucracy has a very active role to play in government. Bureaucratic agencies not only implement law, but they make law; they adjudicate; they make policy; and they control the outflow of masses of information to the general public. It is now necessary to proceed to a discussion of the administrative structures and the organizational forms which have evolved to perform these functions.

THE STRUCTURE OF THE CANADIAN BUREAUCRACY

It has already been explained that the term bureaucracy refers to a kind of organization with certain structural characteristics. We asserted that prime among its characteristics is its large size; most of the other factors of bureaucratic structure have evolved to accommodate the preeminent problem of "bigness." Bureaucratic structures feature a well-developed division of labour whereby the officials occupying roles within the organization perform clearly defined functions. Ideally there is no duplication of effort and no overlapping of roles within a bureaucracy, although this is more difficult to achieve in practice than in the abstract.

Furthermore, it was noted that the bureaucratic role is defined by the office itself and not by the incumbent of the office. This is essential if bureaucratic behaviour is to be predictable in the short run, and if there is to be continuity over time in the performance of the duties of that office. Continuity over time is also facilitated by the keeping of detailed written records of all actions taken by the bureaucratic officers. In this way every decision can be backed up by precedents established in the past, and in turn, itself becomes part of the body of precedents for future decisions. There is no legal rule of precedent in bureaucratic decision making, but the fact is that if someone else has made a certain decision in the past and has "gotten away with it," the chances are that a similar decision today can be justified by the officer responsible. Also contributing to the continuity of bureaucratic decision making is the fact that the holding of a bureaucratic office is a full-time occupation. In recent years, bureaucratic officers have been tenured, rather than holding office merely at the pleasure of the employer.

Finally, although it is not unique to bureaucratic organizations, the basic mechanism of control within a bureaucracy is hierarchical. This means that authority flows downward through the organization with each level of the organization being responsible to the level above.

Before proceeding to describe the bureaucratic structures in the Canadian government, we can look briefly at the reasons for adopting a bureaucratic type of organization; given all of its real or imagined malfunctions, what is good about the bureaucratic form? First of all, because equality is a value of our system of government, it is necessary, when applying the law to specific cases, to treat similar cases in a similar fashion. Bureaucratic organization permits a maximum of impartiality in dealing with the public by *routinizing* the decision-making process. Second, the application of the law must be predictable to be fair, and a bureaucratic system can be made highly predictable. The problem here is that in applying the law equally and impartially, the man with the "special case," who requires an equitable decision instead of an impartial one, is frequently penalized. How many times have we all met with the standard bureaucratic answer that "If we do that for you we will have to do it for everyone else as well"; or, "We are sorry but our regulations do not permit any exceptions." Thus, while bureaucratic procedures are valid for, perhaps, 90 per cent of the cases, for the 10 per cent that may be exceptional, the system imposes difficulties. The justification for such a system is that it is the only way we have of dealing fairly and at reasonable cost with the majority of the vast number of cases that come up.

Modern bureaucracies have, of course, developed some mechanisms for dealing with special cases. Many large programs dealing directly with the public have some form of appeal procedure, and individual bureaucrats at the operating levels do have some discretion in dealing with special cases. We will note too, in our discussions of the functions of Parliament that one of the most important parts of the MP's role is helping constituents who have not been adequately dealt with by the bureaucracy. More and more Canadian governments are utilizing ombudsmen to ensure that special cases are fairly dealt with. Nonetheless, in conclusion we must return to the rather unsatisfactory comment that bureaucratic organization is the best-known way of dealing with bigness in government and that some problems inevitably arise.

The basic organizational form found in the Canadian bureaucracy is the *department*, accounting for almost two-thirds of the employees of the federal government. Most of the rest of the government agencies are classed as Crown Corporations, although there are a few federal government agencies—such as the Bank of Canada, the Canada Council, the Canadian Wheat Board, and the National Arts Centre—which operate in a manner similar to Crown Corporations but which are not formally classified as such. Finally, there are the central control agencies such as the Treasury Board secretariat and the Privy Council Office, discussed above, and the Public Service Commission which will be dealt with briefly below.

The Government Department[8]Several characteristics distinguish the departmental form of organization from other types within the Canadian bureaucracy. First, a government department is answerable directly to a cabinet minister who functions as its formal head and who, conversely, is responsible for the actions of both the department and the departmental officials. The practical effectiveness of the minister in heading his department will depend to a large extent on his personality. While there is a lot of room for him to provide encouragement and to generate excitement within the department, the minister generally will leave the administrative decisions to the permanent officials under him. There is even a theory that the best minister is a man who has ideas and influential stature in the cabinet, but who knows very little about the line functions of the department itself. The minister can then represent the broad interests of the department in cabinet meetings, but he is not motivated to meddle in the internal affairs of the department. Perhaps this theory is just the wishful thinking of public servants who would prefer to keep the political head of the department involved in priority decisions and out of their hair. On the other hand, this situation may occur in reality simply because the minister is too busy with other things to become very involved in administration.

The second distinguishing characteristic of the government department is the fact that it is subject to the estimates system of budgeting, which means simply that the money appropriated to the department by

[8]See A.M. Willms, "Crown Agencies," in W.D.K. Kernaghan (ed.), *Bureaucracy in Canadian Government*, (Methuen, Toronto, 1969), pp. 23–25.

parliament must be spent in the manner directed by parliament. The coming of the system of Planning Programming Budgeting (PPB) has not changed this basic fact of departmental finance, although it permits planning of departmental programs over longer than one-year periods, subject to the approval of the Treasury Board.

The third characteristic of the government department is that it recruits departmental officials through the Public Service Commission. With the exception of some temporary and part-time help in some departments, all of the personnel of government departments are public servants under the Public Service Act and are recruited according to the principle of merit.

The Deputy Minister The administrative head of the department is a deputy minister. His appointment is a prerogative not of the minister of a department but of the Prime Minister, usually advised by a senior "mandarin", normally the Secretary to the Cabinet. This process of appointment gives the Prime Minister some measure of control over individual departments even if a minister becomes recalcitrant or remiss, but since the deputy minister usually works in very close contact with his minister and at arms length from the Prime Minister, this power is more formal than real. The deputy minister (DM), unlike a public servant, holds office "at the pleasure" of the government. He does not have permanent tenure, and it is considered quite proper for a new government to occasionally ask that the DMs in certain key departments resign. Similarly, the DM, in a department such as Finance, may resign without being asked if a different political party takes over after an election. It is essential that the minister have the confidence of the permanent head of the department (and vice versa) if he is to be able to function effectively as its political head; if there are suspicions that the existing DM is still friendly to the old government, it is best that he be replaced. While DMs are not tenured, it must be emphasized that, in most cases, a change in government does not necessitate their removal. Usually the incoming government is glad to have to help of such senior bureaucrats in "learning the ropes," and the DMs are willing to adapt to the needs and programs of their new political masters.

Perhaps the major function of the deputy minister is a *managerial* one; i.e., he must function as the manager of an organization called a department. He must therefore plan, direct, and control the department of which he is the administrative head. Like all managers in large organizations, he must set intradepartmental policy, participate in the selection of officers for senior positions within the department (subject to the merit principle), and coordinate departmental activities through executive leadership. The function of coordination is usually facilitated through the delegation of some managerial functions to subordinates, and in many departments through a *central management committee* or *executive committee*, which consists of the deputy minister as chairman and all of the assistant deputies as members. The minister may occasionally be present; whether or not he is is usually a matter of his personal style or the importance of the agenda items. The management committee sets the broad objectives and priorities of the department and examines any new proposals which may emerge from the bowels of the organization, and deals as well with such "vital" management questions as the date of the departmental picnic. However, properly operated, the committee can do much, together with the budget process, to rationalize intradepartmental priorities, and can be used effectively by the deputy minister as a tool of management.

Figure 16-1

FUNCTIONS OF THE DEPUTY MINISTER

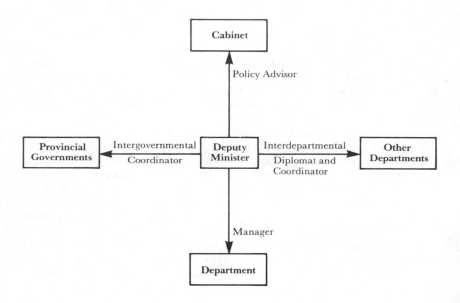

The deputy minister is responsible for the maintenance of liaison with people in other departments. This is necessary partially because each department must depend to some extent on other departments whose function is to provide services for the rest. The most important example of such a service department is the Department of Supply and Services which was created by a 1969 governmental reorganization. This type of liaison is not usually difficult and does not normally require much of the deputy's personal time, but in addition, liaison must be maintained with other departments which have similar or overlapping line responsibilities. All of this is achieved through a semi-institutionalized process of protocol and interdepartmental "diplomacy" which has evolved to meet at least some of the needs of interdepartmental coordination and overall public service efficiency. DMs also act as intergovernmental "diplomats," a function which has already been discussed in detail in Chapter 15.

In terms of the policy process in Canada, the most important function of the deputy minister is to act as the senior departmental advisor to the government. His is the key role in the transmission of policy information from the many people under him with many types of expertise to his minister and through him, to the cabinet. Because of his position in the department itself, and in most cases because of his many years of administrative experience, the deputy minister must go beyond merely transmitting neutral information to his superior. He is expected to interpret and explain the advice flowing from the department; and where political decisions are required by the minister and the cabinet, he must, to the best of his ability, tender political or quasi-political advice when asked. While the DM is but one man, and incapable of total understanding of the specialist decisions made by his administrative underlings, as a professional manager he is in a good position to decide which of several departmental technical advisors the government should put its faith in. It has been mentioned before that one of the important aspects of cabinet decisions at the policy-formulation stage of the policy process is deciding which policy advice to convert into formal outputs. It is in this respect that the advice of the deputy minister is invaluable to the government. Because he knows the advisors, and not only because he understands the substance of their advice, the DM can decide which advice is likely to be better.

In summary, the deputy minister of a Canadian government department basically plays the role of a manager of a very large organization. However, the nature of government organization places unique powers and restrictions on the management function, and the extent to which the DM can exercise those unique powers and cope with those unique restrictions ultimately rests on his own personal ability. Deputy ministers, both in Ottawa and the provinces, hold some of the most difficult and important jobs in Canada, and play a very central role in the entire working of the Canadian political system.

The Interdepartmental Distribution and Responsibilities The interdepartmental distribution of responsibilities and jurisdiction is based on the closely related principles of function and clientele. The Department of Labour and the Department of Agriculture, for instance, exist to perform administrative and policy-making functions in certain specific areas relating to labour and farmers respectively. Basically, the name of a department will give some indication of the function it is intended to perform and the clientele to which it is expected to cater. However, while the distribution of functions between the various departments is intended to eliminate interdepartmental confusion and conflict over who is to do what, there is much overlapping of departmental jurisdiction. The result of this jurisdictional conflict is a process whereby bureaucratic agencies compete with each other for jurisdiction in areas of potential overlap. Thus, the Departments of Energy, Mines and Resources, Indian Affairs and Northern Development, Environment, Transport, National Health and Welfare, and Agriculture all have some responsibility for water-pollution control. Which of these departments actually emerges supreme in the various aspects of this policy area will depend on a process of interdepartmental bargaining cabinet decisions, and the political influence of each department's clientele.

As time passes and conditions change, new departments spring up and other departments disappear. Sometimes the functions of one department are absorbed into another one, and at other times two departments will be amalgamated administratively even though the functions are not very closely related. Often it is apparent that the demands of a certain clientele perpetuate the existence of archaic departments long after their functions should have been absorbed into newer departments. For instance, the Department of Veteran's Affairs, continues to exist even though it is difficult to see why such matters are not merely placed under the jurisdiction of the Department of Health and Welfare.

Some government departments like Secretary of State have a sort of "catch-all" jurisdiction; any matters that are not important enough to be placed in a separate department are administratively lumped together here. Still other departments such as Supply and Services and Public Works perform a number of services for all of the other departments. The Post Office is somewhat unique in that it carries on dealings with the general public on a quasi-commercial basis. On the other hand, some of the more traditional departments of government such as National Defence and External Affairs have responsibilities which are only secondarily concerned with any clientele in Canada.

Hence, the rationale for the interdepartmental distribution of responsibilities in Canada is very difficult to state in any succinct fashion. Departments exist for a number of reasons, and most of them justify their existence through some specific function that they perform or some clientele that they serve. To attempt to simplify or rationalize this situation any further would only serve to confuse the reader and distort the reality of government organization in this country beyond the bounds of academic licence.

The Internal Structure of Departments The internal functions of an organization can broadly be classed as *line* or *staff*. In Canada this distinction is based on the type of relationship between various intradepartmental administrative structures and the goals of the department as a whole. To use the example of a specific department, the goal of the Department of National Revenue, simply stated, is tax collection. Those branches of the department involved directly in collecting tax revenues are said to be performing line functions. On the other hand, there are branches and/or divisions of the same department involved in matters such as personal administration, finance, and legal advice, none of which directly involves the performance of the line function. These branches of the department are said to perform a staff function, and they exist to assist the line managers in an advisory capacity or through the performance of a service.[9]

The basic structure of a government department is hierarchical

[9]Professor Willms makes a distinction between three kinds of functions: line, staff, and service. We have retained the more traditional classification here because, for purposes of explaining the workings of a government department, the important point is to set the line function off from the rest. Service functions are very close conceptually to staff functions, and hence the distinction is more important for public administration than it is for an introductory text in Canadian politics.

with the deputy minister at the top of the pyramid. Under the DM there are a number of subordinate levels. Each of these levels of the departmental organization is itself hierarchical in structure, and each is directly accountable to the level above. The staff role carries no direct authority over the line officers, and the branches of the department involved in the performance of staff functions are usually organized more simply than those of the line, with only two basic organizational levels.

When we come to look at some departments, (such as Finance) which have a constant and very direct connection with policy, and departments (such as Manpower and Immigration or Energy, Mines and Resources) which are deeply involved in the contemporary policy process because of current public interest and political priorities in the areas of immigration, employment and unemployment or energy policy, the line and staff distinction becomes somewhat confused. If there is a policy and planning branch in a government department, the officers in that branch will have a purely advisory relationship with the officers in the various operations or line branches. In other words, the relationship of the policy branch to the line branches of the organization will be a staff relationship. On the other hand, one of the major goals of many modern government departments is to formulate policy for the cabinet. Thus, policy formulation becomes itself a line function of that department. A manager in the policy and planning branch will therefore have a staff relationship with the managers in the operations branches, and a line relationship with other officers in his own branch and with his Deputy Minister. This same line and staff confusion occurs when we look at, for instance, information services in a department. As has already been seen, an important function of a modern bureaucracy is to disseminate information; this is, within one context, a line function. However, the information services division of a department also performs a service and therefore has a staff relationship with the other branches and divisions.

Thus, while it is important to recognize the distinction between line and staff functions within a department, the attempt to classify on the basis of this distinction must fail if carried too far. Modern bureaucratic organizations are far too complicated structurally to permit many broad generalizations. The aim of this section is to set out some of the principles and terms that can be employed when looking at any specific department. If one is really to understand the structure of the Canadian bureaucracy today, however, one must analyse each government department separately, for they are all different, displaying their own organizational quirks and idiosyncrasies. A department-by-department analysis is beyond the scope of this text, so we must be satisfied with the few generalizations and specific comments above.

Crown Corporations The Crown corporation is a bureaucratic institution with a corporate form created by the government to perform a public function. Such institutions aim at combining the need for some degree of public accountability with the freedom of initiative usually associated (rightly or wrongly) with private enterprise. While most Crown corporations must report through a minister to parliament, particularly in budgetary matters, they are not subject to either the estimates system of budgeting or the direct control of a minister in the same way that a government department is. Personnel administration in Crown corporations, furthermore, differs from that within a government department in the extent to which the Public Service Commission regulates recruitment, promotion, and transfer procedures. In the case of the departmental corporation,[10] the employees are public servants. In the other types, however, employees generally are not affected by the terms of the Public Service Act, for personnel matters are dealt with internally and independently.

Basically, Crown corporations differ from government departments in the degree of political control exercised over them. As we noted above, the minister is the formal head of a department, and a deputy minister is the administrative head. However, because the Crown corporation is designed to give a measure of freedom of action, it is usually headed by an independent board which is appointed by the government for a set period of time. The members of this board usually include a full-time chairman or president who functions as the administrative head and chief executive of the corporation, and part-time members who meet as a board only a few times each year. In the case of some Crown corporations, members of the board include public servants from other governmental agencies. The relationship of the chief executive of the corporation to the board itself will differ depending on the nature of the corporation and the personalities involved.

The activities of Crown corporations, unlike those of government departments, are not supervised directly by a cabinet minister. Indeed, independence from direct ministerial control is one of the major reasons for creating a Crown corporation. Despite this, mainly because it is felt that public enterprises financed by public money should be subjected to at least some parliamentary control, each Crown corporation is assigned to a minister of the Crown through which it must report to parliament. The minister, however, does not in any way direct the activities of the corporation, and conversely, he is in no way personally responsible for the activities of the corporation. Rather, he acts as a communication link between the corporation, which is engaged in public enterprise and which, in most cases, is spending public money, and parliament. The bulk of his work on behalf of a Crown corporation for which he reports will entail piloting the corporation's estimates through the House of Commons. Naturally it is possible for a minister to influence corporation policy informally but this is difficult to document. All that can be said is that informal ministerial control over a Crown corporation will depend largely on the personalities involved and the political circumstances of the times.

The greatest restriction on the activities of a Crown corporation oc-

[10]The best description of the structure and functions of Crown corporation is in C.A. Ashley and R.G.H. Smails, *Canadian Crown Corporations*, (Macmillan, Toronto, 1965), pp. 99–160.

curs through its financial relationship with the Government of Canada, particularly in the case of corporations whose activities are totally financed out of the Consolidated Revenue Fund by parliamentary appropriations. While the estimates for most Crown corporations are voted in far less detailed form than departmental estimates, the fact remains that most of their expenditures do have to be annually and publicly justified. Furthermore, with the exception of a few specified Crown corporations, the accounts of Canadian Crown corporations are subject to audit by the Auditor General. While this is a post-audit control, somewhat analogous to closing the barn door after the horse has run off, the executive of a Crown corporation must still be aware that careless expenditure of public money "this time" may result in a less generous appropriation "next time".

Finally, Crown corporations are controlled by the legislation which creates them. The terms of reference of a Crown corporation are set down in a statute which is subject to amendment or repeal by act of parliament. While this does not in any way approach the directness of control exercised over a government department, it does define jurisdictional limits beyond which the corporation is not competent to act. The Financial Administration Act defines three basic types of Crown corporations: departmental corporations, agency corporations and proprietary corporations. Each of these deserves some additional comment by way of clarification.

Departmental Corporations A departmental corporation is an agency of the government of Canada which is engaged in ". . .administrative, supervisory, or regulatory services. . . ." in much the same way as a department. Schedule B of the Financial Administration Act lists the following as departmental corporations:

> Agricultural Stabilization Board
> Atomic Energy Control Board
> Director of Soldier Settlement
> The Director, The Veterans' Land Act
> Economic Council of Canada
> Fisheries Prices Support Board
> Medical Research Council
> Municipal Development and Loan Board
> National Museums of Canada
> National Research Council
> Science Council of Canada
> Unemployment Insurance Commission

For purposes of the Financial Administration Act, these corporations are exactly the same as regular government departments. For instance, a departmental corporation does not buy, sell, or own any assets in its own name but always in the name of the Crown in right of Canada. Similarly, all of the financial affairs of this type of corporation are carried out through the Consolidated Revenue Fund and are subject to the control of the Treasury Board, Auditor General, etc. However, while the money spent by a departmental corporation must be appropriated by parliament and encumbered from the Consolidated Revenue Fund as with a government department, there is a much greater degree of independence in how the funds appropriated are actually spent. The estimates for a departmental corporation are usually put through parliament in the form of one vote in the estimates of the department through whose minister the corporation must report to parliament. Hence, the National Museums of Canada, which is a departmental corporation reporting to parliament through the Secretary of State, gets its money for any given budgetary year in the form of one item in the main estimates of the Department of Secretary of State. Where the government department must be able to justify through the minister every item of expenditure for the upcoming year to a skeptical parliament, the entire budget for a Crown corporation is debated as one item. The limitation on this independence is the fact that the Treasury Board must examine and approve the estimates for a departmental corporation before they are included in the departmental estimates. Hence, independence from parliamentary control may not mean very much when one considers that the Treasury Board, which exercises much of the real financial control over government expenditure, has as close a look at a corporation's financial needs as it has at a department's.

The boards of departmental corporations and their chairmen are almost all appointed by the Governor General in Council. The tenure of these positions varies from set ten-year periods, as with the Unemployment Insurance Commission, to "the pleasure of her majesty in right of Canada", as with other boards. The employees of departmental corporations are often appointed by the Public Service Commission and hold office during good behaviour. Thus, most of the employees of the Unemployment Insurance Commission are public servants as are the employees of the Director of Soldier Settlement or the Director of the Veterans' Land Act. On the other hand, the employees of some departmental corporations are not public servants, their remuneration and terms of employment being set by the board itself. This is the case with corporations such as the Agricultural Stabilization Board.[11] Other Departmental corporations come somewhere between these two extremes in their employment practices.

Finally, all of the departmental corporations must submit to the minister responsible an annual report which is tabled in the House of Commons within fifteen days. This report is provided for in most of the legislation setting up the various departmental corporations, and its function is essentially to provide publicity for the activities of the organization, acting, perhaps, as a sort of deterrent to abuses of power or squandering of public funds. The effectiveness of the annual reports as a control measure is very difficult to assess, and likely varies with the political sensitivity of the subject matter dealt with by the particular crown corporation.

Agency Corporations An agency corporation is defined in the Financial Administration Act as ". . .a Crown corporation that is an agent of Her Majesty in right of Canada and is responsible for the management of trading or service operations on a quasi-commercial basis, or for the man-

---

[11]Ashley and Smails, *op. cit.*, p. 107.

agement of procurement, construction, or disposal activities on behalf of Her Majesty in right of Canada. . . ."

Schedule C of the Financial Administration Act lists the following as agency corporations:

> Atomic Energy of Canada Limited
> Canadian Arsenals Limited
> Canadian Commercial Corporation
> Canadian Dairy Commission
> Canadian Film Development Corporation
> Canadian Livestock Feed Board
> Canadian National (West Indies) Steamships Limited
> Canadian Patents and Development Limited
> Canadian Saltfish Corporation
> Company of Young Canadians
> Crown Assets Disposal Corporation
> Defence Construction (1951) Limited
> National Battlefields Commission
> National Capital Commission
> National Harbours Board
> Northern Canada Power Commission
> Royal Canadian Mint
> Uranium Canada Limited

Unlike departmental corporations, agency corporations are subject to the sections of the Financial Administration Act that apply specifically to Crown corporations. However, the act itself goes on to state that where there is a conflict between its provisions and those of another act, the latter will prevail. The agency corporations which have "Limited" after their name were set up under the Companies Act and the rest were set up by separate acts. The boards of directors of the "Limited" corporations are formally appointed by the shareholders; but, because the shares are held in trust for the Crown, in fact the Governor General in Council makes the appointments.[12] Most of the other corporations are headed by a board of directors which is appointed for a set term by the Governor General in Council.

The employees of the agency corporations are all appointed by the management of the corporation itself, and the salaries and conditions of work are also determined in a manner similar to private industry. While the National Harbours Board is an exception, agency corporations are empowered to maintain accounts in their own names in any bank which is formally approved by the Minister of Finance. The operating budget of the corporation is scrutinized by the minister through which the corporation reports to parliament, but the actual estimates for operating costs are placed before parliament in the form of one item in departmental estimates. Capital budgets of agency corporations are subject to more detailed scrutiny by parliament, and as with departmental corporations, an annual report including financial statements must be presented to the minister

[12]*Ibid.*, p. 112.

responsible at the end of the financial year. These reports are then tabled in parliament. All of the financial statements of the agency Crown corporations are subject to the scrutiny of the Auditor General.

The agency corporations display a great diversity in terms of their real financial status; for while some such, as Canadian Patents and Development Ltd., operate at a profit, others, like the National Battlefields Commission, operate entirely on parliamentary appropriations. Similarly, while some of these corporations, like the Northern Canada Power Commission, hold large capital assets, others, like Canadian Arsenals Ltd., hold very little in the way of capital assets. Many of these agencies are also subsidized in part through the provision of office facilities and furniture by the Department of Public Works in the same way that a government department is.

The legal position of agency corporations is much the same as any corporation under the Corporations Act. All agency corporations (with the exception of the National Harbours Board and the National Battlefields Commission) can be sued in any court just as if they were not agents of the Crown. This is important in that it places them in much the same legal position *vis-à-vis* their clientele as any firm operating in the private sphere. By making them legally directly responsible for their activities, the government can also afford to grant them a great deal of independence from financial and political control.

Proprietary Corporations   A proprietary corporation is defined as a Crown corporation which is responsible either for the management of lending or financial operations, or for the management of commercial or industrial operations involving the producing of or dealing in goods and the supplying of services to the public. These corporations are furthermore expected to function without the aid of parliamentary appropriations. The following are listed as proprietary corporations in Schedule D of the Financial Administration Act:

> Air Canada
> Canada Deposit Insurance Corporation
> Canadian Broadcasting Corporation
> Canadian Overseas Telecommunication Corporation
> Cape Breton Development Corporation
> Central Mortgage and Housing Corporation
> Eldorado Aviation Limited
> Eldorado Nuclear Limited
> Export Development Corporation
> Farm Credit Corporation
> Freshwater Fish Marketing Corporation
> National Railways, as defined in the Canadian National–
>   Canadian Pacific Act (RSC 1952, c. 39)
> Northern Transportation Company Limited
> Pilotage Authorities:
>   Atlantic Pilotage Authority
>   Laurentian Pilotage Authority
>   Great Lakes Pilotage Authority

Pacific Pilotage Authority
St. Lawrence Seaway Authority
Seaway International Bridge Corporation Limited
   (formerly Cornwall International Bridge Company Limited)

Many of the proprietary corporations in Canada not only have a direct commercial relationship with the public, but also are in competition with private corporations performing the same functions or providing the same services. The best examples of this kind of competitive Crown corporation are Air Canada and the CBC, each of which must compete with other firms in the private sphere. Because these proprietary corporations must compete with private industry, they have been guaranteed a great deal of protection from both parliamentary and public scrutiny. The principle has been established, for instance, that information regarding salaries of individuals will not be released to parliament and the annual reports of the proprietary corporations, unlike those of the agency corporations, are only required to include the sort of information required from a private firm under the Companies Act. Like agency corporations, proprietary corporations are subject to the Financial Administration Act except where the terms of that act conflict with another—in which case the latter legislation applies. Similarly, proprietary corporations are legally liable in the same way that any non-government corporation is.

The directors of the corporations are appointed in much the same way as the directors of agency corporations, by the Governor General in Council. Exceptions here are the Central Mortgage and Housing Corporation, the Export Development Corporation, and the Farm Credit Corporation whose boards of directors are in part composed of senior departmental officials. Ashley and Smails point out that these corporations should likely not be included in Schedule D of the Financial Administration Act for they have far less freedom in the determination of policy than do the other proprietary corporations. While the membership of the boards of these three corporations includes men from several different departments, "...the policies of these corporations cannot but be, as they are meant to be, a reflection of government policy. . . ."[13] The employees of the proprietary corporations, on the other hand, are all appointed by the management of the particular corporation and not through the Public Service Commission.

Financial control over the activities of proprietary Crown corporations is similar to the control exercised through the Financial Administration Act over agency corporations. Each one is required to submit a capital budget to the minister through whom it reports to parliament. This capital budget is subsequently approved by the cabinet and submitted to parliament by the minister. Some of these corporations, such as Air Canada, are required by their individual legislation to also submit an operating budget, although this is not the case with the corporations set up under the provisions of the Companies Act. A form of financial control is also ex-

[13]Ashley and Smails, *op. cit.*, pp. 128–129. See also Royal Commission on Government Organization (Glassco Commission), *Report*, Vol. 5, p. 63.

ercised over the activities of these Crown corporations through the power of parliament to vote special financial assistance to make up deficits. While it is stated in the Financial Administration Act that proprietary corporations are normally expected to operate without appropriations, in fact most of them from time to time (and some of them all the time) require help from parliament to balance their operating-cost budgets. None of the proprietary corporations gets free accommodation or furniture from the Department of Public Works and, as of 1952, like private firms they have to pay corporation income taxes. Many of the proprietary corporations are subject to the scrutiny of the Auditor General, although others such as Air Canada are not. This fact has frequently been a bone of contention introduced in parliamentary debates, although recent developments in the government's attitude to the office of the Auditor General indicate there will likely not be any change in this regard.

"Para"-Crown Corporations There are a large number of government institutions in Canada which are not listed in Schedules B to D of the Financial Administration Act. While these are not classed as departmental, agency, or proprietary corporations, they perform mostly the same kinds of functions as those corporations listed in the Financial Administration Act, and therefore should be considered briefly at this point.

Most of these unclassified Crown corporations are set up by federal legislation to perform functions which require a degree of independence of action; but, for reasons that are usually not clear, they have not been included in the Financial Administnation Act. The best examples of this sort of bureaucratic agency are the Bank of Canada and the Canadian Wheat Board, each of which has been set up by its own special legislation. These corporations display as many varieties of internal organization and procedures for control as there are acts. Because of their structural diversity, that is all that can be said about them here.

There are a number of government corporations in existence which are unique not because of their line functions but rather because they are federal–provincial in structure. The best example of this is the Eastern Rockies Forest Conservation Board which was established by complementary federal and provincial legislation and which is managed by two provincial officials and one federal appointee. Bodies such as this, however, which could become important in the future, are rare today, largely because of the difficulties involved in personnel and financial administration. It should also be mentioned, at this point, that there are many government corporations at the provincial level which function in approximately the same way that their federal counterparts do. Naturally, because of their organizational diversity and great numbers we can do no more in this study than mention the fact of their existence.

Finally it must be pointed out that there are a number of intradepartmental agencies which have a position of relative independence within the department, but which are not strictly Crown corporations. These independent boards and commissions are usually set up by special legislation to perform functions which require a degree of independence from direct political or ministerial control and which come within the organizational boundaries of one of the departments. Basically, these independent boards and commissions function in the same way as departmental corporations. Examples of this type of bureaucratic agency are the National Energy Board, Canadian Pension Commission, the Fisheries Research Board, the Board of Grain Commissioners, and the Canada Labour Relations Board. There are many more such organizations and there are also other important agencies of the government of Canada, such as the Canadian Radio-Television Commission and the Canadian Transport Commission, which function in much the same way as departmental corporations but which have varying relationships with the cabinet, parliament, and the departments. Unfortunately the scope of this text does not permit a more detailed analysis of these structurally diverse and multifunctional bureaucratic agencies.

Central Agencies The Treasury Board and the Privy Council Office have been discussed previously, so it is not necessary to say anything more about them at this juncture. Another central agency, which has been mentioned before and which has a direct influence on a large segment of the bureaucracy, is the Public Service Commission. The creation of the first Civil Service Commission in Canada in 1908 was precipitated by changes that occured in the functions of the bureaucracy and in the attitudes of Canadians concerning the nature of the public service.

At one time there had been a general acceptance of the state of affairs where appointment to bureaucratic office was based not on the qualifications of the applicant and the requirements of the job but on partisan considerations. Liberal governments rewarded party faithfuls by granting them jobs in the public service and Conservative governments did the same.[14] The short-run effect of this practice was to aid the political parties in building strong party organizations in most of the country's constituencies. As the parties built up bases of support, however, they no longer needed the promise of patronage appointments to entice people into working for the party, and the administrative problem of distributing the patronage had become a great headache to the party leader.

People, furthermore, began to consider such tactics morally and ethically improper, and movements sprang up to reform the civil service. Finally, as the role of government expanded, the jobs to be done in the public service began to require a degree of expertise that was often sadly lacking in a person who was appointed for reasons of his political preference. The upshot of all of these changes was that the recruitment practices of the public service were changed from the principle of patronage to the principle of merit. In other words, applicants for public service positions were now to be chosen on the basis of their qualifications and the requirements of the position, and if more than one person fit the same position, the choice between them was to be made on the basis of a competitive examination. The original Civil Service Commission was set up to supervise

[14]Political biographies give many of the details of the development of patronage in Canada. See especially Donald Creighton, *John A. Macdonald*, Vol. 2: *The Old Chieftain, passim.*

the implementation of the merit system of recruitment in the public service.

Today, the Public Service Commission is made up of three Commissioners—all of whom are appointed for a set term by the Governor in Council, with salaries set by parliament—and a large permanent staff. The functions of the Public Service Commission include the overseeing of the merit system and other responsibilities related to staffing the Public Service of Canada, as well as the responsibility for training and development,[15] certain types of appeals concerned with staffing, and the provision of advisory services in the areas of organization analysis, management analysis, and personal services. In short, because of its large measure of control over the people who get into the Canadian Public Service, the Public Service Commission is an important independent agency of the Canadian bureaucracy.

On the other hand, the Public Service Commission is probably not as important today as it has been in the past. Prior to 1966 virtually all hiring into the civil service was carried out by the Commission, but the implementation of many of the recommendations of the Royal Commission on Governmental Organization (the Glassco Report) placed some of the responsibility for hiring in the hands of individual departments and transferred many of the other functions of the Public Service Commission, such as pay research, to the Treasury Board.

Each of the provinces has a body similar to the federal Public Service Commission that supervises recruitment and promotion within the provincial public services. There is no necessary connection, however, between the personnel practices of the provinces and those of the federal government.

This concludes our analysis of the various institutional forms found within the Canadian bureaucracy. Although it has been sketchy, it has pointed to a few of the tentative generalizations that can be made about the structures involved in the formulation stage of the policy process in Canada. We will now turn to the question of how the Canadian bureaucracy is controlled; for if anything is obvious by now, it should be that the bureaucracy has much of the actual power in the political process, and that, if some checks are not provided on its influence, the bureaucracy could entirely dominate the decision-making process in Canada.

THE CONTROL OF BUREAUCRATIC DECISIONS

Control by Cabinet The concern in this section is with the modes of control of the constraints placed on bureaucratic decision making by other governmental institutions. As has already been stated, bureaucratic power flows from the concentration of various kinds of expertise

---

[15]For the best analysis of the Public Service Commission in Canada, see: Hodgetts, J.E. *et al. The Biography of an Institution*, (McGill–Queen's University Press, Montreal, 1972).

within the bureaucracy and from a degree of control over the flow of information to the Cabinet. The bureaucracy influences priority determination and largely dominates policy formulation because it is expected to advise the cabinet on the basis of the information it possesses. However, while the bureaucracy occupies a position of great importance in the policy process, ultimate political power still rests with the cabinet and the Prime Minister. Whether on whim or political exigency, whether wisely or unwisely, the cabinet and the Prime Minister can and do periodically choose to disregard bureaucratic advice, even when that advice was ordered by the government in the first place.

The actual exercise of this ultimate control by the cabinet is usually limited to situations where the action demanded by political expediency is not congruent with the course of action indicated by technical or administrative considerations. When this happens, the political advisors to the cabinet (such as those in the Prime Minister's Office), the party structure, the Privy Council Office, and the cabinet ministers and Prime Minister themselves, tend to be in a position of competition *vis-à-vis* the bureaucracy proper. If the cabinet as a whole or the Prime Minister should become convinced that the political considerations are more important than the technical, financial, or administrative ones, the regular bureaucrats will, at least for the moment, lose out. This situation of competing advice from the political advisors and the bureaucratic advisors can exist at all stages of the decision-making process, although in many cases it is likely that political and other considerations will in fact coincide. The point that must be emphasized in this regard is simply that the political advisors, particularly in the Privy Council and Prime Minister's Offices, or the cabinet ministers themselves may function as an alternate source of information which can—in some instances—place major restrictions on the power of the bureaucracy.

Financial Control: The Budgetary Process[16] Further

mechanisms of control over the policy-making role of the Canadian bureaucracy are employed through the budgetary process.[17] With the gradual implementation of a system of Planning, Programming, and Budgeting, the role of the Treasury Board in the determination of spending priorities has been greatly enhanced. To the extent that the Treasury Board secretariat bears much of the responsibility for controlling government spending, PPBS can be viewed as an aggrandizement of bureaucratic power, for the secretariat is, after all, a part of the bureaucracy. On the other hand, if one views the Treasury Board in terms of its formal composition as a committee of the Privy Council, PPBS can be viewed as placing new restrictions on the priority-setting role of the bureaucracy. Certainly, the power of the individual department in some ways has been

[16]H.R. Balls, "Financial Administration in Canada," in Kernaghan, *Bureaucracy in Canadian Government*, pp. 57–64.
[17]See also Chapter 15 for a discussion of the budgetary process and priority determination.

decreased through the placing of new power in the hands of the more centralized Treasury Board secretariat, and by virtue of the fact that revenues
are now largely tied up for a three-year period leaving less year-to-year
flexibility. However, one might argue that departmental power has been
increased by permitting program planning over a three-year rather than a
one-year period. About all that is really clear here is that the extent to
which the Treasury Board controls bureaucratic expenditure is difficult to
assess.

Additional control over the bureaucracy, is exercised through the
traditional processes of public finance. According to Norman Ward, there
are two basic principles of public finance in Canada: first, that the executive should have no money which is not granted to it or otherwise sanctioned by parliament; and, second, that the executive should make no expenditures except those authorized specifically by parliament.[18] In brief,
therefore, the executive branch and its operational arm, the bureaucracy,
can only get funds through parliamentary appropriation, and it can only
spend those funds for purposes specified by parliament. The implementation of these two basic principles is facilitated by a complicated set of practices and procedures. In the first place, there must be a budget which is a
clear enunciation of the present financial needs of the government, the
plans for the upcoming year and a general statement of the financial "state
of the nation". This is provided at least annually, and it is the responsibility of the government of the day to prepare it and justify its contents to
parliament. More will be said about the budget and the budget debate in
the following chapter.

The basic premise of the entire system of public finance in Canada
is that the public pursestrings are held by parliament. While there are *de
facto* limitations on the power of parliament to control public spending,
these will be dealt with in a subsequent discussion of parliament and the
legislative process. Here it is necessary to describe only the formal process
of appropriating public money through the system of *estimates.* Basically,
this is a system of appropriation of funds by parliament in advance to meet
the estimated costs of the various governmental programs in the next year.

Since the program-review[19] stage of preparing the departmental estimates has been mentioned at several points in our analysis already, the
discussion here commences when the program review has been completed
and the Treasury Board has set *spending targets* based on expenditure
guidelines by the cabinet. At this time—usually in late summer—a letter is
issued asking the departments to prepare their estimates for the upcoming
year. In fact, the various branches and divisions of the department have
already been preparing estimates since the spring in anticipation of the
Treasury Board's letter, and by late September the deputy minister (and
in some cases the departmental policy committee) reviews the total estimates of the department. In late fall the minister himself reviews the de-

[18]N. Ward, *The Public Purse*, (University of Toronto Press, Toronto, 1955), *passim.*
[19]See P.L. Little and C.L. Mitchell, "The Program Budget: Planning and Control
for the Public Sector," in Kernaghan and Willms, *Public Administration in Canada:
Selected Readings*, pp. 188–195.

partmental estimates and gives them his formal approval, usually without making many significant changes. (It must be noted that in discussing this process as a series of distinct stages, we distort the true picture; for in fact, the minister and the deputy minister, the various branch directors and division chiefs, and officials in the Treasury Board staff are in continuous contact. Often this is informal contact, characterized by a phone call from one person to another, but its effect is to keep the people involved in the preparation of the estimates aware of what to expect from the next stage of the process.)

Once the estimates have been approved by the minister, they are sent to the Treasury Board staff who go over them in great detail, with an eye to cutting down on expenses. The Treasury Board's concern at this point is with economy and frugality—not with the overall advisability of the various departmental programs which have already been approved in principle by the Board at the program-review stage of the process.

Having passed the meticulous and penny-pinching staff of the Treasury Board secretariat, the estimates are then handed to the Treasury Board itself whose responsibility it is to put all of the estimates of all of the departments in some kind of a perspective. The concern of the Board itself is not with economy *per se*, but with what resources are actually available and whether or not any priorities set at the program-review stage should be changed. If the spending priorities set at the program-review stage have been reasonably accurate and if, in preparing the estimates, the departments have adhered to the original targets and programs, there should be no significant changes at this stage. However, because the PPB system has not yet been and may never be fully implemented, there are often major changes made at this stage in the preparation of the estimates. Such changes inevitably produce hurt feelings and bitterness on the part of the bureaucrats whose estimates have been reduced or eliminated. However, because of the almost constant informal contact among senior bureaucrats in the Treasury Board, Department of Finance, and the various other government departments, these changes are never completely unanticipated.

Having survived the scrutiny of the Treasury Board, the formal approval of the cabinet as a whole is not usually difficult, or of any interest. It is possible at this stage for a minister whose department has been seriously affected by Treasury Board's frugality to make a final "impassioned plea" to his colleagues, although it is unlikely that they should be very impressed unless they have been equally hard done by.

After Cabinet approval, the *main estimates* are printed up in a form usually referred to as the *Blue Book*, and tabled in the House of Commons. The Blue Book not only lists the actual "votes" which ultimately will be passed in parliament but it also includes supporting details that give an even more specific breakdown of the department's estimated expenses for the coming year. The main estimates themselves ultimately become the *Appropriation Act*, whereas the supporting details are stated merely for the information of the members of parliament and the general public, and as more detailed guidelines for the spending of funds by the department.

The estimates for the various departments are then given to an appropriate standing committee of the House of Commons to be considered in detail. These committees go over the estimates item by item, calling upon the minister of the department whose estimates are being discussed to defend its programs and estimated expenditures. The committees then report back to the House of Commons and the estimates of all the departments are passed through parliament as one bill like any other piece of legislation. When this *Supply Bill* has passed through parliament and has been assented to by the Governor General, it becomes the Appropriation Act, part of the law of the land.[20]

Once the money has been appropriated by parliament, it can be spent only by the executive. Parliament does not spend money, it merely appropriates it. The actual spending of money requires an *encumbrance* of funds from the revenue pool of the government of Canada, the *Consolidated Revenue Fund*. The money is encumbered by the Treasury Board to the Departments as they need it for specific purposes. The *Comptroller of the Treasury*, who is now known as the Deputy Minister of Services and Deputy Receiver General for Canada, acts as a "gatekeeper" for the Consolidated Revenue Fund, insuring that the expenditure for which the money is being encumbered is within the terms of the Appropriation Act, that there are sufficient funds in the Fund to meet the cost, and that appropriate receipts, etc., for the goods and services purchased are forthcoming. The function of the Deputy Minister of Services is, in effect, a pre-audit function. He is assisted by officers located throughout the public service who are responsible not only for operational audit of the financial affairs of the department to which they are attached but also for the preparation of the accounts of the departments. While to an increasing extent (because of the recommendations of the Glassco Commission) the internal-audit or operational-audit function is being performed not by treasury officers seconded to the department but by departmental officials themselves, in the case of the smaller departments and agencies of the government of Canada, the Department of Supply and Services still supplies these financial officers on request to perform operational-audit functions.

When it comes time for the department to spend the money encumbered to it, it must spend it for the exact purposes stated in the Appropriation Act; although, with the approval of the Treasury Board, the department is permitted to deviate somewhat from the more detailed presentation of the estimates in the Blue Book. Normally, however, it is expected that the department will closely adhere even to the supporting details of the Blue Book as well as the votes of the Appropriation Act itself. Of course, all departments are bound by the Appropriation Act and are not permitted to use funds appropriated for one purpose for something else. If a department has estimated a certain amount for personnel and it does not spend it all, the money voted for that purpose never gets spent. Even though the department would have liked to use the extra funds to meet a shortage in money for travel expenses, this is not possible with an estimates system of finance. Furthermore, money voted ·for a certain pur-

[20]See Chapter 17.

pose is voted for one year only. If the money is not spent by the time the next Appropriation Act is passed, it reverts to the Consolidated Revenue Fund.

The discussion up until now has centered on the preparation of the main estimates and the main supply bill, which indeed involves the most important and the most substantial appropriation of public funds. However, there are a few additional kinds of supply which must be mentioned briefly here.

The *supplementary estimates*, which are intended to meet contingencies unforeseen at the time of the preparation of the main estimates, are voted late in the parliamentary session. It is expected that these will not be large, although they seem to increase in amount annually. *Further supplementary estimates* are introduced just before the close of the fiscal year to look after any additional items not covered by the main or supplementary estimates. These are sometimes voted near the end of the parliamentary session, and as a result they are passed without too much fuss by MPs who want to get on with the summer recess.

Interim supply is passed after the current fiscal year, but before the main estimates are approved. A vote of interim supply merely assumes that the main supply bill will pass successfully, and approves expenditures in amounts such as one-twelfth or one-sixth of the main estimates. This permits the departments to continue to carry out their programs even while parliament is considering whether or not to give them the money to do so. An interesting problem would arise if a main supply bill were actually defeated; for, with the longer parliamentary sessions that are frequent today, it is not unusual for the departments to have been voted a significant percentage of the main estimates by the time the main supply bill is actually passed. Such a defeat, however, is highly unlikely and supply is granted virtually automatically by June 30.

Finally, when parliament is not in session the government can spend money through the use of *Governor General's warrants*. These are expected to be used only for emergencies, and are subsequently approved by parliament in the formal way as part of the next supplementary estimates.

The Auditor General also performs a significant control function. He is an officer of parliament, not of the government, and he is responsible only to parliament. His salary is set by statute and he can only be removed from office through a joint address by the House of Commons and the Senate. The office was created in 1878 and its functions today are defined in the Financial Administration Act. Basically, the role of the Auditor General is to check up on all expenditures in the public service to insure that money has been spent efficiently and according to law, and to bring any matter involving the financial affairs of the government which he deems to be relevant to the attention of parliament. In short, he performs the function of post-audit of the public accounts. The basic strength of the Auditor General flows from his power of access to all of the government's financial "books", and his ability to make public any indiscretions found therein. The *Report of the Auditor General* comes out annually, and is tabled in the House of Commons. The normal procedure at this stage is for the

Auditor's report to be handed over immediately to the House of Commons Public Accounts Committee for more detailed study, a procedure which will be dealt with in greater detail in the next chapter. The basic weakness inherent in the office of the Auditor General is that his staff consists of public servants, and not parliamentary officials like himself. This means that the "establishment" of the office of the Auditor General depends on recommendations of cabinet. There is nothing in law to prevent the government of the day from cutting back on the staff of the Auditor General and in this way weakening his effectiveness as a "financial watchdog" for parliament. In fact, however, no government can politically afford to go too far in this regard, for the Auditor General to some extent symbolizes the financial authority of parliament. Any attempt to limit his independence from control by the government of the day, although quite legal, might do political damage to the party that so dared.

Judicial Safeguards Judicial control over the Canadian bureaucracy is exercised not with respect to policy decisions or advice from public servants, but rather with respect to administrative decisions. In the case of most administrative functions, the public official is granted fairly wide discretionary powers with which to carry out his responsibilities. Within the area of discretion granted him by law, the public servant enjoys a significant degree of independence from judicial control. However, the courts will review the administrative decisions of public officials to determine whether or not those decisions were within the jurisdiction granted to the official by law. In other words, if the public official has made a discretionary decision which is lacking in good judgment but is within the jurisdiction granted him by law, the courts will take no action. However, if an official makes a decision or takes administrative action which is beyond his competence, or *ultra vires* his discretionary powers, the courts will step in to quash the decision. Note that this can occur only with respect to administrative decisions—actual outputs of the political system that originate in the bureaucracy. In the case of policy decisions or advice, the bureaucratic official is formally only making a recommendation to the political decision makers in the process. A policy recommendation has no immediate or necessary impact on citizens, for it does not become a system output except at a much later stage.

If administrative decisions are judicial or quasi-judicial in nature, the courts will act to control the bureaucracy in another way. Here the courts question not only the jurisdiction of the administrative official or board, but the procedures followed in coming to the decision. Basically, a judicial control over bureaucratic decisions exists if an individual is affected by that decision and if the administrative official or board in making the decision has not adhered to the principles of *Natural Justice*. The principles of Natural Justice define the standards for fair procedures in coming to decisions that affect the rights and privileges of individuals. The first principle is that no man should be a judge in his own cause. In other words, the administrative officials on the board or tribunal which is making the decision must be impartial and not directly affected themselves by the outcome of the hearing. The second principle is that the individual affected by the decision has a right to be heard. His side must be aired and considered by the board before a decision is made. If either of these principles has been ignored by a bureaucratic agency or by an individual bureaucrat in coming to a judicial or quasi-judicial decision, the court will order that the decisions be quashed.[21]

Dissatisfaction with the effectiveness of judicial remedies in curbing abuses of bureaucratic power is growing. Not only are the courts unable to deal with misuse of discretionary power unless the administrative act is also *ultra vires*, but even in cases where judicial action is appropriate, the backlog of cases means that litigants must often wait years for satisfaction. One solution at the federal level has been to create an explicity administrative court, the *Federal Court*, which has jurisdiction to hear appeals from federal boards and tribunals. A partial solution in some of the provinces has been to appoint an *ombudsman*. His function is to investigate complaints by individuals who feel they have been wronged by some bureaucratic decision. He is an independent official of the legislature and his salary is set by statute. The ombudsman has broad powers of access to most public files and a modest staff to aid in his investigations. Unlike the courts, the ombudsman can investigate cases where the bureaucratic decision has been *intra vires*, but, in terms of equity, a bad decision. However, the ombudsman has the power only to investigate, to publicize abuses of bureaucratic power, and in some cases to initiate legal action much as a private citizen would. The ombudsman cannot himself order a decision be quashed. In the final analysis, the ombudsman can only be an effective check on bureaucratic excesses if the bureaucrats themselves respect or fear the office. Much of his work has to be done by phone call to the official about whom there has been a complaint. The official might agree to reconsider the decision; he might agree to change it somewhat or to rehear the case; and he will, at least, offer reasons for the decision. The ombudsman idea is being considered at present in a number of other provinces, and there is ultimately some possibility that the federal government will adopt the practice for the federal bureaucracy. However, the offices currently existing in Canada have not been operating long enough to permit a valid assessment of their effectiveness.[22]

Intrabureaucratic Controls: Recruitment and Collective Bargaining
Some amount of control over the decisions of bureaucrats is exercised by agencies and procedures that are themselves a part of the bureaucratic process. This is, of course, a different kind of control from that exercised by the courts, which are institutions outside the bureaucracy itself. Perhaps the subtlest form of this "control from within" is imposed through recruitment and training. As pointed out earlier, the kinds of decisions that will be made in the future are in part determined by who is making them. Therefore, the kinds of people who are selected to occupy

[21]See Chapter 6 for a discussion of the Federal Court.
[22]See Donald Rowat, *The Ombudsman*, (University of Toronto Press, Toronto, 1965).

positions in the bureaucracy will very directly affect the kinds of decisions that will emanate from it. This means that the criteria established by the Public Service Commission in assessing the suitability of various candidates for public service employment function as a mechanism of control over the Canadian bureaucracy.

The control from within however, does not cease with recruitment. As with any organization, it is necessary to train the people who are part of it, not only with respect to the technical skills of the specific occupation, but also with respect to the goals of the organization. The employee who has been thoroughly socialized into a bureaucratic organization will likely function more enthusiastically and even more efficiently than the man who looks on his occupation as "just a living." Hence there is an almost constant process of training and development[23] within the Canadian bureaucracy which, by molding the attitudes of public servants, very subtly affects bureaucratic decision making.

Public servants have traditionally been viewed as different from employees in the private sector. In part this is because they are "servants of the public" and should therefore take a highly responsible attitude to their jobs; but by far the greatest justification for treating public servants differently from their counterparts in private industry is simply their proximity to politics. Because they have access to information that the general public does not, and because they are involved in the process of policy formulation, public servants could potentially do a great deal of damage to the government of the day. By leaking information to the opposition parties or by "sabotaging" government projects, the public servant could potentially bring down the government. Thus, the tradition has evolved that while the public servant must be cognizant of his responsibility to the public, if this conflicts with the interests of the government, he must look to the latter first since it is the government—not the bureaucrat—which must ultimately face the public. For instance, when a senior actuary in the public service felt that it was his responsibility to the public to tell them through the media that the government's proposed Canada Pension Plan was unwise and actuarily unsound, he was immediately dismissed.

In order to protect the government from this kind of "betrayal," there are clauses in the Official Secrets Act providing for severe penalties for public servants who make unauthorized statements based on official information. Furthermore, the public servant must take an oath of office upon entering the federal public service in which he swears not to ". . .disclose or make known any matter that comes to my knowledge by reason of such employment. . . ." Violation of this principle can be immediate dismissal, as it did to a senior executive in the Central Mortgage and Housing Corporation who "leaked" a secret cabinet document to some Indian groups.

There are also restrictions on the extent to which a public servant

[23]The Glassco Commission distinguishes between *training,* which teaches people specific skills and technique, and *development,* which provides periodic exposure to broad courses on subjects related only tangentially to the job itself. Each can be important in the process of socializing an employee to the organizational norms.

can become involved in politics. He can vote and he can even contribute money to parties and attend meetings while he is a public servant, but he cannot actively campaign on behalf of a candidate or run for elected office. Since the passage of the most recent Public Service Employment Act, public servants have been permitted to take a leave of absence without pay from their jobs to seek election at the federal, provincial or municipal levels. The restrictions on the political activities of provincial public servants are generally similar to those at the federal level.[24]

One of the newest and potentially more important mechanisms of intrabureaucratic control is the system of collective bargaining that is developing in the federal public service. Until 1966, the public servant, as an employee, had very little in the way of true bargaining rights *vis-à-vis* the government-as-employer. The attitude was that the government, being a sovereign employer, could not constitutionally or morally be coerced in any way by the public service unions, or "staff associations" as they have been euphemistically called. This meant essentially that the public servants could organize in much the same way that any union in the private sector could, but that their relationship with the government employer was a "consultative" one and in no way a bargaining one. In a bargaining relationship, after all, the parties involved each have certain inducements and sanctions with which to threaten or entice the other side into meeting their demands. In private industry, the employer holds the power to raise wages and/or alter working conditions, and, in the last resort, to "lock out" the employees. The employees on the other hand, have the threat of strike action as an ultimate bargaining weapon. In such a situation each side holds certain powers that enable it to bargain with the other side. Up until 1966, therefore, while there were joint councils which facilitated the consultation of the government-as-employer with the staff associations and while the relationship was filled with good intentions, there was no collective bargaining relationship because the staff side had no bargaining power.

Because of the unique situation of staff relations in the public service before the current collective bargaining legislation, a very special kind of quasi-collective bargaining relationship emerged. Given the fact that they had no economic sanctions to bring to bear against the "sovereign employer," the staff associations very slowly began to realize that politically—in terms of the number of votes that they represented in certain constituencies—they did have a real bargaining power. It was not the direct economic sanction of the labour union, but the subtler political sanction of the pressure group. The demand of the public service "union" was not "meet our demands or we will strike" but "meet our demands or our members will vote against you in the next election." While this sort of a bargaining relationship is hardly overwhelming and while it did not in any way give the staff associations the power of labour unions in the private sector, it did permit them to speak with greater authority when mak-

[24]O.P. Dwivedi and J.P. Kyba, "Political Rights of Canada's Public Servants," in F. Vaughan, J.P. Kyba and O.P. Dwivedi, *Contemporary Issues in Canadian Politics*, (Prentice-Hall, Toronto, 1970), pp. 230–240.

ing wage demands on the government. Members of parliament in constituencies with large numbers of public servants, particularly in the Ottawa
area, were forced to become spokesmen for the staff associations; and a
failure to adequately support their demands could very well spell a defeat
at the polls.

With the collective bargaining legislation, the public service staff
associations were given a genuine system of collective bargaining.
Although, with some highly visible exceptions, it has not been exercised
extensively, the staff associations in the public service now possess the right
to strike. There is as well, however, a parallel system of conciliation and
binding arbitration through which collective agreements are now usually
arrived at. A similar system of arbitration which is binding on both sides
was introduced to the handling of employee grievances in the public service. Ultimately, however, the public servants can choose to take strike
action rather than follow the more moderate course ending in binding
arbitration.

We must now return to our first assumption: that the collective-
bargaining relationship in the public service is a form of intrabureaucratic
control. This control exists to the extent that the government employer
(the management side) and the government employee (the staff side) have
power over each other. Each limits the other's freedom of action because
each holds inducements and sanctions with which to convince the other to
at least partially meet its demands. The employer in the modern public
service collective-bargaining relationship is the Treasury Board. In other
words, the Treasury Board is the agency which actually does the "horse
trading" with the staff associations that ends in a compromise collective
agreement. The effect of this rather new power relationship on the complex of interdepartmental politics, is difficult to ascertain at this stage in its
development. Let it suffice to say here that the staff associations, which include among their members men who, in the aggregate, are involved in
policy making, which still retain the residual political power of a pressure
group, and which now possess the right to strike, have the potential for
considerable political power in the Canadian system.

The most effective controls over the bureaucracy are controls over
administrative decisions or spending. With the exception of certain broad
powers exercised by the cabinet (which may decide to disregard its advisors) or by a vigilant press (which may criticize policy formulation on
those rare occasions when it can penetrate the veil of secrecy) there are
very few direct checks over the policy advice provided by bureaucrats. The
press, academics, interest groups, the parliamentary opposition and even
the provincial governments are to a large extent prevented from evaluating the policies formulated by federal bureaucrats by the near monopoly
over information and technical expertise possessed by the large numbers of
federal policy advisors. The situation is exacerbated by strong Canadian
traditions of administrative secrecy and by the Official Secrets Act
described above. It is clear that the Canadian public is not always well
served by this situation; one of the most important reforms which might be
considered by any Canadian government would be the provision of much

freer access for the public to the information necessary to criticize the bureaucratic policy makers.

This concludes our discussion of the Canadian bureaucracy. The reader will have to look further into other sources listed in the bibliography for more detailed information about the structures and processes of this country's bureaucracy. We have attempted to give a perspective on the bureaucracy in the political process, and to demonstrate that, while the bureaucracy is crucial to the process of policy formulation, it is also an important actor in every other aspect of the political process in Canada.

17
Parliament:
The Policy Refinery

Parliament, the legislative branch of government in Canada, is legally supreme. The legal implications of the constitutional principle of parliamentary supremacy have already been discussed at great length and there is no need to reiterate them here. In this chapter our concern is with parliament's role in the policy process. It will be seen that, while parliament is legally supreme, it is functionally subordinate to the cabinet and the bureaucracy in the making of public policy. Today, parliamentary supremacy is largely a mythical expression of the belief that in our system of government ultimate political power *should* reside in the elected representatives of the people. Yet paradoxically, despite the very real functional limitations on parliament's ability to be truly "supreme", the myth remains significant as both a symbol and an operational principle of our form of democratic polity. Moreover, to the extent that the role of the cabinet minister making policy decisions in the cabinet chamber is intertwined with his role as a member of parliament, there is a day-to-day linkage between the myth and the reality of the policy process.

The structure of the Canadian legislature is *bicameral:* that is, Parliament consists of two separate legislative bodies, the House of Commons and the Senate. The House of Commons is the elected branch of parliament and is therefore more important than the Senate which is an appointed body. The bulk of our analysis of the role of parliament in the policy process will focus on the House of Commons, although a few words will be said about the Senate and its place in the Canadian political system.

THE FUNCTIONS OF PARLIAMENT

The Policy Function[1] Chapter 1 sets up a descriptive model of the policy process in Canada which posits policy making as a four-stage process. Generally speaking, parliament is paramount only at the fourth stage (refinement and legitimation) of that process. However, it can and does have some impact at all stages of policy making, and we must com-

[1] For the best overview description of this see: R.J. Jackson and M.M. Atkinson, *The Canadian Legislative System*, (Macmillan, Toronto, 1974).

ment briefly on that before proceeding to the more detailed discussion of parliament as a core institution at the policy-refining and formal output stage.

As an initiator of policy ideas, parliament still has ample opportunity to influence policy decisions. As was pointed out in Chapter 1, the basic problem of policy initiation is one of communication. It is necessary to communicate one's policy idea to the cabinet which functions as the main priority-setting institution in Canadian government. Parliament can and does function as a communication link between the public at large and the cabinet. When people make demands on the political system, they often make such inputs by writing letters or speaking to a member of parliament. This particular input channel was especially important at an early period in Canadian political history when other channels of access to the political decision makers were not as well developed as they are now. As an input channel today, however, parliament is in competition with many other institutions such as interest groups, parties, the media and the bureaucracy, and most of these other institutions can communicate policy ideas to the cabinet as well as, if not better than, parliament. Furthermore, some of the modern techniques such as survey research, and institutions such as task forces or large departmental field organizations have permitted the cabinet and the bureaucracy to go out into the environment of the system and actively seek out new policy ideas. Hence, parliament's role as a communicator of new policy ideas to the system's priority setters has been much diluted. Parliament can still convey demands to the cabinet, but there are many other institutions and many other techniques which achieve the same end and can possibly achieve it more effectively.

It must be remembered that, as intelligent people, MPs periodically come up with good policy ideas themselves. In such cases, the MP can function as policy initiator in a very immediate way by communicating an idea of his own directly to the cabinet. A good example of policy initiation by an individual MP was the abolition of capital punishment. The idea was introduced in parliament originally as a private member's bill and was subsequently picked up by the cabinet and re-introduced as government policy. Perhaps the classic example is the inception of an old-age security scheme in Canada, for the introduction of that idea in the nation was largely the work of W.S. Woodsworth. (Indeed, in an earlier era, Woodsworth used parliament as an effective platform to prompt Liberal governments into much of the social welfare legislation that we have today.) Occurrences such as these are no longer frequent, however, in spite of a cabinet decision in 1973 to have all private member's bills examined by the bureaucracy with a view to allowing some which were in line with government priorities to pass.

An MP's influence on the cabinet will depend on the prestige, knowledge, and background of the individual involved. Where a course of action being considered by the cabinet is likely to affect a particular geographic region of Canada, there is some chance that concerted opposition or support by that region's members will influence the cabinet in setting its priorities. However, the cabinet will probably have independent sources of information about the attitudes of the people in the affected region, and if the independent information contradicts the position of the MPs, the cabinet is just as likely to heed the former. Thus, the role of parliament at the priority-setting stage of policy making depends on the willingness of the cabinet to be influenced by the MPs, and on the availability and substance of competing advice.

Policy formulation is the business of the bureaucracy subject to the control of the cabinet. Parliament's role at this stage is virtually nonexistent, because of the generally technical and complex nature of the problem of formulating policy alternatives. In terms of expertise and available time, the MP is ill-equipped to contribute much at this stage of policy making.

Parliament is the core institution at the *refinement stage* of the policy process. While it is the legislative drafting branch of the Department of Justice which converts the raw policy formulation into a bill, and while the cabinet committee on Legislation and House Planning conducts a clause-by-clause review of pending legislation, it is parliament which "cleans up" and polishes the draft so that it is an accurate reflection of what was in the minds of the policy formulators, and so that it does not have unintended and perverse consequences. In the House of Commons, and more specifically in the standing committees, the MPs go over government policy proposals, tightening up the wording, criticizing the weaknesses, suggesting amendments, and through public debate, publicizing the inherent advantages and disadvantages of the bill. In subsequent discussion of parliament, we will focus mainly on this aspect of its policy function.

Finally, parliament is one of the institutions involved in the ultimate conversion of government policy to system output. While the formal votes in the House of Commons and the Senate may appear to be merely *pro forma* steps akin to executive *proclamation*[2] and the Governor General's *assent*, this final ratification or rejection of government policy proposals may, in fact, be a most significant function of parliament. It is true that the number of government proposals actually defeated in parliament is very small, but this is partially the result of the existence of a watchful parliament which may have discouraged governments from introducing intemperate legislation in the first place, and of the fact that many a controversial piece of legislation is simply allowed to die on the order paper without any government attempt to bring it forward for second or subsequent readings. The ultimate power to reject a government's legislative proposals may be significant as a deterrent, but its exercise has been extremely rare.

Functional Limitations on Parliamentary Supremacy

The functional subordination of parliament to the cabinet in policy making has been mentioned previously, but we have yet to say why this is the case. To examine this point, it is necessary to look first at the control exer-

---

[2]The power to proclaim a law or to not do so is potentially an authority in the hands of the PM. Before a law can be implemented it must be proclaimed and this is an executive prerogative. If the PM does not like a law or part of a law passed by

cised by the cabinet over its own backbenchers, and then to consider the cabinet control exercised over the opposition MPs, particularly in the minority government situation.

Party Discipline: Government Control Over Government Backbenchers The control by the Prime Minister and cabinet over the government backbenchers is one aspect of what is usually known as *party discipline.* It is maintained by threat of the various sanctions and by the various inducements cited below, although it is indeed seldom that the government is forced to overtly impose a sanction or withhold a promise in order to enforce discipline. Usually these powers of the parliamentary leadership are tacitly recognized and accepted by the government MPs so that party discipline is maintained without resort to specific sanctions.

Perhaps the most important single factor facilitating the cabinet's control over its own backbenchers in the House of Commons is the simple fact that the cabinet ministers are the parliamentary leaders of the party. There is a natural tendency and willingness in each MP to accept the control of a Prime Minister who has been selected as party leader at a convention and who is responsible to a large extent, in this era of "leadership politics," for the party's success at the polls. Besides this, the very fact that backbenchers and cabinet ministers are members of the same political party provides at least limited grounds for a consensus. This point should not be overemphasized, however, for as has been pointed out in an earlier chapter, the major Canadian political parties are "omnibus" or "brokerage" parties which attempt to aggregate large numbers of interests, and are often, therefore, characterized by much intraparty conflict. Nevertheless, the obvious fact remains that the government of the day will more likely be able to control its *own* backbenchers than the opposition members. And, where a majority of MPs are from the government party the ability to control the government side of the House is naturally, all that is needed to control parliament.

The power of dissolution is the basic constitutional control the Prime Minister possesses over the backbench MP. According to this constitutional convention, the Prime Minister has the sole power to advise the Governor General to dissolve parliament and call an election. In a general election, every MP must put his job on the line, and for most members, this means a tough struggle. Not very many MPs have seats so "safe" that they can afford to campaign without great energy and large outlays of money, and the "typical" Canadian federal election will see some 30 to 40 per cent of them losing their jobs. Thus, although parliament has never been dissolved in order to force dissident backbenchers into line, the fact that most MPs do not enjoy fighting for their jobs probably has some effect on their attitudes to the government's policies. While it would be unwise for a government to call an election to whip its own backbenchers into line—it would show the public that there was a split in the party's

parliament, he can exercise an effective veto by simply not proclaiming it or by delaying proclamation. Whether this will be necessary will depend upon factors such as the prevalence of minority parliaments and the consistency of party discipline.

ranks—the threat of dissolution can be very important in controlling the House of Commons in a minority government situation.[3]

X A subtler but very real power of the government to control its own members flows from the control over the party purse strings. Fighting elections today, in the era of TV campaigns and "Madison Avenue" techniques, is an expensive proposition, and an individual candidate who is not supported by one of the political parties will usually be unable to afford the kind of campaign that will ensure him high probability of success. Thus, the PM and cabinet, and to a certain extent the leaders of the opposition parties, can control maverick backbenchers through either explicit or implicit threat of withdrawal of party financial assistance in the next election campaign.

There are non-financial elements of party support in an election which can be almost as important to the MP as assistance from the party treasurer. The MP who has been a "good boy" and supported the government in parliament will be assured of a visit to his constituency by one of the party's notables to assist him in his campaign. In the 1968 election campaign, for example, the visit to a constituency of Trudeau himself might well have been critical in determining the outcome of that riding's contest. Furthermore, while the party leaders must beware of overtly meddling with the autonomy of the constituency nominating process, if it is known that a sitting member is unlikely to get support from the national level of the party, the local people might be influenced to "ditch" him.

Expulsion from the party caucus is a technique of control that can be exercised by the leadership of a parliamentary party if a maverick MP becomes more trouble than he is worth. The case of Ralph Cowan, a Liberal member from Toronto during the 1960s, is a good example. By constantly levelling bitter criticism at the Liberal government, Cowan became such an embarrassment to the party that he was finally expelled from the caucus. This meant that he was not informed of the party's plans and policies, and thus had to sit as a virtual independent in the House of Commons. When the next election was called, Cowan tried to get the Liberal nomination in his constituency again and failed. (Mr. Cowan ran instead as an independent and was defeated.) However, while it is possible to use the rather drastic measure of expulsion from caucus in the case of a single MP, this technique cannot be used to control the opposition of large numbers of government MPs, for the simple reason that it publicizes the party's internal disunity and could, if party standings are close in the House, result in the government's defeat.

The major inducement available to a government to control its backbenchers is the promise that the well-behaved and efficient member may be promoted to the cabinet, or at least to a temporary sojourn as parliamentary assistant to a minister. Since these positions bestow both income and prestige, potential dissidents may consider them sufficiently desirable incentives to keep themselves in line.

Party discipline is similarly applied in the relationship of the

---

[3]We will provide more detailed description of minority government below.

opposition leaders to their backbenchers. The situation varies from party to party, but with the exception of the power of dissolution, the sanctions and inducements available to the government to control its backbenchers are also available to the leaders of opposition parties. But while party discipline is a factor in the relationship of the leaders of the opposition parties to their backbenchers, it is not as important here as it is for the government party. The leaders of the opposition party can afford to tolerate a degree of dissension and disagreement among their MPs because the fate of a government does not hang in the balance; if a few opposition backbenchers split with the leaders of the party "*on division*" (formal vote in the House of Commons) the result will be little more than embarrassment for the opposition leader. Furthermore, when criticising the government, an opposition MP can "oppose" in a number of ways. As long as he is against the policy of the government, the leaders of the opposition will generally permit deviation from the party line.

The primary focus of the analysis thus far has been on the relationship of the government to the government backbenchers, for in a majority government situation, the basic problem of maintaining control over the House of Commons is coextensive with the problem of government party discipline. If the cabinet in a majority government situation can control its own backbenchers, it can stay in power. In fact, there has never been a case of a majority government's defeat in Canada by a vote in the House of Commons, and the likelihood of that eventuality in the future is virtually nil. While legally in control of the House of Commons, the government MPs are functionally disqualified from opposing government policy in the House through the rigid enforcement of the principle of party discipline. As a Liberal backbencher from Toronto was quoted as saying, "We're on call sometimes 14 or 16 hours a day just to support legislation that usually we didn't have any part in framing and sometimes don't even particularly like".

Government Control Over the Parliamentary Opposition In a majority government situation, the basic strengths and weaknesses of the opposition parties in parliament are determined primarily by the procedures of the House of Commons. Since they are never going to be able to outvote the government on any policy proposal, the opposition parties must content themselves with using subtler techniques to attempt to influence policy.

The basic power of the opposition in the House of Commons stems from its ability to control *time* through debate. The House rules of procedure are founded on a balance between two conflicting principles of parliamentary democracy. The first is that the government should be able to get on with the business of governing in an efficient and expeditious fashion, and the second is that the opposition should have ample time to criticize the government's proposals. In other words, the opposition should be able to "oppose", but not to the extreme of obstructionism; and the government should be able to get its programs through the House of Commons efficiently, but not without permitting thorough and often tiresome debate. Until recently, the bias of House of Commons procedures was towards the needs of the opposition parties at the expense of government. If every opposition member were to speak as long as the rules permitted on every stage of the debate, most legislation would be debated almost endlessly. Given this situation, the opposition, although unable to vote down the government's legislation, could achieve the same end by the technique of filibuster, or endless debate. However, in order to prevent filibustering, the procedures of the House of Commons have always provided for *closure*, which is a counter-technique whereby the government party, with the aid of the Speaker, can unilaterally terminate a debate. While these techniques have long been a part of the rules of debate in the House, they have not often been used; it is bad politically for the opposition to filibuster and be branded "obstructionist", or for the government to apply closure and be branded dictatorial or "heavy-handed". In practice, the government will often make deals with the opposition regarding the specifics of the legislation being debated. In return for a minor change in the legislation, the opposition parties will often agree to limit their criticism to a few spokesmen for the party, and thus speed up the passage of the bill in question. The government will seldom agree to a change in the substance of legislation in return for this kind of agreement, and this fact is generally respected by the opposition parties.

In the spring of 1969, a fundamental change in the Standing Orders of the House of Commons was passed after long debate and, ultimately, only after the government was forced to invoke closure. The point of contention at that time was Standing Order (S.O.) 75 (c) which provides for unilateral limitation of debate at each stage of the passage of a bill through the House. If the government cannot achieve the agreement of all parties or at least of a majority of the parties in setting time limits for debate, it is permitted to unilaterally impose the desired time limits. Initially it was feared that this would take away the fundamental source of opposition influence in the House of Commons, the control of time. However, the extensive use of S.O. 75 (c) by a government would be a very unpopular tactic with the public, for its effect is to "gag" the opposition almost as effectively as closure. It is still far better for both the government and the opposition to seek some sort of mutually acceptable agreement on the limitation of debate. Hence, while procedurally the balance has shifted from the opposition to the government, actual practice indicates that the government–opposition relationship has not substantially altered as a result of the passage of S.O. 75 (c).

The great flaw in the argument that the opposition can influence policy through control over parliamentary time is that this power is a negative one. It is indeed possible to stall the government, and it is possible even to influence the government to make minor changes in its legislation, but if the government is committed to it, the substance of the legislation is non-negotiable. Furthermore, the government can usually stand firm even on the minor demands of the opposition if it chooses, and the opposition can merely balk temporarily.

Other than its control over the time to be used up in the passage of government legislation, the opposition has only one fundamental strength in attempting to influence the government. This is the traditional power to publicly criticize the government's policy proposals. In debates in the House of Commons, and increasingly in the lobby of parliament before the TV cameras, the opposition MPs do their very best to make the government's policies appear foolhardy, irresponsible, dangerous, opportunistic, or just plain silly. The arguments they present to back this up are designed to convince the voting public that a new government should be put in power at the earliest opportunity. Unfortunately, the great weakness of the opposition parties in endeavouring to convince the public that the government policy is bad is—once again—their lack of information and expertise. By the time the opposition parties are involved in the policy process, the legislation they are considering has usually been the object of intensive research by an innumerable experts in task forces, royal commissions, interdepartmental committees, government departments, the PMO and the PCO—all of whom have probably taken into account the recommendations of interest groups and other private institutions. The likelihood is slim that a handful of MPs, with little time to spare for even cursory research, will be able to add much substantial criticism of such heavily studied proposals.

Thus, while the opposition can criticize government policy both publicly and in the House, the impact of this criticism is not likely to be great. Empowered and expected to criticize the government, the opposition in the House of Commons is functionally disqualified from doing so through its lack of information and expertise. The really significant arguments will have been made and met already by competing experts in the various institutions vested with the responsibility for advising the government, (although, because of the Canadian tradition of government secrecy, these arguments may never see the light of day).

Minority Government The relationship of the cabinet to parliament is significantly altered when there is a minority government situation in the House of Commons. Minority government occurs when the government party does not have a majority of the seats in the House of Commons; in order to stay in power, it must at all times be able to secure the support of some members of other parties. The government in this case is usually formed by the party which holds a plurality of seats, although it is conceivable that a party standing second in number of seats could form the government with the voting support of a third party. In Canada, a minority situation normally means that either the Liberals or the Conservatives will form the government, with the other one forming the official opposition. The third parties hold the balance of power in the House, and can choose either to defeat the government by voting against it, or to maintain the government by siding with it. As was pointed out earlier, the government can often be sustained at length in this situation.

The Liberals have been particularly successful in maintaining minority governments, most notably in the period of 1963–68 when they managed to stay in power with little difficulty. Throughout this time, the minority Liberal government needed only a few opposition votes to retain control of the House of Commons, and with thirty to fifty seats in the hands of the NDP, Ralliement Créditiste and Social Credit, it was usually a simple matter to find them. The real strength of the Liberal government during this period was that it stood pretty much "in the middle" on most issues, with the NDP and Créditistes taking positions to the left and right of the government respectively. Virtually all of the government's policy proposals were opposed by the Conservative official opposition "on principle", and by either the Créditistes or the NDP. However, the two minor parties were never able to vote on the same side because of their radically different points of view, and because through much of that period, the third-party MPs feared an election as much as the Liberals did. Again, in the period from 1972 to 1974, the Liberals formed a minority government and successfully stayed in power by consistently acquiring support from the NDP. They were eventually defeated in a vote of no confidence when the NDP finally abandoned them, but in the subsequent election the Liberals were swept to power with a majority, and the ranks of the NDP were seriously depleted, confirming a fear of third-party MPs that the forcing of elections such circumstances could well cost them their seats.

The lesson of these two examples is not only that the problem of controlling the House of Commons in a minority government situation is much more complicated and difficult than it is in the majority situation, but that it is still quite possible to govern if some adjustments are made. In the 1972–74 period, for example, it was common practice for cabinet ministers to consult opposition spokesmen before bringing bills forward, and ministers could be certain that they would have great difficulty in getting their bills on the order paper at all if they could not convince their cabinet colleagues and the Prime Minister that sufficient discussions had taken place with the opposition to assure passage of the legislation. Meetings between government and opposition House Leaders, weekly events in any case, became much more frequent and the views of the opposition House Leaders were given much more weight both in House scheduling and in cabinet deliberations.

In the spring of 1968 a constitutional issue arose and was settled in a manner which may become a precedent, altering the status of minority governments. The Liberal Government was defeated, quite by accident, because of a very high rate of absenteeism on the part of the government backbenchers. The vote had been on the third reading of an important piece of financial legislation, and such a defeat of an important government bill would normally have meant the resignation of the government and an immediate election. At this time the Liberals were embroiled in a leadership campaign, and the opposition parties were not prepared to fight an election either. The solution was for the government to introduce a motion of confidence in itself at the next sitting of the House, essentially asking the House of Commons if it "really" wanted an immediate election. The government was given a vote of confidence by a majority of the House and was permitted to stay in power. The significance of this is that whereas previously a minority government could force unpalatable legislation on the opposition by threat of election, now, perhaps, the legislation can be defeated without forcing the resignation of the government.[4]

[4]See also Chapter 6.

To conclude this section it can be re-emphasized that while there is a potential for greater policy-making power in the hands of the opposition in the situation of minority government, there remain severe limitations on the ability of the opposition to exercise this power. First of all, the fact remains that the opposition does not have the access to expert advice as does the cabinet, and cannot therefore deal as meaningfully with policy issues. Secondly, procedure in the House of Commons is such that the legislative program, the agenda of parliament, is controlled by the PM and his cabinet. This means that any control that is exercised by the opposition is largely negative in nature. Thirdly, as has been pointed out above, the existing alignment of political parties in Canada militates against any concerted opposition effort. The minor opposition parties are usually too divided among themselves ever to unite to defeat the government in a minority situation. Finally, majority government has become a sort of norm of our system of government, and, in spite of its prevalence, a minority situation is always viewed as atypical and merely temporary. In fact the 1965 election which was called by the Liberal minority government was fought in part on the issue of a return to majority government, although in that case the electorate was not convinced.

Restraints on the Government Party Caucus It has been seen that party discipline prevents the government MP from either voting against the government on division, or from actively criticizing government policy in debates in the House of Commons. Where the government MP is alleged to have his say on the policies of the government is in the caucus where, it is traditionally held, he can influence policy through concerted criticism and articulate dissent. Caucus consists of all of the supporters of a political party in the House of Commons and is intended to establish a communication link between the party leaders and the rank and file. While all parties have a caucus, the one which is most potentially significant in the policy process is that of the government. The meetings of government caucus occur weekly while the House is sitting: they are attended by the cabinet ministers and they are held *in camera*. The tradition of caucus procedure is that decisions are not made by a formal vote, but rather that a consensus is achieved through dialogue and a willingness to seek mutually satisfactory agreement. Because the meetings are held *in camera*, the MP can speak his mind freely, with no fear of endangering the image of party unity. When there is backbench solidarity in caucus it is possible for the members to stall or even completely arrest legislative proposals put forward by the cabinet but this happens very seldom. The odds that a group as diverse in its interests as the caucus will ever be unanimous in opposition to the cabinet are very slight. For the most part, the cabinet can bank on divergencies of opinion among the backbenchers in caucus being at least as wide as the gulf between the cabinet and the rank and file. The most basic weakness of the caucus, however, stems from its relative lack of information. The minister who is proposing and defending a given policy in caucus has a fund of facts and figures on which to draw, while the MP with limited research facilities and limited personal expertise, cannot compete with the vast array of expert advice that the minister has at his finger tips.

A secondary argument about the caucus's utility as a policy organ of the party posits the role of the MP as a representative of interests. The argument is that the cabinet can "test" its legislative proposals by submitting them for the consideration of a representative body. In most cases today, however, the MP is not as well equipped as the Prime Minister and his political advisors to speak authoritatively about the wishes of Canadians and the feasibility, in political terms, of any particular policy proposal. Again, the problem is not so much that the articulation of interests has been avowedly taken away from parliament or, more specifically, from the caucus, but that other institutions such as the bureaucracy and the centralized political advisory bodies are competing with the MP in the performance of this function.

After a great deal of criticism from Liberal backbenchers, a new set of ground rules for caucus procedure and a major reorganization of the federal Liberal caucus itself was approved by the cabinet and introduced in the fall of 1969. Basically, the new rules bind the ministers to introduce all legislative proposals in caucus before introducing them in the House. Previously, it had been a fairly common practice to discuss the policy proposals in caucus after the legislation had actually been introduced and the government had already been publicly committed to it. While there has been little to suggest that the new rules have made the caucus any more effective as an organ for changing the government's mind about policy proposals, at least the Liberal backbenchers are now "the first to know" when the cabinet is about to introduce a policy. [5]

In an attempt to permit a degree of specialization in caucus deliberations, the same 1969 reorganization also divided the Liberal caucus into functional sub-committees roughly paralleling the Standing Committees of the House itself. Each of these sub-committees of the caucus is given some research assistance to enable it to develop a measure of expertise in a particular area of concern. While this is generally a good idea, and has in fact been adopted by the opposition parties in the House, the fact remains that one or two graduate students working on a given policy area will not enable a caucus sub-committee to compete with a minister who has an entire government department to provide him with research assistance. While these changes will make the discussions in caucus marginally more meaningful, they are not going to alter fundamentally the relationship between the caucus and the cabinet in the policy process.

Basically, then, the caucus is neither sufficiently united nor equipped with expertise and research personnel to effectively initiate substantive changes in government policy proposals. More and more, the function of the caucus is to assist the government in scheduling the parliamentary speeches of the Liberal members, and to inform them what to expect in the upcoming parliamentary week.

The General Audit Function[6] Perhaps, because of the func-

---

[5] Jackson and Atkinson cite two examples. See *op. cit*, p. 70.

[6] Jackson and Atkinson refer to this as the "Surveillance" function of parliament. (*op. cit.*, pp. 86–95.)

tional limitations on the role of the parliament in the policy process, the most important function of parliament today is what we might call the *general audit function*. This is not a financial audit, although, through the Public Accounts Committee parliament does, in a sense, audit the financial affairs of the government. Rather, the general audit function of the Canadian parliament involves broadly based public criticism of the total record of the government. This process goes on almost constantly, and brings to the attention of the press and the public many of the shortcomings and potential shortcomings of the government of the day. Because of party discipline and loyalty, the general audit of the overall record of the government is performed primarily by the opposition parties and not by the government backbenchers. Furthermore, the focus of this kind of criticism is not specific policy proposals but the "state of the nation" in broad terms. While the general audit of the government's record goes on at all stages of government legislation, the bulk of such criticism comes out through various procedural devices and special debates which occur intermittently during each parliamentary session. Each of these deserves more detailed mention.

The Throne Speech Debate   The Standing Orders of the House of Commons provide for a debate on the Address in Reply to His Excellency's Speech. [7] The Speech from the Throne is prepared by the Prime Minister and read by the Governor General to a joint sitting of the House of Commons and the Senate. In this speech, which is delivered at the opening of parliament, there is a review of the "state of the nation" and a statement of the legislative program of the government in the coming session. Eight days are set aside for opposition criticism and comment on the record of the government, and on these days the normal rules of "relevance" that apply in debates in the House are suspended. The backbench member has the opportunity to speak his mind on anything that has been bothering him or any matter which is of special concern to his constituents. The tendency is for the backbenchers to make special pleas for local needs and interests, and for the opposition frontbenchers to use the debate to introduce motions of non-confidence in the government. The subject matter of the Throne Speech Debate, while varied, does not usually involve specific policy proposals of the government but tends, rather, to be devoted to broad criticisms of the record. To the extent that the speeches of the various MPs are reported in their home newspapers, this debate is helpful in showing the voters back home that their man in Ottawa is working on their behalf. Similarly, to the extent that the frontbench speeches of the opposition parties are reported in the news media, the throne speech debate functions to publicize the real and imagined shortcomings of the government as seen through opposition eyes.

The Business of Supply and Ways and Means   A total of twenty-five days spread over three separate *supply periods* is allotted to the opposition for debating the business of supply. On these *allotted days*, or *opposition days*, opposition motions take precedence over government business, and debates on the motions are limited to twenty minutes per speaker with the

[7]Standing Order 38 (1)

exception of the mover and seconder. The function of these allotted days is to permit the opposition an ample opportunity to criticize the government's spending policy. The debates on these days constitute an important part of the general audit function of parliament in that they force the government to publicly defend its spending policy against tough opposition criticism.

The Budget Debate is the second 'free-for-all' debate that occurs during the parliamentary year—the first being the Throne Speech Debate—during which the backbenchers are permitted to put on the record their own comments on the government's over-all financial policy for the benefit of their constituents and the nation. The Budget Debate begins after the Minister of Finance has brought down the budget in the House of Commons, and it lasts for six days. As with the Throne Speech Debate, the relevancy rule for speeches is relaxed and MPs can wander fairly far afield in seeking to embarrass the government or to make themselves look good, although one is encouraged to speak to the *ways and means* proposals set down in the budget.

"S.O. 26" Debates   Standing Order 26 of the House of Commons provides for a motion to adjourn the House ". . .for the purpose of discussing a specific and important matter requiring urgent consideration." If a matter has arisen suddenly which is not likely to be brought before the House of Commons in any other way, and which is not a purely administrative matter, this Standing Order permits a special debate to consider it immediately. The Speaker is given final say as to whether or not the matter is urgent and whether it is a matter for consideration under S.O. 26. If the Speaker decides that the matter is deserving of further consideration, the motion to adjourn is held over until the evening sitting of the House, at which time the matter is debated. There is no formal time limit on this form of debate, although the Speaker can declare the motion to adjourn "carried" when he ". . .is satisfied that the debate has been concluded. . ." and forthwith adjourn the House until the next day.

A time limit of 20 minutes is placed on speeches in an S.O. 26 debate. While such debates are not granted frequently, we are seeing more and more of them since the 1969 rules revisions. Basically these debates function to permit the opposition to raise issues with which the government is not dealing in the House, and to make public their opinion that the government should be doing something. While an S.O. 26 debate will not be granted to discuss something the government has already done but with which the opposition disagrees, it is an important means for pointing out something the government should be doing but is not. Moreover, it is not necessary that the Speaker grant the request for a debate in order for S.O. 26 to serve its purpose. Simply by requesting a debate, the opposition can suggest that something is amiss and requires attention.

A procedure which is akin to S.O. 26 and which is being used more and more frequently is defined by Standing Order 43. This is a procedure whereby a member can ask for leave of the House to present a motion without the standard "notice". The obvious intention of S.O. 43 is to permit the house to set aside regular business in order to deal with genuine emergency circumstances, and its use requires unanimous consent. This procedure has been seized upon by the opposition backbenchers as an opportunity to raise an issue even though there is little hope that they will achieve the necessary unanimity to permit an actual debate. As Jackson and Atkinson have pointed out, this probably is not a good tactic for the opposition to employ because a "43" precedes Question Period and possibly detracts from the "keynote" first question of the leader of the opposition which sets the theme for that first hour of the daily business: ". . .The abuse of this rule restricts the time parliament has at its disposal and, because they directly precede the oral question period, such motions detract attention from the main questions of the day. . . ."[8]

The Question Period The question period provides the most interesting and lively interchange between ministers and opposition members in the daily routine of the House of Commons. It is the question period which is covered most closely by the press gallery, and in the public eye it is likely that the question period is viewed as the most important opportunity for the opposition to attack the government. Any backbencher, including those on the government side of the House, can ask a question of a minister, but because of party discipline, because the government backbencher can usually get the information he wants without a formal question, and because the Speaker traditionally recognizes opposition members more often than government members, the question period has become a time almost exclusively for opposition questions.

Questions simply seeking information from a minister of the Crown are normally written down and placed on the Order Paper. The answers to such written questions are in turn handed to the clerk of the House and subsequently printed in *Hansard*. The function of this form of question is to assist the individual MP in gathering information relevant to his interests and those of his constituents. However, in some cases the opposition will ask questions simply in order to get "on the record" information that might be embarrassing to the government in the future. Sometimes, if the answer is potentially embarrassing, an opposition member will ask for an *oral answer*. Oral answers are requested by placing an asterisk beside the written question. No member may have more than three "starred" questions in the Order Paper at the same time.

More important, however, than either the written question or the starred questions, are those asked during the daily 40-minute *Oral Question Period*. Its purpose is to permit a member to ask a minister ". . .questions on matters of urgency. . . ."[9] or questions that should be answered immediately rather than placed on the Order Paper. The Speaker is formally empowered to direct that an oral question is not urgent and therefore should be placed on the Order Paper, although in practice, this stipulation is seldom invoked. Generally the Oral Question Period is an opportunity for the opposition to ask questions which could potentially embarrass the government. The question must be very carefully phrased in order to force the

---

[8]Jackson and Atkinson, *op. cit.*, p. 93.
[9]S.O. 39 (5).

minister to answer it on the opposition's terms, for there is no debate permitted during the question period. Sometimes a member will receive the permission of the Speaker to ask a "supplementary" question if the minister has evaded the point of the main question, although even then it is difficult to pin down the minister if he is determined to be evasive. One of the interesting features of the Oral Question Period is the seemingly random banter that is carried on by members who have not been recognized by the Speaker. Such heckling and wisecracking, which is often reported verbatim in *Hansard*, provides some opportunity for backbenchers on both sides of the House to put a few comments on the record on behalf of their side. What usually ensues is a verbal fencing match with precocious opposition members sparring with the ministers, attempting to bait them into saying something that is an embarrassment to the government. The minister must "keep his cool" and not allow himself to be goaded into saying anything more than is necessary to provide factual information or, as is often the case, to gracefully evade the question.

If a member is not satisfied with the answer to a question, he may serve notice that he intends to raise the matter "on the adjournment" of the House. This procedure provides for a thirty minute debate at the termination of the daily sitting wherein the member raising the question is given seven minutes to speak, and other members must limit their comments to three minutes each. Questions asked on the adjournment are more important in the U.K. than in Canada, but they provide an opportunity to debate a question which would not be debatable in the Oral Question Period. Generally, adjournment debates are simply another opportunity for the opposition members to attempt to embarrass the government, and for all members to raise questions involving the interests of their particular constituencies or regions.

Questions in the House thus perform two functions. First, they can provide the MP with information. Second, they can give the opposition MPs an opportunity to expose the shortcomings of the government. However, the limitations on questions as a device for parliamentary criticism of the government are many. In the first place, the minister may refuse to answer the question on the grounds that a government policy statement is forthcoming, or that to answer would be a breach of national security. Secondly, in the case of questions on the Order Paper, the minister can take a long time to answer the question or he may even choose not to answer at all. At the end of each session of parliament there is always a long list of questions on the Order Paper which have not been answered and which probably never will be. Finally, the minister can simply refuse to answer the question, even in the Oral Question Period. There is nothing which compels a minister to answer parliamentary questions, although for political reasons a minister cannot afford to treat parliament with indifference or disdain. Furthermore, unanswered questions get asked over and over again until either an answer is obtained or the public is made aware of the fact that a minister is "covering up" or "withholding information from the Canadian people".

Perhaps the most important limitation of the question period as a tool that facilitates the general audit function of parliament is the simple fact that most of the exchanges that occur between opposition members and ministers deteriorate to a mere banter. Often this is a relatively friendly session of wisecracks and "in jokes" which does not become elevated to the discussion of any matters of substance. The questions asked are "loaded" and the answers given are usually evasive and designed to "defuse" the question rather than to answer it. Once in a while the question period provides truly bitter exchanges between members, with much name-calling by the principals and jeering by the rest. Sometimes such an exchange causes a minister to blurt out information which the government would have preferred to keep quiet. The best example of this was the exchange between members of the opposition and Justice Minister Cardin which ultimately precipitated the so-called Munsinger Scandal in 1966.

Thus, while at times the question period does not accomplish anything of substance, it functions to keep the government alert. Corruption in high places is sometimes uncovered through the opposition's use of the question period and the threat of such public exposure perhaps serves as a conscience for the government. Despite its limitations, therefore, the question period remains one of parliament's most important procedural devices for criticizing the cabinet and for auditing the record of the government.

Opportunity for broad criticism of government policy comes up during the proceedings on public bills and at almost all stages of parliamentary debate, but on these occasions the debate is usually restricted to the specific legislation being considered. In other words, the Speaker will enforce the relevancy requirement for all speeches at all stages in the normal process of passing public bills. Thus, the best opportunity for broadly criticizing the cabinet and publicly auditing the government's record occurs in the various special debates and in the question period. The effectiveness of the opposition in parliament as an auditor of the record of the government is lessened by that lack of information and expertise which is the fundamental weakness of the MP in the policy process. Nevertheless, there is still an important function to be performed here, and it is hoped that with the addition of research assistants in the research offices of the various parties, and through the other means such as the "parliamentary internship" program whereby young university graduates serve for one year as assistants to individual MPs, the MP can remain an effective political auditor even though he can no longer be an effective policy maker.

The Representative Function: The MP and his Constituency

It has been seen that parliament as an institution and individual MPs as actors in that institution are functionally disqualified from having a substantive impact on government policy decisions. The primary policy role of parliament is to refine and polish government policy and not to set priorities or formulate policy outputs. Because of this limitation on parliament's policy role, we hypothesize that the most important aspects of the MP's representative role must be limited to non-policy matters. The MP today is acting more and more as a channel through which the individual constituent can register and seek redress for grievances. The types of problems being dealt with by MPs do not require large-scale policy decisions in order to effect a remedy; they involve inequities in the application of existing policies to individual cases, which can be remedied by specific administrative action. The redress of many individual grievances can be achieved through simple means such as a telephone call to the minister or public official involved, or, if that should fail, through a question in the House of Commons which has the effect of publicizing an injustice or inequity being perpetrated by the administration. This function of the MP is like that of an ombudsman. Because the MP has some official status in Ottawa and because he has the power to publicly assert the case in parliament, he is in a good position to act as an ombudsman for his constituents, or at least for those constituents who have the initiative to approach him.

This same concern with the inequities and injustices inevitably committed by large government administrations probably also affects the individual MP's role in the policy-refining stage of the policy process, where parliament can and does take a positive and active role. At this stage, administrative consequences missed by the cabinet and the bureaucracy are sometimes seen by parliament. Because of the MP's familiarity with the sorts of problems created by carelessly drafted legislation, he can attempt to minimize the number of grievances likely to arise from the administration of an act while it is at the refining stage of the policy process. Thus, the MP represents the interests of individual constituents not only in seeking to redress grievances, but also in attempting to prevent their occurrence.

The ombudsman function of the MP is important to the system, for it creates support for the system among people who might otherwise feel that they have no access to the authorities. While many MPs still feel that their most important role is to represent the interests of their constituencies, their regions, or the country as a whole in the policy process, it is unlikely that backbench MPs will ever again be able to take a very positive policy role. However, as long as the MP remains alert to the injustices and inadequacies in the implementation of public policy, particularly as they affect individual Canadians, such unfortunate concomitants of "big government" can perhaps be minimized.

Summary and Conclusions: The Functions of Parliament

The functions of parliament include the positive functions of refining policy and converting it into legislative outputs of the system. However, in relation to the political system as a whole, parliament's more negative ratification/rejection and general audit functions are of much greater importance. In the extreme case, if it is clear that the PM is losing his marbles—if he should grow a little moustache, comb his hair down over one eye and start wearing a uniform to work—it is still open to parliament to say, "party discipline be damned," and to reject his proposals. More routinely, it is through day-by-day criticism and comment by the opposition parties in the House of Commons that the government is kept on its toes. Cabinet ministers are constantly called upon to publicly justify the government's record through procedural devices such as the question period and a number of special debates. Finally, what may be a very important aspect of the role of the individual MP but one which has not been extensively studied,is the ombudsman function. The MP in this regard is both an elected "watchdog" and a communication link between the anonymous bureaucrat and the individual citizen.

More could be said here about secondary functions of parliament in the Canadian political system. For instance, parliament is a symbol of some of the things we believe in, like representative democracy and responsible government. It could be argued that this symbolic function of parliament is as important as the policy, audit and ombudsman functions discussed above, if not more so; after all, parliament and the provincial legislatures are the symbols around which most Canadians centre their perceptions of politics. On the other hand, a more cynical argument suggests that parliament is no longer of any significance in the Canadian political process and that it functions purely as an "electoral college" through which we indirectly elect a Prime Minister on the pattern of a U.S. presidential election. This, however, is a textbook and not a polemic. There are many points of view about the function and importance of parliament in our political system today; we have tried to state some of them and to take a middle ground in describing them. The reader must decide for himself just how important parliament is in the process.

THE ORGANIZATION OF PARLIAMENT

The House of Commons *Officers of the House* The most important office of the House of Commons is the *Speakership*.[10] The office of Speaker of the House was created by the BNA Act, Section 44, which states that:

> The House of Commons on its first assembling after a General Election shall proceed with all practicable speed to elect one of its members to be speaker. . . .

The main function of the Speaker, to preside over the debates in the House of Commons, is also defined by the BNA Act, although the elaboration of the duties of this role are left to the Standing Orders. Constitutionally it is clear that the Speaker is an officer of the House who is selected by the House itself and not by the cabinet. In practice, however, because of the functional supremacy of the cabinet in the parliamentary process, the Speaker is nominated by the Prime Minister and is usually elected without opposition. Invariably, the Speaker is a member from the government side of the House, although it is expected that he will function in a non-partisan and impartial manner. More recently, the tradition of impartiality has become more firmly established. Since 1963, the Speaker has been nominated by the PM with the leader of the opposition as the seconder. In 1968

[10]See W.F. Dawson, *Procedure in the Canadian House of Commons*, (University of Toronto Press, Toronto, 1962), Ch. 2, for a detailed description of the office of the Speaker of the Canadian House of Commons.

the Conservatives went one step further by indicating that they were willing to permit Mr. Lamoureux to continue as the Speaker even if they won the election, despite the fact that he had originally been elected as a Liberal. To facilitate this, the Speaker ran as an Independent and the Conservatives did not run a candidate against him in his own riding. This has paved the way for procedural changes that have streamlined debate in the House by making most procedural rulings by the Speaker not subject to appeal to the House.[11]

The response of the first Speaker to possess this grant of final authority in procedural matters was to take an extremely fair and impartial stand, often in opposition to the wishes of the government. Whereas in the past, the rulings of the Speaker were viewed with suspicion by the members of the oppostion, the fact that the Speaker from 1968–1974 was an Independent member of the House, and not a member of the government party, helped to establish his legitimacy as a truly impartial arbitrator.[12] The Speaker does not participate in debates except where necessary to defend the internal estimates of the House of Commons. Furthermore, Standing Orders are explicit that the Speaker cannot vote except to break a tie.

Thus far all that has been discussed is the Speaker's function as a presiding officer of the House. A secondary function of the office is to act as the administrative head of the House of Commons. The Speaker is responsible for the internal economy of the House, for the staffing of the House with permanent employees such as secretaries, and for preparing the estimates of internal costs and piloting them through the House of Commons. Thus, in some ways, the Speaker is like a minister of a small department who is responsible in a formal way for the administrative policies of that department.

The *Deputy Speaker* of the House is elected at the same time as the Speaker.[13] His functions are to take the place of the Speaker when he is not able to be present and to act as the Chairman of Committees of the Whole. Like the Speaker, the Deputy Speaker is elected for the duration of a parliament. He is expected to be proficient in whichever of the official languages is not the first language of the Speaker. The general practice is that the Deputy Speaker is selected from among the members of the government party although, with the office of the Speaker becoming less partisan than in the past, there is some possibility that the office of the Deputy Speaker will be affected as well.

In the absence of the Deputy Speaker, Standing Orders provide for the temporary appointment by the Speaker of any member to chair the

[11]Mr. Lamoureux did not contest the 1974 election, and after that election, a Liberal backbencher was appointed Speaker. Thus, in effect we are no closer now to a permanent speakership than we were before Mr. Lamoureux took office.
[12]Whether the new Speaker, James Jerome, will be able to sustain them will depend upon his demonstrated impartiality. See also D.S. Macdonald, "Changes in the House of Commons—New Rules", *Canadian Public Administration*, Vol. 13, Spring 1970, p. 32.
[13]See S.O. 53 (1).

Committee of the Whole.[14] However, it is more common today, for a *Deputy Chairman of Committees* (appointed for the duration of the session) to function as the Chairman of the Committees of the Whole in the absence of the Deputy Speaker. He can take over as Speaker in the unlikely case that both the Speaker and the Deputy Speaker are absent.[15] This appointment is made by the House and is invariably a member of the government party.

The *Clerk of the House*[16] is the permanent head of the House of Commons staff. His function is to supervise all permanent officers and staff of the House of Commons, to ensure that the Order Paper for the day is prepared and delivered to the Speaker, to print up certain documents for the distribution to all members of the House, and to ensure that two copies of every bill presented in the House are forwarded to the Minister of Justice.[17] In short, the Clerk of the House is a "deputy minister" of the House of Commons. His "department" is the permanent staff of the House, and his "minister" is the Speaker. He is the most important permanent officer of the House of Commons.

In this discussion of the officers of the House of Commons we must also say a word about the *Party Whips.*[18] While they are not strictly officers of the House, but rather officers of the various political parties represented there, they must be included in this section because of the important role they play in the organization of the business of the House. They are appointed by the parties to represent their respective interests in the Striking Committee (which assigns individual MPs to committees), and to maintain party discipline. They ensure that the members are all present when there is to be a recorded vote in the House, and they check to see that the members vote the "right" way on division. Finally, arrangements between parties, for instance concerning the limitation of debate and the agenda for the sitting day, are sometimes worked out through the whips. Thus, while the whips are in no way official House of Commons officers, they do have an integral part to play in the day-to-day workings of the House, and particularly, in enforcing party discipline.

The *House Leaders* of the various parties are responsible for the overall in-House conduct of their own MPs, and consequently for the overall flow of business through the House. The government House Leader is a member of the cabinet, and with his office is responsible for seeing that the business of the government gets through the House as quickly as possible. Each opposition House Leader acts as formal spokesman of his caucus to negotiate with the government House Leader the apportioning of the

[14]See S.O. 53 (4).
[15]See S.O. 53 (5).
[16]See S.O. 80–83.
[17]This latter provision is to comply with the provisions of the Canadian Bill of Rights. (See Chapter 6).
[18]A. Herbert Morrison, *Government and Parliament: A Survey From the Inside*, (Oxford University Press, New York, 1964); Robert J. Jackson, *Rebels and Whips: An Analysis of Discipline and Cohesion in British Political Parties*, (St. Martin's Press, New York, 1968).

scarce time of the House. The high prestige of House Leaders and the fact that they are really chosen by the party leaders to take much of the legislative load off their own backs insure that they can usually direct the caucus to do what they think is necessary to expedite the legislative process.

The Committee of the Whole Standing Order 75 (3) states that ". . .any Bill based on a supply or ways and means motion after second reading thereof shall stand referred to Committee of the Whole." The Committee of the Whole is composed of all the members of the House sitting as a committee with the Speaker out of the Chair and the Deputy Speaker presiding. Standing Orders generally apply when the House is sitting as a Committee of the Whole, with the exceptions that speeches have a shorter time limit, relevancy criteria are more strictly enforced, and debate is less formalized. Today, the function of the Committee of the Whole is primarily symbolic. Traditionally, all legislation was considered clause by clause in the Committee of the Whole after second reading or approval in principle had been passed. Now, however, the clause-by-clause consideration of non-money bills is given bills in the appropriate Standing Committee, thus making the Committee-of-the-Whole stage a perfunctory one. Similarly, special Committees of the Whole—the Committee of Supply and the Committee of Ways and Means—were once required to give clause-by-clause consideration of all financial legislation. The Committee of Supply was responsible for the detailed consideration of the estimates before a supply bill could be introduced; this is a task now left to the Standing Committees.[19] The Committee of Ways and Means was required to deal separately with taxation proposals before introducing the actual bills in the House; but now this is achieved through a blanket motion by the Minister of Finance that "the House approve in general the budgetary policy of the Government." In 1969, the Committee of Supply and the Committee of Ways and Means were abolished. Thus, the function of the Committee of the Whole is today mostly symbolic, as its main substantive functions have been taken over by the Standing Committees.

Division Debates in the House of Commons which have been commenced by a specific motion inevitably end in a vote. The basic rule in a parliamentary system is that a majority of those present in the House decide the outcome of a motion. When debate on a question has been concluded, the Speaker "puts the question" to the House by reading the main motion and any amendments. Those in agreement say "aye" and those against say "nay", and the Speaker announces which side has won— according to his interpretation. If at least five members rise to demand a recorded vote or a "division" (and they usually do in the case of important votes), the "division bells" are rung, to inform members not sitting in the House at the time that a division is about to occur. Sometimes the division bells are rung for more than 20 minutes in order to allow the Party Whips to round up as many votes as they can, although, in most cases, ten minutes is sufficient to summon members from offices and other places within the parliament buildings. When the whips of the various parties are con-

[19]Macdonald, "Changes in the House of Commons—New Rules", p. 33.

tent that they have as many as possible of their members present, the doors of the House are closed and the vote is taken. Members register their votes by standing in their places in the House of Commons to be counted by the Clerk of the House. When the vote is counted and recorded, the Speaker announces the outcome.

Recorded votes in the House are very time-consuming, but fortunately most votes in the House are settled without a formal division; in most circumstances it is obvious to all members that the government has a majority of the members in the House, so that there is never any real question that the government will be able to carry any motion. In recognition of this, the opposition parties force a recorded vote only on non-confidence motions, second reading of important bills, etc. For the most part, the question is decided by a voice vote with the Speaker declaring the government side to have carried the motion.

If a member is going to be absent from the House for a time, he often will arrange to "pair" himself with a member of the opposition party. This means that both members agree not to vote on division if one is absent from the House. This practice, while based only on a gentleman's agreement, means that even if many members are absent from the House, there is no danger that the government will fall by mistake. The practice of pairing is obviously more important in the situation of a minority government than when the government has a healthy majority. Frequently after a division, a member who abstained from voting will rise in his place and state the way he would have voted had he not been paired. The supervision of pairing in the House is usually left to the whips, who organize pairs for members and who ensure that their own members who are paired do not vote on division. It is interesting to note that on one occasion in 1926 the government was defeated in the House by one vote because of a "broken pair" and although everyone was embarrassed, the vote stood and the government was forced to resign.[20]

Rules of Debate Some discussion has already been devoted to the basic functions of the Canadian parliament. However, what has been left unsaid until now is the fact that the general method or technique whereby parliament performs all of these functions is *debate*. Above all else, the House of Commons would appear to an uninitiated observer primarily as a forum of debate, for it is debate which occupies the bulk of time in the parliamentary day. The rules of debate are consequently an important aspect of the parliamentary process.

The rules of debate, as already pointed out, are enforced by the Speaker, Deputy Speaker, or Deputy Chairman of Committees. The chair does not exercise control over debate in an arbitrary fashion; there are definite rules and procedures which the Speaker is called upon to apply from time to time in the course of debate. It is a basic principle that every member who wishes to speak to a question should be permitted to do so. The problem faced by the Speaker is, therefore, not who should be permitted to speak, but who should be permitted to speak first. The procedure for being

[20]See W.F. Dawson, *op. cit.*, Chapter 10.

recognized by the Speaker, or for catching his eye, is for the member wishing to speak to rise in his place[21] in the House. The Speaker attempts to switch his attention from the government side of the House to the opposition side, to permit a fair alternation of speakers by party. The Speaker's job has been greatly simplified through the practice of the Party Whips supplying the Speaker with a daily list of members who wish to speak on that day. In the question period, it is traditional that the Speaker first recognizes the official opposition leader and then turns to the leader of one of the minor opposition parties.[22] In debates, however, the basic rule is that the parties have themselves worked out which of their members they wish to have heard and in which order, and the Speaker merely rotates from one party to another. If the whips have done their job, there will be only one man from a given party rising to address the House at any given time.

Speeches in the House have a time limit of 40 minutes when the Speaker is in the chair,[23] and no member may speak more than once on any question. The exceptions to this rule are the PM, the leader of the official opposition, any minister moving a Government Order, and any member making a motion of non-confidence in the government, all of whom may speak more than once, and for longer than 40 minutes. A 20-minute time limit applies to speeches during Private Members' Hour[24] and during various extraordinary types of debates such as those under Standing Order 26.

It is a convention of parliamentary debate that members should not read their speeches but should deliver them extemporaneously.[25] This is not a written rule, however, and cannot be enforced by the Speaker. The result is that any member who so desires will read his speech with some kidding and heckling from other members who observe the practice. The stock reply by a member who is chided for reading his speech is that he is merely following his extensive notes very closely. There is a similar rule that the member may not repeat himself in a speech and that he may not repeat arguments made previously by other members.[26] The former is applied infrequently by the Speaker, and the latter never; it defies enforcement. There are also rules requiring relevance[27] in debate, which are similarly difficult to apply. The major impetus for relevance in speeches comes from the Party Whips, who try to ensure that time is not wasted during important debates. As already seen, there are certain debates, such as the Throne Speech Debate and the Budget Debate, to which the requirement of relevance does not apply at all.

In addition to the more explicit rules of debate, there is a general rule that members should not use what is euphemistically called "unparliamentary language". What this means is that the members should

[21]S.O. 28–29.
[22]See Dawson, *op.cit.*, pp. 103–104.
[23]S.O. 31 (1).
[24]S.O. 31 (2).
[25]Dawson, *op. cit.*, p. 104.
[26]*Ibid.*, p. 108.
[27]*Ibid.*, p. 109.

treat each other with politeness and should not revert to the name-calling or *ad hominem* arguments in debate. Generally the members do abide by this rule, and it is seldom that the speaker is called upon to rebuke a member for the use of unparliamentary language.[28] Unparliamentary comments by members other than the member who has the floor usually go unrecognized formally, and appear in *Hansard* as "Some Hon. Members: Oh, Oh!" The phrase "Oh, Oh!" is a cryptic euphemism for earthy comments ranging from those which cast aspersions on the Honourable Member's ancestry to harmless but quaint colloquilisms such as "yer mother wears army boots!" or "fuddle-duddle".

Privilege Parliamentary privilege is the sum of the rights and privileges of both Houses of the Canadian parliament which function to place parliament in a position above all other institutions and individuals in the land. These rights are held by parliament as a whole and by each individual MP. They include such rights as freedom from arrest arising out of civil action while the House is in session, exemption from jury duty or from subpoena as a witness, the protection from libel actions for the content of speeches in the House and publications of the House. Another part of parliamentary privilege in Canada is the right of parliamentary committees to hear witnesses under oath. Breaches of privilege are considered to be analogous to contempt of court, and are punishable by imprisonment, fine, or simply censure by the House itself. For matters of privilege, the House can act as a court, calling witnesses "before the Bar of the House of Commons."

The real importance of parliamentary privilege has waned. Its significance today is primarily as a symbolic reminder of the principles of freedom of speech and freedom from arrest which were at one time not so widely accepted as they are today. Occasionally today, a member will rise in the House on a *question of privilege* to complain about statements made about him in the press, or to complain about the conduct of another member, but in most cases the question raised has very little to do with privilege as such, and sometimes is merely a stalling technique. As Professor W.F. Dawson has pointed out:

> At the root of the problem is the ignorance of the Canadian House of the true meaning of privilege, which is essentially the defensive weapon of a legislature which has been used to protect itself against interference. The Canadian House has never had to fear such trouble and has never bothered to develop a defence.[29]

Sporadic attempts to raise questions of privilege in the Canadian House of Commons have been motivated by purely partisan needs and not by genuine threats to the security and freedom of the House. Parliamentary privilege, therefore, while important for its historical meaning, is not an important aspect of the modern parliamentary process in Canada.[30]

Committees in the House of Commons One of the first

[28]*Ibid.*, pp. 110–114.
[29]*Ibid.*, p. 54.
[30]See Dawson, *op. cit.*, Chapter 3, for a general discussion of privilege in Canada.

responsibilities of the House of Commons at the beginning of the first session of each parliament is to appoint a *Committee of Selection*, or as it is usually known, a *Striking Committee*. The Striking Committee is made up of six or seven MPs, usually including the chief whips of the opposition parties, a representative of the ministry, and the Chief Government Whip who acts as the chairman. The function of the Striking Committee is to select the members of the Standing Committees of the House within ten days of the commencement of the session, and to ensure that all committees have a full complement of members throughout the session.

At the present time, there are eighteen Standing Committees of the Canadian House of Commons, thirteen of which are the *Specialist Committees* in various substantive areas of government policy. The thirteen are as follows:

Agriculture
Broadcasting, Films and Assistance to the Arts
External Affairs and National Defence
Finance, Trade and Economic Affairs
Fisheries and Forestry
Health, Welfare and Social Affairs
Indian Affairs and Northern Development
National Resources and Public Works
Justice and Legal Affairs
Labour, Manpower and Immigration
Regional Development
Transport and Communications
Veterans Affairs

In addition to these Specialist Committees, there are five Standing Committees of the House responsible for various matters outside the realm of government legislation *per se*. These are as follows:

1. Miscellaneous Estimates
2. Miscellaneous Private Bills and Standing Orders
3. Privileges and Elections
4. Public Accounts
5. Procedure and Organization

The Striking Committee is also responsible for appointing the House members of the four *Joint Standing Committees* of the Senate and House of Commons, which are as follows:

1. Printing
2. The Library of Parliament
3. Regulations and other Statutory Instruments
4. The Restaurant of Parliament

Special Committees, such as the present Committee on Egg Marketing, and *Special Joint Committees*, such as the Committee on Employer–Employee Relations in the Public Service, are set up from time to time to deal with specific problems in specific policy areas. The Striking Committee is also responsible for assigning members to these.

Membership on the Standing Committees is usually limited to a maximum of twenty, but the Committee on Agriculture and the Committee on External Affairs and National Defence have as many as thirty members, while the Procedure and Organization, the Miscellaneous Private Bills and the Standing Orders Committees are limited to only twelve. Standing Order 65(5) specifies that Special Committees should consist of not more than fifteen members. The guiding principle for selection of committee members by the Striking Committee is that the parties should have representation proportional to their membership in the House itself. Thus, in a twenty-member committee, a typical distribution by party in 1975 might be: Liberals, eleven; Conservatives, six; NDP, two; and Créditistes, one. In the case of the Liberals and Conservatives, each Party Whip assigns his party's allotment of members to the various committees according to the membership on the Party Caucus Committees which correspond roughly to the Specialist Committees of the House. Thus, if a Conservative MP is a member of the Caucus Committee on Agriculture, it is likely that he will also be a member of the House Committee on Agriculture. The two smaller parties in the House usually determine their men in a less formal way, depending largely upon which committees the MP wishes to sit on, and his seniority in the party caucus. It is generally accepted that the Striking Committee bases its selection of committee membership entirely on the recommendation of the Party Whips, and does not interfere with a party's wishes except with regard to the number of members allocated to each party for each committee.

Membership on committees is subject to change simply through notification of the Clerk of the House by the Chief Whips. Such changes are granted to the opposition parties as a matter of course, on request. Cabinet ministers are never selected as members of the Standing Committees, but Parliamentary Secretaries are often temporarily appointed to committees dealing with the policy areas that concern their ministers. Although a minister may testify before a committee, the Parliamentary Secretary is expected to speak on his behalf when a piece of legislation which the minister has introduced in the House is being considered by the relevant Specialist Committee. Conversely, the Parliamentary Secretary is expected to keep the minister posted on developments in the committee hearings.

The Chairmen and Vice Chairmen of Standing Committees are elected by the committees themselves, and because the government has a majority of the members of the committees, these officers are normally government MPs. The single exception to this rule is the Public Accounts Committee which in recent years, has been chaired by a member of the opposition. From time to time, an opposition committee man with unique interest or expertise in the area of the committee's responsibility will be elected Vice Chairman, but such occurrences are, as yet, relatively rare in Canada. The function of the chair in Canadian committees is primarily to preside over the hearings of the committee and not to assume the aggressive and dominant role of the chairmen of U.S. Congressional committees. While this is a general rule, the practice of committees in this regard varies widely from committee to committee and from chairman to chairman.

Procedure in the Standing Committees of the Canadian House of Commons is basically the same as that for the House itself, with the exception that Standing Orders restricting the length of speeches and the number of times of speaking do not apply, in order to insure a less formal discussion of the issues. The committees hear witnesses, mainly from the public service but frequently from the private sector and the academic community, and they report back to the House of Commons. All committee hearings are public in Canada, although neither the press nor the general public seems to give very much attention to the proceedings of most committees.

Committees of the House are all staffed by clerks who are permanent employees of the House of Commons. While there is a potential for these men to acquire some degree of power vis-à-vis their committees, simply by virtue of their continuance in the same roles for a number of parliaments, they tend to be rather junior people with purely clerical responsibilities.

The Functions of the House Committees A. *Refining Government Policy: The Legislative Function* The most important function of Committees of the House of Commons as regards the policy process is the detailed scrutiny and polishing of government bills. After a bill has been given second reading, it is normally referred to the appropriate Standing Committee. The committee studies the legislative proposal, hears witnesses from the public service and experts from other sectors, and proposes changes that it feels would have the effect of improving the quality of the final legislative output. The committees can perform this function much more effectively than the House itself because their pattern of debate is more open and procedurally less restrictive. It is possible for the committee members simply to discuss the issues involved, rather than debate them, as is the case in the House.

Furthermore, the principle of the legislation has already been accepted by the House at second reading, and consequently, the focus of the committee's deliberations is genuinely on improving the end product, although the opposition parties may still try to sneak substantive changes into an act under the guise of improving the wording. Whereas in the House debate on second reading the opposition parties perform the negative role of opposition, in committee they can concentrate on more positive criticism of the form of the legislation and they often propose useful amendments to the bills before them. The argument that committees are to a lesser extent partisan forums for debate than the House of Commons must be qualified by the fact that the matters they discuss (the details) are less likely to lend themselves to partisan divisions. However, it must be remembered that partisanship runs deep in the House of Commons, and most divisions, even in committees, tend to go along party lines. It is quite clear that if a contentious aspect of a bill should be discussed in the committee stage, party discipline would be enforced by the government much in the same way that it is in House debates. If an opposition member proposes in committee an amendment with which the government does not agree, the amendment will be defeated on division in the committee. Nevertheless, it is not uncommon for an opposition proposal in committee to be accepted by the government if it is agreed that the suggestion would genuinely improve the bill.

There are some limitations and weaknesses in the committee system which must be considered to clarify its role in the policy process. The first and most obvious is that a committee considering a government bill reports back to the House of Commons. In other words, all decisions made in committee are merely decisions to recommend something to the House, and have no final or binding effect by themselves. At the report stage, a recommendation of the committee can be simply reversed by a vote of the whole House. Paradoxically, a further limitation on the effectiveness of committees is the fact that, although they are intended to be specialist bodies which develop some expertise in certain subject matters of legislation, there is, in practice, a very high turnover both in the membership of committees and in the membership of the House itself; consequently, the average committeeman does not have time to become very much of an expert. [31] Members of parliament tend to be generalists and not specialists; they often become interested in a specific issue which perhaps concerns their constituency or region, but their interests rarely extend to the entire subject area of any one committee's specialization.[32] While the majority of MPs will remain on a committee for a full session, quite a number will move from one committee to another, according to which committee is studying which bill and where the party wishes to concentrate its best committeemen.

The basic tasks of committees in dealing with government bills, then, are to refine the legislation, to attempt to foresee difficulties that might arise in the administration of the legislation, and to make such amendments as are necessary to achieve the desired improvements. Committees dealing with bills that have already passed second reading are precluded by the rules of procedure from making substantive changes in the legislation, and are precluded by party discipline and the recommendatory nature of their decisions from making even small changes with which the government does not agree.

B. Detailed Scrutiny of Estimates: The Business of Supply. Before the procedural changes of 1969 abolished the Committee of Supply, it was that committee's responsibility to go over the departmental estimates in detail. Now the estimates for a particular department go instead to the appropriate Standing Committee for detailed consideration. Thus, for instance, the estimates of the Department of National Health and Welfare are reviewed by the Committee on Health, Welfare and Social Affairs, the Department of National Defence estimates are reviewed by the Committee on External Affairs and National Defence, and so forth. This has meant a large saving of time for the House of Commons, but it has increased commensurately the amount of time each member must spend in committee.

[31]C.E.S. Franks, "The Committee System of the House of Commons", (Unpublished paper at the C.P.S.A. Conference, 1969), pp. 26–27.
[32]Not only is turnover very high but attendance is extremely sporadic. See Jackson and Atkinson, *op. cit.*, Ch. 6.

Currently, by far the largest part of the time spend in committees is devoted to a consideration of the departmental estimates.[33]

The ability of a Standing Committee to effectively criticize the tures in committees probably prevents carelessness in the preparation of independent expertise in the committee. The witnesses called to back up the estimates of the department are themselves departmental officials and furthermore, by the time the estimates reach parliament, they have already run the gauntlet of criticism from the cabinet, cabinet committees, Treasury Board, Treasury Board staff, and the departmental financial experts themselves.[34] It is unlikely that the Standing Committee will be able to improve substantially or reduce the estimates; of course, the fact that the minister of each department must publicly justify estimated expenditures in committees probably prevents carelessness in the preparation of the estimates in the first place.

Finally, it must be mentioned that the opposition parties can, to some extent, use the consideration of the estimates in committee as an additional forum for criticism of the government's programs and policy priorities. In this sense, the committee stage of the estimates is at least as important for the general audit function of parliament as it is for improving the detailed estimates.

C. *Pre-legislative Functions: Policy Committees.* It is becoming more common in Canada for House committees to be used as investigatory bodies to examine policy proposals before the legislative stage. In this way, the committees can play a role at both the priority-setting and formulation stages of the policy process. In the priority-setting stage, the House committee may travel across the country hearing briefs submitted by interested parties in order, apparently, to gather information that ultimately can be used by the cabinet in setting priorities. The recommendations that the committee comes up with are not as important as the data it gathers about the attitudes of the public towards the particular problem. At the policy-formulation stage, the committees again act as information gatherers but usually with respect to a specific set of policy alternatives such as those set down in a government white or "coloured" paper. In this case the priority has already been set and the problem faced by the committee is to discover public attitudes to the various alternatives. Again, the committee itself lacks the expertise to make substantive recommendations, but by hearing the views of interested parties across the country, the committee is put in a position to state something about the public's attitudes to the proposals.

There are Standing Committees capable of taking on investigatory duties in most policy areas, although it is in this area of committee work that one most frequently sees the creation of Special Committees. The contribution that committees of the House of Commons can bring to the policy process at the pre-legislative stages is the ability to conduct hearings and listen sympathetically to the submissions of the public. Here the com-

[33]Franks, "The Committee System of the House of Commons," pp. 26–27.
[34]In fact, there is never enough time to consider the estimates thoroughly in Committee and S.O. 58 (14) states that they "shall be deemed to have been reported" by May 31 whether the committee is through with them or not.

mittees can augment the government-sponsored task forces and royal commissions, and the political advisory bodies such as the PMO and PCO in sounding public attitudes before any concrete policy commitments have been made.

Investigatory committees, although they report back to the House of Commons, can afford to be less partisan than committees involved in the refining of government legislation. At the pre-legislative phase the government is not firmly committed to any policy, and if the findings of the committee differ from the government's attitudes to the problem being studied, the government can still back down without losing face. Furthermore, whereas a Standing Committee's report on a government bill is subject to debate in the House at the report stage, the reports of committee investigations need not be debated at all.

An obvious latent function of the pre-legislative use of House committees is the stimulation of wider participation in the policy process and the creation of feelings of efficacy among the public and the MPs. The extent to which investigatory committees will actually affect policy will depend entirely on the quality of the information gathered and the consistency of that information with that gathered through other agencies. In short, there is a definite potential for additional input to the policy process through the use of parliamentary committees at the earlier stages of the process. The development of that potential will depend on the willingness of the government to utilize it fully and on the recognition by the public and the committees themselves that such non-expert inputs can seldom be accepted without the additional input of expert advice. There must be a realistic understanding that simple committee recommendation of a policy alternative does not necessarily ensure its implementation, particularly if there exists a mass of technical advice which contradicts the committee findings.

D. The Public Accounts Committee: The Post Audit Function. The Canadian Public Accounts Committee is perhaps the most specialized of the Standing Committees of the House of Commons, and it is in some ways the most effective. It consists of twenty members, and, like other committees, is controlled numerically by the government party. However, unlike the other Standing Committees, Public Accounts has had, since 1957, an opposition member as its chairman. Furthermore, the Auditor General, who is an independent officer of parliament, makes the job of the committee easier by providing it with expert assistance in scrutinizing the accounts of the government's expenditures. The functions of the Public Accounts Committee are to investigate the financial shortcomings of the government—as pointed out by the Auditor General, and as discovered through independent examination of the Public Accounts by the committee members themselves—and to make recommendations to the government as to how it should improve its spending practices.

The basic weakness of this procedure as a meaningful exercise of control over the financial affairs of the government is that the government usually chooses not to heed the recommendations. Each year the Auditor General lists a number of recommendations, made over the past years by the Public Accounts Committee, which have never been implemented by the government. Furthermore, the government frequently releases the Public Accounts to the committee only very late in the session and this has the effect of making the recommendations of the committee seem out of date by the time they are presented. This situation could be improved by making automatic the referral of the Public Accounts to the committee instead of waiting for a specific referral by the government. As it stands today, it is not uncommon for the committee to fail to make any inquiries at all before the prorogation of parliament.[35]

To summarize, the Public Accounts Committee has considerable potential for investigating and publicizing the financial bungling and sleight-of-hand of the government and government officials, but as yet it has not been very successful. The committee reports directly to the House, as do all Standing Committees, but the report does not produce any debate; the report is simply received by the House and forgotten or ignored by the government. This committee could be made more effective by instituting certain procedural reforms, and by creating a public consciousness of the importance of its role and the relevance to the citizen of its recommendations.

E. Miscellaneous Committee Functions.   Finally, mention must be made of the fact that there are a number of Standing Committees whose functions are basically outside the realm of government policy. The Commons Committee on Miscellaneous Private Bills, for instance, exists primarily to look at private bills already approved by the Senate. The bulk of the work here has usually been performed by the Senate and the Senate committees, and the Commons committee merely gives its approval to the legislation.

The Committees on Privileges and Elections and on Procedure and Organization are concerned primarily with the internal affairs of the House of Commons. They are relatively inactive most of the time, becoming active only when specific circumstances necessitate. The Joint Committees are mainly concerned with mundane business such as running the parliamentary restaurant, the library of parliament, and the printing services; while these committees are actually quite active, their role is not critical to the workings of the Canadian political system and hence does not deserve more than this cursory mention.

The exception to this rule is the newly established Joint Standing Committee on Regulations and other Statutory Instruments which was set up in 1972 pursuant to the Statutory Instruments Act of 1971. The function of this committee is to scrutinize all subordinate legislation in much the same way that the "Scrutiny Committee" in the U.K. does. Given the amount of subordinate legislation and the general extent of delegation of legislative functions to executive and bureaucratic officers, such a committee could come to perform an invaluable control function *vis-à-vis* the bureaucracy. Moreover, it could in some ways aggrandize the general audit function of parliament and give to the Senate a new and genuine responsibility. The success or failure of this committee, however, will depend on

[35]See Franks, "The Committee System of the House of Commons," p. 38; also Ward, *The Public Purse*, Chapters 3 and 13, *passim.*

the way in which its mandate is carried out, and not on the principles stated in its charter. No assessment of the role of the Committee on Regulations and Statutory Instruments can be made until it has had a few years of operation.

This concludes the discussion of the functions of parliamentary committees. The verdict, briefly, is that they are necessary to streamline the parliamentary process, and that they are central actors in the refining of government legislation. They have some positive role to play in assessing government policy proposals through the investigation of the public's attitudes via public hearings, etc. However, for most of the same reasons that parliament as a whole has a restricted role in the policy process, the committees of the House of Commons do not occupy a very important place at the most critical stages of policy making.

The Senate The Canadian parliament is bicameral in structure, consisting of the House of Commons and the Senate. The House of Commons (or "lower house") functions virtually exclusively as the effective legislative branch of the Canadian political system, while the Senate (or "upper house") plays a relatively insignificant role in the legislative process. While it is likely that the Senate was always intended to be a minor partner in the business of passing legislation, its legislative role was once seen as more significant than it has become today. The Senate was originally viewed as the representative of the various regions of the federation, with the Maritimes, Quebec, Ontario and the West allotted 24 Senators each. The entry of Newfoundland added 6 more Senators to make up today's total of 102. The importance of the Senate today as a regional and provincial representative is essentially nil; other institutions such as the cabinet and the federal–provincial conferences, which are more deeply involved in the policy process, are much better equipped to perform this function.

The second function of the Senate as perceived by the Fathers of Confederation was to act as a conservative restraint on the young, the impressionable and the impulsive in the House of Commons. In order to secure this more sober voice in the legislative process, Senators are required to be at least thirty years of age and to own property valued at a minimum of $4,000 in the province they represent. Unlike the members of the lower house who are elected, Senators are appointed by the Governor General in Council and enjoy permanent tenure until age 75.[36]

Most of the factors which function to restrict the role of the House of Commons in the policy process apply also to the Senate. Specifically, the Senate cannot compete with the cabinet as a priority-setter, and it lacks the expertise to become deeply involved in policy formulation. There are, however, even more handicaps placed on the policy role of the Senate than on that of the House of Commons. First of all, a Senator is not elected to office as is an MP, but is appointed by the government at the time when

---

[36]Until 1965, tenure was for life. Senators appointed before that date have the option today of staying on or retiring at age 75. Any Senator appointed since 1965 must retire at age 75.

a vacancy occurs. This has meant traditionally that the party in power appoints people who have shown themselves to be faithful: Liberal governments have appointed Liberals, and Conservative governments have appointed Conservatives, much to the annoyance of the NDP which is virtually unrepresented in the upper house. The effect of this partisan pattern of Senate appointments has been to deny the Senate both the legitimacy enjoyed by the House by virtue of popular election and the respect of a body which is independent of partisanship. Furthermore, the tendency has been to offer people Senate posts only when their useful political lives have terminated. As a reward for many years of faithful service to the party, an old politician is "retired" by being put in the Senate. Because of this tendency, the image of the Senate is that of an "old folks' home" for tired and retired party faithfuls, an image which severely restricts the prestige of the upper house.

The Senate is not permitted constitutionally to introduce money bills, and in practice it cannot amend or defeat money bills either. (There is still some question as to the constitutionality of Senate amendments of money bills, but in practical terms the Senate does not even attempt to amend them today.) With the exception of the government leader in the Senate, there are no cabinet ministers sitting in the upper house. While in the past even Prime Ministers have been senators, by now it is generally accepted that ministers must all have seats in the House of Commons and cannot be drawn from the Senate. Because of this circumstance, virtually all government bills are introduced in the House of Commons. It is increasingly rare for the Senate even to attempt to amend a government bill that has been passed by the lower house, let alone to defeat it. While the Senate is legally empowered to make substantive amendments to or even to defeat government legislation passed by the House of Commons, the legitimacy of such courses of action is questionable in a system that values popular sovereignty.

Despite the fact that the Senate is not a very active institution in the Canadian policy process today, there are a few items on the positive side of the ledger. Most important, the Senate does most of the parliamentary work involved in private bills, giving the overworked House of Commons more time for dealing with government legislation. Secondly, committees of the Senate are becoming more and more involved in investigations of political problems that might otherwise be left to royal commissions. An example of the use of a Senate committee in a pre-legislative investigatory role is the 1970–71 study done on the mass media in Canada. Because the Senate is less involved in the politics of the day, it can conduct such studies without the danger of sensationalism and "grandstanding" on the part of the committeemen which might occur if the same investigation were undertaken by the more "political" House of Commons. Also, of course, the House of Commons simply would not have the time to conduct hearings in the leisurely fashion typical of the Senate. Thus, through Senate committees, the Canadian upper house can contribute some meaningful inputs to the policy process and simultaneously relieve the House for the consideration of government legislative proposals.

The Senate also performs an important function for the Canadian party system, in that it permits the party in power to retire party faithfuls without too seriously alienating them, or imposing on them financial disaster. The Senate is, in this sense, a convenient place for stacking "over-age pols" who might cause political embarrassment if permitted to continue in the House of Commons, or who might be forced back into the private sector at a rather advanced age. While there have been some recent appointments of relatively young men to the Senate, the fact remains that a large number of Senators still belong to the category of "retired pol". The importance of this function of the Senate should not be minimized, for it provides some slight job security for the politician. If a politician, particularly a cabinet minister, can manage to retire while his party is in office, he is likely to get either a Senate seat or some other patronage position. As a consequence, he need not constantly pander to private interests in the hope that they might give him a job when his days in politics are done.

In a similar vein, appointment to the Senate is sometimes used to provide an Ottawa address and an office close to those of cabinet ministers for key organizers of the party in power. The clearest example of this is Senator Keith Davey, a central figure in several elections in the 1960s, who re-emerged as the dominant tactician in the Liberal party's 1974 election victory.

By way of conclusion to these brief remarks about the Senate, it should be mentioned that reform or abolition of the upper house has been considered continually since 1867. Some reforms have been tried, such as compulsory retirement at age 75, but functionally, the Senate has not changed significantly since Confederation. Basically, there is little that can be done in the way of structural or procedural reform which will improve the Senate. If it is made elective, all that will happen is that the House of Commons will be duplicated. We have an elected House already, and although the American system has a bicameral elective legislature, there is no reason to assume that one is needed here. If the Senate were abolished, there are functions that it performs today which would have to be taken over by the already overworked House of Commons. The hope for improvement, therefore, seems to rest in functional changes. It is incumbent upon the government of the day to recognize the fact that the Senate is closer to being politically neutral than the elected house, and to make use of the Senate and Senate committees for investigatory studies. If, instead of proliferating commissions and bureaucratic task forces to undertake investigations that should be non-partisan in focus and visible to the public, the government would delegate still more investigatory powers to the Senate and appoint more Senators who are capable of taking a vigorous role in this respect, the upper house might be given a more meaningful role in the policy process.[37]

[37]For further enlightenment on the role of the Senate, see F.A.Kunz, *The Modern Senate of Canada 1925–1963*, (University of Toronto Press, Toronto, 1965); R.A. MacKay, *The Unreformed Senate of Canada*, (Carleton Library, McClelland and Stewart, Toronto, 1963); and R.M. Dawson, *The Government of Canada*, Ch. 15.

THE LEGISLATIVE PROCESS: PARLIAMENT AND GOVERNMENT POLICY

Before proceeding with a specific illustration of parliament's role in the policy process, some terminological clarification is necessary. Once a policy has been formulated and a draft of the proposed legislation has been completed by the Department of Justice, it is then introduced in the House of Commons by the minister responsible for that particular subject area of policy. At this stage the policy proposal takes the form of a *bill*. When a bill has been passed by parliament it becomes an *act*, and after formal assent by the Governor General and proclamation, an act becomes *law*. The involvement of parliament in the policy process, therefore, is formally limited to converting bills introduced by the government into acts. This process naturally includes the refining of government policies and their ultimate conversion to formal outputs of the political system.

All bills introduced in parliament can be classed as either *public* or *private*, depending on whether their effect is intended to be general or specific. Private bills are aimed at altering the law only insofar as it affects an individual or a corporate individual. Examples of this kind of legislation are laws altering the charters of companies or incorporating companies. Most such private bills are introduced in the Senate where they are discussed and revised in detail by committees. Passage by the House of Commons is usually more or less perfunctory, with first, second and third reading virtually simultaneous. Private bills that have been passed by the Senate are frequently passed by the House of Commons in packages rather than individually, a practice which speeds up the process considerably.

Public bills, on the other hand, are intended to have a general effect and to alter the law as it affects all Canadians. Public bills take up by far the largest amount of parliamentary time, for it is by such measures that government policies are converted to outputs of the system. Most of the legislation passed by parliament can be classed as public, examples being the Canada Water Act, the Canada Pension Act, the Canada Grain Act, etc. Public bills, because they generally involve the implementation of government policy, are introduced in the House of Commons by the minister concerned. In contrast with private bills, public bills provide the focal points for heated partisan debate in the House of Commons.

As noted above, most public bills originate with the government and hence are referred to as *government bills*. There are, however, provisions in the rules and procedures of the House of Commons for the introduction of public bills by individual MPs. This type of public bill is usually referred to as a *private member's bill*, signifying that it is the creation of an individual MP and has nothing to do with the government or government policy. [Note here that "private members' " bills are completely different from "private" bills, the former term signifying the originators of the legislative proposals and the latter signifying their intended applications.] Private members' bills, although procedurally a part of the parliamentary process, seldom go very far in the House of Commons. In fact, it is rare indeed for a private member's bill to go beyond first reading, unless the government likes the idea and adopts it as its own policy. This does not happen often, and it is possible to say with confidence that consideration of private members' bills does not constitute an important part of the policy role of parliament.

The high mortality rate of private members' bills results from the fact that only four hours per week (one hour each day except Wednesday) are devoted to private members' business.[38] There is usually a long list of private members who wish to introduce their "pet bills", and they all must take turns in spending the allotted one-hour units of private members' time debating their proposals. Once a member has used a private members' hour to introduce his bill, his name drops to the bottom of the long list and he doesn't get another chance until everyone else has had his turn. The result is that most private members' bills are introduced, debated for one hour, and never dealt with again. Bills accorded this treatment are said to have been "talked out." At the end of the parliamentary session, any government or private members' bills which are not completely passed by parliament lapse and must be reintroduced at the next session.

It would be misleading, however, to limit our assessment of private members' bills to their function in the policy process. The more important function of the private member's bill is that it permits the MP to state publicly the policy proposals he considers important, and those he feels the government is ignoring. Such bills are often passed down the line for consideration by bureaucrats, who may eventually incorporate the ideas in government bills. The MP can, in other words, put on the record his point of view on a certain policy area. Furthermore, by introducing a bill which favours his constituency's interests, he can publicize problems which exist there and are, perhaps, unique. In this way, the MP can use the private member's bill as a device to assist him in the performance of the representative, or ombudsman's, function that was discussed earlier. In the past, opposition members have often utilized the private members' hours to perform the general audit function of parliament. By raising contentious issues through the introduction of a private member's bill, an opposition member can embarrass the government without committing his party as a whole to a firm stand on the issue. Thus it can be concluded that, although the private member's bill is not important as a category of legislative proposals to be considered by parliament, it is a useful device for criticizing the government's policy priorities and for publicizing special problems and needs within certain regions and constituencies of the country.[39]

Government bills occupy the lion's share of the time available in the Canadian House of Commons, and it is the passage of these bills which must be considered at greater length as part of the policy process. The procedures for dealing with government bills differ slightly depending on

[38]S.O. 15 (4).
[39]For an excellent discussion of the significance of Private Members' Bills, see Stewart Hyson, "The Role of the Backbencher—an Analysis of Private Members' Bills in the Canadian House of Commons," *Parliamentary Affairs*, vol. XXVII, no. 3, Summer 1974, pp. 262–272.

whether or not the legislation in question involves the spending or raising of public money. Money bills, such as the Supply Bill or tax amendments, cannot constitutionally be introduced in the Senate, and while there is no similar restriction on *non-money bills*, virtually all government bills are introduced in the House of Commons simply because most of the cabinet members sit there. With these few points by way of introduction, let us now follow the passage of a typical government bill through parliament.

Passing the Canada Water Act[40] The Canada Water Act was one of the major pieces of government legislation passed during the 1969–70 session of parliament. Before the legislation ever arrived on parliament's doorstep, it has been subjected to many of the processes which we described earlier. Considerable public demand and a certain amount of bureaucratic "withinput" had caused the cabinet to attach a high priority to the provision of an act for the overall coordination of water management problems in Canada. Alternatives had been proposed by the bureaucracy and the cabinet had chosen the one most highly recommended by the senior bureaucrats in charge of policy formulation. A tentative form of the act had been "trial-ballooned," and discussions with several provincial governments had resulted in a few modest changes. The bill was then drafted by the Department of Justice and approved by the Water Sector of the federal Department of Energy, Mines and Resources, by the Interdepartmental Committee on Water, and finally by cabinet. It was then ready for consideration by the House of Commons, and on November 5, 1969, first reading was given.

First reading of a bill in the House is a perfunctory affair. The first mention of a bill in the House occurs when the House is asked to give leave to introduce it. The motion specifies the title of the bill and is virtually always decided without debate. Although the member introducing it may be permitted to give a succinct explanation of its provisions, in practice this occurs only with private members' bills. When the House has granted leave, the bill is given first reading, whereupon the House agrees "that this bill be read a first time and printed" (S.O. 70[1]). There is no debate at this stage and the vote merely involves the Speaker mumbling, "Is it the pleasure of the House to adopt the said motion? Carried, Adopted," and the Clerk of the House rising to declare the bill to have passed first reading.

Following first reading, a bill is assigned a number (the Water Bill was C-144) which will be used in referring to that bill for the rest of its legislative passage. Depending on its importance and on how much business the House faces, the bill is then scheduled for second reading. The decision about when second reading will occur is made primarily by the Government House Leader, sometimes in consultation with the Opposition House Leaders.

Second reading of the Water Bill began November 26, 1969 and went

[40]We are indebted to Mr. J.G. Yanover, special assistant to the Government House Leader, for briefly checking this section. Although the Water Act was passed in 1970, the procedures have not changed substantially since.

on for one sitting, after which it was put aside in favour of more urgent business until mid-January when second reading was completed in four further sittings. The length of time taken at second reading varies greatly from bill to bill and depends mainly on how many opposition speakers wish to debate the legislation. The debate on the motion that the bill be given a second reading and that it be referred to a relevant standing committee is begun by the member who introduced the bill—in the case of a government bill, by a minister. In the case of Bill C-144, the debate was led off by J.J. Greene, Minister of Energy, Mines and Resources, who read an impassioned speech prepared by bureaucratic minions and polished by himself for this occasion. The chief opposition critic of the minister's department replies to the minister's speech, followed by members of the smaller parties and then by other opposition members and a few government backbenchers. When all or most of those who want to speak in the debate have finished, the motion is put, second reading is granted and the bill is referred to a committee. Second reading is usually taken as approval in principle, but since no amendments which do not have the effect of killing the bill can be introduced at second reading, and since the granting of second reading is a foregone conclusion, opposition parties often try to introduce amendments in principle at later stages in the proceedings under the guise of changes in details.

If a bill is one of supply or of ways and means, it is referred to the Committee of the Whole after second reading. The Canada Water Bill was not such a bill and it was, consequently, referred to the Standing Committee on National Resources and Public Works for detailed consideration. Standing Committees do two things when deliberating a bill: they listen to briefs presented by various organizations and individuals, and they conduct a clause-by-clause examination of the legislation. Before they hear briefs, however, they often listen to testimony by the minister who has introduced the bill and they question officials of the department which is sponsoring the bill about its intent and effect. Committee deliberations on the Water Bill took some 21 days, with about 3 days being taken up listening to official testimony, and 10 or 11 days on briefs from organizations as disparate as the Electric Reduction Company, which manufactures virtually all of the phosphate used in detergents in Canada, and the Consumers' Association of Canada. The remaining sitting days were taken up with clause-by-clause analysis.

The opposition's first chance to introduce amendments to a bill is at the clause-by-clause analysis stage of the hearings, and at this point an attempt will often be made to change the substance of the legislation by introducing sweeping amendments. Since the government has a majority on all committees there is no chance of success for an amendment which the government would not want to see in the act. At least, this has been true in the past. However, party lines do sometimes break down in voting in committees, and since the 1969–70 session observers have noted an increasing independence on the part of government backbenchers. It is most unlikely that major changes could be successfully introduced by anyone without government sanction at the clause-by-clause stage. For example, in the case of the Canada Water Bill one amendment was introduced without government sanction by a government member and subsequently was defeated at the report stage in the House of Commons.

The opposition members usually introduce a number of minor amendments at the clause-by-clause stage, and not all are rejected. Some of them genuinely improve the wording of the bill and some of the changes of administrative detail suggested by the opposition are also valuable. It also often happens that the government amends its own bill at this stage. In the case of Bill C-144, almost twenty government amendments were introduced and accepted by the committee. These amendments came about as a result of public and parliamentary criticism of the legislation, second thoughts of bureaucrats and, because water management is a field of divided jurisdiction, criticisms by the provinces. Two of the government amendments, (providing for loans to water management agencies and for the control of nutrients such as phosphates in detergents) were ruled by the committee chairman to be changes in principle, and these consequently had to be introduced by the government at the next stage in the legislative passage when the bill reported back to the House of Commons.

Before leaving the discussion of the committee stage of legislation, it must be noted that most decisions about an amendment's acceptability are made, in fact, not by the committee but by senior bureaucrats and the minister. During clause-by-clause analysis there is always a senior member of the sponsoring department at the hearings and he sits as a witness at the committee table. The Parliamentary Secretary to the minister is also present and he, advised quietly by the witness, comments on amendments as they arise. From his words, government members of the committee take their cue about how to vote on each amendment.

When the committee has completed its deliberations, it reports the bill back to the House of Commons with the recommended amendments. The House debate at the *report stage* can be extensive, for any MP is free to offer amendments at this stage, and the opposition often introduces the same amendments at the report stage as it introduced during clause-by-clause consideration of the legislation in committee. Any major changes which the government makes in its legislation must also be introduced at this stage. For the Canada Water Bill, debate at this stage took four days, following which all the amendments were voted on. The government ones were carried and the opposition ones defeated. When all amendments have been considered, a motion that the reported bill be concurred in as amended is passed without further debate.

Third reading of a bill, which usually occurs as quickly as possible after the report stage (normally after one day), is often perfunctory. Usually the bill is simply sent on to the Senate or to the Governor General, depending on whether it was introduced in the Senate or the House of Commons. But debate can occur at this stage. If the opposition is in an obstreperous mood, it can give notice of a motion to introduce a series of amendments and start the whole debate again, but unless the relations between the government and the opposition are bad or the opposition feels very strongly about a particular piece of legislation, this does not usually happen.

When a bill reaches the Senate its treatment is again usually per-functory. First reading is granted with appropriate mumblings and mur-murs, and the debate on second reading, if there is any, is usually good-humoured, imprecise and mercifully brief. If the Senate is going to do any-thing to a bill it will do so in committee, but action here is also rather rare. In the case of the Canada Water Bill, one of the honourable Senators de-cided that the bill required amendment to provide for appeal procedures, but overwhelming pressure against this was brought on him by one or two cabinet ministers and assorted party leaders, because if an amendment were passed by the Senate, the bill would have to go back to the House, and the delay, so near the June 26th end of the session, might have blocked the legislation. In true senatorial fashion, the honourable gentle-man acceded and the bill raced through the Senate committee with very brief testimony by departmental officials and a quick clause-by-clause analysis. Senate committee hearings took one day.

Just as in the House of Commons, the bill then returns to the floor of the Senate where it is usually given instantaneous passage through the report and third-reading stages, and is then passed on to the Governor General for royal assent. Royal assent is always granted automatically, and is usually given to many bills at the same time on the last day of the session.

The Canada Water Bill, now the Canada Water Act, was under more-or-less continuous legislative scrutiny from November to June. Sev-eral amendments were made to this bill, and it is important to note that the major amendments were put forward by the bureaucracy, agreed to by the cabinet, and rubber-stamped by parliament. Parliament played its role in polishing the legislation but, as suggested earlier, its role at the other stages of the policy process was a sharply circumscribed one. Parlia-ment is important as an ombudsman, as an electoral college, and as an auditor of the government's record. Its symbolic position as the focus—around which revolve the more active parts of the policy-making process—is vital to the way Canadians relate to their political system, but one must be careful not to base the evaluation of parliament as an institu-tion on a misapprehension about its role in the policy process. Parliament plays a central role in Canadian politics, but it is not the role usually as-cribed to it at service club luncheons.

A Consolidation of the British North America Acts, 1867–1964*

FOREWORD

The law embodied in the *British North America Act, 1867* has been altered many times otherwise than by direct amendment, not only by the Parliament of the United Kingdom, but also by the Parliament of Canada and the legislatures of the provinces in those cases where provisions of the British North America Act are expressed to be subject to alteration by Parliament or the legislatures, as the case may be. A consolidation of the British North America Acts with only such subsequent enactments as directly alter the text of the Act would therefore not produce a true statement of the law.

In preparing this consolidation an attempt has been made to reflect accurately the substance of the law contained in the series of enactments known as the British North America Acts and other enactments modifying the provisions of the original *British North America Act, 1867*.

The various classes of enactments modifying the original text of the *British North America Act, 1867*, have been dealt with as follows.

I. Direct Amendments

1. Repeals

Repealed provisions (e.g. section 2) have been deleted from the text and quoted in a footnote.

2. Amendments

Amended provisions (e.g. section 4) are reproduced in the text in their amended form and the original provisions are quoted in a footnote.

3. Additions

Added provisions (e.g. section 51A) are included in the text.

---

* *The Amendment of the Constitution of Canada*, (Queen's Printer, Ottawa, 1965), pp. 54-97. Reproduced by permission of Information Canada.

4. *Substitutions*

Substituted provisions (e.g. section 18) are included in the text, and the former provision is quoted in a footnote.

II. Indirect Amendments

1. *Alterations by United Kingdom Parliament*

Provisions altered by the United Kingdom Parliament otherwise than by direct amendment (e.g. section 21) are included in the text in their altered form, and the original provision is quoted in a footnote.

2. *Additions by United Kingdom Parliament*

Constitutional provisions added otherwise than by the insertion of additional provisions in the British North America Act (e.g. provisions of the *British North America Act, 1871* authorizing Parliament to legislate for any territory not included in a province) are not incorporated in the text, but the additional provisions are quoted in an appropriate footnote.

3. *Alterations by Parliament of Canada*

Provisions subject to alteration by the Parliament of Canada (e.g. section 37) have been included in the text in their altered form, wherever possible, but where this was not feasible (e.g. section 40) the original section has been retained in the text and a footnote reference made to the Act of the Parliament of Canada effecting the alteration.

4. *Alterations by the Legislatures*

Provisions subject to alteration by legislatures of the provinces (e.g. sections 70, 72, 83, 84) have been included in the text in their original form, but the footnotes refer to the provincial enactments effecting the alteration. Amendments to provincial enactments are not referred to; these may be readily found by consulting the indexes to provincial statutes. The enactments of the original provinces only are referred to; there are corresponding enactments by the provinces created at a later date.

III. Spent Provisions

Footnote references are made to those sections that are spent or are probably spent. For example, section 119 became spent by lapse of time and the footnote reference so indicates; on the other hand, section 140 is probably spent, but short of examining all statutes passed before Confederation there would be no way of ascertaining definitely whether or not the section is spent; the footnote reference therefore indicates the section as being probably spent.

THE BRITISH NORTH AMERICA ACT, 1867
30 & 31 Victoria, c. 3.
(Consolidated with amendments)

An Act for the Union of Canada, Nova Scotia, and New Brunswick, and the Government thereof; and for Purposes connected therewith.

(29th March, 1867.)

WHEREAS the Provinces of Canada, Nova Scotia and New Brunswick have expressed their Desire to be federally united into One Dominion under the Crown of the United Kingdom of Great Britain and Ireland, with a Constitution similar in Principle to that of the United Kingdom:

And whereas such a Union would conduce to the Welfare of the Provinces and promote the Interests of the British Empire:

And whereas on the Establishment of the Union by Authority of Parliament it is expedient, not only that the Constitution of the Legislative Authority in the Dominion be provided for, but also that the Nature of the Executive Government therein be declared:

And whereas it is expedient that Provision be made for the eventual Admission into the Union of other Parts of British North America: (1)

I.—PRELIMINARY.

Short title.

1. This Act may be cited as The British North America Act, 1867.

2. Repealed. (2)

II.—UNION.

Declaration of Union.

3. It shall be lawful for the Queen, by and with the Advice of Her Majesty's Most Honourable Privy Council, to declare by

---

(1) The enacting clause was repealed by the *Statute Law Revision Act, 1893,* 56-57 Vict., c. 14 (U.K.). It read as follows:

> Be it therefore enacted and declared by the Queen's Most Excellent Majesty, by and with the Advice and Consent of the Lords Spiritual and Temporal, and Commons, in this present Parliament assembled, and by the Authority of the same, as follows:

(2) Section 2, repealed by the *Statute Law Revision Act, 1893,* 56-57 Vict., c. 14 (U.K.), read as follows:

Application of Provisions referring to the Queen.

> **2.** The Provisions of this Act referring to Her Majesty the Queen extend also to the Heirs and Successors of Her Majesty, Kings and Queens of the United Kingdom of Great Britain and Ireland.

Proclamation that, on and after a Day therein appointed, not being more than Six Months after the passing of this Act, the Provinces of Canada, Nova Scotia, and New Brunswick shall form and be One Dominion under the Name of Canada; and on and after that Day those Three Provinces shall form and be One Dominion under that Name accordingly. (3)

4. Unless it is otherwise expressed or implied, the Name Canada shall be taken to mean Canada as constituted under this Act. (4)

Construction of subsequent Provisions of Act.

5. Canada shall be divided into Four Provinces, named Ontario, Quebec, Nova Scotia, and New Brunswick. (5)

Four Provinces.

6. The Parts of the Province of Canada (as it exists at the passing of this Act) which formerly constituted respectively the Provinces of Upper Canada and Lower Canada shall be deemed to be severed, and shall form Two separate Provinces. The Part which formerly constituted the Province of Upper Canada shall constitute the Province of Ontario; and the Part which formerly constituted the Province of Lower Canada shall constitute the Province of Quebec.

Provinces of Ontario and Quebec.

7. The Provinces of Nova Scotia and New Brunswick shall have the same Limits as at the passing of this Act.

Provinces of Nova Scotia and New Brunswick.

8. In the general Census of the Population of Canada which is hereby required to be taken in the Year One thousand eight hundred and seventy-one, and in every Tenth Year thereafter, the respective Populations of the Four Provinces shall be distinguished.

Decennial Census.

III.—EXECUTIVE POWER.

9. The Executive Government and Authority of and over Canada is hereby declared to continue and be vested in the Queen.

Declaration of Executive Power in the Queen.

---

(3) The first day of July, 1867, was fixed by proclamation dated May 22, 1867.

(4) Partially repealed by the *Statute Law Revision Act, 1893*, 56-57 Vict., c. 14 (U.K.). As originally enacted the section read as follows:

> **4.** The subsequent Provisions of this Act shall, unless it is otherwise expressed or implied, commence and have effect on and after the Union, that is to say, on and after the Day appointed for the Union taking effect in the Queen's Proclamation; and in the same Provisions, unless it is otherwise expressed or implied, the Name Canada shall be taken to mean Canada as constituted under this Act.

(5) Canada now consists of ten provinces (Ontario, Quebec, Nova Scotia, New Brunswick, Manitoba, British Columbia, Prince Edward Island, Alberta, Saskatchewan and Newfoundland) and two territories (the Yukon Territory and the Northwest Territories).

Application of Provisions referring to Governor General.

10. The Provisions of this Act referring to the Governor General extend and apply to the Governor General for the Time being of Canada, or other the Chief Executive Officer or Administrator for the Time being carrying on the Government of Canada on behalf and in the Name of the Queen, by whatever Title he is designated.

Constitution of Privy Council for Canada.

11. There shall be a Council to aid and advise in the Government of Canada, to be styled the Queen's Privy Council for Canada; and the Persons who are to be Members of that Council shall be from Time to Time chosen and summoned by the Governor General and sworn in as Privy Councillors, and Members thereof may be from Time to Time removed by the Governor General.

All Powers under Acts to be exercised by Governor General with Advice of Privy Council, or alone.

12. All Powers, Authorities, and Functions which under any Act of the Parliament of Great Britain, or of the Parliament of the United Kingdom of Great Britain and Ireland, or of the Legislature of Upper Canada, Lower Canada, Canada, Nova Scotia, or New Brunswick, are at the Union vested in or exerciseable by the respective Governors or Lieutenant Governors of those Provinces, with the Advice, or with the Advice and Consent, of the respective Executive Councils thereof, or in conjunction with those Councils, or with any Number of Members thereof, or by those Governors or Lieutenant Governors individually, shall, as far as the same continue in existence and capable of being exercised after the Union in relation to the Government of Canada, be vested in and exerciseable by the Governor General, with the Advice or with the Advice and Consent of or in conjunction with the Queen's Privy Council for Canada, or any Member thereof, or by the Governor General individually, as the Case requires, subject nevertheless (except with respect to such as exist under Acts of the Parliament of Great Britain or of the Parliament of the United Kingdom of Great Britain and Ireland) to be abolished or altered by the Parliament of Canada. (6)

Application of Provisions referring to Governor General in Council.

13. The Provisions of this Act referring to the Governor General in Council shall be construed as referring to the Governor General acting by and with the Advice of the Queen's Privy Council for Canada.

Power to Her Majesty to authorize Governor General to appoint Deputies.

14. It shall be lawful for the Queen, if Her Majesty thinks fit, to authorize the Governor General from Time to Time to appoint any Person or any Persons jointly or severally to be his Deputy or Deputies within any Part or Parts of Canada, and in that Capacity to exercise during the Pleasure of the Governor General such of the Powers, Authorities, and Functions of the Governor General as the Governor General deems it necessary or expedient to assign to him or them, subject to any Limitations or Directions expressed or given by the Queen; but the Appointment of such a Deputy or Deputies shall not affect the Exercise by the Governor General himself of any Power, Authority or Function.

15. The Command-in-Chief of the Land and Naval Militia, and of all Naval and Military Forces, of and in Canada, is hereby declared to continue and be vested in the Queen. Command of armed Forces to continue to be vested in the Queen.

16. Until the Queen otherwise directs, the Seat of Government of Canada shall be Ottawa. Seat of Government of Canada.

IV.—LEGISLATIVE POWER.

17. There shall be One Parliament for Canada, consisting of the Queen, an Upper House styled the Senate, and the House of Commons. Constitution of Parliament of Canada.

18. The privileges, immunities, and powers to be held, enjoyed, and exercised by the Senate and by the House of Commons, and by the Members thereof respectively, shall be such as are from time to time defined by Act of the Parliament of Canada, but so that any Act of the Parliament of Canada defining such privileges, immunities, and powers shall not confer any privileges, immunities, or powers exceeding those at the passing of such Act held, enjoyed, and exercised by the Commons House of Parliament of the United Kingdom of Great Britain and Ireland, and by the Members thereof. (7) Privileges, etc., of Houses.

19. The Parliament of Canada shall be called together not later than Six Months after the Union. (8) First Session of the Parliament of Canada.

---

(6) See the notes to section 129, *infra*.

(7) Repealed and re-enacted by the *Parliament of Canada Act*, 1875, 38-39 Vict., c. 38 (U.K.). The original section read as follows:

> **18.** The Privileges Immunities, and Powers to be held, enjoyed, and exercised by the Senate and by the House of Commons and by the Members thereof respectively shall be such as are from Time to Time defined by Act of the Parliament of Canada, but so that the same shall never exceed those at the passing of this Act held, enjoyed, and exercised by the Commons House of Parliament of the United Kingdom of Great Britain and Ireland and by the Members thereof.

(8) Spent. The first session of the first Parliament began on November 6, 1867.

Yearly
Session of the
Parliament
of Canada.

20. There shall be a Session of the Parliament of Canada once at least in every Year, so that Twelve Months shall not intervene between the last Sitting of the Parliament in one Session and its first Sitting in the next Session. (9)

The Senate.

Number of
Senators.

21. The Senate shall, subject to the Provisions of this Act, consist of One Hundred and Two Members who shall be styled Senators. (10)

Representation
of Provinces
in Senate.

22. In relation to the Constitution of the Senate Canada shall be deemed to consist of Four Divisions:—

1. Ontario;

2. Quebec;

3. The Maritime Provinces, Nova Scotia and New Brunswick, and Prince Edward Island;

4. The Western Provinces of Manitoba, British Columbia, Saskatchewan, and Alberta;

which Four Divisions shall (subject to the Provisions of this Act) be equally represented in the Senate as follows: Ontario by twenty-four senators; Quebec by twenty-four senators; the Maritime Provinces and Prince Edward Island by twenty-four senators, ten thereof representing Nova Scotia, ten thereof representing New Brunswick, and four thereof representing Prince Edward Island; the Western Provinces by twenty-four senators, six thereof representing Manitoba, six thereof representing British Columbia, six thereof representing Saskatchewan, and six thereof representing Alberta; Newfoundland shall be entitled to be represented in the Senate by six members.

---

(9) The term of the twelfth Parliament was extended by the *British North America Act, 1916*, 6-7 Geo. V. c. 19 (U.K.), which Act was repealed by the Statute Law Revision Act, 1927, 17-18 Geo. V, c. 42 (U.K.).

(10) As amended by the *British North America Act, 1915*, 5-6 Geo. V, c. 45 (U.K.), and modified by the *British North America Act, 1949*, 12-13 Geo. VI, c. 22 (U.K.).

The original section read as follows:

> **21.** The Senate shall, subject to the Provisions of this Act, consist of Seventy-two Members, who shall be styled Senators.

The *Manitoba Act* added two for Manitoba; the Order in Council admitting British Columbia added three; upon admission of Prince Edward Island four more were provided by section 147 of the *British North America Act, 1867*; The *Alberta Act* and *The Saskatchewan Act* each added four. The Senate was reconstituted at 96 by the *British North America Act, 1915*, and six more Senators were added upon union with Newfoundland.

In the Case of Quebec each of the Twenty-four Senators representing that Province shall be appointed for One of the Twenty-four Electoral Divisions of Lower Canada specified in Schedule A. to Chapter One of the Consolidated statutes of Canada. (11)

23. The Qualification of a Senator shall be as follows:

(1) He shall be of the full age of Thirty Years:

(2) He shall be either a natural-born Subject of the Queen, or a Subject of the Queen naturalized by an Act of Parliament of Great Britain, or of the Parliament of the United Kingdom of Great Britain and Ireland, or of the Legislature of One of the Provinces of Upper Canada, Lower Canada, Canada, Nova Scotia, or New Brunswick, before the Union, or of the Parliament of Canada, after the Union:

(3) He shall be legally or equitably seised as of Freehold for his own Use and Benefit of Lands or Tenements held in Free and Common Socage, or seised or possessed for his own Use and Benefit of Lands or Tenements held in Franc-alleu or in Roture, within the Province for which he is appointed, of the Value of Four thousand Dollars, over and above all Rents, Dues, Debts, Charges, Mortgages, and Incumbrances due or payable out of or charged on or affecting the same.

(4) His Real and Personal Property shall be together worth Four thousand Dollars over and above his Debts and Liabilities:

(5) He shall be resident in the Province for which he is appointed:

(6) In the Case of Quebec he shall have his Real Property Qualification in the Electoral Division for which he is appointed, or shall be resident in that Division.

---

(11) As amended by the *British North America Act, 1915*, and the *British North America Act, 1949*, 12-13 Geo. VI, c. 22 (U.K.). The original section read as follows:

Representation of Provinces in Senate.

22. In relation to the Constitution of the Senate, Canada shall be deemed to consist of Three Divisions:

1. Ontario;
2. Quebec;
3. The Maritime Provinces, Nova Scotia and New Brunswick;

which Three Divisions shall (subject to the Provisions of this Act) be equally represented in the Senate as follows: Ontario by twenty-four Senators; Quebec by twenty-four Senators; and the Maritime Provinces by Twenty-four Senators, Twelve thereof representing Nova Scotia, and Twelve thereof representing New Brunswick.

In the Case of Quebec each of the Twenty-four Senators representing that Province shall be appointed for One of the Twenty-four Electoral Divisions of Lower Canada specified in Schedule A. to Chapter One of the Consolidated Statutes of Canada.

Summons of
Senator.

24. The Governor General shall from Time to Time, in the Queen's Name, by Instrument under the Great Seal of Canada, summon qualified Persons to the Senate; and, subject to the Provisions of this Act, every Person so summoned shall become and be a Member of the Senate and a Senator.

25. Repealed. (12)

Addition of
Senators in
certain cases.

26. If at any Time on the Recommendation of the Governor General the Queen thinks fit to direct that Four or Eight Members be added to the Senate, the Governor General may by Summons to Four or Eight qualified Persons (as the Case may be), representing equally the Four Divisions of Canada, add to the Senate accordingly. (13)

Reduction of
Senate to
normal
Number.

27. In case of such Addition being at any Time made, the Governor General shall not summon any Person to the Senate, except upon a further like Direction by the Queen on the like Recommendation, to represent one of the Four Divisions until such Division is represented by Twenty-four Senators and no more. (14)

Maximum
Number of
Senators.

28. The Number of Senators shall not at any Time exceed One Hundred and ten. (15)

Tenure of Place
in Senate.

29. A Senator shall, subject to the Provisions of this Act, hold his Place in the Senate for Life.

---

(12) Repealed by the *Statute Law Revision Act, 1893*, 56-57 Vict., c. 14 (U.K.). The section read as follows:

Summons of
First Body
of Senators.

25. Such Persons shall be first summoned to the Senate as the Queen by Warrant under Her Majesty's Royal Sign Manual thinks fit to approve, and their Names shall be inserted in the Queen's Proclamation of Union.

(13) As amended by the *British North America Act, 1915*, 5-6 Geo. V, c. 45 (U.K.). The original section read as follows:

Addition of
Senators in
certain cases.

26. If at any Time on the Recommendation of the Governor General the Queen thinks fit to direct that Three or Six Members be added to the Senate, the Governor General may by Summons to Three or Six qualified Persons (as the Case may be), representing equally the Three Divisions of Canada, add to the Senate accordingly.

(14) As amended by the *British North America Act, 1915*, 5-6 Geo. V, c. 45 (U.K.). The original section read as follows:

Reduction of
Senate to
normal
Number.

27. In case of such Addition being at any Time made the Governor General shall not summon any Person to the Senate, except on a further like Direction by the Queen on the like Recommendation, until each of the Three Divisions of Canada is represented by Twenty-four Senators and no more.

(15) As amended by the *British North America Act, 1915*, 5-6 Geo. V, c. 45 (U.K.). The original section read as follows:

Maximum
Number of
Senators.

28. The Number of Senators shall not at any Time exceed Seventy-eight.

30. A Senator may be Writing under his Hand addressed to the Governor General resign his Place in the Senate, and thereupon the same shall be vacant.

31. The Place of a Senator shall become vacant in any of the following Cases:

(1) If for Two consecutive Sessions of the Parliament he fails to give his Attendance in the Senate:

(2) If he takes an Oath or makes a Declaration or Acknowledgment of Allegiance, Obedience, or Adherence to a Foreign Power, or does an Act whereby he becomes a Subject or Citizen, or entitled to the Rights or Privileges of a Subject or Citizen, of a Foreign Power:

(3) If he is adjudged Bankrupt or Insolvent, or applies for the Benefit of any Law relating to Insolvent Debtors, or becomes a public Defaulter:

(4) If he is attainted of Treason or convicted of Felony or of any infamous Crime:

(5) If he ceases to be qualified in respect of Property or of Residence; provided, that a Senator shall not be deemed to have ceased to be qualified in respect of Residence by reason only of his residing at the Seat of the Government of Canada while holding an Office under that Government requiring his Presence there.

32. When a Vacancy happens in the Senate by Resignation, Death, or otherwise, the Governor General shall by Summons to a fit and qualified Person fill the Vacancy.

33. If any Question arises respecting the Qualification of a Senator or a Vacancy in the Senate the same shall be heard and determined by the Senate.

34. The Governor General may from Time to Time, by Instrument under the Great Seal of Canada, appoint a Senator to be Speaker of the Senate, and may remove him and appoint another in his Stead. (16)

---

(16) Provision for exercising the functions of Speaker during his absence is made by the *Speaker of the Senate Act*, R.S.C. 1952, c. 255. Doubts as to the power of Parliament to enact such an Act were removed by the *Canadian Speaker (Appointment of Deputy) Act, 1895*, 59 Vict., c. 3, (U.K.).

Quorum of Senate.

35. Until the Parliament of Canada otherwise provides, the Presence of at least Fifteen Senators, including the Speaker, shall be necessary to constitute a Meeting of the Senate for the Exercise of its Powers.

Voting in Senate.

36. Questions arising in the Senate shall be decided by a Majority of Voices, and the Speaker shall in all Cases have a Vote, and when the Voices are equal to Decision shall be deemed to be in the Negative.

The House of Commons.

Constitution of House of Commons in Canada.

37. The House of Commons shall, subject to the Provisions of this Act, consist of Two Hundred and sixty-five Members of whom Eighty-five shall be elected for Ontario, Seventy-five for Quebec, Twelve for Nova Scotia, Ten for New Brunswick, Fourteen for Manitoba, Twenty-two for British Columbia, Four for Prince Edward Island, Seventeen for Alberta, Seventeen for Saskatchewan, Seven for Newfoundland, One for the Yukon Territory and One for the Northwest Territories. (17)

Summoning of House of Commons.

38. The Governor General shall from Time to Time, in the Queen's Name, by Instrument under the Great Seal of Canada, summon and call together the House of Commons.

Senators not to sit in House of Commons.

39. A Senator shall not be capable of being elected or of sitting or voting as a Member of the House of Commons.

Electoral districts of the Four Provinces.

40. Until the Parliament of Canada otherwise provides, Ontario, Quebec, Nova Scotia, and New Brunswick shall, for the Purposes of the Election of Members to serve in the House of Commons, be divided into Electoral Districts as follows:

1.—ONTARIO.

Ontario shall be divided into the Counties, Ridings of Counties, Cities, Parts of Cities, and Towns enumerated in the First Schedule to this Act, each whereof shall be an Electoral District, each such District as numbered in that Schedule being entitled to return One Member.

---

(17) As altered by the *Representation Act, R.S.C.* 1952, c. 334, as amended by S.C. 1962, c. 17. The original section read as follows:

37. The House of Commons shall, subject to the Provisions of this Act, consist of the One hundred and eighty-one Members, of whom Eighty-two shall be elected for Ontario, Sixty-five for Quebec, Nineteen for Nova Scotia, and Fifteen for New Brunswick.

Quebec shall be divided into Sixty-five Electoral Districts, composed of the Sixty-five Electoral Divisions into which Lower Canada is at the passing of this Act divided under Chapter Two of the Consolidated Statutes of Canada, Chapter Seventy-five of the Consolidated Statutes for Lower Canada, and the Act of the Province of Canada of the Twenty-third Year of the Queen, Chapter One, or any other Act amending the same in force at the Union, so that each such Electoral Division shall be for the Purposes of this Act an Electoral District entitled to return One Member.

3.—NOVA SCOTIA

Each of the Eighteen Counties of Nova Scotia shall be an Electoral District. The County of Halifax shall be entitled to return Two Members, and each of the other Counties One Member.

4.—NEW BRUNSWICK

Each of the Fourteen Counties into which New Brunswick is divided, including the City and County of St. John, shall be an Electoral District. The City of St. John shall also be a separate Electoral District. Each of those Fifteen Electoral Districts shall be entitled to return One Member. (18)

41. Until the Parliament of Canada otherwise provides, all Laws in force in the several Provinces at the Union relative to the following Matters or any of them, namely,—the Qualifications and Disqualifications of Persons to be elected or to sit or vote as Members of the House of Assembly or Legislative Assembly in the several Provinces, the Voters at Elections of such Members, the Oaths to be taken by Voters, the Returning Officers, their Powers and Duties, the Proceedings at Elections, the Periods during which Elections may be continued, the Trial of controverted Elections, and Proceedings incident thereto, the vacating of Seats of Members, and the Execution of new Writs in case of Seats vacated otherwise than by Dissolution,— shall respectively apply to Elections of Members to serve in the House of Commons for the same several Provinces. *Continuance of existing Election Laws until Parliament of Canada otherwise provides.*

Provided that, until the Parliament of Canada otherwise provides, at any Election for a Member of the House of Commons for the District of Algoma, in addition to Persons qualified by the Law of

---

(18) Spent. The electoral districts are now set out in the *Representation Act*, R.S.C. 1952, c. 334, as amended.

the Province of Canada to vote, every Male British Subject, aged Twenty-one Years or upwards, being a Householder, shall have a Vote. (19)

42. Repealed. (20)

43. Repealed. (21)

As to Election of Speaker of House of Commons.

44. The House of Commons on its first assembling after a General Election shall proceed with all practicable Speed to elect One of its Members to be Speaker.

As to filling up Vacancy in Office of Speaker.

45. In case of a Vacancy happening in the Office of Speaker by Death, Resignation, or otherwise, the House of Commons shall with all practicable Speed proceed to elect another of its Members to be Speaker.

Speaker to preside.

46. The Speaker shall preside at all Meetings of the House of Commons.

Provision in case of Absence of Speaker.

47. Until the Parliament of Canada otherwise provides, in case of the Absence for any Reason of the Speaker from the Chair of the House of Commons for a Period of Forty-eight consecutive Hours, the House may elect another of its Members to act as Speaker, and

---

(19) Spent. Elections are now provided for by the *Canada Elections Act*, S.C. 1960, c. 38; controverted elections by the *Dominion Controverted Elections Act*, R.S.C. 1952, c. 87; qualifications and disqualifications of members by the *House of Commons Act*, R.S.C. 1952, c. 143 and the *Senate and House of Commons Act*, R.S.C. 1952, c. 249.

(20) Repealed by the *Statute Law Revision Act, 1893*, 56-57 Vict., c. 14 (U.K.). The section read as follows:

Writs for First Election.

42. For the First Election of Members to serve in the House of Commons the Governor General shall cause Writs to be issued by such Person, in such Form, and addressed to such Returning Officers as he thinks fit.

The Person issuing Writs under this Section shall have the like Powers as are possessed at the Union by the Officers charged with the issuing of Writs for the Election of Members to serve in the respective House of Assembly or Legislative Assembly of the Province of Canada, Nova Scotia, or New Brunswick; and the Returning Officers to whom Writs are directed under this Section shall have the like Powers as are possessed at the Union by the Officers charged with the returning of Writs for the Election of Members to serve in the same respective House of Assembly or Legislative Assembly.

(21) Repealed by the *Statute Law Revision Act, 1893*, 56-57 Vict., c. 14 (U.K.). The section read as follows:

As to Casual Vacancies.

43. In case a Vacancy in the Representation in the House of Commons of any Electoral District happens before the Meeting of the Parliament, or after the Meeting of the Parliament before Provision is made by the Parliament in this Behalf, the Provisions of the last foregoing Section of this Act shall extend and apply to the issuing and returning of a Writ in respect of such vacant District.

the Member so elected shall during the Continuance of such Absence of the Speaker have and execute all the Powers, Privileges, and Duties of Speaker. (22)

48. The Presence of at least Twenty Members of the House of Commons shall be necessary to constitute a Meeting of the House for the Exercise of its Powers, and for that Purpose the Speaker shall be reckoned as a Member.

Quorum of House of Commons.

49. Questions arising in the House of Commons shall be decided by a Majority of Voices other than that of the Speaker, and when the Voices are equal, but not otherwise, the Speaker shall have a Vote.

Voting in House of Commons.

50. Every House of Commons shall continue for Five Years from the Day of the Return of the Writs for choosing the House (subject to be sooner dissolved by the Governor General), and no longer.

Duration of House of Commons.

51. (1) Subject as hereinafter provided, the number of members of the House of Commons shall be two hundred and sixty-three and the representation of the provinces therein shall forthwith upon the coming into force of this section and thereafter on the completion of each decennial census be readjusted by such authority, in such manner, and from such time as the Parliament of Canada from time to time provides, subject and according to the following rules:

Readjustment of representation in Commons.

1. There shall be assigned to each of the provinces a number of members computed by dividing the total population of the provinces by two hundred and sixty-one and by dividing the population of each province by the quotient so obtained, disregarding, except as hereinafter in this section provided, the remainder, if any, after the said process of division.

Rules.

2. If the total number of members assigned to all the provinces pursuant to rule one is less than two hundred and sixty-one, additional members shall be assigned to the provinces (one to a province) having remainders in the computation under rule one commencing with the province having the largest remainder and continuing with the other provinces in the order of the magnitude of their respective remainders until the total number of members assigned is two hundred and sixty-one.

3. Notwithstanding anything in this section, if upon completion of a computation under rules one and two, the number of members to be assigned to a province is less than the number of senators

---

(22) Provision for exercising the functions of Speaker during his absence is now made by the *Speaker of the House of Commons Act*, R.S.C. 1952, c. 254.

representing the said province, rules one and two shall cease to apply in respect of the said province, and there shall be assigned to the said province a number of members equal to the said number of senators.

4. In the event that rules one and two cease to apply in respect of a province then, for the purposes of computing the number of members to be assigned to the provinces in respect of which rules one and two continue to apply, the total population of the provinces shall be reduced by the number of the population of the province in respect of which rules one and two have ceased to apply and the number two hundred and sixty-one shall be reduced by the number of members assigned to such province pursuant to rule three.

5. On any such readjustment the number of members for any province shall not be reduced by more than fifteen per cent below the representation to which such province was entitled under rules one to four of this subsection at the last preceding readjustment of the representation of that province, and there shall be no reduction in the representation of any province as a result of which that province would have a smaller number of members than any other province that according to the results of the then last decennial census did not have a larger population; but for the purposes of any subsequent readjustment of representation under this section any increase in the number of members of the House of Commons resulting from the application of this rule shall not be included in the divisor mentioned in rules one to four of this subsection.

6. Such readjustment shall not take effect until the termination of the then existing Parliament.

Yukon Territory and other part not comprised within a province.

(2) The Yukon Territory as constituted by chapter forty-one of the statutes of Canada, 1901, shall be entitled to one member, and such other part of Canada not comprised within a province as may from time to time be defined by the Parliament of Canada shall be entitled to one member. (23)

---

(23) As enacted by the *British North America Act, 1952*, R.S.C. 1952, c. 304, which came into force on June 18, 1952. The section, as originally enacted, read as follows:

Decennial Re-adjustment of Representation.

51. On the Completion of the Census in the Year One Thousand eight hundred and seventy-one, and of each subsequent decennial Census, the Representation of the Four Provinces shall be readjusted by such Authority, in such Manner, and from such Time, as the Parliament of Canada from Time to Time provides, subject and according to the following Rules:

(1) Quebec shall have the fixed Number of Sixty-five Members:

(2) There shall be assigned to each of the other Provinces such a Number of Members as will bear the same Proportion to the

Number of its Population (ascertained at such Census) as the Number Sixty-five bears to the Number of the Population of Quebec (so ascertained):

(3) In the Computation of the Number of Members for a Province a fractional Part not exceeding One Half of the whole Number requisite for entitling the Province to a Member shall be disregarded; but a fractional Part exceeding One Half of that Number shall be equivalent to the whole Number:

(4) On any such Re-adjustment the Number of Members for a Province shall not be reduced unless the Proportion which the Number of the Population of the Province bore to the Number of the aggregate Population of Canada at the then last preceding Re-adjustment of the Number of Members for the Province is ascertained at the then latest Census to be diminished by One Twentieth Part or upwards:

(5) Such Re-adjustment shall not take effect until the Termination of the then existing Parliament.

The section was amended by the *Statute Law Revision Act, 1893,* 56-57 Vict., c. 14 (U.K.) by repealing the words from "of the census" to "seventy-one and" and the word "subsequent".

By the *British North America Act, 1943,* 6-7 Geo. VI, c. 30 (U.K.) redistribution of seats following the 1941 census was postponed until the first session of Parliament after the war. The section was re-enacted by the *British North America Act, 1946,* 9-10 Geo. VI, c. 63 (U.K.) to read as follows:

51. (1) The number of members of the House of Commons shall be two hundred and fifty-five and the representation of the provinces therein shall forthwith upon the coming into force of this section and thereafter on the completion of each decennial census be readjusted by such authority, in such manner, and from such time as the Parliament of Canada from time to time provides, subject and according to the following rules:—

(1) Subject as hereinafter provided, there shall be assigned to each of the provinces a number of members computed by dividing the total population of the provinces by two hundred and fifty-four and by dividing the population of each province by the quotient so obtained, disregarding, except as hereinafter in this section provided, the remainder, if any, after the said process of division.

(2) If the total number of members assigned to all the provinces pursuant to rule one is less than two hundred and fifty-four, additional members shall be assigned to the provinces (one to a province) having remainders in the computation under rule one commencing with the province having the largest remainder and continuing with the other provinces in the order of the magnitude of their respective remainders until the total number of members assigned is two hundred and fifty-four.

(3) Notwithstanding anything in this section, if upon completion of a computation under rules one and two, the number of members to be assigned to a province is less than the number of senators representing the said province, rules one and two shall cease to apply in respect of the said province, and there shall be assigned to the said province a number of members equal to the said number of senators.

(4) In the event that rules one and two cease to apply in respect of a province then, for the purpose of computing the number of members to be assigned to the provinces in respect of which rules one and two continue to apply, the total population of the provinces shall be reduced by the number of the population of the province in respect of which rules one and two have ceased to apply and the number two hundred and fifty-four shall be reduced by the number of members asigned to such province pursuant to rule three.

(5) Such readjustment shall not take effect until the termination of the then existing Parliament.

(2) The Yukon Territory as constituted by Chapter forty-one of the Statutes of Canada, 1901, together with any Part of Canada not comprised within a province which may from time to time be included therein by the Parliament of Canada for the purposes of representation in Parliament, shall be entitled to one member.

Constitution
of House of
Commons.

51A. Notwithstanding anything in this Act a province shall always be entitled to a number of members in the House of Commons not less than the number of senators representing such province. (24)

Increase of
Number of
House of
Commons.

52. The Number of Members of the House of Commons may be from Time to Time increased by the Parliament of Canada, provided the proportionate Representation of the Provinces prescribed by this Act is not thereby disturbed.

Money Votes; Royal Assent.

Appropriation
and Tax Bills.

53. Bills for appropriating any Part of the Public Revenue, or for imposing any Tax or Impost, shall originate in the House of Commons.

Recommenda-
tion of Money
Votes.

54. It shall not be lawful for the House of Commons to adopt or pass any Vote, Resolution, Address, or Bill for the Appropriation of any Part of the Public Revenue, or of any Tax or Impost, to any Purpose that has not been first recommended to that House by Message of the Governor General in the Session in which such Vote, Resolution, Address, or Bill is proposed.

Royal Assent
to Bills, etc.

55. Where a Bill passed by the Houses of the Parliament is presented to the Governor General for the Queen's Assent, he shall declare, according to his Discretion, but subject to the Provisions of this Act and to Her Majesty's Instructions, either that he assents thereto in the Queen's Name, or that he withholds the Queen's Assent, or that he reserves the Bill for the Signification of the Queen's Pleasure.

Disallowance
by Order in
Council of Act
assented to
by Governor
General.

56. Where the Governor General assents to a Bill in the Queen's Name, he shall by the first convenient Opportunity send an authentic Copy of the Act to one of Her Majesty's Principal Secretaries of State, and if the Queen in Council within Two Years after Receipt thereof by the Secretary of State thinks fit to disallow the Act, such Disallowance (with a Certificate of the Secretary of State of the Day on which the Act was received by him) being signified by the Governor General, by Speech or Message to each of the Houses of the Parliament or by Proclamation, shall annul the Act from and after the Day of such Signification.

Signification
of Queen's
Pleasure on
Bill reserved.

57. A Bill reserved for the Signification of the Queen's Pleasure shall not have any Force unless and until, within Two Years from the Day on which it was presented to the Governor General for the Queen's

---

(24) As enacted by the *British North America Act, 1915,* 5-6 Geo. V, c. 45 (U.K.).

Assent, the Governor General signifies, by Speech or Message to each of the Houses of the Parliament or by Proclamation, that it has received the Assent of the Queen in Council.

An Entry of every such Speech, Message, or Proclamation shall be made in the Journal of each House, and a Duplicate thereof duly attested shall be delivered to the proper Officer to be kept among the Records of Canada.

V.—PROVINCIAL CONSTITUTIONS.

Executive Power.

58. For each Province there shall be an Officer, styled the Lieutenant Governor, appointed by the Governor General in Council by Instrument under the Great Seal of Canada. *Appointment of Lieutenant Governors of Provinces.*

59. A Lieutenant Governor shall hold Office during the Pleasure of the Governor General; but any Lieutenant Governor appointed after the Commencement of the First Session of the Parliament of Canada shall not be removeable within Five Years from his Appointment, except for Cause assigned, which shall be communicated to him in Writing within One Month after the Order for his Removal is made, and shall be communicated by Message to the Senate and to the House of Commons within One Week thereafter if the Parliament is then sitting, and if not then within One Week after the Commencement of the next Session of the Parliament. *Tenure of Office of Lieutenant Governor.*

60. The Salaries of the Lieutenant Governors shall be fixed and provided by the Parliament of Canada. (25) *Salaries of Lieutenant Governors.*

61. Every Lieutenant Governor shall, before assuming the Duties of his Office, make and subscribe before the Governor General or some Person authorized by him Oaths of Allegiance and Office similar to those taken by the Governor General. *Oaths, etc., of Lieutenant Governor.*

62. The Provisions of this Act referring to the Lieutenant Governor extend and apply to the Lieutenant Governor for the Time being of each Province, or other the Chief Executive Officer or Administrator for the Time being carrying on the Government of the Province, by whatever Title he is designated. *Application of provisions referring to Lieutenant Governor.*

---

(25) Provided for by the *Salaries Act*, R.S.C. 1952, c. 243 as amended by S.C. 1963, c. 41.

Appointment of Executive Officers for Ontario and Quebec.

63. The Executive Council of Ontario and of Quebec shall be composed of such Persons as the Lieutenant Governor from Time to Time thinks fit, and in the first instance of the following Officers, namely,— the Attorney General, the Secretary and Registrar of the Province, the Treasurer of the Province, the Commissioner of Crown Lands, and the Commissioner of Agriculture and Public Works, with in Quebec the Speaker of the Legislative Council and the Solicitor General. (26)

Executive Government of Nova Scotia and New Brunswick.

64. The Constitution of the Executive Authority in each of the Provinces of Nova Scotia and New Brunswick shall, subject to the Provisions of this Act, continue as it exists at the Union until altered under the Authority of this Act. (26A)

Powers to be exercised by Lieutenant Governor of Ontario or Quebec with Advice, or alone.

65. All Powers, Authorities, and Functions which under any Act of the Parliament of Great Britain, or of the Parliament of the United Kingdom of Great Britain and Ireland, or of the Legislature of Upper Canada, Lower Canada, or Canada, were or are before or at the Union vested in or exerciseable by the respective Governors or Lieutenant Governors of those Provinces, with the Advice or with the Advice and Consent of the respective Executive Councils thereof, or in conjunction with those Councils, or with any Number of Members thereof, or by those Governors or Lieutenant Governors individually, shall, as far as the same are capable of being exercised after the Union in relation to the Government of Ontario and Quebec respectively, be vested in and shall or may be exercised by the Lieutenant Governor of Ontario and Quebec respectively, with the Advice or with the Advice and Consent of or in conjunction with the respective Executive Councils, or any Members thereof, or by the Lieutenant Governor individually, as the Case requires, subject nevertheless (except with respect to such as exist under Acts of the Parliament of Great Britain, or of the Parliament of the United Kingdom of Great Britain and Ireland,) to be abolished or altered by the respective Legislatures of Ontario and Quebec. (27)

---

(26) Now provided for in Ontario by the *Executive Council Act*, R.S.O. 1960, c. 127, and in Quebec by the *Executive Power Act*, R.S.Q. 1941, c. 7.

(26A) A similar provision was included in each of the instruments admitting British Columbia, Prince Edward Island, and Newfoundland. The Executive Authorities for Manitoba, Alberta and Saskatchewan were established by the statutes creating those provinces. See the footnotes to section 5, *supra.*

(27) See the notes to section 129, *infra.*

66. The Provisions of this Act referring to the Lieutenant Governor in Council shall be construed as referring to the Lieutenant Governor of the Province acting by and with the Advice of the Executive Council thereof. Application of Provisions referring to Lieutenant Governor in Council.

67. The Governor General in Council may from Time to Time appoint an Administrator to execute the Office and Functions of Lieutenant Governor during his Absence, Illness, or other Inability. Administration in Absence, etc. of Lieutenant Governor.

68. Unless and until the Executive Government of any Province otherwise directs with respect to that Province, the Seats of Government of the Provinces shall be as follows, namely,—of Ontario, the City of Toronto; of Quebec, the City of Quebec; of Nova Scotia, the City of Halifax; and of New Brunswick, the City of Fredericton. Seats of Provincial Governments.

Legislative Power.

1.—ONTARIO.

69. There shall be a Legislature for Ontario consisting of the Lieutenant Governor and of One House, styled the Legislative Assembly of Ontario. Legislature for Ontario.

70. The Legislative Assembly of Ontario shall be composed of Eighty-two Members, to be elected to represent the Eighty-two Electoral Districts set forth in the First Schedule to this Act. (28) Electoral districts.

2.—QUEBEC.

71. There shall be a Legislature for Quebec consisting of the Lieutenant Governor and of Two Houses, styled the Legislative Council of Quebec and the Legislative Assembly of Quebec. Legislature for Quebec.

72. The Legislative Council of Quebec shall be composed of Twenty-four Members, to be appointed by the Lieutenant Governor. in the Queen's Name, by Instrument under the Great Seal of Quebec, One being appointed to represent each of the Twenty-four Electoral Constitution of Legislative Council.

---

(28) Spent. Now covered by the *Representation Act*, R.S.O. 1960, c. 353, as amended by S.O. 1962-63, c. 125, which provides that the Assembly shall consist of 108 members, representing the electoral districts set forth in the Schedule to that Act.

Divisions of Lower Canada in this Act referred to, and each holding Office for the Term of his Life, unless the Legislature of Quebec otherwise provides under the Provisions of this Act. (29)

Qualification of Legislative Councillors.

73. The Qualifications of the Legislative Councillors of Quebec shall be the same as those of the Senators for Quebec. (30)

Resignation, Disqualification, etc.

74. The Place of a Legislative Councillor of Quebec shall become vacant in the Cases, *mutatis mutandis*, in which the Place of Senator becomes vacant.

Vacancies.

75. When a Vacancy happens in the Legislative Council of Quebec by Resignation, Death, or otherwise, the Lieutenant Governor, in the Queen's Name, by Instrument under the Great Seal of Quebec, shall appoint a fit and qualified Person to fill the Vacancy.

Questions as to Vacancies, etc.

76. If any Question arises respecting the Qualification of a Legislative Councillor of Quebec, or a Vacancy in the Legislative Council of Quebec, the same shall be heard and determined by the Legislative Council.

Speaker of Legislative Council.

77. The Lieutenant Governor may from Time to Time, by Instrument under the Great Seal of Quebec, appoint a Member of the Legislative Council of Quebec to be Speaker thereof, and may remove him and appoint another in his Stead. (31)

Quorum of Legislative Council.

78. Until the Legislature of Quebec otherwise provides, the Presence of at least Ten Members of the Legislative Council, including the Speaker, shall be necessary to constitute a Meeting for the Exercise of its Powers.

Voting in Legislative Council.

79. Questions arising in the Legislative Council of Quebec shall be decided by a Majority of Voices, and the Speaker shall in all Cases have a Vote, and when the Voices are equal the Decision shall be deemed to be in the Negative.

---

(29) Spent. Now covered by the *Legislature Act*, R.S.Q. 1941, c. 4 as amended by S.Q. 1963, c. 12; the membership remains at twenty-four, representing the divisions set forth in the *Territorial Division Act*, R.S.Q. 1941, c. 3, as amended.

(30) Altered by the *Legislature Act*, R.S.Q. 1941, c. 4, s. 7, which provided that it shall be sufficient for any member to be domiciled, and to possess his property qualifications, within the Province of Quebec.

(31) Spent. Now covered by the *Legislature Act*, R.S.Q. 1941, c. 4, s. 9.

80. The Legislative Assembly of Quebec shall be composed of Sixty-five Members, to be elected to represent the Sixty-five Electoral Divisions or Districts of Lower Canada in this Act referred to, subject to Alteration thereof by the Legislature of Quebec: Provided that it shall not be lawful to present to the Lieutenant Governor of Quebec for Assent any Bill for altering the Limits of any of the Electoral Divisions or Districts mentioned in the Second Schedule to this Act, unless the Second and Third Readings of such Bill have been passed in the Legislative Assembly with the Concurrence of the Majority of the Members representing all those Electoral Divisions or Districts, and the Assent shall not be given to such Bill unless an Address has been presented by the Legislative Assembly to the Lieutenant Governor stating that it has been so passed. (32)

Constitution of Legislative Assembly of Quebec.

3.—ONTARIO AND QUEBEC.

81. Repealed. (33)

82. The Lieutenant Governor of Ontario and of Quebec shall from Time to Time, in the Queen's Name, by Instrument under the Great Seal of the Province, summon and call together the Legislative Assembly of the Province.

Summoning of Legislative Assemblies.

83. Until the Legislature of Ontario or of Quebec otherwise provides, a Person accepting or holding in Ontario or in Quebec any Office, Commission, or Employment, permanent or temporary, at the Nomination of the Lieutenant Governor, to which an annual Salary, or any Fee, Allowance, Emolument, or Profit of any Kind or Amount whatever from the Province is attached, shall not be eligible as a Member of the Legislative Assembly of the respective Province, nor shall he sit or vote as such; but nothing in this Section shall make ineligible any Person being a Member of the Executive Council of the respective Province, or holding any of the following Offices, that is to say, the Offices of Attorney General, Secretary and Registrar of the Province, Treasurer of the Province, Commissioner of Crown Lands, and Com-

Restriction on election of Holders of offices.

---

(32) Altered by the *Legislature Act*, R.S.Q. 1941, c. 4 as amended by S.Q. 1959-60, c. 28, s. 10, and the *Territorial Division Act*, R.S.Q. 1941, c. 3 as amended by S.Q. 1959-60, c. 28; there are now 95 members representing the districts set out in the *Territorial Division Act*.

(33) Repealed by the *Statute Law Revision Act, 1893*, 56-57 Vict., c. 14 (U.K.). The section read as follows:

First Session of Legislatures. **81.** The Legislatures of Ontario and Quebec respectively shall be called together not later than Six Months after the Union.

missioner of Agriculture and Public Works, and in Quebec Solicitor General, or shall disqualify him to sit or vote in the House for which he is elected, provided he is elected while holding such Office. (34)

Continuance of existing Election Laws. **84.** Until the Legislatures of Ontario and Quebec respectively otherwise provide, all Laws which at the Union are in force in those Provinces respectively, relative to the following Matters, or any of them, namely,—the Qualifications and Disqualifications of Persons to be elected or to sit or vote as Members of the Assembly of Canada, the Qualifications or Disqualifications of Voters, the Oaths to be taken by Voters, the Returning Officers, their Powers and Duties, the Proceedings at Elections, the Periods during which such Elections may be continued, and the Trial of controverted Elections and the Proceedings incident thereto, the vacating of the Seats of Members and the issuing and execution of new Writs in case of Seats vacated otherwise than by Dissolution,—shall respectively apply to Elections of Members to serve in the respective Legislative Assemblies of Ontario and Quebec.

Provided that, until the Legislature of Ontario otherwise provides, at any Election for a Member of the Legislative Assembly of Ontario for the District of Algoma, in addition to Persons qualified by the Law of the Province of Canada to vote, every male British Subject, aged Twenty-one Years or upwards, being a Householder, shall have a vote. (35)

Duration of Legislative Assemblies. **85.** Every Legislative Assembly of Ontario and every Legislative Assembly of Quebec shall continue for Four Years from the Day of the Return of the Writs for choosing the same (subject nevertheless to either the Legislative Assembly of Ontario or the Legislative Assembly of Quebec being sooner dissolved by the Lieutenant Governor of the Province), and no longer. (36)

---

(34) Probably spent. The subject-matter of this section is now covered in Ontario by the *Legislative Assembly Act,* R.S.O. 1960, c. 208, and in Quebec by the *Legislature Act,* R.S.Q., 1941, c. 4.

(35) Probably spent. The subject-matter of this section is now covered in Ontario by the *Election Act,* R.S.O. 1960, c. 118, the *Controverted Elections Act,* R.S.O. 1960, c. 65 and the *Legislative Assembly Act,* R.S.O. 1960, c. 208, and in Quebec by the *Quebec Election Act,* 1945, c. 15, the *Quebec Controverted Elections Act,* R.S.Q. 1941, c. 6, and the *Legislature Act,* R.S.Q. 1941, c. 4.

(36) The maximum duration of the Legislative Assembly for Ontario and Quebec has been changed to five years by the *Legislative Assembly Act,* R.S.O. 1960, c. 208, and the Legislature Act, R.S.Q. 1941, c. 4, respectively.

86. There shall be a Session of the Legislature of Ontario and of that Yearly Session of Legislature. of Quebec once at least in every Year, so that Twelve Months shall not intervene between the last Sitting of the Legislature in each Province in one Session and its first Sitting in the next Session.

87. The following Provisions of this Act respecting the House of Speaker, Quorum, etc. Commons of Canada shall extend and apply to the Legislative Assemblies of Ontario and Quebec, that is to say,—the Provisions relating to the Election of a Speaker originally and on Vacancies, the Duties of the Speaker, the Absence of the Speaker, the Quorum, and the Mode of voting, as if those Provisions were here re-enacted and made applicable in Terms to each such Legislative Assembly.

4.—NOVA SCOTIA AND NEW BRUNSWICK.

88. The Constitution of the Legislature of each of the Provinces Constitutions of Legislatures of Nova Scotia and New Brunswick. of Nova Scotia and New Brunswick shall, subject to the Provisions of this Act, continue as it exists at the Union until altered under the Authority of this Act. (37)

89. Repealed. (38)

6.—THE FOUR PROVINCES.

90. The following Provisions of this Act respecting the Parliament Application to Legislatures of Provisions respecting Money Votes, etc. of Canada, namely,—the Provisions relating to Appropriation and Tax Bills, the Recommendation of Money Votes, the Assent to Bills, the Disallowance of Acts, and the Signification of Pleasure on Bills reserved,—shall extend and apply to the Legislatures of the several

---

(37) Partially repealed by the *Statute Law Revision Act, 1893,* 56-57 Vict., c. 14 (U.K.) which deleted the following concluding words of the original enactment: and the House of Assembly of New Brunswick existing at the passing of this Act shall, unless sooner dissolved, continue for the Period for which it was elected.

A similar provision was included in each of the instruments admitting British Columbia, Prince Edward Island, and Newfoundland. The Legislatures of Manitoba, Alberta and Saskatchewan were established by the statutes creating those provinces. See the footnotes to section 5, *supra*.

(38) Repealed by the *Statute Law Revision Act, 1893,* 56-57 Vict., c. 14 (U.K.). The section read as follows:

5.—ONTARIO, QUEBEC, AND NOVA SCOTIA.

First Elections. **89.** Each of the Lieutenant Governors of Ontario, Quebec and Nova Scotia shall cause Writs to be issued for the First Election of Members of the Legislative Assembly thereof in such Form and by such Person as he thinks fit, and at such Time and addressed to such Returning Officer as the Governor General directs, and so that the First Election of Member of Assembly for any Electoral District or any Subdivision thereof shall be held at the same Time and at the same Places as the Election for a Member to serve in the House of Commons of Canada for that Electoral District.

Provinces as if those Provisions were here re-enacted and made applicable in Terms to the respective Provinces and the Legislatures thereof, with the Substitution of the Lieutenant Governor of the Province for the Governor General, of the Governor General for the Queen and for a Secretary of State, of One Year for Two Years, and of the Province for Canada.

VI.—DISTRIBUTION OF LEGISLATIVE POWERS.

Powers of the Parliament.

Legislative Authority of Parliament of Canada.

91. It shall be lawful for the Queen, by and with the Advice and Consent of the Senate and House of Commons, to make Laws for the Peace, Order, and good Government of Canada, in relation to all Matters not coming within the Classes of Subjects by this Act assigned exclusively to the Legislatures of the Provinces; and for greater Certainty, but not so as to restrict the Generality of the foregoing Terms of this Section, it is hereby declared that (notwithstanding anything in this Act) the exclusive Legislative Authority of the Parliament of Canada extends to all Matters coming within the Classes of Subjects next herein-after enumerated; that is to say,—

1. The amendment from time to time of the Constitution of Canada, except as regards matters coming within the classes of subjects by this Act assigned exclusively to the Legislatures of the provinces, or as regards rights or privileges by this or any other Constitutional Act granted or secured to the Legislature or the Government of a province, or to any class of persons with respect to schools or as regards the use of the English or the French language or as regards the requirements that there shall be a session of the Parliament of Canada at least once each year, and that no House of Commons shall continue for more than five years from the day of the return of the Writs for choosing the House: provided, however, that a House of Commons may in time of real or apprehended war, invasion or insurrection be continued by the Parliament of Canada if such continuation is not opposed by the votes of more than one-third of the members of such House. (39)

1A. The Public Debt and Property. (40)

---

(39) Added by the *British North America (No. 2) Act, 1949*, 13 Geo. VI, c. 81 (U.K.).

(40) Re-numbered by the *British North America (No. 2) Act, 1949*.

2. The Regulation of Trade and Commerce.

2A. Unemployment insurance. (41)

3. The raising of Money by any Mode or System of Taxation.

4. The borrowing of Money on the Public Credit.

5. Postal Service.

6. The Census and Statistics.

7. Militia, Military and Naval Service, and Defence.

8. The fixing of and providing for the Salaries and Allowances of Civil and other Officers of the Government of Canada.

9. Beacons, Buoys, Lighthouses, and Sable Island.

10. Navigation and Shipping.

11. Quarantine and the Establishment and Maintenance of Marine Hospitals.

12. Sea Coast and Inland Fisheries.

13. Ferries between a Province and any British or Foreign Country or between Two Provinces.

14. Currency and Coinage.

15. Banking, Incorporation of Banks, and the Issue of Paper Money.

16. Savings Banks.

17. Weights and Measures.

18. Bills of Exchange and Promissory Notes.

19. Interest.

20. Legal Tender.

21. Bankruptcy and Insolvency.

22. Patents of Invention and Discovery.

23. Copyrights.

24. Indians, and Lands reserved for the Indians.

25. Naturalization and Aliens.

26. Marriage and Divorce.

27. The Criminal Law, except the Constitution of Courts of Criminal Jurisdiction, but including the Procedure in Criminal matters.

---

(41) Added by the *British North America Act, 1940*, 3-4 Geo. **VI**, c. **36** (U.K.).

28. The Establishment, Maintenance, and Management of Penitentiaries.

29. Such Classes of Subjects as are expressly excepted in the Enumeration of the Classes of Subjects by this Act assigned exclusively to the Legislatures of the Provinces.

And any Matter coming within any of the Classes of Subjects enumerated in this Section shall not be deemed to come within the Class of Matters of a local or private Nature comprised in the Enumeration of the Classes of Subjects by this Act assigned exclusively to the Legislatures of the Provinces. (42)

---

(42) Legislative authority has been conferred on Parliament by other Acts as follows:

1. The *British North America Act, 1871,* 34-35 Vict., c. 28 (U.K.).

Parliament of Canada may establish new Provinces and provide for the constitution etc., thereof.

2. The Parliament of Canada may from time to time establish new Provinces in any territories forming for the time being part of the Dominion of Canada, but not included in any Province thereof, and may, at the time of such establishment, make provision for the constitution and administration of any such Province, and for the passing of laws for the peace, order, and good government of such Province, and for its representation in the said Parliament.

Alteration of limits of Provinces.

Parliament of Canada may legislate for any territory not included in a Province.

3. The Parliament of Canada may from time to time, with the consent of the Legislature of any Province of the said Dominion, increase, diminish, or otherwise alter the limits of such Province, upon such terms and conditions as may be agreed to by the said Legislature, and may, with the like consent, make provision respecting the effect and operation of any such increase or diminution or alteration of territory in relation to any Province affected thereby.

4. The Parliament of Canada may from time to time make provision for the administration, peace, order, and good government of any territory not for the time being included in any Province.

Confirmation of Acts of Parliament of Canada, 32 & 33 Vict. (Canadian) cap. 3. 33 Vict., (Canadian) cap. 3.

5. The following Acts passed by the said Parliament of Canada, and intituled respectively.—"An Act for the temporary government of Rupert's Land and the North Western Territory when united with Canada"; and "An Act to amend and continue the Act thirty-two and thirty-three Victoria, chapter three, and to establish and provide for the government of "the Province of Manitoba," shall be and be deemed to have been valid and effectual for all purposes whatsoever from the date at which they respectively received the assent, in the Queen's name, of the Governor General of the said Dominion of Canada."

Limitation of powers of Parliament of Canada to legislate for an established Province.

6. Except as provided by the third section of this Act, it shall not be competent for the Parliament of Canada to alter the provisions of the last-mentioned Act of the said Parliament in so far as it relates to the Province of Manitoba, or of any other Act hereafter establishing new Provinces in the said Dominion, subject always to the right of the Legislature of the Province of Manitoba to alter from time to time the provisions of any law respecting the qualification of electors and members of the Legislative Assembly, and to make laws respecting elections in the said Province.

The *Rupert's Land Act, 1868,* 31-32 Vict., c. 105 (U.K.) (repealed by the *Statute Law Revision Act, 1893,* 56-57 Vict., c. 14 (U.K.)) had previously conferred similar authority in relation to Rupert's Land and the North-Western Territory upon admission of those areas.

Exclusive Powers of Provincial Legislatures.

92. In each Province the Legislature may exclusively make Laws in relation to Matters coming within the Classes of Subject next herein-after enumerated; that is to say,—

Subjects of exclusive Provincial Legislation.

1. The Amendment from Time to Time, notwithstanding anything in this Act, of the Constitution of the Province, except as regards the Office of Lieutenant Governor.

2. Direct Taxation within the Province in order to the raising of a Revenue for Provincial Purposes.

3. The borrowing of Money on the sole Credit of the Province.

4. The Establishment and Tenure of Provincial Offices and the Appointment and Payment of Provincial Officers.

5. The Management and Sale of the Public Lands belonging to the Province and of the Timber and Wood thereon.

6. The Establishment, Maintenance, and Management of Public and Reformatory Prisons in and for the Province.

7. The Establishment, Maintenance, and Management of Hospitals, Asylums, Charities, and Eleemosynary Institutions in and for the Province, other than Marine Hospitals.

8. Municipal Institutions in the Province.

9. Shop, Saloon, Tavern, Auctioneer, and other Licences in order to the raising of a Revenue for Provincial, Local, or Municipal Purposes.

10. Local Works and Undertakings other than such as are of the following Classes:—

    (a) Lines of Steam or other Ships, Railways, Canals, Telegraphs, and other Works and Undertakings connecting the Province with any other or others of the Provinces, or extending beyond the Limits of the Province;

---

2. The *British North America Act, 1886,* 49-50 Vict., c. 35 (U.K.).

Provision by Parliament of Canada for representation of territories. 1. The Parliament of Canada may from time to time make provision for the representation in the Senate and House of Commons of Canada, or in either of them, of any territories which for the time being form part of the Dominion of Canada, but are not included in any province thereof.

3. The *Statute of Westminster, 1931,* 22 Geo. V. c. 4, (U.K.).

Power of Parliament of a Dominion to legislate extra-territorially. 3. It is hereby declared and enacted that the Parliament of a Dominion has full power to make laws having extra-territorial operation.

 (b) Lines of Steam Ships between the Province and any British or Foreign Country;

 (c) Such Works as, although wholly situate within the Province, are before or after their Execution declared by the Parliament of Canada to be for the general Advantage of Canada or for the Advantage of Two or more of the Provinces.

11. The Incorporation of Companies with Provincial Objects.

12. The Solemnization of Marriage in the Province.

13. Property and Civil Rights in the Province.

14. The Administration of Justice in the Province, including the Constitution, Maintenance, and Organization of Provincial Courts, both of Civil and of Criminal Jurisdiction, and including Procedure in Civil Matters in those Courts.

15. The Imposition of Punishment by Fine, Penalty, or Imprisonment for enforcing any Law of the Province made in relation to any Matter coming within any of the Classes of Subjects enumerated in this Section.

16. Generally all Matters of a merely local or private Nature in the Province.

Education.

Legislation respecting Education.
93. In and for each Province the Legislature may exclusively make Laws in relation to Education, subject and according to the following Provisions:—

 (1) Nothing in any such Law shall prejudicially affect any Right or Privilege with respect to Denominational Schools which any Class of Persons have by Law in the Province at the Union:

 (2) All the Powers, Privileges, and Duties at the Union by Law conferred and imposed in Upper Canada on the Separate Schools and School Trustees of the Queen's Roman Catholic Subjects shall be and the same are hereby extended to the Dissentient Schools of the Queen's Protestant and Roman Catholic Subjects in Quebec:

 (3) Where in any Province a System of Separate or Dissentient Schools exists by Law at the Union or is thereafter established by the Legislature of the Province, an Appeal shall lie to the Governor General in Council from any Act or Decision of any Provincial Authority affecting any Right or Privilege of the Protestant or Roman Catholic Minority of the Queen's Subjects in relation to Education:

(4) In case any such Provincial Law as from Time to Time seems to the Governor General in Council requisite for the due Execution of the Provisions of this Section is not made, or in case any Decision of the Governor General in Council on any Appeal under this Section is not duly executed by the proper Provincial Authority in that Behalf, then and in every such Case, and as far only as the Circumstances of each Case require, the Parliament of Canada may make remedial Laws for the due Execution of the Provisions of this Section and of any Decision of the Governor General in Council under this Section. (43)

---

(43) Altered for Manitoba by section 22 of the *Manitoba Act*, 33 Vict., c. 3 (Canada), (confirmed by the *British North America Act, 1871*), which reads as follows:

Legislation touching schools subject to certain provisions.

22. In and for the Province, the said Legislature may exclusively make Laws in relation to Education, subject and according to the following provisions:—

(1) Nothing in any such Law shall prejudicially affect any right or privilege with respect to Denominational Schools which any class of persons have by Law or practice in the Province at the Union:

(2) An appeal shall lie to the Governor General in Council from any Act or decision of the Legislature of the Province, or of any Provincial Authority, affecting any right or privilege, of the Protestant or Roman Catholic minority of the Queen's subjects in relation to Education:

Power reserved to Parliament.

(3) In case any such Provincial Law, as from time to time seems to the Governor General in Council requisite for the due execution of the provisions of this section, is not made, or in case any decision of the Governor General in Council on any appeal under this section is not duly executed by the proper Provincial Authority in that behalf, then, and in every such case, and as far only as the circumstances of each case require, the Parliament of Canada may make remedial Laws for the due execution of the provisions of this section, and of any decision of the Governor General in Council under this section.

Altered for Alberta by section 17 of *The Alberta Act*, 4-5 Edw. VII, c. 3 which reads as follows:

Education.

17. Section 93 of The British North America Act, 1867, shall apply to the said province, with the substitution for paragraph (1) of the said section 93 of the following paragraph:—

(1) Nothing in any such law shall prejudicially affect any right or privilege with respect to separate schools which any class of persons have at the date of the passing of this Act, under the terms of chapters 29 and 30 of the Ordinances of the Northwest Territories, passed in the year 1901, or with respect to religious instruction in any public or separate school as provided for in the said ordinances.

2. In the appropriation by the Legislature or distribution by the Government of the province of any moneys for the support of schools organized and carried on in accordance with the said chapter 29 or any Act passed in amendment thereof, or in substitution therefor, there shall be no discrimination against schools of any class described in the said chapter 29.

3. Where the expression "by law" is employed in paragraph 3 of the said section 93, it shall be held to mean the law as set out in the said chapters 29 and 30, and where the expression "at the Union" is employed, in the said paragraph 3, it shall be held to mean the date at which this Act comes into force.

Uniformity of Laws in Ontario, Nova Scotia and New Brunswick.

Legislation for
Uniformity of
Laws in Three
Provinces.

94. Notwithstanding anything in this Act, the Parliament of Canada may make Provision for the Uniformity of all or any of the Laws relative to Property and Civil Rights in Ontario, Nova Scotia, and New Brunswick, and of the Procedure of all or any of the Courts in Those Three Provinces, and from and after the passing of any Act in that Behalf the Power of the Parliament of Canada to make Laws in relation to any Matter comprised in any such Act shall, notwithstanding anything in this Act, be unrestricted; but any Act of the

---

Altered for Saskatchewan by section 17 of *The Saskatchewan Act*, 4-5 Edw. VII, c. 42, which reads as follows:

Education

17. Section 93 of the British North America Act, 1867, shall apply to the said province, with the substitution for paragraph (1) of the said section 93, of the following paragraph:—

(1) Nothing in any such law shall prejudicially affect any right or privilege with respect to separate schools which any class of persons have at the date of the passing of this Act, under the terms of chapters 29 and 30 of the Ordinances of the Northwest Territories, passed in the year 1901, or with respect to religious instruction in any public or separate school as provided for in the said ordinances.

2. In the appropriation by the Legislature or distribution by the Government of the province of any moneys for the support of schools organized and carried on in accordance with the said chapter 29, or any Act passed in amendment thereof or in substitution therefor, there shall be no discrimination against schools of any class described in the said chapter 29.

3. Where the expression "by law" is employed in paragraph (3) of the said section 93, it shall be held to mean the law as set out in the said chapters 29 and 30; and where the expression "at the Union" is employed in the said paragraph (3), it shall be held to mean the date at which this Act comes into force.

Altered by Term 17 of the Terms of Union of Newfoundland with Canada (confirmed by the *British North America Act, 1949*, 12-13 Geo. VI, c. 22 (U.K.)), which reads as follows:

17. In lieu of section ninety-three of the British North America Act, 1867, the following term shall apply in respect of the Province of Newfoundland:

In and for the Province of Newfoundland the Legislature shall have exclusive authority to make laws in relation to education, but the Legislature will not have authority to make laws prejudicially affecting any right or privilege with respect to denominational schools, common (amalgamated) schools, or denominational colleges, that any class or classes of persons have by law in Newfoundland at the date of Union, and out of public funds of the Province of Newfoundland, provided for education,

(a) all such schools shall receive their share of such funds in accordance with scales determined on a non-discriminatory basis from time to time by the Legislature for all schools then being conducted under authority of the Legislature; and

(b) all such colleges shall receive their share of any grant from time to time voted for all colleges then being conducted under authority of the Legislature, such grant being distributed on a non-discriminatory basis.

Parliament of Canada making Provision for such Uniformity shall not have effect in any Province unless and until it is adopted and enacted as Law by the Legislature thereof.

Old Age Pensions.

94A. The Parliament of Canada may make laws in relation to old age pensions and supplementary benefits, including survivors' and disability benefits irrespective of age, but no such law shall affect the operation of any law present or future of a provincial legislature in relation to any such matter. (44)

Legislation respecting old age pensions and supplementary benefits.

Agriculture and Immigration.

95. In each Province the Legislature may make Laws in relation to Agriculture in the Province, and to Immigration into the Province; and it is hereby declared that the Parliament of Canada may from Time to Time make Laws in relation to Agriculture in all or any of the Provinces, and to Immigration into all or any of the Provinces; and any Law of the Legislature of a Province relative to Agriculture or to Immigration shall have effect in and for the Province as long and as far only as it is not repugnant to any Act of the Parliament of Canada.

Concurrent Powers of Legislation respecting Agriculture, etc.

VIII.—JUDICATURE.

96. The Governor General shall appoint the Judges of the Superior, District, and County Courts in each Province, except those of the Courts of Probate in Nova Scotia and New Brunswick.

Appointment of Judges.

97. Until the laws relative to Property and Civil Rights in Ontario, Nova Scotia, and New Brunswick, and the Procedure of the Courts in those Provinces, are made uniform, the Judges of the Courts of those Provinces appointed by the Governor General shall be selected from the respective Bars of those Provinces.

Selection of Judges in Ontario, etc.

98. The Judges of the Courts of Quebec shall be selected from the Bar of that Province.

Selection of Judges in Quebec.

---

(44) Added by the *British North America Act, 1964*, 12-13, Eliz. II, c. 73 (U.K.). Originally enacted by the British North America Act, 1951, 14-15, Geo. VI, c. 32 (U.K.), as follows:

> "94A. It is hereby declared that the Parliament of Canada may from time to time make laws in relation to old age pensions in Canada, but no law made by the Parliament of Canada in relation to old age pensions shall affect the operation of any law present or future of a Provincial Legislature in relation to old age pensions."

Tenure of office of Judges.

99. (1) Subject to subsection two of this section, the Judges of the Superior Courts shall hold office during good behaviour, but shall be removable by the Governor General on Address of the Senate and House of Commons.

Termination at age 75.

(2) A Judge of a Superior Court, whether appointed before or after the coming into force of this section, shall cease to hold office upon attaining the age of seventy-five years, or upon the coming into force of this section if at that time he has already attained that age. (44A)

Salaries etc., of Judges.

100. The Salaries, Allowances, and Pensions of the Judges of the Superior, District, and County Courts (except the Courts of Probate in Nova Scotia and New Brunswick), and of the Admiralty Courts in Cases where the Judges thereof are for the Time being paid by Salary, shall be fixed and provided by the Parliament of Canada. (45)

General Court of Appeal, etc.

101. The Parliament of Canada may, notwithstanding anything in this Act, from Time to Time provide for the Constitution, Maintenance, and Organization of a General Court of Appeal for Canada, and for the Establishment of any additional Courts for the better Administration of the Laws of Canada. (46)

VIII.—REVENUES; DEBTS; ASSETS; TAXATION.

Creation of Consolidated Revenue Fund.

102. All Duties and Revenues over which the respective Legislatures of Canada, Nova Scotia, and New Brunswick before and at the Union had and have Power of Appropriation, except such Portions thereof as are by this Act reserved to the respective Legislatures of the Provinces, or are raised by them in accordance with the special Powers conferred on them by this Act, shall form One Consolidated Revenue Fund, to be appropriated for the Public Service of Canada in the Manner and subject to the Charges in this Act provided.

(44A) Repealed and re-enacted by the *British North America Act, 1960,* 9 Eliz. II, c. 2 (U.K.), which came into force on the 1st day of March, 1961. The original section read as follows:

Tenure of office of Judges of Superior Courts.

99. The Judges of the Superior Courts shall hold Office during good Behaviour, but shall be removable by the Governor General on Address of the Senate and House of Commons.

(45) Now provided for in the *Judges Act,* R.S.C. 1952, c. 159, as amended by S.C. 1963, c. 8.

(46) See the *Supreme Court Act,* R.S.C. 1952, c. 259, and the *Exchequer Court Act,* R.S.C. 1952, c. 98.

103. The Consolidated Revenue Fund of Canada shall be permanently charged with the Costs, Charges, and Expenses incident to the Collection, Management, and Receipt thereof, and the same shall form the First Charge thereon, subject to be reviewed and audited in such Manner as shall be ordered by the Governor General in Council until the Parliament otherwise provides. *Expenses of Collection, etc.*

104. The annual Interest of the Public Debts of the several Provinces of Canada, Nova Scotia, and New Brunswick at the Union shall form the Second Charge on the Consolidated Revenue Fund of Canada. *Interest of Provincial Public Debts.*

105. Unless altered by the Parliament of Canada, the Salary of the Governor General shall be Ten thousand Pounds Sterling Money of the United Kingdom of Great Britain and Ireland, payable out of the Consolidated Revenue Fund of Canada, and the same shall form the Third Charge thereon. (47) *Salary of Governor General.*

106. Subject to the several Payments by this Act charged on the Consolidated Revenue Fund of Canada, the same shall be appropriated by the Parliament of Canada for the Public Service. *Appropriation from Time to Time.*

107. All Stocks, Cash, Banker's Balances, and Securities for Money belonging to each Province at the Time of the Union, except as in this Act mentioned, shall be the Property of Canada, and shall be taken in Reduction of the Amount of the respective Debts of the Provinces at the Union. *Transfer of Stocks, etc.*

108. The Public Works and Property of each Province, enumerated in the Third Schedule to this Act, shall be the Property of Canada. *Transfer of Property in Schedule.*

109. All Lands, Mines, Minerals, and Royalties belonging to the several Provinces of Canada, Nova Scotia, and New Brunswick at the Union, and all Sums then due or payable for such Lands, Mines, Minerals, or Royalties, shall belong to the several Provinces of Ontario, Quebec, Nova Scotia, and New Brunswick in which the same are situate or arise, subject to any Trusts existing in respect thereof, and to any Interest other than that of the Province in the same. (48) *Property in Lands, Mines, etc.*

---

(47) Now covered by the *Governor General's Act*, R.S.C. 1952, c. 139.

(48) The four western provinces were placed in the same position as the original provinces by the *British North America Act, 1930*, 21 Geo. V, c. 26 (U.K.).

Assets connected with Provincial Debts.

110. All Assets connected with such Portions of the Public Debt of each Province as are assumed by that Province shall belong to that Province.

Canada to be liable for Provincial Debts.

111. Canada shall be liable for the Debts and Liabilities of each Province existing at the Union.

Debts of Ontario and Quebec.

112. Ontario and Quebec conjointly shall be liable to Canada for the Amount (if any) by which the Debt of the Province of Canada exceeds at the Union Sixty-two million five hundred thousand Dollars, and shall be charged with Interest at the Rate of Five per Centum per Annum thereon.

Assets of Ontario and Quebec.

113. The Assets enumerated in the Fouth Schedule to this Act belonging at the Union to the Province of Canada shall be the Property of Ontario and Quebec conjointly.

Debt of Nova Scotia.

114. Nova Scotia shall be liable to Canada for the Amount (if any) by which its Public Debt exceeds at the Union Eight million Dollars, and shall be charged with Interest at the Rate of Five per Centum per Annum thereon. (49)

Debt of New Brunswick.

115. New Brunswick shall be liable to Canada for the Amount (if any) by which its Public Debt exceeds at the Union Seven million Dollars, and shall be charged with Interest at the Rate of Five per Centum per Annum thereon.

Payment of interest to Nova Scotia and New Brunswick.

116. In case the Public Debts of Nova Scotia and New Brunswick do not at the Union amount to Eight million and Seven million Dollars respectively, they shall respectively receive by half-yearly Payments in advance from the Government of Canada Interest at Five per Centum per Annum on the Difference between the actual Amounts of their respective Debts and such stipulated Amounts.

Provincial Public Property.

117. The several Provinces shall retain all their respective Public Property not otherwise disposed of in this Act, subject to the Right of Canada to assume any Lands or Public Property required for Fortifications or for the Defence of the Country.

---

(49) The obligations imposed by this section, sections 115 and 116, and similar obligations under the instruments creating or admitting other provinces, have been carried into legislation of the Parliament of Canada and are now to be found in the *Provincial Subsidies Act*, R.C.S. 1952, c. 221.

118. Repealed. (50)

(50) Repealed by the *Statute Law Revision Act, 1950*, 14 Geo. VI, c. 6 (U.K.). As originally enacted, the section read as follows:

Grants to Provinces.

118. The following Sums shall be paid yearly by Canada to the several Provinces for the Support of their Governments and Legislatures:

	Dollars
Ontario	Eighty thousand.
Quebec	Seventy thousand.
Nova Scotia	Sixty thousand.
New Brunswick	Fifty thousand.

Two hundred and sixty thousand;

and an annual Grant in aid of each Province shall be made, equal to Eighty Cents per Head of the Population as ascertained by the Census of One thousand eight hundred and sixty-one, and in the Case of Nova Scotia and New Brunswick, by each subsequent Decennial Census until the Population of each of those two Provinces amounts to Four hundred thousand Souls, at which Rate such Grant shall thereafter remain. Such Grants shall be in full Settlement of all future Demands on Canada, and shall be paid half-yearly in advance to each Province; but the Government of Canada shall deduct from such Grants, as against any Province, all Sums chargeable as Interest on the Public Debt of that Province in excess of the several Amounts stipulated in this Act.

The section was made obsolete by the *British North America Act, 1907*, 7 Edw. VII, c. 11 (U.K.) which provided:

Payments to be made by Canada to provinces.

1. (1) The following grants shall be made yearly by Canada to every province, which at the commencement of this Act is a province of the Dominion, for its local purposes and the support of its Government and Legislature:—

(a) A fixed grant—

where the population of the province is under one hundred and fifty thousand, of one hundred thousand dollars;

where the population of the province is one hundred and fifty thousand, but does not exceed two hundred thousand, of one hundred and fifty thousand dollars;

where the population of the province is two hundred thousand, but does not exceed four hundred thousand, of one hundred and eighty thousand dollars;

where the population of the province is four hundred thousand, but does not exceed eight hundred thousand, of one hundred and ninety thousand dollars;

where the population of the province is eight hundred thousand, but does not exceed one million five hundred thousand, of two hundred and twenty thousand dollars;

where the population of the province exceeds one million five hundred thousand, of two hundred and forty thousand dollars; and

(b) Subject to the special provisions of this Act as to the provinces of British Columbia and Prince Edward Island, a grant at the rate of eighty cents per head of the population of the province up to the number of two million five hundred thousand, and at the rate of sixty cents per head of so much of the population as exceeds that number.

(2) An additional grant of one hundred thousand dollars shall be made yearly to the province of British Columbia for a period of ten years from the commencement of this Act.

(3) The population of a province shall be ascertained from time to time in the case of the provinces of Manitoba, Saskatchewan, and Alberta respectively by the last quinquennial census or statutory estimate of population made under the Acts establishing those provinces or any other

Further Grant to New Brunswick.

119. New Brunswick shall receive by half-yearly Payments in advance from Canada for the Period of Ten Years from the Union an additional Allowance of Sixty-three thousand Dollars per Annum; but as long as the Public Debt of that Province remains under Seven million Dollars, a Deduction equal to the Interest at Five per Centum per Annum on such Deficiency shall be made from that Allowance of Sixty-three thousand Dollars. (51)

Form of Payments.

120. All Payments to be made under this Act, or in discharge of Liabilities created under any Act of the Provinces of Canada, Nova Scotia, and New Brunswick respectively, and assumed by Canada, shall, until the Parliament of Canada otherwise directs, be made in such Form and Manner as may from Time to Time be ordered by the Governor General in Council.

Canadian Manufactures, etc.

121. All Articles of the Growth, Produce, or Manufacture of any one of the Provinces shall, from and after the Union, be admitted free into each of the other Provinces.

Act of the Parliament of Canada making provision for the purpose, and in the case of any other province by the last decennial census for the time being.

(4) The grants payable under this Act shall be paid half-yearly in advance to each province.

(5) The grants payable under this Act shall be substituted for the grants or subsidies (in this Act referred to as existing grants) payable for the like purposes at the commencement of this Act to the several provinces of the Dominion under the provisions of section one hundred

30-31 Vict., c. .3 and eighteen of the British North America Act 1867, or of any Order in Council establishing a province, or of any Act of the Parliament of Canada containing directions for the payment of any such grant or subsidy, and those provisions shall cease to have effect.

(6) The Government of Canada shall have the same power of deducting sums charged against a province on account of the interest on public debt in the case of the grant payable under this Act to the province as they have in the case of the existing grant.

(7) Nothing in this Act shall affect the obligation of the Government of Canada to pay to any province any grant which is payable to that province, other than the existing grant for which the grant under this Act is substituted.

(8) In the case of the provinces of British Columbia and Prince Edward Island, the amount paid on account of the grant payable per head of the population to the provinces under this Act shall not at any time be less than the amount of the corresponding grant payable at the commencement of this Act, and if it is found on any decennial census that the population of the province has decreased since the last decennial census, the amount paid on account of the grant shall not be decreased below the amount then payable, notwithstanding the decrease of the population.

See the *Provincial Subsidies Act*, R.S.C. 1952, c. 221, *The Maritime Provinces Additional Subsidies Act*, 1942-43, c. 14, and the Terms of Union of Newfoundland with Canada, appended to the *British North America Act, 1949*, and also to *An Act to approve the Terms of Union of Newfoundland with Canada*, chapter 1 of the statutes of Canada, 1949.

(51) Spent.

122. The Customs and Excise Laws of each Province shall, subject to the Provisions of this Act, continue in force until altered by the Parliament of Canada. (52) Continuance of Customs and Excise Laws.

123. Where Customs Duties are, at the Union, leviable on any Goods, Wares, or Merchandises in any Two Provinces, those Goods, Wares, and Merchandises may, from and after the Union, be imported from one of those Provinces into the other of them on Proof of Payment of the Customs Duty leviable thereon in the Province of Exportation, and on Payment of such further Amount (if any) of Customs Duty as is leviable thereon in the Province of Importation. (53) Exportation and Importation as between Two Provinces.

124. Nothing in this Act shall affect the Right of New Brunswick to levy the Lumber Dues provided in Chapter Fifteen of Title Three of the Revised Statutes of New Brunswick, or in any Act amending that Act before or after the Union, and not increasing the Amount of such Dues; but the Lumber of any of the Provinces other than New Brunswick shall not be subject to such Dues. (54) Lumber Dues in New Brunswick.

125. No Lands or Property belonging to Canada or any Province shall be liable to Taxation. Exemption of Public Lands, etc.

126. Such Portions of the Duties and Revenues over which the respective Legislatures of Canada, Nova Scotia, and New Brunswick had before the Union Power of Appropriation as are by this Act reserved to the respective Governments or Legislatures of the Provinces, and all Duties and Revenues raised by them in accordance with the special Powers conferred upon them by this Act, shall in each Province form One Consolidated Revenue Fund to be appropriated for the Public Service of the Province. Provincial Consolidated Revenue Fund.

IX.—MISCELLANEOUS PROVISIONS.

General.

127. Repealed. (55)

---

(52) Spent. Now covered by the *Customs Act,* R.S.C. 1952, c. 58, the *Customs Tariff,* R.S.C. 1952, c. 60, the *Excise Act,* R.S.C. 1952, c. 99 and the *Excise Tax Act,* R.S.C. 1952, c. 100.

(53) Spent.

(54) These dues were repealed in 1873 by 36 Vict., c. 16 (N.B.). And see *An Act respecting the Export Duties imposed on Lumber,* etc., (1873) 36 Vict., c. 41 (Canada), and section 2 of the *Provincial Subsidies Act,* R.S.C. 1952, c. 221.

Oath of Allegiance, etc.

128. Every Member of the Senate or House of Commons of Canada shall before taking his Seat therein take and subscribe before the Governor General or some Person authorized by him, and every Member of a Legislative Council or Legislative Assembly of any Province shall before taking his Seat therein take and subscribe before the Lieutenant Governor of the Province or some Person authorized by him, the Oath of Allegiance contained in the Fifth Schedule to this Act; and every Member of the Senate of Canada and every Member of the Legislative Council of Quebec shall also, before taking his Seat therein, take and subscribe before the Governor General, or some Person authorized by him, the Declaration of Qualification contained in the same Schedule.

Continuance of existing Laws, Courts, Officers, etc.

129. Except as otherwise provided by this Act, all Laws in force in Canada, Nova Scotia, or New Brunswick at the Union, and all Courts of Civil and Criminal Jurisdiction, and all legal Commissions, Powers, and Authorities, and all Officers, Judicial, Administrative, and Ministerial, existing therein at the Union, shall continue in Ontario, Quebec, Nova Scotia, and New Brunswick respectively, as if the Union had not been made; subject nevertheless (except with respect to such as are enacted by or exist under Acts of the Parliament of Great Britain or of the Parliament of the United Kingdom of Great Britain and Ireland,) to be repealed, abolished, or altered by the Parliament of Canada, or by the Legislature of the respective Province, according to the Authority of the Parliament or of that Legislature under this Act. (56)

Transfer of Officers to Canada.

130. Until the Parliament of Canada otherwise provides, all Officers of the several Provinces having Duties to discharge in relation to Matters other than those coming within the Classes of Subjects by this

---

(55) Repealed by the *Statute Law Revision Act, 1893,* 56-57 Vict., c. 14 (U.K.). The section read as follows:

As to Legislative Councillors of Provinces becoming senators.

127. If any Person being at the passing of this Act a Member of the Legislative Council of Canada, Nova Scotia, or New Brunswick to whom a Place in the Senate is offered, does not within Thirty Days thereafter, by Writing under his Hand addressed to the Governor General of the Province of Canada or to the Lieutenant Governor of Nova Scotia or New Brunswick (as the Case may be), accept the same, he shall be deemed to have declined the same; and any Person who, being at the passing of this Act a Member of the Legislative Council of Nova Scotia or New Brunswick, accepts a Place in the Senate, shall thereby vacate his Seat in such Legislative Council.

(56) The restriction against altering or repealing laws enacted by or existing under statutes of the United Kingdom was removed by the *Statute of Westminster, 1931,* 22 Geo. V, c. 4 (UK.).

Act assigned exclusively to the Legislatures of the Provinces shall be Officers of Canada, and shall continue to discharge the Duties of their respective Offices under the same Liabilities, Responsibilities, and Penalties as if the Union had not been made. (57)

131. Until the Parliament of Canada otherwise provides, the Governor General in Council may from Time to Time appoint such Officers as the Governor General in Council deems necessary or proper for the effectual Execution of this Act.

Appointment of new Officers.

132. The Parliament and Government of Canada shall have all Powers necessary or proper for performing the Obligations of Canada or of any Province thereof, as Part of the British Empire, towards Foreign Countries, arising under Treaties between the Empire and such Foreign Countries.

Treaty Obligations.

133. Either the English or the French Language may be used by any Person in the Debates of the Houses of the Parliament of Canada and of the Houses of the Legislature of Quebec; and both those Languages shall be used in the respective Records and Journals of those Houses; and either of those Languages may be used by any Person or in any Pleading or Process in or issuing from any Court of Canada established under this Act, and in or from all or any of the Courts of Quebec.

Use of English and French Languages

The Acts of the Parliament of Canada and of the Legislature of Quebec shall be printed and published in both those Languages.

Ontario and Quebec.

134. Until the Legislature of Ontario or of Quebec otherwise provides, the Lieutenant Governors of Ontario and Quebec may each appoint under the Great Seal of the Province the following Officers, to hold Office during Pleasure, that is to say,—the Attorney General, the Secretary and Registrar of the Province, the Treasurer of the Province, the Commissioner of Crown Lands, and the Commissioner of Agriculture and Public Works, and in the Case of Quebec the Solicitor General, and may, by Order of the Lieutenant Governor in Council, from Time to Time prescribe the Duties of those Officers, and of the several Departments over which they shall preside or to which they shall belong, and of the Officers and Clerks thereof, and may also appoint other and additional Officers to hold Office during

Appointment of Executive Officers for Ontario and Quebec.

---

(57) Spent.

Pleasure, and may from Time to Time prescribe the Duties of those Officers, and of the several Departments over which they shall preside or to which they shall belong, and of the Officers and Clerks thereof. (58)

Powers, Duties, etc, of Executive Officers.

135. Until the Legislature of Ontario or Quebec otherwise provides, all Right, Powers, Duties, Functions, Responsibilities, or Authorities at the passing of this Act vested in or imposed on the Attorney General, Solicitor General, Secretary and Registrar of the Province of Canada, Minister of Finance, Commissioner of Crown Lands, Commissioner of Public Works, and Minister of Agriculture and Receiver General, by any Law, Statute, or Ordinance of Upper Canada, Lower Canada, or Canada, and not repugnant to this Act, shall be vested in or imposed on any Officer to be appointed by the Lieutenant Governor for the Discharge of the same or any of them; and the Commissioner of Agriculture and Public Works shall perform the Duties and Functions of the Office of Minister of Agriculture at the passing of this Act imposed by the Law of the Province of Canada, as well as those of the Commissioner of Public Works. (59)

Great Seals.

136. Until altered by the Lieutenant Governor in Council, the Great Seals of Ontario and Quebec respectively shall be the same, or of the same Design, as those used in the Provinces of Upper Canada and Lower Canada respectively before their Union as the Province of Canada.

Construction of temporary Acts.

137. The words "and from thence to the End of the then next ensuing Session of the Legislature," or Words to the same Effect, used in any temporary Act of the Province of Canada not expired before the Union, shall be construed to extend and apply to the next Session of the Parliament of Canada if the Subject Matter of the Act is within the Powers of the same as defined by this Act, or to the next Sessions of the Legislatures of Ontario and Quebec respectively if the Subject Matter of the Act is within the Powers of the same as defined by this Act.

As to Errors in Names.

138. From and after the Union the Use of the Words "Upper Canada" instead of "Ontario," or "Lower Canada" instead of "Quebec," in any Deed, Writ, Process, Pleading, Document, Matter, or Thing, shall not invalidate the same.

---

(58) Spent. Now covered in Ontario by the *Executive Council Act*, R.S.O. 1960, c. 127 and in Quebec by the *Executive Power Act*, R.S.Q. 1941, c. 7.

(59) Probably spent.

139. Any Proclamation under the Great Seal of the Province of Canada issued before the Union to take effect at a Time which is subsequent to the Union, whether relating to that Province, or to Upper Canada, or to Lower Canada, and the several Matters and Things therein proclaimed, shall be and continue of like Force and Effect as if the Union had not been made. (60)

As to issue of Proclamations before Union, to commence after Union.

140. Any Proclamation which is authorized by any Act of the Legislature of the Province of Canada to be issued under the Great Seal of the Province of Canada, whether relating to that Province, or to Upper Canada, or to Lower Canada, and which is not issued before the Union, may be issued by the Lieutenant Governor of Ontario or of Quebec, as its Subject Matter requires, under the Great Seal thereof; and from and after the Issue of such Proclamation the same and the several Matters and Things therein proclaimed shall be and continue of the like Force and Effect in Ontario or Quebec as if the Union had not been made. (61)

As to issue of Proclamations after Union.

141. The Penitentiary of the Province of Canada shall, until the Parliament of Canada otherwise provides, be and continue the Penitentiary of Ontario and of Quebec. (62)

Penitentiary.

142. The Division and Adjustment of the Debts, Credits, Liabilities, Properties, and Assets of Upper Canada and Lower Canada shall be referred to the Arbitrament of Three Arbitrators, One chosen by the Government of Ontario, One by the Government of Quebec, and One by the Government of Canada; and the Selection of the Arbitrators shall not be made until the Parliament of Canada and the Legislatures of Ontario and Quebec have met; and the Arbitrator chosen by the Government of Canada shall not be a Resident either in Ontario or in Quebec. (63)

Arbitration respecting Debts, etc.

143. The Governor General in Council may from Time to Time order that such and so many of the Records, Books, and Documents of the Province of Canada as he thinks fit shall be appropriated and delivered either to Ontario or to Quebec, and the same shall thence-

Division of Records.

---

(60) Probably spent.

(61) Probably spent.

(62) Spent. Penitentiaries are now provided for by the *Penitentiary Act*, S.C. 1960-61, c. 53.

(63) Spent. See pages (xi) and (xii) of the Public Accounts, 1902-03.

forth be the Property of that Province; and any Copy thereof or Extract therefrom, duly certified by the Officer having charge of the Original thereof, shall be admitted as Evidence. (64)

Constitution of Townships in Quebec.

144. The Lieutenant Governor of Quebec may from Time to Time, by Proclamation under the Great Seal of the Province, to take effect from a Day to be appointed therein, constitute Townships in those Parts of the Province of Quebec in which Townships are not then already constituted, and fix the Metes and Bounds thereof.

145. Repealed. (65)

XI.—Admission of Other Colonies

Power to admit Newfoundland, etc., into the Union.

146. It shall be lawful for the Queen, by and with the Advice of Her Majesty's Most Honourable Privy Council, on Addresses from the Houses of the Parliament of Canada, and from the Houses of the respective Legislatures of the Colonies or Provinces of Newfoundland, Prince Edward Island, and British Columbia, to admit those Colonies or Provinces, or any of them, into the Union, and on Address from the Houses of the Parliament of Canada to admit Rupert's Land and the North-western Territory, or either of them, into the Union, on such Terms and Conditions in each Case as are in the Addresses expressed and as the Queen thinks fit to approve, subject to the Provisions of this Act; and the Provisions of any Order in Council in that Behalf shall have effect as if they had been enacted by the Parliament of the United Kingdom of Great Britain and Ireland. (66)

---

(64) Probably spent. Two orders were made under this section on the 24th of January, 1868.

(65) Repealed by the *Statute Law Revision Act, 1893*, 56-57 Vict., c. 14 (U.K.). The section read as follows:

X.—INTERCOLONIAL RAILWAY.

Duty of Government and Parliament of Canada to make Railway herein described.

145. Inasmuch as the Provinces of Canada, Nova Scotia, and New Brunswick have joined in a Declaration that the Construction of the Intercolonial Railway is essential to the Consolidation of the Union of British North America, and to the Assent thereto of Nova Scotia and New Brunswick, and have consequently agreed that Provision should be made for its immediate Construction by the Government of Canada; Therefore, in order to give effect to that Agreement, it shall be the Duty of the Government and Parliament of Canada to provide for the Commencement, within Six Months after the Union, of a Railway connecting the River St. Lawrence with the City of Halifax in Nova Scotia, and for the Construction thereof without Intermission, and the Completion thereof with all practicable Speed.

(66) All territories mentioned in this section are now part of Canada. See the notes to section 5, *supra*.

147. In case of the Admission of Newfoundland and Prince Edward Island, or either of them, each shall be entitled to a Representation in the Senate of Canada of Four Members, and (notwithstanding anything in this Act) in case of the Admission of Newfoundland the normal Number of Senators shall be Seventy-six and their maximum Number shall be Eighty-two; but Prince Edward Island when admitted shall be deemed to be comprised in the Third of the Three Divisions into which Canada is, in relation to the Constitution of the Senate, divided by this Act, and accordingly, after the Admission of Prince Edward Island, whether Newfoundland is admitted or not, the Representation of Nova Scotia and New Brunswick in the Senate shall, as Vacancies occur, be reduced from Twelve to Ten Members respectively, and the Representation of each of those Provinces shall not be increased at any Time beyond Ten, except under the Provisions of this Act for the Appointment of Three or Six additional Senators under the Direction of the Queen. (67)

As to Represen-
tation of
Newfoundland
and Prince
Edward Island
in Senate.

---

(67) Spent. See the notes to sections 21, 22, 26, 27 and 28, *supra*.

Bibliography

GENERAL REFERENCE WORKS

A. Frameworks for the Study of Political Systems

Almond, Gabriel Abraham, and G. Bingham Powell, Jr., *Comparative Politics: A Developmental Approach*, (Little, Brown, Boston, 1966).

Dahl, R.A. *Modern Political Analysis*, (Prentice–Hall, Englewood Cliffs, 1970).

Dahl, R.A., and C.E. Lindblom, *Politics, Economics and Welfare*, (Harper and Row, New York, 1963).

Deutsch, K.W., *The Nerves of Government*, (The Free Press, New York, 1966).

Easton, David, *A Framework for Political Analysis*, (Prentice–Hall, Englewood Cliffs, 1965).

——————— , *A Systems Analysis of Political Life*, (John Wiley and Sons, New York, 1965).

Lasswell, H., *Politics: Who Gets What, When, How?*, (Meridian, Cleveland, 1958).

Parsons, T., and E.A. Shills (eds.), *Toward a General Theory of Action*, (Harper and Row, New York, 1962).

Young, R., (ed.), *Approaches to the Study of Politics*, (Northwestern University Press, Evanston, 1958).

B. General Works on Canada

Blishen, B.R. *et al.* (eds.), *Canadian Society: Sociological Perspectives*, third edition, (Macmillan, Toronto, 1968).

Corry, J.A. and J.E. Hodgetts, *Democratic Government and Politics*, (University of Toronto Press, Toronto, 1959).

Dawson, R.M., *The Government of Canada*, revised by N. Ward, (University of Toronto Press, Toronto, 1970).

Fox, P., *Politics: Canada*, (McGraw–Hill, Toronto, 1970).

Glazebrook. G.P. de T., *A History of Canadian Political Thought*, (McClelland and Stewart, Toronto, 1966).

Khan, R.A., S.A. MacKown, and J.D. McNiven, *An Introduction to Political Science*, (Irwin–Dorsey, Ltd., Georgetown, Ont., 1972).

Kruhlak, O., R. Schultz, and S. Pobihushchy, *The Canadian Political Process: A Reader*, (Holt, Rinehart and Winston, Toronto, 1973), Revised Edition.

Mann, W.E. (ed.), *Canada: A Sociological Profile*, (Copp Clark, Toronto, 1968).

Porter, J., *The Vertical Mosaic*, (University of Toronto Press, Toronto, 1965).

Sabourin, M. Louis (ed.), *Le Système Politique du Canada*, (Edition de l'Université d'Ottawa, 1969).

Taylor, Charles, *The Pattern of Politics*, (McClelland and Stewart, Toronto, 1970).

Urquhart, M.G., (ed.), and K.A.H. Buckley, (assistant ed.), *Historical Statistics of Canada*, (Macmillan, Toronto, 1965).

Vaughan, F., J.P. Kyba, and O.P. Dwivedi (eds.), *Contemporary Issues in Canadian Politics*, (Prentice–Hall, Toronto, 1970).

Warkentin, John (ed.), *Canada: A Geographical Interpretation*, (Methuen, Toronto, 1968).

White, W.L., R.H. Wagenberg, and R.C. Nelson, *Introduction to Canadian Politics and Government*, (Holt, Rinehart and Winston, Toronto, 1972).

C. The Policy Process in Canada

Bauer, R.A., and K.J. Gergen (eds.), *The Study of Policy Formulation*, (The Free Press, New York, 1968), esp. pp. 1–27 and pp. 149–180.

Bell, D., *The End of Ideology*, (Collier–Macmillan, New York, 1960).

Bennis, Warren, "Beyond Bureaucracy" in A. Etzioni (ed.), *Readings on Modern Organizations*, (Prentice–Hall, Englewood Cliffs, 1969), pp. 1–8.

—————— , *Changing Organizations: Essays on the Development of Evolution of Human Organization*, (McGraw–Hill, New York, 1966).

Corbett, David, *Canada's Immigration Policy: A Critique*, (Published under the auspices of the Canadian Institute of International Affairs, University of Toronto Press, Toronto, 1957).

Corry, J.A., "Changes in the Functions of Government" in *The Canadian Historical Association Report of Annual Meeting 1945*, (University of Toronto Press, Toronto, 1945), pp. 15–24.

Doern, G.B., and Peter Aucoin, *The Structures of Policy Making in Canada*, (Macmillan, Toronto, 1971).

—————— , *The Role of Interdepartmental Committees in the Policy Process*, (Carleton University, Unpublished M.A. Thesis, Ottawa, 1966).

—————— , "Recent changes in the philosophy of policy-making in Canada", *Canadian Journal of Political Science*, vol. 4, no. 2, June 1971.

—————— , *Political Policy-Making: A Commentary on the Economic Council's Eighth Annual Review and the Ritchie Report*, (The Private Planning Association of Canada, Montreal, 1972).

Downs, Anthony, *Inside Bureaucracy*, (Little, Brown, Boston, 1967).

Dror, Y., "Muddling Through—Science or Inertia?" in A. Etzioni (ed.), *Readings on Modern Organizations*, (Prentice–Hall, Englewood Cliffs, 1969), pp. 166–171. See also C.E. Lindblom's reply, pp. 171–173.

—————— , *Public Policy Making Re-examined*, (Chandler Publishing Co., San Francisco, 1968).

Drucker, Peter, *The Age of Discontinuity*, (Harper and Row, New York, 1969).

Ellul, J., *The Technological Society*, (Vintage Books, New York, 1967).

Etzioni, A., The Active Society, (The Free Press, New York, 1968).

—————— , "Toward a Keynesian Theory of Social Process," in A. Etzioni (ed.), *Readings on Modern Organizations*, (Prentice–Hall, Englewood Cliffs, 1969, pp. 190–196.

—————— , "Mixed Scanning: A Third Approach to Decision Making," *Public Administration Review*, vol. 27, Dec., 1967, pp. 385–392.

Ferkiss, V., *Technological Man*, (Braziller, New York, 1969), (see bibliography on p. 295).

Forbes, R.J., *The Conquest of Nature: Technology and its Consequences*, (Praeger, New York, 1968).

Friedrich, C.J., and T. Cole, *Responsible Bureaucracy: A Study of the Swiss Civil Service,* (Russell and Russell, New York, 1967).

Galbraith, John Kenneth, *The New Industrial State,* (Houghton–Mifflin, Boston, 1969).

Hawkins, Freda, *Canada and Immigration: Public Policy and Public Concern,* (McGill-Queen's University Press, Montreal, 1972).

Hockin, Thomas A., (ed.), *Apex of Power: the Prime Minister and Political Leadership in Canada,* (Prentice–Hall, Scarborough, Ont., 1971).

Hodgetts, J.E., "The Civil Service and Policy Formation". in J.E. Hodgetts and D.C. Corbett (eds.), *Canadian Public Administration,* (Macmillan, Toronto, 1960).

Jantsch, E., "From Forecasting and Planning to Policy Sciences," *Policy Sciences,* vol. 1, 1970, pp. 31–47.

——————— , *Perspectives in Planning,* (O.E.C.D., Paris, 1969).

Katz, D., and Robert L. Kahn, *The Social Psychology of Organizations,* (Wiley, New York, 1966).

Kornhauser, W., *The Politics of Mass Society,* (The Free Press, Glencoe, 1959).

Lasswell, Harold D., "The Emerging Conception of The Policy Sciences," *Policy Sciences,* vol. 1, 1970, pp. 3–14.

Leiss, W., "The Social Consequences of Technological Progress: Critical Comments on Recent Theories," *Canadian Public Administration,* vol. 13, no. 3, Fall, 1970, p. 246 ff.

Levitt, Kari, *Silent Surrender: The Multi-National Corporation in Canada,* (Macmillan, Toronto, 1970).

Lindblom, Charles E., *The Policy-Making Process,* (Prentice–Hall, Englewood Cliffs, 1968).

——————— , "The Science of Muddling Through" in A. Etzioni (ed.), *Readings on Modern Organizations,* (Prentice–Hall, Englewood Cliffs, 1969), pp. 154–165.

Lowi, T., "Decision Making vs. Policy Making: Toward An Antidote For Technocracy," *Public Administration Review,* May–June, 1970, pp. 314–325.

——————— , *The End of Liberalism,* (W.W. Norton, New York, 1969).

Lyden, F. J., G. A. Shipman, and M. Kroll, *Policies, Decisions and Organizations,* (Appleton–Century–Crofts, New York, 1969).

Mills, C.W., *The Power Elite,* (Oxford University Press, New York, 1956).

Mitchell, Wm. C., "The New Political Economy," *Social Rsearch,* vol. 35, no. 1, Spring, 1968, pp. 76–110.

Ortega y Gasset, J., *The Revolt of the Masses,* (W.W. Norton, New York, 1957).

Ranney, Austin, (ed.), *Political Science and Public Policy,* (Markham, Chicago, 1968), pp. 3–22.

Riesman, D., *The Lonely Crowd,* (Yale University Press, New Haven, 1961).

Rowan, M., "A Conceptual Framework for Government Policy-Making," *Canadian Public Administration,* vol. 13, no. 3, Fall, 1970, pp. 277–296.

Salisbury, Robert H., "The Analysis of Public Policy: A Search for Theories and Roles" in A. Ranney (ed.), *Political Science and Public Policy,* (Markham, Chicago, 1968).

Sayeed, K.B., "Public policy analysis in Washington and Ottawa," *Policy Sciences,* vol. 4, no. 1, March 1973.

Sharkansky, Ira (ed.), *Policy Analysis in Political Science,* (Markham, Chicago, 1970).

Shonfield, A., *Modern Capitalism: The Changing Balance of Public and Private Power,* (Oxford University Press, London, 1965).

Simon, Herbert Alexander, *Administrative Behavior,* 2nd ed., (Macmillan, New York, 1957).

Taylor, M.G., "Quebec medicare: policy formulation in conflict and crisis," *Canadian Public Administration*, vol. 15, no. 2, Summer 1972.

Thompson, V.A., "Bureaucracy and Innovation,"*Administrative Science Quarterly*, June, 1965.

_____ , *Bureaucracy and Innovation*, (University of Alabama Press, 1968).

Whyte, W.H., *The Organization Man*, (Simon and Schuster, New York, 1956).

Young, M., *The Rise of the Meritocracy*, 1870–2033, (Thames and Hudson, London, 1958).

THE ENVIRONMENT

A. Geographical and Economic Cleavages

Alford, R.R., "The Social Bases of Political Cleavage in 1962," in John Meisel (ed.), *Papers on the 1962 Election*, (University of Toronto Press, Toronto, 1965), pp. 203–234.

Armstrong, Muriel, *The Canadian Economy and its Problems*, (Prentice–Hall, Scarborough, 1970).

Brewis, T.N., H.E. English, Anthony Scott, and Pauline Jewett, *Canadian Economic Policy*, (Macmillan, Toronto, 1965), revised edition.

Brewis, Thomas Newton, *Regional Economic Policies in Canada*, (Macmillan, Toronto, 1969).

Brewis, Thomas Newton, and G. Paquet, "Regional Development in Canada: An Exploratory Essay," *Canadian Public Administration*, vol. 11, no. 2, Summer, 1968.

Buckley, Helen, and Eva Tihan, *Canadian Policies for Rural Adjustment*, (Queen's Printer, Ottawa, 1967).

Canada, Economic Council of Canada, *Annual Reviews: 6, 7, 8, 9, 10*

Classen, H.B., "The Chimera of the Homogeneous State," *Queen's Quarterly*, vol. 79, no. 4, Winter, 1972.

Dehem, R. *et al.*, "Concepts of Regional Planning," *Canadian Public Administration*, vol. 11, no. 2, Summer, 1968.

Easterbrook, W.T., and M.H. Watkins, *Approaches to Canadian Economic History*, (McClelland and Stewart, Toronto, 1967).

Economic Council of Canada, 5th Annual Review, *The Challenge of Growth and Change*, (Queen's Printer, Ottawa, Sept., 1968).

Ferguson, C.B., "Maritime Union," *Queen's Quarterly*, vol. 77, no. 2, Summer, 1970.

Guindon, Hubert, "Two Cultures: an Essay on Nationalism, Class and Ethnic Tension" in *Contemporary Canada*, Richard H. Leach (ed.), (Duke University Press, Durham, 1968), pp. 33–59.

Howland, R.D., *Some Regional Aspects of Canada's Economic Development*, (Queen's Printer, Ottawa, 1957).

Innis, H., *Essays in Canadian Economic History*, (University of Toronto Press, Toronto, 1956).

Krueger, R., F. Sargent, A. de Vos, and N. Pearson (eds.), *Regional and Resource Planning in Canada*, (Holt, Rinehart and Winston, Toronto, 1963).

Lipset, S.M., "Social Structure and Political Activity," in B.R. Blishen *et al.* (eds.), *Canadian Society: Sociological Perspectives*, 3rd ed., (Macmillan, Toronto, 1968), pp. 396–409.

Macpherson, C. Brough, *Democracy in Alberta: Social Credit and the Party System*, 2nd ed., (University of Toronto Press, Toronto, 1962).

Myers, Gustavus, *A History of Canadian Wealth*, (Argosy–Antiquarian, New York, 1968).

Nelson, J.G., and M.J. Chambers, *Process and Method in Canadian Geography*, 4 vols., (Methuen, Toronto, 1969, 1970).

Officer, L.H., and L.B. Smith (eds.), *Canadian Economic Problems and Policies*, (McGraw–Hill, Toronto, 1970).

Raynauld, André, *The Canadian Economic System*, (Macmillan, Toronto, 1967).

Rea, K. J., and J. T. McLeod (eds.), *Business and Government in Canada*, (Methuen, Toronto, 1969).

Reid, T.E., (ed.), *Contemporary Canada: Readings in Economics*, (Holt, Rinehart and Winston, Toronto, 1969).

Schwartz, Mildred A., *Politics and Territory*, (McGill–Queen's University Press, 1974).

Warkentin, John (ed.), *Canada: a Geographical Interpretation*, (Methuen, Toronto, 1968).

B. Stratification—Cleavages and Poverty

Abella, Irving, (ed.), *On Strike: Six Key Labour Struggles in Canada, 1919–1949*, (James, Lewis & Samuel, Toronto, 1974).

Adams, Ian, *The Real Poverty Report*, (McClelland and Stewart, Toronto, 1970).

—————— , *The Poverty Wall*, (McClelland and Stewart, Toronto, 1970).

Allan, Richard, *The Social Passion: Religion and Social Reform in Canada, 1914–28*, (University of Toronto Press, Toronto 1971).

Bendix, Reinhard, and S.M. Lipset (eds.), *Class, Status, and Power; Social Stratification in Comparative Perspective*, 2nd ed., (The Free Press, New York, 1966).

Canada, Parliament, Senate Special Committee on Poverty, *Proceedings: 28th Parliament*, (Ottawa, 1969).

—————— , Privy Council Office, Special Planning Secretariat, *Meeting Poverty*, 1965. (Hereafter referred to as "MP" issues.)

—————— , "Social Aspects of Poverty," by Daniel Thursz. (MP–30).

—————— , "The Nature of Poverty in Canada," by D.R. Richmond. (MP–26).

—————— , "Profile of Poverty in Canada." (MP–6).

—————— , "Statistical Profile and Graphic Presentation of Urban Poverty." (MP–15).

Canadian Labour, vol. 9, no. 6, June, 1964.

Chi, N.H., "Class Voting in Canadian Politics," in O. Kruhlak, R. Schultz, and S. Pobihushchy, *The Canadian Political Process: A Reader*, revised edition, (Holt, Rinehart and Winston, Toronto, 1973).

Cooley, Charles Horton, "Poverty" in C.H. Cooley, *Social Organization: a Study of the Larger Mind*, (Schocken Books, New York, 1962), pp. 290–300.

Coser, Lewis, "The Sociology of Poverty," *Social Problems*, vol. 13, no. 2, Fall 1965, pp. 140–148.

Curtis, James E., *Social Stratification in Canada*, (Prentice–Hall, Scarborough, 1973).

Finkel, A. *et al.*, "The 'Beautiful People' of Winnipeg," *Canadian Dimension*, vol. 8, no. 4.

Galbraith, J.K., "Let Us Begin: An Invitation to Action on Poverty," *Harper's Magazine*, vol. 228, no. 1366, March 1964.

Godfrey, Patricia, *The Sixties: Poverty in Our Society*, (Canadian Association for Adult Education, Toronto, 1965).

Goffman, I.J., "Canadian Social Welfare Policy" in Richard H. Leach (ed.), *Contemporary Canada*, (Duke University Press, Durham, 1968).

Gouldner, A.W., "The Sociologist as Partisan: Sociology and the Welfare State," *The American Sociologist*, vol. 3, no. 2, May, 1968, pp. 103–116.

Grayson, J. Paul, and L.M. Grayson, "The Social Base of Interwar Political Unrest in Urban Alberta," in the *Canadian Journal of Political Science*, vol. 7, no. 2, June 1974.

Grossman, L.A., "Safe Seats: The Rural–Urban Pattern in Canada" in John Courtney (ed.), *Voting in Canada*, (Prentice–Hall, Toronto, 1967), pp. 99–103.

Guindon, Hubert, "Social Unrest, Social Class and Quebec's Bureaucratic Revolution," *Queen's Quarterly*, vol. 71, Summer, 1964, pp. 150–162.

Harrington, Michael, *Poverty in Affluence*, (Council of Jewish Federations and Welfare Funds, New York, 1964). (The Herbert R. Abeles memorial address.)

Kent, Thomas Worrall, *Social Policy for Canada: Towards a Philosophy of Social Security*, (Policy Press, Ottawa, 1962).

Laycock, J.E., "New Directions for Social Welfare Policy" in A. Rotstein (ed.), *The Prospect of Change: Proposals for Canada's Future*, (McGraw–Hill, Toronto, 1965), pp. 308–327.

Lorimer, James, and Myfanwy Phillips, *Working People*, (James, Lewis & Samuel, Toronto, 1971).

Mann, W.E., *Poverty and Social Policy in Canada*, (Copp Clark, Toronto, 1970).

Morgan, John S., "Social Welfare Services in Canada" in Michael Oliver (ed.), *Social Purpose for Canada*, (University of Toronto Press, Toronto, 1961).

Osborne, J.E., "Canada Combats Poverty Through Social Policy," *Public Welfare*, vol. 24, no. 2, April, 1966, pp. 131–139.

Paltiel, Freda L., *Poverty: An Annotated Bibliography and References*, (Canadian Welfare Council, Ottawa, 1966). Supplement I—March, 1967. Supplement II—October, 1967.

Pinard, M. "Poverty and Political Movements" in B.R. Blishen *et al.* (eds.), *Canadian Society: Sociological Perspectives*, 3rd ed., (Macmillan, Toronto, 1968), p. 462 ff.

Porter, John, "The Economic Elite and the Social Structure in Canada" in B.R. Blishen *et al.* (eds.), *Canadian Society: Sociological Perspectives*, 3rd ed., (Macmillan, Toronto, 1968, p. 754 ff).

"Profile of Poverty in Canada," *Labour Gazette*, vol. 66, May, 1966. Digest of papers prepared for the Federal–Provincial Conference on Poverty and Opportunity.

Schlesinger, Benjamin, *Poverty in Canada and the United States: Overview and Annotated Bibliography*, (University of Toronto Press, Toronto, 1966).

Smith, David C., *Incomes Policies—Some Foreign Experiences and their Relevance for Canada*, (Queen's Printer, Ottawa, 1966). Economic Council of Canada Special Study no. 4.

Teeple, Gary, (ed.), *Capitalism and the National Question in Canada*, (University of Toronto Press, Toronto, 1972).

Truman, T., "A Critique of Seymour M. Lipset's article 'Value differences, absolute or relative: the English-speaking democracies,'" in the *Canadian Journal of Political Science*, vol. 4, no. 4, December 1971.

Van Ober, Hadley, "Canadian Approaches to Rural Poverty", *Journal of Farm Economics*, vol. 49, no. 5, Dec., 1967, pp. 1209–1224.

Whyte, Donald R., *Social Determinants of Inter-Community Mobility*, (Rural Development Branch, Dept. of Forestry, Ottawa, 1966).

—————— , "Sociological Aspects of Poverty: A Conceptual Analysis," *Canadian Review of Sociology and Anthropology*, vol. 4, Nov., 1965, pp. 175–189.

Wilson, J., "Politics and Social Class in Canada," *Canadian Journal of Political Science*, vol. I, Sept., 1968, p. 288.

—————— , "Sociological Aspects of Poverty: A Conceptual Analysis," *Canadian Review of Sociology and Anthropology*, vol. 2, no. 4, Nov. 1965, pp. 175–189.

C. Ethnic and Religious Cleavage and "The French-Canadian Question"

(NOTE: There is a large bibliography on French Canada in vol. 1, no. 1 of the
Canadian Journal of Political Science. It constitutes the most complete
material readily available for the period up to November, 1967.)

Ali, M., "The Problem of Quebec," *Pakistan Horizon*, vol. 24, no. 3, 1971.

Allard, M., *The Last Chance, The Canadian Constitution and French Canadians* , (Editions
Ferland, Quebec, 1964).

d'Allemagne, A., *Le colonialisme au Québec*, (Editions Renaud et Bray, Montréal,
1966).

Barbeau, R., *Le Québec, est-il une colonie?*, (Editions de l'homme, Montréal, 1962).

Bergeron G., *Le Canada Français après deux siècles de patience*, (Sevil, Paris, 1967).

Bonenfant, J.C., "Le bicaméralisme dans le Québec," *C.J.E.P.S.*, vol. 29, no. 4,
Nov., 1963.

Bonenfant, J.C., and J.C. Falardeau, "Cultural and Political Implications of
French-Canadian Nationalism," *Canadian Historical Association Annual
Report*, (Ottawa, 1946).

Bourgault, P., *Québec Quitte ou Double*, (Ferron, Montréeal, 1970).

Bourque, G., and N. Laurin-Frenette, "Classes sociales et idéologies nationalistes
au Québec 1960–1970", in *L'Homme et la Société* (Paris), 1972.

Brachet, B., "La crise du fédéralisme canadien et le problème québecois," in *Revue
du Droit publique et de la Science politique*, vol. 88, no. 2, 1972.

Brady, A., "Quebec and Canadian Federalism," *C.J.E.P.S.*, vol. 25, no. 3, Aug.
1959.

Breton, R., "The socio-political dynamics of the October events," in *Canadian Review of Sociology and Anthropology*, vol. 9, no. 1, February 1972.

Brichant, A., *Option Canada; The Economic Implications of Separatism for the Province of
Quebec*, (The Canada Committee, Montreal 1968).

Canada, *A Preliminary Report of the Royal Commission on Bilingualism and Biculturalism*,
(Queen's Printer, Ottawa, 1965).

Canadian Broadcasting Corporation, *Quebec: Year Eight*, Glendon College Forum,
(CBC, Toronto, 1968).

Chaput, M., *Why I am a Separatist*, (Ryerson, Toronto, 1962).

Chaput-Rolland, S., *My Country: Canada or Québec*, (Macmillan, Toronto, 1966).

Chodos, Robert, and Nick Auf Der Maur (eds.), *Quebec—A Chronicle, 1968–1972*,
(James, Lewis & Samuel, Toronto, 1972).

Clark, S.D., *Church and Sect in Canada*, (University of Toronto Press, 1948).

Cohen, R.I., *Quebec Votes*, (Saje Publications, Montreal, 1965).

Cook, R., *Canada and the French-Canadian Question*, (Macmillan, Toronto, 1966).

Cook, R. (ed.), *French-Canadian Nationalism: An Anthology*, (Macmillan, Toronto,
1969).

Corbett, E.M., *Quebec Confronts Canada*, (Copp Clark, Toronto, 1967).

Dawson, Robert MacGregor, *The Conscription Crisis of 1944*, (University of Toronto
Press, Toronto, 1961).

Desbarats, P. *The State of Quebec*, (McClelland and Stewart, Toronto, 1965).

Dion, G., "Secularization in Quebec," *Journal of Canadian Studies*, vol. 3, no. 1. Feb.
1968.

Dion, Léon, *Le bill 60 et la société Québecoise*, (Editions H.M.H., Montréal, 1967).

Dooley, D.J., "Quebec and the Future of Canada," *The Review of Politics*, vol. 27,
no. 1, Jan. 1965.

Drache, Daniel, (ed.), *Québec—Only the Beginning: The Manifestos of the Common Front*,
(New Press, Toronto, 1972).

Dumont, F., et Y. Martin, *Situation de la recherche sur le Canada français*, (Les Presses
de l'Université Laval, Québec, 1962).

Dumont, Fernand, et Jean-Paul Montminy (eds.), *Le Pouvoir dans la société canadienne-française*, (Les Presses de l'Université Laval, Québec, 1966).

Elkin, F., "Ethnic Revolutions and Occupational Dilemmas," the *International Journal of Comparative Sociology*, vol. 13, no. 1, March 1972.

Even, A., "Domination et développement au Nouveau-Brunswick," in *Recherches Sociographiques*, vol. 12, no. 3, 1971.

Forsey, E.A., "Canada: Two Nations or One?", *C.J.E.P.S.*, vol. 28, no. 4, Nov. 1962.

——————, "The B.N.A. Act and Biculturalism," *Queen's Quarterly*, vol. 71, no. 2, Summer 1964.

Garigue, P., *L'option politique du Canada français*, (Editions du Lévrier, Montréal, 1963).

——————, *Bibliographie du Québec*, 1955–1965, (Les Presses de l'Université de Montréal, Montréal, 1967).

Gélinas, A., "Les parlementaires et l'administration publique au Québec", *C.J.P.S.*, vol. 1, no. 2, June, 1968.

Gérin-Lajoie, P., *Pourquoi le bill 60*, (Editions du Jour, Montréal, 1963).

Gow, J.I., "Les Québecois, la guerre et la paix, 1945–60," *C.J.P.S.*, vol. 3, no. 1, March 1970.

Grant, D. (ed.), *Quebec Today*, (University of Toronto Press, Toronto, 1960).

Groupe des Recherches Sociales, *Les électeurs québecois*, (Montréeal, 1960).

Guindon, Hubert, "Social Unrest, Social Class, and Quebec's Bureaucratic Revolution," *Queen's Quarterly*, vol. 71, no. 2, Summer 1964.

——————, "The Church in French-Canadian Society," *Canadian Dimension*, vol. 4, no. 3, Mar.–Apr. 1967, pp. 29–31.

——————, "Two Cultures: an Essay on Nationalism, Class and Ethnic Tension in Contemporary Canada" in O. Kruhlak, R. Schultz, and S. Pobihushchy, *The Canadian Political Process: A Reader*, (Holt, Rinehart and Winston, Toronto, 1970).

Hughes, Everett Cherrington, *French Canada in Transition*, (University of Chicago Press, Chicago, 1943).

Jones, R., *Community in Crisis—French-Canadian Nationalism in Perspective*, (McClelland and Stewart, Toronto, 1967).

Jutras, R., *Québec libre*, (Les éditions actualité, Montréal, 1965).

Keyfitz, N., "Canadians and Canadiens," *Queen's Quarterly*, vol. 70, no. 2, Summer 1963.

Kwavnick, D., "The Roots of French-Canadian Discontent," *C.J.E.P.S.*, vol. 31, no. 4, Nov. 1965.

——————, (ed.), *The Tremblay Report*, (Carleton Library, McClelland and Stewart, Toronto, 1972).

Lamontagne, L., *Le Canada français d'aujourd'hui*, (University of Toronto Press, Toronto, 1970).

Laurendeau, André, *La crise de la conscription, 1942*, (Les éditions du jour, Montréal, 1962).

Laurin, C., *Ma Traversée du Québec*, (Les éditions du jour, Montréal, 1970).

Lévesque, R., *Option Québec*, (Les éditions de l'homme, Montréal, 1968). (English edition: McClelland and Stewart, Toronto, 1968).

——————, *La souveraineté et l'économie*, (Les éditions du jour, Montréal, 1970).

——————, *La solution: le programme du Parti Québécois*, (Les éditions du jour, Montréal, 1970).

Levitt, J. (ed.), *Henri Bourassa on Imperialism and Biculturalism*, 1900–1918, (Copp Clark, Toronto, 1970).

Lijphart, Arend, "Cultural Diversity and Theories of Political Integration", in *Canadian Journal of Political Science*, vol. 4, no. 1.

MacRae, C.F., (ed.), *French Canada Today*, (Report of the Mount Allison 1961 Summer Institute, Sackville, 1961).

Maheux, A., "French Canadians and Democracy," *University of Toronto Quarterly*, vol. 27, April, 1958, p. 345 ff.

Mallory, J.E., "The Canadian dilemma: French and English," *Political Quarterly*, vol. 41, no. 3, 1970.

Marier, R., "Les objectifs sociaux du Québec," *Canadian Public Administration*, vol. 12, no. 2, Summer, 1969.

McRae, K.D., "The Structure of Canadian History," in L. Hartz, *The Founding of New Societies*, (Longmans, Toronto, 1964).

Meisel, J., "Religious Affiliation and Electoral Behaviour: a Case Study," in John Courtney (ed.), *Voting in Canada*, (Prentice–Hall, Toronto, 1967), pp. 144–161.

Meyers, H.B., *The Quebec Revolution*, (Harvest House, Montreal, 1964).

Milner, Henry and Sheilagh Hodgins Milner, *The Decolonization of Quebec, An Analysis of Left-Wing Nationalism*, (McClelland and Stewart, 1973).

Noel, S.J.R., "Consociational Democracy and Canadian Federalism" in *Canadian Journal of Political Science*, vol. 4, no. 1.

Oliver, M., "Quebec and Canadian Democracy", *C.J.E.P.S.*, vol. 23, no. 4, Nov. 1957

Orban, E., *Le conseil L'égislatif de Québec*, (Bellarmin, Montréal, 1967).

——————— , "La Fin du bicaméralisme au Québec," *C.J.P.S.*, vol. 2, no. 3, Sept. 1969.

Paré, G., *Au-délà du séparatisme*, (Collection les idées du jour Montréal, 1966).

Parti Pris, *Les Québecois*, (Maspéro, Paris, 1967).

Pelletier, R., "Le militant du R.I.N. et son parti," in *Recherches sociographiques*, vol. 13, no. 1, 1972.

Pinard, Maurice, "Working Class Politics: An Interpretation of the Quebec Case" in *Canadian Review of Sociology and Anthropology*, vol. 7, no. 2, 1970.

Premier Congrès des Affaires Canadiennes, *The Canadian Experiment, Success or Failure?*, (Les Presses de l'Université Laval, Québec, 1962).

Québec, *Le rapport de la commission royale d'enquête sur l'enseignement*, (le rapport Parent, (L'imprimeur de la reine, Québec, 1963–1966), 3 vols.

——————— , *Le rapport de la commission royal d'enquête sur la fiscalité*, (le rapport Bélanger), (L'imprimeur de la reine, Québec, 1966).

——————— , *Report of the Royal Commission of Inquiry on Constitutional Problems*, (Tremblay Report), (Quebec, 1956), 4 vols.

Quinn, Herbert Furlong, *The Union Nationale: a Study in Quebec Nationalism*, (University of Toronto Press, Toronto, 1963).

Raynauld, A., "Les implications économiques de l'option Québec," *Le Devoir*, 24 avril, 1970.

Reid, Malcolm, *The Shouting Signpainters: A Literary and Political Account of Quebec Revolutionary Nationalism*, (McClelland and Stewart, Toronto, 1972).

Rioux, Marcel, "Conscience ethnique et conscience de classe au Québec," *Recherches sociographiques*, vol. 6, no. 1, 1965.

Rioux, M. (ed.), *L'église et le Québec*,(Les textes du réunion de l'Institut Canadien des affaires Publiques, 1961), (Les éditions du jour, Montréal, 1961).

Rioux, M., and Y. Martin, *French-Canadian Society*, (McClelland and Stewart, Toronto, 1964).

Rotstein, A. (ed.), *Power Corrupted: The October Crisis and the Repression of Quebec*, (New Press, 1971).

Rutan, G.F., "Two views of the concept of sovereignty: Canadian–Canadien," in *Western Political Quarterly*, vol. 24, no. 3, September 1971.

Schwartz, M., "Political Behaviour and Ethnic Origin," in John Meisel (ed.),

Papers on the 1962 Election, (University of Toronto Press, Toronto, 1965), pp. 253–71.

Scott, F.R., and M. Oliver (eds.), *Quebec States her Case*, (Macmillan, Toronto, 1964).

_____, "Canada et Canada-Français," *Esprit*, vol. 21, Aug.–Sept., 1953, p. 185.

Séguin, M., "Genése et historique de l'idée séparatiste au Canada français," *Laurentie*, no. 119, 1962.

Siegfried, A., *The Race Question in Canada*, (McClelland and Stewart, Toronto, 1966).

Simeon, R., "Quebec 1970: the dilemma of power," *Queen's Quarterly*, vol. 79, no. 1, Spring 1972.

Sloan, T., *Quebec, The Not-So-Quiet Revolution*,(Ryerson, Toronto, 1965).

La Société St. Jean Baptiste de Montréal, *Le fédéralisme, l'acte de l'Amérique du Nord britannique et les Canadiens français*, Mémoire au comité parlementaire de la constitution du gouvernement du Québec, (Les éditions de l'agence Duvernay, Montréal, 1964).

Smith, Denis, *Bleeding Hearts—Bleeding Country: Canada and the Quebec Crisis*, (Hurtig, Edmonton, 1971).

Stein, Michael B., *The Dynamics of Right-Wing Protest: A Political Analysis of Social Credit in Quebec*, (University of Toronto Press, Toronto, 1973).

Thomson, Dale, *Quebec Society and Politics: Views from the Inside*, (McClelland and Stewart, Toronto, 1973).

Troisième Congrès des Affaires Canadiennes, *Les nouveaux Québecois*, (les Presses de l'Université Laval, Québec, 1964).

Trudeau, P.E., "Some Obstacles to Democracy in Quebec," *C.J.E.P.S.*, vol. 24, no. 3, Aug. 1958.

_____, *Federalism and the French Canadians*, (Macmillan, Toronto, 1968).

Trudeau, P.E. (ed.), *The Asbestos Strike*, (James, Lewis & Samuel, Toronto, 1974).

Vallières, Pierre, *Choose!*, (New Press, Toronto, 1972).

_____, *Nègres blancs d'Amérique*, (Editions Parti Pris, Montréal, 1968).

_____, *White Niggers of America*, translated by Joan Pinkham, (McClelland and Stewart, Toronto, 1971).

Wade, M. (ed.), *Canadian Dualism: Studies of French-English Relations*, (University of Toronto Press, Toronto, 1960).

_____, *The French-Canadian Outlook: A Brief Account of the Unknown North Americans*, (McClelland and Stewart, Toronto, 1964).

_____, *The French Canadians*, vol. 1, *1760–1911*, vol. 2, *1912–1967*, (Macmillan, Toronto, 1968).

POLITICAL ATTITUDES

A. Political Socialization

Abrams, Philip, and Alan Little, "The Young Voter in British Politics," *British Journal of Sociology*, vol. 16, 1965, pp. 95–110.

Abramson, Paul, "The Differential Political Socialization of English Secondary School Students," *Sociology of Education*, vol. 40, 1967, pp. 246–269.

Argyle, Michael, and Peter Delin, "Non-Universal Laws of Socialization," *Human Relations*, vol. 18, 1965, pp. 77–86.

Bender, Gerald J., "Political Socialization and Political Change," *The Western Political Quarterly*, vol. 20, part I, 1967, pp. 722–727.

Bone, Hugh A., "Political Socialization," in *American Politics and the Party System*, 3rd ed., (McGraw–Hill, New York, 1965), pp. 23–39.

Clausen, John A., "Recent Developments in Socialization Theory and Research," *The Annals of the American Academy of Political and Social Science*, vol. 377, 1968, pp. 139–155.

Dawson, Richard, and Kenneth Prewitt, *Political Socialization*, (Little, Brown, Boston, 1968).

Dennis, Jack, "Major Problems of Political Socialization Research," *Midwest Journal of Political Science*, vol. 12, 1968, pp. 85–114.

Easton, D., "The Theoretical Relevance of Political Socialization," *C.J.P.S.*, vol. 1, 1968, pp. 124–146.

Easton, D., and Jack Dennis, *Children in the Political System*, (McGraw–Hill, New York, 1969).

Erikson, Erik H., *Childhood and Society*, 2nd ed., revised and enlarged, (Norton, New York, 1963).

Froman, Lewis A., Jr., "Learning Political Attitudes," *Western Political Quarterly*, vol. 15, 1962, pp. 304–313.

Greenstein, Fred I., "The Benevolent Leader: Children's Images of Political Authority," *American Political Science Review*, vol. 54, 1960, pp. 934–943.

——————— , *Children and Politics*, (Yale University Press, New Haven, 1965).

Hess, Robert D., and Judith V.Torney, *The Development of Political Attitudes in Children*, (Aldine Publishing Co., Chicago, 1967).

Hess, Robert D., and David Easton, "The Role of the Elementary School in Political Socialization," *The School Review*, vol. 70, 1962, pp. 257–265.

Hill, John L.A., "Political Socialization of Children in a Rural Environment," (Unpublished B.A. thesis, Queen's University, 1969).

Hodgetts, A., *What Culture; What Heritage: A Study of Civic Education in Canada*, (Ontario Institute for Studies in Education, Toronto, 1970).

Hyman, Herbert H., *Political Socialization*, (The Free Press, Glencoe, 1959).

Jahoda, Gustav, "The Development of Children's Ideas about Country and Nationality, Part I: The Conceptual Framework," *The Journal of Educational Psychology*, vol. 33, 1963, pp. 47–60.

——————— , "The Development of Children's Ideas about Country and Nationality, Part II: National Symbols and Themes," *The British Journal of Educational Psychology*, vol. 33, 1963, pp. 143–153.

Jaros, Dean, *Socialization to Politics*, (Praeger, New York, 1973).

Jennings, M. Kent, "Pre-adult Orientations to Multiple Systems of Government," *Midwest Journal of Political Science*, vol. 11, 1967, pp. 291–317.

Johnstone, John C., *Young People's Images of Canadian Society*, (Queen's Printer, Ottawa, 1969).

Kornberg, A. and J. Smith, "Self-concepts of American and Canadian party officials," in *Polity*, vol. 3, no. 1, Fall 1970.

Kornberg, Allan and Norman Thomas, "The Political Socialization of National Legislative Elites in the United States and Canada," *Journal of Politics*, vol. 27, 1965, pp. 761–775.

Lane, Robert E., *Political Life*, (Free Press, Glencoe, Ill., 1959).

Langton, K.P., *Political Socialization* (Oxford University Press, New York, 1969).

Lippitt, G.L. (ed.), "Training for Political Participation," *Journal of Social Issues*, vol. 16, 1960.

Lipset, Seymour Martin, "Students and Politics in Comparative Perspective," *Daedalus*, vol. 97, 1968, pp. 1–20.

Litt, Edgar, "Political Cynicism and Political Futility," *Journal of Politics*, vol. 25, 1963, pp. 312–323.

Marvick, Dwaine, "The Political Socialization of the American Negro," *The Annals of the American Academy of Political and Social Science*, vol. 361, 1965, pp. 112–127.

MacPherson, C.B., "The Social Sciences" in Julian Park (ed.), *The Culture of Contemporary Canada*, (Ryerson Press, Toronto, 1957).

Pammett, J.H., and M.S. Whittington (eds.) *Foundations of Political Culture: Readings on Political Socialization in Canada*, (Macmillan, Toronto, 1976).

Pammett, J.H., "The development of political orientations in Canadian school children," *Canadian Journal of Political Science*, vol. 4, no. 1, March 1971.

Patrick, John J., *Political Socialization of American Youth*, (National Council for the Social Studies, Washington, 1967).

Prewitt, Kenneth, Heinz Eulau, and Betty K. Zisk, "Political Socialization and Political Roles," *Public Opinion Quarterly*, vol. 30, 1966, pp. 569–582.

Richert, J.P., "English- and French-Canadian children's perception of the October crisis," *Journal of Social Psychology*, vol. 89, no. 1, February 1973.

——————— , "Political Socialization in Quebec: Young People's Attitudes toward Government," *Canadian Journal of Political Science*, vol. 6, no. 2, June 1973.

Sigel, Roberta (ed.), *Learning about Politics: A Reader in Political Socialization*, (Random House, New York, 1970).

Smith, J.A., A. Kornberg, and D. Bromley, "Patterns of early political socialization and adult party affiliation," *Canadian Review of Sociology and Anthropology*, vol. 5, no. 3, August 1968.

Smith, J., and A. Kornberg, "Self concepts of American and Canadian party officials: their development and consequences," *Social Forces*, vol. 49, no. 1, December 1970.

Solberg, Patricia Anne, "Attitudes of Canadian Veterans to Political Economic Issues," *Journal of Social Psychology*, vol. 38, 1953, pp. 73–86.

Steintrager, James, "Political Socialization and Political Theory," *Social Research*, vol. 35, 1968, pp. 111–129.

Tolley, Howard, *Children and War: Political Socialization to International Conflict*, (Teachers College Press, New York, 1973).

Trudel, Marcel, and Geneviève Jain, *Canadian History Textbooks*, (Queen's Printer, Ottawa, 1970). Canada, Royal Commission on Bilingualism and Biculturalism, Studies no. 5.

Zeligs, Rose, "Children's Concepts and Stereotypes of Turk, Portuguese, Roumanian, Arab, Chinese, French-Canadian, Mulatto, South American, Hawaiian, and Australian," *Journal of Genetic Psychology*, vol. 83, 1953, pp. 171–178.

Ziblatt, David, "High School Extracurricular Activities and Political Socialization," *The Annals of the American Academy of Political and Social Science*, vol. 361, 1965, pp. 20–31.

B. Public Opinion

Albig, W., *Modern Public Opinion*, (McGraw-Hill, New York, 1956).

Alford, R.R., "The Social Bases of Political Cleavage in 1962," in J. Meisel (ed.), *Papers on the 1962 Election*, (University of Toronto Press, Toronto, 1964).

Almond, G., and S. Verba, *The Civic Culture*, (Princeton University Press, Princeton, 1963).

Armstrong, J. "Canadians in crisis: the nature and source of support for leadership in a national emergency," *Canadian Review of Sociology and Anthropology*, vol. 9, no. 4, November 1972.

Christenson, R.M., and R.O. McWilliams (eds.), *Voice of the People*, McGraw–Hill, New York, 1962).

Converse, Philip E., "The Nature of Belief Systems in Mass Publics," in D. Apter (ed.), *Ideology and Discontent*, (The Free Press, New York, 1964), pp. 206–262.

Converse, Philip E., Georges Dupeux, and John Meisel, "Continuities in Popular Political Culture: French and Anglo-Saxon Contrasts in Canada," (paper prepared for the International Conference on Comparative Electoral Behaviour, Ann Arbor, Michigan, April, 1967).

Devall, W.B., "Support for civil liberties among English-speaking Canadian university students," *Canadian Journal of Political Science*, vol. 3, no. 3, September 1970.

Dion, L., "Democracy as Perceived by Public Opinion Analysts," *C.J.E.P.S.*, Vol. 28, no. 4, Nov., 1962.

——————, "Régimes d'opinions publiques et systèmes idéologiques," *Ecrits du Canada Français*, vol. 12, 1962.

Katz, D., *et al.* (eds.), *Public Opinion and Propaganda*, (Holt Rinehart and Winston, New York, 1960).

Key, V.O., *Public Opinion and American Democracy*, (Alfred A. Knopf, New York, 1961).

Lane, R.E., and D.O. Sears, *Public Opinion*, (Prentice–Hall, Englewood Cliffs, 1964).

Lippman, W., *Public Opinion*, (Macmillan, New York, 1960).

Lipset, S.M., *Political Man*, (Anchor–Doubleday, Garden City, 1969).

Lipset, S.M., Paul Lazarsfeld, Allen Barton and Juan Linz, "The Psychology of Voting," in Lindzey Gardner (ed.), *Handbook of Social Psychology*, II, (Addison–Wesley, Cambridge, 1965), pp. 1124–1175.

Luttbeg, Norman R. (ed.), *Public Opinion and Public Policy: Models of Political Influence*, (The Dorsey Press, Homewood, Ill., 1968).

McDonald, L., "Attitude organization and voting behaviour in Canada," *Canadian Review of Sociology and Anthropology*, vol. 8, no. 3, August 1971.

Qualter, T.H., "The Manipulation of Popular Impulse, Graham Wallas Revisited," *C.J.E.P.S.*, vol. 25, no. 2, May, 1969.

Regenstreif, S.P., *The Diefenbaker Interlude: Parties and Voting in Canada, An Interpretation*, (Longmans, Toronto, 1965).

Reilly, W.G., "Political attitudes among law students in Quebec," *Canadian Journal of Political Science*, vol. 4, no. 1, March 1971.

Schwartz, M., *Public Opinion and Canadian Identity*, (Fitzhenry and Whiteside, Toronto, 1967).

Winham, G., "Attitudes on pollution and growth in Hamilton, or 'There's an awful lot of talk these days about ecology'," *Canadian Journal of Political Science*, vol. 5, no. 3, September 1972.

C. The Mass Media

Breed, W., "Social Control in the Newsroom: a Functional Analysis," *Social Forces*, vol. 33, May, 1955.

Bruce, C., *News and the Southams*, (Macmillan, Toronto, 1968).

Canada, Committee on Broadcasting, *Report*, (Queen's Printer, Ottawa, 1965).

——————, Royal Commission on Broadcasting, *Report*, (Queen's Printer, Ottawa, 1957), 2 vols.

——————, Royal Commission on Publications, *Report*, [The O'Leary Report], (Queen's Printer, Ottawa, 1961), 2 vols.

Canada, Senate, *Report of the Senate Committee on the Mass Media*, (Queen's Printer, Ottawa, 1971), 3 volumes, esp. *The Uncertain Mirror*, vol. III.

Cater, D., *The Fourth Branch of Government*, (Houghton Mifflin, Boston, 1959).

Compton, Neil, "The Mass Media," in Michael Oliver (ed.), *Social Purpose for Canada*, (University of Toronto Press, Toronto, 1961), pp. 50–87.

Cook, R., *The Politics of John W. Dafoe and the Free Press*, (University of Toronto Press, Toronto, 1963).

Dahrin, R., "The Media and the Rise of P.E. Trudeau," *Canadian Dimension*, vol. 5, no. 5, June–July, 1968, p. 5.

Dexter, Lewis Anthony, and David Manning White (eds.), *People, Society and Mass Communications*, (The Free Press, New York, 1964).

Donnelly, M., *Dafoe of the Free Press*, (Macmillan, Toronto, 1968).

Eggleston, W., "The Press in Canada," *The Royal Commission on National Development in the Arts, Letters and Sciences* [Massey Report], (King's Printer, Ottawa, 1951).

Engelmann, Frederick C., and Mildred A. Schwartz, "The Mass Media and Elites," in *Political Parties and the Canadian Social Structure*, (Prentice–Hall, Toronto, 1967).

Ferguson, George Victor, *Press and Party in Canada: Issues of Freedom*, (Ryerson, Toronto, 1955).

Gordon, D.R., *Language, Logic and the Mass Media*, (Holt, Rinehart and Winston, Toronto, 1966).

Hamlin, D.L.B. (ed.), *The Press and the Public*, (University of Toronto Press, Toronto, 1962).

Harkness, R., *J.E. Atkinson of the Star*, (University of Toronto Press, Toronto, 1963).

Hornby, Robert, *The Press in Modern Society*, (Muller, London, 1965).

Irving, John Allan (ed.), *Mass Media in Canada*, (Ryerson, Toronto, 1962).

Kesterton, Wilfred H., *A History of Journalism in Canada*, (McClelland and Stewart, Toronto, 1967).

Krugman, H.E., "The Impact of Television Advertising: Learning Without Improvement," *Public Opinion Quarterly*, vol. 29, no. 3, Fall, 1965, pp. 349–356.

Lloyd, Trevor Owen, and Jack McLeod (eds.), *Agenda 1970*, (University of Toronto Press, Toronto, 1968).

Morton, Desmond, "Democracy and the Mass Media," *The Canadian Forum*, vol. 49, July, 1969, pp. 82–84.

Ogle, Marbury Bladen, *Public Opinion and Political Dynamics*, (Houghton Mifflin, Boston, 1950).

Peers, R., *The Politics of Canadian Broadcasting, 1920–1951*, (University of Toronto Press, Toronto, 1969).

Qualter, T.H., and K.A. MacKirdy, "The Press of Ontario and the Election," in John Meisel, *Papers on the 1962 Election*, (University of Toronto Press, Toronto, 1964), pp. 145–168.

Seymour-Ure, Colin Knowlton, "The Parliamentary Press Gallery in Ottawa," *Parliamentary Affairs*, vol. 16, no. 1, Winter, 1962.

Singer, B.D., "Violence, protest, and war in television news: the U.S. and Canada," in *Public Opinion Quarterly*, vol. 34, no. 4, Winter 1970–71.

Stursberg, Peter, *Mr. Broadcasting: The Ernie Bushnell Story*, (Peter Martin Associates, Toronto, 1971).

Weir, E.A., *The Struggle for National Broadcasting in Canada*, (McClelland and Stewart, Toronto, 1965).

Wilson, H.H., "Techniques of Pressure: Anti-nationalization Propaganda in Britain," *Public Opinion Quarterly*, vol. 15, no. 3, Summer, 1951, pp. 225–242.

Windlesham, David J.G.H., *Communication and Political Power*, (Cape, London, 1966).

514   Bibliography

D. Political Participation

Agger, R.E., and V. Ostrom, "Political Participation in a Small Community," in H. Eulau *et al.* (eds.), *Political Behavior*, (The Free Press, Glencoe, 1956), pp. 138–148.

Alford, R.R., *Party and Society*, (Rand-McNally, Chicago, 1963).

Campbell, Angus, "The Passive Citizen," *Acta Sociologica*, vol. 6, (fasc. 1–2), pp. 9–21.

————, *et al., Elections and the Political Order*, (John Wiley and Sons, New York, 1966).

Converse, Philip E., "The Shifting Role of Class in Political Behavior and Attitudes," in Eleanor Maccoby, *et al.* (eds.), *Readings in Social Psychology*, (Holt, Rinehart and Winston, New York, 1958), pp. 388–399.

Davies, James, *Human Nature in Politics*, (John Wiley and Sons, New York, 1963).

Dean, Dwight G., "Alienation and Political Apathy," *Social Forces*, vol. 38, March, 1960, pp. 185–189.

Dennis, Jack, "Support for Party Systems by the Mass Public," *American Political Science Review*, vol. 60, no. 3, Sept., 1966, pp. 600–613.

Dion, L., "Participation in the Political Process," *Queen's Quarterly*, vol. 75, no. 3, Autumn, 1968, pp. 432–437.

Douvan, Elizabeth, and A. Walker, "The Sense of Effectiveness in Public Affairs," *Psychological Monographs*, vol. 70, no. 22, 1956.

Draper, James A., *Citizen Participation: Canada*, (New Press, Toronto, 1971).

Erbe, William, "Social Involvement and Political Activity," *American Sociological Review*, vol. 29, April, 1964, pp. 198–215.

Eulau, Heinz, and Peter Schneider, "Dimensions of Political Involvement," *Public Opinion Quarterly*, vol. 20, Spring, 1956, pp. 128–142.

Eyzenck, H.J., *The Psychology of Politics*, (Routledge and Kegan Paul, London, 1954).

Foskett, J.M., "Social Structure and Social Participation," *American Sociological Review*, vol. 20, Aug., 1955, pp. 431–438.

Frenkel-Brunswik, Else, "The Interaction of Psychological and Sociological Factors in Political Behavior," *American Political Science Review*, vol. 46, March, 1952, pp. 44–65.

Glaser, William A., "The Family and Voting Turnout," *Public Opinion Quarterly*, vol. 23, Winter, 1959, pp. 563–570.

Hennessy, Bernard, "Politicals and Apoliticals: Some Measurements of Personality Traits," *Midwest Journal of Political Science*, vol. 3, Nov., 1959, pp. 336–355.

Himmelstrand, Ulf, "A Theoretical and Empirical Approach to Depoliticization and Political Involvement," *Acta Sociologica*, vol. 6, (fasc. 1–2), 1962, pp. 83–111.

Katz, Daniel, and Samuel Eldersveld, "The Impact of Local Party Activity Upon the Electorate," *Public Opinion Quarterly*, vol. 25, Spring, 1961, pp. 1–24.

Katz, Elihu, and Paul Lazarsfeld, *Personal Influence*, (The Free Press, Glencoe, 1955).

Kim, Y.C., "The Concept of Political Culture in Comparative Politics," *Journal of Politics*, vol. 26, no. 2, May, 1964, pp. 313–336.

Lane, R.E., *Political Life*, (The Free Press, Glencoe, 1959).

————, *Political Ideology*, (The Free Press, New York, 1962).

Levin, Murray B., *The Alienated Voter*, (Holt, Rinehart and Winston, New York, 1960).

Lipset, S.M., *Agrarian Socialism*, (University of California Press, Berkeley, 1950).

Litt, Edgar, "Political Cynicism and Political Futility," *The Journal of Politics*, vol. 25, May, 1963, pp. 312–323.

MacInnis, Grace, "Women in Politics," *The Parliamentarian*, vol. 53, no. 1, January 1972.

MacKinnon, Frank, *Posture and Politics: Some Observations on Participatory Democracy*, (University of Toronto Press, Toronto, 1973).

McDill, Edward L., and Jeanne C. Ridley, "Status, Anomie, Political Alienation and Political Participation," *American Journal of Sociology*, vol. 68, Sept., 1962, pp. 205–217.

Meisel, John, *The Canadian General Election of 1957*, (University of Toronto Press, Toronto, 1962).

——————, *Papers on the 1962 Election*, (University of Toronto Press, Toronto, 1964).

Milbrath, L. *Political Participation*, (Rand–McNally, Chicago, 1965).

Milbrath, Lester, and Walter Klein, "Personality Correlates of Political Participation," *Acta Sociologica*, vol. 6, (fasc. 1–2), 1962, pp. 53–66.

Neal, A.G., and Solomon Rettig, "On the Multidimensionality of Alienation," *American Journal of Sociology*, vol. 32, no. 1, Feb., 1967, pp. 54–64.

Nie, N.H., K. Prewitt, and C.B. Powell, "Social Structure and Political Participation," *American Journal of Political Science*, vol. 63, June and Sept. 1969.

Polsby, Nelson W., *Community Power and Political Theory*, (Yale University Press, New Haven, 1963).

Presthus, Robert, *Men at the Top: A Study in Community Power*, (Oxford Press, 1968).

Riesman, David, and Nathan Glazer, "Criteria for Political Apathy," in Alvin, Gouldner (ed.), *Studies in Leadership*, (Harper and Row, New York, 1950), pp. 540–547.

Robinson, W.S., "The Motivational Structure of Political Participation," *American Sociological Review*, vol. 17, April, 1952, pp. 151–156.

Rokkan, Stein, "Electoral Activity, Party Membership and Organizational Influence," *Acta Sociologica*, vol. 4 (fasc. 1), 1959, pp. 25–37.

——————, "Mass Suffrage, Secret Voting and Political Participation," *European Journal of Sociology*, vol. 2, no. 1, 1961, pp. 132–152.

——————, "Approaches to the Study of Political Participation," *Acta Sociologica*, vol. 6, (fasc. 1–2), 1960, pp. 1–8.

——————, "The Comparative Study of Political Participation," in Austin Ranney (ed.), *Essays on the Behavioral Study of Politics*, (University of Illinois Press, Urbana, 1962), pp. 47–90.

Rokkan, Stein, and Svennick Hoyer, "Comparative Research on Citizen Participation in Politics," *International Social Science Journal*, vol. 14, no. 2, 1962, pp. 351–363.

Rose, Arnold M., "Alienation and Participation: A Comparison of Group Leaders and the Mass,'" *American Sociological Review*, vol. 27, Dec., 1962, pp. 834–838.

Rosenberg, Morris, "Some Determinants of Political Apathy," *Public Opinion Quarterly*, vol. 18, Winter, 1954–55, pp. 394–396

——————, "Self-Esteem and Concern with Public Affairs," *Public Opinion Quarterly*, vol. 16, Summer, 1962, pp. 201–211.

Scarrow, Howard A., "Patterns of Voter Turnout in Canada," *Midwest Journal of Political Science*, vol. 5, Nov., 1961, pp. 351–365.

Scheff, T.J., "Towards a Sociological Model of Consensus," *American Journal of Sociology*, vol. 32, Feb., 1967, pp. 32–46.

Seeman, Melvin, "On the Meaning of Alienation," *American Sociological Review*, vol. 24, 1959, pp. 783–791.

——————, "Alienation Membership and Political Knowledge," *Public Opinion Quarterly*, vol. 30, Fall, 1966, p. 353 ff.

Sewell, John, *Up Against City Hall*, (James, Lewis & Samuel, Toronto, 1972).

Sproule-Jones, Mark, and Kenneth D. Hart, "A Public-Choice Model of Political Participation," in *Canadian Journal of Political Science*, vol. 6, no. 2, June, 1973.

Templeton, Frederick, "Alienation and Political Participation," *Public Opinion Quarterly*, vol. 30, Summer 1966, p. 249.

Thompson, Wayne E., and John E. Horton, "Political Alienation as a Force in Political Action," *Social Forces*, vol. 38, March 1960, pp. 190–195.

Van Loon, R.J., "Political Participation in Canada: The 1965 Election," *Canadian Journal of Political Science*, vol. 3, no. 3, Sept. 1970.

E. Canadian Nationalism

Abella, Irving M., *Nationalism, Communism and Canadian Labour: The C.I.O., the Communist Party and the Canadian Congress of Labour 1935–1956*, (University of Toronto Press, Toronto, 1973).

"Blair Fraser—Canadian," *Maclean's*, vol. 81, no. 8, Aug., 1968.

Blishen, B.R., *et al.*, (eds.), *Canadian Society: Sociological Perspectives*, (Macmillan, Toronto, 1968).

Camp, Dalton C., "Canadian-American Interdependence: How Much?" *The Canadian Forum*, vol. 48, Feb., 1969, pp. 242–244.

Canada, Prime Minister, *The Constitution and the People of Canada*, (Queen's Printer, Ottawa, 1969).

Canada, Prime Minister, *Federalism for the Future*, (Queen's Printer, Ottawa, 1968).

Canada, Privy Council Office, *White Paper on a Domestic Satellite Communication System for Canada*, (Queen's Printer, Ottawa, 1968).

Canada, Royal Commission on Bilingualism and Biculturalism, *Preliminary Report*, (Queen's Printer, Ottawa, 1965).

Canada, Royal Commission on Publications, *Report*, (Queen's Printer, Ottawa, 1961), 2 vols.

Canada, Task Force on the Structure of Canadian Industry, *Foreign Ownership and the Structure of Canadian Industry*, [The Watkins Report], (Queen's Printer, Ottawa, 1968).

Clarkson, Stephen (ed.), *An Independent Foreign Policy for Canada?*, The University League for Social Reform, (McClelland and Stewart, Toronto, 1968).

Cook, Ramsay, *The Maple Leaf Forever: Essays on Nationalism and Politics in Canada*, (Macmillan, Toronto, 1971).

Crispo, John H., *International Unionism: a Study in Canadian–American Relations*, (McGraw–Hill, Toronto, 1967).

Easterbrook, William Thomas, and Hugh G.J. Aitkin, *Canadian Economic History*, (Macmillan, Toronto, 1956).

Eayrs, James George, *The Art of the Possible: Government and Foreign Policy in Canada*, (University of Toronto Press, Toronto, 1961).

Gordon, Walter Lockhart, *A Choice for Canada*, (McClelland and Stewart, Toronto, 1966).

Grant, George Parkin, *Lament for a Nation: the Defeat of Canadian Nationalism*, (McClelland and Stewart, Toronto, 1970).

——————, *Technology and Empire*, (House of Anansi, Toronto, 1969).

Horowitz, Gad, *Canadian Labour in Politics*, (University of Toronto Press, Toronto, 1968).

Johnson, Harry Gordon, *The Canadian Quandary*, (McGraw-Hill, Toronto, 1963).
_____ , "The Economics of the 'Brain Drain': the Canadian Case," *Minerva*, vol. 3, Spring, 1965, pp. 299–311.
_____ , "Problems of Canadian Nationalism," *International Journal*, vol. 16, 1961, pp. 238–249.
_____ , "The Watkins Report: Towards a New National Policy," *International Journal*, vol. 23, Autumn, 1968, pp. 615–622.
Kierans, Eric W., *Challenge of Confidence: Kierans on Canada*, (McClelland and Stewart, Toronto, 1967).
Lermer, G., "Safarian's Survey of Subsidiaries," *Canadian Dimension*, vol. 4, no. 4, May–June, 1967, pp. 36–37.
Levitt, Kari, *Silent Surrender: The Multi-National Corporation in Canada*, (Macmillan, Toronto, 1970).
Logan, Harold Amos, *Trade Unions in Canada*, (Macmillan, Toronto, 1948).
Lower, Arthur R.M., "Canadian Values and Canadian Writing," *Mosaic*, vol. 1, no. 1, Oct., 1967, p. 79. (See also section on Bilingualism and Biculturalism.)
Lumsden, Ian (ed.), *Close the 49th Parallel; The Americanization of Canada*, (University of Toronto Press, Toronto, 1970).
McInnis, Edgar, *Canada, a Political and Social History*, (Holt, Rinehart and Winston, New York, 1959).
Morton, W.L., *The Canadian Identity*, (University of Toronto Press, Toronto, 1972).
Parai, Louis, *Immigration and Emigration: of Professional and Skilled Manpower During the Post-war Period*, (Queen's Printer, Ottawa, 1965).
Pearson, L.B., "Canada's Role as a Middle Power," in J. King Gordon (ed.), *Canada's Role as a Middle Power*, (Canadian Institute of International Affairs, Toronto, 1966).
Safarian, A.E., *Foreign Ownership of Canadian Industry*, (McGraw–Hill, Toronto, 1966).
Schwartz, Mildred A., *Public Opinion and Canadian Identity*, (University of California Press, Berkeley, 1967).
Smiley, Donald Victor, *The Canadian Political Nationality*, (Methuen, Toronto, 1967).
Underhill, Frank Hawkins, *In Search of Canadian Liberalism*, (Macmillan, Toronto, 1960).
United Nations Educational Scientific and Cultural Organization, *Communication in the Space Age: the Use of Satellites by the Mass Media*, (Paris, 1968).
Wyman, Ken, Robin Mathews, and G. Lermer, "The Task Force Report on Foreign Ownership," *Canadian Dimension*, vol. 5, no. 4, April–May, 1968, pp. 15–20.

THE CANADIAN CONSTITUTION

A. General Materials

Cairns, A.C., "The Living Canadian Constitution," *Queen's Quarterly*, vol. 77, no. 4, Winter 1970.
Cheffins, R.I., *The Constitutional Process in Canada*, (McGraw–Hill, Toronto, 1969).
Clokie, H.M., "Basic Problems of the Canadian Constitution," *C.J.E.P.S.*, vol. 8, 1942.
Corry, J.A., "The Prospects for the Rule of Law," *C.J.E.P.S.*, vol. 21, no. 4, Nov. 1955.
Corry, J.A., and J.E. Hodgetts, *Democratic Government and Politics*, (University of Toronto Press, Toronto, 1959).

Dawson, R.M., *The Government of Canada*, revised by N. Ward, (University of Toronto Press, Toronto, 1970).

Dicey, A.V., *Introduction to the Study of the Law of the Constitution*, (Macmillan, London, 1966).

Jennings, W.I., *The British Constitution*, (Cambridge University Press, London, 1966).

——————, *The Law and the Constitution*, (University of London Press, London, 1959).

Keith, A.B., *The Governments of the British Empire*, (Macmillan, London, 1935).

Kennedy, W.P.M., *The Constitution of Canada, 1534–1937*, (Oxford University Press, London, 1938).

B. Democratic Values

Clarke, S.D., "The Frontier and Democratic Theory," in Royal Society of Canada, *Proceedings and Transactions*, June, 1954, p. 65.

Cnudde, C.F., and D.E. Neubaur (eds.), *Empirical Democratic Theory*, (Markham, Chicago, 1969).

Corry, J.A., and J.E. Hodgetts, *Democratic Government and Politics*, (University of Toronto Press, Toronto, 1959).

Dahl, R.A., *A Preface to Democratic Theory*, (University of Chicago Press, Chicago, 1963).

MacIver, R.M., *The Web of Government*, (The Free Press, New York, 1965).

Macpherson, C.B., *The Real World of Democracy*, (C.B.C., Toronto, 1965).

Mayo, H.B., *An Introduction to Democratic Theory*, (Oxford University Press, New York, 1960).

Sartori, G., *Democratic Theory*, (Praeger, New York, 1965).

Schumpeter, J.A., *Capitalism, Socialism and Democracy*, (Harper and Row, New York, 1950).

Underhill, F.H., "Some Reflections on the Liberal Tradition," in F.H. Underhill, *In Search of Canadian Liberalism*, (Macmillan, Toronto, 1960).

UNESCO, *Democracy in a World of Tension*, (Paris, 1951).

C. Civil Liberties

Batshaw, H., "A landmark decision against discrimination in Canada," *Revue des Droits de l'Homme*, vol. 4, July 1971.

British Columbia, *Protection of Personal Privacy Act*, 1968.

Canada, Parliament, Special Joint Committee on Human Rights and Fundamental Freedoms, *Minutes of Proceedings and Evidence*, (King's Printer, Ottawa, 1947), no. 1–7 and (1947–8), no. 1–11.

——————, *Proceedings*, (King's Printer, Ottawa, 1950), no. 1–10.

——————, *Minutes of Proceedings and Evidence Concerning Bill C–79*, (Queen's Printer, Ottawa, 1960).

——————, *Royal Commission on Security*, (Abridged), (Queen's Printer, Ottawa, June, 1969), *passim*.

Canada, *Protection of Privacy Act*, 1973.

Canadian Bar Review, vol. 37, 1959.

       Articles by:
       (A) Laskin, p. 77.
       (B) Lederman, p. 4.
       (C) Bowker, p. 43.
       (D) Pigeon, p. 66.
       (E) Scott, p. 135.

Cheveldayoff, W., "Computers Can be Robbed," *Toronto Globe & Mail*, May 3, 1974, p. 1.

Clokie, H.M., "Basic Problems of the Canadian Constitution", *Canadian Bar Review*, vol. 20, May 1942, pp. 395–429; Dec. 1942, pp. 817–840.

Crook, F., "Police Need More Men," *Toronto Star*, May 18, 1974.

Dewdney, J., "The Data Bank Society," *Canadian Chartered Accountant*, 1971.

Gopalakrishna, K.C., "The Canadian Bill of Rights," *Journal of Constitutional and Parliamentary Studies*, vol. 5, no. 2, April–June 1971.

How, W.G., "The Case for a Canadian Bill of Rights," *Canadian Bar Review*, vol. 36, 1958, pp. 750–796.

Kinsella, N.A., "The Canadian model for the protection from discrimination," *Revue des Droits de l'Homme*, vol. 4, July 1971.

Lawford, Hugh, "Privacy vs. Freedom of Information," *Queen's Quarterly*, vol. 78, Fall 1971.

Lowman, R., "New Wiretap Law. . ." *Toronto Star*, May 18, 1974, p. 4.

MacGuigan, Mark R., "Civil Liberties in Canada," *Queen's Quarterly*, vol. 72, 1965, p. 270.

Manitoba, *Personal Investigations Act*, 1971.

McWilliams, P., "Safeguard Against False Police Records," *Toronto Globe & Mail*, May 3, 1974, p. 7.

Ontario, Royal Commission on Civil Rights, *Report Number One*, (Queen's Printer, 1968), 3 vols.

—————— , *Report Number Two*, (Queen's Printer, Toronto, 1968).

—————— , "A Democratic Approach to Civil Liberties," *University of Toronto Law Journal*, vol. 119, 1969, pp. 109–131.

Ontario, *Credit Information Act*, 1974.

Ottawa Citizen, "Saskatchewan Invasion of Privacy Bill," May 8, 1974.

Ottawa Citizen, "Police Files—Juveniles," May 3, 1974.

Quebec, *Consumer Protection Act*, 1972.

Russell, Peter H. (ed.), *Leading Constitutional Decisions*, (McClelland and Stewart, Toronto, 1965).

—————— , "Mr. Trudeau's Bill of Rights: Disadvantages," *The Canadian Forum*, vol. 49, March, 1969, pp. 274–276.

Ryan, S., "Charting Our Liberties," *Queen's Quarterly*, vol. 66, 1959, pp. 389–404.

Saskatchewan, *Credit Reporting Agencies Act*, 1972.

—————— , *Invasion of Privacy Act*, 1974

Schmeiser, Douglas, A., *Civil Liberties in Canada*, (Oxford University Press, London, 1964).

Scott, Francis Reginald, *Civil Liberties and Canadian Federalism*, (University of Toronto Press, Toronto, 1959).

Sharp, T.M., "Consumers and Privacy Law," *Canadian Consumer*, April 1973.

Tarnopolsky, Walter Surma, *The Canadian Bill of Rights*, (Carswell, Toronto, 1963).

The Toronto *Globe & Mail*, Ottawa Bureau, "Ottawa Tightens Security," May 3, 1974, p. 3.

Toronto Star, "Wiretap Law Ambiguous," May 18, 1974, p. 1.

Trudeau, Pierre Elliott, *A Canadian Charter of Human Rights*, (Queen's Printer, Ottawa, 1968).

Winsor, H., "Wiretap Bill—Indirect Evidence," *Toronto Globe & Mail*, November 26, 1973, p. 7.

D. Operative Principles Of The Constitution

Cheffins, R.I., *The Constitutional Process in Canada*, (McGraw–Hill, Toronto, 1969).

520 Bibliography

Cobham, Viscount, "The Governor General's Constitutional Role," *Political Science*, vol. 15, no. 2, Sept., 1963.

Corry, J.A., "The Prospects for the Rule of Law," *C.J.E.P.S.*, vol. 21, no. 4, 1955.

Corry, J.A., and J.E. Hodgetts, *Democratic Government and Politics*, (University of Toronto Press, Toronto, 1959).

Cronkite, B.C., "Canada and the Abdication," *C.J.E.P.S.*, vol. 4, 1938.

Dawson, R.M. (ed.), *Constitutional Issues in Canada 1900–1931*, (Oxford University Press, London, 1933).

———, *The Government of Canada*, revised by N. Ward, (University of Toronto Press, Toronto, 1970).

Dawson, W.F., *Procedure in the Canadian House of Commons*, (University of Toronto Press, Toronto, 1962).

Esberey, J.E., "Personality and Politics: A New Look at the King–Byng Dispute," *Canadian Journal of Political Science*, vol. 6, no. 1, March 1973.

Evalt, H.V., "The Discretionary Authority of Dominion Governors," *Canadian Bar Review*, vol. 28, 1940.

———, *The King and the Dominion Governors; A Study of the Reserve Powers of the Crown in Great Britain and the Dominions*, (Cass, London, 1967).

Forsey, E.A., "The Extension of the Life of Legislatures," *C.J.E.P.S.*, vol. 26, no. 4, Nov., 1960.

———, *Essays on Freedom and Order*, (McClelland and Stewart, 1973).

———, *The Royal Power of Dissolution of Parliament in the British Commonwealth*, (Oxford University Press, Toronto, 1943).

———, "Independence of the Judiciary," *Canadian Bar Review*, 1957.

Franck, T., "The Governor General and the Head of State Functions," *Canadian Bar Review*, vol. 32, no. 10, Dec., 1954.

Graham, Roger (ed.), *The King–Byng Affair, 1926: A Question of Responsible Government*, (Copp Clark, Toronto, 1967).

Hendry, J. McL., *Memorandum on the Office of Lieutenant-Governor of a Province: Its Constitutional Character and Functions*, (Department of Justice, Ottawa, 1955).

Kennedy, W.P.M., "The Office of Governor General of Canada," *Canadian Bar Review*, vol. 31, no. 9, Nov., 1953.

LaForest, G.V., *Disallowance and Reservation of Provincial Legislation*, (Department of Justice, Ottawa, 1955).

Laskin, B., *Canadian Constitutional Law*, (Carswell, Toronto, 1969).

Lederman, W.R., "The Independence of the Judiciary," *Canadian Bar Review*, 1956.

Mallory, J.R., "Disallowance and the National Interest: The Alberta Social Credit Legislation of 1937," *C.J.E.P.S.*, vol. 14, no. 3, Aug., 1943.

———, *Social Credit and the Federal Power in Canada*, (University of Toronto Press, Toronto, 1954).

———, "The Lieutenant-Governor as a Dominion Officer: The Reservation of The Three Alberta Bills in 1937," *C.J.E.P.S.*, vol. 14, no. 4, Nov., 1948.

———, "The Royal Prerogative in Canada: The Selection of Successors to Mr. Duplessis and Mr. Sauvé," *C.J.E.P.S.*, vol. 26, May, 1960.

———, "Canada's Role in the Appointment of the Governor General," *C.J.E.P.S.*, vol. 26, no. 1, Feb., 1960.

———, "Seals and Symbols: From Substance to Form in Commonwealth Equality," *C.J.E.P.S.*, vol. 22, no. 3, Aug., 1956.

———, "The Election and the Constitution," *Queen's Quarterly*, vol. 64, no. 4, Winter, 1957.

_____ , "The Appointment of the Governor-General: Responsible Government, Autonomy and the Royal Prerogative," *C.J.E.P.S.*, vol. 26, 1960.

McGregor, D.A., *They Gave Royal Assent: The Lieutenant-Governors of British Columbia*, (Mitchell Press, Vancouver, 1967).

McWhinney, E., J.R. Mallory, and E.A. Forsey, "Prerogative Powers of the Head of State (The Queen or Governor General)," *Canadian Bar Review*, vol. 35, nos. 1, 2, 3, Jan., Feb., March, 1957.

_____ , *Judicial Review in the English Speaking World*, (University of Toronto Press, Toronto, 1969).

Morton, W.L., "Meaning of Monarchy in Confederation" in Royal Society of Canada, *Transactions*, Fourth Series, vol. 1, 1963.

Saywell, J.T., "The Crown and the Politicians: The Canadian Succession Question, 1891–1896," *Canadian Historical Review*, vol. 37, no. 4, Dec., 1956.

_____ , *The Office of Lieutenant-Governor*, (University of Toronto Press, Toronto, 1957).

Stanley, G.F.G., "A 'Constitutional Crisis' in British Columbia," *C.J.E.P.S.*, vol. 21, no. 3, Aug., 1955.

Strayer, B., *Judicial Review of Legislation in Canada*, (University of Toronto Press, Toronto, 1969).

Ward, N., *The Public Purse: A Study in Canadian Democracy*, (University of Toronto Press, Toronto, 1962).

_____ , *The Canadian House of Commons: Representation*, (University of Toronto Press, Toronto, 1963).

Willis-O'Connor, H., *Inside Government House*, (Ryerson, Toronto, 1954).

CONSTITUTIONAL AND LEGAL PROCESSES

A. The Process of Change

1. Revolution

Amman, P., "Revolution: A Definition," *Political Science Quarterly*, vol. 77, March, 1962.

Brinton, C., *The Anatomy of Revolution*, (Random House, New York, 1965).

Calvert, P., "Revolution: The Politics of Violence," *Political Studies*, vol. 15, 1967.

Davies, J.C., "Toward a Theory of Revolution," *American Sociological Review*, vol. 27, 1962.

Jackson, R.J., and M. Stein, *Issues in Comparative Politics*, (Macmillan, Toronto, 1971), Chapter 5.

Leiden, C., and K.M. Schmitt, *The Politics of Violence: Revolution in the Modern World*, (Prentice–Hall, Englewood Cliffs, 1968).

Stone, L., "Theories of Revolution," *World Politics*, vol. 18, 1966.

Yoder, P., "Current Definitions of Revolution," *The American Journal of Sociology*, vol. 32, 1926.

2. Amendment in Canada

Alexander, E.R., "A Constitutional Strait Jacket for Canada," *Canadian Bar Review*, vol. 43, no. 3, March, 1965.

Angers, F.A., "Le problème du repatriement de la constitution," *L'Action Nationale*, vol. 54, Nov., 1964.

Brady, A., "Constitutional Amendment and the Federation," *C.J.E.P.S.*, vol. 29, 1963, pp. 486–494.

Canada, Prime Minister, *The Constitution and the People of Canada*, (Queen's Printer, Ottawa, 1969).

The Canadian Bar Review, vol. 45, no. 3, Sept., 1967, (Special issue on the Constitution, "Canada 1867–1967").

Clokie, H.M., "Basic Problems of the Canadian Constitution," *C.J.E.P.S.*, vol. 8, 1942, pp. 1–32.

Cook, Ramsay, *Provincial Autonomy, Minority Rights and the Compact Theory, 1867–1921*, Studies of the Royal Commission on Bilingualism and Biculturalism, no. 4, (Queen's Printer, Ottawa, 1969).

Efrat, E.S., "Federations in crisis—The failure of the old order," *Western Political Quarterly*, vol. 25, no. 4, December 1972.

Favreau, Guy, *The Amendment of the Constitution of Canada*, (Department of Justice, Ottawa, 1965).

Gérin-Lajoie, P., *Constitutional Amendment in Canada*, (University of Toronto Press, Toronto, 1950).

Laskin, B., "Amendment of the Constitution: Applying the Fulton–Favreau Formula," *McGill Law Journal*, vol. 11, no. 1, Jan., 1965.

Lederman, W.R., "The Process of Constitutional Amendment for Canada," *McGill Law Journal*, vol. 12, no. 4, 1966. Reprinted in Ontario Advisory Committee, *Background Papers*, pp. 77–87.

Livingstone, W.S., "The Amending Power of the Canadian Parliament," *American Political Science Review*, vol. 34, 1951, pp. 437–439.

Lower, A.R.M., "Two Ways of Life: The Spirit of Our Institutions," *Canadian Historical Review*, vol. 28, 1947, pp. 383–400.

MacDonald, V.C., "The Constitution in a Changing World," *Canadian Bar Review*, vol. 26, Jan., 1948, pp. 21–45.

Morin, J.Y., "Le repatriement de la constitution," *Cité Libre*, vol. 26, no. 2, décembre, 1964.

O'Hearn, Peter J.T., *Peace, Order and Good Government*, (Macmillan, Toronto, 1964).

Rowat, D.C., "Recent Developments in Canadian Federalism," *C.J.E.P.S.*, vol. 18, Feb., 1952.

Stanley, G.F.G., "Act or Pact? Another Look at Confederation," in *Canadian Historical Association Annual Report*, (Ottawa, 1956).

B. The Judicial Process

Angus, W.H., "Judicial Selection in Canada—the Historical Perspectives," Address to Association of Canadian Law Teachers, Sherbrooke, June 10, 1966.

Clark, J.A., "Appointments to the Bench," *Canadian Bar Review*, vol. 30, no. 1, Jan., 1952, pp. 28–36.

Cunningham, W.B., "Labour Relations Boards and the Courts," *Canadian Journal of Political Science*, November 1964.

Dahl, Robert, "Decision Making in a Democracy: the Supreme Court as a National Policy-Maker," *Journal of Public Law*, vol. 6, 1958.

————— , "The Too Limited Jurisdiction of the Supreme Court," *Canadian Bar Review*, vol. 25, June–July, 1947, pp. 573–586.

Fera, N., "The Federal Court," *Canadian Public Administration*, 1972.

Fouts, D., "The Supreme Court of Canada, 1950–60," in Glendon A. Schubert and David J. Danelski (eds.), *Comparative Judicial Behaviour*, (Oxford University Press, New York, 1969), ch. 10.

Kinnear, H., "The County Judge in Ontario," *Canadian Bar Review*, vol. 32, Jan., 1954, Feb., 1954.

Laskin, Bora, "The Supreme Court of Canada: a Final Court of and for Canadians," *Canadian Bar Review*, vol. 29, Dec., 1951, pp. 1038–1079.

_____, "Our Civil Liberties—the Role of the Supreme Court," *Queen's Quarterly*, vol. 61, 1954–55, pp. 455–471.

_____, *Canadian Constitutional Law, Cases, Text and Notes on Distribution of Legislative Power*, 4th ed., (Carswell, Toronto, 1973).

Lederman, William Ralph, *The Courts and the Canadian Constitution*, (McClelland and Stewart, Toronto, 1964), pp. 106–175.

_____, "Thoughts on Reform of the Supreme Court of Canada," in Ontario Advisory Committee on Confederation, *Background Papers and Reports*, Volume II, (Queen's Printer of Ontario, Toronto, 1970).

_____, "Thoughts on Reform of the Supreme Court of Canada," *Alberta Law Review*, vol. 8, no. 1, 1970, pp. 1–17.

Logan, G.R., "Historical Sketch of the Supreme Court of Canada," *Osgoode Hall Law Journal*, vol. 3, 1964.

Lyon, J. Noel, "A Fresh Approach to Constitutional Law: Use of a Policy-Science Model," *Canadian Bar Review*, vol. 45, Sept., 1967, pp. 554–577.

MacDonald, V.C., "The Privy Council and the Canadian Constitution," *Canadian Bar Review*, Dec., 1951.

MacKinnon, F., "The Establishment of the Supreme Court of Canada," *Canadian Historical Review*, 1946.

McWhinney, Edward, "Federal Supreme Courts and Constitutional Review," *Canadian Bar Review*, vol. 45, Sept., 1967, pp. 578–607.

_____, "A Supreme Court in a Bicultural Society," in Ontario, Advisory Committee on Confederation, *Background Papers and Reports*, (Queen's Printer, Toronto, 1967), pp. 91–99.

Millward, P.J., "Judicial Review of Administrative Authorities in Canada," *Canadian Bar Review*, 1961.

Morin, Jacques-Yvan, "Le Québec et l'arbitrage constitutionnel: De Charybde en Scylla," *Canadian Bar Review*, vol. 45, Sept., 1967, p. 608.

Peck, S.R., "The Supreme Court of Canada, 1958–1966. . .," *Canadian Bar Review*, vol. 45, 1967, pp. 666–725.

_____, "A Behavioural Approach to the Judicial Process: Scalogram Analysis," *Osgoode Hall Law Journal*, vol. 1, April, 1967.

Read, H., "The Judicial Process in Common Law Canada," *Canadian Bar Review*, vol. 37, 1959.

Russell, Peter H., *Bilingualism and Biculturalism in the Supreme Court of Canada*, (Queen's Printer, Ottawa, 1969).

_____, "The Jurisdiction of the Supreme Court of Canada; Present Policies and a Programme for Reform," *Osgoode Hall Law Journal*, vol. 6, no. 1, Oct., 1968.

_____, "Constitutional Reform of the Canadian Judiciary", (paper delivered at the A.C.L.T. meetings in Calgary, June, 1968).

_____, "Constitutional Reform of the Canadian Judiciary", *Alberta Law Review*, vol. 8, no. 1, 1970, pp. 1–17.

Strayer, B.L., *Judicial Review of Legislation in Canada*, (University of Toronto Press, Toronto, 1968).

FEDERALISM

Aitchison, J.H., "Interprovincial Cooperation" in James Hermiston Aitchison (ed.), *The Political Process in Canada*, (University of Toronto Press, Toronto, 1963), pp. 153–170.

Angus, H.F., "Two Restrictions on Provincial Autonomy," *C.J.E.P.S.*, vol. 21, 1955, pp. 445–446.

524 Bibliography

Beck, J.M., "Canadian Federalism in Ferment" in Richard H. Leach (ed.), *Contemporary Canada*, (Duke University Press, Durham, 1968), pp. 148–176.

Bissonnette, B., *Essai sur la constitution du Canada*, (Editions du jour, Montréal, 1963).

Black, Edwin R., and Alan C. Cairns, "A Different Perspective on Canadian Federalism," *Canadian Public Administration*, vol. 9, March, 1966, pp. 27–44.

Black, E.R., "Federal Strains Within a Canadian Party", in H. Thorburn (ed.), *Party Politics in Canada*, 3rd ed., (Prentice–Hall, Toronto, 1972).

Brachet, B., "La crise du fédéralisme canadien et le problème québécois", *Revue du Droit public et de la Science politique*, vol. 88, no. 2, 1972.

Brady, Alexander, "Quebec and Canadian Federation," *C.J.E.P.S.*, vol. 25, 1959, pp. 259–270.

Brossard, J., *L'immigration: Les droits et pouvoirs du Canada et du Québec*, (Presses de l'Université de Montréal, Montréal, 1967).

Browne, G.P., *The Judicial Committee and the BNA Act*, (University of Toronto Press, Toronto, 1967).

Buck, Arthur Eugene, *Financing Canadian Government*, (Public Administration Service, Chicago, 1949), chs. 10, 13.

Burns, R.M., "The Royal Commission on Dominion–Provincial Relations: the Report in Retrospect," in Robert Mills Clark (ed.), *Canadian Issues*, University of Toronto Press, Toronto, 1961), pp. 143–157.

————, *One Country or Two?*, (McGill–Queen's University Press, Montreal, 1971).

Canada Committee, The, *Declaration by English and French-Speaking Canadians*, (Montreal, 1966).

Canada, Senate, *Report to the Honourable Mr. Speaker Relating to the Enactment of the BNA Act 1867* [O'Connor Report], (Queen's Printer, Ottawa, 1939).

Caplan, Neil, "Some Factors Affecting the Resolution of a Federal–Provincial Conflict," *C.J.E.P.S.*, vol. 2, no. 2, June, 1969, pp. 173–186.

Cheffins, R.I., *The Constitutional Process in Canada*, (McGraw–Hill, Toronto, 1969).

Cole, Taylor, *The Canadian Bureaucracy and Federalism, 1947–1965*, (University of Denver, Denver, 1966).

Cook, R., *Provincial Autonomy, Minority Rights and the Compact Theory, 1867–1921*, (Queen's Printer, Ottawa, 1969), Royal Commission on Bilingualism and Biculturalism, Studies, no. 4.

Creighton, D.G., *Canada's First Century: 1867–1967*, (Macmillan of Canada, Toronto, 1970).

Creighton, D.G., *The Road to Confederation: The Emergence of Canada, 1863–1867*, (Macmillan, Toronto, 1964).

Crépeau, Paul André, and C.B. Macpherson (eds.), *The Future of Canadian Federalism; l'Avenir du fédéralisme canadien*, (University of Toronto Press, Toronto; les Presses de l'Université de Montréal, Montréal, 1965).

Dawson, Robert M. (ed.), *Constitutional Issues in Canada, 1900–1931*, (Oxford University Press, London, 1933), ch. 9.

Doern, G.B., "Vocational Training and Manpower Policy: a Case Study in Intergovernmental Liaison," *Canadian Public Administration*, vol. 12, March, 1969, pp. 63–71.

Dubuc, A., "Une interprétation économique de la constitution," *Socialisme 66, Revue du socialisme internationale et Québecois*, no. 7, janvier, 1966. English translation in *Canadian Forum*, vol. 45, no. 542, March, 1966.

Dufour, André, "Le statut particulier," *Canadian Bar Review*, vol. 45, Sept., 1967, pp. 437–453.

Eggleston, Wilfred, "Recent Trends in Federal–Provincial Relations," *The Canadian Banker*, vol. 59, Winter, 1952, pp. 66–78.

_____ , *The Road to Nationhood; a Chronicle of Dominion-Provincial Relations*, (Oxford University Press, Toronto, 1946).

Faribault, M., and R. Fowler, *Ten to One, The Confederation Wager*, (McClelland and Stewart, Toronto, 1965).

Forsey, E., "Canada: Two Nations or One?," *C.J.E.P.S.*, vol. 28, Nov., 1962.

Gelinas, A., "Trois modes d'approche à la détermination de l'opportunité de la décentralisation de l'organisation politique principalement en système fédéral," *Canadian Public Administration*, vol. 9, no. 1, March, 1966.

Gettys, Cora Luella, *The Administration of Canadian Conditional Grants: a Study in Dominion–Provincial Relationships*, (Public Administration Service, Chicago, 1938).

Hare, F.K., "Regionalism and Administration: North American Experiments," *C.J.E.P.S.*, vol. 13, 1947, pp. 563–571.

Hawkins, G. (ed.), *Concepts of Federalism*, Proceedings of 34th Couchiching Conference, (Canadian Institute on Public Affairs, Toronto, 1965).

_____ , *The Idea of Maritime Union*, Report of a Conference sponsored by the Canadian Institute on Public Affairs and Mount Allison University, Sackville, N.B., 1965.

Johnson, A.W., "The Dynamics of Federalism in Canada," *C.J.P.S.*, vol. 1, no. 1, March, 1968, pp. 18–39.

Kear, A.R., "Cooperative Federalism: a Study of the Federal–Provincial Continuing Committee on Fiscal and Economic Matters," *Canadian Public Administration*, no. 1, March, 1963, pp. 43–56.

LaForest, G.V., *Natural Resources and Public Property Under the Canadian Constitution*, (University of Toronto Press, Toronto, 1969).

Lamontagne, M. *Le fédéralisme canadien*, (Les presses universitaires Laval, Quebec, 1954).

La Societé St. Jean Baptiste de Montréal, *le Fédéralisme, l'acte de l'Amérique du Nord britannique et les Canadiens français*, Mémoire au comité parlementaire de la constitution du gouvernement du Québec, (Les éditions de l'agence Duvernay, Montréal, 1964).

Leach, R.H., "Interprovincial Co-operation: Neglected Aspects of Canadian Federalism," *Canadian Public Administration*, vol. 2, 1969, pp. 83–99.

Leach, R.H. (ed.), *Contemporary Canada*, (University of Toronto Press, Toronto, 1968).

Lederman, William Ralph, *The Courts and the Canadian Constitution*, (McClelland and Stewart, Toronto, 1964).

_____ , "Some Forms and Limitations of Cooperative Federalism," *Canadian Bar Review*, vol. 45, Sept., 1967, pp. 409–436.

_____ , "The Concurrent Operation of Federal and Provincial Laws in Canada," *McGill Law Journal*, vol. 9, 1963.

_____ , "Cooperative federalism: constitutional revision and parliamentary government in Canada," *Queen's Quarterly*, vol. 78, no. 1, Spring 1971.

Livingston, W.S., *Federalism and Constitutional Change*, (Oxford University Press, Oxford, 1963).

Lower, A.R.M., F.R. Scott, *et al.*, *Evolving Canadian Federalism*, (Duke University Press, Durham, 1958).

Macmahon, A.W., *Administering Federalism in a Democracy*, (Oxford University Press, New York, 1972).

McLeod, T.H., "Federal Provincial Relations, 1958," *Canadian Public Adminis-*

tration, vol. 1, no. 8, 1958, pp. 1–25.

McRae, K.D., *The Federal Capital: Government Institutions*, (Queen's Printer, Ottawa, 1969), Royal Commission on Bilingualism and Biculturalism Studies, no. 1.

——, *Switzerland: Example of Cultural Co-existence*, (Canadian Institute of International Affairs, Toronto, 1964).

McWhinney, E., *Comparative Federalism, States' Rights and National Power*, (University of Toronto Press, Toronto, 1962).

——, "The 'Quiet Revolution' in French Canada and its constitutional implications for Canadian federalism," *Jahrbuch des Öffentlichen Richts der Gegenwart*, vol. 19, 1970.

Mallory, J.R., *The Structure of Canadian Government*, (Macmillan, Toronto, 1971).

Maxwell, James Ackley, *Federal Subsidies to the Provincial Governments in Canada*, (Harvard University Press, Cambridge, 1937).

May, R.J., "Decision-making and Stability in Federal Systems," *C.J.P.S.*, vol. 3, no. 1, March 1970.

Meekison, J. Peter (ed.), *Canadian Federalism: Myth or Reality*, (Methuen, Toronto, 1968).

Moore, A. Milton, and J. Harvey Perry, *Financing Canadian Federation: the Federal–Provincial Tax Agreements*, (Canadian Tax Foundation, Toronto, 1953).

Morin, Claude, *Le Pouvoir Québécois... en Négociation*, (Boreal Express, Quebec, 1972).

Noel, S.J.R., "Consociational Democracy and Canadian Federalism," *Canadian Journal of Political Science*, vol. IV, no. 1, p. 15.

O'Hearn, P., *Peace, Order and Good Government*, (Macmillan, Toronto, 1964).

Oliver, Michael (ed.), *Social Purpose for Canada*, (University of Toronto Press, Toronto, 1961).

Olmsted, R.A., *Decisions Relating to the BNA Act, 1867, and the Canadian Constitution, 1867–1954*, (Queen's Printer, Ottawa, 1954), 3 vols.

Pearson, L.B., *Federalism for the Future*, (Queen's Printer, Ottawa, 1968).

Pépin, G., *Les Tribunaux Administratifs et La Constitution: Etude des articles 96 à 101 de l'A.A.N.B.*, (Les presses de l'Université de Montréal, Montréal, 1969).

Perry, J.H., "Conditional Grants" in Institute of Public Administration of Canada, *Proceedings of the Annual Conference*, (Toronto, 1953), pp. 352–386.

Riker, W.H., *Federalism: Origin, Operation, Significance*, (Little, Brown, Boston, 1964).

Rioux, Marcel, *Quebec in Question*, (James, Lewis & Samuel, Toronto, 1971).

Robinson, Albert J., and James Cutt, *Public Finance in Canada: Selected Readings*, (Methuen, Toronto, 1968).

Rowat, D.C., "Recent Developments in Canadian Federalism," *C.J.E.P.S.*, vol. 18, 1952, pp. 1–16.

Russell, P., *Leading Constitutional Decisions*, (McClelland and Stewart, Toronto, 1965).

——, (ed.), *Nationalism in Canada*, (McGraw–Hill, Toronto, 1966).

——, *The Supreme Court of Canda as a Bilingual and Bicultural Institution*, (Information Canada, Ottawa, 1970). Royal Commission on Bilingualism and Biculturalism, Documents, no. 1.

Ryerson, S.B., *Unequal Union: Confederation and the Roots of Conflict in the Canadas 1815–1873*, 2nd ed., (Progress, Toronto, 1973).

Ryerson, S., *et al.* (eds.), "The Two Canadas: Towards a New Confederation? A Symposium," *The Marxist Quarterly*, no. 15, Autumn, 1965.

Smiley, Donald Victor, *The Canadian Political Nationality*, (Methuen, Toronto, 1967).

——, *Conditional Grants and Canadian Federalism*, (Canadian Tax Foundation, Toronto, 1963).

_____ , *The Rowell–Sirois Report*, (Carleton Library, McClelland and Stewart, Toronto, 1963).

_____ , "Rationalism or Reason: Alternative Approaches to Constitutional Review in Canada," (paper delivered at the Progressive Conservative "Priorities for Canada" Conference, Niagara Falls, Ontario, Oct. 12, 1969).

_____ , "The Two Themes of Canadian Federalism," *C.J.E.P.S.*, vol. 31, no. 1, Feb., 1965.

_____ , *Canada in Question: Federalism in the Seventies*, (McGraw–Hill Ryerson, Toronto, 1972).

_____ , *Constitutional Adaptation and Canadian Federalism Since 1945*, (Queen's Printer, Ottawa, 1970). Royal Commission on Bilingualism and Biculturalism, Documents, no. 4.

_____ , "The structural problem of Canadian federalism", *Canadian Public Administration*, vol. 14, no. 3, Fall 1971.

Smith, Denis, *Bleeding Hearts, Bleeding Country*, (M.G. Hurtig, Edmonton, 1971).

Soucy, E., "Confédération ou 'fédéralisme co-opératif?" *L'Action nationale*, vol. 54, octobre, 1964.

Taylor, M.G., "Government Planning: the Federal–Provincial Health Survey Reports," *C.J.E.P.S.*, vol. 19, 1963, pp. 501–510.

Tremblay, A., *Les compétences législatives au Canada et les pouvoirs provinciaux en matière de propriété et de droits civils*, (Editions de l'Université, Ottawa, 1967).

Trudeau, Pierre Elliott, *Federalism and the French Canadians*, (Macmillan, Toronto, 1968).

_____ , *The Constitution and the People of Canada*, (Queen's Printer, Ottawa, 1969).

Underhill, F.H., *The Image of Confederation*, (CBC, Toronto, 1964).

Waines, W.J., "Dominion–Provincial Financial Arrangements: an Examination of Objectives," *C.J.E.P.S.*, vol. 19, 1953, pp. 304–315.

Waite, P.B., *The Life and Times of Confederation*, (University of Toronto Press, 1967).

Wheare, K.C., *Federal Government*, 4th ed., (Oxford University Press, London, 1963).

PARTIES AND ELECTIONS IN CANADA

Note: No attempt has been made to section this part of the bibliography as most studies of parties bear, at least incidentally, on many themes. For example, it is difficult to discuss minor parties in Canada without also discussing the major ones and vice versa. As well, discussing elections without also discussing parties is virtually impossible.

Abella, Irving M., *Nationalism, Communism and Canadian Labour: The C.I.O., the Communist Party and the Canadian Congress of Labour 1935–1956*, (University of Toronto Press, Toronto, 1973).

Aitchison, J.H. (ed.), *The Political Process in Canada*, (University of Toronto Press, 1963).

Alford, Robert R., *Party and Society: The Anglo-American Democracies*, (Rand McNally, Chicago, 1963).

Anderson, Grace M., "Voting Behavior and the Ethnic Religious Variables: A Study of a Federal Election in Hamilton, Ontario," *C.J.E.P.S.*, vol. 32, 1966.

Aubé, N.R., Hudon, and V. Lemieux, "L'étude du patronage des partis provinciaux du Québec de 1944 à 1970," *Recherches Sociographiques*, vol. 13, no. 1, January–April 1972.

Beck, J.M., "The Electoral Behaviour of Nova Scotia in 1965," *Dalhousie Review*, vol. 43, 1966.

————, *Pendulum of Power: Canada's Federal Elections*, (Prentice–Hall, Toronto 1968).

————, "Socialist or Democratic Party?" *Dalhousie Review*, vo. 41, 1961; and D.J. Dooley, "Labour Parties New and Old," *Dalhousie Review*, vol. 40, 1960.

Beeching, W.C., and M. Lazarus, "Le socialisme en Saskatchewan—trop ou trop peu," *Socialisme 64, Revue du socialisme international et Québecois*, no. 2, automne, 1964.

Bergeron, G., "Political Parties in Quebec," *University of Toronto Quarterly*, vol. 17, 1958.

Blais, Andre, "Third Parties in Canadian Provincial Politics," *Canadian Journal of Political Science*, vol. 6, no. 3, September 1973.

Blais, A., H. Cantin, and J. Crete, "Les élections comme phénomène de décision collective: les élections fédérales de 1957 à 1965 au Québec," *Canadian Journal of Political Science*, vol. 3, no. 4, December 1970.

Blake, D.E., "The measurement of regionalism in Canadian voting patterns, *Canadian Journal of Political Science*, vol. 5, no. 1, March 1972.

Borden, H., (ed.), *Robert Laird Borden: His Memoirs*, (Macmillan, New York, 1938).

Brady, Alexander, *Democracy in the Dominions*, 3rd ed., (University of Toronto Press, Toronto, 1958).

Burnet, Jean, "Town–Country Relations and the Problem of Rural Leadership," *C.J.E.P.S.*, vol. 13, 1947.

Cairns, A.C., "The Electoral System and the Party System in Canada," *C.J.E.P.S.*, vol. 1, no. 1, March, 1968.

Canada, *Report of the Committee on Election Expenses*, (Queen's Printer, Ottawa, 1966).

Canadian Dimension, Special Supplement, "The NDP and the Waffle," vol. 8, no. 8, April 1971.

Caplan, Gerald L., *The Dilemma of Canadian Socialism: The CCF in Ontario*, (McClelland and Stewart, Toronto, 1973).

Careless, J.M.S., *Brown of the Globe*, vol. 1, *The Voice of Upper Canada 1818–1859*, (Macmillan, Toronto, 1959); vol. II, *Statesmen of Confederation, 1860–1880*, (Macmillan, Toronto, 1963).

Carrigan, D., *Canadian Party Platforms, 1867–1968*, (Copp Clark, Toronto, 1968).

Carter, Gwendolyn M., "Commonwealth Overseas, Variations on a British Theme" in Sigmund Neumann (ed.), *Modern Political Parties*, (University of Chicago Press, Chicago, 1956).

Casstevens, T.W., and W.A. Denham, "III—Turnover and tenure in the Canadian House of Commons, 1867–1968," *Canadian Journal of Political Science*, vol. 3, no. 4, December 1970.

Cherwinski, W.J., "Bibliographical Note, The Left in Canadian History, 1911–1969," *Journal of Canadian Studies*, vol. 9, no. 4, Nov., 1969.

Churchill, G., "Recollections and comments of election strategy," *Queen's Quarterly*, vol. 77, no. 4, Winter 1970.

Clark, S.D., *Movements of Political Protest in Canada 1640–1840*, (University of Toronto Press, Toronto, 1959).

Clarkson, Stephen, *City Lib: Parties and Reform*, (A.M. Hakkert, Toronto, 1972).

Comeau, Paul-André, "La transformation du parti libéral québécois," *C.J.E.P.S.*, vol. 31, 1965.

Cook, Ramsay, *The Politics of John W. Dafoe and the Free Press*, (University of Toronto Press, Toronto, 1966).

————, (ed.), *Politics of Discontent*, (University of Toronto Press, Toronto, 1962).

Copes, D., "The fisherman's Vote in Newfoundland," *Canadian Journal of Political Science*, vol. 3, no. 4, December 1971.

Cornell, Paul G., *The Alignment of Political Groups in Canada, 1841–1957*, (University of Toronto Press, Toronto, 1962).

Courtney, J.C., *The Selection of National Party Leaders in Canada*, (Macmillan, Toronto, 1973).

——————, *Voting in Canada*, (Prentice–Hall, Scarborough, Ont., 1967).

Croisat, M., "Centralisation et décentralisation au sein des partis politiques canadiens," *Revue française de Science politique*, vol. 20, no. 3, June 1970.

Cunningham, R., "The impact of the local candidate in Canadian federal elections," *Canadian Journal of Political Science*, vol. 4, no. 2, June 1971.

Davis, Morris, "Ballot Behaviour in Halifax Revisited," *C.J.E.P.S.*, vol. 30, 1964.

Dawson, R.M., *The Government of Canada*, 5th ed., (University of Toronto Press, Toronto, 1970).

——————, *The Conscription Crisis of 1944*, (University of Toronto Press, Toronto, 1961).

Denman, N., *How to Organize an Election*, (Les éditions du jour, Montréal, 1962).

Dion, l'Abbé G., et l'Abbé L. O'Neill, *Le chrétien et les élections*, (Les éditions de l'homme, 8me éd., Montréal, 1960).

——————, *Le chrétien en démocratie*, (Les éditions de l'homme, Montréal, 1961).

Dion, L., "The Concept of Political Leadership," *C.J.P.S.*, vol. 1, no. 1, March, 1968.

——————, "A la recherche d'une méthode d'analyse des partis et des groupes d'intérêt," *C.J.P.S.*, vol. 2, no. 1, March, 1969.

——————, "Politique consultative et système politique," *C.J.P.S.*, vol. 2, no. 2, June, 1969.

Engelmann, Frederick C., "Membership Participation in Policy Making in the CCF," *C.J.E.P.S.*, vol. 22, 1956.

Engelmann, F., and Mildred Schwartz, *Political Parties and the Canadian Social Structure*, (Prentice–Hall, Toronto, 1967).

Epstein, L., "A Comparative Study of Canadian Parties," *The American Political Science Review*, vol. 58, no. 1, March, 1964.

Epstein, L.D., *Political Parties in Western Democracies*, (Praeger, New York, 1967).

Ferguson, G.V., and F.H. Underhill, *Press and Party in Canada: Issue of Freedom*, (Ryerson, Toronto, 1955).

Filley, Walter O., "Social Structure and Canadian Political Parties: The Quebec Case," *Western Political Quarterly*, vol. 9, 1956.

Fox, Paul, "Early Socialism in Canada" in J.H. Aitchison (ed.), *The Political Process in Canada*, (University of Toronto Press, Toronto, 1963).

——————, *Politics: Canada*, 3rd ed., (McGraw-Hill, Toronto, 1970).

——————, "Canada's Most Decisive Federal Election," *Parliamentary Affairs*, vol. 40, 1958.

Gagne, Wallace, and Peter Regenstreif, "Some Aspects of New Democratic Party Urban Support in 1965," *C.J.E.P.S.*, vol. 33, 1967.

Granatstein, J.E., *The Politics of Survival: The Conservative Party of Canada, 1939–1945*, (University of Toronto Press, Toronto, 1967).

Grossman, L.A., "Safe Seats: The Rural Urban Pattern in Ontario," *C.J.E.P.S.*, vol. 29, 1963.

——————, Groupe de Recherches Sociales, *Les électeurs Québecois*, (Groupe de Recherches Sociales, Montréal, 1960).

Gwyn, R., *The Shape of Scandal, A Study of a Government in Crisis*, (Clarke Irwin, Toronto, 1965).

Hagy, J.W., "Le Parti québecois in the 1970 election," *Queen's Quarterly*, vol. 77, no. 2, Summer 1970.

Hamelin, Jean, Jacques Letarte, and Marcel Hamelin, "Les élections provinciales dans le Québec," *Cahiers de Géographie de Québec*, vol. 4, 1958–60.

Harbron, J.D., "The Conservative Party and National Unity," *Queen's Quarterly*, vol. 69, no. 3, Autumn 1962.

Havel, J.E., *Les citoyens de Sudbury et la politique*, (Laurentian University Press, Sudbury, 1966).

Heasman, D.J., "Parliamentary Developments: The Politics of Canadian Nationhood," *Parliamentary Affairs*, vol. 19, no. 2, Spring 1966.

——————, "Political Alignments in Canada: The Fragmentation of Canadian Politics," *Parliamentary Affairs*, vol. 16, no. 4, Autumn 1963 and vol. 17, no. 1, Winter, 1963–64.

Higginbotham, C.H., *Off the Record: The C.C.F. in Saskatchewan*, (McClelland and Stewart, Toronto, 1968).

Hoffman, David, "Intra-Party Democracy: A Case Study," *C.J.E.P.S.*, vol. 27, 1961.

Hogan, G., *The Conservative in Canada*, (McClelland and Stewart, Toronto, 1963).

Holloban, G.M., "Canada First: A Minor Party in Microcosm," *C.J.E.P.S.*, vol. 19, 1953.

Hooke, Alf, *Thirty Plus Five: I Know, I Was There*, (Institute of Applied Arts, Edmonton, 1971).

Horowitz, G., "Tories, Socialists and the Demise of Canada," *Canadian Dimension*, vol. 2, no. 4, May–June, 1965.

——————, "Conservatism, Liberalism, and Socialism in Canada: an Interpretation," *C.J.E.P.S.*, vol. 32, no. 2, May, 1966.

——————, *Canadian Labour in Politics*, (University of Toronto Press, Toronto, 1968).

——————, "Toward the Democratic Class Struggle" in Trevor Lloyd and Jack McLeod (eds.), *Agenda 1970*, (University of Toronto Press, Toronto, 1968).

Hunter, W.D.G., "The New Democratic Party: Antecedants, Policies, Prospects," *Queen's Quarterly*, vol. 69, no. 3, Autumn 1962.

Irving, J.A., *The Social Credit Movement in Alberta*, (University of Toronto Press, Toronto, 1959).

Jacek, H., J. McDonough, R. Shimizu, and P. Smith, "The Congruence of Federal–Provincial Campaign Activity in Party Organizations: the Influence of Recruitment Patterns in Three Hamilton Ridings," *Canadian Journal of Political Science*, vol. 5, no. 2, June 1972.

Jackman, R.W., "Political parties, voting and national integration," *Comparative Politics*, vol. 4, no. 4, July 1972.

Jenson, J., and P. Regenstreif, "Some dimensions of partisan choice in Quebec, 1969," *Canadian Journal of Political Science*, vol. 3, no. 3, June 1970.

Jewett, Pauline, "Voting in the 1960 Federal By-Elections at Peterborough and Niagara Falls: Who Voted New Party and Why?" *C.J.E.P.S.*, vol. 28, 1962.

Johnpoll, Bernard K., "Two Aspects of Voter Behaviour in Saskatchewan." (Prepared for delivery to the 1966 Annual Meeting of the Canadian Political Science Association, Sherbrooke, Quebec, June 8, 1966).

Joyce, J.G. and H.A. Hosse, *Civic Parties in Canada*, (Canadian Federation of Mayors and Municipalities, Toronto, 1970).

Kamin, Leon, "Ethnic and Party Affiliations of Candidates as Determinants of Voting" in *Introductory Readings in Political Behaviour*, S. Sidney Ulmer (ed.), (Rand McNally, Chicago, 1961).

Knowles, S., *The New Party*, (McClelland and Stewart, Toronto, 1961).

Kornberg, A., J. Smith, and D. Bromley, "Some Differences in the Political Socialization Patterns of Canadian and American Party Officials: A Preliminary Report," *C.J.P.S.*, vol. 2, no. 1, March, 1969.

Kornberg, A., J. Smith and H. Clarke, "Attributes of ascribed influence in local party organization in Canada and the United States," *Canadian Journal of Political Science*, vol. 5, no. 2, June 1972.

Lakeman, E., and J.D. Lambert, *Voting in Democracies*, 2nd ed., (Faber, London, 1959).

Land, Brian, *Eglinton: The Election Study of a Federal Constituency*, (Peter Martin Associates, Toronto, 1965).

Laponce, J.A., "Non-voting and Non-Voters: A Typology," *C.J.E.P.S.*, vol. 33, 1967.

_____, "Canadian Party Labels: An Essay in Semantics and Anthropology," *C.J.E.P.S.*, vol. 2, 1969.

_____, *People vs. Politics*, (University of Toronto Press, Toronto, 1969).

_____, "Post-dicting electoral cleavages in Canadian federal elections, 1949–1968: material for a footnote." *Canadian Journal of Political Science*, vol. 5, no. 2, June 1972.

Laporte, Pierre, *The True Face of Duplessis*, (Harvest House, Montreal, 1960).

Lavau, G., "Parties et systèmes politiques; interactions et fonctions," *C.J.P.S.*, vol. 2, no. 1, March, 1969.

Laxer, J., "The Socialist Tradition in Canada", *Canadian Dimension*, vol. 6, no. 6, December–January 1969–70.

League for Social Reconstruction, *Social Planning for Canada*, (Nelson, Toronto, 1935).

Lederle, John W., "Liberal Convention of 1893," *C.J.E.P.S.*, vol. 16, 1950.

_____, "The Liberal Convention of 1919 and the Selection of Mackenzie King," *Dalhousie Review*, vol. 27, 1947–1948.

Leduc, L., "Party decision-making: some empirical observations on the leadership selection process," *Canadian Journal of Political Science*, vol. 4, no. 1, March 1971.

Leduc, L., and Walter L. White, "The Role of the Opposition in a One-Party Dominant System: The Case of Ontario," *Canadian Journal of Political Science*, vol. 7, no. 1, March 1974.

Lemieux, F., "Lobbying Plus—The CMA," in P. Fox, *Politics: Canada*, 2nd ed., (McGraw–Hill, Toronto, 1966).

Lemieux, Vincent, "La Composition des préférences partisanes," *C.J.P.S.*, vol. 2, 1969.

_____, "Le patronage politique dans l'Ile d'Orléans," *L'Homme*, vol. 10, no. 2, April–June 1970.

Leslie, Peter M., "The Role of Parties in Promoting the Interests of Ethnic Minorities," *C.J.P.S.*, vol. 2, 1969.

Lightbody, J., "Swords and ploughshares: the election prerogative in Canada", *Canadian Journal of Political Science*, vol. 5, no. 2, June 1972.

Lipset, S.M., *Political Man, The Social Bases of Politics*, (Doubleday, New York, 1963).

_____, *Agrarian Socialism: The Cooperative Commonwealth Federation in Saskatchewan*, (Anchor Books, Doubleday, New York, 1968).

_____, "Democracy in Alberta," *Canadian Forum*, vol. 34, 1954.

Long, J.A., "Maldistribution in Western Provincial Legislatures: The Case of Alberta," *C.J.P.S.*, vol. 2, no. 3, Sept. 1969.

Lorimer, James, *A Citizen's Guide to City Politics*, (James, Lewis and Samuel, Toronto, 1972).

_____, *The Real World of City Politics*, (James, Lewis and Samuel, Toronto, 1970).

Lovink, J.A.A., "On analysing the impact of the electoral system on the party system in Canada," *Canadian Journal of Political Science*, vol. 3, no. 4, December 1970.

――――――― , "Is Canadian Politics Too Competitive?" *Canadian Journal of Political Science*, vol. 6, no. 3, September 1973.

Lyons, W.E., *One Man—One Vote*, (McGraw-Hill, Toronto, 1970).

Macpherson, C.B., *Democracy in Alberta: the Theory and Practice of a Quasi-Party System*, (University of Toronto Press, Toronto, 1953).

MacQuarrie, Heath N., "Robert Borden and the Election of 1911," *C.J.E.P.S.*, vol. 25, 1959.

――――――― , *The Conservative Party*, (McClelland and Stewart, Toronto, 1965).

Mayer, L., "Federalism and party behaviour in Australia and Canada," *Western Political Quarterly*, vol. 23, no. 4, December 1970.

McDonald, L., "Social class and voting: a study of the 1968 Canadian federal election in Ontario," *British Journal of Sociology*, vol. 22, no. 4, December 1971.

McGeer, Pat, *Politics in Paradise*, (Peter Martin Associates, Toronto, 1972).

McGuigan, M., and T. Lloyd, *Liberalism and Socialism*, (Exchange for Political Ideas in Canada, Toronto, 1964), [pamphlet].

McHenry, D.E., *The Third Force in Canada: The Cooperative Commonwealth Federation, 1932–1948*, (University of California Press, Berkeley, 1950).

McIlwraith, M., "Misrepresentative Government," *Canadian Commentator*, March, 1963.

MacKenzie, W.J., *Free Election*, (Allen and Unwin, London, 1958).

McNaught, Kenneth W., "CCF: Town and Country," *Queen's Quarterly*, vol. 61, 1954.

――――――― , *A Prophet in Politics*, (University of Toronto Press, Toronto, 1959).

Meisel, John, *The Canadian General Election of 1957*, (University of Toronto Press, Toronto, 1962).

――――――― , "The Stalled Omnibus: Canadian Parties in the 1960's," *Social Research*, vol. 30, no. 3, Sept., 1963.

――――――― , "The June 1962 Election: Break-up of Our Party System," *Queen's Quarterly*, vol. 69, 1962.

――――――― , (ed.), *Papers on the 1962 Election*, (University of Toronto Press, Toronto, 1964).

――――――― , "Religious Affiliation and Electoral Behaviour," *C.J.E.P.S.*, vol. 22, 1956.

――――――― , "Formulation of Liberal and Conservative Programs in 1957 Canadian General Election," *C.J.E.P.S.*, vol. 26, 1960.

――――――― , *L'évolution des partis politiques canadiens*, Cahiers de la Société canadienne de Science politique, no. 2, 1966.

――――――― , *Les transformations des partis politiques canadiens*, Cahiers de la Société canadienne de Science politique, no. 2, 1966.

――――――― , "Canadian Parties and Politics" in R.H. Leach, *Contemporary Canada*, (University of Toronto Press, Toronto, 1968).

――――――― , "Cleavages, Parties and Values in Canada." *IPSA*, World Congress, August 1973.

――――――― , *Working Papers on Canadian Politics*, rev. ed., (McGill–Queen's University Press, Montreal, 1973).

Meynaud, J., *Agent et politique*, (Le centre de documentation et de recherches politique, Collége Jean-de-Brébeuf, Montréal, 1966).

Morrison, K.L., "The Businessman Voter in Thunder Bay: The Catalyst to the Federal–Provincial Voting Split?" *Canadian Journal of Political Science*, vol. 6, no. 2, June 1973.

Mortin, D., *With Your Help, An Election Manual*, (New Democratic Party, Ottawa, 1966).

——————, "The Effectiveness of Political Campaigning: The NDP in the 1967 Ontario Election," *Journal of Canadian Studies*, vol. 4, no. 3, Aug., 1969.

Morton, W.L., *The Progressive Party in Canada*, (University of Toronto Press, Toronto, 1950).

Muller, S., "Massive Alternation in Canadian Politics," *Foreign Affairs*, vol. 36, 1958.

——————, "Federalism and the Party System in Canada" in J.P. Meekison, *Canadian Federalism: Myth or Reality*, (Methuen, Toronto, 1968).

Neill, R.F., "Social Credit and National Policy in Canada," *Journal of Canadian Studies*, vol. 3, no. 1, Feb., 1968.

Neumann, S., *Modern Political Parties*, (University of Chicago Press, Chicago, 1956).

Newman, P.C., *The Distemper of Our Times: Canadian Politics in Transition, 1963–1968*, (McClelland and Stewart, Toronto, 1968).

——————, *Renegade in Power: The Diefenbaker Years*, (McClelland and Stewart, Toronto, 1963).

Nicholson, P., *Vision and Indecision: Diefenbaker and Pearson*, (Longman Canada, Toronto, 1968).

Nixon, Robert, (ed.), *The Guelph Papers*, (Ontario Liberal Party Conference, Toronto, 1968).

Oliver, M., (ed.), *Social Purpose for Canada*, (University of Toronto Press, Toronto, 1961).

Paltiel, K.Z., "Federalism and Party Finance," (Address to the 38th Annual Meeting of the Canadian Political Science Association, Sherbrooke, Quebec, June 8, 1966).

——————, *Financing Political Parties in Canada*, (McGraw–Hill, Toronto, 1970).

Peacock, D., *Journey to Power: The Story of a Canadian Election*, (Ryerson, Toronto, 1968).

Penner, Norman, (ed.), *Winnipeg 1919: The Strikers' Own History of the Winnipeg General Strike*, (James, Lewis & Samuel, Toronto, 1973).

Perlin, G., and P. Peppin, "Variations in party support in federal and provincial elections: some hypotheses," *Canadian Journal of Political Science*, vol. 4, no. 2, June 1971.

Pickersgill, J.W., *The Liberal Party*, (McClelland and Stewart, Toronto, 1962).

Pinard, Maurice, "One Party Dominance and Third Parties," *C.J.E.P.S.*, vol. 33, no. 3, Aug., 1967, pp. 358–373.

——————, *The Rise of a Third Party: A Study in Crisis Politics*, (Prentice–Hall, Englewood Cliffs, N.J., 1971).

——————, "Third Parties in Canada Revisited: A Rejoinder and Elaboration of the Theory of One-Party Dominance," *Canadian Journal of Political Science*, vol. 6, no. 3, September 1973.

Punnett, R.M., "Leadership selection in Opposition: the Progressive Conservative party of Canada," *Australian Journal of Politics and History*, vol. 17, no. 2, August 1971.

Qualter, T.H., "Representation by Population: A Comparative Study," *C.J.E.P.S.*, vol. 33, no. 2, May, 1967.

——————, "Seats and Votes: An Application of the Cube Law to the Canadian Electoral System," *C.J.P.S.*, vol. 1, no. 3, Sept., 1968.

——————, *The Election Process in Canada*, (McGraw–Hill, Toronto, 1970).

Quinn, H.F., "The Role of the Liberal Party in Recent Canadian Politics," *Political Science Quarterly*, vol. 68, no. 3, Sept., 1953.

——————, *The Union Nationale: A Study in Quebec Nationalism*, (University of Toronto Press, Toronto, 1963).

——————, "Third National Convention of the Liberal Party," *C.J.E.P.S.*, vol. 17, 1951.

Rasmussen, Jorgen, "A Research Note on Canadian Systems," *C.J.E.P.S.*, vol. 33, 1967.

Regenstreif, Peter, "Ideology and Leadership in the Canadian Party System," (prepared for delivery to the 1964 Annual Meeting of the American Political Science Association, Chicago, Illinois, Sept., 1964).

——————, "Note on the 'Alternation' of French and English Leaders in the Liberal Party of Canada," *C.J.P.S.*, vol. 2, no. 1, March, 1969.

——————, "The Canadian General Election of 1958," *Western Political Quarterly*, vol. 13, 1960.

——————, *The Diefenbaker Interlude: Parties and Voting in Canada*, (Longman Canada, Toronto, 1965).

——————, "Some Aspects of National Party Support in Canada," *C.J.E.P.S.*, vol. 29, 1963.

Reid Escott, M., "Canadian Political Parties: A Study of the Economics and Racial Basis of Conservatism and Liberalism in 1930," *Contributions to Canadian Economics*, vol. 6, 1933.

Richardson, B.T., *Canada and Mr. Diefenbaker*, (McClelland and Stewart, Toronto, 1962).

Ricketts, E.F., and H. Waltzer, "Electoral arrangements and the party system: the case of Canada," *Western Political Quarterly*, vol. 23, no. 4, December 1970.

Robin, M., *Radical Politics and Canadian Labour, 1880–1930*, (Queen's University, Kingston, 1968).

——————, "The Social Basis of Party Politics in British Columbia," *Queen's Quarterly*, vol. 72, 1965.

——————, *The Rush for Spoils: The Company Province 1871–1933*, (McClelland and Stewart, Toronto, 1972).

——————, *Pillars of Profit: The Company Province 1934–1972*, (McClelland and Stewart, Toronto, 1973).

——————, (ed.), *Canadian Provincial Politics: The Party Systems of the Ten Provinces*, (Prentice–Hall, Scarborough, Ont., 1972).

Rodney, W., *Soldiers of the International: A History of the Communist Party of Canada, 1919–1929*, (University of Toronto Press, Toronto, 1968).

Roussopoulus, D. (ed.), *The New Left in Canada*, (Our Generation Press, Montreal, 1970).

Rowat, D.C. (ed.), *Provincial Government and Politics: Comparative Essays*, 2nd ed., (Department of Political Science, Carleton University, Ottawa, 1973).

Sancton, Andrew, "The Application of the 'Senatorial Floor' Rules to the Latest Redistribution of the House of Commons: The Peculiar Case of Nova Scotia," *Canadian Journal of Political Science*, vol. 6, no. 1, March 1973.

Sankoff, David, and Koula Mellos, "La régionalisation électorale et l'amplification des proportions," *Canadian Journal of Political Science*, vol. 6, no. 3, September 1973.

Santos, C.R., "Some collective characteristics of the delegates to the 1968 Liberal Party Leadership Convention," *Canadian Journal of Political Science*, vol. 3, no. 2, June 1970.

Scarrow, Howard A., "By-Elections and Public Opinion in Canada," *Public Opinion Quarterly*, vol. 25, 1961.

——————, "Federal–Provincial Voting Patterns in Canada," *C.J.E.P.S.*, vol. 26, 1960.

_____ , *Canada Votes: A Handbook of Federal and Provincial Election Data*, (The Hauser Press, New Orleans, 1962).

_____ , "Distinguishing Between Political Parties—The Case of Canada," *Midwest Journal of Political Science*, vol. 9, 1965.

_____ , "Patterns of Voter Turnout in Canada," *Midwest Journal of Political Science*, vol. 5, 1961.

_____ , "Voting Patterns and the New Party," *Political Science*, vol. 14, 1962.

Schindeler, F., "One Man, One Vote: One Vote, One Value," *Journal of Canadian Studies*, vol. 3, no. 1, Feb., 1968.

Schindeler, F., and David Hoffman, "Theological and Political Conservatism," *C.J.P.S.*, vol. 2, 1968.

Schultz, H.J., "The Social Credit Back-Benchers' Revolt, 1937," *Canadian Historical Review*, vol. 45, 1964.

_____ , "Portrait of a Premier: William Aberhart," *Canadian Historical Review*, vol. 41, no. 1, March 1960.

Schwartz, Mildred A., *Politics and Territory*, (McGill–Queen's University Press, Montreal, 1974).

Simmons, James W., "Voting Behaviour and Socio-economic Characteristics: The Middlesex East Federal Election," *C.J.E.P.S.*, vol. 33, 1967.

Smiley, Donald V., "Canada's Poujadists: A New Look at Social Credit," *Canadian Forum*, vol. 42, 1962.

_____ , "The Two-Party System and One-Party Dominance in the Liberal Democratic State," *C.J.E.P.S.*, vol. 24, no. 3, Aug., 1958.

_____ , "Consensus Conflict and the Canadian Party System," *Canadian Forum*, vol. 40, Jan., 1961.

_____ , "The National Party Leadership Convention in Canada: A Preliminary Analysis," *C.J.P.S.*, vol. 1, no. 4, Dec., 1968.

Smith, D.E., "A Comparison of Prairie Political Developments in Saskatchewan and Alberta," *Journal of Canadian Studies*, vol. 40, no. 1, Feb., 1969.

Sniderman, Paul M., H.D. Forbes, and Ian Melzer, "Party Loyalty and Electoral Volatility: A Study of the Canadian Party System," *Canadian Journal of Political Science*, vol. 7, no. 2, June 1974.

Stewart, Walter, *Divide and Con: Canadian Politics at Work*, (New Press, Toronto, 1973).

Stein, Michael, *The Dynamics of Right-Wing Protest: A Political Analysis of the Social Credit in Quebec*, (University of Toronto Press, 1973).

Swainson, Donald, "Manitoba's Election: Patterns Confirmed", *Canadian Forum*, September 1973.

Taylor, Charles, *The Pattern of Politics*, (McClelland and Stewart, Toronto, 1970).

Teeple, Gary (ed.), *Capitalism and the National Question in Canada*, (University of Toronto Press, Toronto, 1972).

Thomas, L.G., *The Liberal Party in Alberta: A History of Politics in the Province of Alberta, 1905–1921*, (University of Toronto Press, Toronto, 1959).

Thorburn, H.G., *Politics in New Brunswick*, (University of Toronto Press, Toronto, 1961).

_____ , (ed.), *Party Politics in Canada*, (Prentice–Hall, Toronto, 1961).

Tyre, R., *Douglas in Saskatchewan: The Story of a Socialist Experiment*, (Mitchell Press, Vancouver, 1962).

Underhill, F.H., *Canadian Political Parties*, Canadian Historical Association Booklet, no. 8, (Ottawa, 1957).

_____ , "The Revival of Conservatism in North America," *Transactions of the Royal Society of Canada*, vol. 52, series 3, June, 1958.

_____ , *In Search of Canadian Liberalism*, (Macmillan, Toronto, 1960).

Vallières, P., "Le Parti Socialiste du Québec à l'heure de la révolution tranquille," *Cité libre*, vol. 15, no. 1, janvier, 1964.

Ward, N., "A Century of Constituencies," *Canadian Public Administration*, vol. 10, no. 1, March, 1967.

Ward, N., and D. Spafford (eds.), *Politics in Saskatchewan*, (Longman Canada, Toronto, 1968).

Wearing, J., "How to Predict Canadian Elections," *Canadian Commentator*, February, 1963.

———, "Party Leadership and the 1966 Conventions," *Journal of Canadian Studies*, vol. 2, no. 1, Feb. 1967.

———, "A Convention for Professionals: The PCs in Toronto," *Journal of Canadian Studies*, vol. 2, no. 4, Nov., 1967.

———, "The Liberal Choice," *Journal of Canadian Studies*, vol. 3, no. 2, May, 1968.

———, "The Trudeau Phenomenon," *C.J.P.S.*, vol. 2, no. 3, Sept. 1969.

Westell, Anthony, *Paradox: Trudeau as Prime Minister*, (Prentice–Hall, Scarborough, 1972).

Whalen, H., "Social Credit Measures in Alberta," *C.J.E.P.S.*, vol. 18, no. 4, Nov. 1952.

White, Graham, "One-Party Dominance and Third Parties: The Pinard Theory Reconsidered," *Canadian Journal of Political Science*, vol. 6, no. 3, September 1973.

Williams, J.R., *The Conservative Party in Canada, 1920–1949*, (Duke University Press, Durham, 1956).

Wilson, J., and D. Hoffman, "The Liberal Party in contemporary Ontario politics," *Canadian Journal of Political Science*, vol. 3, no. 2, June 1970.

Winham, G.R., and R.B. Cunningham, "Party Leader Images in the 1968 Federal Election," *C.J.P.S.*, vol. 3, no. 1, March, 1970.

Winn, Conrad and John McMenemy, "Political Alignment in a Polarized City: Electoral Cleavages in Kitchener, Ontario," *Canadian Journal of Political Science*, vol. 6, no. 2, June 1973.

Wrong, Denis H., "Ontario Provincial Elections 1934–1955: A Preliminary Survey of Voting," *C.J.E.P.S.*, vol. 23, 1957.

———, "The Pattern of Party Voting in Canada," *Public Opinion Quarterly*, vol. 21, 1957.

Young, Walter D., "The Peterborough By-Election: The Success of a Party Image," *Dalhousie Review*, vol. 40, 1961.

———, *The Anatomy of a Party: The National CCF 1932–1961*, (University of Toronto Press, Toronto, 1969).

———, *Democracy and Discontent: Progressivism, Socialism and Social Credit in the Canadian West*, (Ryerson, Toronto, 1969).

Zakuta, L., *A Protest Movement Becalmed: A Study of Change in the C.C.F.*, (University of Toronto Press, 1964).

Political Biographies

Political biographies and memoirs are a valuable source of information about political parties and elections. The following list is originally from Paul Fox, *Politics: Canada*, third edition, (McGraw–Hill, Toronto, 1970), pp. 251–253 and is updated to 1974.

Barrette, A., *Mémoires*, vol. 1, (Librairie Beauchemin, Montréal, 1966).

Beal, J.R., *The Pearson Phenomena*, (Longman Canada, Toronto, 1964).

Beck, J.M., *Joseph Howe: Voice of Nova Scotia*, (Carleton Library, McClelland and Stewart, Toronto, 1964).

Benson, N.A., *None of It Came Easy: The Story of J.G. Gardiner*, (Burns and MacEachern, Toronto, 1955).

Bourassa, A., A. Bergevin, and C. Nish (eds.), *Henri Bourassa, Biography, Bibliographical Index and Index of Public Correspondence, 1895–1924*, (les editions de l'Action Nationale, Montréal, 1966).

Bourassa; A. (ed.), *Henri Bourassa*, (les éditions de l'Action Nationale, Montréal, 1966).

Careless, J.M.S., *Brown of the Globe*, vol. 1, *The Voice of Upper Canada, 1818–1859*, (Macmillan, Toronto, 1959); vol. 2, *Statesman of Confederation, 1860–1880*, (Macmillan, Toronto, 1963).

Creighton, D., *John A. Macdonald*, vol. 1, *The Young Politician*, (Macmillan, Toronto, 1952); vol. 2, *The Old Chieftain*, (Macmillan, Toronto, 1955).

Dafoe, J.W., *Laurier: A Study in Canadian Politics*, (Carleton Library, McClelland and Stewart, Toronto, 1963).

Dawson, R.M., *William Lyon Mackenzie King: A Political Biography, 1874–1923*, vol. 1, (University of Toronto Press, Toronto, 1958).

Dempson, P., *Assignment Ottawa*, (General Publishing, Toronto, 1968).

Donaldson, G., *Fifteen Men: Canada's Prime Ministers from Macdonald to Trudeau*, (Doubleday, Toronto, 1969).

Drury, E.C., *Farmer Premier: The Memoirs of the Hon. E.C. Drury*, (McClelland and Stewart, Toronto, 1966).

Ferns, H.S., and B. Ostry, *The Age of Mackenzie King: The Rise of the Leader*, (Heinemann, London, 1955).

Graham, R., *Arthur Meighen*, vol. 1, *The Door of Opportunity*, (Clarke Irwin, Toronto, 1960); vol. 2, *And Fortune Fled*, (Clarke Irwin, Toronto, 1963); vol. 3, *No Surrender*, (Clarke Irwin, Toronto, 1965).

Gwyn, R., *Smallwood, The Unlikely Revolutionary*, (McClelland and Stewart, Toronto, 1968).

Hunt, Russell, and Robert Campbell, *K.C. Irving, The Art of the Industrialist*, (McClelland and Stewart, Toronto, 1973).

Hutchison, B., *The Incredible Canadian*, (Longmans Green, Toronto, 1952).

_____ , *Mr. Prime Minister, 1867–1964*, (Longmans Canada, Toronto, 1964).

Institut canadien des affaires publiques, *Nos Hommes politiques*, (Editions du jour, Montréal, 1964).

Johnson, L.P.V., and Ola MacNutt, *Aberhart of Alberta*, (Institute of Applied Arts, Edmonton, 1970).

LaMarsh, Judy, *Memoirs of a Bird in a Gilded Cage*, (McClelland and Stewart, Toronto, 1969).

Laporte, P., *The True Face of Duplessis*, (Harvest House, Montreal, 1960).

La Roque, H., *Camillien Houde, le p'tit gars de Ste Marie*, (Les éditions de l'homme, Montréal, 1961).

MacInnis, G., *J.S. Woodsworth, A Man to Remember*, (Macmillan, Toronto, 1953).

MacQuarrie, Heath (ed.), *Robert Laird Borden*, (Carleton Library, McClelland and Stewart, Toronto, 1969), 2 vols.

McGregor, F.A., *The Fall and Rise of Mackenzie King: 1911–1919*, (Macmillan, Toronto, 1962).

McKenty, N., *Mitch Hepburn*, (McClelland and Stewart, Toronto, 1967).

McNaught, K., *A Prophet in Politics: A Biography of J.S. Woodsworth*, (University of Toronto Press, Toronto, 1959).

Neatby, H.B., *William Lyon Mackenzie King, 1924–1932: The Lonely Heights*, vol. 2, (University of Toronto Press, 1963).

Newman, P.C., *Renegade in Power: The Diefenbaker Years*, (McClelland and Stewart, Toronto, 1963).

Pearson, Lester B., *Mike: The Memoirs of the Rt. Hon. Lester B. Pearson*, vol. 1: 1897–1948, (University of Toronto Press, Toronto, 1972), vol. 2 (1973), vol. 3 (1975).

Pickersgill, J.W., *The Mackenzie King Record*, (University of Toronto Press, Toronto), vol. 1, 1939–1944, (1960); with D. Forster, vol. 2, 1944–1945, (1968), vol. 3, (1970).

Roberts, L., *C.D.: The Life and Times of Clarence Decatur Howe*, (Clarke, Irwin, Toronto, 1957).

——————, *The Chief: A Political Biography of Maurice Duplessis*, (Clarke, Irwin, Toronto, 1963).

Schull, J., *Laurier, The First Canadian*, (Macmillan, Toronto, 1965).

Schultz, H.J., "Portrait of a Premier: William Aberhart," *Canadian Historical Review*, vol. 45, no. 3, Sept., 1964.

Sévigny, P., *This Game of Politics*, (McClelland and Stewart, Toronto, 1965).

Shaw, B. (ed.), *The Gospel According to Saint Pierre*, (Trudeau), (Pocket Books, Simon and Schuster, Richmond Hill, 1969).

Sherman, P., *Bennett*, (McClelland and Stewart, Toronto, 1966).

Smith, Denis, *Gentle Patriot: A political biography of Walter Gordon*, (Hurtig, Edmonton, 1973).

Smallwood, Hon. J.R., *I Chose Canada: The Memoirs of the Honourable Joseph R. "Joey" Smallwood*, (Macmillan, Toronto, 1973).

Steeves, D.G., *The Compassionate Rebel: Ernest E. Winch and His Times*, (Evergreen Press, Vancouver, 1960).

Stevens, Geoffrey, *Stanfield*, (McClelland and Stewart, Toronto, 1973).

Stewart, M., and D. French, *Ask No Quarter: A Biography of Agnes MacPhail*, (Longmans Green, Toronto, 1959).

Thomson, D.C., *Alexander Mackenzie: Clear Grit*, (Macmillan, Toronto, 1960);

——————, *Louis St. Laurent: Canadian*, (Macmillan, Toronto, 1967).

Van Dusen, T., *The Chief*, (Diefenbaker), (McGraw–Hill, Toronto, 1968).

Wallace, W.S., *The Macmillan Dictionary of Canadian Biography*, 3rd ed., (Macmillan, Toronto, 1963).

Ward, N. (ed.), *A Party Politician: The Memoirs of Chubby Power*, (Macmillan, Toronto, 1966).

Watkins, E., *R.B. Bennett*, (Kingswood House, Toronto, 1963).

INTEREST GROUPS

Almond, Gabriel, "Interest Groups and the Political Process" in R.C. Macridis and B.E. Brown, *Comparative Politics*, (Dorsey Press, Homewood, Ill., 1964).

Axworthy, Lloyd, "The Housing Task Force—A New Policy Instrument," (Unpublished paper read at the Canadian Political Science Association, Winnipeg, June 4, 1970).

Badgley, Robin F., and Samuel Wolff, *Doctors' Strike*, (Macmillan, Toronto, 1967), pp. 133–153.

Beland, F., "L'Anti-Congrès", *Recherches Sociographiques*, vol. 13, no. 3, 1972.

Belanger, P.R., and L. Maheu, "Pratique politique étudiante au Québec", *Recherches Sociographiques*, vol. 13, no. 3, 1972.

Bentley, A.F., *The Process of Government*, (Belknap Press of Harvard University Press, Cambridge, 1967). Edited by Peter Odegard.

Cameron, *et al.*, "A Crisis in the Organization of Health Care" in Richard Laskin (ed.), *Social Problems: a Canadian Profile*, (McGraw-Hill, New York, 1964), pp. 330–360.

Cardinal, Harold, *The Unjust Society*, (Hurtig, Edmonton, 1969).

Clark, S.D., "Group Interests in Canadian Politics," in J.H. Aitchison, *The Political Process in Canada*, (University of Toronto Press, Toronto, 1963).

_____ , *The Canadian Manufacturers' Association*, (University of Toronto Press, Toronto, 1939).

Corbett, D.C., "The Pressure Groups and the Public Interest" in R.E. Hodgetts and D.C. Corbett (eds.), *Canadian Public Administration*, (Macmillan, Toronto, 1960).

Dawson, H.J., "The Canadian Federation of Agriculture," *Canadian Public Administration*, vol. 3, 1960, pp. 134–149.

_____ , "The Consumers' Association of Canada," *Canadian Public Administration*, vol. 6, no. 1, March 1963.

_____ , "Relations Between Farm Organizations and the Civil Service in Canada and Great Britain," *Canadian Public Administration*, vol. 10, no. 4, Dec. 1967.

Dion, Léon, *Société et politique—le Vie des Groupes: Tome 1, Fondements de la société libérale; Tome 2, Dynamique de la société libérale*, (Les Presses de l'Université Laval, Québec, 1971).

Doern, G.B., *Science and Politics in Canada*, (McGill–Queen's Press, Montreal, 1971).

Eckstein, Harry, *Pressure Group Politics*, (Allen and Unwin, London, 1960).

_____ , "Group Theory and the Comparative Study of Pressure Groups" in H. Eckstein and D. Apter (eds.), *Comparative Politics*, (The Free Press, Glencoe, 1963).

Engelmann, Frederick C., and Mildred A. Schwartz, *Political Parties and the Canadian Social Structure*, (Prentice–Hall, Toronto, 1967), ch. 5, pp. 92–114.

Finer, S.E., *Anonymous Empire*, (Pall Mall Press, London, 1958).

Goffman, Irving, "Canadian Social Welfare Policy" in Nathan Keyfitz, *Contemporary Canada*, Richard H. Leach (ed.), Duke University Press, Durham, 1968), pp. 191–224.

Gouldner, Janet W., "The Doctors Strike: Change and Resistance to Change in Saskatchewan" in Seymour Martin Lipset (ed.), *Agrarian Socialism*, (Anchor Books, Doubleday, Garden City, 1968), pp. 393–404.

Horowitz, Gad, *Canadian Labour in Politics*, (University of Toronto Press, Toronto, 1968).

Krueger, Cynthia, "Praise Protest: the Medicare Conflict in Saskatchewan" in Seymour Martin Lipset (ed.), *Agrarian Socialism*, (Anchor Books, Doubleday, Garden City, 1968), pp. 405–434.

Kwavnick, D., "Pressure Group Demands and the Struggle for Organizational Status: The Case of Organized Labour in Canada," *C.J.E.P.S.*, vol. 3, no. 1, March, 1970.

_____ , *Organized Labour and Pressure Politics: The Canadian Labour Congress: 1956–1968*, (McGill–Queen's University Press, Montreal and London, 1972).

Lowi, T.M., *The End of Liberalism*, (W.W. Norton, New York, 1969).

Macridis, Roy, "Groups and Group Theory" in R.C. Macridis and B.E. Brown, *Comparative Politics*, (Dorsey Press, Homewood, Ill., 1964).

Manzer, R., "Selective Inducements and the Development of Pressure Groups," *C.J.P.S.*, vol. 2, March, 1969, p. 103.

Park, L.C. and F.W. Park, *Anatomy of Big Business in Canada*, (James, Lewis & Samuel, Toronto, 1973).

Porter, John, *The Vertical Mosaic*, (University of Toronto Press, Toronto, 1965), ch. 17, pp. 520–558.

Presthus, Robert, "Interest groups and the Canadian Parliament: activities, interaction, legitimacy and influence," *Canadian Journal of Political Science*, vol. 4, no. 4, December 1972.

——————, *Elite Accommodation in Canadian Politics*, (Macmillan, Toronto 1973).

Pross, A. Paul, *Pressure Group Behaviour in Canadian Politics*, (McGraw–Hill Ryerson, Toronto, 1975).

Taylor, Malcolm G., "The Role of the Medical Profession in the Formulation and Execution of Public Policy," *Canadian Public Administration*, vol. 3, 1960, pp. 233–55.

Thorburn, H.G., "Pressure Groups in Canadian Politics," *C.J.E.P.S.*, vol. 30, 1964, pp. 157–174.

Truman, David Bicknell, *The Governmental Process*, (Knopf, New York, 1951).

Zeigler, Harmon, *Interest Groups in American Society*, (Prentice–Hall, Englewood Cliffs, 1964).

THE AUTHORITIES AND ELITES OF THE CANADIAN POLITICAL SYSTEM

Many of the political biographies listed on pp. 492–494 are relevant here since they present descriptions and background information on many of Canada's more important politicians. In addition, see:

Dion, Leon, "The Concept of Political Leadership: An Analysis," *Canadian Journal of Political Science*, vol. 1, no. 1, March 1968.

Fox, Paul, "The Representative Nature of the Canadian Cabinet" in Paul Fox (ed.), *Politics: Canada*, (McGraw–Hill, Toronto, 1970).

Gibson, F.W. (ed.), *Cabinet Formation and Bicultural Relations*, Royal Commission on Bilingualism and Biculturalism, Study no. 6, (Queen's Printer, Ottawa, 1970).

Hockin, Thomas A., *Apex of Power: The Prime Minister and Political Leadership in Canada*, (Prentice–Hall, Scarborough, Ont., 1971).

Irvine, William P., *Cultural Conflict in Canada: the Erosion of Consociational Politics*, (University Microfilms, Ann Arbor, Mich., 1973).

Kornberg, Allan, *Canadian Legislative Behavior: a Study of the 25th Parliament*, (Holt, Rinehart and Winston, New York, 1967).

——————, "Parliament in Canadian Society" in A. Kornberg, Lloyd A. Musolf *et al.*, *Legislatures in Developmental Perspective*, (Duke University Press, Durham, 1970).

——————, "The Social Basis of Leadership in a Canadian House of Commons," *Australian Journal of Politics*, Dec. 1965.

Kornberg, Allan, and Norman C. Thomas, "The Political Socialization of National Legislative Elites in the United States and Canada," *Journal of Politics*, Nov., 1965.

——————, "Representative Democracy and Political Elites in Canada and the United States," *Parliamentary Affairs*, Winter, 1966.

Kornberg, Allan, and H.H. Winsbrough, "The Recruitment of Canadian Members of Parliament," *American Political Science Review*, Dec. 1968.

Laponce, J.A., "The Religious Background of Canadian M.P.'s," *Political Studies*, vol. 1, 1958.

MacQuarrie, H.N., "The Formation of Borden's First Cabinet," *C.J.E.P.S.*, vol. 23, 1957.

McRae, K.D. (ed.), *Consociational Democracy*, (McClelland and Stewart, Toronto, 1974).

Noel, S.J.R., "Consociational democracy and Canadian federalism," *C.J.P.S.*, vol. 4, no. 1, March 1971.

Porter, John, *The Vertical Mosaic*, (University of Toronto Press, Toronto, 1965).

Presthus, Robert, *Elite Accommodation in Canadian Politics*, (Macmillan, Toronto, 1974).

Royal Commission on Bilingualism and Biculturalism—many of the studies and working papers prepared for the Royal Commission bear incidentally on the composition of decision-making elites in Canada. Studies such as

Beattie, C., J. Desy, and S. Longstaff, *Bureaucratic Careers, Anglophones and Francophones in the Canadian Public Service*,

or

Chartrand, P.J., and K.L. Pond, *A Study of Executive Career Paths in the Public Service of Canada*,

or

Van Loon, R.J., *The Structure and Membership of the Canadian Cabinet*,

are particularly relevant. Five copies of all internal studies have been deposited in the National Library, Ottawa and a complete listing is available there. In addition a nearly complete listing together with a short description of each report can be found in Volume 1 of the Report of the Royal Commission. Some studies have been published separately by the Queen's Printer. These are listed under the authors' names in the appropriate parts of this bibliography.

Schindeler, F., "The Ontario Cabinet: Definition, Size and Representative Nature," *Canadian Public Administration*, vol. 9, 1966.

Ward, Norman, *The Canadian House of Commons: Representation*, 2nd ed., (University of Toronto Press, Toronto, 1963).

Ward, Norman, and David Hoffman, *Bilingualism and Biculturalism in the Canadian House of Commons*, Royal Commission on Bilingualism and Biculturalism, Study no. 3, (Queen's Printer, Ottawa, 1970).

CABINET AND POLICY

Abel, Albert S., "Administrative Secrecy," *Canadian Public Administration*, vol. 11, no. 4, 1968, pp. 440–448.

Banks, M.A., "Privy Council, Cabinet, and Ministry in Britain and Canada: a Story of Confusion," *C.J.E.P.S.*, vol. 31, May, 1965, See also: "Comments," *ibid.*, vol. 31, no. 4, and vol. 32, no. 1.

Barbe, Raoul P., "Le contrôle parlementaire des enterprises au Canada," *Canadian Public Administration*, vol. 12, no. 4.

Barlow, J.S., "Cybernetics, Technology and the Humanities: a View from the Threshold," *Technology Review*, Oct.–Nov., 1968.

Birch, Anthony Harold, *Representative and Responsible Government*, (University of Toronto Press, Toronto, 1964).

Burke, Sister T.A., "Mackenzie and His Cabinet, 1873–1878," *Canadian Historical Review*, vol. 41, no. 2, June, 1960.

Canada, Department of Justice, *The Composition of Legislation*, by Elmer A. Driedger, (Queen's Printer, Ottawa, 1957).

Canada, Parliament, House of Commons, Standing Committee on Miscellaneous

Estimates, *Minutes of Proceedings and Evidence Respecting Bill C-172, an Act to Amend the Financial Administrative Act*, (Queen's Printer, Ottawa, 1969).

——————, *Planning, Programming, Budgeting Guide*, (Queen's Printer, Ottawa, 1968).

——————, Royal Commission on Government Organization, *Report*, (Queen's Printer, Ottawa, 1962–1963), vol. 1.

Canada, Parliament, House of Commons, 28th Parliament, *Report of the Committee on Statutory Instruments*, (Queen's Printer, Ottawa, 1969).

Corry, J.A., "The Prospects for the Rule of Law: Some Recent Developments in the Machinery of the Central Executive," *C.J.E.P.S.*, vol. 21, 1955, pp. 405–415.

Dawson, Robert M., "Cabinet, Position and Personnel," *C.J.E.P.S.*, vol. 12, 1946, pp. 261–281.

——————, *William Lyon Mackenzie King: a Political Biography*, (University of Toronto Press, Toronto, 1958–63), vol. 1, ch. 13.

Doern, G.B., *Scientists and the Making of Science Policies in Canada*, (Unpublished Ph.D. thesis, Queen's University, 1969).

——————, "Mr. Trudeau, the Science Council and P.P.B.: Recent Changes in the Philosophy of Policy Making in Canada." (A paper prepared for the Annual Meeting of the Canadian Political Science Association, June 3, 1970, Winnipeg, Manitoba).

——————, *Political Policy-Making: A Commentary on the Economic Council's Eighth Annual Review and the Ritchie Report*, (Private Planning Association, Montreal, 1972).

——————, "Recent Changes in the Philosophy of Policy-Making in Canada," *Canadian Journal of Political Science*, vol. 4, no. 2, June 1971.

Doern, G.B., and Peter Aucoin, *The Structures of Policy Making in Canada*, (Macmillan, Toronto, 1971).

Doern, G.B. and V.S. Wilson, *Issues in Canadian Public Policy*, (Macmillan, Toronto, 1974).

Dror, Yehenzkel, "Policy Analyst: a New Professional Role in Government Service," *Public Administration Review*, vol. 27, Sept., 1967, pp. 197–203.

——————, *Public Policy Making Reexamined*, (Chandler Publishing Co., San Francisco, 1968).

Etzioni, A., "Mixed Scanning: a 'Third' Approach to Decision-making," *Public Administration Review*, vol. 27, Dec., 1967, pp. 385–392.

Forsey, Eugene, "Mr. King and Parliamentary Government," *C.J.E.P.S.*, vol. 17, 1951, pp. 451–467.

——————, "Meetings of the Queen's Privy Council for Canada, 1867–1882." (Address to the 38th Annual Meeting of the Canadian Political Science Association, Sherbrooke, Quebec, June 8, 1966).

Gibson, F.W. (ed.), *Cabinet Formation and Bicultural Relations: Seven Case Studies*, Studies of the Royal Commission on Bilingualism and Biculturalism, no. 6, (Queen's Printer, Ottawa, 1970).

Golembiewski, Robert T. (ed.), *Public Budgeting and Finance*, (Peacock Publishers, Ithaca, Ill., 1968).

Gow, Donald John Lutton, *Canadian Federal Administration and Political Institutions: a Role Analysis*, (unpublished Ph.D. dissertation, Queen's University, Kingston, 1967).

Halliday, W.E.D., "The Executive and the Government of Canada," *Canadian Public Administration*, vol. 2, Dec., 1959, pp. 229–241.

——————, "The Privy Council Office and Cabinet Secretariat" in J.E. Hodgetts, and D.C. Corbett (eds.), *Canadian Public Administration*, (Macmillan, Toronto, 1960), pp. 108–119.

Harris, J.P., "Legislative Control of Expenditure : the Public Accounts Committee of the British House of Commons, *Canadian Public Administration*, vol. 2, Sept., 1959, pp. 113–131.

Hawkins, Freda, *Canada and Immigration: Public Policy and Public Concern*, (McGill–Queen's University Press, Montreal, 1972).

Heeney, A.D.P., "Cabinet Government in Canada," *C.J.E.P.S.*, vol. 12, 1946, pp. 282–301.

_____ , "Mackenzie King and the Cabinet Secretariat," *Canadian Public Administration*, vol. 10, 1967, pp. 366–375.

Hockin, Thomas A. (ed.), *Apex of Power: the Prime Minister and Political Leadership in Canada*, (Prentice–Hall, Scarborough, Ont., 1971).

Hodgetts, J.E., "Parliament and the Powers of the Cabinet," *Queen's Quarterly*, vol. 52, 1945, pp. 465–477.

_____ , "The Civil Servant and Policy Formulation," *C.J.E.P.S.*, vol. 23, no. 4, pp. 470–473.

Hopkins, E.R., "Administrative Justice in Canada," *Canadian Bar Review*, vol. 17, 1939, pp. 619–637.

Jackson, Robert J. and Michael M. Atkinson, *The Canadian Legislative System*, (Macmillan, Toronto, 1975).

Johnson, A.W., "The Treasury Board of Canada and the Machinery of Government of the 1970's," *Canadian Journal of Political Science*, vol. 4, no. 3, September 1971.

Jones, G.W., "The Prime Minister's Powers," *Parliamentary Affairs*, vol. 18, no. 2, Spring, 1965.

Kersell, John E., *Parliamentary Supervision of Delegated Legislation; the United Kingdom, Australia, New Zealand and Canada*, (Stevens, London, 1960).

_____ , "Parliamentary Debate of Delegated Legislation," *Canadian Public Administration*, vol. 2, 1959, pp. 132–144.

Knight, K.W., "Administrative Secrecy and Ministerial Responsibility," *C.J.E.P.S.*, vol. 32, no. 1, 1966, pp. 77–83.

Lalonde, M., "The changing role of the Prime Minister's Office," *Canadian Public Administration*, vol. 14, no. 4, Winter, 1971.

LaMarsh, Judy, *Memoirs of a Bird in a Gilded Cage*, (McClelland and Stewart, Toronto, 1969).

Lamontagne, M., "The Influence of the Politician," *Canadian Public Administration*, vol. 11, no. 3, 1968, pp. 263–271.

Lévesque, R., *Program Budgeting in the Canadian Government*, (M.A. thesis, Carleton University, 1969).

Lipset, Seymour Martin, *Agrarian Socialism*, (Anchor Books, Doubleday, Garden City, 1968), ch. 12.

Lloyd, T., "The Reform of Parliamentary Proceedings" in Abraham Rotstein, *The Prospect of Change*, (McGraw–Hill, Toronto, New York, 1965).

MacQuarrie, H.N., "The Formation of Borden's First Cabinet," *C.J.E.P.S.*, vol. 23, no. 1, Feb., 1957.

Mallory, J.R., "Cabinet Government in Canada," *Political Studies*, vol. 2, pp. 142–153.

_____ , "Delegated Legislation in Canada: Recent Changes in Machinery," *C.J.E.P.S.*, vol. 19, 1953, pp. 462–67.

_____ , "The Minister's Office Staff: an Unreformed Part of the Public Service," *Canadian Public Administration*, vol. 10, no. 1, 1967, pp. 25–34.

McIlwain, C.H., "Constitutional History and the Present Crisis of Constitutionalism," *C.J.E.P.S.*, vol. 7, 1941, pp. 147–153.

McKeough, W. Darcy, "The Relations of Ministers and Civil Servants," *Canadian Public Adminstration*, vol. 12, no. 1.

Millward, R.E., "P.P.B.S.: Problems of Implementation," *Journal of the American Institute of Planners*, March, 1968, p. 88.

Morton, W.L., "The Formation of the First Federal Cabinet," *Canadian Historical Review*, vol. 36, no. 2, June, 1955.

Newman, Peter Charles, *The Distemper of Our Times; Canadian Politics in Transition, 1963–1968*, (McClelland and Stewart, Toronto, 1968).

——————, *Renegade in Power; the Diefenbaker Years*. (McClelland and Stewart, Toronto, 1963).

O'Leary, D., "The Cabinet Revolt—How They Tried to Get Rid of Diefenbaker," *Canadian Commentary*, July–August, 1963.

Ondaatje, C., and D. Swainson, *The Prime Ministers of Canada, 1867–1968: Macdonald to Trudeau*, (General Publishing, Toronto, 1967).

"Planning-Programming-Budgeting System: A Symposium," *Public Administration Review*, vol. 26, 1966.

Porter, John, *The Vertical Mosaic*, (University of Toronto Press, Toronto, 1965), pp. 386–416.

Robertson, R.G., "The Canadian Parliament and Cabinet in the Face of Modern Demands," *Canadian Public Administration*, vol. 11, 1968, p. 272.

——————, "The Changing Role of the Privy Council Office," *Canadian Public Administration*, vol. 14, no. 4, Winter 1971.

Robinson, Albert J., and James Cutt, *Public Finance in Canada: Selected Readings*, (Methuen, Toronto, 1968).

Rowan, M., "A Conceptual Framework for Government Policy-Making," *Canadian Public Administration*, vol. 13, no. 3, pp. 277–296.

Rowat, D.C., "Administrative Secrecy and Ministerial Responsibility: a Reply," *C.J.E.P.S.*, vol. 32, no. 1, 1966, pp. 84–87.

——————, "How Much Administrative Secrecy?" *C.J.E.P.S.*, vol. 32, no. 4, 1965, pp. 479–498.

Rutherford, G.S., "Delegation of Legislative Power to the Lieutenant-Governors in Council," *Canadian Bar Review*, vol. 26, 1948, pp. 533–544.

Schindeler, F., "The Prime Minister and the Cabinet" in T. Hockin (ed.), *Apex of Power*, (Prentice–Hall, Toronto, 1971).

Schindeler, Fred, and C.M. Lamphier, "Social Science Research and Participatory Democracy in Canada," *Canadian Public Administration*, vol. 12, no. 4, Winter, 1969, pp. 481–498.

Scott, F.R., "Administrative Law: 1923–1947," *Canadian Bar Review*, vol. 26, 1948, pp. 268–285.

Sharp, Mitchell, "The Bureaucratic Elite and Policy Formation," in W.D.K. Kernaghan (ed.), *Bureaucracy in Canadian Government*, (Methuen, Toronto, 1969).

Silk, E.H., "The Publication of Regulations and other Delegated Legislation," *Canadian Bar Review*, vol. 20, 1942, pp. 604–615.

Smith, Denis, "President and Parliament: The Transformation of Parliamentary Government in Canada," in O. Kruhlak *et al.* (eds.), *The Canadian Political Process*, (Holt, Rinehart and Winston, Toronto, 1970).

Ward, Norman, *The Public Purse*, (University of Toronto Press, Toronto, 1962).

White, W.L., and J.C. Strick, *Policy, Politics and the Treasury Board in Canadian Government*, (Science Research Associates, Don Mills, Ont., 1971).

Wildavsky, Aaron B., *The Politics of the Budgetary Process*, (Little, Brown, Boston, 1964).

Willms, Abraham M., and W.D.K. Kernaghan (eds.), *Public Administration in Canada*, (Methuen, Toronto, 1968), pp. 168–215.

FEDERALISM AND PUBLIC POLICY

A. Intergovernmental Institutions

Atkey, R.G., "The role of the provinces in international affairs," *International Journal*, vol. 26, no. 1, Winter 1970–71.

Black, E.R., and A.C. Cairns, "A Different Perspective on Canadian Federalism," *Canadian Public Administration*, vol. 9, no. 1, 1966, pp. 27–44.

Brewis, T.N., and Gilles Paquet, "Regional Development and Planning in Canada: an Exploratory Essay," *Canadian Public Administration*, vol. 11, Summer, 1968, pp. 123–162.

Canada, Constitutional Conference, Ottawa, February 5–7, 1968, *Proceedings*, (Queen's Printer, Ottawa, 1968).

_____ , February 10–12,1969, *Proceedings*, (Queen's Printer, Ottawa, 1969).

Canada, Constitutional Conference, *Report of the Continuing Committee of Officials to the Constitutional Conference*, Privy Council Office, December, 1968.

_____ , Secretariat of the Constitutional Conference, *A Briefing Paper on Discussion Within the Continuing Committee of Officials*, December, 1968.

_____ , Constitutional Conference, First Working Session, *Report of the Conclusions of the Meeting*, June 11–12, 1969.

Canada, Federal–Provincial Relations Division, *Federal–Provincial Grants and the Spending Power of Parliament*, (Queen's Printer, Ottawa, June, 1969).

_____ , *Taxing Power and the Constitution of Canada*, (Queen's Printer, Ottawa, June 1969).

Canada, Prime Minister, *Federalism for the Future; a Statement of Policy by the Government of Canada*, (Queen's Printer, Ottawa, 1968).

Cole, Taylor, *The Canadian Bureaucracy and Federalism*, 1947–1965, (University of Denver, Denver, 1966).

Cole, R.T., "The universities and governments under Canadian federalism," *Journal of Politics*, vol. 34, no. 2, May 1972.

Dehem, R., *Planification économique et fédéralisme*, (Laval, Quebec, 1968).

Doern, G.B., "Canadian Intergovernmental Liaison: Tax Agreements, Fiscal Policy and Conditional Transfers," (a paper prepared in the Institute of Intergovernmental Relations, Queen's University).

Dupré, J. Stefan, Graeme McKechnie, David M. Cameron, and Theodore B. Rotenberg, *Federalism and Policy Development, The Case of Adult Occupational Training in Ontario*, (University of Toronto Press, Toronto, 1973).

Gallant, Edgar, "The Secretariat to the Constitutional Conference," in W.D.K. Kernaghan (ed.), *Bureaucracy in Canadian Government*, (Methuen, Toronto, 1969).

Gallant, E., and R.M. Burns, "The Machinery of Federal–Provincial Relations: I and II," *Canadian Public Administration*, vol. 8, no. 4, 1965, pp. 515–534.

Goffman, Irving J., "Canadian Social Welfare Policy," in Richard H. Leach (ed.), *Contemporary Canada*, (Duke University Press, Durham, 1968), pp. 191–224.

Groisat, M., "Planification et fédéralisme," *Canadian Public Administration*, vol. 11, no. 3.

Guindon, H. "The Social Evolution of Quebec Reconsidered," *C.J.E.P.S.*, vol. 26, 1960, p. 533.

Hodgetts, J.E., "Regional Interests and Policy in a Federal Structure," *C.J.E.P.S.*, vol. 32, no. 1, Feb., 1966, pp. 3–14.

546 Bibliography

Johnson, A.W., "The Dynamics of Federalism in Canada," *C.J.P.S.*, vol. 1, March, 1968, pp. 18–39.

Jones, Richard, *Community in Crisis: French-Canadian Nationalism in Perspective*, (McClelland and Stewart, Toronto, Montreal, 1967).

Macdonald, John B., *et al.*, *The Role of the Federal Government in Support of Research in Canadian Universities*, (Queen's Printer, Ottawa, 1969). (Canada, Science Secretariat, Special Study, no. 7.)

MacDonald, V.C., *Legislative Power and the Supreme Court in the Fifties*, (Butterworth, Toronto, 1961).

Manzer, Ronald A., "The National Organization of Canadian Education," *Canadian Public Administration*, vol. 11, no. 4, Winter, 1968, pp. 492–508.

Martin, Hon. Paul Joseph James, *Federalism and International Relations*, (Queen's Printer, Ottawa, 1968).

McLarty, R.A., "Organizing for a Federal–Provincial Fiscal Policy," *Canadian Tax Journal*, vol. 15, no. 4, 1967, pp. 412–420.

McWhinney, E., "The New Pluralistic Federalism in Canada," *La Revue Juridique Thémis*, vol. 2, 1967.

Ontario Advisory Committee on Confederation, *The Confederation Challenge, Background Papers and Reports*, Volumes I and II.

Paltiel, K.Z., "Federalism and Party Finance: a Preliminary Sounding," in Canada, Committee on Election Expenses, *Studies in Canadian Party Finance*, (Queen's Printer, Ottawa, 1966), pp. 1–22.

Porter, J., "Post-industrialism, post-nationalism and post-secondary education," *Canadian Public Administration*, vol. 14, no. 1, Spring 1971.

Le Québec dans le Canada de demain, vol. 1, *Avenir constitutionnel et statut particulier*, vol. 2, *Vers un nouveau partage des pouvoirs*, (Editions du Jour, Montréal, 1967). (Editions du Jour, Publication 62, 63.)

Reagan, M.D., *New Federalism*, (Oxford University Press, New York, 1972).

The Report on Maritime Union Commissioned by the Governments of Nova Scotia, New Brunswick and Prince Edward Island, (Queen's Printer, Fredericton, Halifax, Charlottetown, 1970).

Rowat, D.C., "Relations between universities and governments in Canada," *Journal of Constitutional and Parliamentary Studies*, vol. 5, no. 1, January–March 1971.

Russell, Peter H., *Leading Constitutional Decisions*, rev. ed., (McClelland and Stewart, Toronto, 1973).

Rutan, G.R., "Provincial Participation in Canadian Foreign Relations," *Comparative Political Studies*, Spring 1971.

Scott, F.R., "Centralization and Decentralization in Canadian Federalism," *Canadian Bar Review*, vol. 29, no. 10, Dec., 1951.

Sharp, M., *Federalism and International Conferences on Education*, (Queen's Printer, Ottawa, 1968).

Simeon, Richard E.B., *Federal–Provincial Diplomacy: The Making of Public Policy in Canada*, (University of Toronto Press, Toronto, 1972).

Smiley, Donald Victor, *Conditional Grants and Canadian Federalism*, (Canadian Tax Foundation, Toronto, 1963).

Stein, S.B., "Environment control and different levels of government," *Canadian Public Administration*, vol. 14, no. 1, Spring 1971.

"Symposium on Intergovernmental Relations," *Public Administration Review*, vol. 23, Jan.–Feb., 1968.

Torrelli, M., "Les relations extérieures du Québec," *Annuaire français de Droit international*, vol. 16, 1970.

Weidner, E.W., "Decision-Making in a Federal System" in Aaron B. Wildavsky (ed.), *American Federalism in Perspective*, (Little, Brown, Boston, 1967), pp. 229–255.

B. Federal–Provincial Finance

Benson, E.J., *The Taxing Powers and the Constitution of Canada*, (Queen's Printer, Ottawa, 1969).

Birch, A.H., *Federalism, Finance, and Social Legislation in Canada, Australia, and the United States*, (Clarendon, Oxford, 1955).

Break, G.F., *Intergovernmental Fiscal Relations in the U.S.*, (Brookings Institute, Washington, 1967).

Breton, A., "A Theory of Government Grants," *C.J.E.P.S.*, vol. 31, no. 2, May, 1965. (See also "Notes," *ibid.*, vol. 32, no. 2, May, 1966; A. Breton, "A Theory of the Demand for Public Goods," *ibid.*, vol. 32, no. 4, Nov., 1966, and "Notes," *ibid.*, vol. 33, no. 1, Feb., 1967.

Brydon, Marion H., *Occupancy of Tax Fields in Canada*, (Canadian Tax Foundation, Toronto, 1965).

Canada, *Dominion–Provincial Conference on Reconstruction: Submission and Plenary Conference Discussion*, (King's Printer, Ottawa, 1946).

Canada, Minister of Finance, *Report of the Tax Structure Committee to the Federal–Provincial Conference of Prime Ministers and Premiers*, Ottawa, February 16–17, 1970.

Canada, *Report of the Royal Commission on Dominion–Provincial Relations* [Rowell–Sirois Report], Book I, *Canada: 1867–1939*, Book II, *Recommendations*, Book III, *Documentation*, (King's Printer, Ottawa, 1940). (Reprinted in one volume, 1954), also Appendices 1–8.

Canada, *Report of the Royal Commission on Taxation*, [Carter Commission], (Queen's Printer, Ottawa, 1966), 6 vols.

Canadian Tax Foundation, *The National Finances. 1965–66* (to 1969–70), Toronto.

Carter, G.C., *Canadian Conditional Grants Since World War II*, (Canadian Tax Foundation, Toronto, 1971).

Clark, D.H., *Fiscal Need and Revenue Equalization Grants*, Canadian Tax Papers No. 49, (Canadian Tax Foundation, Toronto, 1969).

Dehem, R., and J.N. Wolfe, "The Principles of Federal Finance and the Canadian Case," *C.J.E.P.S.*, vol. 21, no. 1, Feb., 1955.

Dupré, J.S., "Tax-Powers vs. Spending Responsibilities: An Historical Analysis of Federal–Provincial Finance," in A. Rotstein (ed.), *The Prospect of Change*, (McGraw–Hill, Toronto, 1965).

—————, "Contracting Out: A Funny Thing Happened on the Way to the Centennial," *Report of the Proceedings of the Eighteenth Annual Tax Conference*, (Canadian Tax Foundation, Toronto, 1965).

Graham, J.F., A.W. Johnson, and J.F. Andrews, *Inter-Government Fiscal Relationships*, Canadian Tax Papers No. 40, (Canadian Tax Foundation, Toronto, Dec. 1964).

Grey, R., "Conditional Grants in Aid," *Proceedings of the Fifth Annual Conference*, (The Institute of Public Administration of Canada, Toronto, 1953).

Hanson, E.J., *Fiscal Needs of the Canadian Provinces*, Canadian Tax Papers No. 23, (Canadian Tax Foundation, Toronto, Feb., 1961).

Johnson, J.A. "Provincial–Municipal Intergovernmental Fiscal Relations," *Canadian Public Administration*, vol. 12, no. 2, Summer, 1968.

Institute of Intergovernmental Relations, *Intergovernmental Liaison on Fiscal and Economic Matters: Report*, (Queen's Printer, Ottawa, 1968).

LaForest, G.V., *Natural Resources and Public Property under the Canadian Constitution*, (University of Toronto Press, Toronto, 1969).

——————— , *The Allocation of Taxing Powers Under the Canadian Constitution*, (Canadian Tax Foundation, Toronto, 1967).

Mackintosh, W.A., "Federal Finance (Canada)," in G. Sawer (ed.), *Federalism: an Australian Jubilee Study*, (F.W. Cheshire, Melbourne, 1952).

——————— , *The Economic Background of Dominion–Provincial Relations*, (McClelland and Stewart, Toronto, 1964).

May, R., *Federalism and Fiscal Adjustment*, (Queen's Printer, Ottawa, 1968).

Moore, A.M., J.H. Perry, and D.I. Beach, *The Financing of Canadian Federation: The First Hundred Years*, Canadian Tax Paper No. 43, (Canadian Tax Foundation, Toronto, 1966).

Musgrave, R.A., *The Theory of Public Finance*, (McGraw–Hill, New York, 1959), Ch. 8.

Nowlan, D.M., "Centrifugally Speaking: Some Economics of Canadian Federalism," in T. Lloyd and J.T. McLeod (eds.), *Agenda 1970*, (University of Toronto Press, Toronto, 1968).

Officer, L.H., and L.B. Smith, *Canadian Economic Problems and Policies*, (McGraw–Hill, Toronto, 1970).

Ontario, Department of Treasury and Economics, *Intergovernmental Policy Coordination and Finance*, Staff Papers, Toronto, 1970.

Ontario, *Report of the Committee on Taxation* [Smith Committee], (Queen's Printer, Toronto, 1967), 3 vols.

Perry, J.H., *Taxation in Canada*, 3rd ed., (University of Toronto Press, Toronto, 1961).

——————— , *Taxes, Tariffs and Subsidies: A History of Canadian Fiscal Development*, (University of Toronto Press, Toronto, 1955), 2 vols.

——————— , "What Price Provincial Autonomy?" *C.J.E.P.S.*, vol. 21, no. 4, Nov., 1955.

Quebec, *Report of the Royal Commission on Taxation*, [Bélanger Report], (Queen's Printer, Quebec, 1965).

Robinson, A.J., and J. Cutt, (eds.), *Public Finance in Canada: Selected Readings*, (Methuen, Toronto, 1968).

Salyzyn, V., "Federal–Provincial Tax Sharing Schemes," *Canadian Public Administration*, vol. 10, no. 2, June, 1967.

Saskatchewan, *Report of the Royal Commission on Taxation*, (Queen's Printer, Regina, 1965).

Saunders, S.A., and E. Back, *The Rowell–Sirois Commission Part 1, A Summary of the Report*, (Ryerson, Toronto, 1940).

Shearer, Ronald (ed.), *Exploiting our Economic Potential*, (Holt, Rinehart and Winston, Toronto, 1968).

Smiley, D.V., "The Rowell–Sirois Report, Provincial Autonomy, and Post-War Canadian Federalism," *C.J.E.P.S.*, vol. 28, no. 1, Feb., 1962.

——————— , *Conditional Grants and Canadian Federalism*, Canadian Tax Paper No. 32, (Canadian Tax Foundation, Toronto, Feb., 1962).

——————— , "Block Grants to the Provinces: A Realistic Alternative?" *Report of the Proceedings of the Eighteenth Annual Tax Conference*, (Canadian Tax Foundation, Toronto, 1965).

——————— , *Constitutional Adaptation and Canadian Federalism Since 1954*, Document 4 of the Royal Commission on Bilingualism and Biculturalism, (Queen's Printer, Ottawa, 1970).

Smiley, D.V., and R.M. Burns, "Canadian Federalism and the Spending Power: Is Constitutional Restriction Necessary?" *Canadian Tax Journal*, vol. 17, no. 6, Nov.–Dec., 1969.

Trudeau, P.E., *Federal–Provincial Grants and the Spending of Power of Parliament*, (Queen's Printer, Ottawa, 1969).
_____ , *Income Security and Social Services*, (Queen's Printer, Ottawa, 1969).

C. The Provinces

Beck, J.M., *The Government of Nova Scotia*, (University of Toronto Press, Toronto, 1957).
Benjamin, J., "La rationalization des choix budgétaires: les cas québecois et canadien," *Revue canadienne de Science politique*, vol. 5, no. 3, September 1972.
Canada, *Report of the Advisory Commission on the Development of Government in the Northwest Territories* [Carrothers' Report], (Queen's Printer, Ottawa, 1966).
Donnelly, M.S., *The Government of Manitoba*, (University of Toronto Press, Toronto 1963).
Duprat, J.-P., "Les institutions québécois," *Revue juridique et économique de Sud-Ouest, Série juridique*, vol. 22, 1971.
Dussault, R., and R. Bernatchez, "La fonction publique canadienne et québecoise," *Canadian Public Administration*, vol. 15, no. 1, Spring 1972.
Dussault, R., and R. Bernatchez, "La fonction publique canadienne et québecoise: suite," *Canadian Public Administration*, vol. 15, no. 2, Summer 1972.
Elton, D.K., (ed.), *One Prairie Province?*, (Lethbridge Herald, Lethbridge, 1970).
Gow, J.I., "Histoire administrative du Québec et théorie administrative," *C.J.P.S.*, vol. 4, no. 1, March 1971.
_____ , "The Modernization of the Quebec Civil Service," *International Review of Administrative Sciences*, vol. 36, no. 3, 1970.
Guindon, H., "Social Unrest, Social Class and Quebec's Bureaucratic Revolution," *Queen's Quarterly*, vol. 17, 1964.
Krueger, R.R., "The Provincial–Municipal Government Revolution in New Brunswick," Canadian Public Administration, vol. 13, no. 1, Spring, 1970.
Kwavnick, David (ed.), *The Tremblay Report*, (McClelland and Stewart, Toronto, 1973).
MacKinnon, F., *The Government of Prince Edward Island*, (University of Toronto Press, Toronto, 1951).
Manitoba, *Report of the Royal Commission on Local Government and Finance*, [Michener Report], (Winnipeg, 1964).
Mathias, Philip, *Forced Growth*, (James, Lewis & Samuel, Toronto, 1971).
Mayo, H.B., "Newfoundland's Entry into the Dominion," *C.J.E.P.S.*, vol. 15, no. 4, Nov., 1949.
Nelles, H.V., *The Politics of Development: Forests, Mines and Hydro Electric Power in Ontario 1849–1941*, (Macmillan, Toronto, 1974).
"Newfoundland, Nation and Province," *Canadian Forum*, Special Issue, March 1974.
Noel, S.J.R., *Politics in Newfoundland*, (University of Toronto Press, Toronto, 1971).
Perry, Robert L., *Galt U.S.A.*, (Maclean–Hunter, Toronto, 1971).
Price, Trevor, (ed.), *Regional Government in Ontario*, (Science Research Associates, Don Mills, 1971).
Schindeler, F.F., *Responsible Government in Ontario*, (University of Toronto Press, 1969).
Swainson, Donald, (ed.), *Oliver Mowat's Ontario*, (Macmillan, Toronto, 1972).
Zaslow, M., "Recent Constitutional Developments in Canada's Northern Territories," *Canadian Public Administration*, vol. 10, no. 2, June, 1967.

CANADIAN BUREAUCRACY

A. The Administrative Process

Baker, W.A., "Management by Objectives: A Philosophy and Style of Management for the Public Sector," *Canadian Public Administration*, vol. 12, 1969.

Balls, H.R., "Improving Performance of Public Enterprise through Financial Management and Control," *Canadian Public Administration*, vol. 13, no. 1, Spring, 1970.

Benning, J.A., "Canadian University Service Overseas and Administrative Decentralization", *Canadian Public Administration*, vol. 12, no. 4.

Bieler, J.H., R.M. Burns, and A.W. Johnson, "The Role of the Deputy Minister," *Canadian Public Administration*, vol. 4, no. 4, Dec., 1961.

Bridges, The Rt. Hon. Lord, "The Relationship Between Ministers and the Permanent Departmental Head," *Canadian Public Administration*, vol. 7, no. 3, Sept., 1964.

DesRoches, J.M., "The Evolution of the Organization of Federal Government in Canada," *Canadian Public Administration*, vol. 5, no. 4, Dec., 1962.

Donnelly, M.S., *et al.*, "Aspects of Municipal Administration: A Symposium," *Canadian Public Administration*, vol. 11, no. 1, Spring, 1968.

Forrest, D.G., "Performance Appraisal in Government Service," *Canadian Public Administration*, vol. 12, no. 3, Fall, 1969.

Gérin-Lajoie, P., "CIDA in a changing government organization," *Canadian Public Administration*, vol. 15, no. 1, Spring, 1972.

Heeney, Arnold D.P., *Things that are Ceasar's: Memoirs of a Canadian Public Servant*, (University of Toronto Press, Toronto, 1972).

Hodgetts, J.E., *Canadian Public Service: A Physiology of Government 1867–1970*, (University of Toronto Press, Toronto, 1973).

Hodgetts, J.E., and D.C. Corbett (eds.), *Canadian Public Administration*, (Macmillan, Toronto, 1960).

Kernaghan, W.D., Kenneth, *Bureaucracy in Canadian Government*, 2nd ed., (Methuen, Toronto, 1973).

————, "An Overview of Public Administration in Canada Today," *Canadian Public Administration*, vol. 11, no. 3, Fall, 1968.

Kernaghan, W.D.K., and A.M. Willms (eds.), *Public Administration in Canada: Selected Readings, 2nd ed., (Methuen, Toronto, 1971)*.

Laframboise, W.L., "Administrative Reform in the federal public service: signs of a saturation psychosis," *Canadian Public Administration*, vol. 14, no. 3, Fall, 1971.

Legault, A., "L'organisation de la défense au Canada," *Études internationales*, vol. 3, no. 2, June, 1972.

Mallory, J.R., "The Minister's Office Staff: An Unreformed Part of the Public Service," *Canadian Public Administration*, vol. 10, no. 1, March, 1967.

McKeough, W. Darcy, "The Relations of Ministers and Civil Servants," *Canadian Public Administration*, vol. 12, no. 1, Spring, 1969.

Rea, K.J., and J.T. McLeod (eds.), *Business and Government in Canada: Selected Readings*, (Methuen, Toronto, 1969).

Ritchie, R.S., A.D.P. Heeney, M.W. MacKenzie, and M.G. Taylor, "The Glassco Commission Report," *Canadian Public Administration*, vol. 5, no. 4, Dec., 1962.

Rowat, Donald C., *The Ombudsman Plan: Essays on the Worldwide Spread of an Idea*, (McClelland and Stewart, Toronto, 1973).

Santos, C.R., "Public Administration as Politics," *Canadian Public Administration*, vol. 12, no. 2, Summer, 1969.

School of Public Administration, *Approaches to the Study of Federal Administrative and Regulatory Agencies, Boards, Commissions and Tribunals*, (Carleton University, Ottawa, 1974).

Shoyama, T.K., "Advisory Committees in Administration," *Proceedings of the Ninth Annual Conference*, (The Institute of Public Administration of Canada, Toronto, 1957).

Stead, G.W., "The Treasury Board of Canada," *Proceedings of the Seventh Annual Conference*, (The Institute of Public Administration of Canada, Toronto, 1955).

Steele, G.G.E., "The Treasury Board as a Control Agency," *Canadian Public Administration*, vol. 4, no. 2, June, 1961.

Tellier, P.M., "Pour une réforme des cabinets de ministres fédéraux," *Canadian Public Administration*, vol. 11, no. 4, Winter, 1968.

Willis, J., J.E. Eades, H.F. Angus, *et al.*, "The Administrator as Judge," *Proceedings of the Eighth Annual Conference*, (The Institute of Public Administration of Canada, Toronto, 1956).

Willms, A.M., "The Administration of Research in the Government of Canada," *Canadian Public Administration*, vol. 10, no. 4, Dec., 1967.

B. The Public Service: Personnel Administration

Armstrong, R., "Some Aspects of Policy Determination in the Development of the Collective Bargaining Legislation in the Public Service of Canada," *Canadian Public Administration*, vol. 11, no. 4, Winter, 1968.

Bauer, F., "The Public Service Staff Relations Act and Collective Bargaining 1967–1969," *Civil Service Review*, vol. 43, no. 2, June, 1970.

Blackburn, G.A., "A Bilingual and Bicultural Public Service," *Canadian Public Administration*, vol. 12, no. 1, Spring, 1969.

Callard, K.B., *Advanced Training in the Public Service*, Governmental Studies Number 1, (The Institute of Public Administration of Canada, Toronto, 1958).

Canada, *Canadian Industrial Relations: The Report of the Task Force on Labour Relations*, (Queen's Printer, Ottawa, 1968).

Canada, *Report of the Preparatory Committee on Collective Bargaining in the Public Service of Canada*, (Queen's Printer, Ottawa, 1965).

Carson, J.J., "The Changing Scope of the Public Servant," *Canadian Public Administration*, vol. 11, no. 4, Winter, 1968.

Civil Service Commission, *Personnel Administration in the Public Service*, Report of the Civil Service Commission of Canada [Heeney Report], 1958.

Cloutier, S., "Le Statut de la Fonction publique du Canada: Son histoire," *Canadian Public Administration*, vol. 10, no. 4, Dec., 1967.

_____ , "Senior Public Service Officials in a Bicultural Society," *Canadian Public Administration*, vol. 11, no. 4, Winter, 1968.

Cole, Taylor, *The Canadian Bureaucracy, 1939–1947*, (Duke University Press, Durham, 1949).

_____ , *The Canadian Bureaucracy and Federalism, 1947–1965*, (University of Denver, Denver, 1966).

Côté, E.A., "The Public Services in a Bicultural Community," *Canadian Public Administration*, vol. 11, no. 3, Fall, 1968.

Coulson, Herbert H., "The Professional Worker and Collective Bargaining," *Civil Service Review*, vol. 41, no. 4, December, 1968.

Crispo, John H.B., (ed.), *Collective Bargaining and the Professional Employee*, (Centre for Industrial Relations: University of Toronto, Toronto, 1965).

DesLauriers, R.C., "First Collective Agreements in the Public Service of Canada," *Civil Service Review*, vol. 41, no. 2, June, 1968.

Deutsch, J.J., "Some Thoughts on the Public Service," *C.J.E.P.S.*, vol. 23, no. 1, Feb., 1957.

—————, "The Public Services in a Changing Society," *Canadian Public Administration*, vol. 11, no. 1, Spring, 1968.

Dowdell, R.H., "Personnel Administration in the Federal Public Service," in A.M. Willms and W.D.K. Kernaghan (eds.), *Public Administration in Canada: Selected Readings*, (Methuen, Toronto, 1968).

Edwards, Claude, "Address to the Conference on Collective Bargaining in Public Employment, San Francisco," *Civil Service Review*, vol. 42, November, 1969.

—————, "Collective Bargaining in Canada between the Federal Government and its Employees," *Civil Service Review*, vol. 43, June, 1970.

—————, "Effects of Collective Bargaining on Staff Associations," *Civil Service Review*, vol. 41, September, 1968.

Finkelman, Jacob, "Some Aspects of Public Service Bargaining in Canada," *Civil Service Review*, vol. 43, no. 1, March, 1970.

Frankel, S.J., *A Model for Negotiation and Arbitration between the Canadian Government and Its Civil Servants*, (McGill University Press, Montreal, 1962).

—————, *Staff Relations in the Civil Service: The Canadian Experience*, (McGill University Press, Montreal, 1962).

Gosselin, E., G. Lalande, G. Dozois, and R. Boyd, "L'administration publique dans un pays bilingue et bicultural: actualités et propos," *Canadian Public Administration*, vol. 6, no. 4, Dec., 1963.

Gow, Donald, "Public Administration Training for Whom? for What?" *Optimum*, vol. 1, no. 3, 1970.

Heeney, Arnold, *The Things that are Caesar's: The Memoirs of a Canadian Public Servant*, (University of Toronto Press, Toronto, 1972).

—————, "Civil Service Reform 1958," *C.J.E.P.S.*, vol. 25, no. 1, Feb., 1959.

Hodgetts, J.E., *Pioneer Public Service: An Administrative History of the United Canadas, 1841–1867*, (University of Toronto Press, Toronto, 1955).

—————, "Challenge and Response: A Retrospective View of the Public Service of Canada," *Canadian Public Administration*, vol. 6, no. 4, Dec., 1964.

—————, William McCloskey, Reginald Whitaker, and V. Seymour Wilson, *The Biography of an Institution: The Civil Service Commission of Canada, 1908–1967*, (McGill–Queen's University Press, Montreal, 1972).

Hodgetts, J.E., and O.P. Dwivedi, "The Growth of Government Employment in Canada," *Canadian Public Administration*, vol. 12, no. 2, Summer, 1969.

Kwavnick, D., "French Canadians and the Civil Service of Canada," *Canadian Public Administration*, vol. 11, no. 1, Spring, 1968.

Laberge, E.P., "Collective Bargaining in the Public Service of Canada," *International Review of Administrative Sciences*, vol. 36, no. 3, 1970.

Robinson, K.R., "Labour Unions in the Armed Forces," *Civil Service Review*, vol. 43, no. 3, September, 1970.

Slivinski, L.W. and B. Desbiens, "Managerial Job Dimensions and Job Profiles in the Canadian Public Service: A Pilot Study," *Studies in Personnel Psychology*, vol. 2, no. 2, October, 1970.

Subramaniam, V., "Representative Bureaucracy: A Reassessment," *American Political Science Review*, December, 1967.

Swettenham, John, and David Kelly, *Serving the State: A History of the Professional In-*

stitute of the Public Service of Canada 1920–1970, (Le Droit, Ottawa, 1970).

"Symposium on Collective Negotiations in the Public Service," *Public Administration Review*, March–April, 1968.

Tunnoch, G.V., "The Bureau of Government Organization," *Canadian Public Administration*, vol. 8, no. 4, Dec., 1965.

Vaison, R.A., "Collective Bargaining in the Federal Public Service: The Achievement of a Milestone in Personnel Relations," *Canadian Public Administration*, vol. 12, no. 1, 1969.

Wilson, V. Seymour, *Staffing in the Canadian Federal Bureaucracy*, (Queen's University, unpublished Ph.D. Thesis, Kingston, 1970).

C. The Budgetary Process

Balls, H.R., "New Techniques in Government Budgeting: Planning, Programming and Budgeting in Canada," *Public Administration*, vol. 48, no. 3, Autumn, 1970.

Bird, Richard M., *The Growth of Government Spending in Canada*, Canadian Tax Papers, no. 51, (Canadian Tax Foundation, Toronto, July, 1970).

Botner, S.B., "Four Years of PPBS: An Appraisal," *Public Administration Review*, July/August, 1970, pp. 423–431.

Brownstone, M., "The Canadian System of Government in the Face of Modern Demands," *Canadian Public Administration*, vol. 11, no. 5, p. 428.

Canada, *Estimates, The Blue Book for the Fiscal Year Ending March 31, 1971*, (Queen's Printer, Ottawa, 1970), or any other year; they have a certain sameness.

Canada, Parliament, House of Commons, Standing Committee on Miscellaneous Estimates, *Minutes of Proceedings and Evidence Respecting Bill C-172—an Act to Amend the Financial Administration Act*, nos. 10–12, (Queen's Printer, Ottawa, 1969).

Canada, Royal Commission on Government Organization, *Report*, vol. 1, (Queen's Printer, Ottawa, 1962–63).

Canada, Task Force on Government Information, *To Know and Be Known*, (Queen's Printer, Ottawa, 1969).

Canadian Tax Foundation, *The National Finances—An Analysis of the Revenues and Expenditures of the Government of Canada*, published annually by the Canadian Tax Foundation, Toronto.

Canada, Treasury Board, *Program Forecast and Estimates Manual*, Program Branch, August 1969. (Includes Revisions 5, 6 and 7.)

Cutt, James, "The Programming Budgeting Approach to Public Expenditure: A Conceptual Review," *Canadian Public Administration*, vol. 13, no. 4.

Doern, G.B., "Mr. Trudeau, The Science Council and P.P.B.: Recent Changes in the Philosophy of Policy Making in Canada." (Paper presented to 42nd Annual Meeting of Canadian Political Science Association, June, 1970).

Harper, E.L., *et al.*, "Implementation and Use of P.P.B. in Sixteen Federal Agencies," *Public Administration Review*, vol. 29, no. 6, pp. 623–632.

Hinrichs, Harley H., and G.M. Taylor (eds.), *Program Budgeting and Cost Benefit Analysis*, (Goodyear Publishing Co., Pacific Palisades, 1969).

Hodgetts, J.E., "The Civil Servant and Policy Formation," *C.J.E.P.S.*, vol. 23, no. 4, 1957, pp. 470–473.

Johnson, A.W., "PPB and Decision Making in the Government of Canada." (Speech to 50th Anniversary Conference of Society of Industrial Accountants, June 18, 1970).

——————— , "The Treasury Board of Canada and the Machinery of Government of the 1970's," *Canadian Journal of Political Science*, vol. 4, no. 3, September, 1971.

Lamontagne, M., "The Influence of the Politician," *Canadian Public Administration*, vol. 11, no. 3, pp. 263–271.

Lévesque, R., *Program Budgeting in the Canadian Government*, (M.A. thesis, Carleton University, 1969).

Lyden, F.J., *Planning, Programming, Budgeting: a Systems Approach to Management*, (Markham, Chicago, 1967).

Millward, R.E., "P.P.B.S.: Problems of Implementation," *Journal of American Institute of Planners*, March, 1968, p. 88.

Normanton, E.L., *The Accountability and Audit of Governments*, (Manchester University Press, Manchester, Eng.; Praeger, New York, 1966).

Novick, David (ed.), *Program Budgeting*, (Harvard University Press, Cambridge, 1965).

"Planning–Programming–Budgeting System: a Symposium," *Public Administration Review*, vol. 26, 1966.

Robinson, A.J., and James Cutt, *Public Finance in Canada: Selected Readings*, (Methuen, Toronto, 1968).

Sharkansky, Ira, *Public Administration Policy Making in Government Agencies*, (Markham, Chicago, 1970).

Strick, J.C., "Recent Development in Canadian Administration," *Public Administration*, vol. 48, Spring, 1970, pp. 69–85.

Ward, Norman, *The Public Purse*, (University of Toronto Press, Toronto 1962).

White, W.L., and J.C. Strick, *Policy, Politics and the Treasury Board in Canadian Government*, (Science Research Associates, Don Mills, Ontario, 1970).

Wildavsky, Aaron B., *The Politics of the Budgetary Process*, (Little, Brown, Boston, 1964).

Willms, Abraham Martin, and W.D.K. Kernaghan, *Public Administration in Canada*, (Methuen, Toronto 1968), pp. 168–215.

D. Crown Corporations

Ashley, C.A., *The First Twenty-five Years: A Study of Trans-Canada Air Lines*, (Macmillan, Toronto, 1963).

Ashley, C.A., and R.G.H. Smails, *Canadian Crown Corporations*, (Macmillan, Toronto, 1965).

Barbe, R.P., "Le contrôle parlementaire des entreprises au Canada," *Canadian Public Administration*, vol. 12, no. 4, Winter, 1969.

Canada, *Report of the Committee on Broadcasting*, [The Fowler Report], (Queen's Printer, Ottawa, 1965).

Corbett, D., *Politics and the Airlines*, (University of Toronto Press, Toronto 1965).

Friedman, W. (ed.), *The Public Corporation: A Comparative Symposium*, (Carswell, Toronto, 1954).

Hull, W.H.N., "The Public Control of Broadcasting: The Canadian and Australian Experiences," *C.J.E.P.S.*, vol. 28, no. 1, February, 1962.

—————— , "The Fowler Report Revisited: A Broadcasting Policy for Canada," (Address to the 38th Annual Meeting of the Canadian Political Science Association, Sherbrooke, Quebec, June, 1966).

Kristjanson, K., "Crown Corporations: Administrative Responsibility and Public Accountability," *Canadian Public Administration*, vol. 11, no. 4, Winter, 1968.

Shea, A.A., *Broadcasting, The Canadian Way*, (Harvest House, Montreal, 1963).

Spry, G., "The Decline and Fall of Canadian Broadcasting," *Queen's Quarterly*, vol. 68, no. 2, Summer, 1961.

Weir, E.A., *The Struggle for National Broadcasting in Canada*, (McClelland and Stewart, Toronto, 1965).

E. Task Forces and Royal Commissions

Axworthy, L., "The Housing Task Force—A New Policy Instrument." (A paper prepared for the 42nd Meeting of the Canadian Political Science Association, Winnipeg, June 4, 1970).

Bryden, M., and M. Gurney, "Royal Commission Costs," *Canadian Tax Journal*, vol. 14, no. 2, 1966.

Courtney, J.C., "Judges as Royal Commissioners," *Dalhousie Review*, vol. 44, no. 4, Winter, 1964–65.

_____ , "In Defense of Royal Commissions," *Canadian Public Administration*, vol. 12, no. 2, 1969.

Cronin, Thomas E., and Sanford D. Greenberg (eds.), *The Presidential Advisory System*, (Harper and Row, New York, 1969).

Dion, Léon, "Politique consultative et système politique," *C.J.P.S.*, vol. 2, no. 2, June, 1969, pp. 226–244.

Doern, G.B., "The Role of Royal Commissions in the General Policy Process and in Federal–Provincial Relations," *Canadian Public Administration*, vol. 10, Dec., 1967.

_____ , "Scientists and Science Policy Machinery" in W.D.K. Kernaghan (ed.), *Bureaucracy in Canadian Government*, (Methuen, Toronto, 1969).

Fowke, V.C., "Royal Commissions and Canadian Agricultural Policy," *C.J.E.P.S.*, vol. 14, 1948.

Gillespie, W.I., "Decision Making by Official Commission" in A.J. Robinson and James Cutt (eds.), *Public Finance in Canada: Selected Readings*, (Methuen, Toronto, 1968), pp. 57–60.

Hanser, Charles J., *Guide to Decision: The Royal Commission*, (Bedminster Press, Totawa, N.J. 1965).

Hanson, H.R., "Inside Royal Commissions," *Canadian Public Administration*, vol. 12, no. 3, 1969.

Henderson, G.F., *Federal Royal Commissions in Canada, 1867–1966: A Checklist*, (University of Toronto Press, Toronto, 1967).

Hodgetts, J.E., "Public Power and Ivory Power" in Trevor Owen Lloyd and Jack McLeod (eds.), *Agenda 1970*, (University of Toronto Press, Toronto, 1968), pp. 256–280.

_____ , "The Role of Royal Commissions in Canadian Government" in Institute of Public Administration of Canada, *Proceedings of the 3rd Annual Conference*, (Toronto, 1951).

_____ , "Should Canada be De-commissioned? A Commoner's View on Royal Commissions," *Queen's Quarterly*, vol. 70, no. 4, Winter 1964.

Lermer, Arthur, "The Case for Social Economic Councils in Canada," (Paper prepared for the Harrison Liberal Conference, Harrison Hot Springs, B.C., Nov. 21–23, 1969).

Lithwick, N.H., "Housing: in Search of a Crisis," *The Canadian Forum*, vol. 49, Feb., 1969, pp. 250–251.

McLeod, T.H., "Glassco Commission Report," *Canadian Public Administration*, vol. 6, 1963.

Mitchell, H., *et al.*, "To Commission or Not to Commission," *Canadian Public Administration*, vol. 5, no. 3, 1962.

New Brunswick, *Participation and Development: The New Brunswick Task Force Report on Social Development and Social Welfare*, (Queen's Printer, Fredericton, 1971).

Rose, Albert, "Paul Hellyer on Housing: Fact or Fiction?" Toronto *Globe and Mail*, Feb. 4 & 5, 1969, p. 7.

Saywell, John T., "The Royal Commission on Bilingualism and Biculturalism," *International Journal*, vol. 20, no. 3, 1965, p. 381.

Schindeler, Fred, and C.M. Lamphier, "Social Science and Participatory Democracy in Canada," *Canadian Public Administration*, vol. 12, no. 4, Winter, 1969, pp. 481–498.

Silcox, P., "The Proliferation of Boards and Commissions" in T. Lloyd, *et al.* (eds.), *Agenda 70*, (University of Toronto Press, Toronto, 1968), p. 115.

Tunnoch, G.V., "The Glassco Commission: Did It Cost More Than It Was Worth?," *Canadian Public Administration*, vol. 7, no. 3, 1964.

Walls, C.E.S., "Royal Commissions—Their Influence on Public Policy," *Canadian Public Administration*, vol. 12, no. 3, 1969.

Willms, A.M., "The Administration of Research on Administration in the Government of Canada," *Canadian Public Administration*, vol. 10, Dec., 1967, pp. 405–416.

Wyman, Ken, Robin Mathews, and G. Lermer, "Articles Reviewing the Task Force Report on Foreign Ownership,'" *Canadian Dimension*, vol. 5, no. 4, April–May, 1968, pp. 15–20.

F. Advisory Councils

Babbitt, John D., *Science in Canada*, (University of Toronto Press, Toronto, 1965).

Burns, R.M., "The Economic Council of Canada: Reflections Prompted by the Fourth Review," *Canadian Tax Journal*, vol. 16, 1968, pp. 600–605.

Canada, Parliament, Senate, Special Committee on Science Policy, *Proceedings*, Phase 1, 27th Parl., 1967–68, and 28th Parl., nos. 1–30 plus subsequent proceedings, (Queen's Printer, Ottawa).

Carter, L.A., "Canadian Science Policy: Doubts Raised About Advisory Apparatus," *Science*, Aug., 1968, p. 450.

Cook, Ramsay, "Loyalism, Technology and Canada's Fate," *Journal of Canadian Studies*, Aug. 1970, pp. 50–59.

Doern, G. Bruce, "The National Research Council: The Causes of Goal Displacement," *Canadian Public Administration*, vol. 13, no. 2, June, 1970.

——————, *Science and Politics in Canada*, (McGill–Queen's University Press, Montreal, 1972).

——————, "The Senate Report on Science Policy: A Political Assessment," *Journal of Canadian Studies*, May, 1971.

——————, "Scientists and Science Policy Machinery," in W.D.K. Kernaghan (ed.), *Bureaucracy in Canadian Government*, (Methuen, Toronto, 1969), chs. 6–11.

——————, "The Political Realities of Science Policy Making in the Federal Government," *Science Forum*, vol. 3, no. 15, June, 1970.

Gilpin, Robert, and Christopher Wright (eds.), *Scientists and National Policy-Making*, (Columbia University Press, New York, 1964).

——————, "Technological Strategies and National Purpose," *Science*, vol. 169, July 31, 1970, pp. 441–448.

Glassco Commission, *Scientific Research and Development*, vol. 4, Report 23, (Queen's Printer, Ottawa, 1962–3).

Gunning, Harry E., "Canadian Science Policy and the OECD Report: a Critical Analysis," *Science Forum*, Dec., 1969, pp. 3–6.

Heller, Walter W., "Economic Policy Advisers," in Thomas E. Cronin and S.D. Greenberg (eds.), *The Presidential Advisory System*, (Harper and Row, New York, 1969), pp. 29–39.

Jackson, R.W., "Major Programs in R & D: Where the Means Justify the Ends," *Science Forum*, vol. 2, no. 2, April, 1969, pp. 10–14.

Kaliski, S.F. (ed.), *Canadian Economic Policy Since The War*, (Canadian Trade Committee, Montreal, 1966).

Line, Richard J., and Arthur J.R. Smith, "Economic Planning For Canada" in M.H. Watkins, and D.F. Forster (eds.), *Economics Canada*, (McGraw–Hill, Toronto, 1963), pp. 35–46. See also pp. 161–167.

Mesthene, E.G., *Technological Change: Its Impact on Man and Society*, (Harvard University Press, Cambridge, 1970).

Organization for Economic Cooperation and Development (OECD), *Reviews of National Science Policy Canada*, (OECD, Paris, 1969).

Paquet, Gilles, "The Economic Council as Phoenix" in Trevor Owen Lloyd, and Jack McLeod (eds.), *Agenda 1970*, (University of Toronto Press, Toronto, 1968), pp. 135–158.

Reid, T.E.H., (ed.), *Economic Planning in a Democratic Society*, Canadian Institute on Public Affairs, 9th Winter Conference, (University of Toronto Press, Toronto, 1963).

Science Council of Canada, *Annual Reports*, 1966 to 1970 inclusive, (Queen's Printer, Ottawa).

Science Council of Canada, Report No. 4, *Towards a National Science Policy for Canada*, Information Canada, Ottawa, 1968).

Skolnikoff, E.B., "The Difficult Political Choices of Science," *World Politics*, April, 1968.

Taylor, K.W., "Fiscal Policy and Economic Growth" in M.H. Watkins and D.F. Forster, *Economics: Canada*, (McGraw–Hill, Toronto, 1963), pp. 161–167.

Thistle, Mel, *The Inner Ring: The Early History of the National Research Council of Canada*, (University of Toronto Press, Toronto, 1966).

Thompson, Wm. I., "Technological Liberalism," *Canadian Forum*, Sept., 1970, pp. 213–214.

Trainor, Lynn, "The Americanization of Canadian Science: How We Lose By Default," *Science Forum*, vol. 3, April, 1970, pp. 3–8.

Watkins, M., "Technology and Nationalism" in Peter Russell (ed.), *Nationalism in Canada*, (McGraw–Hill, Toronto, 1966), pp. 284–302.

PARLIAMENTARY PROCESS

Abel, A.S., "Administrative Secrecy," *Canadian Public Administration*, vol. 11, no. 4, 1968.

Abrams, Matthew J., *The Canada–United States Parliamentary Group*, (Parliamentary Centre for Foreign Affairs/Canadian Institute for International Affairs, Toronto, 1973).

Aitchison, J.H., "The Speakership of the Canadian House of Commons" in Robert Mills Clark (ed.), *Canadian Issues*, (University of Toronto Press, Toronto, 1961), pp. 23–56.

Albinski, H.S., "The Canadian Senate: Politics and the Constitution," *American Political Science Review*, vol. 57, no. 2, June, 1963.

Anderson, S.V., *Canadian Ombudsman Proposals*, (University of California Press, Berkeley, 1966).

Balls, H.R., "The Public Accounts Committee," *Canadian Public Administration*, vol. 6, no. 1, March, 1963.

Bishop, P.V., "Restoring Parliament to Power," *Queen's Quarterly*, vol. 77, no. 2, Summer, 1970.

Blair, Ronald, "What Happens to Parliament" in Trevor Owen Lloyd, and Jack McLeod (eds.), *Agenda 1970*, (University of Toronto Press, Toronto, 1968), pp. 217–240.

Briggs, E.D., "The Senate: Reform or Reconstruction?" *Queen's Quarterly*, vol. 75, no. 1, Spring, 1968.

Brownstone, M., "The Canadian System of Government in the Face of Modern Demands," *Canadian Public Administration*, vol. 11, no. 4, Winter, 1968.

Byers, R.B., "Perceptions of Parliamentary Surveillance of the Executive: The Case of Canadian Defence Policy," *Canadian Journal of Political Science*, vol. 5, no. 2, June, 1972.

Byrne, D., "Some Attendance Patterns Exhibited by Members of Parliament During the 28th Parliament," *Canadian Journal of Political Science*, vol. 5, no. 1, March, 1972.

Cairns, A.C., "The Judicial Committee and Its Critics," *Canadian Journal of Political Science*, vol. 4, no. 3, September, 1971.

Canada, Parliament, House of Commons, *Debates*, (special debate on the broadcasting of House and committee proceedings by television and radio, March 26, 1969), pp. 7158–7179.

————, *Standing Orders of the House of Commons*, Canada, 1962, (Queen's Printer, Ottawa, 1962).

————, Special Committee on Procedure, *Third Report*, (Queen's Printer, Ottawa, 1968).

————, Standing Committee on Procedure and Organization, *Second Report*, (dealing with the establishment of an internship program in the House of Commons). See Votes and Proceedings of House of Commons, no. 138, Apr. 29, 1969.

————, Special Committee on Statutory Instruments, *Proceedings: 28th Parl., 1st Sess.*, (Queen's Printer, Ottawa, 1969).

Canada, *Rules of the Senate of Canada*, (Queen's Printer, Ottawa, 1964).

Connolly, J.J., "The Senate of Canada," *The Parliamentarian*, vol. 53, no. 2, April, 1972.

Corry, J.A., "Adaptation of Parliamentary Processes to the Modern State," *C.J.E.P.S.*, vol. 20, 1954, pp. 1–9.

————, "Arms and the Man," *Queen's Quarterly*, vol. 62, 1955–56, pp. 315–328.

Dawson, Robert MacGregor (ed.), *Constitutional Issues in Canada, 1900–1931*, (Oxford University Press, London, 1933), pp. 218–230.

Dawson, William Foster, *Procedure in the Canadian House of Commons*, (University of Toronto Press, Toronto, 1962). (Canadian government series, 12.)

————, "Parliamentary Privilege in the Canadian House of Commons," *C.J.E.P.S.*, vol. 25, no. 4, Nov. 1959.

————, "Parliamentary Privilege in the Senate of Canada." (Address to the 38th Annual Meeting of the Canadian Political Science Association, Sherbrooke, Quebec, June 8, 1966).

Driedger, E.A., "Legislative Drafting," *Canadian Bar Review*, vol. 27, no. 3, March, 1949, pp. 291–317.

————, "Public Administrators and Legislation," *Canadian Public Administration*, vol. 1, no. 2, 1958, pp. 14–26.

Forsey, Eugene, "The Problem of 'Minority' Government in Canada," *C.J.E.P.S.*, vol. 30, no. 1, Feb., 1964, pp. 1–11.

————, "The Extension of the Life of Legislatures," *C.J.E.P.S.*, vol. 26, no. 4, Nov., 1960.

————, "Parliament's Power to Advise," *C.J.E.P.S.*, vol. 29, no. 2, May, 1963.

Franks, C.E.S., "The Committee Clerks and the Canadian House of Commons," *The Parliamentarian*, vol. 50, no. 2, April, 1969.

_____ , "The Committee System of the Canadian House of Commons." (Paper presented to the Annual Meeting of the Canadian Political Science Association, Toronto, June, 1969).

_____ , "The Legislature and Responsible Government" in Norman Ward and Stafford Duff (eds.), *Politics in Saskatchewan*, (Longman Canada, Toronto, 1968).

_____ , "The Reform of Parliament," *Queen's Quarterly*, vol. 76, no. 1, Spring, 1969.

_____ , "The Dilemma of the Standing Committees of the Canadian House of Commons," *Canadian Journal of Political Science*, vol. 4, no. 4, December, 1971.

Fulton, D., P. Jewett, *et al.*, "Parliament and the Public" in Gordon Hawkins (ed.), *Order and Good Government*, 33rd Couchiching Conference, Canadian Institute on Public Affairs, (University of Toronto Press, Toronto, 1965), pp. 43–90.

Gellhorn, Walter, *When Americans Complain: Governmental Grievance Procedures*, (Harvard University Press, Cambridge, 1966).

Hastings, Sen. Earl A., "Just How the Canadian Senate Spends its Time," Toronto *Globe and Mail*, May 20, 1969, p. 7.

Hawkins, G. (ed.), *Order and Good Government*, Proceedings of a 33rd Couchiching Conference, Canadian Institute on Public Affairs, Toronto, 1965.

Hockin, T.A., "The Advance of Standing Committees in Canada's House of Commons: 1965 to 1970," *Canadian Public Administration*, vol. 13, no. 2, Summer, 1970.

_____ , *Apex of Power: The Prime Minister and Political Leadership in Canada*, (Prentice–Hall, Scarborough, Ontario, 1971).

Hoffman, D., and N. Ward, *Bilingualism and Biculturalism in the Canadian House of Commons*, Document #3 of the Royal Commission on Bilingualism and Biculturalism, (Queen's Printer, Ottawa, 1970).

Hopkins, E.R., "How Parliament Works," *Canadian Banker*, vol. 58, no. 1, Winter, 1951, pp. 69–81.

_____ , "Financial Legislation in the Senate," *Canadian Tax Journal*, vol. 6, no. 5, Sept.–Oct., 1958.

_____ , "Streamlining Parliament," *Canadian Banker*, vol. 60, no. 2, Spring, 1953, pp. 37–48.

Jackson, Robert J., and Michael M. Atkinson, *The Canadian Legislative System*, (Macmillan, Toronto, 1975).

Jennings, Sir William Ivor, *Parliament*, 2nd ed., (Cambridge University Press, Cambridge, 1957), chs. 4–6, 10–11.

Jewett, P., "The Reform of Parliament," *Journal of Canadian Studies*, vol. 1, 1966.

Johnson, H., "Parliamentary Questions and the Conduct of Administration," *Public Administration*, vol. 20, Summer, 1961.

Johnson, J.K. (ed.), *The Canadian Directory of Parliament, 1867–1967*, (Public Archives of Canada, Ottawa, 1968).

Kersell, John E., *Parliamentary Supervision of Delegated Legislation*, (Stevens, London, 1960).

Knowles, Stanley Howard, *The Role of the Opposition in Parliament*, (Woodsworth Memorial Foundation, Ontario, 1957).

Kornberg, Allan, *Canadian Legislative Behavior; a Study of the 25th Parliament*, (Holt, Rinehart and Winston, New York, 1967), ch. 3, pp. 42–62.

_____ , "The Rules of the Game in the Canadian House of Commons," *Journal of Politics*, vol. 26, 1964, pp. 358–80.

——————— , "The Social Bases of Leadership in a Canadian House of Commons," *Australian Journal of Politics and History*, vol. 11, 1965, pp. 324–334.

——————— , *Some Differences in Role Perceptions Among Canadian Legislators*, (University of Michigan Press, Ann Arbor, 1964).

——————— , "Caucus and Cohesion in Canadian Parliamentary Parties," *The American Political Science Review*, vol. 60, no. 1, March, 1966.

——————— , "Parliament in Canadian Society" in Allan Kornberg and Lloyd D. Musolf (eds.), *Legislatures in Comparative Perspective*, (McKay, New York, 1973).

Kornberg, Allan, David Falcone and William Mischler, "Socio-economic Change, Legislative Composition, and Political System Outputs in Canada 1867–1968" in *Sage Series in Comparative Legislatures*, no. 1, November, 1972.

Kornberg, Allan, and N. Thomas, "The Purposive Roles of Canadian and American Legislators: Some Comparisons," *Political Science*, vol. 18, no. 2, Sept., 1965.

Kornberg, A., and N. Thomas, "Representative Democracy and Political Elites in Canada and the United States," *Parliamentary Affairs*, vol. 19, no. 1, Winter, 1965–66.

Krislov, Samuel, and Lloyd D. Musolf (eds.), *The Politics of Regulation: a Reader*, (Houghton Mifflin, Boston, 1964).

Kunz, E.A., *The Modern Senate of Canada, 1925–1963: A Re-appraisal*, (University of Toronto Press, Toronto, 1965).

Lambert, N., "Reform of the Senate," (Winnipeg Free Press, April 1950), pamphlet no. 30.

Lamontagne, M., "The Influence of the Politician," *Canadian Public Administration*, vol. 11, no. 3, Fall, 1968.

Laponce, Jean, "The Religious Background of Canadian MP's," *Political Science*, vol. 6, 1958, pp. 253–58.

Laundry, P., "The Future of the Canadian Speakership," *The Parliamentarian*, vol. 53, no. 2, April, 1972.

Laundry, Philip, "Procedural Reform in the Canadian House of Commons," *The Parliamentarian*, vol. 50, no. 2, April, 1969.

——————— , "Procedural Reform in the Canadian House of Commons," in R.S. Lankster, and D. Dewor (eds.), *The Table: Being the Journal of the Society of Clerks-at-the-Table in Commonwealth Parliaments for 1965*, vol. 34, (Butterworth, London, 1966).

Lee, B., "Age and Criticism Do Not Weary Them," Toronto, *Globe and Mail*, February 7, 1966.

Lees, J.D., "Legislative Review and Bureaucratic Responsibility," *Public Administration*, vol. 26, Winter, 1967.

Lloyd, Trevor, "The Reform of Parliamentary Proceedings" in A. Rotstein (ed.), *The Prospect of Change: Proposals for Canada's Future*, (McGraw–Hill, Toronto, New York, 1965), pp. 23–39.

Lovink, J.A.A., "Who Wants Parliamentary Reform?," *Queen's Quarterly*, vol. 79, no. 4, Winter, 1972.

Lyon, P.V., "A New Idea for Senate Reform," *Canadian Commentator*, July–August, 1962.

Macdonald, Donald S., "Change in the House of Commons—New Rules," *Canadian Public Administration*, vol. 13, no. 1, Spring, 1970.

Mallory, J.R., "Delegated Legislation in Canada: Recent Changes in Machinery," *C.J.E.P.S.*, vol. no. 4, Nov., 1953.

_____ , "The use of Legislative Committees," *Canadian Public Administration*, vol. 6, no. 1, March, 1963.

_____ , "Vacation of Seats in the House of Commons: The Problem of Burnaby-Coquitlam," *C.J.E.P.S.*, vol. 30, no. 1, Feb., 1964.

_____ , "Parliamentary Scrutiny of Delegated Legislation in Canada: A Large Step Forward and a Small Step Back," *Public Law*, Spring, 1972.

Mallory, J.R., and B.A. Smith, "The Legislative Role of Parliamentary Committees in Canada: The Case of the Joint Committee on the Public Service Bills," *Canadian Public Administration*, vol. 15, no. 1, Spring, 1972.

McDonald, D.C., "The Alberta Ombudsman Act," *University of Toronto Law Journal*, vol. 19, 1969, p. 257.

MacKay, R.A., *The Unreformed Senate of Canada*, rev. ed., (McClelland and Stewart, Toronto, 1963).

McKeown, Robert, "Protector of the Public," *Weekend Magazine*, (The Ottawa Journal), May 24, 1969, pp. 6–10.

McNaught, Kenneth, "Parliamentary Control of Foreign Policy?" *International Journal*, vol. 11, 1956, pp. 251–260.

Morin, J.-Y., "Un nouveau rôle pour un Sénat moribond," *Cité libre*, vol. 15, juin–juillet, 1964.

Munro, William Bennett, and Morley Ayerst, *The Governments of Europe*, 4th ed., (Macmillan, New York, 1954).

Newman, P.C., "Pearson's Senate Choices—Odd Kind of 'New' Politics," Toronto *Daily Star*, November 17, 1964.

Normandin, P.G. (ed.), *The Canadian Parliamentary Guide, 1968*, (Queen's Printer, Ottawa, 1968), (annual).

Orban, E., *Le Conseil législatif de Québec*, (Bellarmin, Montréal, 1967).

Page, D., "Steamlining the Procedures of the Canadian House of Commons," *C.J.E.P.S.*, vol. 33, no. 1, Feb., 1967, pp. 27–49.

Porter, John, *The Vertical Mosaic: an Analysis of Social Class and Power in Canada*, (University of Toronto Press, Toronto, 1965), pp. 386–416.

Power, C.G., D.R. Michener, *et al.*, "Focus on Parliament," *Queen's Quarterly*, vol. 43, no. 4, Winter, 1957.

Premont, J., "Publicité de documents officiels," *Canadian Public Administration*, vol. 11, no. 4, Winter, 1968.

Regenstreif, S.P., "Some Aspects of National Party Support in Canada," *C.J.E.P.S.*, vol. 29, 1963, pp. 59–74.

Reid, Alan D., "The New Brunswick Ombudsman Act," *University of Toronto Law Journal*, vol. 18, no. 4, 1968, p. 361.

Robertson, R.G., "The Canadian Parliament and Cabinet in the Face of Modern Demands," *Canadian Public Administration*, vol. 11, no. 3, Fall, 1968.

Rowat, Donald Cameron, "An Ombudsman Scheme for Canada," *C.J.E.P.S.*, vol. 27, no. 4, Nov., 1963.

Rowat, Donald Cameron, and Henry J. Lambias, "Canadian-Proposed Ombudsman Schemes" in Donald Cameron Rowat (ed.), *The Ombudsman: Citizen's Defender*, (University of Toronto Press, Toronto, 1965).

_____ , "How Much Administrative Secrecy?" *C.J.E.P.S.*, vol. 31, no. 4, Nov., 1965. (See also "Comments," *ibid.*, vol. 32, no. 1, Feb., 1966.)

_____ , *The Ombudsman: Citizen's Defender*, (University of Toronto Press, Toronto, 1965).

_____ , "Recent Developments in Ombudsmanship," *Canadian Public Administration*, vol. 10, no. 1, March, 1967.

Schindeler, F., "The Role of the Opposition in Ontario." (Address to the 38th Annual Meeting of the Canadian Political Science Association, Sherbrooke, Quebec, June 10, 1966).

Smith, D., "The Speakership of the Canadian House of Commons: Some Proposals." (A paper prepared for the House of Commons' Special Committee on Procedure and Organization), (Queen's Printer, Ottawa, 1965).

Thorburn, H.G., "Parliament and Policy-Making: the Case of the Trans-Canada Gas Pipeline," *C.J.E.P.S.*, vol. 23, 1957, pp. 516–31.

Turner, J., *Politics of Purpose*, (McClelland and Stewart, Toronto, 1968), ch. 2.

Turner, J.N., "The Senate of Canada—Political Conundrum" in R.M. Clark (ed.), *Canadian Issues: Essays in Honour of Henry F. Angus*, (University of Toronto Press, Toronto, 1961).

Van Loon, R.J., "The Frustrating Role of the Ottawa Backbencher," Toronto *Globe & Mail*, April 5, 1971.

Walker, H.W., "Parliamentary Procedure," *Queen's Quarterly*, vol. 58, 1951–52, pp. 228–236.

——————, "Question Time in Parliament," *Queen's Quarterly*, vol. 59, 1952–53, pp. 64–71.

Ward, Norman, "Called to the Bar of the House of Commons," *Canadian Bar Review*, vol. 35, 1957, pp. 529–546.

——————, "Parliamentary Bilingualism in Canada," *Parliamentary Affairs*, vol. 10, no. 2, Spring, 1957, pp. 155–164.

——————, "The Committee on Estimates," *Canadian Public Administration*, vol. 6, no. 1, March, 1963.

——————, *The Canadian House of Commons: Representation*, (University of Toronto Press, Toronto, 1950).

——————, *The Public Purse: a Study in Canadian Democracy*, (University of Toronto Press, Toronto, 1962). Canadian Government Series, 11.

INDEX